# GALILEE
## IN THE LATE SECOND TEMPLE
## AND MISHNAIC PERIODS

### Volume 1
*Life, Culture, and Society*

# GALILEE

## IN THE LATE SECOND TEMPLE AND MISHNAIC PERIODS

### Volume 1
### *Life, Culture, and Society*

**David A. Fiensy and James Riley Strange**

*Editors*

Fortress Press
Minneapolis

GALILEE IN THE LATE SECOND TEMPLE AND MISHNAIC PERIODS
Volume 1: Life, Culture, and Society
David A. Fiensy and James Riley Strange, Editors

Cover images, from right to left: Mona Lisa of the Galilee, flik47/iStock/Thinkstock. Olive Branch, Ryan Rodrick Beiler/iStock/Thinkstock. Roman Road, © Doug Oakman; reprinted by permission. Sea of Galilee, Naive/iStock/Thinkstock. Tomb with niches (Khirbet Qana) © David A. Fiensy; reprinted by permission.
Cover design: Laurie Ingram

*Library of Congress Cataloging-in-Publication data is available*

**ISBN:** 978-1-4514-6674-4
**eISBN:** 978-1-4514-8958-3

The paper used in this publication meets the minimum requirements of American National Standard for Information Sciences—Permanence of Paper for Printed Library Materials, ANSI Z329, 48-1984. Manufactured in the U.S.A.

IN MEMORIAM

Seán Freyne

# CONTENTS

Archaeological Chronology                                                    ix

Events and Rulers in Galilee and Judea in the Late Second Temple
    through Mishnaic Periods                                                 xi

Maps and Galilee Photo Gallery

Preface                                                                     xvii

OVERVIEW OF GALILEAN STUDIES

Introduction to *Galilee*: Volumes 1 and 2
*David A. Fiensy and James Riley Strange*                                     3

1. Galilee and the Historical Jesus in Recent Research
   *Roland Deines*                                                           11

HISTORY

2. The Political History in Galilee from the First Century BCE
   to the End of the Second Century CE
   *Morten Hørning Jensen*                                                   51

3. Religious Practices and Religious Movements in Galilee: 100 BCE–200 CE
   *Roland Deines*                                                           78

4. The Ethnicities of Galileans
   *Mark A. Chancey*                                                        112

5. The Synagogues of Galilee
   *Lee I. Levine*                                                          129

6. Notable Galilean Persons
   *Thomas Scott Caulley*                                                   151

7. Social Movements in Galilee
   *Richard Horsley*                                                        167

VILLAGE LIFE

8. The Galilean Village in the Late Second Temple and Mishnaic Periods
   *David A. Fiensy*                                                        177

 9. Household Judaism
    *Andrea M. Berlin*                                                    208

10. The Galilean House in the Late Second Temple and Mishnaic Periods
    *David A. Fiensy*                                                     216

11. Mortality, Morbidity, and Economics in Jesus' Galilee
    *Jonathan L. Reed*                                                    242

12. Education/Literacy in Jewish Galilee: Was There Any and at What Level?
    *John C. Poirier*                                                     253

Economics

13. The Galilean Road System
    *James F. Strange*                                                    263

14. Urbanization and Industry in Mishnaic Galilee
    *Ze'ev Safrai*                                                        272

15. Never the Two Shall Meet? Urban–Rural Interaction in Lower Galilee
    *Agnes Choi*                                                          297

16. Inner Village Life in Galilee: A Diverse and Complex Phenomenon
    *Sharon Lea Matilla*                                                  312

17. Debate: Was the Galilean Economy Oppressive or Prosperous?
    A. *Late Second Temple Galilee: Socio-Archaeology and Dimensions of Exploitation
       in First-Century Palestine*
       *Douglas E. Oakman*                                               346
    B. *Late Second Temple Galilee: A Picture of Relative Economic Health*
       *J. Andrew Overman*                                               357

18. Taxation and Other Sources of Government Income
    in the Galilee of Herod and Antipas
    *Fabian Udoh*                                                        366

Contributors                                                             389
Abbreviations                                                            391
Index of Ancient Sources                                                 395
Index of Subjects                                                        407

# Archaeological Chronology*

| ARCHAEOLOGICAL PERIOD | ABBREVIATION | DATES |
|---|---|---|
| Iron I | I1 | 1200–1000 BCE |
| Iron II | I2 | 1000–586 BCE |
| Persian | P | 586–333 BCE |
| Hellenistic I | H1 | 333–152 BCE |
| Hellenistic II | H2 | 152–37 BCE |
| Early Roman | ER | 37 BCE–70 CE |
| Middle Roman | MR | 70–250 CE |
| Late Roman | LR | 250–363 CE |
| Early Byzantine | Byz 1 | 363–451 CE |
| Late Byzantine | Byz 2 | 451–640 CE |
| Early Islamic | EI | 640–950 CE |
| Late Islamic | LI | 950–1291 CE |

* This chronology is taken from James F. Strange, Thomas R.W. Longstaff, and Dennis E. Groh with revisions by James Riley Strange, *The Excavations at Shikhin: Manual for Area Supervisors* (unpublished manuscript). The archaeological periods are those seen at Sepphoris and Shikhin.

# Events and Rulers in Galilee and Judea in the Late Second Temple through Mishnaic Periods

## Key Events

| | |
|---|---|
| 110 BCE? | John Hyrcanus conquers parts of Galilee? |
| 104 BCE | Aristobulus I annexes Galilee |
| 104 BCE | Ptolemy IX Lathyros attacks Sepphoris |
| 63 BCE | General Pompey of Rome conquers Judea |
| 55 BCE | Gabinius locates a regional Sanhedrin at Sepphoris |
| 47–37 BCE | Herod the Great governs the Galilee |
| 49/38 BCE | Herod makes Sepphoris his northern headquarters |
| 4 BCE | Death of Herod; Sepphoris revolts; Roman legions destroy it |
| 4 BCE | Antipas, *tetrarch* of Galilee and Perea, rebuilds Sepphoris as his Galilean capital |
| 20 CE | Antipas builds Tiberias as his new capital |
| 30–33 CE | Jesus' ministry |
| 66–70 CE | First Jewish Revolt: Vespasian invades Galilee; destruction of Yodefat, Magdala, and Gamla; destruction of Jerusalem and the temple; migration of Judeans to Galilee |
| 70–225 CE | Era of the Tannaim |
| 80–140 CE | Sanhedrin moves to Usha |
| 132–135 CE | Bar Kokhba Revolt; expulsion of Jews from Jerusalem; migration to Galilee |
| 140 CE | Sanhedrin moves to Shefarʿam |
| 163 CE | Sanhedrin moves to Beit Sheʿarim, then to Sepphoris |
| 193 CE | Sanhedrin moves to Tiberias |
| 200–220 CE | Rabbi Judah the Prince completes the codification of the Mishnah at Sepphoris |

## Rulers of Judea from Hellenistic Times**

| Hellenistic Dynasties | Dates of Reign |
|---|---|
| Alexander III of Macedon | 333–323 BCE |
| Ptolemy I Soter ("Savior") | 300–282 BCE |
| Ptolemy II Philadelphus ("Brother-loving") | 285–246 BCE |
| Ptolemy III Euergetes ("Benefactor") | 246–221 BCE |
| Ptolemy IV Philopator ("Father-loving") | 221–204 BCE |
| Ptolemy V Epiphanes ("[God] Manifest") | 204–180 BCE |
| Antiochus III ("The Great") | 223–187 BCE (takes control of Palestine in 198) |
| Seleucus IV Philopator | 18–175 BCE |
| Antiochus IV Epiphanes | 175–164 BCE |

| Hasmonean Dynasty | Dates of Control |
|---|---|
| Mattathias | d. 166 BCE |
| Judas, son of Mattathias | 165–160 BCE |
| Jonathan, son of Mattathias | 160–142 BCE |
| Simon, son of Mattathias | 142–135 BCE |
| John Hyrcanus I, son of Simon | 135–104 BCE |
| Judah Aristobulus I, son of John Hyrcanus I | 104–103 BCE |
| Alexander Jannaeus, son of John Hyrcanus I | 103–76 BCE |
| Salome Alexandra, wife of Alexander Jannaeus | 76–67 BCE |
| Aristobulus II, son of Alexander Jannaeus and Alexandra | 67–63 BCE |
| John Hyrcanus II, son of Alexander Jannaeus and Alexandra | 63–40 BCE (high priest) |
| Mattathias Antigonus II, son of Aristobulus II | 40–37 BCE (Parthian rule) |

---

** Information compiled and expanded from Michael D. Coogan, ed., *New Oxford Annotated Bible: New Revised Standard Version with the Apocrypha,* 4th ed. (Oxford and New York: Oxford University Press, 2010), 2260–61; John Roberts, ed., *Oxford Dictionary of the Classical World* (Oxford, U.K.: Oxford University Press, 2005), 848.

| Herodian Dynasty | Dates of Reign |
|---|---|
| Herod the Great | |
| governor of the Galilee | 47–37 BCE |
| king of the Jews | 37–4 BCE |
| | |
| Archelaus, son of Herod, *ethnarch* ("ruler of a people") of Judea, Samaria, Idumea | 4 BCE–6 CE[1] |
| | |
| Antipas, son of Herod, *tetrarch* ("ruler of a fourth") of Galilee and Perea | 4 BCE–39 CE |
| | |
| Philip, son of Herod, *tetrarch* of Batanea, Trachonitis, Auranitis | 4 BCE–34 CE |
| | |
| Agrippa I, grandson of Herod and son of Aristobulus IV and Berenice, | |
| king of Batanea, Trachonitis, Aurantis, | 37–44 CE |
| and of Judea, Galilee, and Perea | 41–44 CE |
| | |
| Herod Agrippa II, son of Herod Agrippa I, king of Chalcis (north of Judea), | |
| king of Batanea, Trachonitis, Auranitis, Galilee, | 50–53 CE |
| and Perea | 53–ca. 93 CE |

---

1. In 6 CE Herod Archelaus was deposed and Judea, Samaria, and Idumea became the Roman province Judaea with its capital at Caesarea.

| Roman Emperors | Dates of Reign |
|---|---|
| Octavian (Augustus) | 27 BCE–14 CE |
| Tiberius | 14–17 CE |
| Caius Caligula | 37–41 CE |
| Claudius | 41–54 CE |
| Nero | 54–68 CE |
| Galba | 68–69 CE |
| Otho | 69 CE |
| Vitellius | 69 CE |
| Vespasian | 69–79 CE |
| Titus | 79–81 CE |
| Domitian | 81–96 CE |
| Nerva | 96–98 CE |
| Trajan | 98–117 CE |
| Hadrian | 117–138 CE |
| Antoninus Pius | 138–161 CE |
| Marcus Aurelius | 161–180 CE |
| Lucius Verus | 161–166 CE |
| Commodus | 180–192 CE |
| Pertinax | 192–193 CE |
| Didius Julianus | 193 CE |
| Septimius Servus | 193–211 CE |
| Aurelius Antoninus (Caracalla) | 198–217 CE |
| Geta | 211 CE |
| Macrinus | 217–218 CE |
| Diadumenius | 218 CE |
| Elagabalus | 218–222 CE |
| Aurelius Severus Alexander | 222–235 CE |

| Roman Governors of Judea | Dates of Governorship |
|---|---|
| Coponius | 6–8 CE |
| M. Ambivius | 9–12 CE |
| Annius Rufus | 12–15 CE |
| Valerius Gratus | 15–26 CE |
| Pontius Pilate | 26–36 CE |
| Marcellus | 36–37 CE |

| | |
|---|---|
| Marullus | 37–41 CE[2] |
| Cuspius Fadus | 44–46 CE |
| Tiberius Julius Alexander | 46–48 CE |
| Ventidius Cumanus | 48–52 CE |
| M. Antonius Felix | 52–60 CE |
| Porcius Festus | 60–62 CE |
| Clodius Albinus | 62–64 CE |
| Cessuis Florus | 64–66 CE |
| Vettulenes Cerialis | 70–72 CE |
| M. Salvienus | 75–86 CE |
| Pompeius Longinus | 86 CE |
| Lusius Quietus | 117 CE |
| Tineius Rufus | 130–132 CE |

2. Herod Agrippa I ruled Judea as part of his kingdom beginning in 41. Judea became a Roman province again after Agrippa's death in 44. Emperor Hadrian renamed the province Syria Palaestina after the Bar Kokhba revolt (132–135), and he renamed Jerusalem Aelia Capitolina after his clan name (Aelius) combined with Jupiter Capitolinus.

PALESTINE AT THE END OF THE SECOND TEMPLE PERIOD

Map 1

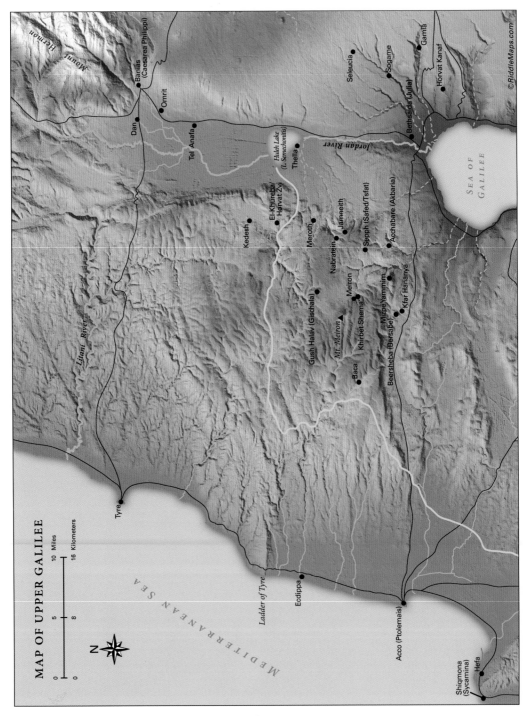

Map 2

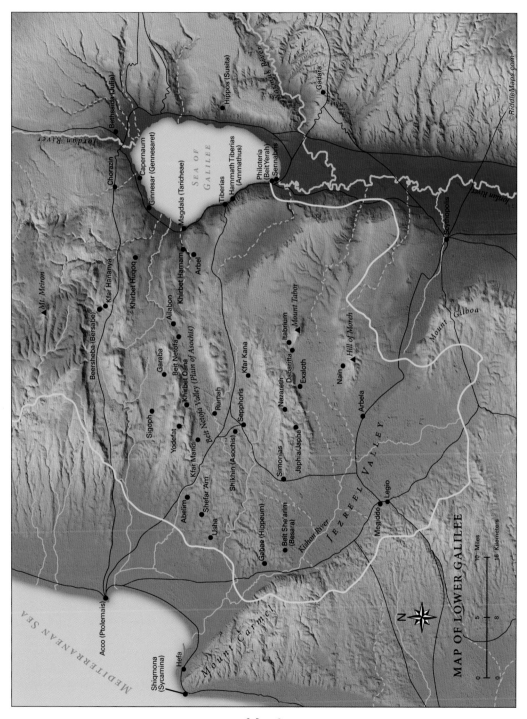

MAP OF LOWER GALILEE

Map 3

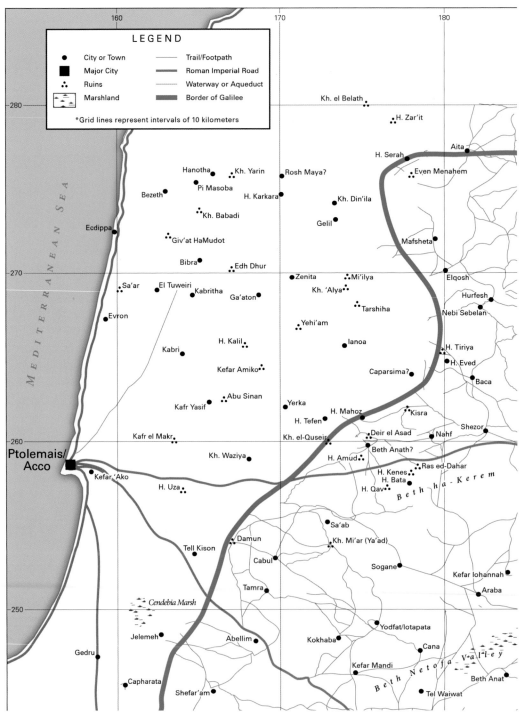

LEGEND

| | | | |
|---|---|---|---|
| ● | City or Town | —— | Trail/Footpath |
| ■ | Major City | ▬▬ | Roman Imperial Road |
| ∴ | Ruins | —— | Waterway or Aqueduct |
| 🏞 | Marshland | ▬▬ | Border of Galilee |

*Grid lines represent intervals of 10 kilometers

MEDITERRANEAN SEA

160   170   180

—280—
—270—
—260—
—250—

Kh. el Belath
H. Zar'it
Aita
H. Serah
Even Menahem
Rosh Maya?
Hanotha  Kh. Yarin
Pi Masoba
Kh. Din'ila
Bezeth  H. Karkara
Kh. Babadi
Gelil
Mafsheta
Ecdippa
Giv'at HaMudot
Bibra  Edh Dhur
Zenita  Mi'ilya  Elqosh
Sa'ar  El Tuweiri  Kh. 'Alya  Hurfesh
Kabritha  Tarshiha
Ga'aton  Nebi Sebelan
Evron  Yehi'am
H. Tiriya
Kabri  H. Kalil  Ianoa  H. Eved
Kefar Amiko  Baca
Caparsima?
Abu Sinan
Kafr Yasif  Yerka
H. Mahoz  Kisra
H. Tefen  Shezor
Kafr el Makr.  Kh. el-Quseir  Deir el Asad  Nahf
Beth Anath?
Kh. Waziya  H. Amud  Ras ed-Dahar
Ptolemais/  H. Kenes
Acco  H. Bata
Kefar 'Ako  H. Qav  Beth ha-Kerem
H. Uza
Sa'ab
Kh. Mi'ar (Ya'ad)
Damun
Tell Kison  Cabul  Sogane  Kefar Iohannah
Araba
Tamra
Cendebia Marsh  Yodfat/Iotapata
Jelemeh  Abellim  Kokhaba  Cana
Kefar Mandi  Beth Netofa Valley
Gedru  Beth Anat
Capharata  Tel Waiwat
Shefar'am

Composite map of Galilee adapted for use by RiddleMaps.com from original maps by James F. Strange.

Map 4A: Galilee, NW

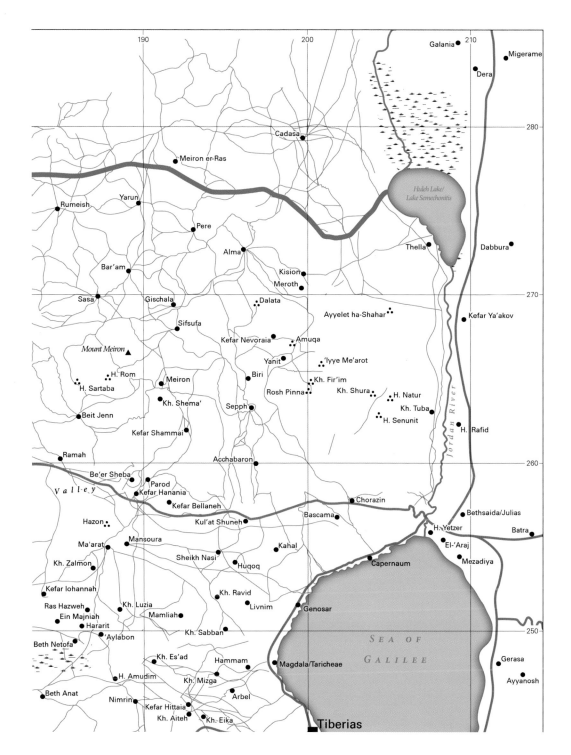

190                    200              Galania ● 210        Migerame ●

Dera ●

Cadasa ●                                              ● 280

Meiron er-Ras ●

                                         *Huleh Lake/*
                                         *Lake Semechonitis*

Yarun ●
Rumeish ●

Pere ●                              Thella ●        Dabbura ●

Alma ●

Bar'am ●        Kision ●                                    ● 270
                Meroth ●

Sasa ●    Gischala ●    Dalata ●        Ayyelet ha-Shahar ●●   Kefar Ya'akov ●

         Sifsufa ●
                      Kefar Nevoraia ●  Amuqa ●●
*Mount Meiron* ▲                Yanit ●   'Iyye Me'arot ●●

         H. Rom ●       Meiron ●    Biri ●   Kh. Fir'im ●●
H. Sartaba ●●                          Rosh Pinna ●●  Kh. Shura ●●   H. Natur ●●
                Kh. Shema' ●                                Kh. Tuba ●●
Beit Jenn ●              Sepph ●                     H. Senunit ●●   H. Rafid ●
         Kefar Shammai ●

Ramah ●              Acchabaron ●                              ● 260
    Be'er Sheba ●
*V a l l e y*    Parod ●
           Kefar Hanania ●
              Kefar Bellaneh ●           Chorazin ●
Hazon ●●      Kul'at Shuneh ●        Bascama ●      ● Bethsaida/Julias
Ma'arat ●   Mansoura ●                        H. Yetzer ●       Batra ●
                      Kahal ●              El-'Araj ●
Kh. Zalmon ●   Sheikh Nasi ●  Huqoq ●              Mezadiya ●
Kefar Iohannah ●                    Capernaum ●
Ras Hazweh ●   Kh. Luzia ●  Kh. Ravid ●
Ein Majniah ●   Mamliah ●    Livnim ●   Genosar ●
Hararit ●                                                  ● 250
Beth Netofa ●  'Aylabon ●  Kh. Sabban ●
            Kh. Es'ad ●         *S E A   O F*          Gerasa ●
         H. Amudim ●  Hammam ●   *G A L I L E E*     Ayyanosh ●
Beth Anat ●  Nimrin ●  Kh. Mizga ●  Magdala/Taricheae ●
         Kefar Hittaia ●  Arbel ●
            Kh. Aiteh ●  Kh. Eika ●
                              ■ **Tiberias**

Map 4B: Galilee, NE

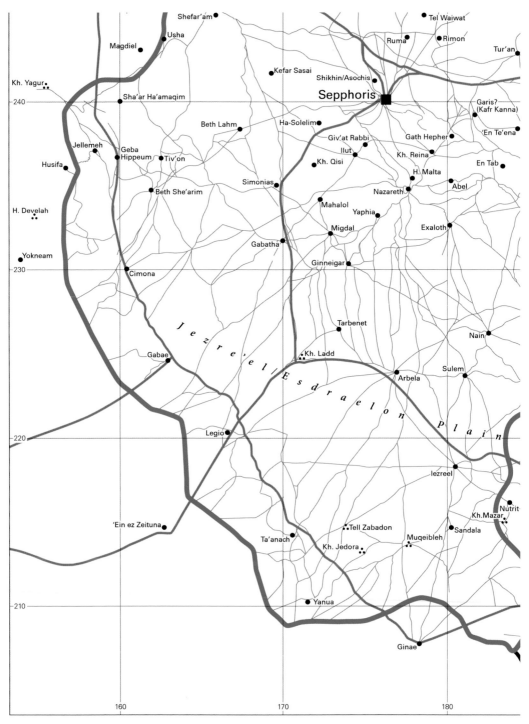

Map 4C: Galilee, SW

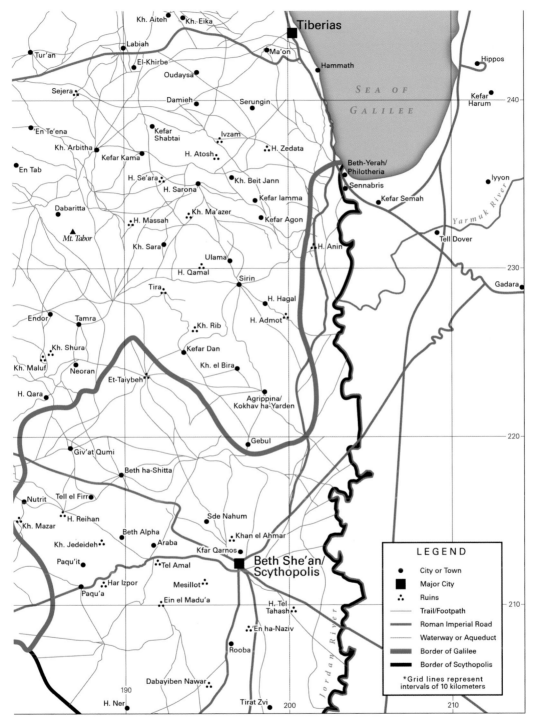

Map 4D: Galilee, SE

A view of the Sea of Galilee from Arbel Pass. Photo courtesy David Fiensy.

Valley of Jezreel from Mount Precipice. © Stock/Thinkstock.

Theater at Sepphoris. Photo courtesy Douglas Oakman.

The hill of Nazareth. © Stock/Thinkstock.

Cooking pots in reconstructed Nazareth village. Photo: BiblePlaces.com/ Nazareth Village. Copyright © Todd Bolen. Used by permission.

Oil lamp in reconstructed Nazareth village. Photo: BiblePlaces.com/ Nazareth Village. Copyright © Todd Bolen. Used by permission.

Jordan River below the Sea of Galilee. Photo courtesy David Fiensy.

Basalt olive crusher at Capernaum. Photo courtesy Douglas Oakman.

Basalt grinding stones at Capernaum. Photo courtesy Douglas Oakman.

A view of the Bet Netofa Valley from Cana. Photo courtesy David Fiensy.

Capernaum, looking north from the Sacra Insula toward Insula II and the synagogue in Insula V. Photo by Zoonar RF.

Mona Lisa of the Galilee, Zippori. © Stock/Thinkstock.

Curbstones of Roman road, Shikhin. Photo courtesy James Riley Strange.

The slopes of Mount Meiron from Khirbet Shema. Photo: Todd Bolen/
BiblePlaces.com. Copyright © Todd Bolen. Used by permission.

Hiking trail in Upper Galilee. © Stock/Thinkstock.

Olive harvest in Upper Galilee.
© Stock/Thinkstock.

The Huleh Valley, Northern Galilee. Photo courtesy Douglas Oakman.

Gischala mausoleum side room with *kokhim*.
Photo: Todd Bolen/
BiblePlaces.com.
Copyright © Todd Bolen.
Used by permission.

Upper Galilee near Gischala.
Photo courtesy
Douglas Oakman.

Aerial view of Tel Kedesh.
© Richard Cleve.

# PREFACE

In the summer of 1971, excavations began at the village site of Khirbet Shemaʿ in the hills of Upper Galilee. This project was noteworthy because the village was located in an area that had received little attention from archaeologists, because the excavators focused on the Hellenistic through the Roman and Byzantine periods, and because the team dug village ruins rather than a tell. That venture became the Meiron Excavation Project, which lasted from 1971 to 1984 and expanded to include three more Jewish villages of the Upper Galilee: Meiron, Gush Halav, and Nabratein. It is fair to say that this project inaugurated a new period in the archaeology of Palestine, in which men and women trained in the tell archaeology of Judea expended considerable energy in a region and time period critical for understanding Formative Judaism (Judaism of the sages of rabbinic literature) and the birth of Christianity.

Beginning in the mid-1980s, attention began to shift to the urban environment of the Lower Galilee. Some dig directors reasoned that having gained a new understanding of social and religious institutions among Galilean Jewish villages, it was time to investigate a city of the same period. Lower Galilee was home to two cities in the Roman through Byzantine periods, Sepphoris and Tiberias, both built by Antipas. Tiberias was heavily built over by modern construction, whereas the hilltop of Sepphoris was largely untouched by development. A team from the University of Michigan had excavated on the acropolis in 1931. Systematic and stratigraphic excavations of the city began in 1983 with the University of South Florida Excavations at Sepphoris, followed in 1985 by the Joint Expedition to Sepphoris (Duke University and Hebrew University of Jerusalem). Eventually Duke and Hebrew University sponsored separate excavations, and the University of Haifa excavated the city waterworks.

It is difficult to overstate the importance of Sepphoris for the history of the archaeology of Galilee, as well as for understanding Formative Judaism and nascent Christianity. Because of what they learned about Sepphoris, coupled with their knowledge of Upper Galilee, scholars began to reevaluate their understandings of the origins of Galilee's population, village and city relations, economy, Jewish social identity, and even how to read the New Testament Gospels, Josephus, the writings of the sages, and other texts that talk about the region.

During the years Sepphoris has been excavated (1983–present), the Lower Galilee has seen its share of village excavations by both Israeli and foreign teams, including Yodefat/Jotapata, Khirbet Qana, Hamam, Huqoq, and Migdal/Magdala, to name a few. Our picture of Hellenistic and Roman (and Byzantine and Islamic) Galilee continually grows, and archaeologists and textual scholars alike keep up their debates about how to understand the data.

The editors of these volumes think that the time is ripe to offer readers—whom we envision as interested laypeople as well as college and seminary students, but also scholars who study other topics—both the evidence and the debates about the evidence that are shaping what people say about Galilee between 100 bce and 200 ce, what we are calling the Late Second Temple period through the Mishnaic period. This is the period and the region that birthed two Judaisms: the one that became the Christianities we know today, and the other that became the Judaisms of the Talmud. We have aimed to present chapters written by leaders in the field and, whenever possible, by the archaeologists responsible for excavating the sites they talk about.

When the idea for this two-volume work was still in its germination phase, it was shared with two veteran archaeologists from the Meiron Excavation Project: Eric Meyers and Jim Strange (both of whom are contributors). Their suggestions and guidance at that time have proven very helpful in the ongoing planning and execution of the idea. The editors wish to express their gratitude for the combined wisdom of these "notable Galileans."

We also wish to thank our editor at Fortress, Scott Tunseth, for his encouragement, for facilitating our work, and for the ease of our working relationship.

Our graduate assistant, Sarah Bottomley, helped check the footnoting style of many of the essays and composed bibliographies for several of the contributions as well. Many thanks to her for this assistance.

We are indebted to the authors of the chapters, our colleagues and friends in the field, for the quality of what they offer to you here.

Finally, of course, we also wish to thank our spouses—Molly Fiensy and Laura Strange—for their love, support, and tolerance of our absences while we both dig in Israel and bury ourselves in our offices to finish this editing.

David Fiensy　　　　　　　　　　　　　　　　　　　　　　James Riley Strange
Grayson, Kentucky　　　　　　　　　　　　　　　　　　　Birmingham, Alabama

# Overview of Galilean Studies

# INTRODUCTION TO GALILEE: VOLUMES 1 AND 2

## David A. Fiensy and James Riley Strange

Galilee has fascinated historians for the last 150 years. Ernest Renan, the nineteenth-century biographer of Jesus, thought that ancient Galilee must have been a paradise. He referred to the area around Nazareth as "This enchanted circle. . . ." Galilee was "charming and idyllic" and was characterized by green, shade, beautiful flowers, and small, gentle animals. "In no country in the world do the mountains spread themselves out with more harmony. . . ." Galilee, he thought, "spiritualised itself in ethereal dreams—in a kind of poetic mysticism, blending heaven and earth."[1] It was here in Renan's dreamlike never-never-land that he pictured Jesus' youth.

What we need is a more sober appraisal of ancient Galilee. The research in the last thirty years has sought to do that, but, nevertheless, the current study of Galilee is fraught with conflicting conclusions. If the Sermon on the Mount is known for its six Antitheses (Matt. 5:21-48), scholars may look back on this period of research as the Antitheses of Galilee: (1) Some look at Galilee through the lenses of cultural anthropology and macro-sociology;[2] others look at Galilee through the lenses of archaeology and reject the use of social theories.[3] (2) Some

---

1. Ernest Renan, *The Life of Jesus* (London: Trübner, 1867), 51, 74–76.
2. See the analyses of Richard A. Horsley, "The Historical Jesus and Archaeology of the Galilee: Questions from Historical Jesus Research to Archaeologists," *SBL 1994 Seminar Papers* (Atlanta: Scholars Press, 1994), 91–135; Douglas E.. Oakman, "The Archaeology of First-Century Galilee and the Social Interpretation of the Historical Jesus," in ibid., 220–51; and Seán V. Freyne, "Archaeology and the Historical Jesus," in *Archaeology and Biblical Interpretation* (ed. John R. Bartlett; London: Routledge, 1997), 129.
3. J. Andrew Overman, "Jesus of Galilee and the Historical Peasant," in *Archaeology and the Galilee: Texts and Contexts in the Graeco-Roman and Byzantine Periods* (ed. Douglas R. Edwards and C. Thomas McCollough;

maintain that the relations between rural villages and the cities were hostile;[4] others propose that the relationship was one of economic reciprocity and good will.[5] (3) Some suggest that Galilee was typical of other agrarian societies, with poor peasants who lived in the rural areas and exploitative wealthy people who lived mostly in the cities;[6] others respond that life was pretty good for everyone in Galilee and that it was an egalitarian society.[7] (4) Some regard Galilee as so hellenized (Greek-like) that there were Cynic philosophers running around;[8] others retort that Galilee was thoroughly Jewish.[9] (5) Some think Sepphoris, one of the cities of Lower Galilee, was rather large for an ancient city (up to 30,000 persons); others think it was a small "city" (around 7,500).[10] (6) Some think that the theater ruins in Sepphoris

---

Atlanta: Scholars Press, 1997), 67–73; and, in the same volume, Dennis E. Groh, "The Clash between Literary and Archaeological Models of Provincial Palestine," 29–37.

4. Oakman, "Archaeology of First-Century Galilee"; Richard A. Horsley, *Archaeology, History, and Society in Galilee: The Social Context of Jesus and the Rabbis* (Valley Forge, Pa.: Trinity Press International, 1996), 70–83; Gerhard E. Lenski, *Power and Privilege: A Theory of Social Stratification* (New York: McGraw-Hill, 1966), 206.

5. See David Adan-Bayewitz, *Common Pottery in Roman Galilee: A Study of Local Trade* (Bar-Ilan Studies in Near Eastern Languages and Culture; Ramat-Gan: Bar-Ilan University Press, 1993), 23–41, 216–36; Adan-Bayewitz,"Kefar Hananya, 1986," *IEJ* 37 (1987): 178–79; Adan-Bayewitz and Isadore Perlman, "The Local Trade of Sepphoris in the Roman Period," *IEJ* 40 (1990): 153–72; James F. Strange, "First Century Galilee from Archaeology and from the Texts," in Edwards and McCollough, *Archaeology and the Galilee*, 41; Douglas R. Edwards, "First-Century Urban/Rural Relations in Lower Galilee: Exploring the Archaeological and Literary Evidence," in *SBL 1988 Seminar Papers* (ed. David J. Lull; Atlanta: Scholars Press, 1997), 169–82; Edwards, "The Socio-Economic and Cultural Ethos of the Lower Galilee in the First Century: Implications for the Nascent Jesus Movement," in *The Galilee in Late Antiquity* (ed. Lee I. Levine; New York: Jewish Theological Seminary of America, 1992), 53–73; Eric M. Meyers, "Jesus and His Galilean Context," in Edwards and McCollough, *Archaeology and the Galilee*, 57–66.

6. John Dominic Crossan and Jonathan L. Reed, *Excavating Jesus: Beneath the Stones, Behind the Texts* (San Francisco: HarperSanFrancisco, 2001), 70; Richard A. Horsley, "Jesus and Galilee: The Contingencies of a Renewal Movement," in *Galilee through the Centuries: Confluence of Cultures* (ed. Eric M. Meyers; Duke Judaic Studies Series 1; Winona Lake, Ind.: Eisenbrauns, 1999), 65.

7. Groh, "Clash between Literary and Archaeological Models," 29–37.

8. Howard Clark Kee, "Early Christianity in the Galilee: Reassessing the Evidence from the Gospels," in Levine, *Galilee in Late Antiquity*, 3–22, esp. 15; Robert W. Funk, *Honest to Jesus: Jesus for a New Millennium* (San Francisco: HarperSanFrancisco, 1996), 58; Burton L. Mack, *A Myth of Innocence: Mark and Christian Origins* (Philadelphia: Fortress Press, 1988), 64, 66.

9. See Jonathan L. Reed, *Archaeology and the Galilean Jesus: A Re-Examination of the Evidence* (Harrisburg, Pa.: Trinity Press International, 2000), 49–51; Mark A. Chancey and Eric M. Meyers, "How Jewish Was Sepphoris in Jesus' Time?" *BAR* 26, no. 4 (2000): 18–41, 61; Eric M. Meyers, "Jesus and His World: Sepphoris and the Quest for the Historical Jesus," in *Saxa loquentur: Studien zur Archäologie Palästinas/Israels: Festschrift für Volkmar Fritz zum 65. Geburtstag* (ed. Cornelis G. den Hertog; Ulrich Hübner, and Stefan Münger; AOAT 302; Münster: Ugarit, 2003), 191–95; Mark A. Chancey, *The Myth of a Gentile Galilee* (SNTSMS 118; Cambridge: Cambridge University Press, 2002), 79–90.

10. Compare the figures in Reed, *Archaeology and the Galilean Jesus*, 117. Meyers suggests 18,000 for Sepphoris and 24,000 for Tiberias ("Jesus and His Galilean Context," 59). J. Andrew Overman offered 30,000 to 40,000 for Tiberias and 30,000 for Sepphoris ("Who Were the First Urban Christians?" in *SBL Seminar 1988 Seminar Papers*, 160–68); Horsley maintained that both cities together had a population of 15,000 (*Archaeology, History, and Society in Galilee*, 45).

of Galilee (only five kilometers or four miles from Nazareth) indicate that Jesus could have attended theatrical performances; others maintain that the theater was not constructed until after Jesus' time.[11]

These contradictory viewpoints have made it a cliché that the quest for the historical Jesus is at the same time a quest for the historical Galilee.[12] The geographical and cultural location of Jesus' youth, it is surmised, may help us understand his later message and/or his pattern of ministry. Certainly scholars of the past have thought as much; the current group seems to have the same opinion.[13]

Today Galilee studies are having an influence on several areas of New Testament studies. In addition to the study of the historical Jesus, mentioned above, many today see Galilee as the context for the composition of the sayings source commonly called Q.[14] Others add that the Gospel of Mark was also composed in Galilee.[15] Research in the New Testament Gospels mandates that we have an up-to-date assessment of ancient Galilee.

Students of ancient Judaism also have an interest in Galilee. As archaeological surveys are demonstrating, Judeans began to immigrate into Galilee during the Hasmonean period (early first century BCE) and, consequently, Galilee became a very Jewish territory.[16] When the great Jewish War erupted in 66 CE, Galilee was the focal point. It was there that the Roman army first attacked, defeating Josephus's army and laying waste to several cities (*J. W.* 2.566–3.203). After the war, Judaism eventually reorganized there. The Sanhedrin moved at first to Yavneh (Jamnia) on the coast, then to Usha, to Beth She'arim, to Sepphoris, and finally to Tiberias (all in Galilee).[17] It was in Galilee, in Sepphoris, that Rabbi Yehudah ha-Nasi lived and redacted

---

11. For a date in the early first century (thus the time of Antipas and Jesus), see James F. Strange, "Six Campaigns at Sepphoris," in Levine, *Galilee in Late Antiquity*, 342; and Richard A. Batey, *Jesus and the Forgotten City: New Light on Sepphoris and the Urban World of Jesus* (Grand Rapids: Baker, 1991), 83–103. For a date of late first century or early second century for the theater, see Ze'ev Weiss and Ehud Netzer, "Hellenistic and Roman Sepphoris: The Archaeological Evidence," in *Sepphoris in Galilee: Crosscurrents of Culture* (ed. Rebecca Martin Nagy, Carol L. Meyers, Eric M. Meyers, and Ze'ev Weiss; Raleigh: North Carolina Museum of Art, 1996; distributed by Eisenbrauns, Winona Lake, Ind.), 32; Carol L. Meyers and Eric M. Meyers, "Sepphoris," *OEANE* 4:533; and Meyers, "Jesus and His World," 188–90.

12. Seán Freyne, "The Geography, Politics, and Economics of Galilee and the Quest for the Historical Jesus," in *Studying the Historical Jesus: Evaluations of the State of Current Research* (ed. Bruce Chilton and Craig A. Evans; NTTS 19; Leiden: Brill, 1994), 76; and Halvor Moxnes, "Construction of Galilee," *BTB* 31 (2001): 26–37, 64–77.

13. See the surveys in Moxnes, "Construction of Galilee"; and Mark Rapinchuk, "The Galilee and Jesus in Recent Research," *Currents in Biblical Research* 2 (2004): 197–222.

14. Reed, *Archaeology and the Galilean Jesus*, 170–96; John Kloppenborg Verbin, *Excavating Q: The History and Setting of the Sayings Gospel* (Minneapolis: Fortress Press, 2000), 170–75, 214–61.

15. Joel Marcus, "The Jewish War and the *Sitz im Leben* of Mark," *JBL* 111 (1992): 441–62; Werner H. Kelber, *Mark's Story of Jesus* (Philadelphia: Fortress Press, 1979), 13.

16. See the chapters by Jensen and Chancey in this volume.

17. See *b. Roš Haš.* 31b and E. Mary Smallwood, *The Jews under Roman Rule: From Pompey to Diocletian. A Study in Political Relations* (SJLA 20; Leiden: Brill, 1976), 474.

the Mishnah.[18]   Several other important rabbis also lived in Galilee.[19]   Galilee, therefore, has played an important role in both the formation of early Christianity and the reformulation of the Judaism that arose after the destruction of the temple to become the ancestor of the Judaisms we know today.

The Galilee at the time of Jesus and the Mishnah has received intense scrutiny in the past thirty years.   Scholars have combed through the texts (especially Josephus) and the material remains to form an increasingly complete and complex picture. Archaeologists have reopened sites already dug and have sunk their spades into previously unexcavated sites. During this time, several useful collections of articles have appeared.[20]   These collections are certainly full of very helpful information, and they have expanded the knowledge of the region during our period of interest. The authors of the present volume owe a great debt to these previous contributions to the field, yet some of the conclusions and hypotheses may now need reevaluation, and the information can certainly always be updated.   What we propose in these two volumes is to offer the general reader a somewhat full report of the status of Galilean studies.

These two volumes consolidate a great deal of information that has been brought to light in various journals, field reports, and essays over the past thirty years.   Our goal has been to make this information easily accessible to New Testament scholars and Mishnah scholars not familiar with these materials, and also usable to the average intelligent reader.   The volumes will integrate the various excavations (for example, the three excavations at Sepphoris) and will also integrate the archaeological and textual data where possible.

We have sought to hear all voices: archaeologists, historians, biblical scholars, and social-science interpreters; Christians, Jews, and secular scholars; North Americans, Europeans, and Israelis; those who have devoted a significant amount of time and energy to this research (especially those who have excavated in Galilee for many years), a few newcomers, and even "outsiders" who offer a new look at the data. As noted above, there is—and this is hardly surprising—no unanimity with respect to several issues. It has not been the editors' goal to harmonize opinions or reduce disagreements. We present them as they exist and let the reader make decisions.

Volume 1 has collected chapters on the life and culture of ancient Galilee.  After surveys of the modern study of Galilee and of Galilean history, there are specialized studies on ethnicity,  on religious practices of Galilee (including synagogues), on notable personalities, and on important social movements. Village life is featured in one essay on the village, followed by one

---

18. Smallwood, *Jews under Roman Rule*, 499. See the chapter by Caulley in this volume.

19. For example, Rabbi Ḥanina lived in Sepphoris (*y. Taʿan.* 3:4; *y. Peʾah* 7:1). See also Shaye J. D. Cohen, "The Place of the Rabbi in Jewish Society," in Levine, *Galilee in late Antiquity*, 157–73.

20. See Levine, *Galilee in late Antiquity*; Nagy et al., *Sepphoris in Galilee*; Edwards and McCollough, *Archaeology and the Galilee*; Eric M. Meyers, *Galilee through the Centuries*; and Jürgen Zangenberg, Harold W. Attridge, and Dale B. Martin, eds., *Religion, Ethnicity, and Identity in Ancient Galilee: A Region in Transition* (WUNT 210; Tübingen: Mohr Siebeck, 2007).

on household Judaism, and then one on the village houses. This section of the volume ends with essays on education and diseases and health. There follow offerings on the road system, trade and markets, the urban–rural divide, and the economic life of the village. In relation to these latter is the chapter—consisting of two companion essays—that forms a debate on the standard of living of the average villager during our time period. Were they destitute, living modestly, or prosperous? A chapter on taxation rounds out part four of volume 1.

Volume 2 collects reports on all the archaeological excavations of Galilee at which significant remains from our period of time have been found. Among the sites we discuss, some have seen significant excavation (Capernaum, Sepphoris); in some the excavators focused on synagogues (Meiron, Khirbet Shema‘, Gischala/Gush Ḥalav); others have seen limited excavation either because of modern construction (Nazareth, Tiberias) or because the dig began recently (Shikhin). Those sites with remains only before or after our time period (100 BCE–200 CE) find no discussion here.[21] Also, generally speaking, those sites only surveyed but not excavated will not be covered, even though there may be strong evidence of occupation during our time period. The editors thought it important to include chapters on both cities (such as Sepphoris and Tiberias) and villages, because it is the social, economic, religious, and cultural interactions between village and city that provide the basis for so much of the discussion in volume 1.

In both volumes, the reader has the opportunity to watch both textual scholars and archaeologists attempt to make sense of the ancient texts that talk about, and the material culture used and left by the inhabitants of, the Galilee. This is no light task, for it requires making inferences about human institutions and values. Those more ephemeral realities do leave their imprints in material culture and texts, but usually in an oblique way, and scholars are forced to interpret.

That observation provides one of the most valuable offerings of these two volumes: the chance to see how scholars make arguments, while assessing the arguments of others. In this way we take our readers seriously as conversation partners, for we offer up the strengths and weaknesses of our conclusions for their assessment as well. The other value of the volumes is to be found in the bibliographies at the end of each chapter: they are gold mines for people who want to do further reading on their own.

The editors invite readers into the ongoing conversations captured, in part, in these volumes. If you have read this far, it is clear that you are interested in the subject. It is our hope that the curious will find some answers here, and that others will learn how important the questions are. After all, we are looking at the birth of two of the world's great religions: Christianity and the Judaism of the Sages of Blessed Memory.

---

21. Therefore, towns and villages such as Philoteria, Horvat Kur, Bethlehem of Galilee, Kefar Reina, Chorazin, and Gabara will not be treated in vol. 2.

## Bibliography

Adan-Bayewitz, David. *Common Pottery in Roman Galilee: A Study of Local Trade.* Bar-Ilan Studies in Near Eastern Languages and Culture. Ramat-Gan: Bar-Ilan University Press, 1993.

———. "Kefar Hananya, 1986." *IEJ* 37 (1987): 178–79.

Adan-Bayewitz, David, and Isadore Perlman. "The Local Trade of Sepphoris in the Roman Period." *IEJ* 40 (1990): 153–72.

Batey, Richard A. *Jesus and the Forgotten City: New Light on Sepphoris and the Urban World of Jesus.* Grand Rapids: Baker, 1991.

Chancey, Mark A. *The Myth of a Gentile Galilee.* SNTSMS 118. Cambridge: Cambridge University Press, 2002.

Chancey, Mark A., and Eric M. Meyers. "How Jewish Was Sepphoris in Jesus' Time?" *BAR* 26, no. 4 (2000): 18–41, 61.

Cohen, Shaye J. D. "The Place of the Rabbi in Jewish Society." In *The Galilee in Late Antiquity*, edited by Lee I. Levine, 157–73. New York: Jewish Theological Seminary of America, 1992.

Crossan, John Dominic, and Jonathan L. Reed. *Excavating Jesus: Beneath the Stones, Behind the Texts.* San Francisco: HarperSanFrancisco, 2001.

Edwards, Douglas R. "First Century Urban/Rural Relations in Lower Galilee: Exploring the Archaeological and Literary Evidence." *SBL 1988 Seminar Papers*, edited by David J. Lull, 169–82. Atlanta: Scholars Press, 1988.

———. "The Socio-Economic and Cultural Ethos of the Lower Galilee in the First Century: Implications for the Nascent Jesus Movement." In *The Galilee in Late Antiquity*, edited by Lee I. Levine, 53–91. New York: Jewish Theological Seminary of America, 1992.

Edwards, Douglas R., and C. Thomas McCollough, eds. *Archaeology and the Galilee: Texts and Contexts in the Graeco-Roman and Byzantine Periods.* South Florida Studies in the History of Judaism 143. Atlanta: Scholars Press, 1997.

Freyne, Seán. "Archaeology and the Historical Jesus." In *Archaeology and Biblical Interpretation*, edited by John R. Bartlett, 117–44. London: Routledge, 1997.

———. "The Geography, Politics, and Economics in Galilee and the Quest for the Historical Jesus." In *Studying the Historical Jesus: Evaluations of the State of Current Research*, edited by Bruce Chilton and Craig A. Evans, 75–122. NTTS 19. Leiden: Brill, 1994.

Funk, Robert W. *Honest to Jesus: Jesus for a New Millennium.* San Francisco: HarperSanFrancisco, 1996.

Groh, Dennis E. "The Clash between Literary and Archaeological Models of Provincial Palestine." In *Archaeology and the Galilee: Texts and Contexts in the Graeco-Roman and Byzantine Periods*, edited by Douglas R. Edwards and C. Thomas McCollough, 29–37. South Florida Studies in the History of Judaism 143. Atlanta: Scholars Press, 1997.

Horsley, Richard A. *Archaeology, History, and Society in Galilee: The Social Context of Jesus and the Rabbis*. Valley Forge, Pa.: Trinity Press International, 1996.

———. "The Historical Jesus and Archaeology of the Galilee: Questions from Historical Jesus Research to Archaeologists." In *SBL 1994 Seminar Papers*, 91–135. Atlanta: Scholars Press, 1994.

———. "Jesus and Galilee: The Contingencies of a Renewal Movement." In *Galilee through the Centuries: Confluence of Cultures*, edited by Eric M. Meyers, 57–74. Winona Lake, Ind.: Eisenbrauns, 1999.

Kee, Howard Clark. "Early Christianity in the Galilee: Reassessing the Evidence from the Gospels." In *The Galilee in Late Antiquity*, edited by Lee I. Levine, 3–22. New York: Jewish Theological Seminary of America, 1992.

Kelber, Werner H. *Mark's Story of Jesus*. Philadelphia: Fortress Press, 1979.

Kloppenborg Verbin, John. *Excavating Q: The History and Setting of the Sayings Gospel*. Minneapolis: Fortress Press, 2000.

Lenski, Gerhard E. *Power and Privilege: A Theory of Social Stratification*. New York: McGraw Hill, 1966.

Levine, Lee I., ed. *The Galilee in Late Antiquity*. New York: Jewish Theological Seminary of America, 1992.

Mack, Burton L. *A Myth of Innocence: Mark and Christian Origins*. Philadelphia: Fortress Press, 1988.

Marcus, Joel. "The Jewish War and the *Sitz im Leben* of Mark." *JBL* 111 (1992): 441–62.

Meyers, Carol L., and Eric M. Meyers. "Sepphoris." *OEANE* 4:533.

Meyers, Eric M., ed. *Galilee through the Centuries: Confluence of Cultures*. Winona Lake, Ind.: Eisenbrauns, 1999.

———. "Jesus and His Galilean Context." In *Archaeology and the Galilee: Texts and Contexts in the Graeco-Roman and Byzantine Periods*, edited by Douglas R. Edwards and C. Thomas McCollough, 57–66. South Florida Studies in the History of Judaism 143. Atlanta: Scholars Press, 1997.

———. "Jesus and His World: Sepphoris and the Quest for the Historical Jesus." In *Saxa loquentur: Studien zur Archäologie Palästinas/Israels. Festschrift für Volkmar Fritz zum 65. Geburtstag*, edited by Cornelis G. den Hertog, Ulrich Hübner, and Stefan Münger. AOAT 302. Münster: Ugarit, 2003.

Moxnes, Halvor. "The Construction of Galilee as a Place for the Historical Jesus." *BTB* 31 (2001): 26–37, 64–77.

Nagy, Rebecca M., Carol L. Meyers, Eric M. Meyers, and Ze'ev Weiss, eds. *Sepphoris in Galilee: Crosscurrents of Culture*. Raleigh: North Carolina Museum of Art, 1996. Distributed by Eisenbrauns, Winona Lake, Ind.

Oakman, Douglas E. "The Archaeology of First-Century Galilee and the Social Interpretation of the Historical Jesus." In *SBL 1994 Seminar Papers*, 220–51. Atlanta: Scholars Press, 1994.

Overman, J. Andrew. "Jesus of Galilee and the Historical Peasant." In *Archaeology and the Galilee: Texts and Contexts in the Graeco-Roman and Byzantine Periods*, edited by Douglas R. Edwards and C. Thomas McCollough, 67–73. South Florida Studies in the History of Judaism 143. Atlanta: Scholars Press, 1997.

———. "Who Were the First Urban Christians?" In *SBL 1988 Seminar Papers*, 160–68. Atlanta: Scholars Press, 1988.

Rapinchuk, Mark. "The Galilee and Jesus in Recent Research." *CBR* 2 (2004): 197–222.

Reed, Jonathan L. *Archaeology and the Galilean Jesus.* Harrisburg, Pa.: Trinity Press International, 2000.

Renan, Ernest. *The Life of Jesus.* London: Trübner, 1867.

Smallwood, E. Mary. *The Jews under Roman Rule: From Pompey to Diocletian. A Study in Political Relations.* SJLA 20. Leiden: Brill, 1976.

Strange, James F. "First Century Galilee from Archaeology and from the Texts." In *Archaeology and the Galilee: Texts and Contexts in the Graeco-Roman and Byzantine Periods*, edited by Douglas R. Edwards and C. Thomas McCollough, 39–48. South Florida Studies in the History of Judaism 143. Atlanta: Scholars Press, 1997.

———. "Six Campaigns at Sepphoris: The University of South Florida Excavations, 1983–1989." In *The Galilee in Late Antiquity*, edited by Lee I. Levine, 339–56. New York: Jewish Theological Seminary of America, 1992.

Weiss, Ze'ev, and Ehud Netzer. "Hellenistic and Roman Sepphoris: The Archaeological Evidence." In *Sepphoris in Galilee: Crosscurrents of Culture*, edited by Rebecca Martin Nagy, Carol L. Meyers, Eric M. Meyers, and Ze'ev Weiss, 29–37. Raleigh: North Carolina Museum of Art, 1996.

Zangenberg, Jürgen, Harold W. Attridge, and Dale B. Martin, eds. *Religion, Ethnicity, and Identity in Ancient Galilee: A Region in Transition.* WUNT 210. Tübingen: Mohr Siebeck, 2007.

# 1

# GALILEE AND THE HISTORICAL JESUS IN RECENT RESEARCH

*Roland Deines*

### The Scholarly Legacy

"You too were with Jesus the Galilean"—Peter is confronted with this allegation in the court of the palace of the high priest in Jerusalem, having secretly followed Jesus after he was arrested (Matt. 26:69). This little sentence not only reflects the prejudice of a city-dweller against someone from rural Galilee, with its steady stream of troublemakers beginning with the "chief robber" Ezekias (Hezekiah) in 47 BCE,[1] but also throws light on the shifting history of the

This article is an edited and abridged version of "Jesus the Galilean: Questioning the Function of Galilee in Recent Jesus Research," in Roland Deines, *Acts of God in History: Studies Towards Recovering a Theological Historiography* (ed. Christoph Ochs and Peter Watts; WUNT 317; Tübingen: Mohr Siebeck, 2013), 53–93; used with permission. The German original appeared as "Galiläa und Jesus: Anfragen zur Funktion der Herkunftsbezeichnung 'Galiläa' in der neueren Jesusforschung," in *Jesus und die Archäologie Galiläas* (ed. Carsten Claussen and Jörg Frey; 2nd ed.; Biblisch-theologische Studien 87; Neukirchen-Vluyn: Neukirchener Verlag, 2009), 271–320.

1. Josephus, *J.W.* 1.204; *Ant.* 14.159 (cf. 14.167–74). On this Ezekias, who potentially had roots in Jewish nobility, and his role in the Galilean revolt against Herod, see Martin Hengel, *The Zealots: Investigations into the Jewish Freedom Movement in the Period from Herod I until 70 A.D.* (trans. David Smith; Edinburgh: T&T Clark, 1989), 313–17. See also Uriel Rappaport, "How Anti-Roman was the Galilee?" in *The Galilee in Late Antiquity* (ed. Lee I. Levine; New York: Jewish Theological Seminary of America, 1992), 95–101. Against reading the term *Galileans* as insurrectionists, see esp. Louis H. Feldman, "The Term 'Galileans' in Josephus," *JQR* 72 (1981–82): 50–52; Seán Freyne, "The Galileans in the Light of Josephus' *Life*," *NTS* 26 (1980): 397–413 (reprinted in Freyne, *Galilee and Gospel: Collected Essays* [WUNT 125; Tübingen: Mohr Siebeck, 2000], 27–44); Freyne, "Behind the Names: Galileans, Samaritans, *Iudaioi*," in *Galilee through the Centuries: Confluence of Cultures* (ed. Eric M. Meyers; Duke Judaic Studies Series 1; Winona Lake, Ind.: Eisenbrauns, 1999), 39–55 (reprinted in Freyne, *Galilee and Gospel*, 113–31); Folker Siegert, Heinz Schreckenberg, and Manuel Vogel, eds., *Flavius Josephus, Aus meinem Leben* (Vita): *Kritische Ausgabe, Übersetzung und Kommentar* (Tübingen: Mohr Siebeck, 2001), 164–65, Appendix

reception of Jesus the Galilean from his ministry in the first century to the present. Probably no other element of Jesus' biography is used more extensively to explain his message, his demeanor, his impact, and his "success." There is an impressive list of books and articles that make direct or indirect reference to Jesus' Galilean origins even in their titles,[2] and there is hardly a book on Jesus that does not discuss Galilee at length. The present "Third Quest for the Historical Jesus" is to no small extent Galilee research: whoever wants to say something about the earthly Jesus does so with reference to Galilee. Accordingly, Galilee has become one of the most important keys for the understanding of Jesus of Nazareth in modern Jesus research, or as the late doyen of Galilee research Seán Freyne (1935–2013) remarked in one of his last comments on the topic: "More than once I have been tempted to make the fairly obvious comment that the search for the historical Galilee is about to replace the quest for the historical Jesus."[3]

---

4; for an overview, see Mark Rapinchuk, "The Galilee and Jesus in Recent Research," *Currents in Biblical Research* 2 (2004): 197–222, esp. 208–10.

2. This is only a phenomenon of the last few decades, however. If one looks through the bibliography of Albert Schweitzer's *Geschichte der Leben-Jesu-Forschung* (2nd ed.; Tübingen: Mohr Siebeck, 1913; Eng. trans.: *The Quest of the Historical Jesus: First Complete Edition* [ed. John Bowden; London: SCM, 2000]), one will find a number of works that use Nazareth in their title, but as far as I can see there is not one that explicitly refers to Galilee in the title (the only exception is the subtitle in Albert Dulk, *Der Irrgang des Lebens Jesu*, vol. 1, *Die historischen Wurzeln und die galiläische Blüte* [1884]; see Schweitzer, *Geschichte*, 357 n. 2; *Quest*, 519 n. 28). Galilee is also largely irrelevant in the text itself, with the exception of the presentation of Ernest Renan's contribution (see Schweitzer, *Geschichte*; 181; *Quest*, 159; see also the long n. 1 on Mark 14:28 and 16:7 in *Geschichte*, 433–34; *Quest*, 525–26 n. 26). The same result emerges if one looks through Wolfgang Fenske, *Wie Jesus zum "Arier" wurde: Auswirkungen der Entjudaisierung Christi im 19. und zu Beginn des 20. Jahrhunderts* (Darmstadt: Wissenschaftliche Buchgesellschaft, 2005), 265–88. Apparently, Walter Bauer (1877–1960) was the first who explicitly called Jesus a "Galilean" in the title of his work: "Jesus der Galiläer," in *Festgabe für Adolf Jülicher zum 70. Geburtstag, 26 Januar 1927* (Tübingen: Mohr Siebeck, 1927), 16–27; now in Bauer, *Aufsätze und kleine Schriften* (ed. Georg Strecker; Tübingen: Mohr Siebeck, 1967), 91–108. Strecker writes in his introduction that this essay "represents the much noticed attempt to accentuate the syncretistic element of Jesus' Jewish context before the backdrop of the political and religious situation of Galilee" (p. v). Bauer was followed by Ernst Lohmeyer's study, *Galiläa und Jerusalem* (FRLANT n.s. 34; Göttingen: Vandenhoeck & Ruprecht, 1936), and Walter Grundmann's notorious *Jesus der Galiläer und das Judentum* in 1940 (Leipzig: G. Wigand; see n. 16 below). In the same year Rudolf Meyer published the much more objective *Der Prophet aus Galiläa: Studie zum Jesusbild der ersten drei Evangelien* (Leipzig: Lukenbein, 1940; repr., Darmstadt: Wissenschaftliche Buchgesellschaft, 1970). But it was not before Gerd Theissen's best-seller, *Der Schatten des Galiläers: Historische Jesusforschung in erzählender Form* (Munich: Kaiser, 1986; numerous translations and reprints; Eng. trans.: *The Shadow of the Galilean: The Quest of the Historical Jesus in Narrative Form* [trans. John Bowden; London: SCM, 1987]) that a greater public turned its attention to Galilee, and it is since then that the number of "Galilean" Jesus books has increased. A recent German example is Jens Schröter, *Jesus von Nazareth: Jude aus Galiläa — Retter der Welt* (Biblische Gestalten 15; Leipzig: Evangelische Verlagsanstalt, 2006).

3. Seán Freyne, "Galilean Studies: Old Issues and New Questions," in *Religion, Ethnicity, and Identity in Ancient Galilee: A Region in Transition* (ed. Jürgen Zangenberg, Harold W. Attridge, and Dale B. Martin; WUNT 210; Tübingen: Mohr Siebeck, 2007), 13–29, at 13. This excellent volume appeared after the original chapter was submitted, and for the revision of this article I have added only a few remarks. In the last stages of the preparation of this volume came the sad news of Seán Freyne's death on August 5, 2013. He will be sorely missed. On Galilee and Jesus in recent research, see further Halvor Moxnes, "The Construction of Galilee as a Place for the Historical

This is not entirely new, however. The history of Jesus research shows that from time to time and in certain contexts the emphasis on Jesus' Galilean origins has played an important role.[4] Upon closer examination it can be seen that reference to Galilee nearly always serves either the inner-Jewish *qualification* of Jesus or his *distancing* from his Jewish context, whereby the transition from one position to the other is often rather fluid. The first of these phenomena is already encountered in the New Testament[5] and it appears again in the nineteenth century, especially in the beginnings of modern Jewish study of Jesus.[6] Here Jesus, as a Galilean, is neither a Jerusalemite nor a Judean, but rather is placed on the fringe of the religious and social Jewish centers (where "Jewish" indirectly stands for "Judean"). Heinrich Graetz, in his turn-of-the-century work, maintained that, since Jesus was a Galilean, it is "impossible that his knowledge of the law could match the [Jerusalem] standard," which then explains his conflicts with the Pharisees, being less about his messianic claims than about his ignorance of (and contempt for) *halakhah*. Nevertheless, Jesus' relative "success" among his Jewish contemporaries had to be explained, and the solution offered was that his "intensely sympathetic character" made up for his "deficiency in knowledge." With his enthusiastic and charismatic manner of preaching, he was able to impress the equally ill-educated, but all-the-more-spirited Galilean country folk and later also the gentiles, who were offered his message in Paul's altered form intended for pagans. He made little impression, however, on the real ("true") Judaism as taught by Hillel and Shammai.[7]

---

Jesus," *BTB* 31 (2001): 26–37, 64–77; see also Moxnes, *Putting Jesus in His Place: A Radical Vision of Household and Kingdom* (Louisville: Westminster John Knox, 2003), 19–20, 126–38, 142–57; Rapinchuk, "Galilee and Jesus"; Ben Witherington III, *The Jesus Quest: The Third Search for the Jew of Nazareth* (2nd ed.; Downers Grove: InterVarsity, 1997), 14–41. A good overview of recent Galilee research can be found in Seán Freyne, "Introduction: Galilean Studies: Problems and Prospects," in Freyne, *Galilee and Gospel*, 1–26, esp. 20–25 on "Galilee and the Jesus Movement"; and now also in Freyne, "Jesus of Galilee: Implications and Possibilities," *EC* 1 (2010): 372–405.

4. The following is a summary of a longer study; see Roland Deines, "Jesus der Galiläer: Traditionsgeschichte und Genese eines anti-semitischen Konstrukts bei Walter Grundmann," in *Walter Grundmann: Ein Neutestamentler im Dritten Reich* (ed. Roland Deines, Volker Leppin, and Karl-Wilhelm Niebuhr; Arbeiten zur Kirchen- und Theologiegeschichte 21; Leipzig: Evangelische Verlagsanstalt, 2007), 43–131; see also Volker Lubinetzki, *Von der Knechtsgestalt des Neuen Testaments: Beobachtungen zu seiner Verwendung und Auslegung in Deutschland vor dem sowie im Kontext des "Dritten Reiches,"* (Münster: Lit, 2000), 282–93 ("Jesus der Galiläer, der Nichtjude, der Arier"); Moxnes, "Construction," 27–36.

5. Mark 14:70 par. Matt. 26:69; Luke 23:6; Matt. 26:73 (and also *b. Erub.* 53b; *b. Meg.* 24b); Acts 2:7 (cf. 4:13); John 7:48–52; cf. Seán Freyne, *Galilee, Jesus, and the Gospels: Literary Approaches and Historical Investigations* (Philadelphia: Fortress Press, 1988), 1.

6. Cf. Justin Martyr, *Dialogue with Trypho* 108. Accordingly, even during Justin's time, people warned about the "godless and lawless cult," which "had been started by Jesus, a certain Galilean deceiver" (αἵρεσίς τις ἄθενος καὶ ἐγήγερται ἀπὸ Ἰησοῦ τινος Γαλιλαίου πλάνου).

7. Heinrich Graetz, *Geschichte der Juden von den ältesten Zeiten bis auf die Gegenwart: Aus den Quellen neu bearbeitet*, vol. 3, *Geschichte der Juden von dem Tode Juda Makkabi's bis zum Untergang des jüdischen Staates* (ed. and rev. Marcus Brann; 5th ed.; 2 vols.; Leipzig: Leiner, 1905–6; repr., Berlin: Arani, 1996), 1:276–82. On Paul, see ibid., 2:408–25; the quotations are from 1:282. The pertinent passages in the English translation (based on an

Graetz (1817–1891), who was one of the first representatives of the academic study of Judaism[8] that also studied Jesus, represents fairly well the main thrust of the Jewish contributions to Jesus research in the nineteenth century and beyond, which was adopted in Christian scholarship as well.[9] As a Galilean, Jesus belonged to an uneducated, half-pagan fringe form of Judaism that was guided more by feeling (and therefore also by sentimentality and rash, volatile temperament) than intellect. It was this milieu in which Jesus grew up, and here (and only here!) was he successful, where people were foolish enough to follow him and to consider him to be special.[10] For Jerusalemites and Judeans, however, "humanity's salvation came from Zion and Jerusalem, it had to come from Judean blood."[11] With this sentence from Armand (Aaron) Kaminka (1866–1950) the academic study of Judaism reached its zenith in terms of distancing Jesus from Judaism: as a Galilean, Jesus belonged to a "mixed race," which had the status of a foreign nation to Judea. And with this, although hidden behind a few circumlocutions, on account of his Galilean origins some scholars repudiated the claim that Jesus belonged among the Jewish people.[12]

About half a century later, this topic was resumed by some New Testament scholars,[13] who took it as their task to formulate a "*völkische*," or "German" theology. Their ideologically

---

earlier edition), *History of the Jews: From the Earliest Times to the Present Day*, vol. 2, *From the Reign of Hyrcanus (135 B.C.E.) to the Completion of the Babylonian Talmud (500 C. E.)* (Philadelphia: Jewish Publication Society of America, 1893), can be found on pp. 146–65 (on Paul, see ibid., 219–32). Here the passage in full relates: "The measure of his [= Jesus'] mental culture can only be surmised from that existing in his native province. Galilee, at a distance from the capital and the Temple, was far behind Judaea in mental attainments and knowledge of the Law. The lively interchange of religious thought, and the discussions upon the Law, which made its writings and teachings the common property of all who sought the Temple, were naturally wanting in Galilee." In the preface to the English translation, which appeared in five volumes only, compared to the eleven of the original, Graetz describes it as "a condensed reproduction of the entire eleven volumes" (vol. 1, *From the Earliest Period to the Death of Simon the Maccabee [135 B.C.E.]*; Philadelphia: Jewish Publication Society of America, 1891), vi. Graetz and his contemporaries attributed the enthusiastic elements of Jesus' ministry, among which they numbered his exorcisms and prophetic demeanor, to "Essene" influences. This was motivated by the desire to link Jesus to the charismatic-enthusiastic expressions of contemporary Judaism and to isolate him from the "ideal" Judean guise. Whether "Galilean" *and* "Essene" as simultaneous characterizations were actually historically possible or rather were mutually exclusive was not made a topic of inquiry. One has perhaps to imagine here a two-step process of influence: first Jesus' childhood and youth in Galilee, then the discipleship to John the Baptist, who imparted these "Essene" ideas to Jesus. In this way Jesus was, as it were, influenced by two nonrepresentative fringe forms of Judaism.

8. That is, *Wissenschaft des Judentums*.

9. See Joseph Klausner, *Jesus of Nazareth: His Life, Times, and Teachings* (New York: Macmillan, 1925), 167–68, 171–73.

10. See Graetz, *History*, 2:152.

11. Armand (Aaron) Kaminka, *Studien zur Geschichte Galiläas* (Berlin: Engel, 1889), 59. In contrast, Samuel Klein notes that "Galilee . . . was never a foreign country to those who lived in Judea" (*Galiläa von der Makkabäerzeit bis 67* [Palästina-Studien 4; Vienna: Menorah, 1928], 18).

12. See Klausner, *Jesus of Nazareth*, 100, 233 (Klausner disagrees on the gentile nature of Galilee, especially with Kaminka; see 165 n. 89). For a detailed discussion, see Deines, "Jesus der Galiläer," 58–71.

13. Unmentioned here is the long list of more or less intelligent philosophers, writers, "prophets," and anti-Semites who sought to distance Jesus from Judaism on account of his Galilean origins. But it needs to be pointed out here that the judgment of the large majority of theologians and representatives of the *Wissenschaft des Judentums*

driven and firmer conclusions resulted in, first, the claim that Jesus most likely had non-Jewish origins and, second, the founding of the Institute for the Study of the Jewish Influence on German Church Life,[14] which had the task of making the German church "judenfrei" (that is, free of Jews).[15] Probably the most influential book among the publications of this institute was Walter Grundmann's *Jesus der Galiläer und das Judentum* (Jesus the Galilean and Judaism).[16]

Given this background, an inquiry into the function of "Galilee" as Jesus' place of origin in more recent Jesus research, in which critical inquests have repeatedly been reminded of Grundmann, is warranted.[17] Related to this focus on Jesus' Galilean context is the parallel development that placed special emphasis on a Galilean origin of the sayings source Q,[18]

---

was much more level-headed than that of their more journalistic competitors who were, to some extent, rather successful with their, at times, ludicrous theories. In this respect, little seems to have changed. Wolfgang Fenske ("*Arier*") offers an initial overview of these kinds of aberrations and delusions. Unfortunately, the book lacks a subject index, so it is difficult to find the many passages on Galilee; see, for example, 15, 17, 21, 40, 59–60, 69–70. Yet Fenske and many others miss the importance of the Galilee argumentation in Jewish studies of Jesus in distancing Jesus from the Jewish mainstream of his time.

14. Institut zur Erforschung des jüdischen Einflusses auf das deutsche kirchliche Leben.

15. On the history of this institute, which was based in Eisenach, see Peter von der Osten-Sacken, ed., *Das missbrauchte Evangelium: Studien zu Theologie und Praxis der Thüringer Deutschen Christen* (Studien zu Kirche und Israel 20; Berlin: Institut Kirche und Judentum, 2002); see also Otto Merk, "'Viele waren Neutestamentler': Zur Lage neutestamentlicher Wissenschaft 1933–1945 und ihrem zeitlichen Umfeld," *TLZ* 130 (2005): 106–18; Susannah Heschel, *The Aryan Jesus: Christian Theologians and the Bible in Nazi Germany* (Princeton: Princeton University Press, 2008); and also the essay collection on Walter Grundmann mentioned in n. 5 (with detailed literature).

16. The monograph appeared as part of the *Veröffentlichung des Institut zur Erforschung des jüdischen Einflusses auf das deutsche kirchliche Leben* (Leipzig: G. Wigand, 1940). A second revised edition was printed by the same publisher in 1941, bringing the total to five thousand copies.

17. William E. Arnal, *The Symbolic Jesus: Historical Scholarship, Judaism and the Construction of Contemporary Identity* (London: Equinox, 2005), 16–29; Seán Freyne, "Galilean Questions to Crossan's Mediterranean Jesus," in *Whose Historical Jesus?* (ed. William E. Arnal and Michel Desjardins; Studies in Christianity and Judaism 7; Waterloo, Ont.: Wilfrid Laurier University Press, 1997), 63–91, at 91 (reprinted in *Galilee and Gospel*, 208–29; the last page of the original essay that refers to Grundmann is missing in the reprint); Peter M. Head, "The Nazi Quest for an Aryan Jesus," *JSHJ* 2 (2004): 55–89, esp. 60–61; John Kloppenborg Verbin, *Excavating Q: The History and Setting of the Sayings Gospel* (Minneapolis: Fortress Press, 2000), 434–35; Moxnes, "Construction," 33–34, 68; Birger A. Pearson, "The Gospel according to the Jesus Seminar," *Religion* 25 (1995): 317–38, at 338.

18. Based on Luke 10:13-15 par. Matt. 11:20-24 it is often assumed that Q, or its postulated earliest stratum, has its origins in Galilee (see the list in Paul Hoffmann and Christoph Heil, eds., *Die Spruchquelle Q* [Darmstadt: Wissenschaftliche Buchgesellschaft, 2002], 22 n. 45; Birger A. Pearson, "A Q Community in Galilee?" *NTS* 50 [2004]: 475–94, esp. 489–90; Nicholas H. Taylor, "Q and Galilee?" *Neot* 37 [2003]: 283–311, esp. 284; see also William E. Arnal, *Jesus and the Village Scribes: Galilean Conflicts and the Setting of Q* [Minneapolis: Fortress Press, 2001], 159–64). However, these woes over the two Galilean cities only demonstrate a certain geographic focus of Jesus' ministry. This can rightly be contrasted with Luke 13:34-35 par. Matt. 23:37-39 (cf. Mark 11:9-10) and argued that Q could have its origins in Jerusalem. See Hoffmann and Heil, *Spruchquelle Q*, 22 n. 46; Pearson, "Q Community," 492–93; Marco Frenschkowski, "Galiläa oder Jerusalem? Die topographischen und politischen Hintergründe der Logienquelle," in *The Sayings Source Q and the Historical Jesus* (ed. Andreas Lindemann; BETL 158; Leuven: Peeters, 2001), 535–59; see also Frenschkowski, "Welche biographischen Kenntnisse von Jesus setzt

which—despite all the unanswered questions of Q studies[19]—is doubtless one of the most important sources when it comes to reconstructing the life of the historical Jesus. The aim of the following deliberations is surely not to question the overall importance and usefulness of Galilee studies for historical Jesus research, but only to point out the related pitfalls and perhaps also their limitations with regard to understanding Jesus.

## Recent Galilee Research as the Basis for the Quest of the Historical Jesus

The starting point of recent Galilee research, which was spearheaded by the late Seán Freyne's first monograph on the history of Galilee,[20] is diametrically opposed to the process of alienation of Jesus from Judaism mentioned above. Instead it can be understood as a catalyst for the present ("third") quest for the historical Jesus. Such Galilee research, kick-started by Freyne in the literary realm and archaeologically by Eric Meyers, played a significant role by placing the *Jew* Jesus from Galilee in the spotlight. Whereas the hallmark of the "second" phase of Jesus research (or the "New Quest"), which is generally connected to Ernst Käsemann and Günther

---

die Logienquelle voraus? Beobachtungen zur Gattung von Q im Kontext antiker Spruchsammlungen," in *From Quest to Q: Festschrift James M. Robinson* (ed. Jón Ma. Asgeirsson, Kristin De Troyer, and Marvin W. Meyer; BETL 146; Leuven: Peeters, 2000), 3–42. The emphasis on the Galilean origins of Q is—disregarding some exceptions—a relatively new phenomenon. For the most part, it was thought that Q originated in Palestine (or southern Syria), although without any specifics. John S. Kloppenborg did not discuss the origin or the relationship to Galilee in his first monograph on Q in 1987 at all (*The Formation of Q: Trajectories in Ancient Wisdom Collections* [Studies in Antiquity and Christianity; Philadelphia: Fortress Press, 1987]). In *Excavating Q*, published in 2000, the Galilean origins, however, have become foundational for his influential understanding of Q; see pp. 170–75, 214–61 ("Reading Q in the Galilee"). Kloppenborg especially relies here on Jonathan L. Reed, "The Social Map of Q," in *Conflict and Invention: Literary, Rhetorical, and Social Studies on the Sayings Gospel Q* (ed. John S. Kloppenborg; Philadelphia: Fortress Press, 1995), 17–36, reworked in Reed, *Archaeology and the Galilean Jesus: A Re-examination of the Evidence* (Harrisburg, Pa.: Trinity Press International, 2000), 170–96.

    19. For an overview of the current state of research, see Maurice Casey, *An Aramaic Approach to Q: Sources for the Gospels of Matthew and Luke* (SNTSMS 122; Cambridge: Cambridge University Press, 2002), 1–50; and Peter M. Head and P. J. Williams, "Q Review," *TynBul* 34 (2003): 119–44.

    20. Seán Freyne, *Galilee from Alexander the Great to Hadrian, 323 B.C.E. to 135 C.E.: A Study of Second Temple Judaism* (University of Notre Dame Center for the Study of Judaism and Christianity in Antiquity 5; Wilmington, Del.: Michael Glazier; Notre Dame, Ind.: University of Notre Dame Press, 1980; repr., Edinburgh: T&T Clark, 1998). Freyne stayed true to this subject in the following works (in selection): *Galilee, Jesus, and the Gospels*; *Galilee and Gospel*; *Jesus, a Jewish Galilean: A New Reading of the Jesus-Story* (London: T&T Clark, 2004), and also in his presidential address during the Studiorum Novi Testamenti Societas in 2006 in Aberdeen: "Galilee as Laboratory: Experiments for New Testament Historians and Theologians," *NTS* 53 (2007): 147–64. See also his essay "Die soziale Welt Galiläas aus der Sicht des Josephus," in *Jesus und die Archäologie Galiläas* (ed. Carsten Claussen and Jörg Frey; Biblisch-theologische Studien 87; Neukirchen-Vluyn: Neukirchener Verlag, 2008).

Bornkamm,[21] was the criterion of dissimilarity, according to which authentic Jesus material was only that which was different from contemporary Judaism (and from the nascent church), the representatives of the "Third Quest," in almost opposite fashion, favor the plausibility and similarity criterion.[22] This means that those things that associated Jesus with contemporary Judaism were now deemed most likely to be authentic. But here it had to be asked: With what form, variant, or stream of Judaism? This question became particularly important because, parallel to the "Third Quest," the situation of the study of Second Temple period Judaism had also changed, and dramatically at that, when compared to the state of research during the "Second Quest" (also called the "New Quest). At that time Jesus was seen to be facing a mostly Pharisaic-rabbinic–influenced "nomistic" Judaism,[23] whereas now plurality of form and content is emphasized, together with geographic diversity, not only between the land of Israel and the Diaspora but also within the Jewish motherland itself. In terms of geography, Galilean Judaism is now differentiated from Judean and Samaritan Judaism, and in addition to these regional differences (which are further defined internally, for example, with Upper and Lower Galilee as culturally different regions), there are also sociological (for example, the difference between urban and rural, and foreign dominated and indigenous populations) and cultural variations (for example, level of hellenization, education, religious links). This change in Jewish studies forces one to define carefully any placement of Jesus on this by now rather intricate map of the Jewish world.[24] In this context, Jesus' Galilean origin seems to provide a solid point of contact for the necessary precise classification. The statement "Jesus was a Galilean who preached and healed" belongs, according to E. P. Sanders, to the eight facts and activities known about Jesus that can claim the highest level of historical authenticity.[25] Even for the members of the Jesus

---

21. The time between the end of the "First Quest" and the start of the "New Quest" is strongly influenced by Rudolf Bultmann's existentialist interpretation, which had no interest in the historical Jesus. For this reason, this time is often described as the "no quest" phase. But Bultmann's influence also shaped the "New Quest" of his students, so that at times the whole of the "Second" or "New Quest" is improperly used as a label for the whole phase of Jesus research influenced by Bultmann. The terminology was shaped by James M. Robinson, *A New Quest for the Historical Jesus* (SBT 25; Naperville, Ill.: Allenson, 1959), who called attention to this new trend in Jesus research in the circle of Bultmann's students. For a short overview, see James Carleton Paget, "Quests for Historical Jesus," in *The Cambridge Companion to Jesus* (ed. Markus Bockmuehl; Cambridge: Cambridge University Press, 2001), 138–55.

22. See James D. G. Dunn, *Jesus Remembered* (Christianity in the Making 1; Grand Rapids: Eerdmans, 2003), 73–92; Gerd Theissen and Dagmar Winter, *The Quest for the Plausible Jesus: Question of Criteria* (trans. M. Eugene Boring; Louisville: Westminster John Knox, 2002).

23. See E. P. Sanders, *Paul and Palestinian Judaism: A Comparison of Patterns of Religion* (Philadelphia: Fortress Press, 1977).

24. See Kloppenborg Verbin, *Excavating Q*, 437: It is not enough to say that Jesus was a Jew, but one needs to further define "what kind of Judaism Jesus (or Q) represents," similarly also p. 434. On this task, see also Dunn, *Jesus Remembered*, 255–311.

25. E. P. Sanders, *Jesus and Judaism* (Philadelphia: Fortress Press, 1985), 11. Galilee does not, however, play a special role in this book (it is not even mentioned in the index) since, for Sanders, "first-century Judaism," that is, "Palestinian Judaism" constitutes the primary context for understanding (p. 17). Only in later studies does

Seminar, better known for their generous verdicts against the historicity of most of what the canonical Gospels reveal about Jesus' words and deeds, it belongs to our certain knowledge about Jesus that he was "an itinerant teacher in Galilee," and also, somewhat surprisingly, that he preached in the synagogues of Galilee.[26]

But what is known about Galilee in the time of Jesus? One look at the prevailing literature shows that behind this simple question is not just one but a whole plethora of questions: What do we know about the history of settlement and population of Galilee? Was there a specific Galilean Judaism? Or even several? How far is the piety in the villages of Galilee different from that of the two cities Sepphoris and Tiberias? What differences are there between Jewish life in Upper and Lower Galilee? What is Galilee's relationship to Judea, and to the temple? Were there Pharisees in Galilee? What status did the priests have there? How did the administration of the villages work?[27] And finally—how does Jesus fit into this? What molded and formed him as a Galilean? The range of answers given to these questions is vast and can only be illustrated here with a few representative examples.

The Jewish historian Geza Vermes was one of the first to respond to the "Second Quest" with a book entitled *Jesus the Jew*. In it he describes Jesus as "very much at home" in the company of the Hasidim, since "the unsophisticated religious ambiance of Galilee was apt to produce holy men of the Hasidic type."[28] Some twenty years later, John Dominic Crossan came

he explicitly refer to the Galilee debate. See Sanders, "Jesus' Galilee," in *Fair Play: Diversity and Conflicts in Early Christianity. Essays in Honour of Heikke Räisänen* (ed. Ismo Dunderberg, Christopher M. Tuckett, and Kari Syreeni; NovTSup 103; Leiden: Brill, 2002), 3–42; Sanders, "Jesus in Galilee," in *Jesus: A Colloquium in the Holy Land with James D. G. Dunn, Daniel J. Harrington, Elizabeth A. Johnson, John P. Meier, and E. P. Sanders* (ed. Doris Donnelly; New York: Continuum, 2001), 5–26. See also Moxnes, "Construction," 34–36. On Galilee as a "certain" aspect of Jesus' biography, see Craig A. Evans, "Authenticating the Activities of Jesus," in *Authenticating the Activities of Jesus* (ed. Bruce Chilton and Craig A. Evans; NTTS 28.2; Leiden: Brill, 1999; repr., 2002), 3–29, esp. 3–4, 9–10, 26–27; Peter Richardson, *Building Jewish in the Roman East* (Waco, Tex.: Baylor University Press, 2004), 96–99.

26. Robert W. Funk and the Jesus Seminar, eds., *The Acts of Jesus: What Did Jesus Really Do? The Search for Authentic Deeds of Jesus* (San Francisco: HarperSanFrancisco, 1998), 566. Against the argument that Jesus preached in Galilean synagogues, see esp. Richard A. Horsley, *Archaeology, History, and Society in Galilee: The Social Context of Jesus and the Rabbis* (Valley Forge, Pa.: Trinity Press International, 1996), 131–53. In his view, the New Testament refers to "assemblies of the local communities" and not to respective buildings. Against this skeptical minimalist understanding, see, among others, Sanders, "Jesus in Galilee," 18; James F. Strange, "Archaeology and Ancient Synagogues up to About 200 C.E.," in *The Ancient Synagogue from Its Origins until 200 C.E.* (ed. Birger Olsson and Magnus Zetterholm; ConBNT 39; Stockholm: Almqvist & Wiksell, 2003), 37–62; and further Lee I. Levine, "The First Century Synagogue: Critical Reassessments and Assessments of the Critical," in *Religion and Society in Roman Palestine: Old Questions, New Approaches* (ed. Douglas R. Edwards; New York: Routledge, 2004), 70–102.

27. The best and most comprehensive treatments of these issues are, in my opinion, the two books by Mark A. Chancey, which also offer some excellent insights into the hidden agendas within the history of Galilee research: *The Myth of a Gentile Galilee* (SNTSMS 118; Cambridge: Cambridge University Press, 2002); and *Greco-Roman Culture and the Galilee of Jesus* (SNTSMS 134; Cambridge: Cambridge University Press, 2005). See also Chancey, "The Epigraphic Habit of Hellenistic and Roman Galilee," in Zangenberg et al., *Religion, Ethnicity, and Identity in Ancient Galilee*, 83–99.

28. Geza Vermes, *Jesus the Jew: A Historian's Reading of the Gospels* (London: Collins, 1973), 79–80.

up with the claim that Jesus' Galilean origins allow us to see him as "a peasant Jewish cynic," since his "village was close enough to a Greco-Roman city like Sepphoris." For Jesus, "sight and knowledge of Cynicism are neither inexplicable nor unlikely" even though he avoided the marketplaces of the cities (the primary focus of the Greco-Roman Cynics) and only sought out "the farms and villages of Lower Galilee" in order to preach his message of the kingdom as "the combination of free healing and common eating."[29]

Vermes and Crossan, who in some sense represent the contradictory positions discussed above, nevertheless agree on this one point: they both presume a certain image of Galilee—or reconstruct such—in which they place Jesus and from which they understand his activities. Vermes, in addition to this, emphasizes that the "small group of devotees" who followed Jesus on his journeys consisted of "simple Galilean folk." It was "among the Galilean crowd [that] Jesus was a great success," whereas his popularity in Judea and Jerusalem "did not match that which he enjoyed in his own country" (pp. 30–31). For Vermes, due to its history Galilee represents a "territory *sui generis*" (p. 43) that was integrated into the Hasmonean realm only in the first century BCE and thus had a population with "an overwhelming Jewishness" (p. 44). Vermes only rarely discusses the makeup of this population, but he seemingly assumes that it was predominantly Jewish settlers who, perhaps together with the evacuees mentioned in 1 Maccabees 5:14–23, recolonized Galilee in the first century BCE. He also mentions in this context the violent pressure directed against non-Jewish inhabitants of Galilee and their forced circumcision (Josephus, *Ant.* 12.257–58, 318–19), without clarifying his position on how these actions might have affected people. Although, according to this reconstruction of the historical process, Galilee has to be considered a region settled by Judeans from the first century BCE onwards,[30] they very quickly developed a special "Galilean self-awareness" (p. 45). This was represented particularly (but not solely) by the "rebels," which made Galilee, according to Vermes, into "the most troublesome of all Jewish districts" (p. 46) from the middle of the first century BCE. With passages from Josephus and rabbinic literature (see pp. 52–57), he subsequently demonstrates the contentious and aggressive character of this special Galilean nationalism in the north.[31]

---

29. John Dominic Crossan, *The Historical Jesus: The Life of a Mediterranean Jewish Peasant* (San Francisco: Harper, 1991), 421–22. Despite all the differences, Vermes's influence on Crossan is not insignificant; see ibid, 489, index, s.v. Vermes.

30. Pivotal here is the study by Zvi Gal, *Lower Galilee During the Iron Age* (trans. Marcia Reines Josephy; American Schools of Oriental Research Dissertation Series 8; Winona Lake, Ind.: Eisenbrauns, 1992); see also Mordechai Aviam, "The Hasmonean Dynasty's Activities in the Galilee," in Aviam, *Jews, Pagans, and Christians in the Galilee: 25 Years of Archaeological Excavations and Surveys, Hellenistic to Byzantine Periods* (Land of Galilee 1; Rochester, N.Y.: University of Rochester Press, 2004), 41–50 (Hebrew, 1995). On this Judean settlement during the Hasmonean period see Reed, *Archaeology and the Galilean Jesus*, 28–43 (which also compels a re-evaluation of the compulsory circumcision mentioned in Josephus *Ant.* 13.318–19, which is based on a second- or even third-hand record only); Chancey, *Greco-Roman Culture*, 26–42; Pearson, "Q Community," 491.

31. Vermes, *Jesus the Jew*, 30–46.

The suggested genesis of the particular profile of Jewish Galilee, however, does not fully support the distinctive character of Galilee in comparison to Judea; at least, it does not explain its development. It would seem that it is rather the "preconception" of a special culture in Galilee that affects this depiction, motivated not least by the need for this special culture to explain Jesus' activities. Jesus and the Gospels have to be situated among "the specifically Galilean type," because only among such people could Jesus be understood. Jesus, as a "*campagnard*," felt at home with "the simple people of rural Galilee," and he also shared their "Galilean chauvinism" against non-Jews. But in Jerusalem Jesus "must have felt quite alien" (p. 48), and, in turn, as a "Galilean" he would have been seen as a "political suspect" by the establishment of the capital city: "Moreover, if present-day estimates of Jewish historians concerning Galilean lack of education and unorthodoxy are accepted, his same Galilean descent made him a religious suspect also" (p. 57).[32]

The supposed absence of the Pharisees, or Pharisaic influence, in Galilee serves as an explanation for the "lack of education" there. In later publications Vermes appeals to the famous *dictum* of Yoḥanan ben Zakkai, who is said to have lived eighteen years in Arav, close to Sepphoris: "O Galilee, Galilee, you hate the Torah! Your end will be by 'oppressors'!"[33] Pharisaic or (proto-)rabbinic influence in Galilee is regularly disputed by those who hold the assumption of a specific Galilean culture different from that of Judea, and this argument is used whenever such a difference is needed for the explanation of other issues such as, in our case, the specific form of Jesus' Jewishness as Galilean.[34] To summarize Vermes's notion of the

---

32. Vermes, *Jesus the Jew*, 48-57.

33. See *y. Šabb.* 16.8/3 (15d). On this passage as an argument against Pharisaic-(rabbinic) influence and presence in Galilee, see, among others, Klausner, *Jesus of Nazareth*, 173; Seán Freyne, "The Charismatic," in *Ideal Figures in Ancient Judaism: Profiles and Paradigms* (ed. John J. Collins and George W. E. Nickelsburg; Septuagint and Cognate Studies 12; Chico, Calif.: Scholars Press, 1980), 223–58 (under the title: "Ḥanina Ben Dosa: A Galilean Charismatic," also in Freyne, *Galilee and Gospel*, 132–59, at 153); in later publications Freyne modified his position, which had heavily relied on Vermes; see Freyne, *Galilee, Jesus, and the Gospels*, 202, 217; and n. 38 below. For critiques to such a reading of Yoḥanan's *dictum*, see Shmuel Safrai, "The Jewish Cultural Nature of Galilee in the First Century," in *The New Testament and Christian–Jewish Dialogue: Studies in Honor of David Flusser* (ed. Malcolm F. Lowe; *Immanuel* 24/25; Jerusalem: Ecumenical Theological Research Fraternity in Israel, 1990), 147–86; on this see already Klein, *Galiläa*, 21; Eric M. Meyers, "The Cultural Setting of Galilee: The Case of Regionalism and Early Judaism," *ANRW* 2.19.1 (1979): 686–702, at 691, 698.

34. On the oft-debated problem of the Pharisees in Galilee, or the Pharisaic influence in Galilee, see Dunn, *Jesus Remembered*, 306–8; Freyne, *Galilee, Jesus, and the Gospels*, 202–10; Freyne, *Jesus, a Jewish Galilean*, 83; Horsley, *Archaeology, History, and Society*, 151–52; Horsley, "The Pharisees and Jesus in Galilee and Q," in *When Judaism and Christianity Began: Essays in Memory of Anthony J. Saldarini* (ed. Alan J. Avery-Peck, Daniel J. Harrington, and Jacob Neusner; 2 vols.; JSJSup 85; Leiden: Brill, 2004), 1:117–45 (for Horsley, the Pharisaic influence is a result of the Judean imperialism he presupposes); Dieter Lührmann, "Die Pharisäer und Schriftgelehrten im Markusevangelium," *ZNW* 78 (1987): 169–85; Burton L. Mack, *The Lost Gospel: The Book of Q and Christian Origins* (San Francisco: HarperSanFrancisco, 1993), 60; Robert L. Mowery, "Pharisees and Scribes, Galilee and Jerusalem," *ZNW* 80 (1989): 266–68 (adding to Lührmann); Rapinchuk, "Galilee and Jesus," 214–16; Anthony J. Saldarini, *Pharisees, Scribes and Sadducees in Palestinian Society: A Sociological Approach* (Edinburgh: T&T Clark, 1988; repr., Grand Rapids: Eerdmans, 2001, with a foreword by James C. VanderKam), 291–97.

Judean perspective on a Galilean in the first century: a Galilean would have been characterized as having a politically suspect background, a lack of education, the temperament of a farmer, and a deficiency in orthodoxy. And when such a person also behaved in the provocative way that Jesus did, then, for Vermes, it is at least comprehensible why he was surrendered to the Roman authorities.[35]

It is clear that Vermes's portrayal of Galilee, which was published in 1973, remained deeply rooted in the scientific tradition of the nineteenth century. Parallels to Renan, Graetz, Abraham Geiger, and others are not difficult to discern, the only difference being that in place of the "Essene" influence Vermes sets "charismatic Judaism" (see pp. 58–82). The argument itself remains similar, as he also combines charismatic pietism with Galilean emotionalism against Judean-rabbinic rationalism[36] and understands Jesus exclusively as a healer and an exorcist in the context of the former. This then lays the foundation for an all-too-simple dichotomy between Galilee and Judea. Yet Jesus also experienced rejection in Galilee, to the point that he was threatened with death (Mark 3:6; Luke 4:28–29),[37] and he encountered friendship and acceptance in Judea (Lazarus, Mary, Martha, Nicodemus, Joseph of Arimathea, Cleopas and the other Emmaus disciple, the family of John Mark—all people who appear to be Judean).

Crossan invokes Vermes extensively and explicitly for the depiction of his radically different Jesus, whom he places among the socially exploited peasant class struggling for survival.[38] For, like Vermes, he assumes that Jesus' subversive practice of magic (since it was free) and his offer of a temple-tax-free relation to God exerted such a competitive pressure on "the religious monopoly of the priests" that they tried to get rid of this business spoiler as quickly as possible. "The authorities are trapped in their own theology" (p. 324), he claims, and behind this stands, just as with Vermes, a fundamental difference between Jesus and Jerusalem, between the itinerant Galilean and the locally fixed temple service. According to Crossan, Jesus' relation to the temple and the tradition it stood for was at best ambivalent, but probably completely indifferent. As a Cynic, he stood outside of any such fixed institutions and their hierarchies.[39]

---

35. Vermes, *Jesus the Jew*, 34–36. On his view of Jesus' trial, see Vermes, *The Passion* (London: Penguin, 2005).

36. This is also true for the early portrait of Yoḥanan ben Zakkai by Jacob Neusner, in which the "spontaneous religion of Galilee, which looked for daily miracles, signs, and wonders" is put in contrast with the more sober and rational halakhic practice in Jerusalem; see *A Life of Rabban Yohanan ben Zakkai, Ca. 1–80 C.E.* (StPB 6; Leiden: Brill, 1962), 32; see also the 2nd rev. ed. under the title *A Life of Yohanan Ben Zakkai, Ca. 1–80 C.E.* (1970), 57 (on Yoḥanan in Galilee, see 47–58).

37. Vermes, in fact, takes note of this in another place; see *Jesus the Jew*, 33–34. For a similar schematic differentiation between Galilee and Jerusalem, see Willibald Bösen, *Galiläa als Lebensraum und Wirkungsfeld Jesus: Eine zeitgeschichtliche und theologische Untersuchung* (Biblische Sachbuch; Freiburg: Herder, 1985), 262–74. In some sense, one could say that this division is a continuation of the antagonism between Paul and the Jerusalemite Judaizers postulated by Ferdinand Christian Baur, in which Galilee now takes the role of Paul's Hellenism with its associated "openness" with regard to the Torah and the non-Jewish world.

38. Crossan, *Historical Jesus*, 138–49. Yet, for Crossan, Galilee has no special significance; cf. Freyne, "Galilean Questions," 65–70 (= *Galilee and Gospel*, 213–16).

39. Crossan, *Historical Jesus*, 324–60, esp. 324, 355, 360.

Burton Mack goes even further in his book on Q, published in 1993, in that he rejects a constitutive connection between the historical Jesus and the traditional Jewish identity markers that have been observed since the Hasmonean period (the Torah, Jerusalem, and the temple). On the basis of John Kloppenborg's redaction history of Q, which assumes the existence of a first stratum consisting mainly of wisdom sayings upon which was only later superimposed a "biblical" layer (subduing the original sayings to a "Deuteronomistic understanding"), Mack reconstructed the historical Jesus and his first followers exclusively on the basis of this assumed oldest layer. His goal was nothing less than the restatement of the origins of Christianity:

> If the shift from wisdom to apocalyptic could be explained, it would have tremendous consequences for the quest of the historical Jesus and a revision of Christian origins. As for Jesus, it would mean that he had probably been more the sage, less the prophet. And as for Christian origins, it would mean that something other than an apocalyptic message and motivation may have impelled the new movement and defined its fundamental attraction.[40]

Mack's quest for "Christian origins" brings him to the social and cultural context of the original "people of Q" (p. 38), who were not yet "Christians" but representatives of a Galilean Jesus movement. On account of the discovery of this historical situation,[41] it is now not only necessary, according to Mack, to bid farewell to the traditional image of Jesus, which sees him as messiah or at least an inner-Jewish prophet or reformer, but also to the "image of Judaism in Palestine, based on the Christian gospel" (p. 49). Therefore, in order to substantiate the new understanding of the historical Jesus based on Q, it is also necessary to reconceptualize what we know about Galilee if we leave aside the "christianized" Gospels' portrait. To do this, Mack requires "some basic, up-to-date information about the social and cultural climate of first-century Galilee" (p. 49), which he then purports to lay out in the next chapter, "Galilee Before the War" (pp. 51–68).[42] His introductory sentence already makes clear that he is mostly interested in seeing Galilee as a world that is separate from Judea (and its form of Judaism): "In the world of the Christian imagination Galilee belonged to Palestine, the religion of Palestine

---

40. Mack, *Lost Gospel*, 37–38. On Mack's assumed development of Q, which also implies a geographic migration of Q from Galilee via North Palestine, South and North Syria to Asia Minor; see the diagram on p. 259. This is based on Kloppenborg, *Formation of Q*; cf. Kloppenborg Verbin, *Excavating Q*, 87–111.

41. See the defense of Mack's position by William Arnal, "A Manufactured Controversy: Why the 'Jewish Jesus' Is a Red Herring," in Arnal, *Symbolic Jesus*, 20–38, esp. 24–25. According to this apology, it is because of the inescapability of the historical facts, namely, the oldest Jesus tradition and thus what is most authentic in what we can know about Jesus, that we *cannot* relate him to "Israel's epic tradition" (cf., similarly, Kloppenborg Verbin, *Excavating Q*, 188–89, likewise defending Mack). By necessity this then leads Mack and Kloppenborg to devise a complete reappraisal of early Christianity and its pre-history.

42. However, in his selected bibliography (*Lost Gospel*, 263–67), he does not cite a single recent study on the history of Galilee and its archaeology, which, in the light of the announcement of "up-to-date information," is rather telling. On Mack's outdated image of Galilee, see Moxnes, "Construction," 68–69.

was Judaism, so everyone in Galilee must have been Jewish. Since this picture is wrong, and since Q can make no sense as long as it prevails, the reader needs to have a truer picture in mind" (p. 51).[43]

Mack follows this claim by repeating information that has been around at least since Walter Bauer's famous Galilee essay (see n. 3 above), and was also thoroughly maltreated by Grundmann: "a land of mixed peoples" (p. 53; cf. 56), crisscrossed by international highways (see p. 55), and in close proximity to various realms of diverse ethnic makeup. Galilee itself has no central core, no capital, it is "a no-man's-land reserved for initial skirmishers in larger undertakings. It was a kind of beachhead where the surge of political crosscurrents constantly kept the people on their toes" (p. 53). Therefore, "loyalty to the kings and their gods" is not among the Galilean virtues (ibid.). Since the time of Alexander the Great, Galilee was surrounded by Greek cities with all the characteristics of Hellenistic urban life, but "Samaritans and Galileans did not resist. They did not generate a revolution like that of the Maccabees in Judea" (p. 54). The resistance against foreign Hellenistic cultural influences was, according to Mack, limited to Judea (ibid.). Galilee was "annexed" by the Hasmonean kingdom around 100 BCE, but their rule was only exercised there from 100 to 63 BCE (p. 55). Pompeius took over, which meant for Galilee "another superimposition of military, political, economic, social, and cultural presence with which Galileans had to contend" (p. 55).[44]

In this context, Mack poses the question whether the Galileans can be described as a separate ethnic group, akin to "Jews (from Judea, the land of Judah, with its temple in Jerusalem), Idumeans, Samaritans, Phoenicians, and Syrians" (p. 56). He answers this in the negative on account of the history of Galilee with its many invasions, claiming that it rather has to be understood as the home of a multiethnic mix of peoples (ibid.). Mack further emphasizes the Hellenistic influence on Galilee, which for him is downplayed by many scholars "in the interest of buttressing the picture of Jesus appearing in the midst of a thoroughly Jewish culture" (p. 57).[45] He mentions Gadara ("just across the Jordan, a day's walk from Nazareth") and Scythopolis, with their educational and cultural infrastructure ("theaters, sporting arenas [*gymnasia*], and schools"), and also, of course, Sepphoris ("an hour's walk from Nazareth") as an example of a "thoroughly hellenized city" (p. 58).[46] All of this is not entirely wrong, though it is a rather one-sided portrayal. It turns out to be more problematic, however, when hellenization is used as the

---

43. Mack, *Lost Gospel*, 38–51.

44. Mack, *Lost Gospel*, 53–55.

45. Likewise Kloppenborg Verbin, *Excavating Q*, 437. This position is supported by J. Andrew Overman ("Recent Advances in the Archaeology of the Galilee in the Roman Period," *CurBS* 1 [1993]: 35–57), who interprets the archaeological data quite tendentiously in that "the presence and influence of so-called pagan culture is now widely recognized as a result of excavations in the Galilee" (p. 45). An adequate image of Jesus cannot be reached if "the cultural, religious and socioeconomic issues and development that were part of the larger Greek East" are not sufficiently consulted (p. 47). Thus, in his view, archaeology demonstrates the "cultural and religious plurality" in Galilee, which has the consequence that the "distinction between Jews, non-Jews or gentiles and so-called pagans" is not viable any longer(p. 49).

46. Mack, *Lost Gospel*, 56–58.

opposite of "Jewish culture," as is the case in Mack's work. By way of a long sequence of rhetorical questions addressing speculative social changes in the wake of the process of hellenization of the East, he seems to reveal, finally, what lies at the heart of his agenda:

> What if we let Galilee have its place in the Greco-Roman world? What if the people of Galilee were not isolated from the cultural mix that stimulated thought and produced social experimentation in response to the times? What if Galileans were fully aware of the cultural and intellectual forces surging through the Levant? What if we acknowledged that the compact and convoluted history of foreign conquests in Galilee had created disaffection for many Galileans, and a predisposition for social and cultural critique? . . . What if we thought that Galileans were capable of entertaining novel notions of social identity? What then? Why then we would be ready for the story of the people of Q.[47]

The Jesus movement that is discerned as standing at the beginning of the redaction history of Q turns out to be a society-critical avant-garde that seeks to find a new identity outside of *ethnos* and traditional (that is, Jewish) religiosity[48]—which ultimately sounds more reminiscent of elitist postmodern and post-Christian circles in California than of Galilee in the first century.

Related to this Q hypothesis is the position—which is both older and worthy of discussion—that the life of Jesus that burst the cultural norms of society and the radical discipleship ethos practiced by his followers, can be understood along the lines of itinerant Cynic philosophers and their critique of society.[49] More problematic, however, as many critics of the "Cynic

---

47. Mack, *Lost Gospel*, 68. Despite the rhetorical-suggestive weight of these "what-if" questions, the real scholarly results (at the end of the chapter) are rather thin. Most of them have to be clearly answered in the negative, since any references in the available sources that might give rise to an affirmative answer are wanting. But, in fact, they need not even be answered in the negative, since these questions are simply not conformable to the subject matter. On the assumed specific Galilean-Hellenistic ethos in opposition to a "specifically Jewish sectarian milieu," see also Mack, *A Myth of Innocence: Mark and Christian Origins* (Philadelphia: Fortress Press, 1988), 73. For a similar Q-utopia, see Arnal, *Jesus and the Village Scribes*, 193–202 ("The Social Project of the Q Tradents").

48. See Mack, *Lost Gospel*, 213–14: Behind the original Q movement stood the idea that "a mixed group of people could represent the best of the heritage of several ethnically exclusive cultural traditions and claim to be a new kind of community." See also the last chapter, "The Consequences" (pp. 245–58), which strikingly demonstrates that Mack's analysis of Q is concerned with rooting his "social vision" of a "multicultural world" (whose enemy is imperialist America in collusion with traditional Christianity) in the message of Jesus, which for this reason has to be purged from all disruptive elements.

49. See, among others, Gerd Theissen, "Wanderradikalismus," *ZThK* 70 (1973): 245–71, esp. 255–56 (reprinted in Theissen, *Studien zur Soziologie des Urchristentum* [3rd ed.; WUNT 19; Tübingen: Mohr Siebeck, 1989], 79–105, esp. 89–90). Theissen emphasizes, however, that the analogy between Cynicism and the Jesus movement is based on "structural similarities" and not on "historical links." Freyne also has made mention of this similarity in an early work, see *Galilee, Jesus, and the Gospels*, 241, 249; since then he has clearly distanced himself from this position. See Freyne, *Galilee and Gospel*, 343, index, s.v. Cynics.

Jesus" have repeatedly pointed out, is that the attempt to draw Cynic analogies to Jesus is often used to loosen the basic rooting of Jesus in Judaism.[50] Although the proponents of a "Cynic Jesus" never claimed that Jesus was not a Jew, his Judaism is nevertheless not central for the understanding of Jesus (to be read in the sense of both Jesus' own thinking and of our understanding of him).[51] Jesus' kingdom message, which has been preserved undiluted only in the oldest layer of Q, is not related to "any particular tradition or religious thinking" (p. 128), and neither can his "God" be equated with a particular ethnic or cultural tradition. This, according to Mack, could only come about in Galilee:

> The God in question is not identified in terms of any ethnic or cultural tradition. This fits nicely with Galilean provenance, and since the metaphors of God's rule are largely taken from the realm of nature the conception of God in Q[1] is also compatible with the Cynic tone of the preaching.[52]

What we have in the end is an intersection of several research traditions in the debate about the use of the Galilean origins of Jesus. In the study of Q influenced by Mack and Kloppenborg and their students, Galilee becomes the prerequisite for an original Jesus movement

---

50. For an overview of the debate over the Cynic Jesus, see. F. Gerald Downing, *Christ and the Cynics: Jesus and Other Radical Preachers in the First-Century Tradition* (JSOT Manuals 4; Sheffield: JSOT Press, 1988); Downing, *Cynics and Christian Origins* (Edinburgh: T&T Clark, 1992); Downing, "Deeper Reflections on the Jewish Cynic Jesus," *JBL* 117 (1998): 97–104; John S. Kloppenborg Verbin, "A Dog among the Pigeons: The 'Cynic Hypothesis' as a Theological Problem," in *From Quest to Q: Festschrift James M. Robinson* (ed. Jón Ma. Asgeirsson, Kristen De Troyer, and Marvin W. Meyer; BETL 146; Leuven: Peeters, 1999), 73–117; Burton L. Mack, "Q and a Cynic-Like Jesus," in Arnal and Desjardins, eds., *Whose Historical Jesus?*, 25–36; Mack, "The Case for a Cynic-Like Jesus," in Mack, *The Christian Myth: Origins, Logic, and Legacy* (New York: Continuum, 2001), 41–58; David Seeley, "Jesus and the Cynics Revisited," *JBL* 116 (1997): 704–12; Leif E. Vaage, *Galilean Upstarts: Jesus' First Followers according to Q* (Valley Forge, Pa.: Trinity Press International, 1994). For a critique, see Hans Dieter Betz, "Jesus and the Cynics: Survey and Analysis of a Hypothesis," *JR* 74 (1994): 453–75; Paul R. Eddy, "Jesus as Diogenes? Reflections on the Cynic Jesus Thesis," *JBL* 115 (1996): 449–69; John W. Marshall, "The Gospel of Thomas and the Cynic Jesus," in Arnal and Desjardins, eds., *Whose Historical Jesus?*, 37–60; Arnal, *Jesus and the Village Scribes*, 52–64. It is important to point out that the relationship between what is Jewish and what is Cynic is seen quite differently from author to author. Cf., for example, Freyne, "Galilean Questions," 71–74 (= *Galilee and Gospels*, 218–21) with Downing's position.

51. See Arnal, *Symbolic Jesus*, 20–38, 80–82; Arnal, "The Cipher 'Judaism' in Contemporary Historical Jesus Scholarship," in *Apocalypticism, Anti-Semitism and the Historical Jesus* (ed. John S. Kloppenborg and John W. Marshall; JSNTSup 275; London: Continuum, 2005), 24–54; and the review by Maurice Casey, *JTS* 57 (2006): 655–60.

52. Mack, *Lost Gospel*, 127. In order to arrive at the desired results, he accommodates not only the Q tradition to postmodern beliefs but also Cynicism itself: "The use of the term kingdom of God in Q[1] matches its use in the traditions of popular philosophy, especially in the Cynic tradition of performing social diagnostics in public by means of countercultural behavior. The aphoristic imperatives recommended a stance toward life in the world that could become the basis for an alternative community ethos and ethic among those willing to consider an alternative social vision" (pp. 126–27).

in analogy to a Cynic social critique. In support of this, arguments relating to the strong helle-nization, urbanization, and multiethnicity of Galilee are frequently rehearsed. By contrast, the elements that point to inner-Jewish links and Jewish patterns of behavior are either completely ignored (Mack) or significantly reduced in their validity for coming to an understanding of Galilean identity.[53]

## Archaeology and the Jewish Galilee

The shift in the perception of Galilee away from a rural, secluded landscape toward a more urban "cosmopolitan" region mentioned above is due to an extensive archaeological explo-ration of Galilee and the likewise extensive reception of the results of this in historical and exegetical literature. Galilee research is, as such, a successful example of a fruitful and stimulat-ing cooperation between archaeology and text-based scholarship. Without diminishing any contributions made by other scholars, we should note that Eric Meyers and Seán Freyne are particularly deserving of praise in this regard.

At the beginning of the rediscovery and reassessment of Galilee stands Meyers's epoch-making essay on Galilean regionalism.[54] As a result of his archaeological research from the beginning of the 1970s in Upper Galilee,[55] Meyers came to realize that Upper Galilee (the

---

53. Kloppenborg Verbin, *Excavating Q*, 223–34 ("The Galilee, the Temple, and the Torah"). In his view the adoption of Judean traditions was mostly for economic reasons, since trade with Judea was possible only with products that were kosher and properly tithed. Cf. this with the view of Andrea M. Berlin, "Jewish Life before the Revolt: The Archaeological Evidence," *JSJ* 36 (2005): 417–70; she describes the archaeological finds for Judea and Galilee as relatively consistent, giving shape to what she calls "household-Judaism," present from the first century BCE onward at the latest. Beyond Berlin, I would argue that economic factors alone cannot sufficiently explain such a sweeping process of change that reaches as far as household ceramics, which is why I suggested the Pharisees as the most likely group behind this change in the material culture; see Roland Deines, "Non-literary Sources for the Interpretation of the New Testament: Methodological Considerations and Case Studies Related to the Corpus Judaeo-Hellenisticum," in *Neues Testament und hellenistisch-jüdische Alltagskultur: Wechselseitige Wahrnehmungen. III. Internationales Symposium zum Corpus Judaeo-Hellenisticum Novi Testamenti 21.–24. Mai 2009, Leipzig* (ed. Roland Deines, Jens Herzer, and Karl-Wilhelm Niebuhr; WUNT 274; Tübingen: Mohr Siebeck 2011), 25–66, esp. 31–38.

54. Eric M. Meyers, "Galilean Regionalism as a Factor in Historical Reconstruction," *BASOR* 221 (1976): 93–101. For an expanded version, see Meyers, "Cultural Setting." On Meyers's significance for the field of Galilee studies, see Moxnes, "Construction," 69–70.

55. Eric M. Meyers, James F. Strange, and Dennis E. Groh, "The Meiron Excavation Project: Archaeological Survey in Galilee and Golan, 1976," *BASOR* 230 (1978): 1–24; Eric M. Meyers, A. Thomas Kraabel, and James F. Strange, *Ancient Synagogue Excavations at Khirbet Shema', Upper Galilee, Israel 1970–1972* (AASOR 42; Durham, N.C.: Published for the American Schools of Oriental Research by Duke University Press, 1976); Eric M. Meyers, James F. Strange, and Carol L. Meyers, *Excavations at Ancient Meiron, Upper Galilee, Israel 1971–72, 1974–75, 1977* (Meiron Excavation Project 3; Cambridge, Mass.: American Schools of Oriental Research, 1981); Eric M. Meyers, James F. Strange, and Carol L. Meyers, "Preliminary Report on the 1980 Excavations at en-Nabratein, Israel," *BASOR* 244 (1981): 1–25; Eric M. Meyers, James F. Strange, and Carol L. Meyers, "Second Preliminary Report on the 1981 Excavations at en-Nabratein, Israel," *BASOR* 246 (1982): 35–54; Eric M. Meyers, James F.

region around Mount Meiron) had to be distinguished culturally from Lower Galilee (mostly identical with the main area of Jesus' ministry [p. 95]). The characterization of Galilee as a secluded and backward *hinterland*, as assumed in many depictions from Renan to Vermes,[56] is, in Meyers's view, applicable only to Upper Galilee, which he found to be decidedly different from Lower Galilee in terms of language, pottery, and architecture. Upper Galilee was, in his words, "less Hellenized and more conservative" (p. 100). Jesus, however, was at home in the "more cosmopolitan atmosphere of the great southern Galilean urban centers," which were situated along the main trade routes, to which Sepphoris also belonged (p. 95).[57]

In this short paragraph we have the keywords that have defined the subsequent discussion ever since: the cosmopolitan character of (Lower) Galilee, its urban centers, and the linkage to a transnational and transcultural network, all of which presents Sepphoris as an epitome of modern Galilee. To this he added the expectation that the linguistic profile of this region ought to have "a substantial Greek component," which New Testament scholars have repeatedly set out to prove, without, however, applying a precise and sufficiently clear geographic or chronological differentiation.[58] Meyers's main purpose with his essay was to combat the widespread propensity to equate Galilee with a particularly backward population: "The isolation that one often associates with the Galilean personality, then, can hardly be supported by the evidence from Lower Galilee" (p. 95). Meyers further emphasizes that the "developed" areas of Galilee were, in terms of their religious culture, not particularly different from Judea or Jerusalem. Though this preliminary picture was further refined during the course of subsequent excavations, and even corrected at points, in particular with regard to the relative isolation of Upper

---

Strange, and Carol L. Meyers, *Excavations at the Ancient Synagogue of Gush Halav* (Meiron Excavation Project 5; Winona Lake, Ind.: Published for the American Schools of Oriental Research by Eisenbrauns, 1990). For a summary, see Eric M. Meyers, "The Current State of Galilean Synagogue Studies," in *The Synagogue in Late Antiquity* (ed. Lee I. Levine; Philadelphia: American Schools of Oriental Research, 1987), 127–37.

56. Even at that time, though, there were significant exceptions among those authors who saw, or wanted to see, Jesus as more closely related to a Greek-Hellenistic (and, related to this at times, also Aryan) context.

57. Meyers, "Galilean Regionalism," 95, 100.

58. See the collected data in Meyers, "Galilean Regionalism," 97, with the overview in Chancey, *Greco-Roman Culture*, 122–65. The title of Chancey's chapter is "The Use of Greek in Jesus' Galilee," and he makes it obvious that there is very little evidence for this particular time period in Galilee. Against the occasional exaggeration of the influence of Greek, Chancey tends to confine the finds too much (see now also his "Epigraphic Habit"). Yet one has to take his insistence on geography and chronology seriously. See Mark A. Chancey, "Galilee and Greco-Roman Culture in the Time of Jesus: The Neglected Significance of Chronology," in *SBL 2003 Seminar Papers* (SBLSP 42; Atlanta: Society of Biblical Literature, 2003), 173–88. Stanley E. Porter has argued for a maximal position of the presence of Greek in Galilee ("Jesus and the Use of Greek in Galilee," in *Studying the Historical Jesus: Evaluations of the State of Current Research* [ed. Bruce Chilton and Craig A. Evans; NTTS 19; Leiden: Brill, 1994], 123–54). The extent of the cultural changes that came with the second century CE are still underestimated, and all too often finds from the second to fifth century are projected back into the first; see on this Sanders, "Jesus' Galilee," 39.

Galilee, the main features of this view were nevertheless confirmed.[59] And in the meantime the borders of Jewish and non-Jewish settlements can be determined with relative accuracy due to the different material legacy. In fact, these archaeological borders are mostly congruent with those of the written sources from antiquity.[60]

Parallel to the contributions of Meyers, it was Seán Freyne in particular who made Galilee a prominent focus of New Testament studies. In 1980 his history of Galilee from Alexander the Great to the Bar-Kokhba war appeared, though without covering the Galilean Jesus as a separate topic.[61] He was more elaborate, however, when it came to the question of the urbanization of Galilee (pp. 101–54). He differentiates a first phase, which touched Galilee only marginally (Ptolemais/Akko, Scythopolis/Beth Shean, Philoteria, Antioch, Seleucia, Tyre) from the second phase, in which falls the founding of Jewish cities (Sepphoris, Tiberias). For neither of these periods does he see a lasting influence of these cities beyond their immediately surrounding neighborhood:

> [O]ur survey has shown that the cities had only a limited sphere of influence and no one of them seems to have dominated the cultural life in either phase of urbanization. Sepphoris is the most obvious case in point. It can hardly be said to have

---

59. See E. P. Sanders, *Judaism: Practice and Belief, 63 BCE – 66 CE* (Philadelphia: Trinity Press International, 1992), and on this Roland Deines and Martin Hengel, "E. P. Sanders' *Common Judaism*, Jesus, und die Pharisäer," in Hengel, *Judaica et Hellenistica I: Studien zum antiken Judentum und seiner griechischen Umwelt* (Kleine Schriften 2; WUNT 90; Tübingen: Mohr Siebeck, 1996), 392–479 (this is an expanded version of: "E. P. Sanders' 'Common Judaism,' Jesus, and the Pharisees: A Review Article," *JTS* 46 [1995]: 1–70); Roland Deines, "The Pharisees Between 'Judaisms' and 'Common Judaism,'" in *Justification and Variegated Nomism: A Fresh Appraisal of Paul and Second Temple Judaism*, vol. 1, *The Complexities of Second Temple Judaism* (ed. Donald A. Carson, Peter T. O'Brien, and Mark A. Seifrid; WUNT 2.140; Tübingen: Mohr Siebeck, 2001), 443–504. See also: Eric M. Meyers and James F. Strange, *Archaeology, the Rabbis, and Early Christianity* (Nashville: Abingdon, 1981), 31–47 ("The Cultural Setting of Galilee: The Case of Regionalism and Early Palestinian Judaism"); Eric M. Meyers, "Galilean Regionalism: A Reappraisal," in *Studies in Judaism and Its Greco-Roman Context* (ed. William S. Green; Approaches to Ancient Judaism 5; BJS 32; Atlanta: Scholars Press, 1985), 115–31. This is critiqued by Richard A. Horsley, "Archaeology and the Villages of Upper Galilee: A Dialogue with Archaeologists," *BASOR* 297 (1995): 5–16, and responded to in Eric M. Meyers, "An Archaeological Response to a New Testament Scholar," *BASOR* 297 (1995): 17–26; and again replied to in Richard A. Horsley, "Response," *BASOR* 297 (1995): 27–28. Horsley is supported by Pieter F. Craffert, "Digging up *Common Judaism* in Galilee: *Miqva'ot* at Sepphoris as a Test Case," *Neot* 34 (2000): 39–56, who attempts to denigrate the finds in order to claim that there was a plurality of Jewish identities in Galilee (see his n. 45).

60. Meyers, "Archaeological Response," 23; Mordechai Aviam, "First Century Jewish Galilee: An Archaeological Perspective," in Edwards, *Religion and Society in Roman Palestine*, 7–27; Aviam, "Borders between Jews and Gentiles in the Galilee," in Aviam, *Jews, Pagans, and Christians in the Galilee*, 9–21; Aviam, "Distribution Maps of Archaeological Data from the Galilee: An Attempt to Establish Zones Indicative of Ethnicity and Religious Affiliation," in Zangenberg et al., *Religion, Ethnicity, and Identity in Ancient Galilee*, 115–32; Idan Shaked and Dina Avshalom-Gorni, "Jewish Settlement in the Southeastern Hula Valley in the First Century C.E.," in Edwards, *Religion and Society in Roman Palestine*, 28–36.

61. But cf., for example, Freyne, *Galilee from Alexander*, 373–74.

been a threat to the basic beliefs and value system of the Jewish inhabitants of the province, yet it never became the center despite its geographic location and its administrative role.[62]

Though Freyne recognizes that there was a gradual hellenization, in particular with regard to the influence of Greek language, he still sees in Galilee and its population a mostly unbroken tradition with Israelite roots,[63] which, in his view, also explains the common culture and close

---

62. Freyne, *Galilee from Alexander*, 138–39. In the meantime it has become clear that the surrounding regions had also profited from the founding of the cities, and that Galilee as a whole had experienced an economic upsurge in their wake. See Morten Hørning Jensen, "Herod Antipas in Galilee: Friend or Foe of the Historical Jesus?," *JSHJ* 5 (2007): 7–32, esp. 24–25; Jensen, "Message and Minting: The Coins of Herod Antipas in their Second Temple Context as a Source for Understanding the Religio-Political and Socio-Economic Dynamics of Early First Century Galilee," in Zangenberg et al., *Religion, Ethnicity, and Identity in Ancient Galilee*, 277–313; Jürgen Zangenberg, "Archaeological News from the Galilee: Tiberias, Magdala and Rural Galilee," *Early Christianity* 1 (2010): 471–84.

63. See also Horsley, *Archaeology, History, and Society*. The hallmark of Horsley's position is a special Israelite-Galilean identity, which is directed against the Hasmonean conquest and annexation of Galilee into the Judean sphere of control. Related to this is his description of Judean colonialists who came to Galilee in the first century CE. These colonial overlords, in collusion with the Judean aristocracy and later the Romans, oppressed and exploited the long-established Israelite population. Galileans in the time of Jesus, therefore, considered the Jerusalem temple and priesthood as nothing other than ciphers for foreign imperial oppression under the protection and shadow of Rome, which was interested only in raising exploitative taxation from the "Israelite" population. A simple summary of his position can be found in his short article, "Jesus gegen die neue römische Ordnung," *WUB* 7[24] (2002): 27–31; more in-depth, Horsley, "What Has Galilee to Do with Jerusalem? Political Aspects of the Jesus Movement," *HTS Teologiese Studies* 52 (1996): 88–104; Horsley, "Jesus and Galilee: The Contingencies of a Renewal Movement," in Eric M. Meyers, *Galilee through the Centuries*, 57–74. The historical basis of this position is a modification of Albrecht Alt's (1883–1956) account of the development of the population of Galilee (see Reed, *Archaeology and the Galilean Jesus*, 25; Chancey, *Myth of a Gentile Galilee*, 25). Alt's series of essays titled "Galiläische Probleme" appeared for the first time in *Palästinajahrbuch des Deutschen Evangelischen Instituts für Altertumswissenschaft des Heiligen Landes zu Jerusalem* 33 (1937): 52–88; 34 (1938): 80–93; 35 (1939): 64–82; 36 (1940): 78–92, and then again in Alt, *Kleine Schriften zur Geschichte des Volkes Israel*, vol. 2 (Munich: Beck, 1953), 363–435; see further Alt, "Die Stätten des Wirkens Jesus in Galiläa territorialgeschichtlich betrachtet," *ZDPV* 68 (1949): 51–72, now also in *Kleine Schriften* 2:436–55; these articles were written in the context of Nazi rule in Germany, when "Galilee of the Gentiles" was frequently abused to prove the non-Jewish character of the "Galilean" Jesus. Alt's intention was to demonstrate that at no time was there a majority of non-Jews in Galilee, and moreover that even after the Assyrian period one has to assume the continual presence of an Israelite population. Horsley invokes this, but then—quite contrary to Alt's intention—assumes a deep rift between this old Israelite population and the new Judean colonialists. For a discussion and critique of Horsley's position (which also forms the backdrop of Crossan's view), see, *inter alios*, Moxnes, "Construction," 71; Rapinchuk, "Galilee and Jesus," 198–200, 202–3, 208–18; Reed, "Galileans, 'Israelite Village Communities,' and the Sayings Gospel Q," in E. Meyers, *Galilee through the Centuries*, 87–108; Sanders, "Jesus in Galilee," 17–19; Dunn, *Jesus Remembered*, 293–97. Cf. the historical overview in Freyne, *Galilee from Alexander*, 23–26, where he follows the view of Alt for the most part (on Alt's influence, see 459, index, s.v.). In his newer studies, however, Freyne follows Zvi Gal's population model, which argues that the Assyrian conquest largely depopulated Galilee and assumes the resettlement of Galilee in the Hasmonean period.

links with Judea and Jerusalem. Despite all the emphasis on Galilee's peculiarities, it neverthe-less remained a thoroughly Jewish region in close contact with the developments in Judea.[64] Freyne, furthermore, gives an in-depth account of the economic situation, which he—in con-trast to others—does not judge to be that gloomy for the majority of the rural population. In his view, the landscape was marked by small and mid-sized farms owned by families, who could govern their settlements and affairs largely on their own, despite suffering under heavy taxation. Large farm estates, which were run by laborers and slaves, he views as the exception rather than the norm.[65]

Related to the economic question is that of social stratification, which likewise features heavily in Galilee research since Freyne. In his view, the economic situation of the rural popu-lation was not so drastic that it would have ignited a socially motivated uprising, particularly because Galilee had a long tradition of being largely autonomous under foreign rule. Against the image of an all-out insurrectionist landscape reeling under social convulsions, he emphasizes the relative freedom and independence of Galilee, which was more characterized by loyalty to Jerusalem than a particular militant or enthusiastic-apocalyptic "national character" (see Jose-phus, *J. W.* 3.41–42). The question of how revolutionary Galilee was is, therefore, in his view, "a religious rather than a purely social question."[66] With this Freyne distanced himself from influential older studies, which argued for a close relationship between Galilee (and Jesus) and mostly economically motivated social revolutionaries.[67] In the study of the Jewish revolution-ary movements, these two poles—namely, social banditry or religious, messianic-apocalyptic

---

64. See esp. chapter 7, "The Galileans and the Temple" (Freyne, *Galilee from Alexander*, 259–304), and chapter 8.I, "Galilee and the Halakha Prior to 70 C.E." (ibid., 309–23); Freyne, "Galilee–Jerusalem Relations according to Josephus' *Life*," *NTS* 33 (1987): 600–9 (= *Galilee and Gospel*, 73–85); Freyne, "The Geography of Restoration: Galilee–Jerusalem in Early Jewish and Christian Experience," *NTS* 47 (2001): 289–311; for critiques, see Horsley, *Archaeology, History, and Society*, 33–34, 94–95; Horsley, "What Has Galilee to Do with Jerusalem?"; Kloppenborg Verbin, *Excavating Q*, 256–58. According to Freyne, the Pharisees were not least among those who made a lasting impact on the religious and halakhic character of Galilee (see n. 36 above). For an overview, see Rapinchuk, "Galilee and Jesus," 211–12.

65. Freyne, *Galilee from Alexander*, 155–207; cf. Freyne, *Galilee, Jesus, and the Gospels*, 135–75 ("The Social World of First-Century Galilee"); Freyne, "The Geography, Politics, and Economics of Galilee and the Quest for the Historical Jesus," in Chilton and Evans, *Studying the Historical Jesus*, 75–121. He receives support from E. P. Sanders, "Jesus in Galilee," 19–22; F. Gerald Downing, "In Quest of First-Century C.E. Galilee," *CBQ* 66 (2004): 78–97, esp. 95; Karl-Heinrich Ostmeyer, "Armenhaus oder Räuberhöhle? Galiläa zur Zeit Jesu," *ZNW* 96 (2005): 147–70. According to Jensen ("Herod Antipas in Galilee," 8–9, 32), Freyne's social portrait of Galilee is still overly determined by economic hardship. For a more recent summary of Freyne's position see idem, "Jesus of Galilee," 388–94.

66. Freyne, *Galilee from Alexander*, 245 (see the whole chapter, 208–55); also Freyne, "Bandits in Galilee: A Contribution to the Study of the Social Conditions in First-Century Palestine," in *The Social World of Formative Christianity and Judaism: Essays in Tribute to Howard Clark Kee* (ed. Jacob Neusner et al.; Philadelphia: Fortress Press, 1988), 50–68; Freyne, *Galilee, Jesus, and the Gospels* (163–67: debate with Richard A. Horsley; see also n. 70 below).

67. William R. Farmer, *Maccabees, Zealots, and Josephus: An Inquiry into Jewish Nationalism in the Greco-Roman Period* (New York: Columbia University Press, 1956; 2nd ed., 1958); S. G. F. Brandon, *Jesus and the Zealots: A Study of the Political Factor in Primitive Christianity* (Manchester: Manchester University Press, 1967); David M.

motivation—determine the debate to this very day.[68] The arguments for Galilee as an exploited and poverty-stricken poorhouse at the time of Jesus are further refuted by newer archaeological finds, which point to a relatively prosperous situation. This also has consequences for the interpretation of the Jesus tradition, for example, for the parables, where the narrated reality cannot simply be taken to be a mirror image of the social reality. Furthermore, it is important to follow up a remark Mordechai Aviam made in one of his essays regarding the fact that the area settled by Jews in Galilee shrank (that is, it was decreased by Roman administration) after the banishment of Herod Antipas. The subsequent pressure exerted by the expelled on the remaining Jewish territories has, as far as I know, never been considered a trigger for social unrest and tension, either within the Jewish population itself or with their non-Jewish neighbors. More research should be done on this question, because this could mean that the social context at the time of Jesus was radically different from that a few years after his death.

## The Limits of Knowledge about Galilee

Modern Galilee studies, of which I have presented only a sketch, have produced a plethora of insights, which no serious research will want to ignore. The soil and history of Galilee and its inhabitants have been thoroughly ploughed through with all the tools of the historical sciences (although many sites still await thorough archaeological exploration). No stone has been left unturned; no line of an ever-so-obscure author has not been studied in detail wherever a

---

Rhoads, *Israel in Revolution 6–74 C.E.: A Political History Based on the Life of Josephus* (Philadelphia: Fortress Press, 1976); see also Rhoads, "Zealots," *ABD* 6: 1043–54.

68. For the first position, see esp. the works of Richard A. Horsley: "The Sicarii: Ancient Jewish 'Terrorists,'" *JR* 59 (1979): 435–58; "The Zealots: Their Origin, Relationship, and Importance in the Jewish Revolt," *NovT* 28 (1985): 159–92; "Menahem in Jerusalem: A Brief Messianic Episode among the Sicarii—Not 'Zealot Messianism,'" *NovT* 27 (1985): 334–48; *Jesus and the Spiral of Violence: Popular Jewish Resistance in Roman Palestine* (San Francisco: Harper & Row, 1987); Horsley and John S. Hanson, *Bandits, Prophets, and Messiahs: Popular Movements in the Time of Jesus* (New Voices in Biblical Studies; San Francisco: Harper & Row, 1988). In addition, see Terence L. Donaldson, "Rural Bandits, City Mobs and the Zealots," *JSJ* 21 (1990): 19–40; Crossan, *Historical Jesus*, 168–206 ("Bandit or Messiah?"). Of interest in this context is Peter A. Brunt, "Josephus on Social Conflicts in Roman Judea," *Klio* 59 (1977): 149–53; now in Brunt, *Roman Imperial Themes* (Oxford: Oxford University Press, 1990), 282–87 (with addenda, 517–31). In the extensive addenda Brunt completely alters the argument advanced in his original essay. Social factors are removed from the foreground in favor of religious. Thus also Thomas Grünewald, *Räuber, Rebellen, Rivalen, Rächer: Studien zu Latrones im Römischen Reich* (Forschungen zur antiken Sklaverei 31; Stuttgart: Steiner, 1999), esp. 130–56; on "ΛΗΣΤΑΙ in Judäa: Antike Sozialbanden?" Grünewald's result is clear: "in no way were the Jewish λῃσταί social bandits" (p. 156). See also William Klassen, "Jesus and the Zealot Option," in *The Wisdom of the Cross: Essays in Honor of John Howard Yoder* (ed. Stanley Hauerwas et al.; Grand Rapids: Eerdmans, 1999), 131–49; Richardson, *Building Jewish*, 17–38 ("Jesus and Palestinian Social Protest in Archaeological and Literary Perspective"); Roland Deines, "Zeloten," *TRE* 36: 626–30; Deines, "Gab es eine jüdische Freiheitsbewegung? Martin Hengels 'Zeloten' nach 50 Jahren," in Martin Hengel, *Die Zeloten: Untersuchungen zur jüdischen Freiheitsbewegung in der Zeit von Herodes I. bis 70 n. Chr.* (ed. and rev. Roland Deines and Claus-Jürgen Thornton; 3rd rev. ed.; WUNT 283; Tübingen: Mohr Siebeck, 2011), 403–48.

relationship to Galilee is evident. Even Galilean kitchen ceramics are studied with the most modern scientific methods to determine their origin, distribution, and the trade routes they traveled.[69] And yet, with all these immense scientific efforts that are focused on this relatively unimportant region, our knowledge of the everyday life and thinking of *individuals* at a certain period of time is essentially very small. Thus, it is worthwhile also to think about what we do *not* know about Galilee and its population at the time of Jesus.[70]

While we can reconstruct the household ceramics used in a Galilean village in the first century quite well and can also speak with some confidence on the appearance of houses, villages, and cities, as soon as we come to a description of everyday life we run into difficulties. To name just some rather general aspects: What impact did the seasons have on everyday life, a question that has to be further refined based on region, profession, social strata, political and religious affiliations? How did the Jewish festal calendar (or that of Judea or Jerusalem?) influence professional life, at least of the Jewish farmers, craftsmen, fishermen, and their families? If we combine the few remarks found in the New Testament and Josephus and allow for some generalizations, there is a recognizable geographical orientation toward Jerusalem with its pilgrimage festivals, and also a chronological orientation toward the Sabbath, the feasts, and the Sabbath year. Archaeology can, with some limitations, support this picture. Among other things, the presence of *mikva'ot* and stone vessels are indicative of a halakhic practice of piety, which likewise is oriented toward Jerusalem, or which is at least identical with the Judean practice in terms of material culture. Less clear, however, is whether the absence of such elements is indicative of the lack of such an orientation.[71]

The analysis of the material remains of everyday life provides valuable insights into the "inner life" of a society. Thanks to these studies, it is now no longer possible to seriously dispute the predominantly Jewish character of Sepphoris and Galilee in the first century.[72] What has remained controversial, however, is how far the material similarities between Judea and Galilee also imply an "inner" coherence between the two regions, as, for example, assumed by Seán

---

69. See esp. the work by David Adan-Bayewitz, *Common Pottery in Roman Galilee: A Study of Local Trade* (Bar-Ilan Studies in Near Eastern Languages and Culture; Ramat-Gan: Bar-Ilan University Press, 1993); Adan Bayewitz et al., "Pottery Manufacture in Roman Galilee: Distinguishing Similar Provenance Groups Using High-Precision X-Ray Fluorescence and Instrumental Neutron Activation Analysis," in *Modern Trends in Scientific Studies on Ancient Ceramics: Papers Presented at the 5th European Meeting in Ancient Ceramics, Athens 1999* (ed. Vassilis Kilikoglou, Anno Hein, and Yannis Maniatis; BAR International Series 1011; Oxford: Archaeopress, 2002), 361–70.

70. See also Downing, "In Quest of First-Century C.E. Galilee," 97: "We should for now admit, then, that we know enough only to know how little we know, how much we may only conjecture."

71. See the important article by Berlin, "Jewish Life before the Revolt." On the *miqva'ot*, see ibid., 451–53; and Stefanie Hoss, "Die Mikwen der späthellenistischen bis byzantinischen Zeit in Palästina," *ZDPV* 123 (2007): 49–79.

72. James F. Strange, "Recent Discoveries at Sepphoris and Their Relevance for Biblical Research," *Neot* 34 (2000): 125–41, esp. 127–28, 137–39; and esp. Chancey, *Myth of a Gentile Galilee*; and Overman, "Recent Advances," 45–46, 49–51.

Freyne and vehemently disputed by Richard A. Horsley in presenting widely differing social models for imperial Judea and Israelite Galilee.[73]

Furthermore, in pertinent Galilee-oriented Jesus research it is much debated what Jesus' relation to Sepphoris was.[74] The city, built on a hill, which Herod Antipas made into the capital of Galilee at the beginning of his reign (an honor he transferred from Sepphoris to Tiberias around 20 CE) lies only about six kilometers north of Nazareth. When it was made into the capital, various larger building projects ensued, which, as is often assumed, would also have given employment to the craftsmen in the surrounding villages. And thus, with some degree of regularity, Jesus books will point out how Jesus would have accompanied his father to Sepphoris to work there with him, and in this manner would have learned about the life and the rich culture of a city influenced by Hellenism.[75] This is quite possible, but that is all. In any case, Jesus would have encountered not a "half-pagan" city but a Jewish one of which there were not a few in Judea—yet all of them were unrivaled by Jerusalem, which would not have been unfamiliar to Jesus if one accepts Luke 2:41–50 as historical. What was Sepphoris, which was still under construction, able to offer to the eye that Jerusalem (and possibly Jericho and

---

73. For a discussion on Horsley, see above. Horsley's own agenda is anti-imperialist and postcolonial. To this end, he bases his argument on the Jewish rebel movement, the Judean "colonization" of Galilee, and the Galilean resistance to it, for which he finds traces in the Jesus tradition, Paul, Q, and the Gospel of Mark. For a critical rebuttal, see Robert H. Gundry, "Richard A. Horsley's *Hearing the Whole Story*: A Critical Review of Its Postcolonial Slant," *JSNT* 26 (2003): 131–49.

74. For a short overview of this issue, see Reed, *Archaeology and the Galilean Jesus*, 103–8. The possible influence of "half-gentile Sepphoris" (*halbheidnischen Sepphoris*) led Walter Bauer in 1927 to postulate that Jesus was able to disentangle himself from Pharisaism and "the racking fear of impurity transferred through the presence of gentiles" (*Aufsätze und kleine Schriften*, 102). Shirley Jackson Case used the "cosmopolitan atmosphere of Sepphoris" and its population, which "in Jesus's days . . . included both Jews and foreigners," to explain Jesus' friendly, cosmopolitan, and pro-gentile character. "The unconventionality of Jesus in mingling freely with the common people, his generosity toward the stranger and the outcast, and his conviction of the equality of all classes before God" — all were due "in no slight degree to the proximity of Nazareth to Sepphoris" ("Jesus and Sepphoris," *JBL* 45 [1926]: 14–22, here 17, 19). For if Jesus had grown up "in a remote village and strictly Jewish surroundings," the probability would have been much lower that he would have been able "to acquire these generous attitudes which later characterized his public career." Case also uses—although not in so clearly noticeable a manner as Bauer—a distorted image of contemporary Judaism (at least that of a "remote village") as a contrast for the urban, humane, and educated cosmopolitanism of a city such as Sepphoris.

75. See Case, "Jesus and Sepphoris," 17–18: Jesus as the oldest son, responsible for his widowed mother and at least six younger siblings, would hardly have not taken advantage of the opportunity of finding work in neighboring Sepphoris. This would have put him in contact "with the many-sided life in a commercial and political center ranking in importance second only to Jerusalem." More recent literature sees Sepphoris's general influence on Jesus and Galilee very similarly. See, for example, Richard Batey, "Is This Not the Carpenter?" *NTS* 30 (1984): 249–58; Batey, "Jesus and the Theater," *NTS* 30 (1984): 563–74; Batey, *Jesus and the Forgotten City: New Light on Sepphoris and the Urban World of Jesus* (Grand Rapids: Baker, 1991); Batey, "Sepphoris and the Jesus Movement," *NTS* 46 (2001): 401–9; F. Gerald Downing, "The Social Context of Jesus the Teacher: Construction and Reconstruction," *NTS* 33 (1987): 439–51; Horsley, *Archaeology, History, and Society*, 511–53; Mack, *Lost Gospel*, 57–58; Crossan, *Historical Jesus*, 18–19.

other cities on the way from Galilee to Jerusalem) did not have a wealth of?[76] Just as Sepphoris and Tiberias as Jewish cities were unable to compete with those in Judea in the time of Jesus, so too were they unable to stand out against the Hellenistic cities in Galilee's vicinity (Hippos, Gadara, Scythopolis, Caesarea) in which the "normal" religious and philosophical culture of the Eastern Mediterranean world under Roman rule was much more at home. Morten Jensen rightly calls attention to the fact that Sepphoris and Tiberias in comparison are "small-scale cities," which brought only a limited measure of urbanization into the region.[77] So far no reliable data exist that allow us to say with any certainty if and what influence the Hellenistic cities had on the Jewish population of Galilee.

While the Jewish religious-cultural character of Galilee at the time of Jesus is indisputable, many questions about those aspects of life that do not "materialize" still remain unanswered. Although we have literary texts available that originate in this time and mention Galilee, these come with their own set of interpretative difficulties that are common to literary sources. They are not simply a mirror image of reality; their purpose is to affect their audience. Generally they are not interested in describing Galilee and life in Galilee, or the life of Galileans per se. Rather, these texts, whose focus lies always outside of Galilee, and mostly on Jerusalem, refer to Galilee only when the course of the narrative demands it.[78] This is the case not only with the Gospels but also with the numerous comments on Galilee by Josephus. There is no study of Galilee that does not refer to his extensive excursus in the *Jewish War* (*J.W.* 3.35–44; cf. 2.527–75; 3.516–20; and *Life* 235: 204 cities and villages are part of Jewish Galilee).[79] But even here one has to pay attention to the fact that this passage is part of a work about the Jewish uprising

---

76. Although relatively little is known of how Sepphoris looked and what its cultural and religious makeup was like before the year 28/29 CE, the archaeological and literary finds contradict the notion of a religiously (and, as such, also ethnically) mixed population; the vast majority of those who lived in Sepphoris were Jews. The city's Hellenistic character is not different from that of Herodian Jerusalem or Jericho; in fact, in terms of splendor and infrastructure it is far behind them.  See the precise and chronologically differentiated listing in Chancey, *Myth of a Gentile Galilee*, 69–83; Chancey, *Greco-Roman Culture*, 82–86, 221–22. It is much debated whether the theater that was discovered during excavations in 1931 (the excavation was directly related to the newly discovered and assumed importance of Sepphoris for Jesus research) already existed during Jesus' lifetime. On this, see Chancey, *Greco-Roman Culture*, 84–85, who leaves this question unanswered; and Reed, *Archaeology and the Galilean Jesus*, 119–20, who clearly answers it in the negative. James F. Strange dates the theater in the time of Herod Antipas, if not in the time of his father Herod. See "Recent Discoveries," 128, 132; Strange, "Eine Stadt des Herodes Antipas: Sepphoris," *WUB* 7 (2002): 22–25. See also chapters by James F. Strange and Ze'ev Weiss in vol. 2 of this series. According to Richard A. Batey, one has to distinguish two building phases, of which the older goes back to Antipas ("Did Antipas Build the Sepphoris Theater?" in *Jesus and Archaeology* [ed. James H. Charlesworth; Grand Rapids: Eerdmans, 2006], 111–19).

77. Morten H. Jensen, *Herod Antipas in Galilee: The Literary and Archaeological Sources on the Reign of Herod Antipas and Its Socio-Economic Impact on Galilee* (WUNT 2.215; Tübingen: Mohr Siebeck, 2006), 26. See also Moxnes, "Construction," 74–75.

78. Ruth Vale, "Literary Sources in Archaeological Description: The Case of Galilee, Galilees and Galileans," *JSJ* 18 (1987): 209–26.

79. On the number of towns, see Siegert, Schreckenberg, and Vogel, *Flavius Josephus: Aus meinem Leben*, 101 n. 219, appendix 4. For an overview, see Rapinchuk, "Galilee and Jesus," 208–10. See also Freyne, "Die soziale Welt Galiläas aus der Sicht des Josephus."

against Rome that is interested in Galilee only because it was one of the key locations of this conflict and parts of the population of Galilee were involved in various ways in the war. So too, the one who wrote this account was one of the main actors in this conflict, at least while the war was raging in Galilee. The lack of focus on Galilee proper in our available accounts does not diminish their value, and without Josephus's writings our image of Galilee would lack much color and detail. But it shows how much of the available knowledge of Galilee came about by pure chance.

A further gap in our knowledge is the *institutional and administrative history* of Galilee, which is largely unknown from the village to the city level even if some studies give the opposite impression.[80] We do not have any details of the kind that are, for example, supplied in Egyptian papyri, so that we can fill in the picture only with the help of texts from comparable contexts.[81] The resulting image, however, is "typical" not for Galilee in particular but for all Jewish territories in the Eastern Mediterranean.

Similarly, when it comes to *education and schooling*, very little is known if one looks for geographical details. We do not know of particular schools or about the course of schooling that individuals underwent specifically in Galilee. From Josephus (*Ant.* 13.322), Samuel Klein has deduced that "at the time of John Hyrcanus there were men in Galilee who could be entrusted with the education of one's son,"[82] since it is reported there that John Hyrcanus sent his son Alexander Jannaeus to be educated in Galilee in order that he would not threaten the future rule of his older brother. But one cannot deduce, on the basis of this singular note, that there was a system of schooling in Galilee, which only shows how fragmentary and incidental our knowledge in this regard really is. On the other hand, much has been researched and written about *Jewish* schools at the time of Jesus.[83] But whether there was a school in Nazareth, or

---

80. Horsley assumes that before the Judean "colonization" the village leadership and clan leaders were autonomous and handled their affairs with social balance; however, this balanced social situation was gradually marginalized by the Hasmoneans, Romans, and Herodians. The ethos of Q is siding with these small social and local circles and is directed against the functionaries aligned with Jerusalem (which he links to Pharisees and scribes). See Richard A. Horsley, *Sociology and the Jesus Movement* (2nd ed.; New York: Continuum, 1994), 76–80, 134–37; Horsley, "Jesus gegen die neue römische Ordnung," 28. According to Arnal (*Jesus and the Village Scribes*, 151–52, etc.), the representatives and scribes of the villages were pushed out through the ongoing urbanization under Herod Antipas (pp. 146–55), since they had to hand over their influence and authority to the cities. For Horsley and Arnal, this construed conflict between city and countryside is as such also an ideological conflict between grassroots democracy and imperialism.

81. See Seán Freyne, "Town and Country Once More: The Case of Roman Galilee," in *Archaeology and the Galilee: Texts and Contexts in the Graeco-Roman and Byzantine Period* (ed. Douglas R. Edwards and C. Thomas McCollough; South Florida Studies in the History of Judaism 143; Atlanta: Scholars Press, 1997), 49–56 (= Freyne, *Galilee and Gospel*, 59–72, esp. 65–66).

82. Klein, *Galiläa*, 15; cf. 18.

83. See chapter 12 in this volume. See esp. Rainer Riesner, *Jesus als Lehrer: Eine Untersuchung zum Ursprung der Evangelien-Überlieferung* (2nd ed.; WUNT 2.7; Tübingen: Mohr Siebeck, 1984), 182–245. Against this maximal position stands the study of Catherine Hezser, who has attempted to disprove the widespread existence of a Jewish elementary education in the time before 70 CE. She argues instead that this was only the case from the third

whether Jesus went to one, is in the end nothing but a plausible extrapolation, which can base itself on the depiction of Jesus in the Gospels as someone who is able to read and write, and who is familiar with the biblical and religious traditions of his people.[84] Even for Sepphoris nothing is known about schools at the time of Jesus. The only thing that seems certain is that *gymnasia*, the typical Hellenistic educational institutions, are not attested in Sepphoris or Tiberias.[85] We do not know anything about the curriculum or the kind of learning that took place in Galilee, that is, if we understand Jesus only in a Galilean context distinct from Judea. What we know about schools largely originates from Judean sources and rabbinic literature.[86] And although the latter has its origins mostly in Galilee, those who transmitted it were Judeans who came to Galilee in the wake of the anti-Roman uprisings and their respective fallout.[87] That one of them was called "the Galilean" shows how little the rabbis understood themselves as "Galileans," even though later generations were born in Galilee.[88] The other sources on schools

---

century CE, and that before that education mostly took place within the family. See Hezser, *Jewish Literacy in Roman Palestine* (TSAJ 81; Tübingen: Mohr Siebeck, 2001), 39–109. She maintains that the few rabbinic notes related to the Second Temple period are "anachronistic and idealistic depictions" and consequently of no use for the time before 70 CE. For a critique of this minimal position, see my review in *Jahrbuch für evangelikale Theologie* 16 (2002): 276–81. For recent finds that indicate the presence of a stronger literacy and for the significance of Aramaic as the lingua franca in Galilee, see Ester Eshel and Douglas R. Edwards, "Language and Writing in Early Roman Galilee: Social Location of a Potter's Abecedary from Khirbet Qana," in Edwards, *Religion and Society in Roman Palestine*, 49–55.

84. See the summary of Craig A. Evans, "Context, Family and Formation," in Bockmuehl, *Cambridge Companion to Jesus*, 11–24. Crossan's position, according to which Jesus was illiterate, is the result of a fixation on a particular social model (which Strange ["Recent Discoveries," 136] rightly calls "a deterministic understanding of models") in which a member of the "*peasant* class" to which Jesus belongs has to be illiterate. See Crossan, *Historical Jesus*, 370–71; Crossan, *Jesus: A Revolutionary Biography* (San Francisco: Harper, 1994), 25–26. In contrast, cf. the balanced depiction of Dunn, *Jesus Remembered*, 312–15; and also Alan R. Millard, *Reading and Writing in the Time of Jesus* (New York: New York University Press, 2000); on Galilee, 179–82, 210; 225–26; on Jesus, 146, 155–56, 188.

85. See Chancey, *Myth of a Gentile Galilee*, 83; Reed, *Archaeology and the Galilean Jesus*, 135; Sanders, "Jesus' Galilee," 29–34. In contrast, Antiochus IV Epiphanes' attempt at forced hellenization is related to the construction of a *gymnasium* (1 Macc. 1:15).

86. The various remarks in Josephus, Philo, and the Qumran texts are also not specifically "Galilean." For a summary, see Paul Foster, "Educating Jesus: The Search for a Plausible Context," *JSHJ* 4 (2006): 7–33; Gerhard Büttner, "Wie wurde in biblischer Zeit (in der Schule) gelernt? Fragen einer historischen Bibeldidaktik," *TBei* 43 (2012): 43–48.

87. Vermes has emphasized this: "Nevertheless, an indiscriminate use of these writings ["the Mishnah, . . . the Palestinian Talmud, and the earliest interpretative works on the Pentateuch"] for the reconstruction of the atmosphere in which Jesus lived would be mistaken and create utter confusion. For although it was formulated in the province, the real inspiration of rabbinic Judaism was of Judean provenance" (*Jesus the Jew*, 43).

88. On "Rabbi Yose the Galilean," who belonged to Rabbi Aqiba's generation, see Hermann L. Strack and Günter Stemberger, *Introduction to the Talmud and Midrash* (ed. and trans. Markus Bockmuehl; 2nd ed.; Philadelphia: Fortress Press, 1996), 73; Vermes, *Jesus the Jew*, 57. Worth remembering in this context is Adolf Büchler, *Der galiläische 'Am-Ha'ares des zweiten Jahrhunderts: Beiträge zur inneren Geschichte des palästinischen Judentums in den ersten zwei Jahrhunderten* (Vienna: Israelitisch-Theologische Lehranstalt, 1906; repr., Hildesheim:

at the time of Jesus that are often used are likewise not as easily related to Galilee. The best-known founder of such a school, Ben Sira, is to be located in Jerusalem, and the roots of the Qumran sect are also there and in Judea. Nothing certain can be gleaned from this for Galilee at the time of Jesus.

When it comes to the level of the *individual*, our ability to come to know anything for certain is even more restricted. How individual people, like Joseph and Jesus, thought and how people in Nazareth felt about Sepphoris, if that was an issue at all, cannot be deduced from the available sources. E. P. Sanders has clearly stressed that geographic proximity does not necessarily mean greater familiarity, or even interest.[89] Nor, however, can either be excluded. What was discussed in the family, what topics were important, what individuals thought and felt, and how they saw themselves and their social, religious, and economic roles—all this remains inaccessible to historians, despite all the sophisticated methods applied in sociohistorical studies, ethnology, and cultural anthropology, which enable access to this past world to a certain extent. They are more able to discern what is typical, the regularities and long-term historical structures (*longue durée*) that can be traced through extended stretches of time and space. Individual characters and biographies, however, resist this kind of access as long as they do not leave any textual evidence.

## Conclusion

After this foray into modern Galilee studies, we can conclude: The special religious and cultural position of Galilee remains in the focus of Jesus research and is used to explain certain elements of his ministry and to identify the oldest (and most reliable) traditions related to him. In this there is quite a similarity to Albert Schweitzer's classic summary of the first phase of the quest for the historical Jesus: "each individual created Jesus in accordance with his own character. There is no historical task which so reveals a man's true self as the writing of a Life of Jesus."[90] So too with the Galilean *origins* of Jesus (or Q), which are seemingly so certain that there is now the danger that everyone is creating his or her own image of Galilee first, onto which then Jesus and his message can be projected. What one wants to find in Jesus is hence to be located in Galilee. This leads to the constant task of questioning the respective heuristic function of the designation "Galilean" in the ongoing research. This is particularly the case when Jesus' Galilean origin is used to position and segregate him within Judaism against other

---

Olms, 1968), 274–338, who has attempted to show that even before 70 CE, and especially between 70 and 135 CE, there were numerous rabbinic teachers of Galilean origin. See also Klein, *Galiläa*, 39–48.

89. E. P. Sanders, "Jesus in Galilee," 15; Sanders, "Jesus' Galilee," 38.

90. Schweitzer, *Quest*, 6. Very similar is Klaus Berger's assessment of Jesus research at the beginning of the twenty-first century, which he characterizes as a "reduction [*Verkleinerung*] of Jesus through historical criticism": "The consequence of reducing Jesus was that what was left could be tuned up and trimmed trendy to one's heart's content" (*Jesus* [Munich: Pattloch, 2004], 13). That "Galiläa" is missing altogether in the subject index of this Jesus book is telling.

forms of Judaism; concretely, this is where the context of a special (which usually means "different from Judean") Galilean culture is used to reason to a portrait of Jesus that dissociates him from Jerusalem and Judea, and the Judaism represented by these ciphers. For, based on what is discernible in the literary and archaeological sources, such a Galilee did not exist. Of course, that does not mean there were no regional peculiarities. What it does mean, however, is that there were no foundational differences when it came to, for example, the attitude toward Torah, non-Jews, or the centrality of Scripture.

## Bibliography

Adan-Bayewitz, David. *Common Pottery in Roman Galilee: A Study of Local Trade.* Ramat-Gan: Bar-Ilan University Press, 1993.

Adan-Bayewitz, David, et al. "Pottery Manufacture in Roman Galilee: Distinguishing Similar Provenance Groups Using High-Precision X-Ray Fluorescence and Instrumental Neutron Activation Analysis." In *Modern Trends in Scientific Studies on Ancient Ceramics: Papers Presented at the 5th European Meeting on Ancient Ceramics, Athens 1999*, edited by V. Kilikoglou, A. Hein, and Y. Maniatis, 361–70. BAR International Series 1011. Oxford: Archaeopress, 2002.

Adler, William. "The Suda and the 'Priesthood of Jesus.'" In *For a Later Generation: The Transformation of Tradition in Israel, Early Judaism, and Early Christianity*, edited by Randal A. Argall, Beverly A. Bow, and Rodney A. Werline, 1–12. Harrisburg, Pa.: Trinity Press International, 2000.

Alt, Albrecht. "Die Stätten des Wirkens Jesu in Galiläa territorialgeschichtlich betrachtet." *ZDPV* 68 (1949): 51–72.

Arnal, William E. "The Cipher 'Judaism' in Contemporary Historical Jesus Scholarship." In *Apocalypticism, Anti-Semitism and the Historical Jesus*, edited by John S. Kloppenborg and John W. Marshall, 24–54. JSNTSup 275. London: Continuum, 2005.

———. *Jesus and the Village Scribes: Galilean Conflicts and the Setting of Q.* Minneapolis: Fortress Press, 2001.

———. *The Symbolic Jesus: Historical Scholarship, Judaism and the Construction of Contemporary Identity.* London: Equinox, 2005.

Aviam, Mordechai. "Distribution Maps of Archaeological Data from the Galilee: An Attempt to Establish Zones Indicative of Ethnicity and Religious Affiliation." In *Religion, Ethnicity, and Identity in Ancient Galilee*, edited by Jürgen Zangenberg, Harold W. Attridge, and Dale B. Martin. WUNT 210; Tübingen: Mohr Siebeck, 2007.

———. "First Century Jewish Galilee: An Archaeological Perspective." In *Religion and Society in Roman Palestine: Old Questions, New Approaches*, edited by Douglas R. Edwards, 7–27. New York: Routledge, 2004.

———. *Jews, Pagans, and Christians in the Galilee: 25 Years of Archaeological Excavations and Surveys, Hellenistic to Byzantine Periods.* Land of Galilee 1; Rochester, N.Y.: University of Rochester Press; Woodbridge, Suffolk: Boydell & Brewer, 2004.

Barrett, C. K. *The Gospel according to St John: An Introduction with Commentary and Notes on the Greek Text.* 2nd ed. London: SPCK, 1978.

Batey, Richard A. "Did Antipas Build the Sepphoris Theater?" In *Jesus and Archaeology*, edited by James H. Charlesworth, 111–19. Grand Rapids: Eerdmans, 2006.

———. "Is This Not the Carpenter?" *NTS* 30 (1984): 249–58.

———. *Jesus and the Forgotten City: New Light on Sepphoris and the Urban World of Jesus.* Grand Rapids: Baker, 1991.

———. "Jesus and the Theater." *NTS* 30 (1984): 563–74.

———. "Sepphoris and the Jesus Movement." *NTS* 46 (2001): 401–9.

Bauer, Walter. *Aufsätze und kleine Schriften.* Edited by Georg Strecker. Tübingen: Mohr Siebeck, 1967.

———. "Jesus der Galiläer." In *Festgabe für Adolf Jülicher zum 70. Geburtstag, 26 Januar 1927*, 16–27. Tübingen: Mohr Siebeck, 1927.

Berger, Klaus. *Jesus.* Munich: Pattloch, 2004.

Berlin, Andrea M. "Jewish Life before the Revolt: The Archaeological Evidence." *JSJ* 36 (2005): 417–70.

Betz, Hans Dieter. "Jesus and the Cynics: Survey and Analysis of a Hypothesis." *JR* 74 (1994): 453–75.

Bockmuehl, Markus. *This Jesus: Martyr, Lord, Messiah.* Edinburgh: T&T Clark, 1994.

Bösen, Willibald. *Galiläa als Lebensraum und Wirkungsfeld Jesu: Eine zeitgeschichtliche und theologische Untersuchung.* Biblische Sachbuch. Freiburg: Herder, 1985.

Brandon, S. G. F. *Jesus and the Zealots: A Study of the Political Factor in Primitive Christianity.* Manchester: Manchester University Press, 1967.

Brown, Raymond E. *The Birth of the Messiah: A Commentary on the Infancy Narratives in the Gospels of Matthew and Luke.* New updated ed. New York: Doubleday, 1993.

Brunt, Peter A. "Josephus on Social Conflicts in Roman Judea." *Klio* 59 (1977): 149–53.

———. *Roman Imperial Themes.* Oxford: Oxford University Press, 1990.

Büchler, Adolf. *Der galiläische 'Am-Ha'ares des zweiten Jahrhunderts: Beiträge zur inneren Geschichte des palästinischen Judentums in den ersten zwei Jahrhunderten.* Vienna: Israelitisch-Theologische Lehranstalt, 1906; Reprint, Hildesheim: Olms, 1968.

Büttner, Gerhard. "Wie wurde in biblischer Zeit (in der Schule) gelernt? Fragen einer historischen Bibeldidaktik." *TBei* 43 (2012): 43–48.

Case, Shirley Jackson. "Jesus and Sepphoris." *JBL* 45 (1926): 14–22.

Casey, Maurice. *An Aramaic Approach to Q: Sources for the Gospels of Matthew and Luke.* SNTSMS 122. Cambridge: Cambridge University Press, 2002.

Chancey, Mark A. "The Epigraphic Habit of Hellenistic and Roman Galilee." In *Religion, Ethnicity, and Identity in Ancient Galilee*, edited by Jürgen Zangenberg, Harold W. Attridge, and Dale B. Martin, 83–98. WUNT 210. Tübingen: Mohr Siebeck, 2007.

———. "Galilee and Greco-Roman Culture in the Time of Jesus: The Neglected Significance of Chronology." In *SBL 2003 Seminar Papers*, 173–88. SBLSP 42. Atlanta: Society of Biblical Literature, 2003.

———. *Greco-Roman Culture and the Galilee of Jesus*. SNTSMS 134. Cambridge: Cambridge University Press, 2005.

———. *The Myth of a Gentile Galilee*. SNTSMS 118; Cambridge: Cambridge University Press, 2002.

Cotton, Hannah M. "The Roman Census in the Papyri from the Judean Desert and the Egyptian κατ᾽ οἰκίαν ἀπογραφή." In *Semitic Papyrology in Context: A Climate of Creativity. Papers from a New York University Conference Marking the Retirement of Baruch A. Levine*, edited by Lawrence H. Schiffman, 105–22. CHANE 14. Leiden: Brill, 2003.

Craffert, Pieter F. "Digging up *Common Judaism* in Galilee: *Miqva'ot* at Sepphoris as a Test Case." *Neot* 34 (2000): 39–56.

Crossan, John Dominic. *The Historical Jesus: The Life of a Mediterranean Jewish Peasant*. San Francisco: Harper, 1991.

———. *Jesus: A Revolutionary Biography*. San Francisco: Harper, 1994. .

Deines, Roland. *Acts of God in History: Studies Towards Recovering a Theological Historiography*. WUNT 317. Tübingen: Mohr Siebeck, 2013.

———. *Die Gerechtigkeit der Tora im Reich des Messias: Mt 5,13–20 als Schlüsseltext der matthäischen Theologie*. WUNT 177. Tübingen: Mohr Siebeck, 2004.

———. "Jesus der Galiläer: Traditionsgeschichte und Genese eines anti-semitischen Konstrukts bei Walter Grundmann." In *Walter Grundmann: Ein Neutestamentler im Dritten Reich*, edited by Roland Deines, Volker Leppin, and Karl-Wilhelm Niebuhr, 43–131. Arbeiten zur Kirchen- und Theologiegeschichte 21. Leipzig: Evangelische Verlagsanstalt, 2007.

———. "Non-literary Sources for the Interpretation of the New Testament: Methodological Considerations and Case Studies Related to the Corpus Judaeo-Hellenisticum." In *Neues Testament und hellenistisch-jüdische Alltagskultur: Wechselseitige Wahrnehmungen. III. Internationale Symposium zum Corpus Judaeo-Hellenisticum Novi Testamenti 21.–24. Mai 2009, Leipzig*, edited by Roland Deines, Jens Herzer, and Karl-Wilhelm Niebuhr. WUNT 274. Tübingen: Mohr Siebeck 2011.

———. "The Pharisees between 'Judaisms' and 'Common Judaism.'" In *Justification and Variegated Nomism: A Fresh Appraisal of Paul and Second Temple Judaism*. Vol. 1, *The Complexities of Second Temple Judaism*, edited by Donald A. Carson, Peter T. O'Brien, and Mark Seifrid, 443–504. WUNT 2.140. Tübingen: Mohr Siebeck, 2001.

Deines, Roland, and Martin Hengel. "E. P. Sanders' *Common Judaism*, Jesus und die Pharisäer." In Martin Hengel, *Judaica et Hellenistica I: Studien zum antiken Judentum und seiner griechischen Umwelt*, 392–479. Kleine Schriften 2. WUNT 90. Tübingen: Mohr Siebeck, 1996.

Donaldson, Terence L. "Rural Bandits, City Mobs and the Zealots." *JSJ* 21 (1990): 19–40.

Downing, F. Gerald. *Christ and the Cynics: Jesus and Other Radical Preachers in the First-Century Tradition*. JSOT Manuals 4. Sheffield: JSOT Press, 1988.

———. *Cynics and Christian Origins*. Edinburgh: T&T Clark, 1992.

———. "Deeper Reflections on the Jewish Cynic Jesus." *JBL* 117 (1998): 97–104.

———. "In Quest of First-Century C.E. Galilee." *CBQ* 66 (2004): 78–97.

———. "The Social Context of Jesus the Teacher: Construction and Reconstruction." *NTS* 33 (1987): 439–51.

Dunn, James D. G. *Jesus Remembered.* Christianity in the Making, vol. 1. Grand Rapids: Eerdmans, 2003.

Eddy, Paul R. "Jesus as Diogenes? Reflections on the Cynic Jesus Thesis." *JBL* 115 (1996): 449–69.

Eshel, Esther, and Douglas R. Edwards. "Language and Writing in Early Roman Galilee: Social Location of a Potter's Abecedary from Khirbet Qana." In *Religion and Society in Roman Palestine: Old Questions, New Approaches,* edited by Douglas R. Edwards, 49–55. New York: Routledge, 2004.

Evans, Craig A. "Authenticating the Activities of Jesus." In *Authenticating the Activities of Jesus,* edited by Bruce Chilton and Craig Evans, 3–29. NTTS 28.2. Leiden: Brill, 1999. Reprint, 2002.

———. "Context, Family and Formation." In *The Cambridge Companion to Jesus,* edited by Markus Bockmuehl, 11–24. Cambridge: Cambridge University Press, 2001.

Farmer, William R. *Maccabees, Zealots, and Josephus: An Inquiry into Jewish Nationalism in the Greco-Roman Period.* New York: Columbia University Press, 1956. 2nd ed., 1958.

Feldman, Louis H. "The Term 'Galileans' in Josephus." *JQR* 72.1 (1981–82): 50–52.

Fenske, Wolfgang. *Wie Jesus zum "Arier" wurde: Auswirkungen der Entjudaisierung Christi im 19. und zu Beginn des 20. Jahrhunderts.* Darmstadt: Wissenschaftliche Buchgesellschaft, 2005.

Fletcher-Louis, Crispin H. T. "Jesus as the High Priestly Messiah." *JSHJ* 4 (2006): 155–75; 5 (2007): 57–79.

Foster, Paul. "Educating Jesus: The Search for a Plausible Context." *JSHJ* 4 (2006): 7–33.

Frenschkowski, Marco. "Galiläa oder Jerusalem? Die topographischen und politischen Hintergründe der Logienquelle." In *The Sayings Source Q and the Historical Jesus,* edited by Andreas Lindemann, 535–59. BETL 158. Leuven: Peeters, 2001.

———. "Welche biographischen Kenntnisse von Jesus setzt die Logienquelle voraus? Beobachtungen zur Gattung von Q im Kontext antiker Spruchsammlungen." In *From Quest to Q: Festschrift James M. Robinson,* edited by Jón Ma. Asgeirsson, Kristin De Troyer, and Marvin W. Meyer, 3–42. BETL 146. Leuven: Peeters, 2000.

Freyne, Seán. "Bandits in Galilee: A Contribution to the Study of the Social Conditions in First-Century Palestine." In *The Social World of Formative Christianity and Judaism: Essays in Tribute to Howard Clark Kee,* edited by Jacob Neusner et al., 50–68. Philadelphia: Fortress Press, 1988.

Freyne, Seán. "Behind the Names: Galileans, Samaritans, *Iudaioi.*" In *Galilee through the Centuries: Confluence of Cultures,* edited by Eric M. Meyers, 39–55. Duke Judaic Studies Series 1. Winona Lake, Ind.: Eisenbrauns, 1999.

———. "The Charismatic." In *Ideal Figures in Ancient Judaism: Profiles and Paradigms,* edited by John J. Collins and George W. E. Nickelsburg, 223–58. Septuagint and Cognate Studies 12. Chico, Calif.: Scholars Press, 1980.

———. "Die soziale Welt Galiläas aus der Sicht des Josephus." In *Jesus und die Archäologie Galiläas*, edited by Carsten Claussen and Jörg Frey, 75–92. Biblisch-Theologische Studien 87. Neukirchen-Vluyn: Neukirchener Verlag, 2008.

———. "Galilean Questions to Crossan's Mediterranean Jesus." In *Whose Historical Jesus?*, edited by William E. Arnal and Michel Desjardins, 63–91. Studies in Christianity and Judaism 7. Waterloo, Ont.: Wilfrid Laurier University Press, 1997.

———. "The Galileans in the Light of Josephus' *Life*." *NTS* 26 (1980): 397–413.

———. "Galilean Studies: Old Issues and New Questions." In *Religion, Ethnicity, and Identity in Ancient Galilee*, edited by Jürgen Zangenberg, Harold W. Attridge, and Dale B. Martin, 13–29. WUNT 210. Tübingen: Mohr Siebeck, 2007.

———. *Galilee and Gospel: Collected Essays*. WUNT 125. Tübingen: Mohr Siebeck, 2000.

———. "Galilee as Laboratory: Experiments for New Testament Historians and Theologians." *NTS* 53 (2007): 147–64.

———. *Galilee from Alexander the Great to Hadrian, 323 B.C.E. to 135 C.E.: A Study of Second Temple Judaism*. University of Notre Dame Center for the Study of Judaism and Christianity in Antiquity 5. Wilmington, Del.: Michael Glazier; Notre Dame, Ind.: University of Notre Dame Press, 1980. Reprint, Edinburgh: T&T Clark, 1998.

———. *Galilee, Jesus, and the Gospels: Literary Approaches and Historical Investigations*. Philadelphia: Fortress Press; Dublin: Gill & MacMillan, 1988.

———. "The Geography, Politics, and Economics of Galilee and the Quest for the Historical Jesus." In *Studying the Historical Jesus: Evaluations of the State of Current Research*, edited by Bruce Chilton and Craig A. Evans, 75–121. NTTS 19. Leiden: Brill, 1994.

———. *Jesus, a Jewish Galilean: A New Reading of the Jesus-Story*. London: T&T Clark, 2004.

———. "Jesus of Galilee: Implications and Possibilities." *EC* 1 (2010): 372–405.

———. "Town and Country Once More: The Case of Roman Galilee." In *Archaeology and the Galilee: Texts and Contexts in the Graeco-Roman and Byzantine Period*, edited by Douglas R. Edwards and C. Thomas McCollough, 49–56. South Florida Studies in the History of Judaism 143. Atlanta: Scholars Press, 1997 (= Freyne, *Galilee and Gospel*, 59–72).

Gal, Zvi. *Lower Galilee during the Iron Age*. American Schools of Oriental Research Dissertation Series 8. Winona Lake, Ind.: Eisenbrauns, 1992.

Graetz, Heinrich. *From the Earliest Period to the Death of Simon the Maccabee (135 B.C.E.)*. Philadelphia: Jewish Publication Society of America, 1891.

———. *Geschichte der Juden von den ältesten Zeiten bis auf die Gegenwart: Aus den Quellen neu bearbeitet*. Vol. 3, *Geschichte der Juden von dem Tode Juda Makkabi's bis zum Untergang des jüdischen Staates*. Edited and revised by Marcus Brann. 5th ed.; Leipzig: Leiner, 1905–6. Reprint, Berlin: Arani, 1996.

———. *History of the Jews: From the Earliest Times to the Present Day. From the Reign of Hyrcanus (135 B. C. E.) to the Completion of the Babylonian Talmud (500 C. E.)*. Philadelphia: Jewish Publication Society of America, 1893.

Grundmann, Walter. "Die Arbeit des ersten Evangelisten am Bilde Jesu." In Grundmann, *Christentum und Judentum*, 55–77. Leipzig: G. Wigand, 1940.

———. *Jesus der Galiläer und das Judentum*. Leipzig: G. Wigand, 1940.

Grünewald, Thomas. *Räuber, Rebellen, Rivalen, Rächer: Studien zu Latrones im Römischen Reich*. Forschungen zur antiken Sklaverei 31. Stuttgart: Steiner, 1999.

Gundry, Robert H. "Richard A. Horsley's *Hearing the Whole Story*: A Critical Review of Its Postcolonial Slant." *JSNT* 26 (2003): 131–49.

Head, Peter M. "The Nazi Quest for an Aryan Jesus." *JSHJ* 2 (2004): 55–89.

Head, Peter M., and P. J. Williams. "Q Review." *TynBul* 34 (2003): 119–44.

Hengel, Martin. *The Zealots: Investigations into the Jewish Freedom Movement in the Period from Herod I until 70 A.D.* Translated by David Smith. Edinburgh: T&T Clark, 1989.

———. *Die Zeloten: Untersuchungen zur jüdischen Freiheitsbewegung in der Zeit von Herodes I. bis 70 n. Chr.* Edited and revised by Roland Deines and Claus-Jürgen Thornton. 3rd ed. WUNT 283. Tübingen: Mohr Siebeck, 2011.

Heschel, Susannah. *The Aryan Jesus: Christian Theologians and the Bible in Nazi Germany.* Princeton: Princeton University Press, 2008.

Hezser, Catherine. *Jewish Literacy in Roman Palestine*. TSAJ 81. Tübingen: Mohr Siebeck, 2001.

Hoffmann, Paul, and Christoph Heil, eds. *Die Spruchquelle Q*. Darmstadt: Wissenschaftliche Buchgesellschaft, 2002.

Horsley, Richard A. "Archaeology and the Villages of Upper Galilee: A Dialogue with Archaeologists." *BASOR* 297 (1995): 5–16.

———. *Archaeology, History, and Society in Galilee: The Social Context of Jesus and the Rabbis.* Valley Forge, Pa.: Trinity Press International, 1996.

———. "Jesus and Galilee: The Contingencies of a Renewal Movement." In *Galilee through the Centuries: Confluence of Cultures*, edited by Eric M. Meyers, 54–74. Duke Judaic Studies Series 1. Winona Lake, Ind.: Eisenbrauns, 1999.

———. *Jesus and the Spiral of Violence: Popular Jewish Resistance in Roman Palestine.* San Francisco: Harper & Row, 1987.

———. "Jesus gegen die neue römische Ordnung." *Welt und Umwelt der Bibel* 7(24) (2002): 27–31.

———. "Menahem in Jerusalem: A Brief Messianic Episode among the Sicarii—Not 'Zealot Messianism.'" *NovT* 27 (1985): 334–48.

———. "The Pharisees and Jesus in Galilee and Q." In *When Judaism and Christianity Began: Essays in Memory of Anthony J. Saldarini*, edited by Alan J. Avery-Peck, Daniel J. Harrington, and Jacob Neusner, 117–45. 2 vols. JSJSup 85. Leiden: Brill, 2004.

———. "Response." *BASOR* 297 (1995): 27–28.

———. "The Sicarii: Ancient Jewish 'Terrorists.'" *JR* 59 (1979): 435–58.

———. *Sociology and the Jesus Movement.* 2nd ed. New York: Continuum, 1994.

———. "What Has Galilee to Do with Jerusalem? Political Aspects of the Jesus Movement." *HTS Teologiese Studies* 52 (1996): 88–104.

———. "The Zealots: Their Origin, Relationship, and Importance in the Jewish Revolt." *NovT* 28 (1985): 159–92.

Horsley, Richard A., and John S. Hanson. *Bandits, Prophets, and Messiahs: Popular Movements in the Time of Jesus.* New Voices in Biblical Studies. San Francisco: Harper & Row, 1988.

Hurtado, Larry W. *Lord Jesus Christ: Devotion to Jesus in Earliest Christianity.* Grand Rapids: Eerdmans, 2003.

Jensen, Morten Hørning. "Herod Antipas in Galilee: Friend or Foe of the Historical Jesus?" *JSHJ* 5 (2007): 7–32.

———. *Herod Antipas in Galilee: The Literary and Archaeological Sources on the Reign of Herod Antipas and Its Socio-Economic Impact on Galilee.* WUNT 2.215. Tübingen: Mohr Siebeck, 2006.

———. "Message and Minting: The Coins of Herod Antipas in their Second Temple Context as a Source for Understanding the Religio-Political and Socio-Economic Dynamics of Early First Century Galilee." In *Religion, Ethnicity, and Identity in Ancient Galilee*, edited by Jürgen Zangenberg, Harold W. Attridge, and Dale B. Martin, 277–313. WUNT 210. Tübingen: Mohr Siebeck, 2007.

Kaminka, Armand (Aaron). *Studien zur Geschichte Galiläas.* Berlin: Engel, 1889.

Klassen, William. "Jesus and the Zealot Option." In *The Wisdom of the Cross: Essays in Honor of John Howard Yoder*, edited by Stanley Hauerwas et al., 131–49. Grand Rapids: Eerdmans, 1999.

Klausner, Joseph. *Jesus of Nazareth: His Life, Times, and Teachings.* New York: Macmillan, 1925.

Klein, Samuel. *Galiläa von der Makkabäerzeit bis 67.* Palästina-Studien 4. Vienna: Menorah, 1928.

Kloppenborg, John S. *The Formation of Q: Trajectories in Ancient Wisdom Collections.* Studies in Antiquity and Christianity. Philadelphia: Fortress Press, 1987.

Kloppenborg Verbin, John S. *Excavating Q. The History and Setting of the Sayings Gospel.* Minneapolis: Fortress Press, 2000.

———. "A Dog among the Pigeons: The 'Cynic Hypothesis' as a Theological Problem." In *From Quest to Q: Festschrift James M. Robinson*, edited by Jón Ma. Asgeirsson, Kristin De Troyer, and Marvin W. Meyer, 73–117. BETL 146. Leuven: Peeters, 2000.

Levine, Lee I. "The First Century Synagogue: Critical Reassessments and Assessments of the Critical." In *Religion and Society in Roman Palestine: Old Questions, New Apporaches*, edited by Douglas R. Edwards, 70–102. New York: Routledge, 2004.

Lohmeyer, Ernst. *Galiläa und Jerusalem.* FRLANT n.s. 34. Göttingen: Vandenhoeck & Ruprecht, 1936.

Lubinetzki, Volker. *Von der Knechtsgestalt des Neuen Testaments: Beobachtungen zu seiner Verwendung und Auslegung in Deutschland vor dem sowie im Kontext des "Dritten Reiches."* Münster: Lit, 2000.

Lührmann, Dieter. "Die Pharisäer und Schriftgelehrten im Markusevangelium." *ZNW* 78 (1987): 169–85.

Mack, Burton L. "The Case for a Cynic-Like Jesus." In Mack, *The Christian Myth: Origins, Logic, and Legacy*, 41–58. New York: Continuum, 2001.

———. *The Lost Gospel: The Book of Q and Christian Origins.* San Francisco: HarperSanFrancisco, 1993.

———. *A Myth of Innocence: Mark and Christian Origins.* Philadelphia: Fortress Press, 1988.

———. "Q and a Cynic-Like Jesus." In *Whose Historical Jesus?*, edited by William E. Arnal and Michel Desjardins, 25–36. Studies in Christianity and Judaism 7. Waterloo, Ont.: Wilfrid Laurier University Press, 1997.

Marshall, John W. "The Gospel of Thomas and the Cynic Jesus." In *Whose Historical Jesus?*, edited by William E. Arnal and Michel Desjardins, 37–60. Studies in Christianity and Judaism 7. Waterloo, Ont.: Wilfrid Laurier University Press, 1997.

Merk, Otto. "'Viele waren Neutestamentler': Zur Lage neutestamentlicher Wissenschaft 1933–1945 und ihrem zeitlichen Umfeld." *TLZ* 130 (2005): 106–18.

Meyer, Rudolf. *Der Prophet aus Galiläa: Studie zum Jesusbild der ersten drei Evangelien.* Leipzig: Lukenbein, 1940. Reprint, Darmstadt: Wissenschaftliche Buchgesellschaft, 1970.

Meyers, Eric M. "An Archaeological Response to a New Testament Scholar." *BASOR* 297 (1995): 17–26.

———. "The Cultural Setting of Galilee: The Case of Regionalism and Early Judaism." *ANRW* 2.19.1 (1979): 686–702.

———. "The Current State of Galilean Synagogue Studies." In *The Synagogue in Late Antiquity*, edited by Lee I. Levine, 127–37. Philadelphia: American Schools of Oriental Research, 1987.

———. "Galilean Regionalism: A Reappraisal." In *Studies in Judaism and Its Greco-Roman Context*, edited by William S. Green, 115–31. Approaches to Ancient Judaism 5. BJS 32. Atlanta: Scholars Press, 1985.

Meyers, Eric M., A. Thomas Kraabel, and James F. Strange, *Ancient Synagogue Excavations at Khirbet Shema', Upper Galilee, Israel 1970–1972.* AASOR 42. Durham, N.C.: Published for the American Schools of Oriental Research by Duke University Press, 1976.

Meyers, Eric M., and James F. Strange. *Archaeology, the Rabbis, and Early Christianity.* Nashville: Abingdon, 1981.

Meyers, Eric M., James F. Strange, and Carol L. Meyers. *Excavations at Ancient Meiron, Upper Galilee, Israel 1971–72, 1974–75, 1977.* Meiron Excavation Project 3. Cambridge, Mass.: American Schools of Oriental Research, 1981.

———. *Excavations at the Ancient Synagogue of Gush Halav.* Meiron Excavation Project 5. Winona Lake, Ind.: Published for the American Schools of Oriental Research by Eisenbrauns, 1990.

———. "Preliminary Report on the 1980 Excavations at en-Nabratein, Israel." *BASOR* 244 (1981): 1–25.

————. "Second Preliminary Report on the 1981 Excavations at en-Nabratein, Israel." *BASOR* 246 (1982): 35–54.

Meyers, Eric M., James F. Strange, and Dennis E. Groh. "The Meiron Excavation Project: Archaeological Survey in Galilee and Golan, 1976." *BASOR* 230 (1978): 1–24.

Michaels, J. Ramsey. "The Itinerant Jesus and His Home Town." In *Authenticating the Activities of Jesus*, edited by Bruce Chilton and Craig A. Evans, 177–93. NTTS 28.2. Leiden: Brill, 1999. Reprint, 2002.

Millard, Alan R. *Reading and Writing in the Time of Jesus*. New York: New York University Press, 2000.

Miller, Robert J. *The Jesus Seminar and Its Critics*. Santa Rosa, Calif.: Polebridge, 1999.

Mowery, Robert L. "Pharisees and Scribes, Galilee and Jerusalem." *ZNW* 80 (1989): 266–68.

Moxnes, Halvor. "The Construction of Galilee as a Place for the Historical Jesus." *BTB* 31 (2001): 26–37 (Part 1), 64–77 (Part 2).

————. *Putting Jesus in His Place: A Radical Vision of Household and Kingdom*. Louisville: Westminster John Knox, 2003.

Osten-Sacken, Peter von der, ed. *Das missbrauchte Evangelium: Studien zu Theologie und Praxis der Thüringer Deutschen Christen*. Studien zu Kirche und Israel 20. Berlin: Institut Kirche und Judentum, 2002.

Overman, J. Andrew. "Recent Advances in the Archaeology of the Galilee in the Roman Period." *Currents in Research: Biblical Studies* 1 (1993): 35–57.

Paget, James Carleton. "Quests for Historical Jesus." In *The Cambridge Companion to Jesus*, edited by Markus Bockmuehl, 138–55. Cambridge: Cambridge University Press, 2001.

Pearson, Birger A. "The Gospel according to the Jesus Seminar." *Religion* 25 (1995): 317–38.

————. "A Q Community in Galilee?" *NTS* 50 (2004): 475–94.

Porter, Stanley E. "Jesus and the Use of Greek in Galilee." In *Studying the Historical Jesus: Evaluations of the State of Current Research*, edited by Bruce Chilton and Craig A. Evans, 123–54. NTTS 19. Leiden: Brill, 1994.

Rapinchuk, Mark. "The Galilee and Jesus in Recent Research." *Currents in Biblical Research* 2 (2004): 197–222.

Rappaport, Uriel. "How Anti-Roman was the Galilee?" In *The Galilee in Late Antiquity*, edited by Lee I. Levine, 95–101. New York: Jewish Theological Seminary of America, 1992.

Reed, Jonathan L. *Archaeology and the Galilean Jesus: A Re-Examination of the Evidence*. Harrisburg, Pa.: Trinity Press International, 2000.

————. "Galileans, 'Israelite Village Communities,' and the Sayings Gospel Q." In *Galilee through the Centuries: Confluence of Cultures*, edited by Eric M. Meyers, 87–108. Duke Judaic Studies Series 1. Winona Lake, Ind.: Eisenbrauns, 1999.

Rhoads, David M. *Israel in Revolution 6–74 C.E.: A Political History Based on the Life of Josephus*. Philadelphia: Fortress Press, 1976.

Richardson, Peter. *Building Jewish in the Roman East*. Waco, Tex.: Baylor University Press, 2004.

Riesner, Rainer. *Jesus als Lehrer: Eine Untersuchung zum Ursprung der Evangelien-Überlieferung.* 2nd ed. WUNT 2.7. Tübingen: Mohr Siebeck, 1984.

Robert W. Funk, ed. *The Acts of Jesus: What Did Jesus Really Do? The Search for Authentic Deeds of Jesus.* San Francisco: Harper, 1998.

Robinson, James M. *A New Quest for the Historical Jesus.* SBT 25. Naperville, Ill.: Allenson, 1959.

Rosen, Klaus. "Jesu Geburtsdatum, der Census des Quirinius und eine jüdische Steuererklärung aus dem Jahr 127 nChr.," *JAC* 38 (1995): 5–15.

Safrai, Shmuel. "The Jewish Cultural Nature of Galilee in the First Century." In *The New Testament and Christian–Jewish Dialogue: Studies in Honor of David Flusser*, edited by Malcolm F. Lowe, 147–86. *Immanuel* 24/25. Jerusalem: Ecumenical Theological Research Fraternity in Israel, 1990.

Saldarini, Anthony J. *Pharisees, Scribes and Sadducees in Palestinian Society.* Edinburgh: T&T Clark, 1988. Reprint, with a foreword by James C. VanderKam, Grand Rapids: Eerdmans, 2001.

Sanders, E. P. *Jesus and Judaism.* Philadelphia: Fortress Press, 1985.

———. "Jesus' Galilee." In *Fair Play: Diversity and Conflicts in Early Christianity: Essays in Honour of Heikke Räisänen*, edited by Ismo Dunderberg, Christopher M. Tuckett, and Kari Syreeni, 3–42. NovTSup 103. Leiden: Brill, 2002.

———. "Jesus in Galilee." In *Jesus: A Colloquium in the Holy Land with James D. G. Dunn, Daniel J. Harrington, Elizabeth A. Johnson, John P. Meier, and E. P. Sanders*, edited by Doris Donnelly, 5–26. New York: Continuum, 2001.

———. *Judaism: Practice and Belief, 63 BCE–66 CE.* Philadelphia: Trinity Press International, 1992.

———. *Paul and Palestinian Judaism: A Comparison of Patterns of Religion.* Philadelphia: Fortress Press, 1977.

Scholtissek, Klaus. "Von Galiläa nach Jerusalem und zurück: Zur theologischen Topographie im Markusevangelium." In *Oleum laetitiae: Festgabe für P. Benedikt Schwank OSB*, edited by Anke Haendler-Kläsner and Gunda Brüske, 56–77. Jerusalemer theologisches Forum 5. Münster: Aschendorff, 2003.

Schröter, Jens. *Jesus von Nazareth: Jude aus Galiläa—Retter der Welt.* Biblische Gestalten 15. Leipzig: Evangelische Verlagsanstalt, 2006.

Schweitzer, Albert. *Geschichte der Leben-Jesu-Forschung.* 2nd ed. Tübingen: Mohr Siebeck, 1913. English translation: *The Quest of the Historical Jesus: First Complete Edition.* Edited by John Bowden. London: SCM, 2000.

Seeley, David. "Jesus and the Cynics Revisited." *JBL* 116 (1997): 704–12.

Shaked, Idan, and Dina Avshalom-Gorni. "Jewish Settlement in the Southeastern Hula Valley in the First Century C.E." In *Religion and Society in Roman Palestine: Old Questions, New Approaches*, edited by Douglas R. Edwards, 28–36. New York: Routledge, 2004.

Siegert, Folker, Heinz Schreckenberg, and Manuel Vogel, eds. *Flavius Josephus, Aus meinem Leben* (Vita): *Kritische Ausgabe, Übersetzung und Kommentar.* Tübingen: Mohr Siebeck, 2001.

Smith, Mark D. "Of Jesus and Quirinius." *CBQ* 62 (2000): 278–93.

Strack, Herman L., and Günter Stemberger. *Introduction to the Talmud and Midrash.* Edited and translated by Markus Bockmuehl. 2nd ed. Philadelphia: Fortress Press, 1996.

Strange, James F. "Archaeology and Ancient Synagogues up to About 200 C.E." In *The Ancient Synagogue from Its Origins until 200 C.E.*, edited by Birger Olsson and Magnus Zetterholm, 37–62. ConBNT 39. Stockholm: Almqvist & Wiksell, 2003.

———. "Recent Discoveries at Sepphoris and Their Relevance for Biblical Research." *Neot* 34 (2000): 125–41.

———. "Eine Stadt des Herodes Antipas: Sepphoris." *WUB* 7 (2002): 22–25.

Studenovský, Zbyněk. "'Dort werdet ihr ihn sehen' (Mark 16:7): Der Weg Jesu nach Galiläa bei Johannes und bei Markus." In *Kontexte des Johannesevangeliums: Das vierte Evangelium in religions- und traditionsgeschichtlicher Perspektive*, edited by Jörg Frey and Udo Schnelle, 517–59. WUNT 175. Tübingen: Mohr Siebeck, 2004.

Taylor, Nicholas H. "Q and Galilee?" *Neot* 37 (2003): 283–311.

Theissen, Gerd. *Der Schatten des Galiläers: Historische Jesusforschung in erzählender Form.* Munich: Kaiser, 1986. English translation: *The Shadow of the Galilean: The Quest of the Historical Jesus in Narrative Form.* Translated by John Bowden; London: SCM, 1987.

———. "Wanderradikalismus." *ZThK* 70 (1973): 245–71 (= Theissen, *Studien zur Soziologie des Urchristentums* [3rd ed.; WUNT 19; Tübingen: Mohr Siebeck, 1989], 79–105).

Theissen, Gerd, and Dagmar Winter. *The Quest for the Plausible Jesus: The Question of Criteria.* Translated by M. Eugene Boring. Louisville: Westminster John Knox, 2002.

Vaage, Leif E. *Galilean Upstarts: Jesus' First Followers according to Q.* Valley Forge, Pa.: Trinity Press International, 1994.

Vale, Ruth. "Literary Sources in Archaeological Description: The Case of Galilee, Galilees and Galileans." *JSJ* 18 (1987): 209–26.

Vermes, Geza. *Jesus the Jew: A Historian's Reading of the Gospels.* London: Collins, 1973.

Wellhausen, Julius. *Das Evangelium Johannis.* Berlin: Reimer, 1908 (= Wellhausen, *Evangelienkommentare: Mit einer Einleitung von Martin Hengel* [Berlin: de Gruyter, 1987]).

Witherington, Ben, III. *The Jesus Quest: The Third Search for the Jew of Nazareth.* 2nd ed. Downers Grove, Ill.: InterVarsity, 1997.

Zangenberg, Jürgen. "Archaeological News from the Galilee: Tiberias, Magdala, and Rural Galilee." *EC* 1 (2010): 471–84.

# HISTORY

# 2

# THE POLITICAL HISTORY IN GALILEE FROM THE FIRST CENTURY BCE TO THE END OF THE SECOND CENTURY CE

*Morten Hørning Jensen*

## History Matters

The task of understanding the history of Galilee involves far more than just lists of battles and rulers. In a distinct way, views of the history of Galilee have fueled and are fueling specific interpretations of Jesus. To illustrate this: When Walter Grundmann in the heyday of the Third Reich in 1940 published his book *Jesus der Galiläer und das Judentum* (Jesus the Galilean and Judaism), he—in an effort to save Jesus from Judaism—made the claim that "Jesus kein Jude war" (Jesus was not a Jew).[1] From a modern viewpoint, such a claim seems equally surprising and untenable. How could a serious researcher from the world-acclaimed German professors' guild make such a statement? The answer is straightforward: From his reading of the history of Galilee! Since the groundbreaking work of Emil Schürer on Jewish history, it had become standard to describe the Hasmonean takeover of Galilee in 104 BCE as a forceful circumcision of the non-Jewish peoples such as the Iturean tribe from the Hermon range, which Schürer believed had settled Galilee after the Assyrian conquest of the northern kingdom in 732 BCE. This resulted in a prevailing view of the Galileans as a kind of "*halbheidnischen Randjudentum*" (half-Jewish quasi Judaism) that stood in relationship to Judea as any other foreign people.[2]

---

1. See Seán Freyne, "Jesus and the Urban Culture of Galilee," in *Texts and Contexts: Biblical Texts in Their Textual and Situational Contexts. Essays in Honor of Lars Hartman* (ed. Tord Fornberg and David Hellholm; Oslo: Scandinavian University Press, 1995), 599.

2. As summarized by Roland Deines, "Galiläa und Jesus: Anfragen zur Funktion der Herkunftsbezeichnung 'galiläa' in der neueren Jesusforschung," in *Jesus und die Archäologie Galiläas* (ed. Carsten Claussen and Jörg Frey; Biblisch-theologische Studien 87; Neukirchen-Vluyn: Neukirchener Verlag, 2008), 275–76.

When the political circumstances called for it during the Third Reich, it only took a small step further down that road to claim that a Galilean "Jew" was really hardly a Jew at all.

Another, more recent and more interesting example of how the history of Galilee feeds the historical Jesus research concerns the growing interest in reading the Gospels as anti-imperial propaganda. Richard A. Horsley, in particular, has utilized the history of Galilee as an argument for his reading of the aims of Jesus as anti-imperial. For this reason it is important for him to establish a view of Galilee as being heavily subdued by the pressure from Rome either directly or through client rulers such as Herod Antipas.[3]

There is, thus, good reason to evaluate the history of Galilee yet again to clarify questions such as the following:

- Who inhabited Galilee on the eve of the Hasmonean conquest, and what is the story of the Judean takeover?
- What is the story of the Roman conquest and subsequent reorganization?
- What is the story of the Herodian house's deeds in Galilee, especially Herod Antipas?
- How was Roman presence felt in Galilee at the time of Jesus?
- What is the story about Galilee and the Jewish War against Rome?
- What happened in Galilee in the wake of the Jewish War?

In the following, I will shed light on these and similar questions by investigating the written and archaeological sources for the various periods from the Hasmoneans to after the Jewish War.

## Galilee Reborn (104–63 BCE)

With his never-failing sense of royal drama, Josephus lingers long around the internal conflicts in the Hasmonean family during the short-lived reign of Aristobulus I (104–103 BCE) before he finally, in a very brief manner, states the following:

> In his reign of one year, with the title of Philhellene, he conferred many benefits on his country, for he made war on the Ituraeans and acquired a good part of their territory of Judaea and compelled the inhabitants, if they wished to remain in their country, to be circumcised and to live in accordance with the laws of the Jews. He had a kindly nature, and was wholly given to modesty, as Strabo also testifies on the authority of Timagenes, writing as follows. "This man was a kindly person and very serviceable to the Jews, for he acquired additional territory for them, and brought

---

3. See most recently Richard A. Horsley, *The Prophet Jesus and the Renewal of Israel: Moving Beyond a Diversionary Debate* (Grand Rapids: Eerdmans, 2012), 79–83.

over to them a portion of the Ituraean nation, whom he joined to them by the bond of circumcision." (*Ant.* 13.318–19)[4]

As short as it is, we begin our search for the history of the Galilee with the important Timagenes fragment. Unfortunately, its brevity leaves a main question open: Who inhabited Galilee on the eve of Aristobulus's campaign against the Itureans? This is, as already mentioned, one of the hotly debated issues. Three views have dominated the discussion. One is that of Schürer, who took the Timagenes fragment to its extreme by interpreting it as saying that Galilee was judaized in much the same way as Idumea had been a generation before, through forceful circumcision of the Iturean tribes that inhabited the Galilean heartland.[5] While this view has been seriously challenged within Galilean research, it still holds ground in New Testament research in general, not least due to the designation in Matt. 4:15 of Galilee as "Galilee of the Gentiles," quoting Isa. 8:23—9:1.[6]

Another view was presented by Albrecht Alt, who instead argued that Galilee had remained largely Israelite in the interiors throughout the centuries and that Tiglath-pileser III's campaign in Galilee in 733/732 BCE (cf. 2 Kgs. 15:29 and 1 Chron. 5:26 and the Assyrian annals) only meant a forceful deportation of the elite of the society.[7] In recent times, Alt's proposal has found a strong supporter in Richard Horsley, who rejects a total exile of the entire Galilean population and holds that only official and skilled personnel were exiled; "the bulk of the Israelite population, however, that is, the vast majority of the peasantry, would have been left on the land."[8]

However, a third option, based on new archaeological material, suggests that the bulk of the population that inhabited Galilee from the Hasmonean time and onward was neither pagan nor Israelite but simply Judean in the sense that the political circumstances from the Maccabean rebellion onward had allowed for a growing Judean settlement in the Galilean heartland. This suggestion is based on the following:

(a) In 1992, Zvi Gal published a surface survey of Lower Galilee that strongly indicates that an abrupt break in the settlement pattern occurred in the eighth century BCE. In the

---

4. Translation from Ralph Marcus, *Josephus: Jewish Antiquities, Books XII–XIII* (LCL; 365; Cambridge, Mass.: Harvard University Press, 1943).

5. See Emil Schürer, *Geschichte des jüdischen Volkes im Zeitalter Jesu Christi* (3 vols.; Leipzig: Hinrichs, 1901–9), vol. 1 (3rd ed.), 275–76; and vol. 2 (4th ed.), 9–12.

6. The Masoretic Text reads: *gĕlil haggôyim* (גְּלִיל הַגּוֹיִם). LXX reads: Γαλιλαία τῶν ἐθνῶν. The designation is repeated in 1 Macc. 5:15 slightly altered: Γαλιλαίαν ἀλλοφύλων. Cf. also Joel 4:4 LXX: Γαλιλαία ἀλλοφύλων, whereas the MT reads: גְּלִילוֹת פְּלָשֶׁת, "the districts of Philistia."

7. Albrecht Alt, *Kleine Schriften zur Geschichte des Volkes Israel* (3 vols.; Munich: Beck, 1953–59), 2:363–435. Alt likewise investigated the etymological background of *gālîl*, connecting it to the Hebrew root *gll*, with the basic meaning "circle." Galilee of the Gentiles should thus be understood as Galilee *encircled* by the gentiles rather than as inhabited by the gentiles.

8. Richard A. Horsley, "Archaeology and the Villages of Upper Galilee: A Dialogue with Archaeologists," *BASOR* 297 (1995): 27.

period 1000–733/732 BCE sixty settlements were counted, whereas the number in the period running 733/732–586 was a mere zero only to rise to thirty in the Persian period (586–322). On the basis of these numbers, Gal writes, "Thus I conclude that the entire northern part of the kingdom of Israel was devastated. . . . It appears as if Lower Galilee was significantly deserted and its inhabitants exiled to Assur."[9] In other words: Galilee had experienced a heavy depopulation some centuries before the Hasmonean conquest.

(b) The Timagenes fragment does not explicitly state that the Itureans occupied Galilee. The tribe resided around the Hermon range, and, though their expansion before the first century BCE into Galilee proper is unknown and therefore possible,[10] it is nevertheless telling that distinct Iturean material culture has not been found in Upper or Lower Galilee but only in the Hermon region as well as in the northern part of Galilee.[11]

(c) Instead, a number of written sources suggest a growing Judean presence in Galilee before the campaign of Aristobulus: First, 1 Maccabees 5:9-23 narrates how Simeon, in the years immediately following 164 BCE, marched to Galilee at the invitation of Jewish settlers who were attacked by people from Ptolemais, Tyre, Sidon, and "all Galilee of the Gentiles" (5:15). Simeon successfully managed to defeat the enemies, pursuing them all the way "to the gate of Ptolemais" (5:22) and to free the Jewish citizens of Arbattis, bringing them home to Judea (5:23). If the text contains reliable historical information,[12] it gives us an impression of local Jewish settlement outposts in Galilee from very early after the Maccabean rebellion, which provoked the native pagan population in the coastal region. Second, according to 1 Maccabees 9:2 and *Ant.* 12.421, the Seleucid generals Bacchides and Alcimus engaged the Jewish population

---

9. Zvi Gal, *Lower Galilee during the Iron Age* (American Schools of Oriental Research Dissertation Series 8; Winona Lake, Ind.: Eisenbrauns, 1992), 108. Gal's survey has influenced a number of scholars to accept a break in the Israelite/Jewish presence in Galilee. Seán Freyne thus changed his view; see the following works by Freyne: "Galilean Questions to Crossan's Mediterranean Jesus," in *Whose Historical Jesus?* (ed. William E. Arnal, and Michel Desjardins; Studies in Christianity and Judaism 7; Waterloo, Ont.: Wilfrid Laurier University Press, 1997), 72; "Archaeology and the Historical Jesus," in *Galilee and Gospel: Collected Essays* (WUNT 125; Tübingen: Mohr Siebeck, 2000), 177; and "Behind the Names, Galileans, Samaritans, *Ioudaioi*," in *Galilee through the Centuries: Confluence of Cultures* (ed. Eric M. Meyers; Duke Judaic Studies Series 1; Winona Lake, Ind.: Eisenbrauns, 1999), 42. The same is true for Jonathan Reed; see the following works by Reed: "Galileans, 'Israelite Village Communities,' and the Sayings Gospel Q," in Meyers, *Galilee through the Centuries*, 96; *Archaeology and the Galilean Jesus: A Re-Examination of the Evidence* (Harrisburg, Pa.: Trinity Press International, 2000), 28–39.

10. See Menahem Stern, *Greek and Latin Authors on Jews and Judaism*, vol. 1, *From Herodotus to Plutarch* (Fontes ad res Judaicas spectantes; Jerusalem: Israel Academy of Sciences and Humanities, 1974), 225.

11. See Reed, *Archaeology and the Galilean Jesus*, 38–39, Mark A. Chancey, *The Myth of a Gentile Galilee* (SNTSMS 118; Cambridge: Cambridge University Press, 2002), 44; and, most recently, Mordechai Aviam, "People, Land, Economy, and Belief in First-Century Galilee and Its Origins: A Comprehensive Archaeological Synthesis," in *The Galilean Economy in the Time of Jesus* (ed. David A. Fiensy and Ralph K. Hawkins; Early Christianity and Its Literature 11; Atlanta: Society of Biblical Literature, 2013), 13.

12. Some scholars have expressed reservations against accepting 1 Maccabees 5 as historical, since Simon's rescue campaign is left out of 2 Maccabees and since it might be a way of glorifying the Maccabean brothers for a prophetic ingathering of the Jews. See Chancey, *Myth of a Gentile Galilee*, 39–40; Richard A. Horsley, *Galilee: History, Politics, People* (Valley Forge, Pa.: Trinity Press International, 1995), 40.

at "Masaloth in Arbela" on their way "through Galgala" to Judea. Unfortunately, we can only be sure of a Galilean location if we follow Josephus's rendering of Galgala as "Galilee" and Arbela as "Arbel" (*Ant.* 12.421).[13] Third, 1 Maccabees 11:63-74 and *Ant.* 13.154–62 recount a battle between Jonathan and the army of the Seleucid king, Demetrius, at the plain of Hazor. Interestingly, Josephus adds to the Maccabean narration that Galilee was Jonathan's ally (συμμαχία) and the Galileans were his own people (13.154). Fourth, in *Ant.* 13.322, Josephus claims that Hyrcanus I (134–104 BCE) hated his younger son, Alexander Jannæus (103–76 BCE) and had him brought up in Galilee. This seems to imply a solid connection between Jerusalem and Galilee before the campaign of Aristobulus. Fifth, shortly after Aristobulus's campaign, Ptolemy Lathyrus was able to take the Galilean city of Asochis by surprise on a Sabbath, according to Josephus (*Ant.* 13.337; cf. *J. W.* 1.86). As Menahem Stern notes, "From this we may conclude that a year or so after the death of Aristobulus the inhabitants of Asochis were devoted Jews, a fact hardly compatible with the suggestion that they had been compelled to become Jews only recently."[14] Ptolemy also tried to take Sepphoris, but without success (13.338).

(d) These written sources are supported by a growing amount of archaeological data pointing to a clear rise in Judean material culture in Galilee in the late second century BCE and onwards. A number of archaeological surveys performed under the umbrella of the Archaeological Survey of Israel project or as independent research projects all uniformly reveal a sudden increase in settlement activity around the beginning of the first century CE. In Upper Galilee a team counted 82 settlements in the Persian period, whereas 106 were found in the Hellenistic period, rising to 170 in the Roman period.[15] Likewise, a survey performed by Dan Urman of parts of the Golan produced similar results, counting 75 settlements in the Hellenistic period rising to as many as 182 in the Roman period.[16]

Most important, however, is the very recent survey performed by Uzi Leibner of a 285 sq km area in Lower Galilee to the northwest of the Sea of Galilee. This survey's pivotal importance for our purposes is due not only to its locality in central eastern Galilee but also to the fact that Leibner, through utilization of David Adan-Bayewitz's meticulous classification of Galilean pottery, was able to obtain a more precise stratification, with subdivisions of the Roman period into early, middle, and late phases. Thus, Leibner counted twenty-two settlements in the Hellenistic period, forty-one in the period 50 BCE–135 CE, and thirty-nine in the period 135–250 CE.[17] Not only did the number of settlements rise dramatically around the

---

13. While the traditional reading accepts a Galilean location, Horsley has, with reference to a study by Bezalel Bar-Kochva, suggested a Judean location based on a different reading. See Horsley, *Galilee: History*, 40.

14. Stern, *From Herodotus*, 225.

15. Rafael Frankel et al., *Settlement Dynamics and Regional Diversity in Ancient Upper Galilee: Archaeological Survey of Upper Galilee* (IAA Reports 14; Jerusalem: Israel Antiquities Authority, 2001).

16. Dan Urman, *The Golan: A Profile of a Region during the Roman and Byzantine Periods* (BAR International Series 269; London: BAR, 1985).

17. See Uzi Leibner, *Settlement and History in Hellenistic, Roman, and Byzantine Galilee: An Archaeological Survey of the Eastern Galilee* (STAJ 127; Tübingen: Mohr Siebeck, 2009); and Leibner, "Settlement and Demography in Late Roman and Byzantine Eastern Galilee," in *Settlements and Demography in the Near East in Late*

time of the Hasmonean takeover, but Leibner's survey also indicates how the earlier settlements were on "fortified sites located on hill-tops near valleys suitable for large scale cultivation" in contrast to the Early Roman period, when a "massive wave of settlement construction" took place at remote insecure "locations with no strategic value."[18] Thus, in all cases the surface surveys point in the direction of growth and expansion in the wake of the Hasmonean takeover and Leibner in particular demonstrates that the political situation allowed for cultivation of rural tracts of land, which in previous times were found less desirable and protectable.[19]

This picture of an increased settlement activity flowing from the South is further corroborated by a detailed study of the coin circulation in Galilee and the Golan made by Danny Syon in 2004. His study clearly demonstrates how profoundly the Hasmonean takeover is marked in the material culture. Syon provides a database of some ten thousand coins collected from 186 kibbutz collections as well as a number of excavations from across Galilee and the Golan. Taken together, these data clearly demonstrate how, with the advent of the Hasmoneans, "a dramatic change takes place" in coin circulation.[20] The percentage of Hasmonean coinage was found to be very high throughout the central Galilee and western Golan in this period. In other words, "the creation of the Hasmonean state considerably reduced the demand for the bronze coinage of Akko-Ptolemais and that of Tyre."[21]

Finally, the ethnic change is suggested also by a number of destruction layers or material changes at sites such as Mitzpe Hayamim, Yodefat, Esh-Shuhara, and Qeren Naftali, including the building of Jewish ritual baths and the desecration of statues and figurines.[22]

To conclude: Though we admittedly are not well informed on the Galilean population situation on the eve of Aristobulus's campaign, though none of the arguments presented above drives home a solid conclusion on its own, and though the Hasmonean takeover may even have been more gradual than the Timagenes fragment suggests,[23] the sum of the written sources and the archaeological data seems to tip the balance in the direction of the Galileans being newcomers to a large extent, rather than old Israelites or forcefully converted Itureans. In particular, the surveys indicate that Galilee was far from settled to its limit in the pre-Roman period, allowing for a relatively large influx of settlers without a large-scale displacement or conversion of the

---

*Antiquity: Proceedings of the Colloquium, Matera, 27–29 October 2005* (ed. Ariel S. Lewin and Pietrina Pellegrini; Biblioteca di Mediterraneo antico 2; Rome: Istituti Editoriali e Poligrafici Internazionali, 2006).

18. Leibner, "Settlement and Demography," 114–15.

19. For a detailed discussion of the developments within the settlement patterns, see Morten Hørning Jensen, "Rural Galilee and Rapid Changes: An Investigation of the Socio-Economic Dynamics and Developments in Roman Galilee," *Bib* 93 (2012): 43–67.

20. Danny Syon, "Tyre and Gamla: A Study in the Monetary Influence of Southern Phoenicia on Galilee and the Golan in the Hellenistic and Roman Periods" (PhD dissertation, Hebrew University, Jerusalem, 2004), 224.

21. Syon, "Tyre and Gamla," 233. The sudden increase of Hasmonean coinage was attested also at Yodefat; see Aviam, "People, Land, Economy," 22.

22. See Aviam, "People, Land, Economy," 6–10.

23. See Aviam, "People, Land, Economy," 11.

region's native population. At the very least it must be concluded that, though some Iturean tribes to the far north were conquered and forcefully judaized, and though some of the pagan population in Galilee might have been converted,[24] it seems certain that the growing Hasmonean kingdom brought with it a wave of settlers from Judea before and after Aristobulus's campaign in 104 BCE, which, in effect, produced a building boom in Galilee of places like Magdala on the lake with a grand harbor, of the citadel at Sepphoris, and of the fortress at Qeren Naftali.[25] In short, the Hasmoneans rejudaized Galilee through settlement and investment.

## Roman Reorganization (63–37 BCE)

The period under Hasmonean rule was to be short-lived. In the 60s BCE, the Roman senate authorized the great general Pompey to undertake a massive campaign in Syria, Mesopotamia, and Egypt that would successfully annex the remaining parts of the Mediterranean area under Roman control. In 63 BCE, Pompey entered not only Jerusalem but also the holy of holies in the temple and thereby established Roman control over Palestine, which was to continue down through the centuries with only minor breaks until the Arab invasion in 638 CE.

Focusing on Pompey's conquest in the 60s, the main question is whether Pompey's ensuing reorganization and downsizing of the Hasmonean kingdom and the accompanying levying of taxes (see *J.W.* 1.155–58; *Ant.* 14.74–76) produced a process of deterioration that became a direct impetus for the rebellion against Rome in 66 CE. This is argued, among others, by Shimon Applebaum and Richard Horsley. According to Applebaum, Pompey's decision to strip Jerusalem of many of its conquered city-states was nothing less than a game-changer that "must have meant the creation of a very considerable class of landless Jewish peasants."[26] The situation plunged the land into a conflict that was "to be continuous until the rebellion of 66, of which it was an important component."[27] Horsley argues along the same lines when he speaks of "Roman devastation and slaughter in Galilee"[28] by way of brute force unleashed in order "to terrorize peoples into submission" through destruction of villages, enslavement of a large number of peoples, and the hanging of hundreds of insurgents along the roads.[29]

---

24. As, for example, is evident in the Zenon papyri, Galilee was of course inhabited throughout the centuries. See the discussion in Jensen, "Rural Galilee."

25. See also Aviam, "People, Land, Economy," 13–15, 42–43.

26. Shimon Applebaum, "Economic Life in Palestine," in *The Jewish People in the First Century: Historical Geography, Political History, Social, Cultural and Religious Life and Institutions* (ed. Shmuel Safrai, and Menahem Stern; 2 vols.; CRINT, section 1; Assen: Van Gorcum, 1976), 2:637.

27. Applebaum, "Economic Life in Palestine," 638.

28. Richard A. Horsley, *Archaeology, History, and Society in Galilee: The Social Context of Jesus and the Rabbis* (Valley Forge, Pa.: Trinity Press International, 1996), 29.

29. Richard A. Horsley, "Jesus and Empire," in *In the Shadow of Empire: Reclaiming the Bible as a History of Faithful Resistance* (ed. Richard A. Horsley; Louisville: Westminster John Knox, 2008), 79.

Josephus comments on these events (in one of his many inserted editorial remarks), stating that it was a great disaster (πάθος) for Jerusalem to lose its freedom (ἐλευθερία) and to be robbed of some ten thousand talents (*Ant.* 14.77–78) in this way. In light of Josephus's words, Applebaum may be right in claiming that the acts of Pompey "must have created a considerable rural proletariat."[30] Nevertheless, it seems to be an exaggeration to claim that Pompey in reality began the process that eventually resulted in the rebellion of 66 CE, since Josephus clearly states that the burdens placed on the Jewish nation by Pompey were later completely removed by Caesar in return for the assistance provided to him by Antipater and Hyrcanus II in his battle against Pompey in Egypt in 49–48 BCE (*Ant.* 14.127–33). Not only did Caesar return a number of the former areas, but he also granted tax relief (see the lists in *J. W.* 1.193–94 and the decrees in *Ant.* 14.190–216), and, according to Josephus, it was his stated intention to return the land to the Jews that had formerly been in their possession (*Ant.* 14.205, 207).

So, the question about the socioeconomic impact on Galilee remains open, as we now turn to an outline of the events as we have them in our main source for this period, Josephus.

To understand the entire period until Herod the Great finally seized the throne firmly in the 30s BCE, we must begin with the internal fight for the Hasmonean throne following the death of Queen Alexandra in 67 BCE. While she intended to leave the throne to her oldest son, Hyrcanus II, his younger brother, Aristobulus II, succeeded in outmaneuvering him shortly after Alexandra's death (*J. W.* 1.120–22). This pushed Antipater into action, initiating decades of continuous conflict with Aristobulus II and his sons, Alexander and Antigonus, who were eventually backed by the Persians. Hyrcanus for his part was backed by Antipater and his sons, who masterfully had read the political signs correctly, allying themselves successfully with the Romans even in a time of civil war between the Roman generals. In terms of understanding the history of Galilee specifically in this period, the following factors are important.

First, when Pompey reorganized the Hasmonean state after his conquest of Jerusalem in 63 BCE, he kept Galilee as part of the Judean state. Samaria, along with the coastline—not to speak of the many conquered city-states, such as Gadara, Hippos, Scythopolis, Pella, Gaza, Joppa, Dora, and the like—were all removed from Judean influence when the Hasmonean state was confined "within its own boundaries" (μόνοις αὐτοὺς τοῖς ἰδίοις ὅροις περιέκλεισεν, *J. W.* 1.155; cf. *Ant.* 14.74). According to Josephus, as far as the Romans were concerned, Galilee was Jewish at this point, even though geographically disconnected from Judea by Samaria.

Second, Galilee became the scene of some of the battles between the two Hasmonean factions: (a) When Alexander, the son of Aristobulus, revolted against Hyrcanus, whom Pompey had left in power in Jerusalem as high priest (*J. W.* 1.153; *Ant.* 14.73), the governor (στρατηγός) of Syria, Gabinius, invaded the country to quell the uprising (*J. W.* 1.160-178; *Ant.* 14.82-91). He afterwards divided the country into five regions, granting Sepphoris capital rights over Galilee (*J. W.* 1.170; *Ant.* 14.91). This happened around 57 BCE, since Gabinius entered his office in Syria in that year. For some reason, we do not hear much about division

---

30. "Economic Life in Palestine," 656.

later on, and it seems as though Jerusalem quickly regained its former status as capital over the entire Jewish state.[31] (b) Later, Gabinius defeated Aristobulus II and Antigonus, who had escaped from Rome and encamped at Alexandreion and Machaerus (*J.W.* 1.171–74; *Ant.* 14.92–97). However, the other son of Aristobulus, Alexander, was still around raising a huge army of thirty thousand men, which Gabinius confronted and defeated in a battle near Mount Tabor (*J.W.* 1.177; *Ant.* 14.101–2). (c) In these years, the eastern frontier was highly insecure, and different Roman generals and governors engaged the Parthians in various battles. One of them, Cassius, who had managed to flee with parts of the army after Crassus had been defeated by the Parthians in Mesopotamia in 53 BCE, fell upon Taricheae at the lake on his way to Jerusalem and enslaved thirty thousand men, according to Josephus (*J.W.* 1.180; *Ant.* 14.120).

Third, it is exactly in these turbulent years that Herod the Great enters the scene. His father, Antipater, successfully supported Caesar against Pompey, and, though Hyrcanus on paper was made high priest and procurator by Caesar, it was Antipater who was the real man in power, placing his sons in all the important positions (*J.W.* 1.193–203; *Ant.* 14.137, 143–44, 156–58). Thus, the young Herod, who according to Josephus was full of energy (δραστήριος, *J.W.* 1.204), was shipped off to Galilee as governor (στρατηγός) in the year 47 BCE (*J.W.* 1.203; *Ant.* 14.158). He immediately engaged and quelled the resistance against Hyrcanus and Antipater in the form of Ezekias, the arch-robber (ἀρχιληστής), who had perpetrated his crimes in an area along the Syrian border. While Herod's vigor was praised by some, he was charged by the Jerusalem council for his execution of Hezekiah (or Ezekias) without trial, only to be acquitted of all charges through the inntervention of the governor of Syria, Sextus Caesar, who had a good eye for Herod's talents (*J.W.* 1.205–11; *Ant.* 14.165–84, where Hyrcanus ensures Herod's escape from Jerusalem). After this, Sextus made Herod governor of Coele-Syria as well as Samaria (*J.W.* 1.213; *Ant.* 14.180). Later, after Caesar had been killed in 44 BCE and the second civil war in decades was swirling across the empire, Herod was the first to meet the demand presented to the Jewish state by Cassius in the form of one hundred talents collected in Galilee (*J.W.* 1.221; *Ant.* 14.280), just as he also drove back a Tyrian offensive that was meant to support Antigonus (*J.W.* 1.238–39; *Ant.* 14.297–99).

Fourth, it became increasingly clear to the Romans that Herod was their future ally, though Antipater actually had placed Herod's older brother, Phasael, in charge of Jerusalem. Herod successfully managed to transfer his support from Cassius to Marcus Antonius and Octavian, later Augustus, after their defeat of Cassius at Philippi in 42 BCE (*J.W.* 1.242; *Ant.* 14.303). When he had to flee the country after Antigonus (son of Aristobulus II) raided Jerusalem backed by the Parthians, he made his way to Rome, where the Senate crowned him king in the year 40 BCE, after which he, flanked by Antonius and Octavian, went to the grand Jupiter temple to sacrifice and to place the decree before the eyes of the Roman

---

31. Freyne argues that this suggests that Galilee really had no interest in parting from Judea, to which it saw itself closely connected; see Seán Freyne, *Galilee from Alexander the Great to Hadrian, 323 B.C.E. to 135 C.E.: A Study of Second Temple Judaism* (University of Notre Dame Center for the Study of Judaism and Christianity in Antiquity 5; Wilmington, Del.: Michael Glazier; Notre Dame: Notre Dame University Press, 1980), 62.

Capitol gods (*J.W.* 1.285; *Ant.* 14.388). Supported by Roman troops, Herod then set sail to retake the land of Israel. Jerusalem was the final destination, and by far the most severe fighting took place there, to the point that Herod had to beg the Roman general Sossius to stop the plundering and massacres, if there should be any city left to be king of (*J.W.* 1.355; *Ant.* 14.484). However, before Jerusalem was finally captured by Herod in 37 BCE, a chain of events took place in which Galilee was involved to some extent, seemingly with a mixed reaction to Herod. On the one hand, Herod was warmly welcomed when he first arrived back in Israel by way of Ptolemais. According to Josephus, "all Galilee went over to him" with just a few exceptions (πλὴν ὀλίγων πᾶσα ἡ Γαλιλαία προσέθετο, *J.W.* 1.291, cf. *Ant.* 14.395). On the other hand, however, pockets of resistance kept their ground in Galilee, forcing Herod to a number of expeditions in the north: (a) First, Sepphoris, which was captured during a snowstorm without resistance (*J.W.* 1.303; *Ant.* 14.414); (b) then Arbela, whose cave dwellers would prove to be much more of a problem, requiring unorthodox methods and successive sieges and battles (*J.W.* 1.305–6, 309–13, 315–16; *Ant.* 14.415–16, 420–30, 430–33; see Figure A); (c) it seems that resistance was more widespread than just a few places (*J.W.* 1.315–16; *Ant.* 14.432), with rebels constantly looking for another chance to resist Herod (see *J.W.* 1.326, 329–30; *Ant.* 14.450, 452–53). This lends support to the view that the resistance against Herod was more than just plain brigandry but a deeply felt aversion among parts of the population.[32] This is evident also in the fierce defense of Jerusalem, which was captured only after months of sieges. Antigonus and the Hasmonean lineage were preferred by many of the Jews (some would not even under torture hail Herod as king; see *Ant.* 15.9–10).

In conclusion, judging from Josephus, there is no doubt that the civil strife between the two factions in the Hasmonean family, the ongoing conflict between Rome and Parthia, the Roman civil wars, and finally the brutal fight between Herod and Antigonus produced decades of serious unrest and numerous personal tragedies in Galilee in the years from 63 to 37 BCE. There is, however, no basis in the sources for claiming any kind of special Galilean tradition of rebellion, as has been suggested in earlier research.[33] To understand these years of unrest, we need to see the broad picture of a bloody civil war between two parties that for many years constantly attacked and killed each other at every opportunity. In all of this, Jerusalem was the focal point, but battles and killings took place all over the country, including Idumea, Jericho, Samaria, and also Galilee.

---

32. Freyne has proposed that the resistance in Galilee against Herod beginning with Hezekiah the arch-robber was more than plain brigandry but ousted Hasmonean nobility who fought in support of Antigonus (Freyne, *Galilee from Alexander*, 63–68). Also Mordechai Aviam suggests that the Hasmonean policy of migration and investment in Galilee had resulted in a heartfelt loyalty to the Hasmoneans against the Herodian up-and-comers (Aviam, "People, Land, Economy," 43). On the other hand, Horsley (*Galilee: History*, 54 n. 61) rejects Freyne's Hasmonean theory.

33. See Morten Hørning Jensen, *Herod Antipas in Galilee: The Literary and Archaeological Sources on the Reign of Herod Antipas and Its Socio-Economic Impact on Galilee* (WUNT 2.215; Tübingen: Mohr Siebeck, 2010), 5–6.

**Figure A. Arbel.** The towering cliffs at Mount Arbel were for centuries the perfect hideout for robbers and freedom fighters alike. Still today, a climb from the valley of Ginnosar takes its toll on visitors, who in turn are granted one of the most magnificent views over the Sea of Galilee. Photo by Morten Hørning Jensen.

## Herodian Hegemony (37 BCE–66 CE)

In 37 BCE, Herod was able to secure his kingdom with massive support from the Roman army (see, for example, *J. W.* 1.327; *Ant.* 14.468). Quite remarkably, we now enter what seems to have been a period of stability during the reign of Herod from 37 to 4 BCE. We have no reports of upheavals in Galilee or, actually, any other activity. Though Herod is often considered to be one of the most prolific builders Israel has ever known,[34] it seems that he deliberately chose not to invest in Galilee, whereas the areas all around were ringed "with temples to the imperial cult and other construction projects."[35] In Galilee he built no monumental institutions, no temples (which he generally avoided in the land of the Jews, according to *Ant.* 15.328), and even no fortifications except perhaps the royal palace at Sepphoris (cf. *Ant.* 17.271). Ostensibly, Herod did not find it necessary to enforce his control over Galilee by a string for fortifications, as was the case in Judea (his royal palace in Jerusalem, the Herodium, Jericho, Alexandreion, Masada).

This all changed drastically upon the death of Herod the Great in 4 BCE, which paved the way for Galilee's first local ruler for centuries: Herod Antipas. It has been much discussed in recent research how Antipas's reign impacted Galilee and the socioeconomic living conditions of the region, and to this question we turn shortly.

---

34. Josephus summarizes Herod's building activity in a number of places just as he evaluates it differently in *Jewish War* (positively) and *Antiquities* (negatively); cf. *Ant.* 15.266–76, 328–41; 16.136–49; *J. W.* 1.401–28.

35. Chancey, *Myth of a Gentile Galilee*, 50. Chancey argues that Herod left Galilee untouched due to sensitivity to Jewish sentiments. According to Aviam, Herod never forgot the Galilean resistance against him and thus decided to leave it alone ("People, Land, Economy," 16). This suggestion has a lot of merit, based on the sources. Besides the aforementioned notions of resistance against Herod, see also *J. W.* 1.256; *Ant.* 14.342. However, as we have also seen, the picture is not uniform. At times Herod is praised for his deeds in Galilee.

First it must be noted that Galilee to some degree became involved in the serious unrest that broke out in Jerusalem upon Herod's death and Archelaus's failed attempt to keep the people of Jerusalem pacified until he had been formally appointed by Augustus in Rome. His massacre of pilgrims in the temple (*J.W.* 2.4–13; *Ant.* 17.213–18) eventually resulted in a serious uprising that spread throughout the country, where local heroes or usurpers such as Simon in Perea and Athronges in Judea laid claim to royal status, burning and plundering estates and cities (*J.W.* 2.55–65; *Ant.* 17.269–85). According to Josephus, "Judea was full of brigandage" (Λῃστηρίων δὲ ἡ Ἰουδαία πλέως ἦν, *Ant.* 17.285; cf. *J.W.* 2.65). Eventually, this rebellion reached Galilee also, where an old enemy of the Herodians resurfaced, namely, the son of the "arch-robber" Ezekias, whom Herod had fought and killed as his first act as governor of Galilee in 47 BCE (see *J.W.* 1.204; *Ant.* 14.159). Judas was his name, and, according to Josephus, he "burned for royal honor" (ζηλώσει βασιλείου τιμῆς), for which reason he led his "gang of senseless men" (πλῆθος ἀνδρῶν ἀπονενοημένων, *Ant.* 17.271) to raze Sepphoris, capturing the royal arms (*J.W.* 2.56; *Ant.* 17.271–72). This forced the Syrian legate, Varus, to bring down his full force from Syria. On his way to Jerusalem, a part of his army led by either his friend Gaius (*J.W.* 2.68) or his son (*Ant.* 17.289) burned Sepphoris to the ground and sold off all its inhabitants as slaves. There are no other reports of battles or unrest in Galilee during this period of upheaval, which after all seems to have been centered around Jerusalem (cf. *J.W.* 2.79; *Ant.* 17.299).

Turning now to the single most important ruler of Galilee throughout the period we are discussing, Herod Antipas, we should mention initially that Galilee really was not Antipas's first priority. According to Josephus, he laid claim to the entire kingdom of his father during the trials in Rome before the emperor but had to see his brother Archelaus sailing away with the lion's share (see *J.W.* 2.20–32; *Ant.* 17.224–27).[36] This supports the picture painted above. Galilee was not considered as priceless as Judea, with Jerusalem and the great seaport of Caesarea. One of the main questions in regard to Antipas, therefore, is whether he was able to change that. Did he equal his father as a builder, or was his impact more modest? How was his rule felt by the local rural population? This complex set of questions has been widely discussed, and the answers provide the immediate background for the historical Jesus. Despite the efforts, it is not fair to say that consensus has been reached. Quite the opposite: Antipas's reign is used as the cornerstone in totally opposite descriptions of Galilee in what could be termed a "picture of conflict" or a "picture of harmony," respectively.[37] At one end of the spectrum, Freyne describes Antipas as a "buffer for Galilee from the excesses of Roman provincial rule,"[38] and he states that "for the ordinary people the advantages of a peaceful reign outweighed the disadvantages of having to support a hellenistic-style monarch."[39] Aviam asserts that Antipas's "39-year

---

36. See Jensen, *Herod Antipas*, 91.
37. See Halvor Moxnes, "The Construction of Galilee as a Place for the Historical Jesus," *BTB* 31 (2001): 64–77.
38. Freyne, "Galilean Questions," 68.
39. Freyne, *Galilee from Alexander*, 192.

reign was peaceful and probably contributed much to the expansion and strengthening of both structures and society in general."[40] Thus, "Galilee developed into a small, prosperous Jewish kingdom under Herod Antipas. Those were almost 40 years of growing and flourishing, probably with almost no domestic turmoil."[41] In this way the reign of Antipas was good news for the rural villages: "They operated fully within a vibrant economic environment under Herod Antipas that witnessed an expansion in population, agricultural activity and a variety of structures ranging from public buildings, to frescoed private dwellings to olive presses and specialty goods like ceramics, stone vessels or dove production."[42] Thus, "Antipas was a good tetrarch" who "undertook large building projects that helped reduce unemployment."[43]

At the other end of the spectrum, Antipas is described as the "immediate historical context"[44] for the Jesus movement, during whose reign "the slide from peasant owner to day-labourer, to brigand was rapid, and all the evidence points to the fact that this was increasingly the case in first-century Galilee."[45] In short, "Antipas intensified the structural political-economic conflict in Galilee,"[46] and therefore "the impact of Antipas's direct rule in Galilee, both political-economic and cultural, must have been intense, particularly during the generation of Jesus and his followers."[47] It is asserted that "it cannot be coincidental . . . that the prophet John the Baptist condemned Antipas (*Ant.* 18.116–19) and that Jesus and his movement emerged in Galilee under Antipas."[48] Antipas was *the* provocative factor behind the emergence of the prophet Jesus: "if anyone was seeking the Kingdom of God, Antipas was eager to show that the era of its fulfilment had arrived."[49]

---

40. Mordechai Aviam, *Jews, Pagans, and Christians in the Galilee: 25 Years of Archaeological Excavations and Surveys, Hellenistic to Byzantine Periods* (Land of Galilee 1; Rochester N.Y.: University of Rochester Press, 2004), 315.

41. Mordechai Aviam, "First Century Jewish Galilee: An Archaeological Perspective," in *Religion and Society in Roman Palestine: Old Questions, New Approaches* (ed. Douglas R. Edwards; London: Routledge, 2004), 21.

42. Douglas R. Edwards, "Identity and Social Location in Roman Galilean Villages," in *Religion, Ethnicity, and Identity in Ancient Galilee: A Region in Transition* (ed. Jürgen Zangenberg, Harold W. Attridge, and Dale B. Martin; WUNT 210; Tübingen: Mohr Siebeck, 2007), 13.

43. E. P. Sanders, *The Historical Figure of Jesus* (London: Penguin, 1993), 21; cf. E. P. Sanders, "Jesus in Historical Context," *Theology Today* 50 (1993): 440.

44. Seán Freyne, "Herodian Economics in Galilee. Searching for a Suitable Model," in *Galilee and Gospel: Collected Essays* (Tübingen: Mohr Siebeck, 2000), 113. Freyne thus changes his position on this issue from that in his earlier works.

45. Seán Freyne, "A Galilean Messiah?," *ST* 55 (2001): 204.

46. Horsley, *Archaeology, History, and Society*, 36.

47. Richard A. Horsley and Jonathan A. Draper, *Whoever Hears You Hears Me: Prophets, Performance, and Tradition in Q* (Harrisburg, Pa.: Trinity Press International, 1999), 58; cf. Richard A. Horsley, *Hearing the Whole Story: The Politics of Plot in Mark's Gospel* (Louisville: Westminster John Knox, 2001), 36.

48. Horsley and Draper, *Whoever Hears*, 59.

49. Richard A. Horsley and Neil Asher Silberman, *The Message and the Kingdom: How Jesus and Paul Ignited a Revolution and Transformed the Ancient World* (Minneapolis: Fortress Press, 1997), 35–36.

Space and focus in this article do not allow for a full treatment of this set of questions.[50] Instead, I will limit myself to outlining a sketch of Antipas's building activity and the known notifications of upheavals in Galilee during his reign. In regard to Antipas's building program, Josephus relates how Antipas, upon his arrival in Galilee, enclosed Sepphoris with a wall, made it the "ornament" (πρόσχημα) of all Galilee, and renamed it Autocratoris (*Ant.* 18.27).[51] Josephus is slightly more detailed when it comes to Antipas's second large building project in Galilee: Tiberias by the lake, founded most likely in Antipas's twenty-fourth regnal year, (19–20 CE, as proclaimed by Antipas's first coin series).[52]

Unfortunately, Josephus is more concerned with blaming Antipas for his impious decision to build the city on a former graveyard, as well as for forcefully dragging a "promiscuous rabble" to live there, than he is with providing actual details on the city's layout (see *Ant.* 18.36–38). More details are added in Josephus's narration of the happenings in Tiberias during the great Jewish War against Rome, and we hear of a palace with splendid golden ceilings and figurative art in the interiors (*Life* 64–69), the royal archive (*Life* 37–38, moved from Sepphoris; cf. *Ant.* 14.92), a stadium (*J.W.* 2.618; 3.539; *Life* 92, 331; see Figure C), a huge synagogue (*Life* 277), and hot baths (*Life* 85). However, none of these buildings is explicitly attributed to Antipas. As regards archaeology, extensive excavations have been carried out especially in Sepphoris but in Tiberias as well. Though *some* urban facilities found can be securely dated to the time of Antipas, it must be concluded that, while Antipas did sponsor a certain amount of building activity, the two cities were during his time in their "urban infancy" compared to their later phases, just as a comparison with his father's grand building projects allows a ranking of Antipas's cities only "in the second tier of urban parlance."[53]

---

50. For the history of research, see Jensen, *Herod Antipas*, 9–30; see also Jensen, "Rural Galilee."

51. It is interesting to consider what can be derived from Antipas's renaming of Sepphoris. According to Louis H. Feldman, "Autocratoris" should be understood as the Greek equivalent of the Latin *Imperatoria*, and thus the renaming was meant to honor the Roman *Imperator* Augustus, just as Antipas's next city was named in honor of Tiberius. However, it could be translated "autonomous" as well (see Feldman, trans., *Josephus: Jewish Antiquities: Books XVII–XIX* (LCL 433; Cambridge, Mass.: Harvard University Press, 1965), 24 note b). Elsewhere Feldman even considers it probable that the new Autocratoris embodied a cult of Augustus ("The Term 'Galileans' in Josephus," *JQR* 72 [1981–82]: 51). This is not likely, however. No trace of a first-century temple has been found in either Sepphoris or Tiberias, which was likewise named in honor of the emperor, just as there is no mention of such an institution in either of the cities. From the time of Emperor Antoninus Pius (138–161 CE), coins from Sepphoris depict Greco-Roman gods standing in a temple, and it is possible that Sepphoris had a temple by then (see Eric M. Meyers and Mark A. Chancey, "How Jewish Was Sepphoris in Jesus' Time?," *BAR* 26, no. 4 [2000]: 24; Ya'akov Meshorer, *City Coins of Eretz-Israel and the Decapolis in the Roman Period* [Jerusalem: Israel Museum, 1985], 37). Still, no archaeological evidence has been found of this temple either. In an important article, Monika Bernett suggests that the city was named in honor of Gaius Caesar, Augustus's grandson, who obtained an *imperium proconsulare* for the eastern part of the empire in 2 BCE. Because of his untimely death in 4 CE, Sepphoris was soon to regain its old name (Bernett, "Roman Imperial Cult in the Galilee: Structures, Functions and Dynamics," in Zangenberg et al., *Religion, Ethnicity, and Identity in Ancient Galilee*, 342–43).

52. Jensen, *Herod Antipas*, 136.

53. Reed, *Archaeology and the Galilean Jesus*, 118; cf. also 77–80.

**Figure B. Antipas coin.** Antipas's first series dated to his twenty-fourth regnal year. The largest denomination is on the left and the smallest on the right. *Obverse:* Date, LKΔ, 19/20 CE; floral plant (the reed); legend, HPWΔOY TETPAPXO ("of Herod the Tetrarch," the smallest denomination abbreviated). *Reverse:* legend, TIBE/PIAC within a wreath. Reproduced by permission from David Hendin, *Guide to Biblical Coins* (5th ed.; New York: Amphora, 2010).

Looking at the known upheavals and disturbances during the reign of Antipas, we actually encounter a rather short list if one at all: (a) The rebellion in 6 CE by Judas the Galilean (so *J.W.* 2.118; *Ant.* 18.23; and Acts 5:37) or Judas of Gamala (so *Ant.* 18.4), who most likely is identical to our previously mentioned Judas, son of Hezekiah, of *J.W.* 2.56, probably did not take place in Galilee since it was a response to the census in Judea carried out by Quirinius after the removal of Archelaus. (b) Likewise, there is nothing in Josephus's records to indicate that the only mention of a war of Antipas, namely, his fight with his former father-in-law, the Nabatean king Aretas, should have taken place in Galilee. Rather, since the fight was partly due to a dispute about boundaries, it seems to have taken place in or near Antipas's other area, Perea, bordering on Aretas's kingdom (see *Ant.* 18.113–15).[54] (c) A better candidate for an actual revolt against Antipas is found in the story about John the Baptist, at least in the report by Josephus, who describes how people gathered together and became enthusiastic to the highest degree (ἥσθησαν ἐπὶ πλεῖστον) at hearing John's words. For this reason, Herod feared that John's great influence on the people would lead to some kind of rebellion (ἀπόστασις), since it seemed that they would follow every council of his (πάντα γὰρ ἐῴκεσαν συμβουλῇ τῇ ἐκείνου πράξοντες). For this reason, Antipas chose to act in advance and execute John rather than see the events spiral out of control (see *Ant.* 18.116–19). The Gospels likewise describe how John drew great crowds around him in the desert (for example, Mark 1:5), which made him a potent messianic threat. However, in both sets of sources, the execution of John is not followed by rebellion, just as it is most likely set in Perea (*Ant.* 18.119).[55] (d) This is likewise the case with Jesus of Nazareth, whom Antipas, according to some sources, sought to kill (Luke 13:31), but when this finally happens in Jerusalem we have no reports of ensuing popular unrest in

---

54. The manuscripts name the district Gamala, but since it was part of the Decapolis and not subject to either Antipas or Aretas, Feldman suggests that it was the district of Gabilis south of Moabitis in Idumea that was the area in dispute (see Feldman, *Josephus: Jewish Antiquities*, 80–81).

55. For more, see Jensen, *Herod Antipas*, 96–97.

**Figure C. Wall of Tiberias stadium.** During two salvage
excavations in 2002 and 2005, Moshe Hartal discovered
some structures that possibly were parts of the first-
century stadium at Tiberias mentioned by Josephus. This
curved wall is 9 m thick and preserved to a height of
2 m. Photo by Jan Højland. Used by permission.

Galilee.[56] This lack of popular unrest during the long reign of Antipas (4 BCE–39 CE) is actually
interesting, since our main source, Josephus, is keenly interested in portraying Antipas in an
unfavorable light as another example of bad Herodian rule. As the story unfolds in *Antiquities*,
Josephus is collecting examples of tyranny and the like from the Herodian house.[57] Obviously,
he was not able to gather much from the reign of Antipas.

---

56. See further Morten Hørning Jensen, "Herod Antipas: A Shadow of Death on Jesus?," *BAR* 38, no. 5
(2012): 42–46.

57. See my discussion in Jensen, *Herod Antipas*, 99–100.

A similar picture emerges from the period after Antipas's banishment and before the war of 66 CE; that is, a picture with a remarkable absence of reported incidents in the existing sources. Agrippa I succeeded Antipas as ruler of Galilee in 39 CE, albeit only for a short period of time until 44 CE (*Ant.* 18.252; 19.350–52; *J.W.* 2.183, 219). No reports of Galilean upheavals or incidents have come down to us from this time, except for protests against Gaius's attempt to erect his statue in the temple, which were brought against Petronius, the legate of Syria, not only at Ptolemais but also in Tiberias (*Ant.* 18.269; *J.W.* 2.193). Nor are there surviving records from the following period, with direct Roman government[58] in 44–66, of actual confrontations in Galilee, except for the assault on Galilean pilgrims in Samaria (*Ant.* 20.118–36; *J.W.* 2.232–35; cf. Tacitus *Ann.* 12.54). Though Galilee was mainly under the jurisdiction of the Roman procurators in this period, Nero granted "a certain portion of Galilee," including Tiberias and Taricheae, to Agrippa II, the son of Agrippa I (see *Ant.* 20.159).

To sum up this part, it is my conclusion that, while Galilee in the Herodian period experienced some political turmoil—especially during the fights between the upcoming Herodian family and the Hasmonean Aristobulus II and his sons (from 63 to 37 BCE) and after Herod the Great's death in 4 BCE—the region had long periods of relative political peace, and, as mentioned, the archaeological record tells of a steady growth in terms of settlement.[59] On the eve of the great rebellion of 66, Galilee was not on the brink of an economic meltdown, but, through migration, trade, and the temple in Jerusalem, was closely connected to Judea.

## Galilee at War (66–67 CE)

The war between the Jewish nation and Rome was by all measures a watershed in Jewish history. Whereas Judea and Jerusalem were where it all started and had its center throughout, Galilee came to play an important minor role in the course of the events—not least due to Josephus Flavius, who came to be the leading general in the defense of Galilee.

The main question in this connection is: Did Galilee really want the war, or was it a Judean affair in which Galilee only reluctantly became involved? And, further, how much did the war impact Galilee compared to Judea?

First, we need to take a look at our two main sources. On the one hand, the intense archaeological activity in Galilee has provided us with a first-hand understanding of the war, not least through the excavations of Gamla (Gamala) and Yodefat (Jotapata), which were both abandoned after their destruction and thus effectively sealed and left undisturbed.[60] On the

---

58. Agrippa II did gain some foothold in Galilee in this period and was granted the city of Tiberias during the reign of Nero (54–68 CE), cf. *Ant.* 20.159; *J.W.* 2.252; *Life* 37–38. For more on the history of Tiberias, see Jensen, *Herod Antipas*, 135-38.

59. See above and Jensen, "Rural Galilee."

60. For a summary of the excavations, see Aviam, "People, Land, Economy," 21–29; Jensen, *Herod Antipas*, 163–66, 175–77.

other hand, Josephus provides two eyewitness accounts of the affairs in Galilee, one in *Jewish War* (2.510–12, 568–654; 3.29–43, 59–63, 110–542; 4.1–120) and one in *Life* (28–413). While this may seem to be an ideal situation, Josephus's two accounts have been a focus of intense debate in research, since they seem to contradict each other. One solution is to use the two accounts to unravel each other and to find out where Josephus is fabricating his story and where he is to be trusted.[61] Generally, *Life* is preferred because, when Josephus wrote the *Jewish War* in the 70s CE, he was sponsored by the Flavian house in Rome and could not write freely. It then happened later in the 90s that opposition rose against Josephus in Rome especially from Justus of Tiberias, who wrote a now lost book on the war that cast doubts on Josephus's *Jewish War* and made him look like a traitor. For this reason, Josephus had to save his neck by writing another account, his *Life*, in which he had to come forward with the truth. However, this view has been called into question, not least by Per Bilde and Steve Mason,[62] who find more similarities than differences, just as it is unconvincing that *Life* was written solely to refute Justus. Rather, it was written as a sequel to Josephus's masterpiece, *Antiquities*, with the objective of establishing Josephus's credentials in terms of ancestry and character. As I have argued elsewhere, in my opinion, this last view has the better argument,[63] but though it provides us with more trust in Josephus as a writer of history, it does not liberate us from his hands. He was heavily involved in the affairs and wrote from his own agenda, which we need to keep in mind.

Judging from Josephus—and there is no reason to question this—the outbreak of the war was more a chaotic series of happenings than a well-orchestrated event. Initially, the aristocracy of Jerusalem tried to hinder the revolt (see, for example, *J.W.* 2.418; *Life* 17–23) and hoped for a quick resubmission to Rome, but all hopes faded after the dramatic defeat of the Syrian legate Cestius Gallus, who tried to retake Jerusalem but decided to pull back, thereby breaking up his flanks and making them vulnerable to the exhilarated Jewish rebels, who chased them all the way downhill to the sea, almost overtaking the entire army at the narrow Bet-Horon pass (see *J.W.* 2.499–556; *Life* 23–24). After this decisive event, a war council was held in Jerusalem during which generals were appointed to take control of the various regions (so *J.W.* 2.568), or—and that is a main point—were sent to calm the situation from spinning out of control (so *Life* 28–29). This seems flatly contradictory. However, while *Jewish War* presents the course of events in a more official way, *Life* delves into the conflicts behind the scenes. Since it also emerges in the *War* how the nobility of Jerusalem hoped for a quick end to the violence (see *J.W.* 2.418–21, 533; *Life* 23), it might very well have been the case that Josephus was

---

61. See, for example, Shaye J. D. Cohen, *Josephus in Galilee and Rome: His Vita and Development as a Historian* (Columbia Studies in the Classical Tradition 8; Leiden: Brill, 1979); Uriel Rappaport, "Where Was Josephus Lying—In His *Life* or in the *War*?," in *Josephus and the History of the Greco-Roman Period: Essays in Memory of Morton Smith* (ed. Fausto Parente and Joseph Sievers; StPB 41; Leiden: Brill, 1994). For discussion and critique, see Per Bilde, *Flavius Josephus between Jerusalem and Rome: His Life, His Works, and Their Importance* (JSPSup 2; Sheffield: JSOT Press, 1988), 135–40.

62. Cf. Bilde, *Flavius Josephus*, 28–46, 137–40, 160–62; Steve Mason, *Flavius Josephus: Translation and Commentary*, vol. 9, *Life of Josephus* (Leiden: Brill, 2001), XXVII–L.

63. See my discussion in *Herod Antipas*, 54–68.

instructed to take control over Galilee in order to ease tension until a peace agreement could be secured.[64]

When Josephus arrived in Galilee, the situation was nothing short of chaotic. According to *Life* 28, the region had not entirely rebelled against the Romans, but the most pressing issues seemed also to be the internal tumults and conflicts bringing the area close to actual civil war. Divisions were everywhere: (a) the two major cities, Sepphoris and Tiberias, fought for supremacy (*Life* 39); (b) at the lake, Tiberias and Taricheae did the same (*J. W.* 2.604–9; *Life* 136–44); (c) in Tiberias, three factions fought for control (*Life* 32); (d) and, not least, "the Galileans," as Josephus calls the people from the countryside,[65] strongly opposed the major cities (see, for example, *Life* 384).

There was especially no uniform alignment to the war council of Jerusalem. Several noteworthy members opposed Josephus's hegemony, and some of the strong cities tried to keep out of the war by upholding the alliance to Rome and Agrippa II, most notably Sepphoris (see, for example, *J. W.* 2.511; 3.30–34, 59–62; *Life* 30–31, 346–48, 394) and Gamala (*Life* 46–61),[66] but also Tiberias, where one of the factions wanted to uphold the alliance with Agrippa (*Life* 34). The bulk of the *Life* is concerned with these internal conflicts and how Josephus managed, with the support mainly of the Galileans, to stay on top, even though a delegation was sent from Jerusalem to release him from his status as general (*Life* 189–335).

Eventually, it seems that Josephus was able to gain the upper hand and secure a kind of internal peace, which gave him the opportunity to prepare Galilee for the coming Roman invasion by constructing massive fortification walls at nineteen mentioned cities and sites (*Life* 187–88; *J. W.* 2.573–75). This is attested not only by Josephus himself but also by archaeology, which according to Mordechai Aviam provides evidence of fortification systems in nearly half of the named sites. According to Aviam, these fortifications are so massive (for example, a 1-km wall at Jotapata, a 2-km wall at Mount Tabor, a 200-m wall at Gamala, and so on) that it could only have been done by a strong central government with the support of the people.[67]

But Josephus could have saved himself the trouble. The army of Vespasian was so frightening that the mere sight of it at the borders of Galilee made people run for cover, including Josephus, who fled to Tiberias (*J. W.* 3.128–31). In *Life*, Josephus only briefly mentions the ensuing battles in Galilee (411–13). His *Jewish War* does offer a narration with a number of details, especially on the siege of Jotapata in the spring of 67, during which Josephus was captured and famously gained ground before Vespasian by prophesying that he would become emperor (*J. W.* 3.401–2). According to *Jewish War*, Vespasian laid siege to and conquered all the major strongholds of Galilee, starting with Gabara and advancing to Jotapata, then Tiberias,

---

64. See Bilde, *Flavius Josephus*, 45–46.

65. See Freyne, *Galilee from Alexander*, 156–66; Mason, *Life of Josephus*, 38 n. 186; Bilde, *Flavius Josephus*, 42; Jensen, *Herod Antipas*, 5–6.

66. Gamala later changed sides, and one of the epic battles was fought there; see Mason, *Life of Josephus*, 49 n. 273.

67. Aviam, "People, Land, Economy," 30–31.

**Figure D: Gamla.** According to Josephus, the city and strong-
hold of Gamla (Gamala) was the only place where the Roman
army of Vespasian met any noteworthy resistance. Excavations
have brought to light the city's protection wall with the round
tower on top. Photo by Morten Hørning Jensen.

Taricheae, Gamala, Tabor, and finally Gischala (3.59–4.120). Judging from the narration, it
was only at Gamala that the Roman army met any noteworthy resistance (*J.W.* 4.11–54,
62–83). Since the entire campaign was short and lasted only for some months in the spring
and summer of 67,[68] there is no reason to believe that Galilee was entirely devastated when
the Romans set their course south. However, the places that were conquered, were in a typical Roman fashion levelled more or less to the ground and many people sold off as slaves (cf.
*J.W.* 3.132-35 for Gabara, 3.304-6, 336-39 for Japha, 3.540-41 for Tiberias and Taricheae,
4.62–83 for Gamala).

Back to our main question: Did Galilee want the war or could it just not avoid it? It is
impossible to answer definitely. On the one hand, we have "the city of peace," Sepphoris,[69]
Gamala, and one of the factions in Tiberias, who at least overtly tried to adhere to Roman
hegemony. On the other hand, we have internal conflicts between the cities, the local chiefs,

---

68. See Bilde, *Flavius Josephus*, 47.

69. There is a highly interesting coin from Sepphoris minted in 68 declaring itself a "peace-city" (*irenopo-
lis*) with the legend: ΕΠΙ ΟΥΕϹΠΑϹΙΑΝΟΥ ΕΙΡΗΝΟΠΟΛΙϹ ΝΕΡΩΝΙϹ ϹΕΠΦΩΡ ("During Vespasian, in
Irenopolis-Neronias-Sepphoris"). See Ya'akov Meshorer, *Ancient Jewish Coinage*, vol. 2, *Herod the Great through
Bar Cochba* (Dix Hills, N.Y.: Amphora, 1982), 167–68; Mark A. Chancey, *Greco-Roman Culture and the Galilee of
Jesus* (SNTSMS 134; Cambridge: Cambridge University Press, 2005), 186–87. In other words, Sepphoris boldly
declares the exact opposite of the Jewish war coins, corresponding to the notion in *Life,* 411 that the inhabitants of
Sepphoris went out to greet Vespasian.

and not least "the Galileans," who opposed the cities. Did they want war or did they just use the opportunity as a game-changer of the power balance? We cannot tell. It does, however, seem certain that, in the end, most of Galilee, with the exception of Sepphoris, did engage in the revolt, perhaps not least driven by a deeply felt allegiance to Jerusalem and the temple. We have a powerful indication of this in a number of rather crudely struck bronze coins from Gamala, which, according to the standard reading,[70] boldly declare *LG'LT*, "for the redemption," and *YR'SLM HQ*, "Jerusalem, the Holy." According to Danny Syon, these inscriptions should be read together: "For the redemption of Jerusalem, the Holy."[71] For some, at least, the objective of the war was clear enough: To redeem and purify Jerusalem from any foreign influence—just as in the old glorious times of the Maccabees.

**Figure E: Gamla coin.** During the excavations of Gamla, a new type of rebel coin was discovered (seven specimens altogether), with legends that, according to Ya'akov Meshorer and Danny Syon, read: "For the redemption of Jerusalem the Holy," thus providing a glimpse of the ideology behind the rebellion. Photo from David Hendin, *Guide to Biblical Coins* (5th ed.; New York: Amphora, 2010). Reproduced by permission.

Still, it is only fair to say that the war in essence was a Jerusalemite affair.[72] It broke out in Jerusalem; the bulk of the Roman campaign was concentrated on the siege of Jerusalem; and most of the destruction, plundering, and murdering took place in Jerusalem. On a relative scale, Galilee fared better and was thus able to reemerge from the rubble of war all the quicker.[73]

### Galilee Reborn—Yet Again (70–200 CE)

After the war, three major changes took place in Galilee that, combined, marked the transition into a new era. First, Roman military presence grew exponentially, as did the urbanization and romanization processes in the cities. We have no indications of Roman camps in Galilee before the war. This all changed during the reign of Hadrian (117–138 CE), who moved the sixth legion, Ferrata, from Syria to a place known as Kaperkotnei (or Kefar 'Othnay) located at Tel

---

70. Yoav Farhi has suggested a different reading of the obverse side, *BGML'* (Gamla [year] 2); see Hendin, *Guide to Biblical Coins*, 364.

71. Danny Syon, "'City of Refuge': The Archaeological Evidence of the Revolt at Gamla," in *The Great Revolt in the Galilee* (in Hebrew; ed. Ofra Guri-Rimon; Haifa: Hecht Museum, University of Haifa, 2008), 62.

72. See the discussion of the events in Freyne, *Galilee from Alexander*, 78–91. According to Martin Goodman, the increased tension in Judea and Jerusalem was due to socioeconomic inequality between rich and poor, caused by the elite's control especially of the temple institution. See Goodman, "The First Jewish Revolt: Social Conflict and the Problem of Debt," *JJS* 33 (1982): 417–27.

73. See Uriel Rappaport, "The Great Revolt: An Overview," in Guri-Rimon, *Great Revolt in the Galilee*, 13.

Megiddo, which came to be called simply "Legio."[74] Small cohorts were also in place at other places such as Sepphoris and Tiberias.[75] Coins from Sepphoris and Tiberias make clear how vividly the new Roman presence was felt. At Sepphoris, coins were minted depicting temples and deities as well as images of emperors.[76] This was never seen before the war. Various building projects also were launched in both places, such as the lower Eastern plateau in Sepphoris and the large temple in Tiberias known as the "Hadrianeum," of which only one large wall has been found.[77]

**Figure F: Coin of Hadrian** depicting the temple in Tiberias, the Hadrianeum, in a tetrastyle fashion. *Obverse*: The bust of Hadrian with a laurel. *Reverse*: Zeus in a temple with the legend at the left reading TIBEP. Photo from David Hendin, *Guide to Biblical Coins* (5th ed.; New York: Amphora, 2010). Reproduced by permission.

Second, at the same time Galilee experienced a new wave of settlement from the south, at least after the Bar Kokhba revolt, which dealt a heavy blow to Jewish settlements throughout Judea. Nothing indicates that Galilee was impacted by the revolt and, as Horsley rightly suggests, also nothing indicates that Galilee was being farmed through large imperial estates.[78] Instead, small-scale farming continued to be practiced and expanded through the influx of Jewish settlers into the region.

Third, during this process Galilee in reality emerged as the new heartland of Judaism. Not only farmers and workers moved to Galilee, but so did the priestly clans and rabbis.[79] From Yavneh (Jamnia), the seat of the leading rabbis was moved to Galilee, where Judah the Prince (Yehudah ha-Nasi) became the leading figure and compiler of the Mishnah according to the tradition. Beth She'arim and Sepphoris were the major cities in the late second century. Ostensibly, Judah even managed to cultivate good relations with the Romans.[80] In the third century, the rabbinic council was moved to Tiberias, where Rabbi Yoḥanan established *beth ha-Midrash ha-Gadol*, the Great Study House, in 235, which eventually produced the Palestinian Talmud.[81]

---

74. The site is presently being surveyed; see: http://www.biblicalarchaeology.org/daily/biblical-sites-places/ biblical-archaeology-sites/legio/. See also Ze'ev Safrai, "The Roman Army in the Galilee," in *The Galilee in Late Antiquity* (ed. Lee I. Levine; New York: Jewish Theological Seminary of America, 1992); Chancey, *Myth of a Gentile Galilee*, 58–60; Chancey, *Greco-Roman Culture*, 63–70.

75. See Horsley, *Galilee: History*, 92.

76. See Meshorer, *City Coins*, 34–37; Chancey, *Greco-Roman Culture*, 186–92.

77. See Jensen, *Herod Antipas*, 146–47; Chancey, *Greco-Roman Culture*, 100–121.

78. See Horsley, *Galilee: History*, 90–91.

79. See Stuart S. Miller, "Priests, Purities, and the Jews of Galilee," in Zangenberg et al., *Religion, Ethnicity, and Identity in Ancient Galilee*, 375–402.

80. See Horsley, *Archaeology, History, and Society*, 62.

81. See Jensen, *Herod Antipas*, 147.

These changes, taken together, make it clear that postwar Galilee was quite different from prewar Galilee and emerged as the new "spiritual center of Judaism"[82] at the same time as it experienced far more intense urbanization and romanization processes.

## Conclusion

We began our investigation by asking how important our understanding of the history of Galilee has been and is for our understanding of the historical Jesus. It is time to conclude by outlining five major trends of the Galilean history in our time frame.

First, there is a solid line of connection between Judea/Jerusalem and Galilee from the Hasmonean era onward. The Hasmonean policy incorporated a mixture of military campaigns, migration, and building activity. Of course, Galilee was inhabited by non-Jews before the Hasmonean takeover, and it is likely that some of them converted to Judaism. But the increase in settlements was probably due to the influx of settlers from the south. This also explains why there is no notion of mixed cities in our sources from the first century in Galilee proper. It was considered Jewish heartland.

Second, during the several power transitions Galilee did experience a number of battles and destructions. This is the case not least during the years of unrest following Pompey's conquest in 63 BCE until Herod's final victory in 37 BCE, after Herod's death in 4 BCE, and later during the war of 66–70, with a number of battles and internal attacks from 66 to 67 CE. However, measured against Judea and Jerusalem, Galilee got off easy, even though there were long periods of unrest in between. The picture of Galilee being caught in a spiral of violence with ever-growing tension and episodes from Pompey through the Herodians to the rebellion against Rome conflates the evidence in a reductionistic manner.

Third, the most important ruler of Galilee was Herod Antipas. He was allotted Galilee after the death of his father, and his arrival at Sepphoris in effect gave Galilee its first kingly ruler since the old Israelite dynasty. While Herod the Great disregarded Galilee—maybe even purposely so, remembering the fierce resistance he had met there in his early years—Antipas launched a number of building campaigns, most notably at Sepphoris and Tiberias. For this reason, Antipas has been described as the main provocation behind the emergence of social protest movements such as those of John the Baptist and Jesus of Nazareth. However, a close investigation of the sources reveals another story. Archaeological material testifies that Galilee flourished in this period, with new settlements being founded on more remote and less defensible plots of land, while old towns grew in size and activity. Compared to his father, Antipas was much less of a builder, and the deteriorating effect he could have had on the Galilean economy was therefore also all the more limited.

---

82. See Chancey, *Myth of a Gentile Galilee*, 61.

Fourth, our investigation of Josephus's description of the events in Galilee during the great war falls in line with this. Galilee was not the center of the revolt, and much energy was spent on internal fighting and positioning and not on a united front against Rome.

Finally, Galilee evolved into the very center of Judaism after the Bar Kokhba revolt. The rabbinic council was moved to Galilee, with major stops at Beth She'arim, Sepphoris, and Tiberias, and it was in Galilee that the two major writings of the rabbinic era were produced: the Mishnah and the Palestinian Talmud.

## Bibliography

Alt, Albrecht. *Kleine Schriften zur Geschichte des Volkes Israe.* 3 vols. Munich: Beck, 1953–59.

Applebaum, Shimon. "Economic Life in Palestine." In *The Jewish People in the First Century: Historical Geography, Political History, Social, Cultural and Religious Life and Institutions*, edited by Shmuel Safrai and Menahem Stern, 2:631–700. CRINT, section 1. 2 vols. Assen: Van Gorcum, 1976.

Aviam, Mordechai. "First Century Jewish Galilee: An Archaeological Perspective." In *Religion and Society in Roman Palestine: Old Questions, New Approaches*, edited by Douglas R. Edwards, 7–27. London: Routledge, 2004.

———. *Jews, Pagans, and Christians in the Galilee: 25 Years of Archaeological Excavations and Surveys, Hellenistic to Byzantine Periods*. Land of Galilee 1. Rochester N.Y.: University of Rochester Press, 2004.

———. "People, Land, Economy, and Belief in First-Century Galilee and Its Origins: A Comprehensive Archaeological Synthesis." In *The Galilean Economy in the Time of Jesus*, edited by David A. Fiensy and Ralph K. Hawkins, 5–48. Early Christianity and Its Literature 11. Atlanta: Society of Biblical Literature, 2013.

Bernett, Monika. "Roman Imperial Cult in the Galilee: Structures, Functions, and Dynamics." In *Religion, Ethnicity, and Identity in Ancient Galilee: A Region in Transition*, edited by Jürgen Zangenberg, Harold W. Attridge, and Dale B. Martin, 337–56. WUNT 210. Tübingen: Mohr Siebeck, 2007.

Bilde, Per. *Flavius Josephus between Jerusalem and Rome: His Life, His Works, and Their Importance*. JSPSup 2. Sheffield: JSOT Press, 1988.

Chancey, Mark A. *Greco-Roman Culture and the Galilee of Jesus*. SNTSMS 134. Cambridge: Cambridge University Press, 2005.

———. *The Myth of a Gentile Galilee*. SNTSMS 118. Cambridge: Cambridge University Press, 2002.

Cohen, Shaye J. D. *Josephus in Galilee and Rome: His Vita and Development as a Historian*. Columbia Studies in the Classical Tradition 8. Leiden: Brill, 1979.

Deines, Roland. "Galiläa und Jesus: Anfragen zur Funktion der Herkunftsbezeichnung 'Galiläa' in der neueren Jesusforschung." In *Jesus und die Archäologie Galiläas*, edited by Carsten

Claussen and Jörg Frey, 271–320. Biblisch-theologische Studien 87. Neukirchen-Vluyn: Neukirchener Verlag, 2008.

Edwards, Douglas R. "Identity and Social Location in Roman Galilean Villages." In *Religion, Ethnicity and Identity in Ancient Galilee: A Region in Transition*, edited by Jürgen Zangenberg, Harold W. Attridge, and Dale B. Martin, 357–74. WUNT 210. Tübingen: Mohr Siebeck, 2007.

Feldman, Louis H., trans. *Josephus: Jewish Antiquities, Books XVIII–XIX*. LCL. Cambridge, Mass.: Harvard University Press, 1965.

———. "The Term 'Galileans' in Josephus." *JQR* 72.1 (1981): 50–52.

Frankel, Rafael, et al. *Settlement Dynamics and Regional Diversity in Ancient Upper Galilee: Arachaeological Survey of Upper Galilee*. IAA Reports 14. Jerusalem: Israel Antiquities Authority, 2001.

Freyne, Seán. "Archaeology and the Historical Jesus." In Freyne, *Galilee and Gospel: Collected Essays*, 160–82. Tübingen: Mohr Siebeck, 2000. Reprinted from *Archaeology and Biblical Interpretation*, edited by John R. Bartlett, 117–44. London: Routledge, 1997.

———. "Behind the Names: Galileans, Samaritans, *Ioudaioi*." In *Galilee through the Centuries: Confluence of Cultures*, edited by Eric M. Meyers, 39–55. Duke Judaic Studies Series 1. Winona Lake, Ind.: Eisenbrauns, 1999.

———. "A Galilean Messiah?" *ST* 55 (2001): 198–218.

———. "Galilean Questions to Crossan's Mediterranean Jesus." In *Whose Historical Jesus?*, edited by William E. Arnal and Michel Desjardins, 63–91. Studies in Christianity and Judaism 7. Waterloo, Ont.: Wilfrid Laurier University Press, 1997.

———. *Galilee From Alexander the Great to Hadrian, 323 B.C.E. to 135 C.E.: A Study of Second Temple Judaism*. University of Notre Dame Center for the Study of Judaism and Christianity in Antiquity 5. Wilmington, Del.: Michael Glazier; Notre Dame: Notre Dame University Press, 1980. Reprint, Edinburgh: T&T Clark, 1998.

———. "Herodian Economics in Galilee: Searching for a Suitable Model." In Freyne, *Galilee and Gospel: Collected Essays*, 86–113. Tübingen: Mohr Siebeck, 2000. Reprinted from *Modelling Early Christianity: Social-scientific studies of the New Testament in Its Context*, edited by Philip F. Esler, 23–46. London: Routledge, 1995.

———. "Jesus and the Urban Culture of Galilee." In *Texts and Contexts: Biblical Texts in Their Textual and Situational Contexts. Essays in Honor of Lars Hartman*, edited by Tord Fornberg and David Hellholm, 597–622. Oslo: Scandinavian University Press, 1995.

Gal, Zvi. *Lower Galilee During the Iron Age*. ASOR Dissertation Series 8. Winona Lake, Ind.: Eisenbrauns, 1992.

Goodman, Martin. "The First Jewish Revolt: Social Conflict and the Problem of Debt." *JJS* 33 (1982): 417–27.

Hendin, David. *Guide to Biblical Coins*. 5th ed. New York: Amphora, 2010.

Horsley, Richard A. "Archaeology and the Villages of Upper Galilee: A Dialogue with Archaeologists." *BASOR* 297 (1995): 5–16, 27–28.

———. *Archaeology, History, and Society in Galilee: The Social Context of Jesus and the Rabbis.* Valley Forge, Pa.: Trinity Press International, 1996.

———. *Galilee: History, Politics, People.* Valley Forge, Pa.: Trinity Press International, 1995.

———. *Hearing the Whole Story: The Politics of Plot in Mark's Gospel.* Louisville: Westminster John Knox, 2001.

———. "Jesus and Empire." In *In the Shadow of Empire: Reclaiming the Bible as a History of Faithful Resistance*, edited by Richard A. Horsley, 75–96. Louisville: Westminster John Knox, 2008.

———. *The Prophet Jesus and the Renewal of Israel: Moving Beyond a Diversionary Debate.* Grand Rapids: Eerdmans, 2012.

Horsley, Richard A., and Jonathan A. Draper. *Whoever Hears You Hears Me: Prophets, Performance, and Tradition in Q.* Harrisburg, Pa.: Trinity Press International, 1999.

Horsley, Richard A., and Neil Asher Silberman. *The Message and the Kingdom: How Jesus and Paul Ignited a Revolution and Transformed the Ancient World.* Minneapolis: Fortress Press, 1997.

Jensen, Morten Hørning. "Herod Antipas: A Shadow of Death on Jesus?," *BAR* 38, no. 5 (2012): 42–46.

———. *Herod Antipas in Galilee: The Literary and Archaeological Sources on the Reign of Herod Antipas and Its Socio-Economic Impact on Galilee.* WUNT 2.215. Tübingen: Mohr Siebeck, 2006. 2nd ed., 2010.

———. "Rural Galilee and Rapid Changes: An Investigation of the Socio-Economic Dynamics and Developments in Roman Galilee." *Bib* 93 (2012): 43–67.

Leibner, Uzi. "Settlement and Demography in Late Roman and Byzantine Eastern Galilee." In *Settlements and Demography in the Near East in Late Antiquity: Proceedings of the Colloquium, Matera, 27–29 October 2005*, edited by Ariel S. Lewin and Pietrina Pellegrini, 105–30. Biblioteca di Mediterraneo antico 2. Pisa: Istituti Editoriali e Poligrafici Internazionali, 2006.

———. *Settlement and History in Hellenistic, Roman, and Byzantine Galilee: An Archaeological Survey of the Eastern Galilee.* TSAJ 127. Tübingen: Mohr Siebeck, 2009.

Marcus, Ralph, trans. *Josephus: Jewish Antiquities: Books XII–XIII.* LCL. Cambridge, Mass.: Harvard University Press, 1943.

Mason, Steve. *Flavius Josephus: Translation and Commentary.* Vol. 9, *Life of Josephus.* Leiden: Brill, 2001.

Meshorer, Ya'akov. *Ancient Jewish Coinage.* Vol. 2, *Herod the Great through Bar Cochba.* Dix Hills, N.Y.: Amphora, 1982.

———. *City Coins of Eretz-Israel and the Decapolis in the Roman Period.* Jerusalem: Israel Museum, 1985.

Meyers, Eric M., and Mark A. Chancey. "How Jewish Was Sepphoris in Jesus' Time?" *BAR* 26, no. 4 (2000): 18–33.

Miller, Stuart S. "Priests, Purities, and the Jews of Galilee." In *Religion, Ethnicity, and Identity in Ancient Galilee: A Region in Transition*, edited by Jürgen Zangenberg, Harold W. Attridge, and Dale B. Martin, 375–402. WUNT 210. Tübingen: Mohr Siebeck, 2007.

Moxnes, Halvor. "The Construction of Galilee as a Place for the Historical Jesus." *BTB* 31 (2001): 26–37, 64-77.

Rappaport, Uriel. "The Great Revolt: An Overview." In *The Great Revolt in the Galilee*, edited by Ofra Guri-Rimon. Haifa: Hecht Museum, University of Haifa, 2008.

———. "Where Was Josephus Lying—In His *Life* or in the *War*?" In *Josephus and the History of the Greco-Roman Period: Essays in Memory of Morton Smith*, edited by Fausto Parente, and Joseph Sievers, 279–89. StPB 41. Leiden: Brill, 1994.

Reed, Jonathan L. *Archaeology and the Galilean Jesus: A Re-Examination of the Evidence.* Harrisburg, Pa.: Trinity Press International, 2000.

———. "Galileans, 'Israelite Village Communities,' and the Sayings Gospel Q." In *Galilee through the Centuries: Confluence of Cultures*, edited by Eric M. Meyers, 87–108. Winona Lake, Ind.: Eisenbrauns, 1999.

Safrai, Ze'ev. "The Roman Army in the Galilee." In *The Galilee in Late Antiquity*, edited by Lee I. Levine, 103–14. New York: Jewish Theological Seminary of America, 1992.

Sanders, E. P. *The Historical Figure of Jesus.* London: Penguin, 1993.

———. "Jesus in Historical Context." *Theology Today* 50 (1993): 429–48.

Schürer, Emil. *Geschichte des jüdischen Volkes im Zeitalter Jesu Christi.* 3 vols. Leipzig: Hinrichs, 1901–7. Vol. 1, 3rd ed., 1901. Vol. 2, 4th ed., 1907.

Stern, Menahem. *Greek and Latin Authors on Jews and Judaism.* Vol. 1, *From Herodotus to Plutarch.* Fontes ad res Judaicas spectantes. Jerusalem: Israel Academy of Sciences and Humanities, 1974.

Syon, Danny. "'City of Refuge': The Archaeological Evidence of the Revolt at Gamla." In Hebrew. In *The Great Revolt in the Galilee*, edited by Ofra Guri-Rimon, 53–66. Haifa: Hecht Museum, University of Haifa, 2008.

———. "Tyre and Gamla: A Study in the Monetary Influence of Southern Phoenicia on Galilee and the Golan in the Hellenistic and Roman Periods. Jerusalem." PhD dissertation, Hebrew University, Jerusalem, 2004.

Urman, Dan. *The Golan: A Profile of a Region during the Roman and Byzantine Periods.* BAR International Series 269. London: BAR, 1985.

# 3

# Religious Practices and Religious Movements in Galilee: 100 bce–200 ce

*Roland Deines*

The aim of this chapter is twofold: (1) to describe the development of Jewish religious move-ments[1] in Galilee over the period of about three hundred years, and (2) to comment on the

---

I owe a heartfelt thanks to my research assistant Dr. Christoph Ochs, who supported me in many ways in the writing of this paper.

1. The most common Greek term used to mark different religious groups or movements within Judaism is αἵρεσις, meaning "choice, inclination," and then also "system of philosophic principles, or those who profess such principles, sect, school" [LSJ], derived from αἱρέομαι ("to choose"). See Acts 5:17 (Sadducees); 15:5 and 26:5 (Pharisees); and 24:5, 14; 28:22 (Christians); Josephus uses αἵρεσις in *J. W.* 2.118 (Fourth Philosophy, founded by the Galilean Judas), 122, 137, 142 (Essenes), 162 (Pharisees), and *Ant.* 13.171 (Pharisees, Sadducees, Essenes), 288 (Pharisees), 293; 20.199 (Sadducees); *Life* 10 (Pharisees, Sadducees, Essenes), 12, 191, 197 (Pharisees); the synonym προαίρεσις is used in *Ant.* 13.293 (Pharisees) and 15.373 (Essenes). Given the fact that the word *sect* has so many unhelpful connotations in its contemporary usage, I prefer the terms *movement*, *school of thought*, or simply *group* to describe these major religious movements within first-century Judaism. In fact, except for the Essenes, no formal membership is attested in the sources. In addition, Josephus's parallel use of the term φιλοσοφίαι for these Jewish groups (*Ant.* 18.9, 11, 23 [for the use of the verb φιλοσοφέω in the description of the schools, see *J. W.* 2.119, 166; *Ant.* 18.11, 25; in *Life* 12]; Josephus compares the Pharisees to the Greek philosophical school of the Stoics) shows that he sees these Jewish parties as religious schools of thought that have their respective, but differing, ways of life and ideas about human choice (see *Life* 10–12). This, then, is why they should not be understood primarily as political interest groups or as closed "sects." See also Anthony J. Saldarini, *Pharisees, Scribes, and Sadducees in Palestinian Society: A Sociological Approach* (Edinburgh: T&T Clark, 1988; repr., with a foreword by James C. VanderKam, Grand Rapids: Eerdmans, 2001), 123–24: "A *hairesis* was a coherent and principled choice of a way of life, that is, of a particular school of thought" (p. 123); Steve Mason, *Flavius Josephus: Translation and Commentary*, vol. 9, *Life of Josephus* (Leiden: Brill, 2001), 15–16; Roland Deines, "The Social Profile of the Pharisees," in *The New Testament and Rabbinic Literature* (ed. Reimund Bieringer, Florentino García Martínez, Didier Pollefeyt, and Peter J. Tomson; JSJSup 136; Leiden: Brill, 2010), 111–32, esp. 127–30 (reprinted in *Acts of God in History: Studies Towards Recovering a Theological Historiography* [ed. Christoph Ochs and Peter Watts; WUNT 317; Tübingen: Mohr

religious practices that can be assumed for these various groups over the same time period. However, the initial fact to appreciate is that nobody in antiquity had any particular interest in Galilee as a separate region, and consequently reports about the regions are very sparse. Its relevance, in particular today, is mainly due to Jesus being a Galilean.

Accepting that a separate history of Galilee was something inconceivable in antiquity because the region was not understood as a decisive factor in history (as Jerusalem and the temple clearly were)[2] helps to clarify the scattered character of our sources about Galilee and its political and religious developments. This also means that neither Josephus, nor any of the authors of the New Testament, nor the compilers of the rabbinic texts, saw any reason to write particularly on Galilee for Galilee's sake. They occasionally mention Galilee in passing when certain events took place there, though these generally had some bearing on Jerusalem or other more "important" places. Galilee alone was not interesting enough.[3] Thus, for

---

Siebeck, 2013], 29–52, esp. 47–50); Hillel Newman, *Proximity to Power and Jewish Sectarian Groups of the Ancient Period: A Review of Lifestyle, Values, and Halakhah in the Pharisees, Sadducees, Essenes, and Qumran* (Brill Reference Library of Judaism 25; Leiden: Brill, 2006), 1–21, on terminology and his preference for "group" as proper label (p. 5). Within this wider definition, Pharisaism can be understood as a movement promulgating and developing a specific understanding of the Torah as true wisdom. Accordingly, the essential elements for the Pharisaic "way of life" are the unwritten traditions ("the traditions of the elders," Mark 7:3, 5 par. Matt. 15:2; or "the traditions of the fathers," *Ant.* 13.297, 408), which were regarded as similarly authoritative and—in a wider sense—based on God's revelation to Moses (see Matt. 23:2; *Ant.* 13.297).

2. An ancient and a contemporary example will demonstrate this: (1) The Roman geographer Strabo, who wrote in the first quarter of the first century CE, describes in his *Geographica* 16.2.21 the area along the Eastern Mediterranean as "Phoenicia," which is the coastal strip from Orthosia to Pelusium, and the area farther inland between Gaza in the south, Arabia (that is, Nabatea) in the east and the Anti-Lebanon in the north as "Judea," though he is aware of the various areas within these borders. Galilee is mentioned by name only twice (16.2.34 and 16.2.40). Strabo has some more detailed knowledge about the south, that is, the area around Jericho, the Dead Sea, and Idumea (16.2.32, 34, 41–45), but he seems to have no first-hand knowledge of Galilee. He mentions Taricheae once as a place for salting fish, but the context is a description of the Dead Sea and not Galilee (16.2.45). When he talks about the people living in Syria (for the borders see 16.1.1), he differentiates between Syrians and Phoenicians as the main population, with whom four other groups lived: the Judeans, Idumeans, Gazeans, and Azotians (16.2.2). He is willing to differentiate the Idumeans from the Judeans but not the Galileans, whom he obviously takes for Judeans. Other Roman authors who mention Galilee, for example, Pliny (who describes it as "the part of Judaea adjoining Syria," *Nat.* 5.70), Tacitus, and Ptolemy, display the same lack of interest and inaccuracy in their scattered remarks. Silvia Cappelletti summarizes her survey of "Non-Jewish Authors on Galilee," in *Religion, Ethnicity, and Identity in Ancient Galilee: A Region in Transition* (ed. Jürgen Zangenberg, Harold W. Attridge, and Dale B. Martin; WUNT 210; Tübingen: Mohr Siebeck, 2007), 69–81, with the sentence: "In the eyes of the Roman world, Galilee was a marginal region." (2) The relative unimportance of Galilee can be deduced also from *The Oxford Handbook of Early Christian Studies* (ed. Susan Ashbrook Harvey and David G. Hunter; Oxford: Oxford University Press, 2008). Subsection IV of the book presents an outline of early Christianity on a regional basis, where "Egypt and Palestine" (pp. 344–63, written by David Brakke) form one chapter and "Syria and Mesopotamia" another (pp. 365–86, by Lucas van Rompay), but nothing has to be or can be said about Galilee, though the name occasionally occurs in the text (for example, p. 345).

3. But the situation is nevertheless much better than for the previous century, where "there is nearly complete absence of historical sources concerning the eastern Galilee during the 550 years between the Eastern conquest and

the three centuries that are the focus of this chapter, we have only fragmented data that we can use to come to an understanding of the religious life and the religious movements in Galilee. In fact, when it comes to the available sources, it is presently impossible to write a *comprehensive* history of religious practices and movements in Galilee from 100 BCE to the early third century. For most of the groups in Galilee known by name, that is, the Pharisees, the anti-Roman rebels (the Fourth Philosophy, or Zealots), the early Christians, or the sages mentioned in the rabbinic texts, only isolated episodes exist. In fact, the term *Galileans* only occasionally occurs as a label for certain people, and then mostly for when they appear *out-side* of Galilee.[4] The modern interest in Galilee is therefore without equivalent in the ancient sources. Nonetheless, the four Gospels, together with the Jewish historian Josephus, who was the military commander of Galilee during the first stage of the Jewish revolt against Rome, are the most important sources for our knowledge about the religious life of Galilee. Rabbinic texts provide additional, albeit stray, evidence but are our only literary source for the second century. Increasing amounts of ever-more-detailed archaeological evidence as the result of diligent surveys and excavations form a vital and thrilling resource without which our understanding of the religious profile of Galilee would be incredibly poorer. The few references to Galilee in the works of Greek and Roman authors add nothing for this topic.

In the following, I will discuss *four religious movements* in Galilee: the Pharisaic movement, the Bar Kokhba war, the Jewish Christian movement, and the early rabbinic movement. In doing so, I will also refer to archaeological remains as an example of how textual and archaeological evidence can be used to support and corroborate each other.[5]

---

the Hasmonean rebellion," as Uzi Leibner remarks (*Settlement and History in Hellenistic, Roman, and Byzantine Galilee: An Archaeological Survey of the Eastern Galilee* (TSAJ 127; Tübingen: Mohr Siebeck, 2009), 315.

4. For literature, see in this volume my "Galilee and the Historical Jesus in Recent Research," n. 1.

5. Helpful methodological discussions include Dennis E. Groh, "The Clash between Literary and Archaeological Models of Provincial Palestine," in *Archaeology and the Galilee: Texts and Contexts in the Graeco-Roman and Byzantine Period* (ed. Douglas R. Edwards and C. Thomas McCollough; South Florida Studies in the History of Judaism 143; Atlanta: Scholars Press, 1997), 29–37; and, in the same volume, James F. Strange, "First Century Galilee from Archaeology and from the Texts," 39–48. See also Catherine Hezser, "Correlating Literary, Epigraphic, and Archaeological Sources," in *The Oxford Handbook of Jewish Daily Life in Roman Palestine* (ed. Catherine Hezser; Oxford: Oxford University Press, 2010), 9–27; Jürgen Zangenberg, "Common Judaism and the Multidimensional Character of Material Culture," in *Redefining First-Century Jewish and Christian Identities: Essays in Honor of Ed Parish Sanders* (ed. Fabian E. Udoh; Christianity and Judaism in Antiquity 16; Notre Dame: University of Notre Dame Press, 2008), 175–93. For my own considerations and further literature, see Roland Deines, "Non-literary Sources for the Interpretation of the New Testament: Methodological Considerations and Case Studies Related to the Corpus Judaeo-Hellenisticum," in *Neues Testament und hellenistisch-jüdische Alltagskultur: Wechselseitige Wahrnehmungen. III. Internationales Symposium zum Corpus Judaeo-Hellenisticum Novi Testamenti 21.–24. Mai 2009, Leipzig* (ed. Roland Deines, Jens Herzer, and Karl-Wilhelm Niebuhr; WUNT 274; Tübingen: Mohr Siebeck, 2011), 25–66, esp. 30–31, and n. 53 below.

## The Pharisaic Movement in Galilee

### *The Beginnings*

The three hundred years covered in this chapter comprise a varied history with changing ruling powers and dynasties. The starting point is the short, ill-fated rule of the Hasmonean high priest and king Aristobulus I (reigned 104–103 BCE). He first conquered the northern territories of Galilee and Iturea and brought most of Galilee under Hasmonean dominion.[6] Josephus briefly describes the conquest and its dramatic consequences for the inhabitants of Galilee:

> He conferred many benefits on his country, for he made war on the Ituraeans and acquired a good part of their territory for Judaea and compelled the inhabitants, if they wished to remain in their country, to be circumcised and to live in accordance with the laws of the Jews. (*Ant.* 13.301)[7]

The parallel text in *Jewish War* says nothing about the Itureans but enigmatically mentions that Antigonus, the younger brother of Aristobulus, had won for himself military honors and a precious armor in Galilee (*J.W.* 1.77). It is therefore not clear whether the Itureans should be regarded as the inhabitants of Galilee at this time, or whether they only exerted some form of rule from their own territory, which was farther north in the Beqaʿ Valley.[8] In any case, Aristobulus's brother and successor, Alexander Jannaeus (ruled 103–76 BCE) expanded the Hasmonean rule over Galilee and as a result (re-)established the close ties of this region with Jerusalem.

Before the Hasmonean conquest, settlement activity in Galilee seems to have been rather low, although more excavations and archaeological surveys may change this picture in the future. Jürgen Zangenberg mentions military (veteran) settlements during the Ptolemaic rule

---

6. Parts of Lower Galilee might have been conquered already by John Hyrcanus after his conquest of Samaria (*J.W.* 1.65).

7. Trans. Ralph Marcus, LCL. For the forced circumcision, which is also mentioned by Strabo, see Andreas Blaschke, *Beschneidung: Zeugnisse der Bibel und verwandter Texte* (TANZ 28; Tübingen: Francke, 1998), 230–33; on Strabo, see Menahem Stern, *Greek and Latin Authors on Jews and Judaism*, vol. 1, *From Herodotus to Plutarch* (Fontes ad res Judaicas spectantes; Jerusalem: Israel Academy of Sciences and Humanities, 1974), 225–26. See also my "Galilee and the Historical Jesus," n. 31. For the conquest of Galilee and its religious implications for the pagan population, see Aryeh Kasher, *Jews and Hellenistic Cities in Eretz-Israel: Relation of the Jews in Eretz-Israel with the Hellenistic Cities during the Second Temple Period (322 BCE–70 CE)* (TSAJ 21; Tübingen: Mohr Siebeck, 1990), 129–70, who also provides detailed maps.

8. See Strabo, *Geogr.* 16.2.10, 18, 20. For a history of scholarship as well as a full treatment of the available sources on the Itureans, see E. A. Myers, *The Ituraeans and the Roman Near East: Reassessing the Sources* (SNTSMS 147; Cambridge: Cambridge University Press, 2010); and Seán Freyne, "Iturea," in *The Eerdmans Dictionary of Early Judaism* (ed. John J. Collins and Daniel C. Harlow; Grand Rapids: Eerdmans, 2010), 779–80.

(ca. 312 BCE–198 BCE) at Philoteria, et-Tell (Bethsaida), and Gamla.[9] These settlements would mean the presence of mainly retired soldiers from Greece and Macedonia, next to Phoenician influence (related to the powerful Phoenician cities along the Mediterranean coast), and a probable, albeit very limited, continuation of Iron Age, that is, Semite, influences in the Upper and northern Lower Galilee.[10] There are traces of non-Jewish cultic traditions, temples, and sacred places, but their activity seems to come to an end during the second century BCE.[11] This does not mean that non-Jewish religious practice did not continue to a smaller, perhaps more private and less publicly visible degree beyond this point in time, but the dominant religious culture is without doubt related to Judean Judaism.

The early decades of the first century BCE,[12] that is, the period of the Hasmonean conquest, clearly mark a new stage for development of Galilee: a few sites ceased to exist, most of them never to be resettled, but, more importantly, a good number of sites were newly started that in due course came to display the typical archaeological features pointing to Jewish identity—from which a clear picture of the Judean-controlled territory emerges.[13] In fact, according to Mordechai Aviam, the situation at the beginning of the first century BCE was that the Hasmoneans "encouraged people to emigrate from crowded Judea to the new open territories,

---

9. Jürgen Zangenberg, "Archaeology, Papyri, and Inscriptions," in Collins and Harlow, *Eerdmans Dictionary of Early Judaism*, 201–35, esp. 205. See also Kasher, *Jews and Hellenistic Cities*, 45–48 and 220, where he describes the inhabitants of the territory of Herod Philip as "a mixture of descendants of Greek military colonists from the Seleucid period, and Hellenized Ituraeans and Phoenicians from the near vicinity."

10. 1 Maccabees 5:14-24 can be mentioned in support; see esp. Kasher, *Jews and Hellenistic Cities*, 68–72. According to Zangenberg, "there is growing material evidence of an indigenous, Semitic population in the hills of Upper and northern Lower Galilee" ("Archaeology, Papyri, and Inscriptions," 205); see also Mordechai Aviam, "The Hasmonaean Dynasty's Activities in the Galilee," in *Jews, Pagans, and Christians in the Galilee: 25 Years of Archaeological Excavations and Surveys, Hellenistic to Byzantine Periods* (Land of Galilee 1; Rochester, N.Y.: University of Rochester Press, 2004), 41–50. He describes the Jewish population in the second century BCE as "a small weak minority of Jewish survivors in the western Lower Galilee, surrounded by Gentiles" (p. 43).

11. The best available evidence is from the temples at Qedesh and Mitzpe Hayamim. For Mitzpe Hayamim, see Leibner, *Settlement and History*, 104–5, and the following articles in *NEAEHL*: Asher Ovadiah, Moshe Fisher, and Israel Roll, "Kedesh (in Upper Galilee): The Roman Temple," 3:855–59; Andrea Berlin and Sharon Herbert, "Kedesh, Tel (in Upper Galilee)," 5:1905–6; Rafael Frankel, "Miẓpe Yammim, Mount," 3:1061–63. Interestingly enough, the sanctuaries farther north in Dan and in Banias/Caesarea Philippi continued well into the Roman period, clearly indicating that the extension of the Hasmonean conquest is the main reason for the abandonment of the other sites.

12. This may have started already at the end of the second century BCE, if *Ant.* 13.322 about Alexander Jannaeus being "brought up in Galilee from his birth" is at all true.

13. See my "Galilee and the Historical Jesus," n. 61, and in addition Mordechai Aviam, "People, Land, Economy, and Belief in First-Century Galilee and Its Origins: A Comprehensive Archaeological Synthesis," in *The Galilean Economy in the Time of Jesus* (ed. David A. Fiensy and Ralph K. Hawkins; Early Christianity and Its Literature 11; Atlanta: Society of Biblical Literature, 2013), 5–48, esp. 5–15; Aviam, "Hasmonaean's Dynasty Activities," 48–49; Deines, "Non-literary Sources," 33–34; Leibner (*Settlement and History*, 306–89) provides for a small but important geographic area west of Tiberias and Taricheae (see maps on pp. 2 and 64) a highly detailed and sophisticated "Settlement History of the Eastern Galilee in Light of the Archaeological Survey."

and that they encouraged veterans of the Hasmonean armies to settle there, joining the minority of the local population which was, in my opinion, a mix of remnant Jews and converted gentiles."[14]

But before either of the Hasmonean brothers had conquered and/or consolidated Galilee, another event took place that may also have had far-reaching effects on the later settlement of Galilee. According to Josephus, it was John Hyrcanus, the father of Aristobulus and Alexander, who broke with the Pharisees after he had been their disciple (μαθητής, *Ant.* 12.289) for some time. The break happened on the occasion of a banquet to which the ruler had invited the Pharisees. One of them advised the king to step down as high priest, referring to rumors against his legitimacy, namely, that his mother once during the reign of the Seleucid king Antiochus IV Epiphanes was said to have been a captive (*Ant.* 12.292) and as a result potentially exposed to rape. In this context, Josephus mentions the popularity of the Pharisees with the people, which is a recurring theme in his description of them. An important corollary of Hyrcanus's break with the Pharisees is that he "dissolved" the legal regulations they had introduced among the people, even punishing those who continued to observe them.[15] This conflict did not necessarily have any *immediate* influence on Galilee, for at the time Galilee was not yet (or only to a limited degree) included in the Hasmonean territory, even though the conquests of Hyrcanus stretched the borders farther north into the Jezreel valley. However, in the long run it may have been a factor in why Galilee became attractive for those who wanted to stay below the radar of the Hasmoneans in Jerusalem.[16]

Immigration in a substantive form from Judea into the region began after the two Hasmonean brothers, Aristobulus and then Alexander, conquered Galilee. The interesting question then becomes: What can we assume about the religious profile of these Judean newcomers in Galilee? The literary sources are silent, so not much can be said with any certainty, but certain deductions might be valid in light of the aforementioned split of the Hasmoneans away from a more Pharisaic orientation toward a stronger Sadducean profile. When Aristobulus came to power, he imprisoned part of his family to secure his position (*J. W.* 1.70), and Josephus reports further plotting and scheming during his short reign. His brother who succeeded him started his reign with the additional murder of one of his brothers (*J. W.* 1.85). His whole reign was

---

14. Aviam, "People, Land, Economy," 15.

15. The word used in *Ant.* 13.296–97 for "dissolve" (καταλύω) is also used in Matt. 5:17, where Jesus defends himself against the charge that he has come "to dissolve the law or the prophets." The parallel in *b. Qidd.* 66a, which mentions the "oral law" as jeopardized as a result of the incident, tells the same story with Alexander Jannai, who occasionally replaces Hyrcanus in rabbinic sources, but scholarly opinion is divided about which version should be preferred; for a review of scholarship up to 1995, see Roland Deines, *Die Pharisäer: Ihr Verständnis im Spiegel der christlichen und jüdischen Forschung seit Wellhausen und Graetz* (WUNT 101; Tübingen: Mohr Siebeck 1997), 76–77 n. 87.

16. The already mentioned story of Alexander Jannaeus being brought up in Galilee (see n. 12 above) could provide a piece of evidence. He was, according to Josephus, the least favorite son of his father but was revealed to him in a dream as his eventual heir. Sending Alexander to Galilee was meant to keep him away from the center of power and probably also to expose him to danger with the prospect of his being killed somehow.

characterised by civil war and military conflicts with the neighboring states.[17] The internal conflict caused many to flee from Judea (*J. W.* 1.98), and the question is: whither? Some left the country and fled "to the land of Damascus" (CD VI, 5), whose rulers, Demetrius III Eukairos and Antiochus XII Dionysos, no doubt incited by those refugees and the anti-Hasmonean opposition, actively fought against Alexander Jannaeus. Others most likely fled to Egypt.[18] But if one needed or wanted to escape the political hornet's nest of Jerusalem and its surroundings without going abroad, the new border territory of Galilee must have been an ideal place to go for those unhappy with the religious reorientation and also those who where politically opposed to the Hasmoneans. It is therefore at least reasonable to ask whether those who started the Judean settlement of Galilee were from the previous followers of the Hasmoneans who regarded the religious and political changes since the end of John Hyrcanus's reign as unfortunate. His sons' subsequent bid for royal power in addition to the high priestly office alienated even more of their previous supporters. Especially the Pharisees are described in the available sources as opposed to this move, and hence it seems plausible that Pharisees were among those settlers who left the Hasmonean capital—voluntarily or by force—bringing their religious profile with them to Galilee. Interestingly enough, the first rabbinic figure from Galilee, Nittai (so the traditional name; the real name according to the manuscript tradition was Mattai) of Arbela or Nittai the Arbelite, is quoted in *m. 'Avot* 1:7 with the saying, "Distance yourself from an evil neighbor; do not associate with a wicked one; do not give up retribution," which can be read as a justification for his living in Arbela. But, more important, one can see in these lines the attitude of those who settled in Galilee not because of the opportunities it offered but because of the dangers they faced in Jerusalem.[19]

There are further good reasons to assume that the Pharisees played an important role in the long and cruelly fought civil war against Alexander Jannaeus.[20] In Josephus, there is at

---

17. For his reign see *J. W.* 1.85–106; *Ant.* 13.320–404.

18. Josephus speaks of eight thousand of his opponents who "fled by night" (*Ant.* 13.383) —obviously meaning from Jerusalem—as a result of Alexander's punitive measure when he broke down the revolt against him, but he does not mention where these fugitives went. Simeon ben Shetach, according to rabbinic traditions a contemporary of Alexander Jannaeus and most likely a Pharisee, was hidden somewhere in the land by his sister (who is identified with Queen Salome Alexandra), while his companion, Joshua ben Perachiah, fled to Alexandria (*b. Sotah* 47a; *b. Sanh.* 107b; see Jacob Neusner, *The Rabbinic Traditions about the Pharisees before 70* [3 vols.; Leiden: Brill, 1971], 1:83–84, 114, 138–41). Josephus mentions that the Pharisees, favored again at the Hasmonean court when Salome Alexandra succeeded her husband in 76 BCE, called back those who had to flee and in turn made others flee (*J. W.* 1.111; *Ant.* 13.409; cf. also 4QpNah 3–4 II, 4–5). See also *Ant.* 14.22 for Judeans fleeing to Egypt as result of civil war. The flight of Jesus' parents to escape Herod, and on their return from Judea to Galilee to avoid troubles from the side of Archelaus, reflects such a situation very well (Matt. 2:13-14, 22-23), and this is true irrespective of the historical accuracy in relation to Jesus' parents.

19. For Mattai, see the brief comments in Neusner, *Rabbinic Traditions*, 1:82–84.

20. Josephus, *Ant.* 13.372–83. This event also left its traces in the *Nahum Pesher* from Qumran (4QpNah). See Martin Hengel and Roland Deines, "E. P. Sanders' 'Common Judaism,' Jesus, and the Pharisees: A Review Article," *JTS* 46 (1995): 1–70, esp. 56–58; especially on the *Nahum Pesher* as source for the Pharisees, see I. R. Tantlevskij, "The Historical Background of the Qumran Commentary on Nahum (4QpNah)," in *Hellenismus:*

least one hint to support the assumption that Galilee was predominantly against Alexander Jannaeus, and this is the report about the campaign of Demetrius III Eukairos. When the Syrian king came to attack Alexander, he combined his forces with those of the Jewish insurgents somewhere close to Shechem in Samaria before advancing farther south (*J. W.* 1.93; *Ant.* 13.377). There was obviously no felt need to secure Galilee even though Jewish settlements were there at the time. In fact, Shechem as rallying point was suitably located for people from Galilee to join. Of course, this scenario is admittedly speculative, and the available evidence does not allow any firm conclusion.

The next decades saw Galilee again and again involved in Judean politics, the most important development undoubtedly the emergence of a religiously motivated revolutionary movement directed against Roman rule, which is covered in another chapter in this volume.[21]

### *Jesus' Encounter with the Pharisees and Their Scribes in Galilee*

A good number of the conflict stories in the Gospels between Jesus and the Pharisees occur in Galilee, and this means that the first three evangelists, Mark, Matthew, and Luke, locate the Pharisees as a distinct religious group in Galilee (in John's Gospel, Pharisees appear only in Jerusalem). The first time Mark mentions them they are described as being related to the scribes (Mark 2:16, "the scribes of the Pharisees"), and in a later passage another group of scribes is shown to be connected with them, this time coming "from Jerusalem" (7:1, 5). This seems to indicate that the evangelist differentiates between local scribes and those coming from Jerusalem, and this distinction should not be overturned by attributing it to two different sources that Mark ignorantly combined.[22] But how reliable is such information for the time of Jesus? Does this not rather reflect the development *after 70*, when adherents of Jesus increasingly faced opposition from the proto-rabbis, who were seen by the evangelists as the successors of the Pharisees in the time of Jesus? Therefore, the evangelists retrospectively created these

---

*Beiträge zur Erforschung von Akkulturation und politischer Ordnung in den Staaten des hellenistischen Zeitalters: Akten des Internationalen Hellenismus-Kolloquiums, 9.–14. März 1994 in Berlin* (ed. Bernd Funck; Tübingen: Mohr Siebeck, 1997), 329–38; Lawrence H. Schiffman, "Pharisees and Sadducees in Pesher Nahum," in *Minḥah le-Naḥum: Biblical and Other Studies Presented to Nahum M. Sarna in Honour of His 70th Birthday* (ed. Marc Brettler and Michael Fishbane; JSOTSup 154; Sheffield: JSOT Press, 1993), 272–90; Schiffman, "The Pharisees and Their Legal Traditions according to the Dead Sea Scrolls," *DSD* 8 (2001): 262–77, esp. 265–67; James C. VanderKam, "Those Who Look for Smooth Things, Pharisees, and Oral Law," in *Emanuel: Studies in Hebrew Bible, Septuagint and Dead Sea Scrolls in Honor of Emanuel Tov* (ed. Shalom M. Paul et al.; VTSup 94; Leiden: Brill, 2003), 465–77.

21. See the contribution of Richard Horsley in this volume, "Social Movements in Galilee," and n. 41 below.

22. This was proposed by Michael J. Cook, *Mark's Treatment of the Jewish Leaders* (NovTSup 51; Leiden: Brill, 1978), who allowed hardly any historical value to the Synoptic Gospels. Against this view, see the balanced and well-argued contribution of Martin Pickup, "Matthew's and Mark's Pharisees," in *In Quest of the Historical Pharisees* (ed. Jacob Neusner and Bruce D. Chilton; Waco, Tex.: Baylor University Press, 2007), 67–112, esp. 437–45 notes.

conflict stories to help their audience in their contemporary struggles against the Pharisees-turned-into-rabbis.

This widely held view, influenced by developments in rabbinic studies beginning in the 1970s and strongly affected by an article by Morton Smith on Josephus's portrait of the Pharisees,[23] suffers from some serious flaws and has come under much pressure in recent years. First of all, the depiction of the Pharisees in Mark and the double tradition (Q) reflects without any doubt a pre-70 CE perspective on the Pharisees. Whether one dates Mark in the early 40s of the first century, as Maurice Casey does,[24] or with the majority view around 70, has no influence on the historical value, as it is clear that between 30 and 70 no dramatic changes with regard to Pharisaic influence are discernible. Further, if writing in the year 70 (or even 75), Mark could not have known how things would develop after the fall of Jerusalem and the destruction of the temple. That the Pharisees would emerge as the main benefactors from this catastrophe was hardly foreseeable, as was the increased importance of Galilee for the rabbinic movement, which became manifest only after the Bar Kokhba war. But even during the time of Luke and Matthew, if one follows the usual dating in around 80–90 CE, neither the Pharisees nor the early rabbis already played a dominant role. In other words, the idea that the evangelists exaggerated the influence of the Pharisees in the time of Jesus to reflect the rabbinic dominance over Judean Jewry in around 80–90 is based on incorrect assumptions and should therefore be abandoned. Instead, the description of the Pharisees in the Gospels and what they relate about their societal stance can be taken as a fairly accurate picture of the time between 30 and 70. On this basis, what can be learned about the Pharisees in Galilee for this period?

From the ninety-nine references to the Pharisees (Φαρισαῖοι) in the New Testament,[25] twenty-five occurrences (eight in Mark, eight in Matthew, at least nine in Luke,[26] and none in John) are in passages describing encounters with them in Galilee,[27] compared to thirty-one

---

23. Morton Smith, "Palestinian Judaism in the First Century," in *Israel: Its Role in Civilization* (ed. Moshe Davis; New York: Jewish Theological Seminary of America, [1956]), 67–81. For the influence of this article, see Deines, *Die Pharisäer*, 32–33; see also Deines, "The Pharisees between 'Judaisms' and 'Common Judaism,'" in *Justification and Variegated Nomism: A Fresh Appraisal of Paul and Second Temple Judaism*, vol. 1, *The Complexities of Second Temple Judaism* (ed. Donald A. Carson, Peter T. O'Brien, and Mark A. Seifrid; WUNT 2.140. Tübingen: Mohr Siebeck, 2001), 443–504, esp. 452–54.

24. Thus Maurice Casey, *Jesus of Nazareth: An Independent Historian's Account of His Life and Teaching* (London: T&T Clark, 2010), 65–74.

25. Compared to fourteen references to the Sadducees and none to the Essenes.

26. Luke's localization of individual pericopes after 9:51-53 is often impossible to discern. He incorporates in Jesus' itinerary to Jerusalem a number of traditions that seem to belong to Galilee. There is no space to go into any details here, but I would definitely count Luke 13:31 as "Galilean" tradition, and probably 14:1, 3; 15:2; 16:14; 17:20, which are oddly placeless. Even the parable about the Pharisee and tax collector in 18:10-11 need not have been told in Jerusalem. Luke 7:30 is in a Galilean context but does not fit there and is rather a reflection about what happened in Judea.

27. Mark 2:15-16 par. Matt. 9:11-13; Luke 5:30-32; Mark 2:23-28 par. Matt. 12:1-8; Luke 6:1-5; Mark 3:1-6 par. Matt. 12:9-14; Luke 6:6-11; Mark 7:1-5, with only 7:1 having a parallel in Matt. 15:1; Mark 8:11-13 par. Matt. 12:38-39 and 16:1-2 (the parallel in Luke 12:54-56 is a saying of Jesus to the crowds, not initiated by

references (two in Mark, six in Matthew, at least four in Luke, and nineteen in John) localized in Jerusalem or Judea.[28] When Jesus (or others) mentions the Pharisees, we find four utterances situated in Galilee (one in Mark, two in Matthew, at least one in Luke, but none in John) compared to fourteen in Jerusalem (Mark, one; Matthew, nine; Luke, at least three; John, one).[29] These figures of course provide only a very rough picture, as they do not account for parallels in the double or triple tradition. Although the evidence from John points to Jerusalem/Judea as the center of Pharisaic activity (as do Matt. 23:1-35 par. Luke 11:37-53), it is decisive that the other evangelists assume that it is "normal" to have debates with the Pharisees in Galilee and talk about them there. Only John's Gospel locates all encounters with the Pharisees in Jerusalem or Judea.

That the evangelists do not randomly introduce interlocutors or groups in the opening sentences of their ideal scenes, as is often assumed in form-critical and redaction-critical studies (with the result that scholars do not give them much weight as historically reliable), can be seen by the fact that the Sadducees appear, with one exception, *only* in Jerusalem.[30] Likewise, priests are never mentioned as interlocutors of Jesus in Galilee; they are only spoken *about* in a few pericopes located in Galilee, where they nevertheless are assumed to be in Jerusalem (Mark 1:44 par. Matt. 8:4; Luke 5:14; Mark 2:26 par. Matt. 12:4-5; Luke 6:4).[31]

The Galilean Pharisees are described as being interested in eating together with like-minded righteous people and not with "tax collectors and sinners" (Mark 2:16 par. Matt. 9:11; Luke 5:30; see also Luke 7:36-39). Related to table fellowship are concerns about purity: the

---

a Pharisaic interlocutor); Matt. 12:22-38 (the whole discourse is directed toward the Pharisees only in Matthew; see already 9:34); 15:1-12; 16:1. Luke adds the Pharisees in his version of the healing of the paralytic, where Mark and Matthew mention only scribes as interlocutors (Luke 5:17-26 par. Mark 2:1-12; Matt. 9:1-8), and he also introduces them as hosts of Jesus (7:36-50; in Luke the geographical context is Galilee, whereas Mark and Matthew have a similar story with Simon the leper located in Bethphage near Jerusalem).

28. Mark 10:2 par. Matt. 19:3; Mark 12:13-17 par. Matt. 22:15-22 (the parallel in Luke 20:20-26 has the scribes and high priests as questioners); Matt. 3:7; 21:45 (here it is the Pharisees and the high priests; the parallel in Luke mentions scribes and high priests); 22:34, 41 (the parallels mention scribes); 27:62; Luke 11:37, 38, 53; 19:39 (for the other Lukan passages, see n. 26 above). All nine references in Acts (5:34; 15:5; 23:6-9; 26:5) relate to Jerusalem as well.

29. Situated in Galilee are Mark 8:15 par. Matt. 16:6; Luke 12:1; Matt. 5:20; 16:11, and in Jerusalem or Judea Matt. 23:1-36 (for references to the Pharisees in the mouths of other people, see Mark 2:18 par. Matt. 9:14; Luke 5:33; Matt. 15:12; see also Matt. 16:12); ambiguous are Luke 12:1; 18:10-11.

30. The exception is Matt. 16:1, where the Sadducees together with the Pharisees ask Jesus for a sign after the feeding of the four thousand. This is only the second pairing of the two groups in Matthew, the first being 3:7, where they jointly go to see John the Baptist. The connection between the two episodes is evident: the Pharisees and Sadducees want to have a sign "from heaven," which was actually given at Jesus' baptism with the voice "from heaven" (3:17). They were unwilling to accept this, together with the other signs Matthew mentioned between 4:17 and 16:21, which for the most part took place in Galilee. With 16:21 the focus is turning to Jerusalem, and the mention of the Sadducees in 16:1 (which is most likely a Matthean redactional cue to the first appearance of this pairing in 3:7) is indicative of this. In the parallel passage, Matt. 12:38-42, the Pharisees appear in the tow of some scribes when they request a sign from Jesus.

31. Interestingly, all references come from the mouth of Jesus.

participants at a meal are expected to be pure and consequently also the dishes and the food itself (Mark 7:1-2 par. Matt. 15:1-2; John 2:6; Mark 7:3-4 is a general remark about Pharisaic purity concerns, which obviously applies also to Galilee). Another important topic is Sabbath *halakhah* (Mark 2:24 par. Matt. 12:2; Luke 6:2; Mark 3:6 par. Matt.12:14; Luke 6:7). Likewise, fasting is associated with the Pharisees, but not exclusively, as the questioners (the disciples of the Baptist) make clear (Mark 2:18 par. Matt. 9:14; Luke 5:33). With Jesus' reply, which emphasizes mercy instead of sacrifices (Matt. 9:13, quoting Hos 6:6, which in 12:7 is quoted a second time, again in a discussion with the Pharisees), Matthew might be hinting at their interest in temple practices (see also Mark 2:25-26 par.). Matthew also introduces them as interested in matters dealing with demonic influence (9:34; 12:28; in Mark this theological expertise is attributed to the scribes from Jerusalem, 3:22), which fits with their otherwise noted belief in angels, demons, and the resurrection (Acts 23:8).

It is also made clear that their opinion has weight with ordinary people, as evinced by Matt. 9:33-34 and 12:23-24 (in Luke 11:14-15 only "some of the crowds" are mentioned), where in both cases the opinion of the people is set against the rejection by the Pharisees. In the end, it was the Pharisees who were able to convince the crowds with their view of Jesus.[32] This explains at least to a certain degree Matthew's antagonism toward them: they lock the gates to the kingdom of heaven and block the way for the people of Israel to enter (see 23:13), and they are accused of having actively consulted with one another about how to get rid of Jesus (12:34). The influence of the Pharisees on synagogues is another highly controversial issue, but for the moment it might be enough to point to those references where the evangelists describe the Pharisees in the context of synagogal gatherings in Galilee: the Pharisees are not described as leaders of the gatherings in the synagogues (but note that no one is actually described as being in charge), nor as their founders, but as those who are present. They or the scribes—and only they—are the interlocutors of Jesus in the synagogues, whereas not once are priests mentioned as being present in synagogal gatherings in the New Testament.[33] Based on the formulation "their synagogues" in Matt. 12:9 immediately after an encounter with the Pharsisees, Anders

---

32. It is noteworthy that a similar scenario can be seen in the *Nahum Pesher* from Qumran. Here two Jewish groups that are hostile to each other but are both—seen from the perspective of the scroll author—wrong with regard to their teaching are described as fighting over the "simple ones of Israel," which is obviously the same group as the Matthean "crowd" (4QpNah 3-4 III, 5; see also 3-4 II, 8-9). The rival factions are addressed using only the ciphered names "Ephraim" and "Manasseh," and there are good reasons to assume that the names stand for the Pharisees and the Sadducees (see n. 20 above), who lead the crowds—from the perspective of the Qumranites—astray. If we take this text at face value for a moment, then the Pharisees are more successful in their hold over the people than the Sadducees, and the Qumranites can only wait and hope that their deception will become obvious at the end of time (which the Qumranites thought was near).

33. Pharisees in a Galilean synagogue setting are mentioned in Mark 3:1-6 par. Matt. 12:9-14; Luke 6:6-11. Pharisaic influence (or at least ambition) in synagogues can also be assumed behind Matt. 6:2, 5 (in Matthew's Gospel, the hypocrites in a synagogue are always the Pharisees and scribes; see Matt. 23:2, 6; cf. further Luke 13:10-17; 20:46). The scribes as the usual teachers of the Galilean crowds are presupposed in Mark 1:22; Matt. 7:28-29; see also Mark 8:15 par. Luke 12:1; Matt. 16:6-12. Again, no priests are mentioned as teachers in Galilee.

Runesson made the suggestion that the Pharisees had their own semipublic synagogues and that the Matthean communities were originally a subgroup of these Pharisaic communities.[34] Dominant in current scholarship, however, is the notion of Lee I. Levine that "the Pharisees had little or nothing to do with the early synagogue, and there is not one shred of evidence pointing to such a connection."[35] Instead, the priests are seen as the driving force behind the synagogues, but this is not convincing. As long as the temple stood, the priests had an interest in maintaining it as the sole focus of religious practice, as the temple was their main source of prestige and income. Regarding the temple cult they had no real competitors, because the Torah prevents nonpriests from any active role. Not so in the synagogue, as far as we can tell from the existing sources. So is it likely that the priests began to establish a rival institution to their main institutions, allowing laypeople to participate in some of their prerogatives? Prestige and hereditary prerogatives are not lightly given away. No class of religious specialists (who make their living normally because they have a special quality or special training) is interested in sharing its prestige, because that would threaten its own position and therefore its income. If everyone can read and explain the Bible, why should one pay for a rabbi, a pastor, or a priest? Because no priest is required for synagogal gatherings and explanations of Scripture that take place there, it is more likely from the outset that the origins and motivations for this institution must be sought outside of the priestly orbit and their representative form of religious observance in circles of those who are focused on religious education and participation of as many as possible. And the only group the sources offer us for such a task is the Pharisees.[36]

For the situation in pre-70 Galilee, however, most interesting are texts in which Pharisees and scribes in Galilee are described in close contact with their peers from Jerusalem, as in Mark 7:1. If one follows Mark's narrative of the Pharisees, the reader of the Gospel knows that the Pharisees and the scribes were closely related (Mark 2:16 speaks of the "scribes *of* the Pharisees"). In addition, the Pharisees are said to have ties to the Herodians, who most likely were supporters of the Herodian dynasty—either merely politically or, more likely, both politically and religiously (see Mark 8:15). Although during Jesus' adult lifetime no Herodian ruled Judea and Jerusalem, their ambitions were surely set on the Jewish metropolis, and mentioning Herodians thus "rings a Judean bell." It is therefore no wonder that Mark brings the same

34. Anders Runesson, "Rethinking Early Jewish–Christian Relations: Matthean Community History as Pharisaic Intragroup Conflict," *JBL* 127 (2008): 95–132.

35. Lee I. Levine, *The Ancient Synagogue: The First Thousand Years* (New Haven: Yale University Press, 2000), 38–39; Shaye J. D. Cohen, "Were Pharisees and Rabbis the Leaders of Communal Prayer and Torah Study in Antiquity? The Evidence of the New Testament, Josephus, and the Early Church Fathers," in *Evolution of the Synagogue: Problems and Progress* (ed. Howard Clark Kee and Lynn H. Cohick; Harrisburg, Pa.: Trinity Press International, 1999), 89–105 (reprinted in Cohen, *The Significance of Yavneh and Other Essays in Jewish Hellenism* [TSAJ 136; Tübingen: Mohr Siebeck, 2010], 266–81).

36. See my "Die Pharisäer und das Volk im Neuen Testament und bei Josephus," in *Josephus und das Neue Testament: Wechselseitige Wahrnehmungen. II. Internationales Symposium zum Corpus Judaeo-Hellenisticum, 25.–28. Mai 2006, Greifswald* (ed. Christfried Böttrich and Jens Herzer; WUNT 209; Tübingen: Mohr Siebeck, 2007), 147–80.

coalition of Pharisees and Herodians to the stage in his last reference to the Pharisees in 12:13, which is situated in Jerusalem. But what precisely does Mark want to tell his readers when he says that "the Pharisees and some of the scribes who had come from Jerusalem" were gathering around Jesus? The sentence is ambiguous insofar as it is possible to relate the coming from Jerusalem to the Pharisees *and* the scribes, or only to the scribes. The Greek allows for both possibilities, as the participial clause "coming from Jerusalem" (ἐλθόντες ἀπὸ Ἱεροσολύμα) can be understood as an adverbial modifier of the main verb: "And after they—that is, Pharisees and scribes—had come from Jerusalem, they gathered around him," or as attributive to τινες, in which case one would translate "And they gathered around him, the Pharisees, and some [τινες] of the scribes who had come from Jerusalem."[37] The parallel in Matt. 15:1 leaves no doubt that Matthew understood both parts of the delegation as coming from Jerusalem. This, then, is further evidence that Galilee was religiously oriented toward Jerusalem, and that in complicated cases—and Jesus can be clearly counted as such in light of Deuteronomy 13—decisions are made in close consultation with Jerusalem, which follows biblical precedents (Deut. 17:8-11; 2 Chron. 19:8-11).

This episode in the Synoptics about the interaction between Jerusalem and Galilee (Mark 7:1 and par.) can be placed alongside three other important pieces of evidence:

*1. The delegation from Jerusalem to replace Josephus.* In his autobiography, Josephus mentions a delegation that was sent from the moderate war party in Jerusalem, comprising the high priests and leading Pharisees, to relieve him of his command as regional commander of the revolt (or, as he wants his readers to believe, as the one sent to prevent it while nevertheless preparing for it). In describing the four members of this delegation, Josephus gives insight into the prestige that Pharisees could expect in Galilee.

Josephus writes that three Pharisees[38] were part of the delegation, and one of them was also a priest (*Life* 196–98). In addition, an envoy of high priestly origin was part of the delegation, and all four of them were trained scribes. Josephus then describes a man named Ioazar as the most influential figure in this group, that is, a priestly Pharisee from Jerusalem—just what Josephus himself happens to be. The least one can glean from this passage is that the Pharisees were regarded as an influential group in Galilee, to whom people were willing to listen for guidance and advice, and there are no indications that, before the war began, the influence of the various "parties" in Galilee was greatly different from this picture. The episode of the

---

37. Commentators are divided on this point, but it seems that a majority favor the idea that Mark refers to a split group with only some scribes joining the local Pharisees; see, for example, Julius Wellhausen, *Das Evangelium Marci* (2nd ed.; Berlin: Reimer, 1909), 54 (= Wellhausen, *Evangelienkommentare* [Berlin: de Gruyter, 1987], 374); Adela Yarbro Collins, *Mark: A Commentary* (Hermeneia; Minneapolis: Fortress Press, 2007), 343–44; R. T. France, *The Gospel of Mark* (NIGTC; Grand Rapids: Eerdmans, 2002), 280.

38. One of them, Simon, is the son of Gamaliel, the teacher of Paul. Simon is described by Josephus as (like his father Gamaliel) a leader of the Pharisaic party in Jerusalem (*Life* 191–92), although the son—unlike the father—is known more for his political actions during the first revolt than for religious or halakhic activities. There was obviously a personal hostility between Josephus and Simon (*Life* 192).

delegation is one of the rare occasions when Josephus connects Pharisaic influence or affiliation with a place outside of Jerusalem.[39] In his well-known summative descriptions of the four Jewish "philosophies," he does not apply regional differentiation when he describes their prestige among the people. When it comes to the influence of religious movements, the standing of the Pharisees in Galilee should thus be regarded as ubiquitous; that is, they are the ones with the support of the crowds. This means not necessarily political but certainly religious power and influence.[40] And although Josephus recounts that the Essenes had "many in each city" (*J.W.* 2.124–25), we hear nothing about them in Galilee. The main competitors of the Pharisees in Galilee were most likely the Fourth Philosophy, founded by Judas, a native of Gamla (east of the Sea of Galilee, on the border to Gaulanitis), whom Josephus also calls a "Galilean" (*J.W.* 2.118; *Ant.* 18.4, 23), together with a Pharisee named Zaddok (according to the name, therefore, of priestly descent). The only subject that differentiated the two groups was the Fourth Philosophy's insatiable "passion for freedom" (ἐλευθέρου ἔρως), which did not allow having a mortal master as long as God was their "leader and lord" (*Ant.* 18.23).[41]

*2. Letters sent from Jerusalem to Galilee regarding the collection of tithes.* In the rabbinic corpus, a small collection of letters is mentioned that were sent from Jerusalem to Galilee (other places that are of no immediate relevance here). These were to inform the inhabitants of Galilee (differentiating between Upper and Lower Galilee) about the time to remove tithes. There are two sets of letters sent from a place close to the temple (the "stairs of the Temple Mount," or somewhere between the Upper Market and the Dung Gate) but not by priestly temple authori-

---

39. From the few named Pharisees apart from the Galilee delegation, all are connected with Jerusalem: Pollio and Sameas (*Ant.* 15.3); Simon, son of Gamaliel (*Life* 191), and of course Josephus himself (*Life* 12). The two teachers, Judas, son of Sepphoraeus, and Matthias, son of Margalus, who instigated the destruction of the golden eagle Herod had made for one of the temple gates, are also most likely Pharisees (*J.W.* 1.648 par. *Ant.* 17.149). The father's name of the first one is slightly different in the two texts (and with variants in the manuscripts), but it is intriguing to see in it a hint at Sepphoris (Σεπφωραῖος = the Sepphorean), formed in the same way as Jesus the Nazarene (Ναζωραῖος; the usual name in Josephus for the inhabitants of Sepphoris is however Σεπφωρῖται; a Rabbi Ḥiya Zipporiya = R. Ḥiya the Sepphorean is mentioned in *y. Shabb.* 2,1 4d); the other possibility is to see in Σαριφαῖος, as the name is given in *Antiquities*, a misspelling (deliberately or not) of Φαρισαῖος (which is at least attested by one manuscript); for a different explanation of the name, see Tal Ilan, *Lexicon of Jewish Names in Late Antiquity*, vol. 1, *Palestine, 330 BCE–200 CE* (TSAJ 91; Tübingen: Mohr Siebeck, 2002), 405. Another possible Galilean Pharisee is a certain Eleazar, who convinced King Izates of Adiabene to convert fully to Judaism through circumcision (*Ant.* 20.43–45, see Blaschke, *Beschneidung*, 233–40).

40. See Deines, "Social Profile of the Pharisees."

41. See Martin Hengel, *The Zealots: Investigations into the Jewish Freedom Movement in the Period from Herod I until 70 A.D.* (trans. David Smith; Edinburgh: T&T Clark, 1989), 76–88, 330–37. Hengel's view of an ideologically coherent freedom movement starting with Judas and Zaddok and traceable until the outbreak of the revolt is contested, and more recent studies even deny the existence of Judas the Galilean. For a defense and update of Hengel's approach in light of his pioneering study's impact on subsequent scholarship, see Roland Deines, "Gab es eine jüdische Freiheitsbewegung? Martin Hengels 'Zeloten' nach 50 Jahren," in Martin Hengel, *Die Zeloten: Untersuchungen zur jüdischen Freiheitsbewegung in der Zeit von Herodes I. bis 70 n. Chr.* (ed. Roland Deines and Claus-Jürgen Thornton; 3rd rev. ed.; WUNT 283; Tübingen: Mohr Siebeck, 2011), 403–48.

ties. They were sent, rather, by Rabban Gamaliel and the elders, according to *t. Sanh.* 2:6 (with parallels), and by Simeon ben Gamaliel and Rabbi Yoḥanan ben Zakkai according to a midrash (commentary) on Deut. 26:13 from the Tannaitic era (that is, before 200 CE).[42] The precise identification of the Gamaliels is uncertain. The name may refer either to the teacher of Paul, a well-known Jerusalem Pharisee (Acts 5:34; 22:3), or to his grandson Gamaliel II, the leader of the emerging rabbinic movement between ca. 80 and 110 CE.[43] Because Pharisaic influence in the temple and priestly matters is often excluded by default for the time before 70, many think that Gamaliel I would be a projection from the situation of the time of his grandson. But actually, the fact that the letters were *not* authorized or sent from a kind of priestly headquarters,[44] but only from a place close to the temple, would make it more likely that Gamaliel, the teacher of Paul, is meant. These letters (or letter-writing practice) would then have to be dated to a time between ca. 30 and 70 CE.[45] Whether they were addressed mainly to adherents of Pharisaic teaching, or whether the Pharisees acted as if they could speak for all, can be left open.[46] Decisive is that the letters reflect a situation similar to the one described in Mark 7:1 (par. Matt.15:1), where Mark undoubtedly reflects a pre-70 context. There is, therefore, evidence for religious consultation going on between Jerusalem and Galilee, with the capital in the position of giving advice.

*3. Yoḥanan ben Zakkai, Rabban Gamaliel, and Ḥanina ben Dosa.* Geza Vermes has repeatedly pointed to the charismatic miracle workers mentioned in rabbinic literature as the closest parallel to Jesus' ministry in Galilee. The more famous one, Ḥoni the Circle-Drawer, who is mentioned also in Josephus (*Ant.* 14.22–30), is sometimes associated with Galilee but without any evidence (and Vermes is very clear about it).[47] Ḥanina ben Dosa, however, is more likely to be

---

42. David Hoffmann, *Midrasch Tannaim zum Deuteronomium* (Berlin: Itzkowski, 1908–9), 175–76.

43. A full discussion of the textual tradition and the scholarly debate regarding identification and authenticity can be found in Lutz Doering, *Ancient Jewish Letters and the Beginning of Christian Epistolography* (WUNT 298; Tübingen: Mohr Siebeck, 2012), 351–64.

44. As presupposed, for example, in Acts 9:1-2 and 22:5, where Paul seeks a letter that gives him the authority to seize the followers of Jesus in Damascus.

45. Interestingly, the letter in the midrash ends with the note "And it is not we who have begun to write to you, but our ancestors used to write to your ancestors" (Doering, *Ancient Jewish Letters*, 357), thus assuming a well-established tradition, which again makes good sense if Pharisaic groups were instrumental in the settling of Galilee a century or more earlier.

46. If one accepts the description of Paul's mission to Damascus in Acts as historical, we then have a case where the high priestly authorities used a zealous Pharisee to undertake an action that was also in their own interest (cf. Acts 4:1-6; 5:17-18). For a discussion of Acts 9:2 (22:5; 26:10), see Martin Hengel and Anna Maria Schwemer, *Paul between Damascus and Antioch: The Unknown Years* (trans. John Bowden; London: SCM, 1997), 50–51; Doering, *Ancient Jewish Letters*, 360, 379, 508; and commentaries on Acts.

47. See, for example, Alan J. Avery-Peck, "The Galilean Charismatic and Rabbinic Piety: The Holy Man in the Talmudic Literature," in *The Historical Jesus in Context* (ed. Amy-Jill Levine et al.; Princeton Readings in Religions; Princeton: Princeton University Press, 2006), 149–65, where Ḥoni is used to illustrate the traits "of the Galilean miracle worker."

a Galilean figure, as at least one tradition mentions him as living in Arav (*y. Ber.* 7c), the same place where Yoḥanan ben Zakkai lived during the eighteen years he spent in Galilee (*y. Šabb.* 16:8 15d). So, first of all, we can see in Yoḥanan another Judean, who settled in Galilee (the reasons for which are not clear) and who only later returned to Jerusalem. According to the young Jacob Neusner, this Galilean episode was "sometime between 20 CE and 40 CE," which would make Yoḥanan a Galilean contemporary of Jesus.[48] According to legend, Ḥanina was Yohanan's student while the latter lived in Galilee. Once, when Yoḥanan's son fell ill, Ḥanina healed him with a powerful prayer (*b. Ber.* 34b). Ḥanina remained in Galilee after Yoḥanan returned to Jerusalem, where his fame as a healer was so great that Gamaliel (out of chronological reasons it must be Gamaliel the Elder, teacher of Paul), when his son was ill, sent two of his disciples to Ḥanina and asked for his prayer on the boy's behalf. After Ḥanina prayed, he sent the messengers back to Gamaliel and assured them that the boy was well. They noted down the exact time of his prayer and when they returned to Jerusalem, they were told that this was exactly the time when the fever broke (*b. Taʿan.* 24b; cf. John 4:43-53). These bits of information about Galilee, made *en passant,* fit well the picture of close Judean–Galilean relations enjoyed by the Pharisees (or rabbis close to them). It also shows that halakhic (legal) and more charismatic forms of Jewish religious practice were not mutually exclusive but supported and supplemented each other, despite some unavoidable frictions. Finally, a miracle worker was a good enough reason to send a delegation from Jerusalem.

### Stone Vessels as an Indication of Pharisaic Influence

The Pharisaic influence on daily religious practice of Jews living in Galilee can best be deduced from the stone vessels found in excavations throughout Galilee. Stone vessels appeared as something practically unprecedented in Israel in the second half of the first century BCE, with a concentration in Jerusalem, but not restricted to it. Wider Judea and Galilee provide further finds, as well as some areas in the coastal plain and in modern-day Jordan (ancient Perea). Only two sites from Samaria are known, but for both of them a Jewish populace is likely.[49] There are no close parallels for this kind of stone vessel in the Greco-Roman world, which makes them clear indicators of the presence of a Jewish population at a given place. The passing remark in John 2:6 about "six stone water jars according to the purification (customs) of the Jews" during the wedding in Cana is the earliest written testimony for stone vessels. The evangelist takes for granted that they belong to the equip-

---

48. Jacob Neusner, *A Life of Yohanan ben Zakkai, Ca. 1-80 C.E.* (2nd rev. ed.; StPB 6; Leiden: Brill, 1970), 47 (on Yoḥanan and Ḥanina, see 51–53); Geza Vermes, *Jesus in the Jewish World* (London: SCM, 2010), 130–73 ("Ḥanina ben Dosa: A Galilean Contemporary of Jesus"); Avery-Peck, "Galilean Charismatic," 157–65.

49. See Roland Deines, *Jüdische Steingefäße und pharisäische Frömmigkeit: Ein archäologisch-historischer Beitrag zum Verständnis von Joh 2,6 und der jüdischen Reinheitshalacha zur Zeit Jesu* (WUNT 2.52; Tübingen: Mohr Siebeck, 1993), 136–40; Izchak Magen, *The Stone Vessel Industry in the Second Temple Period: Excavations at Ḥimza and the Jerusalem Temple Mount* (Judea and Samaria Publications 1; Jerusalem: Israel Exploration Society, Israel Antiquities Authority, 2002), 160.

ment of a house hosting a big social event in Galilee, and findings of stone jars in Galilee that fit John's description indicate that he was familiar with such details.[50] The range of types of vessels diminished after 70 CE, and they were in use at a reduced level at least until the Bar Kokhba period. There are claims that they were used even longer, but so far there is no evidence that they were still *produced* after the second century CE. For the first century CE, production sites are known from Jerusalem and Galilee. With the nearly parallel spread of Jewish ritual baths, synagogues, and other changes in the material culture, one can deduce that there was a widespread concern in the Jewish lands, including Galilee, for keeping certain religious purity laws in a very specific way. In my earlier work,[51] I tried to demonstrate the relatedness of the sudden spread of stone vessels with ossuaries, Jewish ritual baths, and synagogues. Since its publication in 1993, this list of identity markers as an expression of Jewishness has been increased and is now widely accepted in scholarship.[52] All these developments in the religious and material context seem to form part of an interconnected web that began to appear toward the end of the second century BCE with the emergence of the specific Jewish ritual baths (*mikva'ot*), which then spread continuously to include other areas such as burial practices, purity at the table, and new worship and study patterns in connection with the synagogues—to mention only the most outstanding features. Their full blossom can be observed at the beginning of the first century CE during the reign of Herod. There is no doubt about the material developments, but there is some contention about the social and religious forces behind these changes. The fact that stone vessels, especially in connection with *mikva'ot* in private houses, became a common feature of everyday Jewish life in the time between Herod and the destruction of the temple points to a concern for purity matters in individual households, which is not attested by archaeological or literary evidence before the second century BCE. Certain events or developments obviously acted as catalysts to accelerate individual purity concerns beyond the temple and the priesthood (whereby it is

---

50. On the rabbinic sources, see Deines, *Steingefäße*, 192–246; Magen, *Stone Vessel Industry*, 138–47. For the distribution of these vessels, see Deines, *Steingefäße*, 165; and Magen, *Stone Vessel Industry*, 148–62 (for Galilee, see 160–61). Fragments of stone vessels were found in Khirbet Qana and nearby Yodefat, and the number of sites increases with nearly every new excavation in Galilee that digs up first-century layers (see, for example, the very recent archaeological reports by Yardenna Alexandre mentioned in n. 58 below). For the most recent distribution map, see Yonatan Adler, "The Archaeology of Purity: Archaeological Evidence for the Observance of Ritual Purity in Ereẓ-Israel from the Hasmonean Period until the End of the Talmudic Era (164 BCE–400 CE)" (PhD diss., Bar-Ilan University, 2011 [in Hebrew]), maps 10 and 11 (after p. 374).

51. Deines, *Steingefäße*.

52. See n. 13 above, and in addition Jonathan Reed, *Archaeology and the Galilean Jesus: A Re-examination of the Evidence* (Harrisburg, Pa.: Trinity Press International, 2000), 44: "The Galileans' ethnic identity in the first century can best be determined by examining the material culture inside domestic or private space, since it indicates the populace's behavior and selection of artifacts. . . . The archaeological artifacts found in Galilean domestic space are remarkably similar to those of Judea. In particular, they share four indicators of Jewish religious identity: 1) the chalk vessels, 2) stepped plastered pools, 3) secondary burial with ossuaries in loculi tombs, and 4) bone profiles that lack pork." See further Stuart S. Miller, "Stepped Pools, Stone Vessels, and Other Identiy Markers of 'Complex Common Judaism,'" *JSJ* 41 (2010): 214–43.

necessary to recall that the biblical purity regulations were never meant solely for the priests or the temple cult but have always been a requirement for Israel as a whole). In particular, the Hellenistic crisis under Antiochus IV Epiphanes and, connected to this, the dramatic failure of the priestly aristocracy were decisive factors in Judaism for the origin and development of religiously motivated parties with differing interpretations of how a Jewish lifestyle should proceed. As a result, the focus of religious commitment shifted more and more from the nation to the individual, from the temple to the household, from priest to layperson, in that the latter became increasingly important. In other words, religious commitment became, to a large extent, the task of the individual and a matter of choice (see n. 1 above), which was carried out for the sake of the people as a whole, the integrity of the temple, and the land. My own conviction still is that the most probable solution is to read the archaeological evidence in the light of the emerging Pharisaic movement as its formative context,[53] thus combining the textual and the archaeological cues into a coherent picture. Together with the scribes, the Pharisees offer themselves as the most probable group responsible for this new concern among the general population. They were concerned with pots and pans (Mark 7:3–4) and the tithing of kitchen herbs (see Matt. 23:23). They pursued a praxis that allowed *all Israel* to participate in obedience to the law for the benefit of all, and they were successful, not just in Jerusalem but throughout the Jewish territory in Palestine, including Galilee. What is more, the Pharisees are distributed through all socioeconomic levels of Jewish society because the vessels were found in cities like Jerusalem and Sepphoris but also in small villages like Nazareth and Bethany and in isolated farmsteads; they were found in houses of the rich as well as in rather ordinary houses such as those in Capernaum; they were found in Qumran and in large quantities on Masada, as well as (although in a rather limited repertoire of types) in the caves and hiding complexes of the insurgents during the Bar Kokhba revolt. This general picture, which does not allow for a separate Galilean religious practice or identity against Judea,[54] fits well with the hypothesis mentioned above that,

---

53. For short recent summaries, see Roland Deines, "Jüdische Steingefäße aus der Zeit von Herodes bis Bar Kochba," in *Judäa und Jerusalem: Leben in römischer Zeit* (ed. Jürgen Schefzyk and Wolfgang Zwickel; Exhibition Catalogue, Bibelhaus Erlebnis Museum; Stuttgart: Katholisches Bibelwerk, 2010), 134–37; Yonatan Adler, "Religion, Judaism: Purity in the Roman Period," in *The Oxford Encyclopedia of the Bible and Archaeology* (ed. Daniel M. Master; 2 vols.; Oxford: Oxford University Press, 2013), 2:240–49, esp. 245–47; Jodi Magness, *Stone and Dung, Oil and Spit: Jewish Daily Life in the Time of Jesus* (Grand Rapids: Eerdmans, 2011), 70–74. For methodological discussions (including a critique of my position), see Stuart S. Miller, "Some Observations on Stone Vessel Finds and Ritual Purity in Light of Talmudic Sources," in *Zeichen aus Text und Stein: Studien auf dem Weg zu einer Archäologie des Neuen Testaments* (ed. Stefan Alkier and Jürgen Zangenberg; TANZ 42; Tübingen: Francke, 2003), 402–19; and, in the same volume, Jonathan L. Reed, "Stone Vessels and Gospel Texts: Purity and Socio-Economics in John 2," 381–401. See also Shimon Gibson, "Stone Vessels of the Early Roman Period from Jerusalem and Palestine: A Reassessment," in *One Land, Many Cultures: Archaeological Studies in Honour of Stanislao Loffreda OFM* (ed. G. Claudio Bottini et al.; Studium Biblicum Franciscanum Collectio maior 41; Jerusalem: Franciscan Printing Press, 2003), 287–308.

54. This does not mean, of course, that there were no Galilean particularities. A helpful overview on mentioned differences in the rabbinic corpus is provided by Martin Goodman, "Galilean Judaism and Judaean

among those groups who settled in Galilee at the beginning of the first century BCE, we can expect a certain Pharisaic element.

## The Influence of the Bar Kokhba War (132–135 CE) on Galilee

The effects of the Bar Kokhba War on Galilee remain a riddle. The sparse literary sources say nothing about Galilee,[55] and the archaeological evidence is inconclusive at best. Usually three kinds of archaeological evidence are used to reconstruct the geographical range of the revolt: the distribution of Bar Kokhba coinage, the underground tunnels or hiding places (which were mainly found in the Shephelah but can also be visited at the Herodium near Bethlehem), and the place-names mentioned in the written documents found in the caves along the Dead Sea. So far, no Bar Kokhba coins have been found in official excavations in Galilee (the provenance of the many coins from the antiquities market is, in most cases, unknown), but this is true for Jerusalem as well, even though there is some evidence "that Jerusalem was under the control of the insurgents at least for a short period."[56] There is one enigmatic reference to "Galileans" in one of Bar Kokhba's letters, written in Greek to one of his commanders, Yeshua ben Galgoula: "I call the heavens over me as witness: Should harm co[me] to any one of the Galileans who are with you—I will put fetters to your feet as I di[d] to Ben Aflul."[57] This does not, however, necessarily imply that the territory of Galilee was involved in the war, but only that Galileans had joined Bar Kokhba's forces in the south.

Only the hiding places that are occasionally found, and then often as a result of small-scale salvage excavations, point to the presence of revolutionaries in Galilee. These rock-cut underground complexes, however, are hard to date, and it is often impossible to decide whether they were in operation already during the first revolt or were dug only in preparation for or during the Bar Kokhba uprising. Jürgen Zangenberg concludes, therefore, that "material evi-

---

Judaism," in *The Cambridge History of Judaism*, vol. 3, *Early Roman Period* (ed. William Horbury, W. D. Davies, and John Sturdy; Cambridge: Cambridge University Press, 1999), 596–617; see also Lawrence H. Schiffman, "Was There a Galilean Halakhah?," in *The Galilee in Late Antiquity* (ed. Lee I. Levine; Cambridge, Mass.: Harvard University Press, 1992), 143–56.

55. A discussion of the relevant rabbinic texts that are offered as possible indicators of a Galilean involvement can be found in Peter Schäfer, *Der Bar Kokhba-Aufstand: Studien zum zweiten jüdischen Krieg gegen Rom* (TSAJ 1; Tübingen: Mohr Siebeck, 1981), 105–19; for an update, see the excellent collection *The Bar Kokhba War Reconsidered: New Perspectives on the Second Jewish Revolt against Rome* (ed. Peter Schäfer; TSAJ 100; Tübingen: Mohr Siebeck, 2003), in which see Schäfer's own contribution, "Bar Kokhba and the Rabbis," 1–22.

56. Zangenberg, "Archaeology, Papyri, and Inscriptions," 225. Against this position, see Hanan Eshel, Magen Broshi, and Timothy A. J. Jull, "Four Murabbaʿat Papyri and the Alleged Capture of Jerusalem," in *Law in the Documents of the Judaean Desert* (ed. Ranon Katzoff and David Schaps; JSJSup 96; Leiden: Brill, 2005), 45–50.

57. The translation follows Doering, *Ancient Jewish Letters*, 65. For a discussion, see also Schäfer, *Bar Kokhba-Aufstand*, 116–19.

dence from Galilee is not yet sufficient to determine whether the region actively took part in the revolt."[58]

There is, however, some new evidence from Khirbet Wadi Hamam, a site closely related to the famous cliffs and caves of Arbel not far from Tiberias and Magdala. Excavations started in 2007 under the direction of Uzi Leibner, who found not only a third-century synagogue with a mosaic floor but, more importantly, for the first time clear evidence of a battle at the site with a destruction level that clearly dates in the time of the Bar Kokhba revolt. Leibner dates the destruction "in the third or fourth decade" of the second century, "which raise[s] the possibility that the destruction was connected to the Bar-Kokhba revolt." Finds include a catapult arrowhead, a sword, and a spearhead. As this is the first evidence of fighting in Galilee at this time, he cautions against drawing wide-ranging conclusions, however: "More data from larger areas of the site are needed before definitive conclusions can be reached."[59]

What can be said about the Jewish groups in the time until the end of the second revolt? According to Peter Schäfer, the documents of and related to Bar Kokhba "allow us a glimpse of a Jewish society that is still much closer to the Maccabees, the Qumran community, and

---

58. Zangenberg, "Archaeology, Papyri, and Inscriptions," 225; see also Menahem Mor, "The Geographical Scope of the Bar-Kokhba Revolt," in Schäfer, *Bar Kokhba War Reconsidered*, 107–31. For the hiding complexes in general, see the helpful introduction by Amos Kloner and Boaz Zissu, "Judean Hiding Complexes," in *NEAEHL* 5:1892–93; Kloner and Zissu, "Hiding Complexes in Judaea: An Archaeological and Geographical Update on the Area of the Bar Kokhba Revolt," in Schäfer, *Bar Kokhba War Reconsidered*, 181–214 (on Galilee, see 189). For Galilee, see Mordechai Aviam, "Secret Hideaway Complexes in the Galilee," in Aviam, *Jews, Pagans, and Christians*, 123–32; Yardenna Alexandre, "Kafr Kanna (Jebel Khuwweikha): Iron II, Late Hellenistic and Roman Remains," *HA-ESI* 125 (2013): 1–21 (http://www.hadashot-esi.org.il/images//Kafr-Kanna-En-new.pdf); Alexandre, "Yafi'a: Final Report," *HA-ESI* 124 (2012): http://www.hadashot-esi.org.il/report_detail_eng.aspx?id=2084&mag_id=119. Both places represent the "typical" Galilean settlement pattern: disbanded during Iron Age II, and resettled in the late Hellenistic/early Hasmonean period with clear evidence of a Jewish presence, for example, stone vessels and ritual baths. In both cases, subterranean hiding complexes were excavated as well, which Alexandre understands as most likely hewn in preparation for the revolt in 66/67. Against Aviam and Alexandre, Yuval Shahar argues in favor of a date in relation to the Bar Kohkba revolt: Galileans prepared for the war but in the end did not take part in it, at least not in Galilee itself. See Shahar, "The Underground Hideouts in Galilee and Their Historical Meaning," in Schäfer, *Bar Kokhba War Reconsidered*, 217–40.

59. Uzi Leibner, "Excavations at Khirbet Wadi Hamam (Lower Galilee): The Synagogue and the Settlement," *Journal of Roman Archaeology* 23 (2010): 220–37, esp. 225–26; for the mosaic, see Leibner and Shulamit Miller, "A Figural Mosaic in the Synagogue at Khirbet Wadi Hamam," *Journal of Roman Archaeology* 23 (2010): 238–64. Archaeological surveys do not strongly support the view that large numbers of refugees came to Galilee after the Bar Kohkba War, although in the survey area described by Leibner (*Settlement and History*, 345–51), the settled area increased an approximate 10 to 15 percent between 135 and 250. The Jewish ethnic homogeneity during this time remained unchanged; that is, the Jewish territory as defined by a combination of archaeological and literary sources by Aviam and others remained more or less unchanged (see n. 13 above). For the growing influence of pagan cults in the border regions and cities, see Nicole Belayche, *Iudaea-Palaestina: The Pagan Cults in Roman Palestine (Second to Fourth Century)* (Religionen der römischen Provinzen 1; Tübingen: Mohr Siebeck, 2001). For a critical appraisal, see Stuart S. Miller, "Roman Imperialism, Jewish Self-Definition, and Rabbinic Society: Belayche's *Iudaea-Palaestina*, Schwartz's *Imperialism and Jewish Society*, and Boyarin's *Border Lines* Reconsidered," *AJSR* 31 (2007): 1–34.

the Zealots than to the Rabbis."[60] Schäfer does not mention the Pharisees and the Jesus movement, although they are most likely the two religious movements that continued not only after the destruction of the temple in 70 but even after the catastrophe of the Second Revolt. These groups were "inclusive of all Israel and believed that the divine could be experienced anywhere," and they were therefore able to survive by transforming their key values to adapt them to the changed situation.[61]

## Jewish Christians in Galilee[62]

When looking for religious movements in Galilee for the first century CE, Josephus offers very little help after the events related to Judas the Galilean and before the outbreak of the revolt against Rome. The most important sources for the decades in between are the New Testament Gospels, which describe Jesus' conflict with the Pharisees and scribes as an integral part of his public ministry in Galilee. As mentioned earlier, however, it is somewhat surprising that Galilee so quickly was lost sight of in Christian writings, though this development is parallel to how "Jesus of Nazareth" was eclipsed by "Jesus Christ."[63] The book of Acts, which is the only New Testament book outside of the Gospels that mentions Galilee at all, is quite revealing in this respect. The disciples of Jesus are addressed as Galileans by the angels when Jesus returns to his Father in heaven (Acts 1:11), which Luke locates—differently from Mark and Matthew[64]—in Jerusalem. When Peter explains the Gospel to the Roman centurion Cornelius in his house in Caesarea, he points to the beginnings in Galilee (10:37), and Paul, in the first extended sermon attributed to him in Acts, mentions as witnesses of Jesus' resurrection "many of those who came up with him from Galilee to Jerusalem" (13:31). But except for the acknowledgment of Galilee as the place of Jesus' ministry, Luke has nothing to report about the churches in Galilee. They appear only in the summary verse 9:31, which talks about peace among the churches in

---

60. Schäfer, "Bar Kokhba and the Rabbis," 22.

61. So Magness, *Stone and Dung*, 182, in her "Epilogue—The Aftermath of 70," which traces the changes in the religious and related material culture.

62. For a short overview, see Edwin K. Broadhead, *Jewish Ways of Following Jesus: Redrawing the Religious Map of Antiquity* (WUNT 266; Tübingen: Mohr Siebeck, 2010), 90–98. Mention should also be made of the attempt of Anthony J. Saldarini to locate the Gospel of Matthew in post-70 Galilee; see his "The Gospel of Matthew and Jewish–Christian Conflict in the Galilee," in Levine, *Galilee in Late Antiquity*, 23–38; in the same volume, see also Albert I. Baumgarten, "Literary Evidence for Jewish Christianity in the Galilee," 39–50.

63. See Martin Hengel, "Jesus, the Messiah of Israel: The Debate about the 'Messianic Mission' of Jesus," in *Authenticating the Activities of Jesus* (ed. Bruce Chilton and Craig A. Evans; NTTS 28.2; Leiden: Brill, 1999), 323–49, esp. 323–35; Hengel, "Jesus the Messiah of Israel," in Hengel, *Studies in Early Christology* (Edinburgh: T&T Clark, 1995), 1–72; and Hengel, "'Christos' in Paul," in Hengel, *Between Jesus and Paul: Studies in Earliest Christology* (London: SCM, 1983), 65–77 and endnotes, 179–88.

64. Mark 14:28; 16:7; Matt. 28:7, 10. Luke's relocation of the resurrection appearances from Galilee to Jerusalem is indicative for this prioritization of Jerusalem over Galilee.

Judea, Galilee, and Samaria. But whereas Luke provides a number of individual stories located in Judea, and at least one in Samaria, no single event is located in Galilee. The area quickly fades into insignificance, and hardly any Christian individual from Galilee is known in the following centuries.[65]

Archaeologically, the evidence is equally slim, but this is—at least for the time up to the third century—not really a surprise. What would we have to look for in Galilee to clearly identify belief in Jesus? Churches had not yet been built, and for that period the certain identification of Christian artefacts is not straightforward at all. Funeral inscriptions and tombs from the second century are generally rare in Galilee, and no particular Christian material cult is discernible.[66] The oldest definite physical evidence for a Christian presence— if not in Galilee then at least close to its southern border—is the church (or prayer hall) in Megiddo (Kefar 'Othnay) found in 2005, with its wonderful fish mosaic. One of its inscriptions mentions the "God Jesus Christ" and is dated by the excavators to the third century, although there is an intense discussion about this early date and others have proposed a date somewhere in the fourth century. In the immediate context of the Christian site is the camp of the 6th Roman legion, the *Legio VI Ferrata*, finally identified south of Tel Megiddo

---

65. One could suggest that this was perhaps the case, at least initially, because the early followers of Jesus, including his and their families, moved to Jerusalem (or stayed there after Passover) to join and lead the newly forming group of Jesus followers there. This Jewish Christian community might have left Jerusalem early on during the first revolt (the so-called flight to Pella; see Eusebius, *Hist. eccl.* 3.5.2–3), and some might have returned to Jerusalem after the war but seemingly not to Galilee. For the contested issue of the Pella tradition, see Jonathan Bourgel, "The Jewish-Christians' Move from Jerusalem as a Pragmatic Choice," in *Studies in Rabbinic Judaism and Early Christianity: Text and Context* (ed. Dan Jaffé; Ancient Judaism and Early Christianity 74; Leiden: Brill, 2010), 107–38 (the appendix presents all texts related to this event [pp. 136–38]).

66. With regard to missing evidence, Galilee is no exception. William Tabbernee remarks that only from the beginning of the third century "open expressions of Christianity in 'secure' burial locations . . . became common," and "clear evidence of Christianity on *stelai* (gravemarkers)" is available only "from the second half of the second century," even if there is some earlier evidenced that is discussed as being Christian ("Epigraphy," in Harvey and Hunter, *The Oxford Handbook of Early Christian Studies*, 120–39; quotations from 127–28). Tabbernee also relates that during the first three centuries Christians "chose symbols which were part of the wider culture but which also had a special Christian significance" (p. 127); that is, only insiders of the group could "read" the intended meaning of a common symbol. For the full picture (which again offers hardly anything from before the third century), see Mark Humphries, "Material Evidence (1): Archaeology," in ibid., 87–103; Paul Corby Finney, *The Invisible God: The Earliest Christians on Art* (New York: Oxford University Press, 1994), esp. chapter 5, "Christianity before 200: Invisibility and Adaptation," which explains "the absence of Christian Art before 200" (p. 99); but this is not only true for art but for any form of material evidence (cf. p. 108: "Christians produced nothing distinctive in the material realm"). The only exceptions are the early Christian manuscripts and their distinctive features, but here again, most evidence is post-200, and nothing is in any way related to Galilee. On manuscripts as oldest material evidence of Christianity, see Larry W. Hurtado, *The Earliest Christian Artefacts: Manuscripts and Christian Origins* (Grand Rapids: Eerdmans, 2006).

in 2013, and it is therefore likely that the prayer hall is not reflective of an autochthonous Christianity.[67]

The other archaeological remains often noted in this respect are from the house-church in Capernaum, allegedly Peter's former living quarters, but there again firm evidence does not predate the fourth century, though an ongoing presence of Jewish Christians from the earliest time onward cannot be ruled out completely. In a thorough survey of the evidence, James F. Strange allows the assumption for the second half of the first century that the changes made within the house may indicate that we have here indeed "the earliest Christian sanctuary known for the Jesus movement, and that it may indeed have been of Jewish Christian usage."[68]

The most interesting stories relating to Jewish Christians in Galilee during the second century are two (prevented) healing accounts involving the Jewish Christian (*min*) Jacob from Kefar Sama, most likely to be located in Upper Galilee.[69] Rabbi Eleazar ben Dama, the nephew of Rabbi Ishmael, was bitten by a snake and asked Jacob to heal him in the name of "Yeshua ben Pandera" (Jesus), but his uncle interfered and Eleazar died before Jacob could do anything. This must have happened in the first third of the second century CE. No place is mentioned here aside from Jacob's hometown, which assumes a Galilean setting. The immediate continuation in the Tosefta describes the same Jacob (this time as "a man from Sikhnin") as discussing with Rabbi Eliezer ben Hyrkanos, the famous pupil of Rabbi Yoḥanan ben Zakkai, in

---

67. Yotam Tepper, "Legio, Kefar 'Otnay," *HA-ESI* 118 (2006): www. http://www.hadashot-esi.org.il/report_detail_eng.aspx?id=363. For a more detailed report see Yotam Tepper and Leah Di Segni, *A Christian Prayer Hall of the Third Century CE at Kefar 'Othnay (Legio): Excavations at the Megiddo Prison 2005* (Publications of the Israel Antiquities Authority; Jerusalem: Israel Antiquities Authority, 2006). The mosaics were donated by a Roman centurion named Gaianus.

68. James F. Strange, "Archaeological Evidence of Jewish Believers?," in *Jewish Believers in Jesus: The Early Centuries* (ed. Oskar Skarsaune and Reidar Hvalvik; Peabody, Mass.: Hendrickson, 2007), 710–41, esp. 729. For other supportive discussion of the evidence, see, for example, Rainer Riesner, "Kapharnaum und Heptapegon: Zwei byzantinische Pilgerstätten am See Gennesaret," in *Leben am See Gennesaret: Kulturgeschichtliche Entdeckungen in einer biblischen Region* (ed. Gabriele Fassbeck, Sandra Fortner, Andrea Rottloff, and Jürgen Zangenberg; Zaberns Bildbände zur Archäologie; Mainz: Philipp von Zabern, 2003), 173–80, esp. 176–79; Riesner, "What Does Archaeology Teach Us about Early House Churches," *TTKi* 78 (2007): 159–85, esp. 174–78; Roger W. Gehring, *House Church and Mission: The Importance of Household Structures in Early Christianity* (Peabody, Mass.: Hendrickson, 2004), 32–33 and passim (see index s.v. Capernaum); Broadhead, *Jewish Ways*, 334–41. Broadhead also discusses the archaeological evidence for Jewish Christian presence from Nazareth (pp. 323–34; see also 94–95, for the presence of Jesus' relatives in Nazareth until the second century).

69. For this identification, see Gottfried Reeg, *Die Ortsnamen Israels nach der rabbinischen Literatur* (Beihefte zum Tübinger Atlas des Vorderen Orients, B.51; Wiesbaden: Reichert, 1989), 357–58, and the appertaining map in *Israel nach der rabbinischen Literatur/Israel according to Rabbinical Literature* (charted by Angelika Schefter; Beihefte zum Tübinger Atlas des Vorderen Orients, B VI 16; Wiesbaden: Reichert, 1984), coordinates 178264. Peter Schäfer sees in the town name a pun, because otherwise Jacob is described as a man from Kefar Sekhaniah/Sikhnaya (Sikhnin), which is located ca. 12 km north of Sepphoris (*Jesus in the Talmud* [Princeton: Princeton University Press, 2007], 163 n. 14). See Reeg, *Die Ortsnamen Israels*, 356–57, 458–60 (coordinates 177252).

Sepphoris, and both episodes testify to Jewish Christian activities and their close, if somehow compromised, relationship to fellow Jews in the time between the two revolts.[70]

But even then, it would appear that into the early fourth century Galilee seems to have had no noticeable Christian population. According to one of the earliest Christian pilgrim accounts, the *Itinerarium Burdigalense* (333/334 CE), Galilee warranted no visit. Günter Stemberger has therefore raised the question: "Does he [the pilgrim] perhaps fail to visit Galilee precisely because . . . there are hardly any Christian sites to be visited?"[71] Likewise, the church historian Eusebius of Caesarea appears to know of no Christian martyrs in the early fourth century from Galilee; at least he mentions none in his *Martyrs in Palestine*. Telling also is the fact that no bishop from Galilee attended the council of Nicaea in 325 CE.[72] Epiphanius reports in his *Panarion* 30.4.1 that only at the time of Constantine in the fourth century was allowance given to "Count" Joseph of Tiberius, a Jewish convert to Christianity,[73] to erect church buildings in Tiberias and Diocaesarea (Sepphoris) and other places in Galilee.[74] There is as such little external evidence to suppose a significant Christian presence in Galilee before the fourth century, and there is not much evidence to assume that the picture was very different in the second. This is not to say that there were no Christians at all, but they were at best very small communities who left hardly any discernible traces.

---

70. The prevented healing of Eleazar ben Dama is to be found in *t. Ḥullin* 2:22–23; for the discussion with R. Eliezer see *t. Ḥullin* 2:24. On these texts (and their inner-rabbinic parallels), see Schäfer, *Jesus in the Talmud*, 41–48, 52–59; Philip S. Alexander, "Jewish Believers in Early Rabbinic Literature (2d to 5th Centuries)," in Skarsaune and Hvalvik, *Jewish Believers in Jesus*, 659–709, esp. 677–79; Broadhead, *Jewish Ways*, 289–90.

71. See Günter Stemberger, *Jews and Christians in the Holy Land: Palestine in the Fourth Century* (Edinburgh: T&T Clark, 2000), 95. But only a few decades later, Egeria is visiting Galilee and the places of Jesus' ministry.

72. For Christian presence in Palestine in the first four centuries, see also the still valuable survey in Adolf v. Harnack, *Die Mission and Ausbreitung des Christentums in den ersten drei Jahrhunderten* (Leipzig: Hinrichs, 1924), 630–55: the only bishop from the area was Paulus from Maximinianopolis, a city closely related to the camp of the sixth Roman legion in the Megiddo plain.

73. On Count Joseph, see Stemberger, *Jews and Christians in the Holy Land*, 71–72; Oskar Skarsaune, "Evidence for Jewish Believers in Greek and Latin Patristic Literature," in Skarsaune and Hvalvik, *Jewish Believers in Jesus*, 505–67, esp. 528–40.

74. According to Epiphanius (*Panarion* 30.4.5), the Jewish patriarch of Tiberias, Hillel, requested on his deathbed to be secretly baptized, asking to see the bishop who was then closest *near* Tiberias (πλησιόχωρον τῆς Τιβερι<έ>ων). Unfortunately, Epiphanius gives neither the name nor the place for this bishop. Jerome also asserts that, in the middle of the fourth century, Diocaesarea/Sepphoris and Tiberias were Jewish cities (*Chron. ad* 282 *Olympiad*). This, then, might indicate that no bishop (or church building) was to be found *in the cities* of Galilee before this time (though Epiphanius speaks of the Arian bishop Patrophilius residing in Scythopolis [Beth She'an]; see *Panarion* 30.5.5). See David Goldblatt, "Population, Structure, and Jewish Identity," in Hezser, *Oxford Handbook of Jewish Daily Life in Roman Palestine*, 102–21, esp. 108–13. For the first churches in Galilee, see Stemberger, *Jews and Christians in the Holy Land*, 68–71; and Stemberger, *Juden und Christen im spätantiken Palästina* (Hans-Lietzmann-Vorlesungen 9; Berlin: de Gruyter, 2007), 9–12, 20–55. Based on the report of Julius Africanus (in Eusebius *Hist. eccl.* 1.7.14), which places Christians in Nazareth and the nearby Cochaba, others have argued for a more robust Christian presence in Galilee; see Eckhard Schnabel, *Early Christian Mission* (2 vols.; Downers Grove, Ill.: InterVarsity, 2004) 1:747–65.

### Early Rabbinic Traditions in Galilee

Galilee was relatively unscathed by the two wars, which might be one of the reasons why it became the place for the establishment of a new form of representative leadership over the Jewish people. This did not start immediately after the destruction of Jerusalem in 70 CE. The place of choice for reconstituting a form of religious leadership and authority was not in Galilee but in Yavneh (Jamnia), and therefore closer to Jerusalem and the Judean heartland. This does not mean, however, that immediately after 70 CE, Judea and Galilee should be regarded as being more or less completely under the rule of the rabbinic sages, with Yoḥanan ben Zakkai starting the rebuilding of the Jewish nation after the fall of Jerusalem by implementing Pharisaic/rabbinic rule over the leaderless nation and the patriarchate of the Gamaliel family already fully established.[75] This long-standing story of the council or "Synod of Yavneh (Jamnia)," is now regarded to a large degree as a scholarly myth. Critical scholarship in rabbinic studies, starting in the last third of the last century, has dismantled the idea of rabbinic leadership at least for the time between 70 CE and the end of the Bar Kokhba revolt (135 CE). Some scholars even hold the position that "no such institution [that is, the Sanhedrin] is likely to have existed in post-70 CE times."[76] Without doubt, this goes too far, but one has to acknowledge that how precisely this new leadership came into place cannot be establised by simply retelling rabbinic traditions. For here it is sufficient to say that the traditional view of the Sanhedrin moving from Yavneh to Usha in Galilee, then to Beth She'arim, and finally settling in Sepphoris under Rabbi Judah the Prince is at best an abbreviated and idealized version of a rather more complex development. What can be derived from the traditions about the frequent moves of the Sanhedrin (whatever is historically behind it) is the lack of a real center during the second century for the rabbis, who seem to become a more urban phenomenon only in the third century. The reasons for the places in which they chose to live are beyond our grasp, and often there might simply have been personal factors involved that elude verification, such as family relations or land possession, hostility in certain places against the rabbis, and so on, in addition to political issues that would have made it prudent to be decentralized and to keep a low profile for a while—or perhaps the rabbis were just a rather isolated phenomenon for most of the second century.

---

75. For such a traditional and rather simplistic view, see, for example, Lawrence H. Schiffman, *From Text to Tradition. A History of Second Temple and Rabbinic Judaism* (Hoboken, N.J.: Ktav, 1991), 167–70, 174. The new starting point for an evaluation of the Yavneh traditions is now Shaye J. D. Cohen, "The Significance of Yavneh: Pharisees, Rabbis, and the End of Jewish Sectarianism," *HUCA* 55 (1984): 27–53 (reprinted in Cohen, *Significance of Yavneh*, 44–70), although he seems to distance himself slightly from the "positivist approach" taken in his earlier articles (see ibid., Preface, x). On the rise of the Gamaliel family from Pharisaic leadership to the patriarchate, see Alexei Sivertsev, *Private Households and Public Politics in 3rd–5th Century Jewish Palestine* (TSAJ 90; Tübingen: Mohr Siebeck, 2002), 73–93.

76. Hezser, "Correlating Literary, Epigraphic, and Archaeological Sources," 18, based on David M. Goodblatt, *The Monarchic Principle: Studies in Jewish Self-Government in Antiquity* (TSAJ 38; Tübingen: Mohr Siebeck, 1994).

What is often overlooked when it comes to rabbinic rule and influence is the relatively small numbers of rabbis known at all. Shaye Cohen highlights that the Mishnah and other documents give only about one hundred names for the period between ca. 80 CE and Rabbi Judah the Patriarch (end of second century CE), and the majority of them belong to the period before the Bar Kokhba War. Only a small portion of these one hundred or so rabbis can in one way or another be related to Galilee.[77] In other words, even though it is true that rabbinic Judaism had its geographical center in Galilee from the early third century onward, this is not yet the case for most of the second century. In looking at Galilee, one should not forget that the geographical range of Jewish settlements and rabbinic traditions includes other parts of Israel as well—most notably the Judean mountains around Hebron, the Shephelah, and coastal cities with Caesarea as an important center, and also the areas north and east of Galilee on the Golan Heights (Gaulanitis).[78] It is helpful to keep these data in mind when one considers rabbinic influence. Even if the rabbinic literary heritage seems massive, it is nothing but the residue of a numerically rather small group whose real impact and influence on Jewish society, religious agendas, and practices will continue to spark debates.[79] In general, however, and read critically, the rabbinic information about life in Galilee in the second and third century, rather fits than contradicts the archaeological picture. Both source types provide colorful mosaic stones toward an ever-richer Galilean map, as long as one does not mistake individual mosaic tiles for the whole.

## Conclusion

The history of Galilee in the three centuries between 100 BCE and 200 CE is marked by a history of conquest, settlement, wars, and refugees, all of which had their origin in Judean affairs. The religious profile of the territory is therefore largely oriented toward Jersualem. At least some of the first Judean settlers brought with them the specific reasons why they left Jerusalem for good or ill, and Galilee allowed them to cultivate and intensify their attitude toward Jerusalem and her rulers. This might be one of the reasons why Galileans appear sometimes as rather uncompromising and fanatical in the sources. A large number of important figures of Jewish history spent some time in Galilee and left their mark, includ-

---

77. Shaye J. D. Cohen, "The Rabbi in Second-Century Jewish Society," in Horbury et al., *Cambridge History of Judaism*, 3:922–90; see esp. fig. 29.1 (p. 919) on "Rabbinic activity in Galilee." Cohen argues that rabbinic influence on Galilee existed "at least to some extent, even before the Bar Kokhba war" (p. 967). An abridged version of this article is his "The Place of the Rabbi in Jewish Society of the Second Century," in Levine, *Galilee in Late Antiquity*, 157–73 (reprinted in Cohen, *Significance of Yavneh*, 282–96).

78. The already mentioned map (n. 69) provides a most helpful overview.

79. Groundbreaking contributions for a new understanding of the early rabbinic movements are Lee I. Levine, *The Rabbinic Class of Roman Palestine in Late Antiquity* (Jerusalem: Ben Zvi, 1989); Catherine Hezser, *The Social Structure of the Rabbinic Movement in Roman Palestine* (TSAJ 66; Tübingen: Mohr Siebeck, 1997); Stuart S. Miller, *Sages and Commoners in Late Antique 'Erez Israel* (TSAJ 111; Tübingen: Mohr Siebeck, 2006).

ing Alexander Jannaeus, Ezekias the bandit, Herod and his heirs, Judas the Galilean and the Pharisee Zaddok, Jesus, Peter, Yoḥanan ben Zakkai, Ḥanina ben Dosa, Josephus, Jacob of Sikhnaya, and Rabbi Judah the Prince. They all represent religious traditions that influenced larger or smaller segments of the inhabitants of Galilee. What they have in common, despite all obvious differences, is loyalty to the God of Israel and the covenant he made with their forefathers. Whatever they tried to achieve religiously was guided by God's revelation to them. After the loss of Jerusalem and the temple, the Jewish Scriptures became the new focus. And because of this, the promised land and the place Israel's God had chosen "to put his name there" (Deut. 12:5) could never be forgotten.

## Bibliography

Adler, Yonatan. "The Archaeology of Purity: Archaeological Evidence for the Observance of Ritual Purity in Ereẓ-Israel from the Hasmonean Period until the End of the Talmudic Era (164 BCE–400 CE)." PhD diss., Bar-Ilan University, 2011.

———. "Religion, Judaism: Purity in the Roman Period." In *The Oxford Encyclopedia of the Bible and Archaeology*, edited by Daniel M. Master, 240–49. Oxford: Oxford University Press, 2013.

Alexander, Philip S. "Jewish Believers in Early Rabbinic Literature (2d to 5th Centuries)." In *Jewish Believers in Jesus: The Early Centuries*, edited by Oskar Skarsaune and Reidar Hvalvik, 659–709. Peabody, Mass.: Hendrickson, 2007.

Alexandre, Yardenna. "Kafr Kanna (Jebel Khuwweikha): Iron II, Late Hellenistic and Roman Remains." *HA-ESI* 125 (2013): 1–21.

Avery-Peck, Alan J. "The Galilean Charismatic and Rabbinic Piety: The Holy Man in the Talmudic Literature." In *The Historical Jesus in Context*, edited by Amy-Jill Levine et al., 149–65. Princeton Readings in Religions. Princeton: Princeton University Press, 2006.

Aviam, Mordechai. "The Hasmonaean Dynasty's Activities in the Galilee." In Aviam, *Jews, Pagans, and Christians in the Galilee: 25 Years of Archaeological Excavations and Surveys, Hellenistic to Byzantine Periods*, 41–50. Land of Galilee 1; Rochester, N.Y.: University of Rochester Press, 2004.

———. "People, Land, Economy, and Belief in First-Century Galilee and Its Origins: A Comprehensive Archaeological Synthesis." In *The Galilean Economy in the Time of Jesus*, edited by David A. Fiensy and Ralph K. Hawkins, 5–48. Early Christianity and Its Literature 11. Atlanta: Society of Biblical Literature, 2013.

Belayche, Nicole. *Iudaea-Palaestina: The Pagan Cults in Roman Palestine (Second to Fourth Century)*. Religionen der römischen Provinzen 1. Tübingen: Mohr Siebeck, 2001.

Berlin, Andrea M. "Jewish Life before the Revolt: The Archaeological Evidence." *JSJ* 36 (2005): 417–70.

Blaschke, Andreas. *Beschneidung: Zeugnisse der Bibel und verwandter Texte.* TANZ 28. Tübingen: Francke, 1998.

Bourgel, Jonathan. "The Jewish-Christians' Move from Jerusalem as a Pragmatic Choice." In *Studies in Rabbinic Judaism and Early Christianity: Text and Context,* edited by Dan Jaffé, 107–38. Ancient Judaism and Early Christianity 74. Leiden: Brill, 2010.

Broadhead, Edwin K. *Jewish Ways of Following Jesus: Redrawing the Religious Map of Antiquity.* WUNT 266. Tübingen: Mohr Siebeck, 2010.

Cappelletti, Silvia. "Non-Jewish Authors on Galilee." In *Religion, Ethnicity, and Identity in Ancient Galilee: A Region in Transition,* edited by Jürgen Zangenberg, Harold W. Attridge, and Dale B. Martin, 69–82. WUNT 210. Tübingen: Mohr Siebeck, 2007.

Casey, Maurice. *Jesus of Nazareth: An Independent Historian's Account of His Life and Teaching.* London: T&T Clark, 2010.

Cohen, Shaye J. D. "The Place of the Rabbi in Jewish Society of the Second Century." In *The Galilee in Late Antiquity,* edited by Lee I. Levine, 157–73. Cambridge, Mass.: Harvard University Press, 1992.

———. "The Rabbi in Second-Century Jewish Society." In *The Cambridge History of Judaism,* vol. 3, *Early Roman Period,* edited by William Horbury, W. D. Davies, and John Sturdy, 922–90. Cambridge: Cambridge University Press, 1999.

———. "The Significance of Yavneh: Pharisees, Rabbis, and the End of Jewish Sectarianism." *HUCA* 55 (1984): 27–53.

———. *The Significance of Yavneh and Other Essay in Jewish Hellenism.* TSAJ 136. Tübingen: Mohr Siebeck, 2010.

———. "Were Pharisees and Rabbis the Leaders of Communal Prayer and Torah Study in Antiquity? The Evidence of the New Testament, Josephus, and the Early Church Fathers." In *Evolution of the Synagogue: Problems and Progress,* edited by Howard Clark Kee and Lynn H. Cohick, 89–105. Harrisburg, Pa.: Trinity Press International, 1999.

Collins, Adela Yarbro. *Mark: A Commentary.* Hermeneia. Philadelphia: Fortress Press, 2007.

Cook, Michael J. *Mark's Treatment of the Jewish Leaders.* NovTSup 51. Leiden: Brill, 1978.

———. "Gab es eine jüdische Freiheitsbewegung? Martin Hengels 'Zeloten' nach 50 Jahren." In Martin Hengel, *Die Zeloten: Untersuchungen zur jüdischen Freiheitsbewegung in der Zeit von Herodes I. bis 70 n. Chr.,* edited by Roland Deines and Claus-Jürgen Thornton, 403–48. 3rd rev. ed. WUNT 283. Tübingen: Mohr Siebeck, 2011.

———. "Jüdische Steingefäße aus der Zeit von Herodes bis Bar Kochba." In *Judäa und Jerusalem: Leben in römischer Zeit,* edited by Jürgen Schefzyk and Wolfgang Zwickel, 134–37. Exhibition catalogue, Bibelhaus Erlebnis Museum. Stuttgart: Katholisches Bibelwerk, 2010.

———. *Jüdische Steingefäße und pharisäische Frömmigkeit: Ein archäologisch-historischer Beitrag zum Verständnis von Joh 2,6 und der jüdischen Reinheitshalacha zur Zeit Jesu.* WUNT 2.52. Tübingen: Mohr Siebeck, 1993.

———. "Non-literary Sources for the Interpretation of the New Testament: Methodological Considerations and Case Studies Related to the Corpus Judaeo-Hellenisticum." In *Neues Testament und hellenistisch-jüdische Alltagskultur: Wechselseitige Wahrnehmungen. III. Internationales Symposium zum Corpus Judaeo-Hellenisticum Novi Testamenti, 21.–24. Mai, 2009, Leipzig*, edited by Roland Deines, Jens Herzer, and Karl-Wilhelm Niebuhr, 25–66. WUNT 274. Tübingen: Mohr Siebeck 2011.

———. *Die Pharisäer: Ihr Verständnis im Spiegel der christlichen und jüdischen Forschung seit Wellhausen und Graetz*. WUNT 101. Tübingen: Mohr Siebeck, 1997.

———. "Die Pharisäer und das Volk im Neuen Testament und bei Josephus." In *Josephus und das Neue Testament: Wechselseitige Wahrnehmungen. II. Internationales Symposium zum Corpus Judaeo-Hellenisticum, 25.–28. Mai 2006*, edited by Christfried Böttrich and Jens Herzer, 147–80. WUNT 209. Tübingen: Mohr Siebeck, 2007.

———. "The Pharisees between 'Judaisms' and 'Common Judaism.'" In *Justification and Variegated Nomism: A Fresh Appraisal of Paul and Second Temple Judaism*, vol. 1, *The Complexities of Second Temple Judaism*, edited by Donald A. Carson, Peter T. O'Brien, and Mark A. Seifrid, 443–504. WUNT 2.140. Tübingen: Mohr Siebeck; Grand Rapids: Baker, 2001.

———. "The Social Profile of the Pharisees." In *The New Testament and Rabbinic Literature*, edited by Reimund Bieringer, Florentino García Martínez, Didier Pollefeyt, and Peter J. Tomson, 111–32. JSJSup 136. Leiden: Brill, 2010. Reprinted in *Acts of God in History: Studies Towards Recovering a Theological Historiography*, edited by Christoph Ochs and Peter Watts, 29–52. WUNT 317. Tübingen: Mohr Siebeck, 2013.

Doering, Lutz. *Ancient Jewish Letters and the Beginning of Christian Epistolography*. WUNT 298. Tübingen: Mohr Siebeck, 2012.

Eshel, Hanan, Magen Broshi, and Timothy A. J. Jull. "Four Murabbaʿat Papyri and the Alleged Capture of Jerusalem." In *Law in the Documents of the Judaean Desert*, edited by Ranon Katzoff and David Schaps, 45–50. JSJSup 96. Leiden: Brill, 2005.

Finney, Paul Corby. *The Invisible God: The Earliest Christians on Art*. New York: Oxford University Press, 1994.

France, R. T. *The Gospel of Mark*. NIGTC. Grand Rapids: Eerdmans, 2002.

Freyne, Seán. "Iturea." In *The Eerdmans Dictionary of Early Judaism*, edited by John J. Collins and Daniel C. Harlow, 779–80. Grand Rapids: Eerdmans, 2010.

Gehring, Roger W. *House Church and Mission: The Importance of Household Structures in Early Christianity*. Peabody, Mass.: Hendrickson, 2004.

Gibson, Shimon. "Stone Vessels of the Early Roman Period from Jerusalem and Palestine: A Reassessment." In *One Land, Many Cultures: Archaeological Studies in Honour of Stanislao Loffreda OFM*, edited by G. Claudio Bottini et al., 287–308. SBF Collectio maior 41. Jerusalem: Franciscan Printing Press, 2003.

Goldblatt, David. "Population, Structure, and Jewish Identity." In *The Oxford Handbook of Jewish Daily Life in Roman Palestine*, edited by Catherine Hezser, 102–21. Oxford: Oxford University Press, 2010.

Goodblatt, David M. *The Monarchic Principle: Studies in Jewish Self-Government in Antiquity*. TSAJ 38. Tübingen: Mohr Siebeck, 1994.

Goodman, Martin. "Galilean Judaism and Judaean Judaism." In *The Cambridge History of Judaism*, vol. 3, *The Early Roman Period*, edited by William Horbury, W. D. Davies, and John Sturdy, 596–617. Cambridge: Cambridge University Press, 1999.

Groh, Dennis E. "The Clash between Literary and Archaeological Models of Provincial Palestine." In *Archaeology and the Galilee: Texts and Contexts in the Graeco-Roman and Byzantine Period*, edited by Douglas R. Edwards and C. Thomas McCollough, 29–37. South Florida Studies in the History of Judaism 143. Atlanta: Scholars Press, 1997.

Harnack, Adolf von. *Die Mission und Ausbreitung des Christentums in den ersten drei Jahrhunderten*. Leipzig: Hinrichs, 1924.

Harvey, Susan Ashbrook, and David G. Hunter, eds. *The Oxford Handbook of Early Christian Studies*. Oxford: Oxford University Press, 2008.

Hengel, Martin. *Between Jesus and Paul: Studies in Earliest Christology*. London: SCM, 1983.

———. "Jesus, the Messiah of Israel: The Debate about the 'Messianic Mission' of Jesus." In *Authenticating the Activities of Jesus*, edited by Bruce Chilton and Craig A. Evans, 323–49. NTTS 28.2. Leiden: Brill, 1999.

———. *Studies in Early Christology*. Edinburgh: T&T Clark, 1995.

———. *The Zealots: Investigations into the Jewish Freedom Movement in the Period from Herod I until 70 A.D.* Translated by David Smith. Edinburgh: T&T Clark, 1989.

Hengel, Martin, and Roland Deines. "E. P. Sanders' 'Common Judaism,' Jesus, and the Pharisees: A Review Article," *JTS* 46 (1995): 1–70.

Hengel, Martin, and Anna Maria Schwemer. *Paul between Damascus and Antioch: The Unknown Years*. Translated by John Bowden. London: SCM, 1997.

Hezser, Catherine. "Correlating Literary, Epigraphic, and Archaeological Sources." In *The Oxford Handbook of Jewish Daily Life in Roman Palestine*, edited by Catherine Hezser, 9–27. Oxford: Oxford University Press, 2010.

———. *The Social Structure of the Rabbinic Movement in Roman Palestine*. TSAJ 66. Tübingen: Mohr Siebeck, 1997.

Hoffmann, David. *Midrasch Tannaim zum Deuteronomium*. Berlin: Itzkowski, 1908–9.

Hurtado, Larry W. *The Earliest Christian Artefacts: Manuscripts and Christian Origins*. Grand Rapids: Eerdmans, 2006.

Ilan, Tal. *Lexicon of Jewish Names in Late Antiquity*. Vol. 1, *Palestine 330 BCE –200 CE*. TSAJ 91. Tübingen: Mohr Siebeck, 2002.

Kasher, Aryeh. *Jews and Hellenistic Cities in Eretz-Israel: Relation of the Jews in Eretz-Israel with the Hellenistic Cities during the Second Temple Period (322 BCE –70 CE)*. TSAJ 21. Tübingen: Mohr Siebeck, 1990.

Kloner, Amos, and Boaz Zissu, "Hiding Complexes in Judaea: An Archaeological and Geographical Update on the Area of the Bar Kokhba Revolt." In *The Bar Kokhba War Reconsidered: New Perspectives on the Second Jewish Revolt against Rome*, edited by Peter Schäfer, 181–214. TSAJ 100. Tübingen: Mohr Siebeck, 2003.

Leibner, Uzi. "Excavations at Khirbet Wadi Hamam (Lower Galilee): The Synagogue and the Settlement." *Journal of Roman Archaeology* 23 (2010): 220–37.

———. *Settlement and History in Hellenistic, Roman, and Byzantine Galilee.* TSAJ 127. Tübingen: Mohr Siebeck, 2009.

Levine, Lee I. *The Ancient Synagogue: The First Thousand Years.* New Haven: Yale University Press, 2000.

———. *The Rabbinic Class of Roman Palestine in Late Antiquity.* Jerusalem: Ben Zvi, 1989.

Magness, Jodi. *Stone and Dung, Oil and Spit: Jewish Daily Life in the Time of Jesus.* Grand Rapids: Eerdmans, 2011.

Mason, Steve. *Acts of God in History: Studies Towards Recovering a Theological Historiography*, edited by Christoph Ochs and Peter Watts. WUNT 317. Tübingen: Mohr Siebeck, 2013.

———. *Flavius Josephus: Translation and Commentary.* Vol. 9, *Life of Flavius Josephus.* Leiden: Brill, 2001.

Miller, Shulamit. "A Figural Mosaic in the Synagogue at Khirbet Wadi Hamam." *Journal of Roman Archaeology* 23 (2010): 238–64.

Miller, Stuart S. "Roman Imperialism, Jewish Self-Definition, and Rabbinic Society: Belayche's *Iudaea-Palaestina*, Schwartz's *Imperialism and Jewish Society*, and Boyarin's *Border Lines* Reconsidered." *AJSR* 31 (2007): 1–34.

———. *Sages and Commoners in Late Antique 'Erez Israel.* TSAJ 111. Tübingen: Mohr Siebeck, 2006.

———. "Some Observations on Stone Vessel Finds and Ritual Purity in Light of Talmudic Sources." In *Zeichen aus Text und Stein: Studien auf dem Weg zu einer Archäologie des Neuen Testaments*, edited by Stefan Alkier and Jürgen Zangenberg, 402–19. TANZ 42. Tübingen: Francke, 2003.

———. "Stepped Pools, Stone Vessels, and Other Identity Markers of 'Complex Common Judaism.'" *JSJ* 41 (2010): 214–43.

Mor, Menahem. "The Geographical Scope of the Bar-Kokhba Revolt." In *The Bar Kokhba War Reconsidered: New Perspectives on the Second Jewish Revolt against Rome*, edited by Peter Schäfer, 107–31. TSAJ 100. Tübingen: Mohr Siebeck, 2003.

Myers, E. A. *The Ituraeans and the Roman Near East: Reassessing the Sources.* SNTSMS 147. Cambridge: Cambridge University Press, 2010.

Neusner, Jacob. *A Life of Yohanan ben Zakkai, Ca. 1–80 C.E.* 2nd rev. ed. StPB 6. Leiden: Brill, 1970.

———. *The Rabbinic Traditions about the Pharisees before 70.* 3 vols. Leiden: Brill, 1971.

Newman, Hillel. *Proximity to Power and Jewish Sectarian Groups of the Ancient Period: A Review of Lifestyle, Values, and Halakhah in the Pharisees, Sadducees, Essenes, and Qumran.* Brill Reference Library of Judaism 25. Leiden: Brill, 2006.

Pickup, Martin. "Matthew's and Mark's Pharisees." In *In Quest of the Historical Pharisees*, edited by Jacob Neusner and Bruce D. Chilton, 67–112. Waco, Tex.: Baylor University Press, 2007.

Reed, Jonathan. *Archaeology and the Galilean Jesus: A Re-examination of the Evidence.* Harrisburg, Pa.: Trinity Press International, 2000.

Reeg, Gottfried. *Die Ortsnamen Israels nach der rabbinischen Literatur.* Beihefte zum Tübinger Atlas des Vorderen Orients, B.51. Wiesbaden: Reichert, 1989.

Reich, Ronny. "Baking and Cooking at Masada." *ZDPV* 119 (2003): 140–58.

———. "Women and Men at Masada: Some Anthropological Observations Based on the Small Finds (Coins, Spindles)." *ZDPV* 117 (2001): 149–63.

Riesner, Rainer. "Kapharnaum und Heptapegon: Zwei byzantinische Pilgerstätten am See Gennesaret." In *Leben am See Gennesaret: Kulturgeschichtliche Entdeckungen in einer biblischen Region*, edited by Gabriele Fassbeck, Sandra Fortner, Andrea Rottloff, and Jürgen Zangenberg. Zaberns Bildbände zur Archäologie. Mainz: Philipp von Zabern, 2003.

———. "What Does Archaeology Teach Us about Early House Churches?" *TTKi* 78 (2007): 159–85.

Runesson, Anders. "Rethinking Early Jewish–Christian Relations: Matthean Community History as Pharisaic Intragroup Conflict." *JBL* 127 (2008): 95–132.

Saldarini, Anthony J. "The Gospel of Matthew and Jewish–Christian Conflict in the Galilee." In *The Galilee in Late Antiquity*, edited by Lee I. Levine, 23–38. Cambridge, Mass.: Harvard University Press, 1992.

———. *Pharisees, Scribes, and Sadducees in Palestinian Society: A Sociological Approach.* Edinburgh: T&T Clark, 1988. Reprinted, with a foreword by James C. VanderKam. Grand Rapids: Eerdmans, 2001.

Schäfer, Peter. *Der Bar Kokhba-Aufstand: Studien zum zweiten jüdischen Krieg gegen Rom.* TSAJ 1. Tübingen: Mohr Siebeck, 1981.

———, ed. *The Bar Kokhba War Reconsidered: New Perspectives on the Second Jewish Revolt Against Rome.* TSAJ 100. Tübingen: Mohr Siebeck, 2003.

———. *Jesus in the Talmud.* Princeton: Princeton University Press, 2007.

Schefter, Angelika. *Israel nach der rabbinischen Literatur/Israel according to Rabbinical Literature.* Beihefte zum Tübinger Atlas des Vorderen Orients, B VI 16. Wiesbaden: Reichert, 1984.

Schiffman, Lawrence H. *From Text to Tradition. A History of Second Temple and Rabbinic Judaism.* Hoboken, N.J.: Ktav, 1991.

———. "Pharisees and Sadducees in Pesher Nahum." In *Minḥah le-Naḥum: Biblical and Other Studies Presented to Nahum M. Sarna in Honour of His 70th Birthday*, edited by Marc Brettler and Michael Fishbane, 272–90. JSOTSup 154. Sheffield: JSOT Press, 1993.

———. "The Pharisees and Their Legal Traditions according to the Dead Sea Scrolls." *DSD* 8 (2001): 262–77.

———. "Was There a Galilean Halakhah?" In *The Galilee in Late Antiquity*, edited by Lee I. Levine, 143–56. Cambridge, Mass.: Harvard University Press, 1992.

Schnabel, Eckhard. *Early Christian Mission*. 2 vols.. Downers Grove, Ill.: InterVarsity, 2004.

Shahar, Yuval. "The Underground Hideouts in Galilee and Their Historical Meaning." In *The Bar Kokhba War Reconsidered: New Perspectives on the Second Jewish Revolt against Rome*, edited by Peter Schäfer, 217–40. TSAJ 100. Tübingen: Mohr Siebeck, 2003.

Sivertsev, Alexei. *Private Households and Public Politics in 3rd–5th Century Jewish Palestine*. TSAJ 90. Tübingen: Mohr Siebeck, 2002.

Skarsaune, Oskar. "Evidence for Jewish Believers in Greek and Latin Patristic Literature." In *Jewish Believers in Jesus: The Early Centuries*, edited by Oskar Skarsaune and Reidar Hvalvik, 505–67. Peabody, Mass.: Hendrickson, 2007.

Smith, Morton. "Palestinian Judaism in the First Century." In *Israel: Its Role in Civilization*, edited by Moshe Davis. New York: Jewish Theological Seminary of America, [1956].

Stemberger, Günter. *Jews and Christians in the Holy Land: Palestine in the Fourth Century*. Edinburgh: T&T Clark, 2000.

———. *Juden und Christen im spätantiken Palästina*. Hans-Lietzmann-Vorlesungen 9. Berlin: de Gruyter, 2007.

Strange, James F. "Archaeological Evidence of Jewish Believers?" In *Jewish Believers in Jesus: The Early Centuries*, edited by Oskar Skarsaune and Reidar Hvalvik, 710–41. Peabody, Mass.: Hendrickson, 2007.

Tabbernee, William. "Epigraphy." In *The Oxford Handbook of Early Christian Studies*, edited by Susan Ashbrook Harvey and David G. Hunter, 120–39. Oxford: Oxford University Press, 2008.

Tantlevskij, Igor R. "The Historical Background of the Qumran Commentary on Nahum (4QpNah)." In *Hellenismus: Beiträge zur Erforschung von Akkulturation und politischer Ordnung in den Staaten des hellenistischen Zeitalters. Akten des Internationalen Hellenismus-Kolloquiums, 9.–14 März 1994 in Berlin*, edited by Bernd Funck, 329–38. Tübingen: Mohr Siebeck, 1997.

Tepper, Yotam. "Legio, Kefar 'Otnay." *HA-ESI* 118 (2006). Online: www. http://www.hadashot-esi.org.il/report_detail_eng.aspx?id=363.

Tepper, Yotam, and Leah Di Segni. *A Christian Prayer Hall of the Third Century CE at Kefar 'Othnay (Legio): Excavations at the Megiddo Prison 2005*. Publications of the Israel Antiquities Authority. Jerusalem: Israel Antiquities Authority, 2006.

VanderKam, James C. "Those Who Look for Smooth Things, Pharisees, and Oral Law." In *Emanuel: Studies in Hebrew Bible, Septuagint and Dead Sea Scrolls in Honor of Emanuel Tov*, edited by Shalom M. Paul et al., 465–77. VTSup 94. Leiden: Brill, 2003.

Vermes, Geza. *Jesus in the Jewish World*. London: SCM, 2010.

Wellhausen, Julius. *Evangelienkommentare.* Berlin: de Gruyter, 1987.

———. *Das Evangelium Marci.* 2nd ed. Berlin: Reimer, 1909.

Zangenberg, Jürgen. "Archaeology, Papyri, and Inscriptions." In *The Eerdmans Dictionary of Early Judaism*, edited by John J. Collins and Daniel C. Harlow, 201–35. Grand Rapids: Eerdmans, 2010.

———. "Common Judaism and the Multidimensional Character of Material Culture." In *Redefining First-Century Jewish and Christian Identities: Essays in Honor of Ed Parish Sanders*, edited by Fabian Udoh, 175–93. Christianity and Judaism in Antiquity 16. Notre Dame: University of Notre Dame Press, 2008.

# 4

# THE ETHNICITIES OF GALILEANS

## Mark A. Chancey

If *ethnicity* is defined broadly in terms of a sense of shared ancestry, common cultural heritage, and group identity,[1] then the ethnicity of most Galileans in the late Second Temple and early Mishnaic periods was Jewish. Indeed, the past twenty-five years of archaeological and biblical scholarship attest to a growing consensus that "Galilee of the Gentiles" (Isa. 8:31; 9:1; Matt. 4:14-15) was anything but a pagan region at the beginning of the Common Era.[2] At numerous sites, archaeologists have discovered ample evidence of distinctively Jewish practices, finds that corroborate the depictions of Galilee as predominantly Jewish in the writings of Josephus, rabbinic texts, and the Gospels.[3] This article will outline the current state of discussion regarding Galilee's population, explaining how we know that most Galileans were Jews and exploring what we can say about the ethnic identities of Galilee's non-Jewish minority.

---

1. For varying and more detailed interpretations of ethnicity, see John Hutchinson and Anthony D. Smith, eds., *Ethnicity* (Oxford: Oxford University Press, 1996). On understandings of ethnicity in biblical studies, see David Marvin Miller, "Ethnicity Comes of Age: An Overview of Twentieth-Century Terms for *Ioudaios*," *Currents in Biblical Research* 10 (2012): 293–311.

2. What the term *Galilee of the Gentiles* meant in Isaiah's eighth-century BCE context is unclear. In any case, Matt. 28:18-20 appropriates it not to make claims about Galilee's first-century CE population but to connect Jesus' activity there with biblical prophecy and to foreshadow the post-resurrection mission to the gentiles. See Mark A. Chancey, *The Myth of a Gentile Galilee* (SNTSMS 118; Cambridge: Cambridge University Press, 2002), 170–74.

3. On ancient literary depictions, see Seán Freyne, *Galilee from Alexander the Great to Hadrian, 323 B.C.E. to 135 C.E.: A Study of Second Temple Judaism* (University of Notre Dame Center for the Study of Judaism and Christianity in Antiquity 5; Wilmington, Del.: Michael Glazier; Notre Dame: University of Notre Dame Press, 1980; repr., Edinburgh: T&T Clark, 1998); Freyne, *Galilee, Jesus, and the Gospels: Literary Approaches and Historical Investigations* (Philadelphia: Fortress Press, 1988); Chancey, *Myth of a Gentile Galilee*.

## Galilee's Settlement History

At the root of some debates over Galilee's population lie differing understandings of the consequences of Assyria's invasion of the region. Around 732 BCE, the Assyrian ruler Tiglath-pileser III marched into Galilee in retaliation against the kingdom of Israel for impudently attacking its southern neighbor Judah. Second Kings 15:29 notes that the Assyrians "came and captured . . . Galilee, all the land of Naphtali" (one of the twelve tribes associated with Galilee) and "carried the people captive to Assyria" (NRSV). Tiglath-pileser's annals offer a similar account, proclaiming that he deported thousands of Galileans.[4]

Before the availability of corroborating information, modern scholars often questioned these reports. For example, the early-twentieth-century German scholar Albrecht Alt contended that the accounts preserved exaggerated and distorted memories. He rejected the idea of mass deportations and suggested instead that Galilee's population had remained largely unchanged. By this logic, most Galileans of the Hellenistic and Roman periods would have been descendants of earlier Israelites.[5] Much more recently, Richard A. Horsley has echoed these arguments.[6]

## Evidence from Archaeological Surveys

Large-scale surface surveys by Israeli archaeologists have given us a much clearer picture of Galilean settlement.

### Assyrian Conquest (eighth century BCE)

Work done in surveys of Galilee now strongly indicates that the Assyrian conquest seriously ruptured the region's settlement history.[7] Zvi Gal has demonstrated that many Lower Galilean sites were abandoned in the late Iron Age, pointing to the Assyrian takeover as the likely cause. "Lower Galilee," he argued, "was significantly deserted."[8] A survey of Upper Galilee by Rafael

---

4. K. Lawson Younger, Jr., "The Deportations of the Israelites," *JBL* 117 (1998): 201–27.

5. Albrecht Alt, "Galiläische Probleme," in *Kleine Schriften zur Geschichte des Volkes Israel* (Munich: Beck, 1953–64), 2:363–435.

6. Richard A. Horsley, *Archaeology, History, and Society in Galilee: The Social Context of Jesus and the Rabbis* (Valley Forge, Pa.: Trinity Press International, 1996), 22–23; Horsley, *Galilee: History, Politics, People* (Valley Forge, Pa.: Trinity Press International, 1995), 25–29; cf. Horsley, *Covenant Economics: A Biblical Vision of Justice for All* (Louisville: Westminster John Knox, 2009), 126.

7. Jonathan L. Reed, *Archaeology and the Galilean Jesus: A Re-Examination of the Evidence* (Harrisburg, Pa.: Trinity Press International, 2000), 28–34; Chancey, *Myth of a Gentile Galilee*, 30–34; and Markus Cromhout, "Were the Galileans 'Religious Jews' or Ethnic Judeans?" *HTS Teologiese Studies* 64 (2008): 1279–97.

8. Zvi Gal, *Lower Galilee during the Iron Age* (trans. Marcia Reines Josephy; ASOR Dissertation Series 8. Winona Lake, Ind.: Eisenbrauns, 1992), quotation from p. 108.

Frankel, Mordechai Aviam, Nimrod Getzov, and Avi Degani likewise identified a decline in the number of sites in this period.[9] In light of such strong evidence of discontinuity in the region's settlement, it is difficult to maintain the position that most later Galileans were descendants of the Israelites of the northern kingdom. As for the Assyrians, they appear to have maintained only a modest presence in the region.[10]

### *Persian Period*

Not until the Persian period did Galilee experience a resurgence in population, as evidenced by an increase in pottery sherds and the emergence of new sites. The survey of Upper Galilee documented fifty-four new sites that sprang up to join the twenty-eight continuing from the Iron Age II period.[11] Differences in pottery suggest two distinct groups in Upper Galilee, one living in the east in the vicinity of Mount Meiron and as far south as Tiberias,[12] the other dwelling closer to the coast. The settlers in the east used a new, distinctive type of pottery characterized by pink and gray fabric with white grits, dubbed "Galilean Coarse Ware" by archaeologists.[13] The origins of its users are unclear; the surveyors suggested they were gentiles whose ethnic identity and cultural orientations were indeterminable. In contrast, the ceramics of the inhabitants of western Galilee were clearly Phoenician in style, suggesting that those settlers had pushed inward from the coast.[14] The Phoenician character of their pottery is typical, in fact, of contemporary ceramic finds elsewhere in Galilee.[15] Most Persian-era sites in Galilee were small settlements. At the Upper Galilean site of Mizpeh Yammim, a temple was built. An inscription and the vessels used for perfume and oil offerings indicate that its users were Phoenicians.[16]

---

9. Rafael Frankel, Nimrod Getzov, Mordechai Aviam, and Avi Degani, *Settlement Dynamics and Regional Diversity in Ancient Upper Galilee: Archaeological Survey of Upper Galilee* (IAA Reports 14; Jerusalem: Israel Antiquities Authority, 2001).

10. On Assyrian period finds in northern Palestine, see Ephraim Stern, *Archaeology of the Land of the Bible*, vol. 2, *The Assyrian, Babylonian, and Persian Periods (732–332 B.C.E.)* (ABRL; New York: Doubleday, 2001), 46–49.

11. Frankel et al., *Settlement Dynamics*, 107–8, 126.

12. Mordechai Aviam, "People, Land, Economy, and Belief in First-Century Galilee and Its Origins: A Comprehensive Archaeological Synthesis," in *The Galilean Economy in the Time of Jesus* (ed. David A. Fiensy and Ralph K. Hawkins; Early Christianity and Its Literature 11; Atlanta: Society of Biblical Literature, 2013), 5–48, esp. 5–6.

13. Frankel et al., *Settlement Dynamics*, 1, 61–62, 106–10.

14. Ibid., 107–8, 131–32; Andrea M. Berlin, "From Monarchy to Markets: The Phoenicians in Hellenistic Palestine," *BASOR* 306 (1997): 75–88.

15. Stern, *Archaeology of the Land of the Bible*, 373–85.

16. Andrea M. Berlin and Rafael Frankel, "The Sanctuary at Mizpe Yammim: Phoenician Cult and Territory in the Upper Galilee during the Persian Period," *BASOR* 366 (2012): 25–78; Rafael Frankel and Raphael Ventura, "The Mispe Yamim Bronzes," *BASOR* 311 (1998): 39–55.

## *Hellenistic Period*

The Hellenistic period witnessed a continuing increase in the number of inhabitants. Again, this is most clearly documented in Upper Galilee, where some fifty-one sites continued from the Persian period and fifty-five new ones appeared.[17] At the beginning of the Hellenistic period, most Galileans appear to have been pagans, while by the Early Roman period, the evidence is strong that most were Jews. How did this shift happen?

As is well known, Galilee changed hands multiple times in the Hellenistic Era, from the Persians to Alexander the Great to the Ptolemies to the Seleucids. In 167 BCE, Jews rebelled against Seleucid rule in the Maccabean Revolt, which ultimately led to the establishment of the Hasmonean dynasty. First Maccabees reports a Jewish presence in Galilee at this time, describing an incursion by Simon to save Galilean Jews (1 Macc. 5:9-23). Later, his brother Jonathan's forces reached as far as Kedesh (1 Macc. 11:60-74; 12:24-53). The accuracy of these stories is difficult to gauge, although it is tempting to associate the temporary abandonment of a Phoenician government archive at Kedesh with the threat posed by Jonathan.[18]

What does seem clear is that, regardless of what actually happened in Galilee during the Maccabean Revolt itself, at some point the resultant Hasmonean dynasty fully annexed the region to their territory.[19] Literary sources offer no clear testimony as to when this happened. Josephus's report that the future Hasmonean king Alexander Jannaeus (ruled 103–76 BCE) spent his youth in Galilee implies strong ties between the dynasty and the region in the late second century BCE, but we lack any supporting information for this claim (see Josephus, *Ant.* 13.322).

## *Hasmonean Period*

Scholars have sometimes argued that the Hasmoneans must have taken Galilee when Aristobulus I (104–103 BCE) seized territory from the Itureans, converting some of them to Jewish ways (Josephus, *Ant.* 13.318–19).[20] Archaeological research, however, has found no evidence of Itureans in Galilee, typically associating them instead with pottery found north of Galilee around Mount Hermon, Mount Lebanon, and Anti-Lebanon. An attack by Aristobulus on those areas would have required traversing Galilee, but if any such campaign occurred, its impact appears to have been minimal. Habitation at Iturean sites continued without inter-

---

17. Frankel et al., *Settlement Dynamics*, 108.

18. Sharon C. Herbert and Andrea M. Berlin, "A New Administrative Center for Persian and Hellenistic Galilee: Preliminary Report of the University of Michigan/University of Minnesota Excavations at Kedesh," *BASOR* 329 (2003): 13–59.

19. Reed, *Archaeology and the Galilean Jesus*, 45–49; Chancey, *Myth of a Gentile Galilee*, 30–34; Aviam, "People, Land, Economy"; Cromhout, "Were the Galileans 'Religious Jews.'"

20. Emil Schürer, *The History of the Jewish People in the Age of Jesus Christ (175 B.C.–A.D. 135)* (rev. and ed. Geza Vermes, Fergus Millar, Matthew Black, and Martin Goodman; 3 vols. in 4 parts; Edinburgh: T&T Clark, 1973–87), 1:216–18.

ruption, and the appearance of Iturean coinage a few decades later attests to ongoing Iturean political independence.[21] In short, there is little reason to place much weight on this incident for understanding the cultural changes that Galilee was soon to experience.

By the early first century BCE, however, the shift of Galilee to the Hasmoneans was clearly under way. During his reign (103–76 BCE), Alexander Jannaeus expanded Hasmonean territory to its maximum extent, and it is precisely at this time that marked changes become noticeable in Galilean material culture.[22] Coins of Alexander Jannaeus begin appearing at strata from this period and are common finds well into the Roman period. At sites such as Jotapata and Meiron, the transition from Seleucid to Hasmonean coinage, as indicated by the dates of the coins, is particularly striking.[23] Throughout Galilee, many older sites were abandoned and new sites established. Damage to cultic figurines at Beersheba and the now abandoned temple at Mizpeh Yammim might date to this period, reflecting the hostility of new arrivals in the region to pagan practices.[24] Dramatic shifts in settlement patterns are accompanied by notable changes in the ceramic profile. In western Upper Galilee, users of Phoenician jars began slowly leaving behind their inland sites and shifting back toward the coast. Both Upper Galilee and Lower Galilee saw the abandonment of many of the sites that had used Galilean Coarse Ware, which soon disappeared altogether. Many Galilean sites that flourished in the Early Roman period have a thin stratum of Late Hellenistic sherds, suggesting that they appeared at this time.[25]

Just as the Assyrian invasion had resulted in a sharp break in settlement history and the displacement of many earlier inhabitants, so, too, did the Hasmonean conquest. The pagans who lived there prior to the Hasmonean annexation were descended primarily from settlers who had arrived during the Persian, Ptolemaic, or Seleucid periods. The evidence cited above demonstrates that many, probably most, of these pagan inhabitants left the region.

Who were the new inhabitants? The available evidence—the settlement history reviewed above and the artifacts discussed below—overwhelmingly suggests that they were Jews arriving

21. Mark A. Chancey, *Greco-Roman Culture and the Galilee of Jesus* (SNTSMS 134; Cambridge: Cambridge University Press, 2005), 36–38, revising my argument in *Myth of a Gentile Galilee*, 42–45.

22. Josephus, *Ant.* 13.324–97; 14.18; *J.W.* 1.86–87, 104–5; Chancey, *Myth of a Gentile Galilee*, 41–47; Chancey, "Archaeology, Ethnicity, and First-Century C.E. Galilee: The Limits of Evidence," in *A Wandering Galilean: Essays in Honour of Sean Freyne* (ed. Zuleika Rodgers with Margaret Daly-Denton and Anne Fitzpatrick McKinley; JSJSup 132; Leiden: Brill, 2009), 205–18; Reed, *Archaeology and the Galilean Jesus*, 39–43; Aviam, "People, Land, Economy"; Uzi Leibner, *Settlement and History in Hellenistic, Roman, and Byzantine Galilee: An Archaeological Survey of the Eastern Galilee* (TSAJ 127; Tübingen: Mohr Siebeck, 2009), 315–28.

23. David Adan-Bayewitz and Mordechai Aviam, "Iotapata, Josephus, and the Siege of 67: Preliminary Report on the 1992–1994 Seasons," *Journal of Roman Archaeology* 10 (1997): 131–65; Joyce Raynor and Ya'akov Meshorer with Richard Simon Hanson, *The Coins of Ancient Meiron* (Meiron Excavation Project 4; Cambridge, Mass.: ASOR; Winona Lake, Ind.: Eisenbrauns, 1988), 83–85.

24. Aviam, "People, Land, Economy," 7; Berlin and Frankel, "Sanctuary"; Frankel and Ventura, "Mispe Yamim."

25. Frankel et al., *Settlement Dynamics*, 108–10; Leibner, *Settlement and History*, 327–28.

from Hasmonean Judea. These new settlers from the south were thus the primary ancestors of Jews in first-century CE Galilee. While Galilean Jews may have had their own regional customs, in terms of ancestry, cultural orientation, and group identity they shared a common identity with Judean Jews.[26] Additional Jews from Judea would join them by moving north after each of the two failed revolts against Rome.

These facts have tremendous implications for how we understand the ethnic identities of Galileans at the beginning of the Common Era. Before archaeological investigation of the region, it was understandable for scholars to argue variously that Galilean Jews lived alongside numerous gentiles from a variety of backgrounds, that they were largely descendants of pagans forcibly converted by the Hasmoneans, or that they were mostly descendants of ancient Israelites from the northern kingdom.[27] But the sharp changes in settlement patterns documented by archaeologists now make these positions difficult to maintain.

## Who Were the *Ioudaioi*?

These findings are also of import for ongoing debates about the proper translation and interpretation of the Greek terms *Ioudaioi* (Judeans or Jews) and *Galilaioi* (Galileans) in John, Josephus, and elsewhere.[28] Some scholars insist that the two words refer to two distinct ethnic groups, and many prefer to emphasize the geographical sense of *Ioudaioi*, regarding it as a reference to inhabitants of Judea or those whose ancestors hail from there. For them, a translation of *Ioudaios* as "Judean" is preferable to "Jew." For example, Horsley argues on the basis of his belief that Galileans traced their roots all the way back to the northern kingdom that they considered themselves a very different *ethnos* from the Judeans to the south.

Translating *Galilaioi* as "Galileans" is straightforward enough, especially in contexts that suggest a geographical emphasis. "Judeans" is obviously a sensible rendering of *Ioudaioi*. As Robert Doran has pointed out, however, all too often the narrow geographic connotation of the English word *Judean* does not sufficiently convey the interrelatedness of point of origin and cultural practices suggested by ancient ethnic designations. Furthermore, as Amy-Jill Levine emphasizes, it is essential for modern readers to recognize the continuity, however complex,

---

26. On these points, see esp. Morten Hørning Jensen, "Purity and Politics in Herod Antipas's Galilee: The Case for Religious Motivation," *JSHJ* 11 (2013): 3–34; and Andrea M. Berlin, "Jewish Life before the Revolt: The Archaeological Evidence," *JSJ* 36 (2005): 417–70.

27. See reviews of scholarly positions in Chancey, *Myth of a Gentile Galilee*, 1–4; Jensen, "Purity and Politics."

28. David Marvin Miller provides an extremely helpful review of the issue in "The Meaning of *Ioudaios* and Its Relationship to Other Group Labels in Ancient 'Judaism,'" *Currents in Biblical Research* 9 (2010): 98–126; see also Cromhout, "Were the Galileans 'Religious Jews.'"

between ancient *Ioudaioi* and modern Jews. Therefore, in my opinion, "Jew" is a better translation choice for *Ioudaios* than "Judean" in many cases. [29]

Translation issues aside, it now seems clear that Galileans by and large *were* Judeans in terms of identity, ancestry, and cultural orientation if not current place of habitation or shared political governance. To be sure, they may at times have perceived themselves or been perceived as distinct from Judeans, but such a distinction is better understood as an example of a "sub-nesting" of ethnic identities, one within the other, rather than an absolute differentiation between them. [30] It is precisely because of the common ethnic identity and culture of most Galileans and Judeans that it is appropriate to apply the category "Jew" to both, and interpretations and translation choices that completely sever the groups are problematic in light of their shared history and customs.

### The Shared Material Culture of Judean and Galilean Jews

The Jewishness of Galileans and their cultural orientation to the south at the turn of the era are illustrated by several categories of archaeological finds. [31]

#### *Ritual Baths*

The first is that of ritual baths, or *mikva'ot*, which Jews used to remove impurity caused by factors such as menstruation, genital discharges, childbirth, and contact with corpses. *Mikva'ot* first appeared in Judea in the second century BCE during the Hasmonean period. In northern Israel, the earliest examples appear in the following century at Sepphoris, Qeren Naftali, Yodefat, and the nearby Golan site of Gamla. By the first century CE, they were appearing in various contexts in the Jewish parts of Palestine, including private residences, communal settings, near oil presses, and, at Gamla, near a synagogue. [32] Yonatan Adler counts over six hundred ritual

---

29. Robert Doran, *2 Maccabees: A Critical Commentary* (Hermeneia; Minneapolis: Fortress Press, 2012), 24; Amy-Jill Levine, *The Misunderstood Jew: The Church and the Scandal of the Jewish Jesus* (New York: HarperCollins, 2006), 159–66. Cromhout, however, makes a robust argument against rendering *Ioudaioi* as *Jews* ("Were the Galileans 'Religious Jews'").

30. Miller, "Meaning of *Ioudaios*"; see also Cromhout, "Were the Galileans 'Religious Jews.'"

31. On finds in Galilee as indicators of Jewish practices, see Chancey, *Myth of a Gentile Galilee*, 79–112; Reed, *Archaeology and the Galilean Jesus*, 23–61; Jensen, "Purity and Politics"; Mordechai Aviam and Peter Richardson, "Josephus' Galilee in Archaeological Perspective," in *Flavius Josephus: Translation and Commentary*, vol. 9, *Life of Josephus* (ed. Steve Mason; Leiden: Brill, 2001), 177–209; Aviam, "People, Land, Economy." On the shared material culture of Galilee and Judea, see Berlin, "Jewish Life"; Jensen, "Purity and Politics."

32. Jonathan D. Lawrence, *Washing in Water: Trajectories of Ritual Bathing in the Hebrew Bible and Second Temple Literature* (Academia Biblica; Atlanta: Society of Biblical Literature, 2006); Eric M. Meyers, "Aspects of Everyday Life in Roman Palestine with Special Reference to Private Domiciles and Ritual Baths," in *Jews in the Hellenistic and Roman Cities* (ed. John R. Bartlett; London: Routledge, 2002), 193–210.

baths in Judea in the Hasmonean and Early Roman periods and nearly seventy from the same period in Galilee. [33]

### Stoneware Vessels

An even more ubiquitous indicator of Jewish purity practices is that of limestone vessels. These first appeared in Judea during the reign of Herod the Great, soon spreading to Galilean sites and nearby Gamla. Adler notes their discovery at over 250 sites in Israel and Jordan, including more than sixty in Galilee. Like ritual baths, they are rare outside of Jewish areas. They are particularly common in archaeological strata associated with the mid-first century CE and the First Revolt, but they remained in use to some extent until the Bar Kokhba Revolt (132–135 CE) and perhaps even afterwards. [34]

Although some scholars have suggested that the popularity of stone vessels might have been due primarily to stylistic trends or simply their durability, most think that many Jews shared the rabbinic belief that such vessels were not susceptible to ritual impurity. [35] They appeared in a variety of forms, including plates, trays, mugs, goblets, bowls, large pots, and kraters, and in contexts ranging from small residences to the mansions of the wealthy, at rural and urban sites. [36] In Galilee, evidence for large workshops has been found at the villages of Bethlehem and Reina and for smaller-scale production at Nazareth, Capernaum, and Sepphoris. [37] The Gospel of John famously refers to the "six stone water jars for the Jewish rites of purification, each holding twenty or thirty gallons" (John 2:6 NRSV) at the wedding of Cana, jars that Jesus had filled with water before transforming it into wine. These massive jars probably correspond to large storage vessels that archaeologists have found in elite residences (*m. Parah* 3:3).

### Pottery

The ceramic repertoires of both Judea and Galilee also reflect changing preferences following the Hasmonean conquest. In both regions, usage of imported pottery declines significantly in comparison to the pre-Hasmonean period. Local wares largely took their place. [38]

---

33. Yonatan Adler, "Religion, Judaism: Purity in the Roman Period," in *The Oxford Encyclopedia of the Bible and Archaeology* (ed. Daniel M. Master; Oxford: Oxford University Press, 2013), 2:240–47, esp. 243.

34. Ibid.; and Berlin, "Jewish Life."

35. See *m. Oholot* 5:5, *m. Kelim* 4:4, *m. Yadaim* 1:2, *m. Parah* 5:5.

36. Izchak Magen, *The Stone Vessel Industry in the Second Temple Period: Excavations at Ḥizma and the Jerusalem Temple Mount* (Judea and Samaria Publications 1; Jerusalem: Israel Exploration Society, Israel Antiquities Authority, 2002); Eric M. Meyers and Mark A. Chancey, *Archaeology of the Land of the Bible*, vol. 3, *Alexander to Constantine* (Anchor Yale Bible Reference Library; New Haven: Yale University Press, 2012), 78–80, 137, 233–36.

37. Jonathan L. Reed, "Stone Vessels and Gospel Texts: Purity and Socio-Economics in John 2," in *Zeichen aus Text und Stein: Studien auf den Weg zu einer Archäologie des Neuen Testaments* (ed. Stefan Alkier and Jürgen Zangenberg; TANZ 42; Tübingen: Francke, 2003), 381–401; Aviam, "People, Land, Economy," 32–33.

38. Berlin, "Jewish Life"; Adler, "Religion, Judaism: Purity"; Frankel et al., *Settlement Dynamics*, 65.

## Oil Lamps

Lamp finds display a somewhat different trend. On the one hand, a new form identified by its knife-pared nozzle, simplicity of style, and absent or minimal decoration, began displacing older styles, such as round molded lamps.[39] But distribution patterns of the new lamp, often called a Herodian lamp, attest to strong ties between Galilee and Judea. High-precision X-ray fluorescence analysis and neutron activation analysis shows that many of the specimens found in Galilee were made with clay from the vicinity of Jerusalem. To a surprising degree, Galilean Jews chose to import lamps made in Jerusalem rather than utilize only lamps made by Galilean artisans. This preference for lamps made in Jerusalem workshops did not extend to surrounding gentile communities.[40]

## Secondary Burial

Galilean Jews also adopted from their Judean neighbors the use of ossuaries for secondary burial. Ossuaries were small chests of limestone or clay in which the bones of a deceased person were placed about a year after death, a practice known as *ossilegium*. Exactly why some Jews adopted this custom is unclear, although some scholars have suggested theological rationales, such as a belief that the decay of flesh facilitated the expiation of sins or that the regathering of bones constituted preparation for eschatological resurrection. Ossuaries first appeared in Judea in the first century BCE and reached Galilee by the late first century CE. As with *mikva'ot* and stone vessels, their use appears to have been limited to Jews.[41] Ossilegium ceased in the south after the Bar Kokhba revolt but continued in Galilee for the rest of the second century and perhaps even afterwards.[42] Fragments or whole examples have been found at over twenty-five Galilean sites.[43]

---

39. Berlin, "Jewish Life."

40. David Adan-Bayewitz, Frank Asaro, Moshe Wieder, and Robert D. Giauque, "Preferential Distribution of Lamps from the Jerusalem Area in the Late Second Temple Period (Late First Century B.C.E.–70 C.E.)," *BASOR* 350 (2008): 37–85.

41. Rachel Hachlili, *Jewish Funerary Customs, Practices and Rites in the Second Temple Period* (JSJSup 94; Leiden: Brill, 2005), 94–115, 520–28; Byron R. McCane, *Roll Back the Stone: Death and Burial in the World of Jesus* (Harrisburg, Pa.: Trinity Press International, 2003), 39–47; Mordechai Aviam and Danny Syon, "Jewish Ossilegium in Galilee," in *What Athens Has to Do with Jerusalem: Essays on Classical, Jewish, and Early Christian Art and Archaeology in Honor of Gideon Foerster* (ed. Leonard V. Rutgers; Interdisciplinary Studies in Ancient Culture and Religion 1; Leuven: Peeters, 2002), 151–85; L. Y. Rahmani, *A Catalogue of Jewish Ossuaries in the Collection of the State of Israel* (Jerusalem: Israel Antiquities Authority, 1994).

42. Aviam and Syon, "Jewish Ossilegium."

43. Aviam and Syon note twenty-nine sites in northern Palestine, twenty-six of them in Galilee ("Jewish Ossilegium"); see also Aviam and Richardson, "Josephus' Galilee"; Chancey, "Archaeology, Ethnicity," 213; Reed, *Archaeology and the Galilean Jesus*, 51.

## Synagogues

What of distinctively Jewish architecture? The Gospels imply that synagogues were common in Galilee by the late Second Temple period. As Matthew 9:35 puts it, "Jesus went about all the cities and villages, teaching in their synagogues, and proclaiming the good news of the kingdom, and curing every disease and every sickness" (NRSV). Some pericopes mention synagogues in specific communities, such as Nazareth (Luke 4:16; cf. Mark 6:2; Matt. 13:54) and Capernaum (Mark 1:23-29; Luke 4:33-39; 7:5). Josephus uses an alternative word for synagogue for a building at Tiberias, referring to a *proseuchē* (prayer house) (*Life* 277–80).

Although dozens of synagogues from later periods have been found in Palestine,[44] in the Early Roman period the architectural form of the synagogue was still taking shape. Many smaller communities presumably used large houses, rather than special buildings, for assemblies. In other cases, buildings may have been built or designated as synagogues but constructed in such a way as not to be recognizable as such to archaeologists. Nonetheless, archaeologists have identified first-century CE synagogues at Masada, Herodium, Qiryat Sefer, Modiʿin, and Gamla.[45] In Galilee proper, until recently, the most likely contender for a first-century CE synagogue was at Capernaum. Some have suggested that the basalt structures underneath its famous Byzantine-period limestone synagogue came from an earlier synagogue, perhaps even the one mentioned in Luke 7:5. The issue is impossible to resolve at present because excavation would require disturbing the limestone synagogue.[46]

In 2009, however, excavators made a major discovery a few miles south of Capernaum at Magdala (also known as Taricheae), the small town that was the home of Mary Magdalene. Although technical details of the building have not yet been published, the structure's main hall measured approximately 120 square meters, and benches for seating lined its walls. The high level of workmanship and decoration suggests a relatively affluent community or at least the presence of a number of affluent members within that community. Its brightly colored painted walls and black and white mosaic floor with meander designs reflect the artistic trends of the larger Greco-Roman world. The usage of the building by Jews is attested most clearly by a remarkable limestone pedestal carved in the shape of a square with a triangular base. One side of the stone is adorned with one of the earliest available artistic depictions of a menorah, the seven-branched candelabrum that stood in the Jewish temple. The presence of a symbol so closely related to the temple points to the importance of that institution for the Galilean Jews who gathered here.[47]

---

44. Lee I. Levine, *The Ancient Synagogue: The First Thousand Years* (2nd ed.; New Haven: Yale University Press, 2005).

45. Meyers and Chancey, *Alexander to Constantine*, 208–17.

46. James F. Strange and Hershel Shanks, "Synagogue Where Jesus Preached Found at Capernaum," *BAR* 9, no. 6 (1983): 25–28.

47. "One of the Oldest Synagogues in the World Was Exposed at Migdal," Israel Antiquities Authority Press Release, Sept. 13, 2009 (http://www.antiquities.org.il/article_Item_eng.asp?sec_id=25&subj_id=240&id=1601&module_id=#as); Meyers and Chancey, *Alexander to Constantine*, 211–12; Aviam, "People, Land, Economy," 37–41.

Of the many Galilean synagogues built in later centuries, the earliest is at Nabratein in Upper Galilee. Initially constructed in the mid-second century CE in a "broadhouse" design, with the long walls (11.2 meters) running east–west and the shorter ones (9.35 meters) north–south, it was later reconfigured in the basilical style. The placement of the worship platform on the short southern wall would have required worshipers to face toward Jerusalem, as became traditional practice. This synagogue is famous for providing the earliest known evidence of a Torah shrine, a triangular pediment carved with lions that would have stood atop the niche that contained the Torah scroll. The shrine may date to the second century, although it could be later.[48]

Given the abundance and consistency of such evidence, it is difficult to avoid the conclusion that most of the region's population consisted of Jews, especially in light of the lack of comparable evidence for a sizable gentile presence, especially before the second century CE. Legitimate questions remain, however, about halakhic and theological diversity among Galilean Jews, the significance and extent of regional variations, the relative influence of different sects, and the impact on Galilean Judaism of the arrival of additional Judeans after each of the two revolts, among other issues. Likewise, such finds do not demonstrate that every site in Galilee was Jewish or that every site at which such an artifact was discovered was inhabited solely by Jews. Likewise, they leave unanswered many questions about how Jews related to any gentiles in their midst or to those in adjacent areas.

## Gentiles in Galilee

Who constituted the gentile minority living in Galilee in the first centuries BCE and CE? Some may have been descendants of the relatively small number of gentiles who had stayed put through the population shifts, especially that following the Hasmonean annexation. Their ancestors could have been Persian, Ptolemaic, or Seleucid administrators and soldiers stationed in Galilee, though there is no particular reason to regard the contingents of any of those powers, or of the traders who had followed in their wake, as sizable. Some of their ancestors were no doubt more local gentiles, most notably Phoenicians from the coast but also pagans associated with other nearby areas. Various levels of contact between Galilean Jews and gentiles from surrounding areas would have been unavoidable in the border regions especially.

But in general, evidence to answer the question is lacking, not only for specific ethnic groups but also for gentiles in general. From later centuries one can point to the occasional pagan inscription, figurine, artistic depiction of a deity, or image of a deity or temple on a coin minted at Sepphoris or Tiberias. In the first centuries BCE and CE, however, such finds are sparse, consisting of discoveries such as a bronze plaque depicting a winged figure on a horned

---

48. Eric M. Meyers and Carol L. Meyers, *Excavations at Ancient Nabratein: Synagogue and Environs* (Meiron Excavation Project 6; Winona Lake, Ind.: Eisenbrauns, 2009), 34–44.

animal from the first century BCE or CE at Sepphoris;[49] a dedicatory inscription to Athena at the border site of Qeren Naftali, probably dating to 50–150 CE;[50] and a bone figurine at Tiberias from the first or second century CE.[51] More evidence can be found for nearby sites, such as Scythopolis or Paneas (renamed for a while as Caesarea Philippi). Another figurine has been found at et-Tell, which the excavators believe to be biblical Bethsaida, as well as a structure they identify as a temple, though that interpretation has been questioned.[52]

The literary evidence regarding Galilean gentiles in the first centuries BCE and CE is also meager, and what little there is tells us nothing about their specific ethnic identities. Josephus reports that certain Jews attacked Tiberias's gentile minority early in the First Revolt; he uses only the standard Jewish terminology of *Greeks* (*Life* 65–67). While the Gospels' famous reference to a gentile centurion at Capernaum (Matt. 8:5-13; Luke 7:1-10) has often been taken as evidence for a standing Roman garrison in pre-revolt Galilee, this interpretation is unlikely. Roman incursions into the region appear to have been short-lived campaigns undertaken for specific purposes. During the time of Jesus, Galilee was part of the territory of the loyal client king Herod Antipas. Furthermore, usage of the term typically translated as *centurion* (*hekatonarchos*) was not limited to Roman contexts. Thus, if Jesus did indeed encounter a gentile officer in Capernaum, that officer would have been a soldier in the forces of Antipas, not the commander of a Roman army unit. His specific ethnic identity (whether Syrian, Phoenician, or another identity) and those of his solders are complete mysteries.[53]

Circumstances would change in the second century CE. Judean refugees from the south were not the only new arrivals. Though very active in Galilee during the First Revolt, the Roman army does not seem to have left behind much of a garrison there; it was Jerusalem and Judea that received the Legio X Fretensis, not Galilee. Around 120 CE, however, the Legio II Traiana arrived in northern Palestine, marking the beginning of its long-term military occupation. Within a few years, it was replaced by the Legio VI Ferrata. The legion made its headquarters in the Jezreel Valley near the village of Kefar 'Othnay and had smaller outposts elsewhere. The activity of its soldiers in Galilee is attested by inscriptions, milestones, military-produced

---

49. Ellen Reeder, "Relief Plaque with Figural Scene," in *Sepphoris in Galilee: Crosscurrents of Culture* (ed. Rebecca Martin Nagy, Carol L. Meyers, Eric M. Meyers, and Ze'ev Weiss; Raleigh: North Carolina Museum of Art; Winona Lake, Ind.: Eisenbrauns, 1996), 174.

50. Mordechai Aviam, "The Hellenistic and Hasmonaean Fortress and Herodian Siege Complex at Qeren Naftali," in Aviam, *Jews, Pagans, and Christians in the Galilee: 25 Years of Archaeological Excavations and Surveys, Hellenistic to Byzantine Periods* (Land of Galilee 1; Rochester, N.Y.: University of Rochester Press; Woodbridge, Suffolk: Boydell & Brewer, 2004), 559–88; E. W. G. Masterman, "Two Greek Inscriptions from Khurbet Harrawi," *PEQ* 20 (1908): 155–57.

51. Yizhar Hirschfeld, "Tiberias," *Excavations and Surveys in Israel* 9 (1989–90): 107–9.

52. Rami Arav and Richard A. Freund, eds., *Bethsaida: A City by the North Shore of the Sea of Galilee*, vol. 2 (Kirksville, Mo.: Truman State University Press, 1999); R. Steven Notley, "Et-Tell Is Not Bethsaida," *NEA* 70 (2007): 220–30; Chancey, *Greco-Roman Culture*, 90–94.

53. Chancey, *Greco-Roman Culture*, 50–56; Reed, *Archaeology and the Galilean Jesus*, 161–62.

roof tiles, and remains of encampments.[54] While some of the legion's troops may have been from the Italian peninsula, many or most would have been drawn from the areas to which it had been deployed, Arabia, most recently, and before that Syria and Asia Minor.[55]

It is not surprising that evidence for pagan practices also increases in the second century, some of it reflecting the presence of the army and affiliated personnel and some no doubt reflecting the resultant raised social and political clout of indigenous gentiles. The archaeological record of Sepphoris clearly reflects a changed cultural atmosphere. Its coins soon began bearing depictions of deities such as the Capitoline Triad and Tyche and their temples.[56] The foundation of a large building discovered there could be related to one of these temples.[57] Coins also record that by the mid-second century the city was known by a pagan name, Diocaesarea, which honored Caesar as Zeus. Archaeological and rabbinic evidence make clear that it still had a significant Jewish population—indeed, it was a center for rabbinic activity—but the civic elites were clearly oriented toward the Romans. Pagan motifs appear on lamps from the second and third centuries, and figurines of Pan and Prometheus date to the same period. Mosaics also reflect a comfort with depictions of deities; one, from ca. 200 CE, depicts Dionysos, Herakles, and other mythological figures, while another from later in the third century portrays Orpheus.[58]

Such evidence was not limited to Sepphoris. For example, the coins of Tiberias also began depicting temples and deities (Hygeia, Zeus, Tyche, and others) in the second century CE.[59] Cultic activity is well illustrated by finds at sites on Galilee's borders, such as Qeren Naftali, which yielded a third-century dedicatory inscription to the Heliopolitan Zeus, and Kedesh, where a temple and several inscriptions have been found.[60] Such finds attest to the presence of non-Jews but typically do not enable more precise ethnic identification.

Although gentiles became a larger and more visible presence in Galilee in the second century CE, it is difficult to determine even approximately what proportion of the population they constituted. In any case, Jews continued to flourish there. The region was the heart of Jewish life in Palestine after the two revolts and a key arena for the emergence of the rabbis as

---

54. Chancey, *Greco-Roman Culture*, 43–70.

55. J. F. Gilliam, "Romanization of the Greek East: The Role of the Army," in Gilliam, *Roman Army Papers* (Mavors Roman Army Researches 2; Amsterdam: J. C. Gieben, 1986), 281–87.

56. Ya'akov Meshorer, *City Coins of Eretz-Israel and the Decapolis in the Roman Period* (Jerusalem: Israel Museum, 1985), 34–35.

57. Ze'ev Weiss and Ehud Netzer, "Hellenistic and Roman Sepphoris: The Archaeological Evidence," in Nagy et al., *Sepphoris in Galilee*, 29–37.

58. Meyers and Chancey, *Alexander to Constantine*, 269–80.

59. Meshorer, *City Coins*, 36–37.

60. Aviam, "Hellenistic and Hasmonaean Fortress"; Masterman, "Two Greek Inscriptions"; Moshe Fischer, Asher Ovadiah, and Israel Roll, "The Epigraphic Finds from the Roman Temple at Kedesh in the Upper Galilee," *Tel Aviv* 13 (1986): 60–66; Moshe Fischer, Asher Ovadiah, and Israel Roll, "The Roman Temple at Kedesh, Upper Galilee: A Preliminary Study," *Tel Aviv* 11 (1984): 146–72.

significant religious and cultural leaders. Indeed, the region's increased ethnic diversity contributed to the ongoing processes of Jewish self-definition.

## Bibliography

Adan-Bayewitz, David, and Mordechai Aviam. "Iotapata, Josephus, and the Siege of 67: Preliminary Report on the 1992–1994 Seasons." *Journal of Roman Archaeology* 10 (1997): 131–65.

Adan-Bayewitz, David, Frank Asaro, Moshe Wieder, and Robert D. Giauque. "Preferential Distribution of Lamps from the Jerusalem Area in the Late Second Temple Period (Late First Century B.C.E.–70 C.E.)." *BASOR* 350 (2008): 37–85.

Adler, Yonatan. "Religion, Judaism: Purity in the Roman Period." In *The Oxford Encyclopedia of the Bible and Archaeology*, edited by Daniel M. Master, 240–47. New York: Oxford University Press, 2013.

Alt, Albrecht. "Galiläische Probleme." In *Kleine Schriften zur Geschichte des Volkes Israel*, vol. 2. Munich: Beck, 1953–64.

Anon. "One of the Oldest Synagogues in the World Was Exposed at Migdal." Israel Antiquities Authority Press Release, Sept. 13, 2009. Online: http://www.antiquities.org.il/article_Item_eng.asp?sec_id=25&subj_id=240&id=1601&module_id=#as.

Arav, Rami, and Richard A. Freund, eds. *Bethsaida: A City by the North Shore of the Sea of Galilee*. Vol. 2. Kirksville, Mo.: Truman State University Press, 1999.

Aviam, Mordechai. *Jews, Pagans, and Christians in the Galilee: 25 Years of Archaeological Excavations and Surveys, Hellenistic to Byzantine Periods*. Land of Galilee 1. Rochester, N.Y.: University of Rochester Press; Woodbridge, Suffolk: Boydell & Brewer, 2004.

———. "People, Land, Economy, and Belief in First-Century Galilee and Its Origins: A Comprehensive Archaeological Synthesis." In *The Galilean Economy in the Time of Jesus*, edited by David A. Fiensy and Ralph K. Hawkins, 5–48. Early Christianity and Its Literature 11. Atlanta: Society of Biblical Literature, 2013.

Aviam, Mordechai, and Peter Richardson. "Josephus' Galilee in Archaeological Perspective." In *Flavius Josephus: Translation and Commentary*, vol. 9, *Life of Josephus*, edited by Steve Mason, 177–209. Leiden: Brill, 2001.

Aviam, Mordechai, and Danny Syon. "Jewish Ossilegium in Galilee." In *What Athens Has to Do with Jerusalem: Essays on Classical, Jewish, and Early Christian Art and Archaeology in Honor of Gideon Foerster*, edited by Leonard V. Rutgers, 151–85. Interdisciplinary Studies in Ancient Culture and Religion 1. Leuven: Peeters, 2002.

Berlin, Andrea M. "Jewish Life before the Revolt: The Archaeological Evidence." *JSJ* 36 (2005): 417–70.

Berlin, Andrea M., and Rafael Frankel. "The Sanctuary at Mizpe Yammim: Phoenician Cult and Territory in the Upper Galilee during the Persian Period." *BASOR* 366 (2012): 25–78.

Chancey, Mark A. "Archaeology, Ethnicity, and First-Century C.E. Galilee: The Limits of Evidence." In *A Wandering Galilean: Essays in Honour of Seán Freyne*, edited by Zuleika Rodgers with Margaret Daly-Denton and Anne Fitzpatrick McKinley, 205–18. JSJSup 132. Leiden: Brill, 2009.

———. *Greco-Roman Culture and the Galilee of Jesus.* SNTSMS 134. Cambridge: Cambridge University Press, 2005.

———. *The Myth of a Gentile Galilee.* SNTSMS 118. Cambridge: Cambridge University Press, 2002.

Cromhout, Markus. "Were the Galileans 'Religious Jews' or Ethnic Judeans?" *HTS Teologiese Studies* 64 (2008): 1279–97.

Doran, Robert. *2 Maccabees: A Critical Commentary.* Hermeneia. Minneapolis: Fortress Press, 2012.

Fischer, Moshe, Asher Ovadiah, and Israel Roll. "The Epigraphic Finds from the Roman Temple at Kedesh in the Upper Galilee." *Tel Aviv* 13 (1986): 60–66.

———. "The Roman Temple at Kedesh, Upper Galilee: A Preliminary Study." *Tel Aviv* 11 (1984): 146–72.

Frankel, Rafael, and Raphael Ventura. "The Mispe Yamim Bronzes." *BASOR* 311 (1998): 39–55.

Frankel, Rafael, Nimrod Getzov, Mordechai Aviam, and Avi Degani. *Settlement Dynamics and Regional Diversity in Ancient Upper Galilee: Archaeological Survey of Upper Galilee.* IAA Reports 14. Jerusalem: Israel Antiquities Authority, 2001.

Freyne, Seán. *Galilee from Alexander the Great to Hadrian: A Study of Second Temple Judaism.* University of Notre Dame Center for the Study of Judaism and Christianity in Antiquity 5. Wilmington, Del.: Michael Glazier; Notre Dame: University of Notre Dame Press, 1980. Reprint, Edinburgh: T&T Clark, 1998.

———. *Galilee, Jesus, and the Gospels: Literary Approaches and Historical Investigations.* Philadelphia: Fortress Press, 1988.

Gal, Zvi. *Lower Galilee during the Iron Age.* Translated by Marcia Reines Josephy. Winona Lake, Ind.: Eisenbrauns, 1992.

Gilliam, J. F. *Roman Army Papers.* Mavors Roman Army Researches 2. Amsterdam: J. C. Gieben, 1986.

Hachlili, Rachel. *Jewish Funerary Customs, Practices and Rites in the Second Temple Period.* JSJSup 94. Leiden: Brill, 2005.

Herbert, Sharon C., and Andrea M. Berlin. "A New Administrative Center for Persian and Hellenistic Galilee: Preliminary Report of the University of Michigan/University of Minnesota Excavations at Kedesh." *BASOR* 329 (2003): 13–59.

Hirschfeld, Yizhar. "Tiberias." *Excavations and Surveys in Israel* 9 (1989–90): 107–9.

Horsley, Richard A. *Archaeology, History, and Society in Galilee: The Social Context of Jesus and the Rabbis.* Valley Forge, Pa.: Trinity Press International, 1996.

———. *Covenant Economics: A Biblical Vision of Justice for All.* Louisville: Westminster John Knox, 2009.

———. *Galilee: History, Politics, People.* Valley Forge, Pa.: Trinity Press International, 1995.

Hutchinson, John, and Anthony D. Smith, eds. *Ethnicity.* Oxford: Oxford University Press, 1996.

Jensen, Morten Hørning. "Purity and Politics in Herod Antipas's Galilee: The Case for Religious Motivation." *JSHJ* 11 (2013): 3–34.

Lawrence, Jonathan D. *Washing in Water: Trajectories of Ritual Bathing in the Hebrew Bible and Second Temple Literature.* Academia Biblica. Atlanta: Society of Biblical Literature, 2006.

Leibner, Uzi. *Settlement and History in Hellenistic, Roman, and Byzantine Galilee: An Archaeological Survey of the Eastern Galilee.* TSAJ 127. Tübingen: Mohr Siebeck, 2009.

Levine, Amy-Jill. *The Misunderstood Jew: The Church and the Scandal of the Jewish Jesus.* New York: HarperCollins, 2006.

Levine, Lee I. *The Ancient Synagogue: The First Thousand Years.* 2nd ed. New Haven: Yale University Press, 2005.

Magen, Izchak. *The Stone Vessel Industry in the Second Temple Period: Excavations at Ḥizma and the Jerusalem Temple Mount.* Judea and Samaria Publications 1. Jerusalem: Israel Exploration Society, Israel Antiquities Authority, 2002.

Masterman, E. W. G. "Two Greek Inscriptions from Khurbet Harrawi." *PEQ* 20 (1908): 155–57.

McCane, Byron R. *Roll Back the Stone: Death and Burial in the World of Jesus.* Harrisburg, Pa.: Trinity Press International, 2003.

Meshorer, Ya'akov. *City Coins of Eretz-Israel and the Decapolis in the Roman Period.* Jerusalem: Israel Museum, 1985.

Meyers, Eric M. "Aspects of Everyday Life in Roman Palestine with Special Reference to Private Domiciles and Ritual Baths." In *Jews in the Hellenistic and Roman Cities*, edited by John R. Bartlett, 193–210. London: Routledge, 2002.

Meyers, Eric M., and Mark A. Chancey, *Archaeology of the Land of the Bible*, vol. 3, *Alexander to Constantine.* Anchor Yale Bible Reference Library. New Haven: Yale University Press, 2012.

Meyers, Eric M., and Carol L. Meyers. *Excavations at Ancient Nabratein: Synagogue and Environs.* Meiron Excavation Project 6. Winona Lake, Ind.: Eisenbrauns, 2009.

Miller, David Marvin. "Ethnicity Comes of Age: An Overview of Twentieth-Century Terms for *Ioudaios*." *Currents in Biblical Research* 10 (2012): 293–311.

———. "The Meaning of *Ioudaios* and Its Relationship to Other Group Labels in Ancient 'Judaism.'" *Currents in Biblical Research* 9 (2010): 98–126.

Notley, R. Steven. "Et-Tell Is Not Bethsaida." *NEA* 70 (2007): 220–30.

Rahmani, L. Y. *A Catalogue of Jewish Ossuaries in the Collection of the State of Israel.* Jerusalem: Israel Antiquities Authority, 1994.

Raynor, Joyce, and Ya'akov Meshorer, with Richard Simon Hanson. *The Coins of Ancient Meiron.* Meiron Excavation Project 4. Cambridge, Mass: ASOR; Winona Lake, Ind.: Eisenbrauns, 1988.

Reed, Jonathan L. *Archaeology and the Galilean Jesus: A Re-Examination of the Evidence.* Harrisburg, Pa.: Trinity Press International, 2000.

———. "Stone Vessels and Gospel Texts: Purity and Socio-Economics in John 2." In *Zeichen aus Text und Stein: Studien auf den Weg zu einer Archäologie des Neuen Testaments*, edited by Stefan Alkier and Jürgen Zangenberg, 381–401. TANZ 42. Tübingen: Francke, 2003.

Reeder, Ellen. "Relief Plaque with Figural Scene." In *Sepphoris in Galilee: Crosscurrents of Culture*, edited by Rebecca Martin Nagy, Carol L. Meyers, Eric M. Meyers, and Ze'ev Weiss, 174. Raleigh: North Carolina Museum of Art; Winona Lake, Ind.: Eisenbrauns, 1996.

Schürer, Emil. *The History of the Jewish People in the Age of Jesus Christ (175 B.C.–A.D. 135).* Revised and edited by Geza Vermes, Fergus Millar, Matthew Black, and Martin Goodman. 3 vols. in 4 parts. Edinburgh: T&T Clark, 1973–87.

Stern, Ephraim. *Archaeology of the Land of the Bible.* Vol. 2, *The Assyrian, Babylonian, and Persian Periods (732–332 B.C.E.).* Anchor Bible Reference Library. New York: Doubleday, 2001.

Strange, James F., and Hershel Shanks. "Synagogue Where Jesus Preached Found at Capernaum." *BAR* 9, no. 6 (1983): 25–28.

Weiss, Ze'ev, and Ehud Netzer. "Hellenistic and Roman Sepphoris: The Archaeological Evidence." In *Sepphoris in Galilee: Crosscurrent of Culture*, edited by Rebecca Martin Nagy, Carol L. Meyers, Eric M. Meyers, and Ze'ev Weiss, 29–37. Raleigh: North Carolina Museum of Art; Winona Lake, Ind.: Eisenbrauns, 1996.

Younger, K. Lawson, Jr.. "The Deportations of the Israelites." *JBL* 117 (1998): 201–27.

# 5

# THE SYNAGOGUES OF GALILEE

*Lee I. Levine*

We know virtually nothing about the demography of the Galilee prior to 100 BCE or about synagogues generally, be they in the Galilee or the entire province of Judaea. The information available for the post-Israelite, Persian, and early Hellenistic Galilee is woefully meager, and thus the ethnic identity of its inhabitants remains shrouded in mystery. Only with the Hasmonean conquest and annexation of the Galilee in the late second century BCE do we begin to learn something about this region, particularly with respect to its Jewish inhabitants. The significant Jewish presence in Hasmonean Galilee might have resulted from one or more of the following phenomena: a migration northward from the southern regions of Judaea; the conversion of the local inhabitants to Judaism; or, less likely, the fact that most inhabitants in the region during the previous six hundred years were descendants of the earlier population of the Israelite kingdom destroyed in 722 BCE. Whatever the reason, the Jewish character of the Galilee is clearly attested after the second century BCE.

The synagogue made its first appearance in Judaea by the first century CE, although there are a few indications that the institution existed already in the first century BCE. However, theories abound as to when the synagogue emerged in its broader Judaean setting before this date, ranging from virtually every century of the first millennium BCE.[1] When the institution finally makes its appearance in the Galilee, it appears in both archaeological finds and literary sources.

Although a number of synagogues from first-century CE Palestine are attested in the literary sources, they are often mentioned only in passing within the given agenda of each source.[2] These include references in the writings of Flavius Josephus (Tiberias, Dor, and Caesarea), the New Testament (Nazareth, Capernaum, and Jerusalem), rabbinic literature

---

1. For a discussion of the myriad theories regarding the synagogue's origins, see Lee I. Levine, *The Ancient Synagogue: The First Thousand Years* (2nd ed.; New Haven: Yale University Press, 2005), 21–44.

2. We are referring to those buildings that have been regularly identified as synagogues. In certain places, such synagogue/communal gatherings undoubtedly took place in private homes or village squares.

(Jerusalem), and the *Damascus Document* (Qumran). Solid archaeological evidence for the first-century synagogue is attested at eight sites in Judea: Masada, Herodium, Jerusalem (the Theodotos inscription from the City of David), Qiryat Sefer, and Modi'in (both in western Judea), with a possible additional site at Ḥorvat 'Etri, south of Bet Shemesh. In the Galilee, it is found at Gamla, Migdal, and quite probably Khirbet Qana, with considerably less certain remains from Capernaum, Chorazin, and at a second site in Migdal.[3] Below we will review the literary and archaeological data at each site and then discuss some of their social and religious implications.[4]

## Literary References

### *Nazareth*

Jesus' activity in this synagogue, mentioned in each of the Synoptic Gospels,[5] seems to have been regarded as a memorable occasion, for it marked his first appearance in his *patris*. The accounts in Matthew 13:54-58 and Mark 6:1-6 are similar: Jesus teaches at the local synagogue; those gathered are astonished by his words and deeds and immediately identify him as the carpenter's son—the son of Mary and brother of James, Joseph, Simon, Judas, and his sisters. We are told that those in attendance were highly offended by his words, although the reason for this is not made clear. Jesus' reply, that "a prophet is not without honor except in his own country [that is, hometown] and in his own house" (Mark adds: "among his own kin"), may well be what triggered the above account. Both Gospel pericopes add that Jesus did not succeed in performing miracles there owing to his townsmen's disbelief; Mark notes that Jesus nevertheless managed to heal some sick people.

---

3. See Appendix A below.

4. For recent surveys of this material, see Levine, *Ancient Synagogue*, 45–80, 135–73; Donald D. Binder, *Into the Temple Courts: The Place of the Synagogues in the Second Temple Period* (SBLDS 169; Atlanta: Society of Biblical Literature, 1999), 155–204; Carsten Claussen, *Versammlung, Gemeinde, Synagoge: Das hellenistisch-jüdische Umfeld der frühchristlichen Gemeinden* (SUNT 27; Göttingen: Vandenhoeck & Ruprecht, 2002), 168–69; Stephen K. Catto, *Reconstructing the First-Century Synagogue: A Critical Analysis of Current Research* (Library of New Testament Studies 363; London: T&T Clark, 2007), 82–105; Anders Runesson, Donald D. Binder, and Birger Olsson, *The Ancient Synagogue from Its Origins to 200 C.E.: A Source Book* (Ancient Judaism and Early Christianity 72; Leiden: Brill, 2008), 166–91.

5. The bibliography on this episode is enormous. See, for example, Hans J. B. Combrink, "Structure and Significance of Luke 4:16-30," *Neot* 7 (1973): 39–42; Robert L. Brawley, *Luke-Acts and the Jews: Conflict, Apology, and Reconciliation* (SBLMS 33; Atlanta: Scholars Press, 1987), 1–27; James A. Sanders, "From Isaiah 61 to Luke 4," in *Christianity, Judaism and Other Greco-Roman Cults: Studies for Morton Smith at Sixty* (ed. Jacob Neusner; 4 vols.; SJLA 12; Leiden: Brill, 1975), 1:75–106; Jeffrey S. Siker, "'First to the Gentiles': A Literary Analysis of Luke 4:16-30," *JBL* 111 (1992): 73–90. There is no archaeological evidence for a first- or second-century CE synagogue in Nazareth. For a survey of recent first-century domestic and funerary finds in Nazareth, see Ken Dark, "Early Roman-Period Nazareth and the Sisters of Nazareth Convent," *Antiquaries Journal* 92 (2012): 37–64.

Luke's narrative of Jesus' visit to the Nazareth synagogue is markedly different from the other Gospel accounts, so much so that it has even been suggested, in a harmonizing fashion, that Jesus made two different visits to Nazareth, the one described in Mark and Matthew, the other in Luke. Whatever the case in this regard, the importance of Luke's narrative cannot be overestimated for our understanding of the first-century Galilean synagogue.

> When he came to Nazareth, where he had been brought up, he went to the synagogue on the Sabbath day, as was his custom. He stood up to read, and the scroll of the prophet Isaiah was given to him. He unrolled the scroll and found the place where it was written: "The Spirit of the Lord is upon me, because he has anointed me to bring good news to the poor. He has sent me to proclaim release to the captives and recovery of sight to the blind, to let the oppressed go free, to proclaim the year of the Lord's favor" [Isa. 61:1–2]. And he rolled up the scroll, gave it back to the attendant, and sat down. The eyes of all in the synagogue were fixed on him. Then he began to say to them, "Today this scripture has been fulfilled in your hearing." All spoke well of him and were amazed at the gracious words which came from his mouth. They said, "Is this not Joseph's son?" He said to them, "Doubtless you will quote me this proverb, 'Doctor, cure yourself.' And you will say, 'Do here also in your hometown the things we have heard you did at Capernaum.'" And he said, "Truly, I tell you, no prophet is acceptable in his own country [that is, hometown]. But the truth is, there were many widows in Israel in the time of Elijah, when the heaven was shut up three years and six months, and there was a great famine over all the land; yet Elijah was sent to none of them except to a widow at Zarephath in Sidon. There were also many lepers in Israel in the time of Elisha the prophet; and none of them was cleansed except Naaman the Syrian." When they heard this, all in the synagogue were filled with rage. They got up, drove him out of the town, and led him to the crest of the hill on which their town was built, so that they might hurl him off the cliff. But he passed through the midst of them and went on his way. (Luke 4:16-30)

This passage is far longer and more detailed than its parallels; Luke seems to have deliberately placed this account at the very beginning of Jesus' career. Mark and Matthew, in contrast, place their versions of the Nazareth incident later in Jesus' Galilean ministry. The positioning of this tradition is clearly significant for Luke's agenda, as he apparently intended to use Jesus' "inaugural address" in Nazareth to set forth some main themes of both his Gospel and his companion volume, Acts.[6]

---

6. These themes include the following: (1) Jesus' message is rooted in Jewish tradition: the synagogue setting, reading from Scriptures, and preaching; (2) his mission is of a decidedly social, humanitarian nature—helping the poor, releasing captives, curing the blind, and freeing the oppressed—with a distinctly miracle-oriented component;

A number of details regarding the synagogue are noteworthy in this account. According to Luke, Jesus was accustomed to go to the synagogue on the Sabbath either as an ordinary participant, a preacher, or a healer; other Gospel traditions bear this out. Central components of the synagogue liturgy are noted: Jesus stood up to read from the Prophets, was handed the book of Isaiah, read several verses, returned the book to the synagogue official, sat down, and proceeded to address the congregation.

Surprisingly, the Torah-reading ceremony is omitted. However, rather than conclude that this was not part of the usual practice (in Nazareth, at least), it may be more reasonable to assume that Luke omitted the Torah reading and focused only on that of the Prophets because these verses alone were the basis of Jesus' subsequent sermon.[7] The actual selection of the prophetic reading described by Luke raises some interesting questions. Was this selection from Isaiah the prescribed reading for that particular Sabbath? Who made that decision? Luke's account seems to indicate that Jesus himself chose the passage. If so, was this Luke's invention or was it indeed an accepted practice in Nazareth, and perhaps in other Galilean synagogues? Given the absence of parallels, however, no definitive answer can be offered.

The sudden and dramatic change in the people's attitude toward Jesus (vv. 22 and 28) may have resulted from the specific message delivered on this occasion or from the contrasting attitudes of fellow townsmen toward him generally, ranging from sympathetic acceptance to hostile rejection. Luke may well have chosen to condense these reactions into his account of Jesus' programmatic sermon.[8]

### *Capernaum*

Jesus' activity in the Capernaum synagogue is mentioned in all the Gospels (Mark 1:21-29; Matt. 12:9-14; Luke 4:31-38; John 6:35-59). For Mark, and for Matthew as well, this was apparently the beginning of Jesus' ministry. These Gospels focus primarily on Jesus' healing activity while, according to John, Jesus delivered a long exposition regarding his divinity, the Eucharist, and the Mystical Body—clearly a speech setting forth the author's theological agenda, resembling *mutatis mutandis* Luke's "programmatic" account with respect to Nazareth (see above). In contrast, nothing explicit is reported in Mark and Matthew about the content of his teachings in Capernaum, apart from the fact that all who heard him were amazed. Unlike the scribes, Mark adds, Jesus taught with authority. He reputedly exorcised demons, healed a withered hand, and restored full health to a leper as well as to a deaf and lame person. While Jesus' words caused an uproar in Nazareth (per Luke), his deeds, according to Matthew, stirred opposition in Capernaum.

---

(3) fulfillment is to take place imminently, and Jesus himself is the messianic prophet; (4) having been rejected and persecuted by the Jews, Jesus will direct his mission to the gentiles, as did Elijah and Elisha (see also Luke 17:7-24).

7. In Acts 13:15-16, the readings from both the Torah and the Prophets are noted.

8. Opinions vary about the reasons for this anger. See Brawley, *Luke-Acts and the Jews*, 16–18, and bibliography cited there. See Frederic F. Bruce, *The Acts of the Apostles* (repr., Grand Rapids: Eerdmans, 1970), 15–18.

In Capernaum, the reaction of the congregation to Jesus' act of healing on the Sabbath is noteworthy. The Pharisees (as well as the scribes, according to Matthew and Luke, and the Herodians, according to Mark) found his behavior objectionable and sought ways to counter his influence and activity.[9] The historicity of any or all of these particular groups' opposition is questionable though not impossible. Why such traditions developed specifically with regard to Capernaum rather than elsewhere is unclear, unless we assume that this was Jesus' base of operations throughout his Galilean ministry.[10]

Of additional interest regarding Capernaum is the Lucan tradition (7:1-5) that a Roman centurion stationed in the town built this synagogue.[11] This claim is found only in Luke; Matthew (8:5-13) highlights the Roman officer's piety and personal faith, while Luke emphasizes his worthiness as a gentile.[12] Luke's reference to the Roman centurion fits neatly into his overriding interest in portraying gentile openness and receptivity to Jesus' message from the very outset of his ministry in Nazareth. Thus, the centurion's faith and humility, along with his generosity and support of the synagogue, were suitable traditions for Luke to include. Did Luke himself invent this account of the centurion building the Capernaum synagogue (7:5)? Was it a product of an earlier tradition that he inherited? Or is it, in fact, an authentic piece of historical evidence? Once again, the issue of historicity remains moot.

### Tiberias

In anticipation of the Roman invasion following the outbreak of the Jewish revolt in Jerusalem, Josephus was sent to organize resistance in the Galilee (66–67 CE). Tiberias thus figures prominently in Josephus's writings owing either to the city's pivotal role in the region, the lengthy and convoluted process undertaken by the Tiberians in deciding whether or not to join the revolt, Josephus's particular need in the 90s to refute personal attacks by Justus of Tiberias

---

9. On the identity of these groups and how they functioned in each Gospel, see, *inter alios*, Emil Schürer, *The History of the Jewish People in the Age of Jesus Christ (175 B.C.–A.D. 135)* (rev. and ed. Geza Vermes, Fergus Millar, Matthew Black, and Martin Goodman; 3 vols. in 4 parts; Edinburgh: T&T Clark, 1973–87), 2:322–36; Michael J. Cook, *Mark's Treatment of the Jewish Leaders* (NovTSup 51; Leiden: Brill, 1978); Anthony J. Saldarini, *Pharisees, Scribes and Sadducees in Palestinian Society: A Sociological Approach* (Wilmington, Del.: Michael Glazier, 1988; reprint, Grand Rapids: Eerdmans, 2001); Elizabeth Struthers Malbon, "Jewish Leaders in the Gospel of Mark: A Literary Study of Marcan Characterization," *JBL* 108 (1989): 259–81; Daniel R. Schwartz, *Studies in the Jewish Background of Christianity* (WUNT 60; Tübingen: Mohr Siebeck, 1992), 89–101. On the oft-repeated thesis that the Herodians were Essenes, see the judicious comments of Willi Braun, "Were the New Testament Herodians Essenes? A Critique of an Hypothesis," *RevQ* 14 (1989): 75–88, and bibliography cited there.

10. See John Chijioke Iwe, *Jesus in the Synagogue of Capernaum: The Pericope and Its Programmatic Character for the Gospel of Mark: An Exegetico-Theological Study of Mk 1:21-28* (Tesi gregoriana, Serie teologia 57; Rome: Pontificia Università Gregoriana, 1999).

11. On suggested archaeological remains of a first-century synagogue building in Capernaum, see below.

12. On this narrative in its Matthean and Lucan contexts, see Ralph P. Martin, "The Pericope of the Healing of the 'Centurion's' Servant/Son (Matt 8:5-13 par. Luke 7:1-10): Some Exegetical Notes," in *Unity and Diversity in New Testament Theology: Essays in Honor of George E. Ladd* (ed. Robert A. Guelich; Grand Rapids: Eerdmans, 1978), 14–22.

regarding his conduct of the war, or a combination of the above.[13] Whatever the reasons, Josephus's movements in and around Tiberias, his meetings, speeches, and escapes from the city in the face of opposition, as well as the names of local leaders, leave us with a much more detailed picture of this city than of any other at this time.

Josephus mentions a Tiberian *proseuchē* (prayer hall)[14] on three occasions. In the first (*Life* 277), he describes a very large building (*megiston oikēma*, μέγιστον οἴκημα) capable of accommodating a large crowd where deliberations were held one Sabbath morning. Nothing is said about worship, which presumably took place beforehand. The meeting itself consisted of a series of speeches; the participants disbanded only at midday, when, Josephus notes, the Sabbath meal was served (*Life* 279). Another meeting was scheduled for the next day, and very early that morning people again gathered in the *proseuchē* to resume discussions (*Life* 280). A third meeting was called for the following day, which was also proclaimed a day of public fast. The proceedings began with the usual (*ta nomima*, τὰ νόμιμα) service for a fast day, but soon thereafter a confrontation ensued, which quickly became heated and violent (*Life* 290–303).

Josephus's references to the Tiberian *proseuchē* and associated events are noteworthy on several counts. First of all, this is the only instance in which a Judaean synagogue is referred to as a *proseuchē* (although an equivalent Hebrew term does appear in the *Damascus Document*). In Josephus's other accounts, as well as in all the Gospel traditions, the Theodotos inscription, and rabbinic literature, *synagōgē* is invariably used. If, indeed, *proseuchē* was used primarily with regard to the Diaspora institution, is it possible that there was some tie between this Tiberias building and the Diaspora?

In the absence of firm evidence, we can only speculate. Perhaps this term was used because its founder, Herod Antipas, modeled the city after a Hellenistic *polis*. Tiberias was named after an emperor; its local government was structured as a *polis*, replete with archons, *boulē*, and *dēmos*; it boasted a stadium and, later on, acquired an additional name, Claudiopolis, possibly following Claudius's death in 54 CE.[15] The *proseuchē* may well have been constructed by Antipas himself or, alternatively, during the reign of Agrippa I. The latter's contact with the Diaspora, and particularly with Alexandrian Jewry, is well known, especially with regard to the events surrounding the anti-Jewish outbreaks of 38 CE. Finally, it may or may not be coincidental that a later midrash (*Midr. on Psalms* 93, ed. Buber, p. 416) describes a third- or fourth-century Tiberian synagogue as a *dyplastoon* (דיפליא סטיא)—the identical

---

13. Shaye J. D. Cohen, *Josephus in Galilee and Rome: His Vita and Development as a Historian* (Columbia Studies in the Classical Tradition 8; Leiden: Brill, 1979), 114–70.

14. See Levine, *Ancient Synagogue*, 82–89, 127–28.

15. See, for example, Josephus, *J.W.* 2.641 (*boulē* of 600); *Life* 69, 296 (*deka prōtoi*); 134, 271, 278, 294; *J.W.* 2.599 (*archōn*); 2.615 (*hyparchoi*); *Ant.* 18.149 (*agoranomos*). See also "Tiberias" in volume 2 of this series; Michael Avi-Yonah, "Tiberias in the Roman Period" (in Hebrew), in *All the Land of Naphtali* (ed. Hayyim Z. Hirschberg; Jerusalem: Israel Exploration Society, 1967), 154–62; Aryeh Kasher, "The Founding of Tiberias and Her Functioning as the Capital of the Galilee" (in Hebrew), in *Tiberias: From Her Founding until the Muslim Conquest* (ed. Yizhar Hirschfeld; Jerusalem: Yad Izhak Ben-Zvi, 1988), 3–11; Daniel R. Schwartz, *Agrippa I: The Last King of Judaea* (TSAJ 23; Tübingen: Mohr Siebeck, 1990), 137–40.

term the Tosefta (*t. Sukkah* 4:6, ed. Lieberman, p. 273) uses for the first-century Alexandrian synagogue (דפלסטטון). Interestingly, this term appears in rabbinic literature only in conjunction with these two synagogues.

A second noteworthy feature of this Tiberian account is the purportedly large size of the *proseuchē*. Josephus notes explicitly that when not meeting in the *proseuchē*, Tiberians would gather in the local stadium (*Life* 91, 331), much as the *dēmos* of Ephesus (Acts 19:29) and Antioch (*J.W.* 7.47) were wont to meet in their respective theaters.[16] To date, monumental synagogue buildings are known only from the Diaspora: one (perhaps two) in Alexandria, described by Philo and the Tosefta, and another in Sardis, dating from the late third (or fourth) to seventh centuries CE and excavated in the 1960s.[17]

Finally, the Tiberias *proseuchē* served, *inter alia*, as a meeting place for discussing burning political issues of the day and thus played a pivotal communal role. In Josephus's report at least, its religious dimension was decidedly secondary; on those occasions, the Sabbath and fast-day rituals were apparently dwarfed by the pressures of the political agenda.[18]

## Archaeological Evidence

### Gamla (Golan)

Gamla is the earliest synagogue to have been excavated in the Golan.[19] Its construction had but one phase, probably in the early first century CE,[20] although a mid-first-century BCE founda-

16. See also Martin Hengel, "Proseuche und Synagoge: Jüdische Gemeinde, Gotteshaus und Gottesdienst in der Diaspora und in Palästina," in *The Synagogue: Studies in Origins, Archaeology, and Architecture* (ed. Joseph Gutmann; Library of Biblical Studies; New York: KTAV, 1975), 177–78.

17. On the Sardis synagogue see Andrew R. Seager, "The Building History of the Sardis Synagogue," *AJA* 76 (1972): 425–35; Seager and A. Thomas Kraabel, "The Synagogue and the Jewish Community," in *Sardis from Prehistoric to Roman Times: Results of the Archaeological Exploration of Sardis, 1958–1975* (ed. George M. A. Hanfmann; Cambridge, Mass.: Harvard University Press, 1983), 168–90; A. Thomas Kraabel, "The Diaspora Synagogue: Archaeological and Epigraphic Evidence since Sukenik," *ANRW* II.19.1 (1979): 483–88; Lee I. Levine, *Visual Judaism in Late Antiquity: Historical Contexts of Jewish Art* (New Haven: Yale University Press, 2012), 294–314.

18. See Samuel Rocca, "The Purposes and Functions of the Synagogue in Late Second Temple Period Judaea: Evidence from Josephus and Archaeological Investigation," in *Flavius Josephus: Interpretation and History* (ed. Jack Pastor, Pnina Stern, and Menahem Mor; JSJSup 146; Leiden: Brill, 2011), 295–305.

19. Shmaryahu Gutman, "Gamala," *NEAEHL* 2:460–62; Zvi U. Ma'oz, "The Architecture of Gamla and Her Buildings" (in Hebrew), in *Z. Vilnay Jubilee Volume* (ed. Eli Schiller; Jerusalem: Ariel, 1987), 2:152–54; and Zvi Ilan, *Ancient Synagogues in Israel* (in Hebrew; Tel Aviv: Ministry of Defense, 1991), 73–74; Zvi Yavor and Danny Syon, *Gamla: The Shmarya Gutmann Excavations, 1976–1989*, vol. 2, *The Architecture and Stratigraphy of the Eastern and Western Quarters* (IAA Reports 44; Jerusalem: Israel Antiquities Authority, 2010), 40–61, 189–91. See also Binder, *Into the Temple Courts*, 162–72. The building's dimensions differ somewhat in each of the above publications; I have followed those of Yavor and Syon.

20. See, however, Zvi U. Ma'oz ("Four Notes on the Excavations at Gamala," *Tel Aviv* 39 [2012]: 236), who dates the synagogue to ca. 50 CE and the adjacent *mikveh* to 66–67 CE, during the preparations for war against the Romans.

tion, sometime between Alexander Jannaeus (103–76 BCE) and Herod (37–4 BCE), was first suggested by its excavator, Shmaryahu Gutman.

**Figure A. Gamla.** View of the synagogue from a westerly direction. Photo © BiblePlaces.com. Reprinted by permission.

The Gamla building is architecturally impressive (see figure A). Located adjacent to the town's eastern wall, the building is 21.5 x 17.5 m and is positioned on a northeast–southwest axis. The hall itself measures approximately 19.7 (northern and southern walls) x 16.3 (eastern and western walls) m. Near the northwestern corner of this hall (along the northern wall) is a square niche that may have been used for storage (of Torah scrolls?). There are three entrances, one giving access to the northwestern upper level while a second and larger one led directly into the main hall from the middle of the western wall. A third entrance from the southeast opens onto the eastern aisle.

Along all four sides of the main hall stood colonnades surrounded by rows of benches, above which was an elevated landing. Columns surrounded an open space in the middle of an unpaved hall (7.2 x 11.2 m), with the exception of a row of stones laid in a north–south direction on the eastern side of the hall, dividing the room disproportionately into two thirds and one third. The purpose of this row of stones remains undetermined (liturgical? communal?). An additional single bench abutted the eastern wall of the building, and similar ones may have run along the northern and southern walls as well. Those sitting in the synagogue were clearly oriented toward the center of the hall. A small plastered basin (for washing hands?) in the eastern aisle was fed by a plastered channel that cut through the eastern (that is, city) wall.

No inscriptions were discovered in the building, and the only artistic depiction is a stylized palm tree carved into a stone block. East of the synagogue's main hall is a complex of auxiliary rooms, one of which has some sort of opening into the main hall. This room also contains benches, which led the excavator to suggest that it may have served as a study hall or a small meeting room.

Just west of the synagogue entrance is a series of rooms (a vestibule, exedra, and service areas), and farther west is a *mikveh* (ritual bath) along with a plastered basin (possibly an *otzar* containing ritually pure water). A stepped cistern just outside the synagogue's main entrance may have been used as a *mikveh* as well. If our assumptions are correct, namely, that the synagogue of the first century was primarily a communal institution, then this structure at Gamla must have served as the local synagogue.[21]

The building's internal plan is reminiscent of (though not identical to) the Hellenistic public hall, such as the *bouleutērion* or *ekklēsiastērion*, and is similar in its overall plan to synagogues found at other Judaean sites (for instance, Qiryat Sefer and Modi'in). This structure at Gamla was the first building to be identified as a synagogue in the pre-70 Galilee-Golan region.

### Khirbet Qana

On the northern slope of the Bet Netofa Valley, some 8 km north-northeast of Sepphoris, a Jewish village was discovered that has often been identified with Cana mentioned in the New Testament.[22] One building, excavated by Douglas Edwards, measures 20 x 15 m and has been dated to the first or early second century CE on the basis of the ceramic profile at foundation level, the Carbon-14 dating of mortar and plaster from foundation-level walls, and the first-century dating of a capital whose form and decoration are similar to capitals from the Gamla

---

21. In this regard, it is important to mention that another large building dating to the first century CE was found in the western part of the town and has been referred to in archaeological reports as a basilica. Its measurements are very similar to those of the synagogue, featuring unusually wide aisles and an impressive central aisle, large stones in its walls, and wide doorways containing corbels and pilasters. Thus, it appears to have been a public building, but of a very different type than heretofore known. As summarized by its excavators, "It is not a synagogue, for there is no single space within suitable for the assembly of a large group of people. It is an entirely new type of religious and/or secular Jewish public building of the Second Temple period" (Danny Syon and Zvi Yavor, "Gamla 1997–2000," *'Atiqot* 50 [2005]: 52–59; quotation from p. 59).

22. Douglas R. Edwards, "Khirbet Qana: From Jewish Village to Christian Pilgrim Site," in *The Roman and Byzantine Near East*, vol. 3, *Late-antique Petra, Nile Festival Building at Sepphoris, Deir Qal'a Monastery, Khirbet Qana Village and Pilgrim Site, 'Ain-'Arrub Hiding Complex and Other Studies* (ed. John H. Humphrey; Journal of Roman Archaeology Supplementary Series 49; Ann Arbor, Mich.: Journal of Roman Archaeology, 2002), 101–32, specifically 110–15; Peter Richardson, *Building Jewish in the Roman East* (Waco, Tex.: Baylor University Press, 2004), 55–71, specifically 66; Catto, *Reconstructing the First-Century Synagogue*, 102–3; Runesson et al., *Ancient Synagogue from Its Origins*, 22–25; and, most recently, Tom McCollough, "Final Report on the Archaeological Excavations at Khirbet Qana: Field II, the Synagogue," *Albright News* 18 (November 2013): 13.

synagogue. Moreover, a number of remains seem to indicate the existence of a public building: a main hall flanked by two side aisles, plastered benches and floors, large amounts of painted wall plaster on the interior, traces on the floor of eight columns located equidistant from one another and from the adjacent wall. Finally, column bases and drums also were found there in addition to well-executed roof tiles. Although certainty is elusive with regard to the nature of the finds at Khirbet Qana, it seems likely that these are the remains of a synagogue. Unfortunately, owing to the excavator's illness and subsequent passing, work at the site was temporarily aborted, although it has been renewed under the direction of Tom McCollough.

## *Migdal (Magdala)*

Excavations conducted between 2009 and 2013 by Dina Avshalom-Gorni and Arfan Najar in Migdal, on the Sea of Galilee just north of Tiberias, uncovered a building that is widely acknowledged to have been a synagogue.[23] The building dates to the first century CE and consists of two large rooms, a long and narrow vestibule, and a main hall measuring 120 sq m with a presumed entrance from the west. The hall is rectangular in shape and was surrounded by a raised aisle with what appear to be benches along four sides. The eastern part of the hall contains the remains of a mosaic floor displaying a rosette motif surrounded by two meander designs. Remains of parallel stylobates were also found as well as fragments of two basalt columns standing on them *in situ* and fragments of another column on the floor of the hall. The walls of the hall and its columns display colorful fresco paintings. Finally, a small room is located southwest of this hall and is divided by a partition wall into two spaces. The walls of this room are decorated with a colorful fresco, and its floor is paved with mosaics. It has been suggested that this room may have been used for storage.

The pièce de résistance of this excavation was a rectangular limestone block with short legs, about a half-meter on each side (0.4 and 0.6 m) and 0.3 m high (see figure B); it was found in the middle of the floor but its function is unclear. To date, the suggestions put forth for its usage include: a base of a chair, a lectern for reading the Torah, or a prayer table. It is decorated on all four sides and on its top with geometric, architectural, and floral patterns; the front of the stone features a seven-branched menorah with a triangular base standing on a square platform flanked by two amphoras.

It is generally assumed that the stone's decorations, especially the menorah and amphora motifs, relate to the Jerusalem Temple.[24] This is the only instance from the pre-70 era in which a menorah, so ubiquitous in Late Antiquity, is displayed in a synagogue setting.

---

23. The following information is based in large part on the Israel Antiquities Authority's press release (http://www.antiquities.org.il/article_Item_eng.asp?module_id=&sec_id=25&subj_id=240&id=1601—cited July 20, 2014) and my personal communication with the excavator, Dina Avshalom-Gorni)..

24. See the recent article of Mordechai Aviam ("The Decorated Stone from the Synagogue at Migdal: A Holistic Interpretation and a Glimpse into the Life of Galilean Jews at the Time of Jesus," *NovT* 55 [2013]: 205–20), in which creative though rather unsubstantiated and speculative interpretations are presented.

**Figure B. Migdal.** Stone found on the synagogue floor. Note its many decorations, especially the menorah flanked by amphoras on the short side. Courtesy of The Israel Antiquities Authority.

## Galilean Synagogues in Context

The information that can be culled from sources relating to the Galilean synagogue appears to carry a large measure of accuracy. The very term *synagogue*, with one exception (the Tiberias *proseuchē*, as noted above), was used exclusively throughout first-century Judaea, the Galilee included. The Greek term *synagōgē*, meaning "a gathering" or "a place of gathering," thus refers to a Jewish communal setting.

That a communal dimension was indeed intended by the term *synagōgē* is confirmed by two additional considerations. For one, the activities that transpired there (political, religious, and social gatherings, judicial proceedings, the administration of punishment, the occasional presence of a public installation such as a ritual bath, and more) all attest to a multipurpose communal institution.

Second, the buildings discovered to date—with benches surrounding the main hall indicating an orientation toward the center of the room—also point to their public, communal, dimension. The religious dimension, however, is absent altogether from the material finds; there is no provision for a Torah shrine, no orientation toward Jerusalem (as became normative later on), no religious art or symbols (Migdal excepted), and no inscription attesting to the sacred status of the building. Moreover, since the Judaean synagogue of the late Second Temple period does not seem to have enjoyed any particular religious status, it would be all the more reasonable to assume that the synagogue at this stage functioned primarily as a multipurpose community center, with a significant religious component coming to the fore on Sabbaths and holidays.[25]

Nevertheless, the literary sources, for their part, especially the Gospels, consistently emphasize the religious component of synagogue life. Jesus frequented the synagogue on the Sabbath, where the Torah reading, readings from the Prophets (*haftarot*), and teachings/sermons were featured. Is this, then, a contradiction between the literary and archaeological materials, or between the civic and religious dimensions of the synagogue? Or does each type of source simply emphasize what is most appropriate and of interest to its authors or communities, the archaeological material pointing to a communal setting and the textual evidence, such as the New Testament, highlighting a religious focus? If the latter, then we are confronted with the fact that those interested in religious-theological matters invoked synagogue settings that furthered their agenda while those who built the synagogue buildings (that is, the local congregations) were focused on a community center setting.

The religious agenda of the Gospel writers regarding Jesus' activity in the synagogue is quite clear. Mark and Luke speak of Jesus' preaching and healing in synagogues throughout the region; Matthew, of his teaching, preaching, and healing there; and John, of his speaking openly in synagogues and in the Temple.[26] The towns and villages that Jesus frequented (as has often been noted, he seems to have studiously shied away from cities)[27] appear to have had synagogues, whatever their size, character, location, or social-religious configuration (see, for example, Luke 4:44). Jesus' visits to these synagogues on the Sabbath were clearly intended to afford him maximum exposure to the local population; at least the Gospels' narratives purport to convey this message.

On occasion, New Testament sources reveal facets of synagogue life virtually unknown elsewhere. For example, the Gospels mention healings and miracles performed in these settings, while other contemporary sources, whether Josephus, Philo, or rabbinic material, ignore this aspect of synagogue life—possibly because it was too common a phenomenon to require

---

25. Levine, *Ancient Synagogue*, 135–73, 381–411, and bibliography therein.

26. Evidence from each Gospel is referred to respectively: Mark 1:21-28, 39; 3:1; 6:2 (for other settings in Jesus' ministry according to Mark, see David M. Rhoads and Donald Michie, *Mark as Story: An Introduction to the Narrative of a Gospel* [Philadelphia: Fortress Press, 1982], 63–72); Matt. 4:23; 9:35; Luke 4:15-44; 13:10-21; John 6:35-59; 18:20. See also Sylvan D. Schwartzman, "How Well Did the Synoptic Evangelists Know the Synagogue?" *HUCA* 24 (1952–53): 115–32.

27. Seán Freyne, *Galilee, Jesus, and the Gospels: Literary Approaches and Historical Investigations* (Philadelphia: Fortress Press; Dublin: Gill & MacMillan, 1988), 135–55; Richard A. Horsley, *Galilee: History, Politics, People* (Valley Forge, Pa.: Trinity Press International, 1995), 158–255; Douglas R. Edwards, "The Socio-Economic and Cultural Ethos of the Lower Galilee in the First Century: Implications for the Nascent Jesus Movement," in *The Galilee in Late Antiquity* (ed. Lee I. Levine; New York and Jerusalem: Jewish Theological Seminary of America, 1992), 53–73. See also Seán Freyne, "Urban–Rural Relations in First-Century Galilee: Some Suggestions from the Literary Sources," in Levine, *Galilee in Late Antiquity*, 75–91. On urban–rural relations generally in the empire, see Ramsay MacMullen, *Roman Social Relations, 50 B.C. to A.D. 284* (New Haven: Yale University Press, 1974), 28–56.

comment, it may have proved embarrassing to them, or simply it was one of the many dimensions of this institution's agenda that they chose to ignore. Whatever the reason for this silence, there are no compelling grounds to doubt the veracity of such Gospel reports.[28]

In fact, performing miracles was far from uncommon in antiquity, including in Judaea.[29] Exorcising demons, performing wonders, making miraculous signs, and healing the sick would probably not have been considered unusual even in the context of the synagogue, given the institution's centrality in Jewish life. The Gospel authors appear to have emphasized a common rural phenomenon, using healing to enhance Jesus' charisma and popularity. What is highlighted in these narratives, however, is not only the nature and extent of such practices, but also the fact that they took place on the Sabbath. This proved to be controversial and became a bone of contention between Jesus and some of those present in the synagogue. In one case he is reportedly criticized by an *archisynagōgos*, in another by Pharisees (Luke 13:14; Matt. 12:14).

Nevertheless, the historical value of these Gospel narratives regarding first-century Galilee has often been called into question. It has been suggested that all the Gospels, Matthew perhaps excepted, were written in the Diaspora decades later and therefore may reflect a late-first-century CE Diaspora reality that was familiar to these authors, who then projected it onto the earlier Galilean scene.[30] Moreover, the very different literary and theological agendas of each Gospel have further raised doubts as to the material's historical credibility.

In the case of the Galilean synagogue, however, such skepticism should be regarded with extreme caution. Although the Gospels and Acts, those writings most relevant to the subject at hand, may have originated in the Diaspora, they are not so distant chronologically from Jesus' setting; the difference between the latter half of the first century CE and ca. 30 CE is but a generation or two. Furthermore, it is not at all clear whether a Diaspora setting had any sort of impact on these accounts. All the Gospels, no matter when or where they were written, report much the same information regarding the Galilean synagogue. This coincidence may be explained by assuming that Diaspora synagogues—whether in Rome, Alexandria, Antioch, or Asia Minor, where the various Gospels were quite possibly composed—shared identical features. Yet, as demonstrated elsewhere, this was not universally the case; Diaspora synagogues varied considerably from region to region.[31] Moreover, even were we to assume the existence of

---

28. On the fourth-century report of such activity in one or more Antioch synagogues, see John Chrysostom, *Adv. Iud.* 1, 6; Robert L. Wilken, *John Chrysostom and the Jews: Rhetoric and Reality in the Late Fourth Century* (Transformation of the Classical Heritage 4; Berkeley: University of California Press, 1983), 97–98.

29. Howard Clark Kee, *Miracle in the Early Christian World: A Study in Sociohistorical Method* (New Haven: Yale University Press, 1983), 146–70; Freyne, *Galilee, Jesus, and the Gospels*, 227–39; and especially David E. Aune, "Magic in Early Christianity," *ANRW* II.23.2 (1984): 1507–57; See also Edward P. Sanders, *Jesus and Judaism* (Philadelphia: Fortress Press, 1985), 157–73; Morton Smith, *Jesus the Magician* (New York: Harper & Row, 1978), 68–93; and John Dominic Crossan, *The Historical Jesus: The Life of a Mediterranean Jewish Peasant* (New York: HarperCollins, 1992), 303–32.

30. See, for example, Howard Clark Kee, "The Transformation of the Synagogue after 70 C.E.: Its Import for Early Christianity," *NTS* 36 (1990): 18.

31. Levine, *Ancient Synagogue*, 81–134.

some sort of overriding unity among the far-flung first-century Diaspora synagogues, might it not be possible that Galilean synagogues, too, shared that commonality?

Finally, there is significant agreement regarding synagogue liturgy in the New Testament and other sources from this period, and this relates to Judaea, the Galilee, and the Diaspora. For example, Acts refers to Diaspora Jewry's synagogues in Jerusalem, a reality that is reflected also in rabbinic literature and the Theodotos inscription.[32] The centrality of scriptural readings in the synagogue (such as Luke 4) is echoed in the Theodotos inscription, Philo, Josephus, and several early rabbinic traditions (for example, *t. Meg.* 3:17-21, ed. Lieberman, pp. 357–60) and was considered the most distinguishing religious characteristic of synagogues everywhere.[33]

### *The Post-70 CE Era*

Following the end of the Second Temple era in 70 CE, archaeological evidence regarding the synagogue virtually disappears from the Galilee for several centuries.[34] This region thus follows a pattern typical of synagogues found elsewhere both in Palestine and the Diaspora; only in the third century do we begin to find a significant number of synagogue remains, which increase exponentially from the fourth through seventh centuries. A number of explanations have been offered for this absence in Palestine—for example, the obliteration of synagogues as a result of the Hadrianic persecutions of ca. 135–138; the use of domestic facilities at this time instead of public buildings (as had been the norm beforehand and was to be afterwards); the destruction of earlier buildings owing to large-scale synagogue construction throughout late antiquity; the mass influx of Judean migrants only following the Bar Kokhba revolt (135), which subsequently led to synagogue construction in the third century. None, however, has gained widespread support.[35]

---

32. Ibid., 57–59.

33. The fact that the Gospel writers have been characterized of late less as historians than as theologians and literary writers should not be given undue weight for our particular purposes; see Hans Conzelmann, *The Theology of St. Luke* (Philadelphia: Fortress Press, 1961), 34–38; Charles H. Talbert, *Literary Patterns, Theological Themes, and the Genre of Luke-Acts* (SBLMS 20; Missoula, Mont.: Scholars Press, 1974); contra Hugh Anderson, "Broadening Horizons: The Rejection at Nazareth Pericope of Luke 4:16-30 in Light of Recent Critical Trends," *Int* 18 (1964): 261–74. It is rather safe to assume that even those writers using "historical" data in a supposedly biographical or theological narrative (for example, Luke-Acts) would include as much reliable data as possible to make their accounts convincing and compelling. So, for example, Luke 1:1: "It seemed good to me to write an orderly account." On the inclusion of very early (and perhaps relatively authentic and historical) material in much of Luke's narrative, see Heinz Schürmann, *Das Lukasevangelium* (Herders theologischer Kommentar zum Neuen Testament 3; Freiburg: Herder, 1969), 1:223–25; Sharon H. Ringe, *Jesus, Liberation, and the Biblical Jubilee: Images for Ethics and Christology* (Overtures to Biblical Theology 19; Philadelphia: Fortress Press, 1985), 42–45, 107–9; and Bruce D. Chilton, *God in Strength: Jesus' Announcement of the Kingdom* (1976; repr., Biblical Seminar 8; Sheffield: JSOT Press, 1987), 121–32.

34. On the supposed building at Nabratein from the second century, see below.

35. For a discussion of these alternatives, see Levine, *Ancient Synagogue*, 184–86. Moreover, the above explanations are primarily Palestinian oriented. The fact is that there is a notable absence of second-century evidence even in the Diaspora, where archaeological remains are far less ubiquitous.

The absence of such evidence in the archaeological sphere finds partial confirmation in rabbinic sources of the period, particularly in the Mishnah and Tosefta, the former edited at the turn of the third century, the latter about a generation or so later. These early compilations refer to the contemporary synagogue rather infrequently, despite the institution's centrality in Jewish life, and even in discussions addressing liturgical issues the synagogue is often ignored.[36] Interestingly, and conforming to the archaeological finds, it appears that the synagogue is noted far more frequently only in later rabbinic compositions (fourth to sixth/seventh centuries).

While the absence of archaeological evidence for synagogues in the second century CE remains a conundrum, the relative dearth of references to synagogues in early rabbinic literature may be easier to fathom. Tannaitic literature (those writings composed before the early to mid-third century CE) focuses almost exclusively on the rabbis and their activities—developing *halakhah*, interpreting biblical passages, and commenting on rabbinic and, more rarely, non-rabbinic matters, but only to the extent that the latter had relevance to the rabbis themselves; the synagogue was, at best, peripheral to the rabbinic agenda of the second century. Thus, it is not surprising that matters dealing with the synagogue and the community were beyond the rabbinic purview and interest, and therefore the material preserved in this regard is sparse. Whatever the reasons for this silence with regard to second-century Galilean synagogue affairs, this situation began to change from the third century onward. During the next four hundred or so years, the synagogue flourished beyond recognition, gaining an unprecedented religious profile accompanied by a lavish display of architecture, art, and inscriptions side by side with the institution's continued, and presumably enhanced, communal centrality.[37] Rabbinic sources responded accordingly to this new reality, and thus we find that later compositions contain far more references to the synagogue than earlier ones.

## Appendix A: Less-Certain Identifications of Galilean Synagogues

### *Migdal (Magdala)*

In 1971–74, Virgilio C. Corbo and Stanislao Loffreda discovered and identified a building from the first centuries CE as the first stage of a synagogue.[38] The building had an unusual

---

36. The Tosefta mentions the synagogue more often than the Mishnah and includes references to it as a communal institution, and not only with regard to liturgical matters. However, the Tosefta is commonly dated to the mid-third century, at a time when synagogues begin to appear in archaeological remains as well.

37. Levine, *Ancient Synagogue*, passim; Levine, *Visual Judaism*, passim.

38. Virgilio C. Corbo, "La città romana di Magdala," in *Studia Hierosolymitana in onore del P. Bellarmino Bagatti*, vol. 1, *Studi archeologici* (ed. Emmanuele Testa, Ignazio Mancini, and Michele Piccirillo; SBF Collectio maior 22; Jerusalem: Franciscan Printing Press, 1976), 364–72; Dennis E. Groh, "The Stratigraphic Chronology of the Galilean Synagogue from the Early Roman Period through the Early Byzantine Period (ca. 420 C.E.)," in *Ancient Synagogues: Historical Analysis and Archaeological Discovery* (ed. Dan Urman and Paul V. M. Flesher; 2 vols.; StPB 47; Leiden: Brill, 1995), 1:58–59.

shape; it was a small structure (8.2 x 7.2 m); its inner hall measured 6.6 x 5.5 m and had five rows of benches on the north and seven columns along the other three walls. Corbo claims that the building was converted into a water installation in the second century. Subsequently, however, Ehud Netzer demonstrated that the water channels on three sides of the hall were built at the same time as the earlier floor, that is, the original first-century building was intended as a water facility that functioned as a *nymphaeum* in both stages, although the floor of the second stage was raised to correct a problem of flooding.[39]

## *Capernaum*

In the course of excavating the fourth- to fifth-century CE synagogue, Corbo and Loffreda noted black basalt walls beneath the building's white limestone ones, although with a slight discrepancy in direction along the western side. In 1981, following the excavation of trenches to clarify the dating and function of these basalt walls and others under the later building's stylobates, Corbo claimed to have discovered a first-century CE synagogue.[40] Measurements of the earlier building approximate those of the later one, ca. 24.50 x 18.70 m, and its walls are 1.20–1.30 m thick and seem most likely to have been part of a public rather than private building. The dating of the earlier building is based on pottery found in and under a cobbled basalt pavement, some 1.3 m below the level of the later synagogue floor.

Assuming that the basalt walls were built not merely as a foundation for the later building but belonged to an earlier structure, it is quite possible that a first-century CE building stood on this site. The excavators suggest that a layer of basalt stones constituted the floor of an earlier building, although no connection to the walls has been established and no doors or benches have been identified. However, if the existence of an earlier building is granted, then its identification as a synagogue becomes intriguing. A large building located in the center of town could have been a first-century CE synagogue, although it would have been of a different size than the one at Gamla. According to the excavators, this building would have been about 50 percent larger than the Gamla building and more than twice the size of the Masada and

---

39. Ehud Netzer, "Did the Water Installation in Magdala Serve as a Synagogue?" in *Synagogues in Antiquity* (in Hebrew; ed. Aryeh Kasher et al.; Jerusalem: Yad Izhak Ben-Zvi, 1987),165–72. See also Binder, *Into the Temple Courts*, 193–95.

40. Virgilio C. Corbo, "Resti della sinagoga del primo secolo a Cafarnao," *Studia Hierosolymitana* 3 (1982), 313–57. For an English summary of these excavations, see James F. Strange and Hershel Shanks, "Synagogue Where Jesus Preached Found at Capernaum," *BAR* 9, no. 6 (1983): 25–31. Supportive of this suggestion is Binder, *Into the Temple Courts*, 186–93. Cf., however, the reservations of Yoram Tsafrir, "The Synagogues of Capernaum and Meroth and the Dating of the Galilean Synagogue," in *The Roman and Byzantine Near East: Some Recent Archaeological Research*, vol. 1 (ed. J. H. Humphrey; Journal of Roman Archaeology Supplementary Series 14; Ann Arbor, Mich.: Journal of Roman Archaeology, 1995), 155–57; Jodi Magness, "The Question of the Synagogue: The Problem of Typology," in *Judaism in Late Antiquity*, part 3, *Where We Stand: Issues and Debates in Ancient Judaism*, vol. 4, *The Special Problem of the Synagogue* (ed. Alan J. Avery-Peck and Jacob Neusner; Handbook of Oriental Studies; Leiden: Brill, 2001), 19–20.

Herodium buildings. However, given the meager remains, there is little to be learned about the overall plan of this building, and its identification as a synagogue is at present rather tenuous.

## Chorazin

In 1926, the highly regarded archaeologist Jacob Ory reported the discovery of a synagogue at Chorazin, some 200 m west of the later building visible today at the site. Ory's unpublished report states the following: "A square colonnaded building of small dimensions, of a disposition similar to the interior arrangement of the synagogue, 7 columns, 3 on each side (the entrance was afforded through the east wall), were supporting the roof, and the whole space between the colonnade and walls on three sides was occupied with sitting benches in 5 courses."[41] Unfortunately, these remains have never been verified. Multiple visits to the site have yielded no clues as to the whereabouts of this structure. Ory's report has been included on occasion in surveys of first-century synagogues, but the use of such data seems unwarranted for the present.

## Nevoraya (Nabratein)

In contrast to the earlier publications in the Meiron Excavation Project Reports series, the appearance of the volume on the reputed first (that is, second-century) stage of this synagogue was seriously delayed. While earlier excavation reports were published far more expeditiously, with time gaps ranging between five and ten years between excavation and publication, the report for this early building was completed only twenty-four years later and, even then, the actual publication was held up another four years. Another unfortunate happenstance was the unforeseen termination of this excavation after the completion of only two seasons (1980–81). As noted in the volume's preface, vandalism and destructive acts by ultra-Orthodox hooligans, who damaged the excavation camp, as well as the equipment left there overnight, forced the excavators to abort this project prematurely.

As a result, the excavators candidly admit that many questions resulting from the incomplete fieldwork remain unresolved. Moreover, there are a number of mistakes and misidentifications in the final report (some apparently significant), many of which are noted in Jodi Magness's review of the volume.[42] The excavators acknowledge these errors, and they themselves note about ten of them in their response to her.[43] Moreover, it is stated very clearly, both in the final report and again in the response to Magness's comments, that work at the site and the accompanying analyses were seriously hindered by additional factors: the site was disturbed in modern times; the latest synagogue floor was disturbed already in antiquity; other floors,

---

41. Gideon Foerster, "The Synagogues at Masada and Herodium," in *Ancient Synagogues Revealed* (ed. Lee I. Levine; Jerusalem: Israel Exploration Society, 1981), 26.

42. Jodi Magness, "Review Article: The Ancient Synagogue at Nabratein," *BASOR* 358 (2010): 61–68.

43. Eric M. Meyers and Carol L. Meyers, "Response to Jodi Magness's Review of the Final Publication of Nabratein," *BASOR* 359 (2010): 67–76.

along with their underbedding, were preserved only in irregular patches; the irregular sloping of bedrock resulted in the confusion of surfaces "lensing" into one another.[44]

Of interest to us, of course, is the reputed first stage of the building dating to the post–Bar Kokhba era in the second century. This was purportedly a relatively small building with a broadhouse plan, that is, its width was longer than its length. Measuring 11.2 x 9.35 m, it is described as having two benches running along its eastern, northern, and western walls; the southern wall, facing Jerusalem, had no benches since the entrance there was flanked by two *bimot* on the interior, and there may have been a portico outside the building. Another entrance was located in the northeastern corner. The room, it is claimed, had a plastered floor and possibly four columns. The excavators assume that there was once a table or lectern in the middle of this floor that was used for reading the Torah.

Given the problematics of the fragmentary evidence at hand and its unclear interpretations (for example, were there in fact two *bimot*, the evidence for the existence of benches all around the room is incomplete; was there a portico at the southern entrance? Were there indeed interior columns? Could a table have fit into the center of the hall?), it has been suggested that no second-century synagogue ever existed at this site but that the extant remains all come from a considerably later building.[45]

## Bibliography

Anderson, Hugh. "Broadening Horizons: The Rejection at Nazareth Pericope of Luke 4:16-30 in Light of Recent Critical Trends." *Int* 18 (1964): 259–75.

Aune, David E. "Magic in Early Christianity." *ANRW* 23.2.2 (1984): 1507–57.

Aviam, Mordechai. "The Decorated Stone from the Synagogue at Migdal: A Holistic Interpretation and a Glimpse into the Life of Galilean Jews at the Time of Jesus." *NovT* 55 (2013): 205–20.

Avi-Yonah, Michael. "Tiberias in the Roman Period." In Hebrew. In *All the Land of Naphtali*, edited by Hayyim Z. Hirschberg, 154–62. Jerusalem: Israel Exploration Society, 1967.

Binder, Donald D. *Into the Temple Courts: The Place of the Synagogues in the Second Temple Period.* SBLDS 169. Atlanta: Society of Biblical Literature, 1999.

Braun, Willi. "Were the New Testament Herodians Essenes? A Critique of an Hypothesis." *RevQ* 14 (1989): 75–88.

Brawley, Robert L. *Luke-Acts and the Jews: Conflict, Apology, and Reconciliation.* SBLMS 33. Atlanta: Scholars Press, 1987.

Bruce, Frederic F. *The Acts of the Apostles.* Reprint. Grand Rapids: Eerdmans, 1970.

---

44. Ibid., 68.

45. Magness, "Review Article." See my review of Eric M. Meyers and Carol L. Meyers, *Excavations at Ancient Nabratein: Synagogue and Environs* (Winona Lake, Ind.: Eisenbrauns, 2009) in *Journal of Roman Archaeology* 25 (2012): 905-8.

Catto, Stephen K. *Reconstructing the First-Century Synagogue: A Critical Analysis of Current Research.* Library of New Testament Studies 363. London: T&T Clark, 2007.

Chilton, Bruce D. *God in Strength: Jesus' Announcement of the Kingdom.*1976. Reprint, Biblical Seminar 8. Sheffield: JSOT Press, 1987.

Claussen, Carsten. *Versammlung, Gemeinde, Synagoge: Das hellenistisch-jüdische Umfeld der frühchristlichen Gemeinden.* SUNT 27. Göttingen: Vandenhoeck & Ruprecht, 2002.

Cohen, Shaye J. D. *Josephus in Galilee and Rome: His Vita and Development as a Historian.* Columbia Studies in the Classical Tradition 8. Leiden: Brill, 1979.

Combrink, Hans J. B. "Structure and Significance of Luke 4:16-30." *Neot* 7 (1973): 27–42.

Conzelmann, Hans. *The Theology of St. Luke.* Philadelphia: Fortress Press, 1961.

Cook, Michael J. *Mark's Treatment of the Jewish Leaders.* NovTSup 51. Leiden: Brill, 1978.

Corbo, Virgilio C. "La città romana di Magdala." In *Studia Hierosolymitana in onore del P. Bellarmino Bagatti*, vol. 1, *Studi archeologici*, edited by Emmanuele Testa, Ignazio Mancini, and Michele Piccirillo, 355–78. SBF Collectio maior 22. Jerusalem: Franciscan Printing Press, 1976.

———. "Resti della sinagoga del primo secolo a Cafarnao." *Studia Hierosolymitana* 3 (1982): 313–57.

Crossan, John Dominic. *The Historical Jesus: The Life of a Mediterranean Jewish Peasant.* New York: HarperCollins, 1992.

Dark, Ken. "Early Roman-Period Nazareth and the Sisters of Nazareth Convent." *Antiquaries Journal* 92 (2012): 37–64.

Edwards, Douglas R. "Khirbet Qana: From Jewish Village to Christian Pilgrim Site." In *The Roman and Byzantine Near East: Some Recent Archaeological Research*, vol. 3, *Late-Antique Petra, Nile Festival Building at Sepphoris, Deir Qal'a Monastery, Khirbet Qana Village and Pilgrim Site, 'Ain-'Arrub Hiding Complex and Other Studies*, edited by J. H. Humphrey, 101–32. Journal of Roman Archaeology Supplementary Series 49. Ann Arbor, Mich.: Journal of Roman Archaeology, 2002.

———. "Socio-Economic and Cultural Ethos of the Lower Galilee in the First Century: Implications for the Nascent Jesus Movement." In *The Galilee in Late Antiquity*, edited by Lee I. Levine, 53–73. New York and Jerusalem: Jewish Theological Seminary of America, 1992.

Foerster, Gideon. "The Synagogues at Masada and Herodium." In *Ancient Synagogues Revealed*, edited by Lee I. Levine, 24–29. Jerusalem: Israel Exploration Society, 1981.

Freyne, Seán. *Galilee, Jesus, and the Gospels: Literary Approaches and Historical Investigations.* Philadelphia: Fortress Press; Dublin: Gill and MacMillan, 1988.

———. "Urban–Rural Relations in First-Century Galilee: Some Suggestions from the Literary Sources." In *The Galilee in Late Antiquity*, edited by Lee I. Levine, 75–91. New York: Jewish Theological Seminary of America, 1992.

Groh, Dennis E. "The Stratigraphic Chronology of the Galilean Synagogue from the Early Roman Period through the Early Byzantine Period (ca. 420 C.E.)." In *Ancient Synagogues:*

*Historical Analysis and Archaeological Discovery*, edited by Dan Urman and Paul V. M. Flesher, 1:51–69. 2 vols. StPB 47. Leiden: Brill, 1995.

Gutman, Shmaryahu. "Gamala." *NEAEHL* 2:459–63.

Hengel, Martin. "Proseuche und Synagoge: Jüdische Gemeinde, Gotteshaus und Gottesdienst in der Diaspora und in Palästina." In *The Synagogue: Studies in Origins, Archaeology, and Architecture*, edited by Joseph Gutmann, 157–84. Library of Biblical Studies. New York: KTAV, 1975.

Horsley, Richard A. *Galilee: History, Politics, People*. Valley Forge, Pa.: Trinity Press International, 1995.

Ilan, Zvi. *Ancient Synagogues in Israel*. In Hebrew. Tel Aviv: Ministry of Defense, 1991.

Israel Antiquities Authority. http://www.antiquities.org.il/article_Item_eng.asp?module_id=& sec_id=25&subj_id=240&id=1601—cited July 20, 2014.

Iwe, John Chijioke. *Jesus in the Synagogue of Capernaum: The Pericope and Its Programmatic Character for the Gospel of Mark. An Exegetico-Theological Study of Mk 1:21-28*. Tesi Gregoriana, Serie Teologia 57. Rome: Pontificia Università Gregoriana, 1999.

Kasher, Aryeh. "The Founding of Tiberias and Her Functioning as the Capital of the Galilee." In Hebrew. In *Tiberias: From Her Founding until the Muslim Conquest*, edited by Yizhar Hirschfeld, 3–11. Jerusalem: Yad Izhak Ben-Zvi, 1988.

Kee, Howard Clark. *Miracle in the Early Christian World: A Study in Sociohistorical Method*. New Haven: Yale University Press, 1983.

———. "The Transformation of the Synagogue after 70 c.e.: Its Import for Early Christianity." *NTS* 36 (1990): 1–24.

Kraabel, A. Thomas. "The Diaspora Synagogue: Archaeological and Epigraphic Evidence since Sukenik." *ANRW* 19.1.2 (1979): 477–510.

Levine, Lee I. *The Ancient Synagogue: The First Thousand Years*. 2nd ed. New Haven: Yale University Press, 2005.

———. Review of Eric M. Meyers and Carol L. Meyers, *Excavations at Ancient Nabratein: Synagogue and Environs. Journal of Roman Archaeology* 25 (2012): 905–8.

———. *Visual Judaism in Late Antiquity: Historical Contexts of Jewish Art*. New Haven: Yale University Press, 2012.

MacMullen, Ramsay. *Roman Social Relations, 50 b.c. to a.d. 284*. New Haven: Yale University Press, 1974.

Magness, Jodi. "Review Article: The Ancient Synagogue at Nabratein," *BASOR* 358 (2010): 61–68.

———. "The Question of the Synagogue: The Problem of Typology." In *Judaism in Late Antiquity*, part 3, *Where We Stand: Issues and Debates in Ancient Judaism*, vol. 4, *The Special Problem of the Synagogue*, edited by Alan J. Avery-Peck and Jacob Neusner, 1–48. Handbook of Oriental Studies. Leiden: Brill, 2001.

Malbon, Elizabeth Struthers. "Jewish Leaders in the Gospel of Mark: A Literary Study of Marcan Characterization." *JBL* 108 (1989): 259–81.

Ma'oz, Zvi U. "The Architecture of Gamla and Her Buildings." In Hebrew. In *Z. Vilnay Jubilee Volume*, edited by Eli Schiller, 2:147–54. Jerusalem: Ariel, 1987.

————. "Four Notes on the Excavations at Gamala." *Tel Aviv* 39 (2012): 230–37.

Martin, Ralph P. "The Pericope of the Healing of the 'Centurion's' Servant/Son (Matt 8:5-13 par. Luke 7:1-10): Some Exegetical Notes." In *Unity and Diversity in New Testament Theology: Essays in Honor of George E. Ladd*, edited by Robert A. Guelich, 14–22. Grand Rapids: Eerdmans, 1978.

McCollough, Tom. "Final Report on the Archaeological Excavations at Khirbet Qana: Field II, the Synagogue." *Albright News* 18 (November 2013): 13.

Meyers, Eric M., and Carol L. Meyers. "Response to Jodi Magness's Review of the Final Publication of Nabratein." *BASOR* 359 (2010): 67–76.

Netzer, Ehud. "Did the Water Installation in Magdala Serve as a Synagogue?" In Hebrew. In *Synagogues in Antiquity*, edited by Aryeh Kasher et al., 165–72. Jerusalem: Yad Izhak Ben-Zvi, 1987.

Rhoads, David M., and Donald Michie. *Mark as Story: An Introduction to the Narrative of a Gospel*. Philadelphia: Fortress Press, 1982.

Richardson, Peter. *Building Jewish in the Roman East*. Waco, Tex.: Baylor University Press, 2004.

Ringe, Sharon H. *Jesus, Liberation, and the Biblical Jubilee: Images for Ethics and Christology*. Overtures to Biblical Theology 19. Philadelphia: Fortress Press, 1985.

Rocca, Samuel. "The Purposes and Functions of the Synagogue in Late Second Temple Period Judaea: Evidence from Josephus and Archaeological Investigation." In *Flavius Josephus: Interpretation and History*, edited by Jack Pastor, Pnina Stern, and Menahem Mor, 295–313. JSJSup 146. Leiden: Brill, 2011.

Runesson, Anders, Donald D. Binder, and Birger Olsson. *The Ancient Synagogue from Its Origins to 200 C.E.: A Source Book*. Ancient Judaism and Early Christianity 72. Leiden: Brill, 2008.

Saldarini, Anthony J. *Pharisees, Scribes, and Sadducees in Palestinian Society: A Sociological Approach*. Wilmington, Del.: Michael Glazier, 1988. Reprint, with a foreword by James C. VanderKam. Grand Rapids: Eerdmans, 2001.

Sanders, Edward P. *Jesus and Judaism*. Philadelphia: Fortress Press, 1985.

Sanders, James A. "From Isaiah 61 to Luke 4." In *Christianity, Judaism, and Other Greco-Roman Cults: Studies for Morton Smith at Sixty*, edited by Jacob Neusner, 1:75–106. 4 vols. SJLA 12. Leiden: Brill, 1975.

Schürer, Emil. *The History of the Jewish People in the Age of Jesus Christ (175 B.C.–A.D. 135)*. Revised and edited by Geza Vermes, Fergus Millar, Matthew Black, and Martin Goodman. 3 vols. in 4 parts. Edinburgh: T&T Clark, 1973–87.

Schürmann, Heinz. *Das Lukasevangelium*. Herders theologischer Kommentar zum Neuen Testament 3. Freiburg: Herder, 1969.

Schwartz, Daniel R. *Agrippa I: The Last King of Judaea.* TSAJ 23. Tübingen: Mohr Siebeck, 1990.

——. *Studies in the Jewish Background of Christianity.* WUNT 60. Tübingen: Mohr Siebeck, 1992.

Schwartzman, Sylvan D. "How Well Did the Synoptic Evangelists Know the Synagogue?" *HUCA* 24 (1952–53): 115–32.

Seager, Andrew R. "The Building History of the Sardis Synagogue." *AJA* 76 (1972): 425–35.

Seager, Andrew R., and A. Thomas Kraabel. "The Synagogue and the Jewish Community." In *Sardis from Prehistoric to Roman Times: Results of the Archaeological Exploration of Sardis, 1958–1975,* edited by George M. A. Hanfmann, 168–90. Cambridge, Mass.: Harvard University Press, 1983.

Siker, Jeffrey S. "'First to the Gentiles': A Literary Analysis of Luke 4:16-30." *JBL* 111 (1992): 73–90.

Smith, Morton. *Jesus the Magician.* New York: Harper & Row, 1978.

Strange, James F., and Hershel Shanks. "Synagogue Where Jesus Preached Found at Capernaum." *BAR* 9, no. 6 (1983): 25–31.

Syon, Danny, and Zvi Yavor. "Gamla 1997–2000." *'Atiqot* 50 (2005): 37–71.

Talbert, Charles H. *Literary Patterns, Theological Themes, and the Genre of Luke-Acts.* SBLMS 20. Missoula, Mont.: Scholars Press, 1974.

Tsafrir, Yoram. "The Synagogues of Capernaum and Meroth and the Dating of the Galilean Synagogue." In *The Roman and Byzantine Near East: Some Recent Archaeological Research,* vol. 1, edited by J. H. Humphrey, 151–61. Journal of Roman Archaeology Supplementary Series 14. Ann Arbor, Mich.: Journal of Roman Archaeology, 1995.

Wilken, Robert L. *John Chrysostom and the Jews: Rhetoric and Reality in the Late Fourth Century.* Transformation of the Classical Heritage 4. Berkeley: University of California Press, 1983.

Yavor, Zvi, and Danny Syon. *Gamla: The Shmarya Gutmann Excavations, 1976–1989,* vol. 2, *The Architecture and Stratigraphy of the Eastern and Western Quarters.* IAA Reports 44. Jerusalem: Israel Antiquities Authority, 2010.

# 6

# NOTABLE GALILEAN PERSONS

*Thomas Scott Caulley*

The student of the New Testament is accustomed to reading about strong personalities coming from Galilee. The historical sources reveal to us other heroes who originated from this land. Below is a list of thirteen of the most notable ones.

### Hezekiah (Ezekias) the Bandit (d. 46 BCE)

Hezekiah was the leader of a gang of "bandits" (guerrillas?) fighting in Galilee, which raided gentile towns along the Syrian border.[1] Hezekiah has been characterized as a "freedom fighter" against foreign rule[2] and as a bandit taking advantage of the aftermath of civil war and political-economic strife.[3] Richard A. Horsley suggests that the members of Hezekiah's band were "probably victims of, and fugitives from, the shifting political and economic situation."[4] Josephus reported that, as part of Antipater's campaign to bolster support for Hyrcanus and squelch any uprisings, he appointed his eldest son Phasael as governor of Jerusalem, and his next son, Herod, (the Great) he entrusted with Galilee "though a mere lad" (*J. W.* 1.203; Thackeray, LCL).[5] In Galilee, Herod encountered Hezekiah, a brigand chief (*archilēstēs*) at the head of a large horde. Hezekiah was ravaging the district on the Syrian frontier, where Herod caught him and put him and many of the brigands to death (*J. W.* 1.201–5; *Ant.* 14.158–59).

---

1. A. Schalit, "Hezekiah," *EncJud* 8:455.

2. Ibid., 455.

3. Richard A. Horsley and John S. Hanson, *Bandits, Prophets, and Messiahs: Popular Movements at the Time of Jesus* (Minneapolis: Winston, 1985), 63.

4. Ibid.

5. Elsewhere Josephus claims that Herod was only fifteen years old at the time (*Ant.* 14.159).

According to Abraham Schalit, who apparently equates Judas the son of Hezekiah with "Judas the Galilean," Josephus does not give a true picture of Hezekiah's personality—he was of distinguished ancestry; his family was composed of scholars, which may be inferred from the fact that his son Judas was called *sophistēs* (*J.W.* 2.118).[6]

### Judas son of Hezekiah (attacked 4 BCE; same as Judas the Galilean?)

After the death of Herod the Great, Judas the son of Hezekiah "captured the royal arsenal at Sepphoris, armed his followers, and attacked other aspirants to power."[7] According to Josephus, "at Sepphoris in Galilee Judas, son of Ezechias [that is, Hezekiah], the brigand-chief who in former days infested the country and was subdued by King Herod, raised a considerable body of followers, broke open the royal arsenals, and, having armed his companions, attacked the other aspirants to power" (*J.W.* 2.56). "He became an object of terror to all men by plundering those he came across in his desire for great possessions and his ambition for royal rank (*Ant.* 17.271–72; Thackeray, LCL). Judas may have been linked to the royal Maccabean family, which was suppressed by Herod the Great.[8] While Emilio Gabba speculates that Judas's aspiration to kingship may also clarify the reasons that lay behind his father's struggle,[9] and F. J. Foakes-Jackson and Kirsopp Lake objected to Emil Schürer's identification of this Judas with Judas the Galilean because the Judas of 6 CE was "neither a brigand nor an aspirant to a throne,"[10] one should notice that "aspiring to power/sovereignty" is an accusation made repeatedly by Josephus in reference to individuals who resisted the Roman-backed leadership in the region. Although Jacob Neusner also denies that the Judas son of Hezekiah who raided the armory in Sepphoris in 6 CE is connected to Judas the Galilean,[11] several other scholars accept that identification.[12]

---

6. Schalit, "Hezekiah," 455; Schalit, "Judah the Galilean," *EncJud* 10:354–55; but cf. *Dictionary of Judaism in the Biblical Period* (ed. Jacob Neusner and William Scott Green; Peabody, Mass.: Hendrickson, 1996), 353.

7. Neusner and Green, *Dictionary of Judaism,* 352.

8. Harold W. Hoehner, *Herod Antipas* (SNTSMS 17; Cambridge: Cambridge University Press, 1972), 83 n. 5; cf. William R. Farmer, "Jesus, Simon, and Athronges," *NTS* 4 (1958): 150–52.

9. Emilio Gabba, "The Social, Political, and Economic History of Palestine 63 B.C.E.–C.E. 70," in *The Cambridge History of Judaism*, vol. 3, *Early Roman Period* (ed. William Horbury, W. D. Davies, and John Sturdy; Cambridge: Cambridge University Press, 1999), 129.

10. J. Spencer Kennard, "Judas of Galilee and His Clan," *JQR* n.s. 36 (1946): 281–86; F. J. Foakes-Jackson and Kirsopp Lake, *The Acts of the Apostles* (5 vols.; Beginnings of Christianity 1; London: Macmillan, 1920–33; repr., Grand Rapids: Baker, 1979), 1:424; Emil Schürer, *A History of the Jewish People in the Time of Jesus Christ* (5 vols.; New York: Scribner, 1891), 1.2:80.

11. Neusner and Green, *Dictionary of Judaism,* 353; cf. Kennard, "Judas of Galilee and His Clan," 281.

12. Seán Freyne, *Galilee, Jesus, and the Gospels: Literary Approaches and Historical Investigations* (Philadelphia: Fortress Press, 1988), 193–94, 196–97; Martin Hengel, *The Zealots: Investigations into the Jewish Freedom*

### Judas the Galilean/of Gamala. (d. 6 CE)

During the tenure of Coponius (procurator of Judea following Archelaus), a Galilean named Judas "incited his countrymen to revolt, upbraiding them as cowards for consenting to pay tribute to the Romans and tolerating mortal masters, after having God for their lord" (*J. W.* 2.118; Thackeray, LCL). The incitement was in direct response to the census under Quirinius (Cyrenius), governor of Syria. Judas's incitement contained two main arguments, namely, (1) that the census would lead to slavery and that the people should fight for their freedom; and (2) God would help them only if they actively sought to liberate themselves and not lose heart (*Ant.* 18.4–5).[13] Elsewhere Josephus refers to this same man as "a certain Judas, a Gaulanite from the city named Gamala, who had enlisted the aid of Saddok, a Pharisee, [and] threw himself into the cause of rebellion" (*Ant.* 18.4; Feldman, LCL). The only mention of Judas the Galilean outside Josephus is the reference attributed to Gamaliel in Acts 5:37.

Judas the Galilean founded a "Fourth Philosophy" (so Josephus), which, according to Martin Hengel, had not only definite beliefs but also clear organization and a single leadership.[14] Its distinctive character was its break with the Jewish tradition of accommodation to foreign rulers by confessing the "sole rule of God," an eschatological "kingdom of God" theology, which not only allowed but required adherents to enter into a life-and-death struggle with Rome.[15] Hengel ties this directly to Palestinian Judaism's encounter with the cult of the emperor, introduced by Herod the Great.[16] Josephus's seemingly contradictory statements about Judas and his group—saying, on the one hand, that Judas was a "sophist who founded a sect of his own, having nothing in common with the others" (*J. W.* 2.118), but, on the other hand, that all its teachings were in accordance with the Pharisees, except for the group's "love of freedom . . . in that it recognizes only God as ruler and lord" (*Ant.* 18.23–25)—can be explained by the context of the two statements (the first in relation to Zaddok, who was a Pharisee). Josephus's Fourth Philosophy remains without a name, which Hengel argues is out of respect for the "Zealots" of old, originally an honorific title.[17] This group, he says, came to be associated later with the *Sicarii*, who famously made their last stand at Masada during the war in the late 60s and early 70s.

*Movement in the Period from Herod I until 70 A.D.* (trans. David Smith; Edinburgh: T&T Clark, 1989), 76; Josephus, *Ant.* 18.4 (Feldman, LCL); cf. Kennard, "Judas of Galilee and His Clan," 281–86.

13. Hengel, *Zealots*, 76; cf. Solomon Zeitlin, "The Sicarii and Masada," *JQR*, n.s., 57 (1967): 251–70.

14. Hengel, *Zealots*, 86.

15. Ibid., *Zealots*, 91.

16. Ibid., 99, 101.

17. Ibid., 88–89. For a critique of Hengel, see Richard A. Horsley, "Menahem in Jerusalem: A Brief Messianic Episode among the Sicarii—Not 'Zealot Messianism,'" *NovT* 27 (1985): 334–48.

### Ḥoni (Onias) the Circle-Drawer (first century BCE)

The best known of the ancient Hasidim charismatics was a sage called Ḥoni the Circle-Drawer by the rabbis, and Onias the Righteous by Josephus.[18] An important characteristic of these Hasidim was that their prayer was believed to be all-powerful, capable of performing miracles, that is, exerting their will on natural phenomena. During a drought, Ḥoni was said to draw a circle, stand inside it, and refuse to move until it rained the exact quantity needed for the crops (see *Ant.* 14.22–24). To those who had begged him to pray for rain, Ḥoni answered, "go out and bring in the Passover ovens (made of dried clay) that they not be softened" (*m. Ta'an.* 3:8).[19]

The name "Circle-Drawer" is usually explained from this story, although some think it is a place-name or refers to Ḥoni's calling to fix roofs—or ovens—with a "roller" (*megillah*).[20] The Babylonian Talmud connects the name with Habakkuk (Hab 2:1). The Talmud records a legend that Ḥoni slept for seventy years, after which he was no longer recognized by his descendants. At this he was grieved, prayed to die, and died (*b. Ta'an* 23a).

Josephus relates that when Aristobulus II was besieged by Hyrcanus II in Jerusalem (ca. 66 BCE), Hyrcanus's men seized Ḥoni (called Onias by Josephus) and told him to curse Aristobulus, just as by his prayers he had ended the drought. But instead Ḥoni prayed to the Lord not to grant their demand, since these men were his people and those whom they besieged were his priests. Therefore, Hyrcanus's men stoned Onias/Ḥoni to death (*Ant.* 14.22–24).

### Ḥanina ben Dosa (first century CE)

Ḥanina ben Dosa was a first-century tanna who lived in Arav, Lower Galilee, and was a disciple and colleague of Yoḥanan ben Zakkai. Ḥanina was renowned for his piety: once he was praying when a scorpion bit him, but he did not interrupt his prayer. When the scorpion died, he said, "Woe to the man bitten by a scorpion; but woe to the scorpion that bites ben Dosa" (*t. Ber.* 3:20;[21] cf. *b. Ber.* 33a). The sages applied to Ḥanina ben Dosa the phrase "men of truth" from Exodus 18:21.[22] They held him up as a completely righteous man (*b. Ber.* 61b), and described him as "one for whose sake God shows favor to an entire generation"

---

18. See Geza Vermes, *Jesus the Jew: A Historian's Reading of the Gospels* (Philadelphia: Fortress Press, 1973), 69–72.

19. Neusner and Green, *Dictionary of Judaism,* 300.

20. Cecil Roth and Geoffrey Wigoder, "Honi Ha Me'aggel," *EncJud* 8:964–65.

21. Ze'ev Kaplan, "Ḥanina ben Dosa," *EncJud* 7:1265. See Jacob Neusner, *The Tosefta: Translated from the Hebrew with a New Introducton* (2 vols; Peabody, Mass.: Hendrickson, 2002), 1:20; Neusner reads "poisonous lizard" instead of "scorpion."

22. Kaplan, "Ḥanina ben Dosa," 1265.

(*b. Ḥag.* 14a).[23] Ḥanina ben Dosa used to pray over the sick and say, "This one will live and this one will die." When asked how he knew, he responded, "If my prayer is fluent in my mouth I know that he is accepted; and if it is not I know that he is rejected" (*m. Ber.* 5:5). It is said, "When Ḥanina b. Dosa died, men of deeds ceased and piety came to an end" (*m. Soṭah* 9:15). His wife was said to resemble her husband in piety (*b. B. Bat.* 74b).

According to *b. Taʿan.* 24b–25a, Ḥanina ben Dosa was on the road with a bundle of wood when it began to rain. He prayed, "Sovereign of the Universe, the whole world is happy but Ḥanina is suffering. The rain stopped. When he reached home he prayed, Sovereign of the Universe, Ḥanina is happy but the whole world is suffering. It rained again." It is reported that the high priest had prayed for a "hot year" (so that God's people would not depend for livelihood on each other), but Ḥanina's prayer availed against the high priest's prayer.

Ḥanina ben Dosa was known for his austerity. According to the Talmud, on the eve of every Sabbath the wife of R. Ḥanina was accustomed to make fire in her oven and to throw twigs into the stove (*b. Taʿan.* 25a) to prevent the disgrace of being exposed in her poverty. She had, however, one bad neighbor, who said, "I know that they have nothing to cook for the Sabbath, why does she make a fire in her oven? I shall go and see." She straightway knocked at the door. Ḥanina's wife, ashamed, retired to her bedroom. Suddenly a miracle occurred, for the oven became filled with bread, and the kneading basin with dough. In another story, Ḥanina's wife asked him to pray for something since she was weary of poverty: A hand came forth and gave him a leg from a golden table. Then she dreamed that in heaven everyone would eat from a golden table with three legs, except them—their table only had two legs (they had already received the third leg in this life). So she told her husband to pray that God take back the table leg (*b. Taʿan.* 24b–25a).

## Antipas (ruled 4 BCE–39 CE)

Antipas, tetrarch of Galilee and Perea, was the youngest son of Herod the Great, "whom Malthrace, a Samaritan, had borne to him" (ca. 5 BCE).[24] At one point Herod had willed his entire kingdom to Antipas, passing over his older sons Archelaus and Philip because of his hatred for them (*J.W.* 1.646; *Ant.* 17.146). "Only four or five days before his death, Herod ordered (his son) Antipater's (execution), and once again changed his mind about his succession," dividing his realm among the three sons, Archelaus, Philip, and Antipas.[25] Antipas contested the will (*J.W.* 2.20) and Archelaus's accession was strongly resisted by his subjects and others. In the end, Caesar settled the matter, making Archelaus ethnarch over roughly half

---

23. Ibid.
24. Hoehner, *Herod Antipas*, 10.
25. Ibid., 10-11.

of Herod's realm, and Philip and Antipas were each appointed tetrarch of their respective territories.[26] Antipas was to govern Galilee and Perea. Antipas's title, tetrarch, is attested also in inscriptions on Cos and Delos.[27]

Antipas is mentioned in the Gospels as the king who had John the Baptist arrested and executed (Matt. 14:3-12//Mark 6:17-29; Josephus, *Ant.* 18.116–19) and subsequently interrogated Jesus during his trial in Jerusalem (Luke 23:6-12).[28] When his brother Archelaus was deposed in 6 CE, Antipas received the right to use the appellation "Herod," which had become a dynastic title after the death of Herod the Great.[29]

As was customary for Jewish boys, Antipas was first educated at home. If Adolf Deissmann is correct, this may also be inferred from the reference to Antipas's *syntrophos* (σύντροφος) Manaen, his "companion in education."[30] Like his brothers, Antipas completed his education in Rome (Josephus, *Ant.* 17.20).

Antipas is remembered for building three cities early in his career: Sepphoris and Tiberius in Galilee, and Livias in Perea, of which little is known.[31] In particular, he rebuilt Sepphoris[32] and "fortified it to be the ornament of all Galilee, and called it *Autocratoris*" (Josephus, *Ant.* 18.27), a name apparently in honor of Augustus. Antipas used Sepphoris as his residence until he built Tiberius.[33]

Antipas also founded Tiberias, named for the emperor during whose reign it was built. Antipas built Tiberias as a new city on the western slope of the Sea of Galilee,[34] in a central location within his two territories.[35] Tiberias had the status of a *polis*, the first city in Jewish history founded within that municipal framework.[36]

---

26. Nicolaus of Damascus, *De vita sua* 3, in Menahem Stern, *Greek and Latin Authors on the Jews and Judaism*, vol. 1, *From Herodotus to Plutarch* (Fontes ad res Judaicas spectantes; Jerusalem: Israel Academy of Sciences and Humanities, 1974), 254–55; 260; Josephus, *Ant.* 17.224; *J. W.* 2.20–22.

27. David C. Braund, "Herod Antipas," *ABD* 3:160.

28. Frank E. Wheeler, "Antipas," *ABD* 1:272.

29. See Josephus, *J. W.* 2.167; Hoehner, *Herod Antipas,* 105.

30. See Acts 13:1; Adolf Deissmann, *Bible Studies: Contributions Chiefly from Papyri and Inscriptions to the History of the Language, the Literature, and the Religion of Hellenistic Judaism and Primitive Christianity* (Edinburgh: T&T Clark, 1901; repr., Winona Lake, Ind.: Alpha, 1979), 312.

31. Emil Schürer, *The History of the Jewish People in the Age of Jesus Christ, 175 B.C.–A.D. 135* (rev. and ed. Geza Vermes, Fergus Millar, Matthew Black, and Martin Goodman; 3 vols. in 4 parts; Edinburgh: T&T Clark, 1973–87), 1:171–83.

32. During Herod the Great's time Sepphoris was the location of a military post where arms and provisions were stored. Judas son of Hezekiah seized Sepphoris and raided the arsenal (Josephus, *J. W.* 2.56), turning Sepphoris into the main seat of the rebellion (*Ant.* 17.271). In response, the Roman leader Varus burned the town and made slaves of its inhabitants (*Ant.* 17.289; *J. W.* 2.68).

33. Hoehner, *Herod Antipas,* 85.

34. "Tiberias with its salubrious hot springs on the west (of Gennesara)" is mentioned by Pliny the Elder, *Nat.* 5.71; see Stern, *Greek and Latin Authors,* 1:471.

35. Hoehner, *Herod Antipas,* 92. Antipas had the city built over the cemetery (Josephus, *Ant.* 19.36–38).

36. Stern, *Greek and Latin Authors,* 2:570; Hoehner, *Herod Antipas,* 91.

Antipas married the daughter of Aretas, king of neighboring Nabatea. But Antipas's notorious divorce and marriage to his niece, Herodias, attracted the criticism of traditionalists (for example, John the Baptist [Matt. 14:4]) and enraged Aretas. Some Jews saw Antipas's downfall as divine judgment for his execution of John the Baptist (Josephus, *Ant.* 18.116–20).[37]

The new emperor, Gaius Caligula, appointed Antipas's nephew Agrippa as "king," which encouraged Antipas to seek that title for himself. Antipas traveled to Rome but was at the same time denounced to the emperor by envoys from Agrippa, who accused Antipas of treason. Gaius ruled against Antipas, deposed him, and annexed his territory to Agrippa's kingdom. Antipas was exiled to the west (perhaps Lyons or northern Spain). Although Gaius offered to pardon Herodias because she was Agrippa's sister, she chose instead to follow her husband into exile (*Ant.* 18.240–55).

## Agrippa I (11 BCE–44 CE)

Marcus Julius Agrippa[38] was born in 11/10 BCE, son of Berenice (daughter of Salome [Herod the Great's sister] and Costobarus)[39] and Aristobulus (son of Herod the Great and Mariamme I). His father and his uncle were both executed by Herod the Great, as was his paternal grandmother, Mariamme, and his maternal grandfather, Costobus. Agrippa became Herod's only true heir.[40]

After Agrippa's father's death, and before that of Herod the Great, Berenice took Agrippa and moved to Rome, where he was to stay another thirty years.[41] Perhaps Berenice was nervous about Herod the Great's plans for her son, and in any case Augustus preferred future vassal rulers to be educated in Rome.[42] Agrippa's mother was a close friend of Antonia, widow of Drusus the elder (brother of Tiberius). Agrippa was brought up with their son Claudius (the future emperor), and with the son of Tiberius who also was named Drusus, and with the members of the imperial family. Josephus reports that Agrippa "grew up together" (*homotrophias*, ὁμοτροφίας) with Claudius's circle (*Ant.* 18.165), a circle that included all the future legates of Syria during the years 32–45 CE.[43]

After his mother's death, Agrippa spent so freely that he was reduced to poverty.[44] With changes in political circumstances in Rome, Agrippa was forced to retire quietly to Malatha,

---

37. Braund, "Herod Antipas," 3.160.

38. Daniel R. Schwartz, *Agrippa I: The Last King of Judaea* (TSAJ 23; Tübingen: Mohr Siebeck, 1990), 39; the praenomen is nowhere given, but this is Agrippa II's name, which implies that it was also that of his father.

39. Hoehner, *Herod Antipas*, 257–258.

40. Schwartz, *Agrippa I*, 39.

41. Ibid., 40.

42. David C. Braund, *Rome and the Friendly King: The Character of the Client Kingship* (London: Croom Helm; New York: St. Martin's, 1984), 9–21.

43. Schwartz, *Agrippa I*, 42; John Nicols, *Vespasian and the Partes Flavianae* (Historia. Einzelschriften 28; Wiesbaden: Steiner, 1978), 15–19.

44. Schwartz, *Agrippa I*, 45.

a fortress in Idumea, leaving angry creditors behind him in Rome (Josephus, *Ant.* 18.143–47, 165). Through Herodias's influence with Antipas, Agrippa was given a home, a guaranteed income, and a small civil service position as inspector of markets (*agoranomos*, ἀγορανόμος) in Antipas's new capital, Tiberias (*Ant.* 18.149; cf. 14.261).[45] Antipas never let Agrippa forget his indebtedness to him, and hard feelings characterized their subsequent relationship.

After the death of Agrippa's uncle, Philip the tetrach (d. 34 CE), Agrippa tried to convince Tiberius that Antipas had colluded with enemies of Rome and was guilty of treason. Tiberius sided with Antipas, however, and Agrippa further ran afoul of Tiberius and was thrown in prison.[46] To his credit, Agrippa had been able to curry favor with Gaius (also called Caligula), and when Tiberius died six months later, Gaius had Agrippa released from prison and gave him a gold chain equal in weight to the iron chain he had worn in prison. Gaius conferred on Agrippa the territory formerly belonging to Philip, plus the region that had been the tetrarchy of Lysanias. Agrippa was given the title "king" (Josephus, *Ant.* 18.237), and the senate conferred on him the rank of praetor (Philo, *Flacc.* 40), and subsequently consular rank (Dio 60.8.2). Agrippa was allowed to return to Palestine in the second year of Gaius's reign (38–39 CE), probably arriving there in late summer of 38 CE.

Agrippa's favor with Gaius sparked jealousy from Antipas and especially from Herodias, and when Antipas set off for Rome to seek from Gaius the title "king," as Agrippa had done (Josephus, *Ant.* 18.240–46), Agrippa dispatched an emissary to Rome to accuse Antipas.[47] The accusation of collusion was raised and Antipas could not deny it. Gaius exiled Antipas to Gaul (39 CE) and gave his tetrachy and property, as well as that belonging to Herodias, to Agrippa (*Ant.* 18.253–55).[48]

When Gaius attempted to erect his statue in the temple in Jerusalem (ca. 40 CE), Agrippa went to Rome to dissuade him (cf. Tacitus, *Historiae* 5.9.1). Philo's *Embassy to Gaius* has Agrippa write a long plea to Gaius on behalf of Jerusalem and against his plan (*Embassy* 276–329), which Daniel R. Schwartz judges to be a literary composition by Philo himself.[49] Gaius was angry with the Jews for refusing to acknowledge his claim to divinity (Josephus, *Ant.* 18.257–60).[50] Agrippa was reported to be initially successful in persuading Gaius to back down, but both Josephus and Philo say that Gaius later changed his mind. Gaius's assassination in January 41 CE ended the matter.[51]

According to Cassius Dio (60.8.2), "Claudius enlarged the kingdom of Agrippa of Palestine, who had cooperated with him in seeking rule, since he had then happened to be

45. See note in Feldman, LCL; Hoehner, *Herod Antipas*, 257–58.
46. Josephus, *Ant.* 18.161–236; *J.W.* 2.178–80; Cassius Dio 59.8.2; Stern, *Greek and Latin Authors*, 2:366; Hoehner, *Herod Antipas*, 260.
47. Josephus (*J.W.* 2.183) says that Agrippa personally went to Rome. See also Hoehner, *Herod Antipas*, 261.
48. Hoehner, *Herod Antipas*, 262.
49. Schwartz, *Agrippa I*, 200–202.
50. Ibid., 80.
51. Ibid., 78–79.

in Rome." Josephus reports that Claudius increased Agrippa's kingdom to include approximately all of Herod the Great's former territories (*J. W.* 2.215–16; *Ant.* 19.274–75). Suetonius (*Claudius* 11) credited Agrippa with only a minor role in Claudius's accession, although Josephus states that Agrippa's role was crucial in that he played the part of peacemaker between Claudius and the Senate (*Ant.* 19.236–45).[52] Whatever his exact role, the limits of Agrippa's influence became apparent in his failure to secure from Claudius certain political rights for the Jews of Alexandria.[53]

Agrippa returned to Palestine, where he remained for the rest of his life. He is remembered for his favorable attitude toward the Sadducees and the priestly class, which is consistent with the report in Acts that he persecuted the Christians and had James the brother of John killed (Acts 12:1-4).[54] He began construction of a wall around Jerusalem, which, had it been completed, would have "rendered ineffectual all the efforts of the Romans in the subsequent siege" (Thackeray, LCL) He died in Caesarea before work was completed (*J. W.* 2.218–19). According to Josephus, Agrippa ruled for six years—three years over the territories of Philip and Antipas, and three over Judea (*J. W.* 2.219); or he ruled (parts of) seven years (*Ant.* 19.351), four years under Gaius and three under Claudius. He died in the fifty-fourth year of his life (*Ant.* 19.351; Acts 12:20-23).

## Agrippa II (b. 27, d. 93? CE)

Marcus Julius Agrippa, also known as Herod Agrippa II, was the son of Agrippa I and Cypros (Josephus, *J. W.* 2.220; *Ant.* 19.354).[55] Like the other Herods, Agrippa II was educated in Rome. Upon his father's death in 44, because of Agrippa's youth, Claudius returned Judea to a procuratorship (*Ant.* 15.11; 19.363; 20.1). In 48 CE, Agrippa received authority over the temple in Jerusalem (oversight of the high priesthood), and beginning in 50 CE he was ruler of Chalcis in southern Lebanon. This appointment was quickly followed by a reshuffling of duties resulting in Agrippa's leadership over Philip's former tetrarchy; in 54 Nero added to his territory the area around the Sea of Galilee (*Ant.* 20.159; *J. W.* 2.252).

According to Acts 25:13—26:32, Agrippa was present when Paul was questioned by Festus. Acts 26:28 places the Roman slur *Christianos* on the lips of Agrippa, recounting his sarcastic response to Paul, "Are you so quickly persuading me to become a Christian?"[56]

Agrippa II had the unfortunate task of ruling Judea during the uprising of 66 CE. Agrippa failed to stop the revolt, and he himself became a target (Josephus, *J. W.* 2.426). Although

---

52. Schwartz (*Agrippa I*, 99–106) considers the latter a romanticized account and not to be taken too seriously.

53. Schwartz, *Agrippa I*, 91, 99–106.

54. Ibid., 117–19.

55. Schürer, *History of the Jewish People*, rev. ed., 1:471–83.

56. NRSV; see Thomas Scott Caulley, "The Title *Christianos* and Roman Imperial Cult," *RQ* 53 (2011): 196.

Agrippa's concern and advocacy for the Jews are not in doubt,[57] he was still beholden to the Romans, which put considerable military resources at his disposal (*J. W.* 2.500–503, 523–25). To the revolutionaries, Josephus has Agrippa declare, "Fortune has transferred her favors" to Rome (*J. W.*, 2.360; 3.622), and that "without God's aid so vast an empire could never have been built up" (*J. W.* 2.390–91). Agrippa preferred to rule through delegates and spent much of his time outside of the kingdom prior to Vespasian's command.

Upon Vespasian's arrival in Palestine in 67 CE, Agrippa stayed close to him and his son Titus, who had also spent his youth in the court of Claudius.[58] When Vespasian was named emperor, Agrippa stayed with Titus, who was left to deal with the revolt in Palestine.[59] After Rome's victory in Judea, Agrippa was rewarded for his loyalty with additional territory, as well as praetorian rank.

Little else is known about Agrippa. He apparently never married; there were rumors of an incestuous relationship with his sister Bernice, denied by Josephus (*Ant.* 20.145) but accepted by Juvenal (6.158). Agrippa died during the reign of Domitian, in approximately 93 CE.

## Bernice (Berenice) [b. 28 CE; d. after 81 CE]

Julia Bernice was born to Agrippa I and Cypros, one of three daughters and the sister of Agrippa II. Bernice married Marcus Julius Alexander, son of Alexander the Alabarch, and a prominent businessman.[60] "After the death of Marcus . . . , who was her first husband, Agrippa gave her to his own brother Herod (king of Chalcis), after asking Claudius to give him the kingdom of Chalcis" (in the Lebanon Valley). The marriage took place in 43 or 44 CE.[61] Herod of Chalcis died in 48,[62] and Claudius gave the kingdom of Chalcis to Agrippa II (Josephus, *J. W.* 2.221–23). Following the death of her husband, Herod of Chalcis, Bernice lived as a widow with her brother Agrippa II. Josephus refers to her as the "queen" (*J. W.* 2.598; cf. *Life* 49).

Bernice married Polemo of Cilicia, whom—although he underwent circumcision—she soon left and returned to live with her brother (*Ant.* 20.146). According to the New Testament book of Acts she was present when Agrippa II questioned Paul in Caesarea (ca. 60 CE; Acts 25:13, 23; 26:30).

When the Jewish revolt began in 66, Bernice attempted to intercede with the Roman governor but was ignored. At the same time, she and Agrippa II tried to dissuade the revolu-

---

57. Braund, "Agrippa," *ABD* 1:99.

58. Braund, "Agrippa," *ABD* 1:99; Schürer, *History of the Jewish People*, rev. ed., 1:477.

59. Tacitus, *Historiae* 2.1–2; 2.79, 81–88; 5.1–13; Stern, *Greek and Latin Authors*, 2:281.

60. Josephus, *Ant.* 19.276–77; Feldman, LCL, 343 note f.

61. Josephus, *Ant.* 19.277; Feldman, LCL, 343 notes g and h.

62. "The eighth year of the reign of Claudius" (Josephus, *Ant.* 20.104); cf. David C. Braund, "Bernice," *ABD* 1:677–78.

tionaries but to no avail. At one point some of the dissidents threw rocks at Agrippa (Josephus, *J.W.* 2.407), and their residence in Jerusalem was set on fire (*J.W.* 2.426).

Bernice contributed financially to Vespasian's cause during the time of his transition to emperor; in addition, Tacitus comments on "her great youthful beauty" (*Historiae* 2.81.2; Moore, LCL). She began her notorious relationship with Titus during this time, although she and Agrippa did not travel to Rome until 75—perhaps in consideration of the volatile situation in Rome after "the year of the four emperors."[63] While the rumor of incest with her brother Agrippa was a favorite topic of gossip,[64] it was Bernice's relationship with Titus that caused the most consternation among the Roman citizenry.[65]

Of their arrival Cassius Dio wrote:

> Berenice was at the very height of her power and consequently came to Rome along with her brother Agrippa. The latter was given the rank of praetor, while she dwelt in the palace, cohabiting with Titus. She expected to marry him and was already behaving in every respect as if she were his wife; but when he perceived that the Romans were displeased with the situation, he sent her away.[66]

At about the time of his accession, then, Titus sent Bernice away, apparently as part of his campaign to improve his public image.[67] She returned to Rome prior to Titus's death in 81 (Cassius Dio 66.18.1).

### John of Gischala (first century CE)

John of Gischala (Yoḥanan ben Levi) was an important economic figure (Josephus, *Life* 74–75) in Upper Galilee (where the village of Gischala is located, see Map 2) and a leader in the revolt against Rome. His Pharisaic connections brought him into direct conflict with Josephus, who was appointed commander in Galilee, not least because of his Hasmonean background.[68] According to Josephus, John was initially not in favor of revolt (*Life* 43). For his part, John

---

63. See Braund, "Bernice," 678; see also J. A. Crook, "Titus and Bernice," *AJP* 72 (1951): 162–75.

64. In his satire on marriage, Juvenal refers to the relationship of "the barbarian Agrippa to his incestuous sister" (*Satirae* 6.156–58); see Stern, *Greek and Latin Authors*, 2:99–100.

65. See *Epitome de Caesaribus* 10.4.7; Stern, *Greek and Latin Authors*, 2:514.

66. Cassius Dio, *Historia Romana* 64.15.3–5; Stern, *Greek and Latin Authors*, 2:378–79. Crook argues that Titus's relationship to Bernice should be understood in light of the political history of the time, especially in terms of Titus's personal ambitions for leadership after the reign of his father ended. Crook finds a key event in the death (ca. 75) of the "king-maker" Mucianus, whose ambitions clashed with those of Titus (Crook, "Titus and Bernice," 166). For another view of Titus and Mucianus, see P. M. Rogers, "Titus, Bernice, and Mucianus," *Historia* 29 (1980): 86–95.

67. David C. Braund, "Berenice in Rome," *Historia* 33 (1984): 120–23, at 121.

68. Francis Loftus, "The Anti-Roman Revolts of the Jews and the Galileans," *JQR* n.s. 68 (1977): 96; cf. 94.

accused Josephus of disloyalty (based on Josephus's deference to Agrippa, a Roman sympathizer), with the result that Josephus contended that John's demands were heeded because of bribes and the exploitation of John's connections.  As can be gleaned from Josephus's hostile tone, John of Gischala was a daring and skillful leader, yet intolerant of taking orders, ambiguous, and militarily inept—much like Josephus.[69] John failed in his efforts to prepare the region for war, and when Galilee fell to the Romans,[70] John escaped to Jerusalem (Josephus, *J. W.* 4.100–102; cf. Tacitus, *Historiae* 5.2–13).[71]

In Jerusalem, John joined the Jewish resistance against the Romans and became the leader of the Zealots in Jerusalem, overcoming internal dissent and leading them to fortify the city against the coming siege by the Romans.  Josephus describes the period as one of anarchy and disregard for human life, in which John of Gischala allegedly aspired to "despotic power" (*J. W.* 4.389–90),[72] but John's contribution as a resistance leader should not be overlooked.[73]  At the fall of Jerusalem, John was taken to Rome as part of Titus's victory procession.  Simeon ben Giora, whom the Romans considered the commander of the Jerusalem forces, was executed; John of Gischala was sentenced to life in prison.[74]

## Justus of Tiberias (first century CE)

Justus of Tiberias was a historian and a contemporary and rival of Josephus in describing the Jewish War (66–73 CE).  Justus came from a respected and well-to-do Tiberian family whose names suggest Hellenistic influence.  He later served as the private secretary to Agrippa II, during which time he may have composed his history of the Jews, now lost.[75]  Our only source of information about Justus is Josephus.  Josephus accused Justus of steering Tiberius on a path toward revolt (*Life* 37, 41, 341–44), in apparent retaliation for Justus's accusation of the same thing against Josephus (*Life* 340).[76]  As evidence of his anti-Roman activities, Josephus adduced Justus's attacks in 66 CE on Sepphoris, which had recently rejected Tiberias as capital of Galilee, and the raids he led against cities of the Decapolis (*J. W.* 2.457–59).  These conflicts are probably better understood, however, in the context of the rising violence against the Jewish population in those areas.[77]

---

69. Gabba, "Social, Political, and Economic History," 160.

70. Lea Roth, "John of Gischala," *EncJud* 10:163–64.

71. Stern, *Greek and Latin Authors*, 1:510.

72. Richard A. Horsley, "The Zealots: Their Origin, Relationships and Importance in the Jewish Revolt," *NovT* 28 (1986): 159–92, here, 183–84.

73. Roth, "John of Gischala," 164.

74. Stern, *Greek and Latin Authors*, 2:58.

75. Tessa Rajak, "Justus of Tiberias," *CQ* n.s. 23 (1973): 345–68; Stern, *Greek and Latin Authors*, 2:333.

76. Rajak, "Justus of Tiberias," 352.

77. Rajak, "Justus of Tiberias," 352.

In an attempt to crush the opposition against him that he met when he arrived from Jerusalem as commander of Galilee, Josephus imprisoned many of the city's "notables" (*prōtoi*), including Justus and his father (*J. W.* 2.632–34; 5.155). Justus, however, succeeded in escaping from his prison in Taricheae; he fled to the protection of Agrippa at Berytus (Beirut), and henceforth had no further direct contact with the events of the war.[78]

## Menahem (son of Judas the Galilean; first century CE)

Menahem was a rebel leader in the revolt against the Romans.[79] He is known as the "son of Judas," although he may have been Judas's grandson.[80] With other rebels, Menahem broke into the Herodian fortress of Masada and stole arms. It is also possible that he was responsible for the burning of tax records in Jerusalem (Josephus, *J. W.* 2.427–48). Josephus refers to Menahem as the leader of the *Sicarii* (*J. W.* 2.433–35; 7.252–55). Hengel equated the *Sicarii* with Zealots and Josephus's "brigands," an identification that Horsley and others dispute.[81]

Josephus reports that Menahem went to the temple wearing royal robes, an action that provoked his enemies. The people turned on him, and, although he escaped to "Ophlas" (the Ophel) in the lower city, he was caught and killed (*J. W.* 2. 447–48).[82]

While Hengel and others have identified the Zealots with Josephus's Fourth Philosophy and portrayed Menahem as a messianic leader of the dynasty beginning with Judas, Horsley disputes this reading of the evidence.[83]

> Far from Menahem having been the head of a large organized resistance movement which had finally succeeded in provoking a massive rebellion, he was simply one of the principal leaders (perhaps the most important leader) of a group that joined in the revolt apparently only after the initial struggles led by others.[84]

Horsley and others have pointed out that the Zealot movement did not originate with Judas in 6 CE but first appeared in the middle of the revolt against Rome (Josephus, *J. W.* 4.134–61).[85]

---

78. Abraham Schalit, "Justus of Tiberius," *EncJud* 10:479–80.

79. See Stern, *Greek and Latin Authors*, 2.58.

80. Kennard, "Judas of Galilee and His Clan," 281–86; Loftus, "Anti-Roman Revolts," 92–93.

81. Hengel, *Zealots*, 86; Horsley, "Menahem in Jerusalem," 334–36; Horsley and Hanson, *Bandits*, 200–202.

82. Loftus, "Anti-Roman Revolts," 93.

83. Horsley, "Menahem in Jerusalem," 334–36.

84. Ibid., 336.

85. Ibid., 335; contra Hengel, *Zealots*, 89.

## Judah Ha-Nasi (second half of second century/ beginning of third century CE)

Judah Ha-Nasi (Judah the Prince) was a patriarch and redactor of the Mishnah. He was a sixth- or seventh-generation descendant of Hillel.[86] He had had his *yeshiva* (school) at Beth She'arim, but "when he fell ill he was brought to Sepphoris" (*b. Ket.* 103b), where he reportedly lived for seventeen years (*b. Ket.* 35a).

In the Babylonian Talmud Judah Ha-Nasi is venerated as "savior of Israel," as were Mordecai and Esther, (and later) "Simeon the Righteous, Hasmonai and his sons, and Mattathias the high priest" (*b. Meg.* 11a). He was said to exhibit all the characteristics becoming to the righteous (*m. Avot* 6:8). Aspects of his prayer (*b. Ber.* 16b) have been compared to the Qumran liturgical psalms.[87]

Judah Ha-Nasi was said to have close ties to a Roman leader Antoninus (= Marcus Aurelius?). According to aggadic tradition, Judah owned estates both inside and outside the land of Israel, partly as a benefit of this relationship. Antoninus reportedly gave Judah tenancy of estates in the Golan,[88] and the two were partners in cattle breeding.[89]

Judah Ha-Nasi is remembered for his mastery of the tradition and his application to his studies (*b. Ket.*104a), as well as his humility ("When Rabbi died, humility and the shunning of sin ceased" [*m. Soṭah* 9:15]), sound judgment, and strict discipline (*b. Ket.* 103b). Later tradition refers to Judah as *Ha-Kadosh*, "the holy one."[90]

## Bibliography

Braund, David C. "Bernice." *ABD* 1:677–78.

———. "Bernice in Rome." *Historia* 33 (1984): 120–23.

———. "Herod Antipas." *ABD* 3:160.

———. *Rome and the Friendly King: The Character of the Client Kingship*. London: Croom Helm; New York: St. Martin's, 1984.

Crook, J. A. "Titus and Bernice." *AJP* 72 (1951): 162–75.

Freyne, Seán. "Galilee–Jerusalem Relations according to Josephus' *Life*." *NTS* 33 (1987): 600–609.

---

86. "Judah Ha-Nasi." *EncJud* 10:366–72; see Anthony J. Saldarini, "The End of the Rabbinic Chain of Tradition," *JBL* 93 (1974): 97–106, at 104.

87. S. B. Hoenig, "Review of *The Qumran Liturgic Psalms (DJDJ* IV)," *JQR* n.s. 57 (1967): 327–32.

88. Samuel Klein, "The Estates of R. Judah Ha-Nasi and the Jewish Communities in the Trans-Jordanic Region," *JQR* n.s. 2 (1912): 545–56.

89. "Judah Ha-Nasi," *EncJud* 10:367; for literature, see Stern, *Greek and Latin Authors*, 2:626.

90. "Judah Ha-Nasi," *EncJud* 10:367.

———. *Galilee, Jesus, and the Gospels: Literary Approaches and Historical Investigations*. Philadelphia: Fortress Press, 1988.

Gabba, Emilio. "The Social, Political, and Economic History of Palestine 63 B.C.E.-C.E. 70." In *The Cambridge History of Judaism*, vol. 3, *The Early Roman Period*, edited by William Horbury, W. D. Davies, and John Sturdy, 94–167. Cambridge: Cambridge University Press, 1999.

Goodblatt, David, Avital Pinnick, and Daniel R. Schwartz. *Historical Perspectives: From the Hasmoneans to Bar Kokhba in the Light of the Dead Sea Scrolls. Proceedings of the Fourth International Symposium of the Orion Center for the Study of the Dead Sea Scrolls and Associated Literature, 27–31 January, 1999*. STDJ 37. Leiden: Brill. 2001. eBook.

Hengel, Martin. *The Zealots: Investigations into the Jewish Freedom Movement in the Period from Herod I until 70 A.D.* Translated by David Smith. Edinburgh: T&T Clark, 1989.

Hoehner, Harold W. *Herod Antipas: A Contemporary of Jesus Christ*. Contemporary Evangelical Perspectives 17. Grand Rapids: Zondervan, 1983.

Hoenig, Sidney B. "Review of *The Qumran Liturgic Psalms (DJDJ* IV)." *JQR* n.s. 57 (1967): 327–32.

———. "The Sicarii in Masada: Glory or Infamy?" *Tradition* 11 (1970): 5–30.

Horsley, Richard A. "Menahem in Jerusalem: A Brief Messianic Episode among the Sicarii— Not 'Zealot Messianism.'" *NovT* 27 (1985): 334–48.

———. "The Zealots: Their Origin, Relationships and Importance in the Jewish Revolt." *NovT* 28 (1986): 159–92.

Horsley, Richard A., and John S. Hanson. *Bandits, Prophets, and Messiahs: Popular Movements at the Time of Jesus*. Minneapolis: Winston, 1985.

Kennard, J. Spencer. "Judas of Galilee and His Clan." *JQR* n.s. 36 (1946): 281–86.

Klein, Samuel. "The Estates of R. Judah Ha-Nasi and the Jewish Communities in the Trans-Jordanic Region." *JQR* n.s. 2 (1912): 545–56.

Levine, Lee I. "John of Gischala: From Galilee to Jerusalem." *JJS* 33 (1982): 479–93.

Loftus, Francis. "The Anti-Roman Revolts of the Jews and the Galileans." *JQR* n.s. 68 (1977): 78–98.

Neusner, Jacob, and William Scott Green, eds. *Dictionary of Judaism in the Biblical Period: 450 B.C.E. to 600 C.E.* Peabody, Mass.: Hendrickson, 1999.

Rajak, Tessa. "Justus of Tiberias." *CQ* n.s. 23 (1973): 345–68.

Richardson, Peter. *Herod: King of the Jews and Friend of the Romans*. Studies on Personalities of the New Testament. Columbia: University of South Carolina Press, 1996.

Rogers, P. M. "Titus, Bernice, and Mucianus." *Historia* 29 (1980): 86–95.

Roth, Cecil, and Geoffrey Wigoder. "Judah Ha-Nasi." *EncJud* 10:366–72.

Rubenstein, Jeffrey L. "Social and Institutional Settings of Rabbinic Literature." In *The Cambridge Companion to the Talmud and Rabbinic Literature*, edited by Charlotte Elisheva Fonrobert and Martin S. Jaffee, 59–74. Cambridge Companions to Religion. Cambridge: Cambridge University Press, 2007.

Safrai, Shmuel, and Menahem Stern, eds. *The Jewish People in the First Century: Historical Geography, Political History, Social, Cultural and Religious Life and Institutions*, vol. 2. CRINT, section 1, vol. 2. Assen: Van Gorcum, 1976.

Saldarini, Anthony J. "The End of the Rabbinic Chain of Tradition." *JBL* 93 (1974): 97–106.

Schürer, Emil. *The History of the Jewish People in the Age of Jesus Christ (175 B.C.–A.D. 135)*. Revised and edited by Geza Vermes, Fergus Millar, Matthew Black, and Martin Goodman. 3 vols. in 4 parts. Edinburgh: T&T Clark, 1973–87.

Schwartz, Daniel R. *Agrippa I: The Last King of Judaea*. TSAJ 23. Tübingen: Mohr Siebeck, 1990.

Stern, Menachem. *Greek and Latin Authors on the Jews and Judaism*. 3 vols. Jerusalem: Israel Academy of Sciences and Humanities, 1974–84.

Vermes, Geza. "Ḥanina ben Dosa: A Controversial Galilean Saint from the First Century of the Christian Era, " *JJS* 23 (1972): 28–50.

———. *Jesus the Jew: A Historian's Reading of the Gospels*. Philadelphia: Fortress Press, 1973.

Wheeler, Frank E. "Antipas." *ABD* 1:272.

Zeitlin, Solomon. "The Sicarii and Masada." *JQR* n.s. 57 (1967): 251–70.

———. "Who Were the Galileans? New Light on Josephus' Activities in Galilee." *JQR* n.s. 64 (1974): 189–203.

———. "Zealots and Sicarii." *JBL* 81 (1962): 395–98.

# 7

# SOCIAL MOVEMENTS IN GALILEE

## *Richard Horsley*

The principal reason for the upsurge of interest in Galilee is that the area was the historical context both of the mission of Jesus and of the circles of sages who cultivated rulings collected in the Mishnah. Both Jewish and Christian scholars have been eager to "recover" a fuller sense of their origins. This also means, however, that much of the study of things Galilean has been determined by the synthetic theological constructs of "Judaism/Jews," and "Christianity/Christians."

In order to understand social movements in Roman Galilee, it is necessary to avoid allowing information to be filtered through these synthetic constructs. Instead, it is important to understand the historical background, the distinctive regional history of the Galileans prior to the Roman conquest, the fundamental social form in which people lived, their shifting political-economic relations with a succession of rulers, and the cultural tradition out of which they lived and responded to the impact of shifting political conflicts and arrangements.

### Banditry and Guerrilla Warfare[1]

Banditry was a significant symptom and a telling barometer of the difficult economic conditions and impact of political-military violence in Galilee in the mid-first century BCE and the mid-first century CE. The Romans used the term *lēsteia/lēstai* (λῃστεια/λῃσται) for any disrup-

---

1. See esp. Richard A. Horsley,"Josephus and the Bandits," *JSJ* 10 (1979): 37-63; Horsley, "Ancient Jewish Banditry and the Revolt against Rome," *CBQ* 43 (1981): 409–32; Horsley and John S. Hanson, *Bandits, Prophets, and Messiahs: Popular Movements at the Time of Jesus* (Minneapolis: Winston, 1985; repr., Harrisburg, Pa.: Trinity Press International, 1999), 48–87.

tion of the Roman order, and indeed local social banditry could swell into wider insurrection. Oppressive economic pressures could leave desperate peasants with no alternative but to "rob the rich" in order to survive. Depending on the bandits, they might even share with the poor. Small bands of brigands often remained in close contact with villagers, who protected them and viewed them as heroes of resistance. If oppressive conditions persisted or spread, such local banditry might well become epidemic. Judging from the large numbers of brigands Josephus claims to have found in Galilee in the summer of 66, this may be what had happened in the social-economic turmoil of the 50s and 60s. In this context, Josephus's account of John of Gischala (*J. W.* 2.585–94) as leader of a band of brigands that began guerrilla warfare along the Syrian frontier in 66–67 is quite credible. Such village "big-men" who became brigand chiefs were quite capable of making alliances with others and becoming leaders of a wider coalition of insurgents.

Military conquest, civil war, and the repeated battles of political rivals often resulted in the destruction and social disruption that produced large bands of brigands. Rather than wait to be slaughtered by the conquering Roman legions, peasants would "head to the hills" only to find that they had no villages to return to after the military devastation. According to Josephus's accounts, this is what happened in northwest Judea in the Roman reconquest in 67–68, as large bands of brigands coalesced into the insurgent coalition called "the Zealots" (*J. W.* 4.128–61). The Roman troops in effect produced the insurgent forces that resisted their further invasion.

Similarly, over a century before, repeated military invasion and destruction appear to be what produced the banditry in Galilee that Herod suppressed. After the young strongman was appointed military governor over Galilee in 48–47 BCE, he killed a large band led by the brigand chief Hezekiah that was raiding across the Syrian frontier. We may reasonably surmise that the brigands were among the results of the repeated battles between the rival Hasmonean forces and that the situation was compounded by (rival) Roman warlords' military actions in Galilee and Judea. In Josephus's lengthy account of the aftermath, the high-ranking Judeans' attempt to use the killing of the bandits as an occasion to "clip his (i.e., Herod's) wings" cannot be interpreted as sympathy or support. The bandits' relatives' appeal to the high priest Hyrcanus, however, is an illustration of the support that even large bands of brigands have from the villages of their origins.

Again, after the Roman senate appointed Herod "king of the Judeans," he attacked brigands. And again these "brigands" can be understood only in the context of a war of conquest, Herod's three-year-long campaign to conquer his own subjects. From Josephus's preceding narrative it is clear that the fighters and their families who had taken refuge in the caves in the cliffs near the village of Arbela were some of the many Galileans who were waging guerrilla warfare against Herod's army. As Josephus notes in passing exaggeration, they "combined the experience of seasoned warriors with the daring of brigands" (*J. W.* 1.305). Josephus takes great relish in telling the story of how Herod managed to slaughter these "freedom fighters" by lowering his seasoned warriors in baskets to smoke them out and hurl them to their death (*J. W.* 1.304–13; *Ant.* 14.413–30). But more of "the usual promoters of disturbance in Galilee" continued to make attacks, then flee into the marshes and other inaccessible places (*J. W.* 1.314–16; *Ant.* 14.431–33). Such "brigands" were indigenous Galilean villagers waging guerrilla warfare.

Social banditry has been characterized as apolitical, a kind of local self-help by desperate villagers under oppressive conditions. The larger bands of guerrillas thrown up by the Romans' or Herod's devastating military conquest had virtually no choice but to become political, to fight back against the systematic and relentless conquest that would either kill them outright or subject them to ever tighter control and exploitation. Social banditry and guerrilla resistance are not distinctive to Israelite society but are frequently encountered social-political phenomena in many agrarian societies.

In Roman Galilee, however, villagers mounted some movements of resistance and/or renewal against their rulers that took distinctly Israelite form, informed by particular social memories in Israelite popular tradition. Two of these particular Israelite movements had parallels in Judea and/or Samaria, and one is, so far as we know, specific to the Galilean peasants. In all three of these kinds of movements, villagers were deliberately taking political action, in two of them clearly nonviolent.

### The Messianic Movement Led by Judas Son of Hezekiah

When the tightly tyrannical rule of Herod ended with his death in 4 BCE, his security forces quickly lost control of the country to the widespread spontaneous resistance. Longer-range continuing resistance then took a distinctively Israelite form in each of three principal areas, Galilee, Judea, and the trans-Jordan. In each case, followers acclaimed their leader as "king" and the movement managed to maintain the people's independence of the Roman and Jerusalem rulers for months and, in the case of the movement in Judea, for three years before the Roman army could suppress them (Josephus, *J. W.* 2:56, 57–59, 60–65; *Ant.* 17.271–72, 273–77, 278–84). Yet another movement of the same type gathered around Simon bar Giora in Judea in the lull between the spontaneous revolt that drove the Romans out of Jerusalem in the summer of 66 and the Roman campaigns of reconquest in 67–70 (*J. W.* 2.652–53; 4:503–13, 529–34).[2]

The leader of the movement centered in the royal fortress of Sepphoris in Galilee was "Judas son of Hezekiah, the brigand chief who once overran the countryside," who assembled a sizable force of "desperate men." Simon, the leader in Perea, had been a royal servant (military officer?), a man of great size and strength, and in Judea the leader Athronges, also a man of great stature and strength, was a "mere shepherd." In Josephus's hostile accounts the leaders

---

2. For more extensive treatment, with references and analysis, see Richard A. Horsley, "Popular Messianic Movements around the Time of Jesus," *CBQ* 46 (1984) 471–95. See also Horsley and Hanson, *Bandits, Prophets, and Messiahs,* 111–17.

of these movements are all "acclaimed king" by their followers and/or aspire to kingship or to "don the diadem." Although Josephus does not mention the term *messiah*, it is clear that the form taken by all of these movements was influenced by the stories of the young David, who was "messiahed" as king first by the Judahites and then by the elders of all Israel to lead them in their struggle against the Philistines (2 Sam. 2:1-4; 4:1-4). As the stories of the young David go, he had been a mere shepherd and then became an outlaw and bandit chief, as all who were in distress or debt or discontented gathered around him (1 Sam. 22:1-2), prior to his being "messiahed" as king. Stories in the Israelite popular tradition, told and retold for generations in Israelite villages, provided the social memory that informed these movements, the pattern of interaction the villagers followed when they had "breathing room" to organize themselves, to govern themselves in the vacuum of control by their rulers, and to resist the inevitable Roman reconquest.

Judging from Josephus's accounts, these "messianic movements" show little or no influence from the ideology of imperial kingship articulated in Psalms 2 and 110 and some of Isaiah's prophecies at the birth of a royal son. As became increasingly evident a generation ago, there are virtually no Judean texts (apart from *Psalms of Solomon* 17 and a few references to two messiahs in certain Dead Sea Scrolls) that attest any expectation of a "messiah" in elite (scribal or ruling) circles.[3] The Roman overlords would not have looked kindly on any kingship other than that of the Herodian clients of Rome.

Regardless of whether they were called "messiahs" by their followers, Judas and the parallel figures in Judea were popular kings. It is not surprising that villagers in Galilee looked to the son of a famous brigand chief as their leader or "king." As a popular hero, the bandit chief Hezekiah had become a venerated martyr among the Galileans when he was killed by the hated "tyrant" Herod. Judas, the popular king in and around Sepphoris, is clearly a different figure from "Judas of Gamla/Gaulanitis/Galilee," whom Josephus clearly identifies as a scribal teacher (*sophistēs*) and leader of a scribal resistance movement to the Roman tribute in Judea in 6 CE, not the popular messianic movement in Galilee in 4 BCE (Josephus, *J. W.* 2.116; *Ant.* 18.4–6, 9–10, 23–24). It is not surprising that the principal target of Judas son of Hezekiah and his movement that Josephus mentions in Galilee was the royal fortress of Sepphoris. Like Simon in Perea, Judas and his men broke into the royal fortress to obtain arms and to *take back* all of the goods that had been seized (from the people) and stored there. Josephus does not indicate how long Judas and his movement maintained their independence of Roman rule. But it must have been a few months before the Roman general Varus could organize the campaign of military reconquest—which meant enslavement for the people in and around Sepphoris, near the village of Nazareth, a trauma that would surely have resonated into the next generation or two.

---

3. See Marinus de Jonge, "The Use of the Word 'Anointed' in the Time of Jesus," *NovT* 8 (1966): 132–48; Horsley, "Messianic Movements."

## Peasant Strike

One of the more remarkable popular movements in Roman Galilee or in antiquity generally was the "peasant strike" mounted by the villagers in protest against the emperor Gaius's order to install his statue in the Jerusalem temple, a powerful and provocative image of the divinized imperial ruler's domination and demand for tribute.[4] The crisis in Galilee and Judea began in response to charges that the Jews of Alexandria refused the honors to the emperor that all other subject cities and peoples celebrated in temples, shrines, and festivals. According to the lengthy accounts of both the Alexandrian Jewish theologian Philo (*Legatio ad Gaium* 184–373) and the Judean historian Josephus (*Ant.* 18.257–309; *J.W.* 2.183–203), as a way of punitively forcing the issue, Gaius ordered Petronius, the legate of Syria, at the head of a large military expedition, to install his statue in the temple by force, with slaughter of those who might resist. The remarkable, disciplined collective action of the Galilean peasants becomes swallowed up in the elaborate account of Philo, whose rhetorical flourishes picture hundreds of thousands of "the Jews" from all around the eastern Mediterranean and Babylonia flocking to sacrifice their lives in resistance. Josephus also portrays just what a serious crisis it was for the Jews generally. According to Josephus, tens of thousands gathered in Ptolemais, west of Galilee, and then in Tiberias to plead with Petronius. Josephus's account, however, includes what really led Petronius and his Herodian advisors in Tiberias to back away from the expedition, that is, the Galilean peasants' agrarian "strike."[5]

As the Roman army advanced to the west of Galilee, large numbers of peasants refused to plant their fields. They sustained their strike for weeks, insisting that they did not want war but would die rather than violate their customs. As the high-ranking officers of Herod Agrippa's administration pointed out to Petronius, "since the land was unsown, there would be a harvest of banditry because the requirement of the tribute could not be met" (*Ant.* 18.274). The peasants' strategy was to challenge the Roman order economically as well as disrupt it politically. The threatened "harvest of banditry" was a double threat. The Romans would be deprived of their tribute (still taken every second year?). But the peasants were also risking starvation with no crops for themselves, and they would have to resort to banditry, which would only escalate when the Romans, as expected, sent in a punitive military expedition and the peasants fled to the hills. Petronius got the point, agreed to write Gaius, exhorted the people to return to "labor on the land," and ordered the Herodian officers "to attend to agricultural matters and to conciliate the people with optimistic propaganda" (*Ant.* 18.283–84).

The basis of the peasants' refusal to plant the fields, hence to deny the Romans their tribute, was clearly the first two Mosaic covenantal commandments, that is, that God, not Gaius,

---

4. Horsley and Hanson, *Bandits, Prophets, and Messiahs*, 39–41.

5. For a fuller analysis of the peasant strike in the context of the broader crisis, see Richard A. Horsley, *Jesus and the Spiral of Violence: Popular Jewish Resistance in Roman Palestine* (San Francisco: Harper & Row, 1987), 110–16.

was their exclusive Lord and Master ("no other gods . . .") and that they were prohibited from "bowing down and serving" with their produce (the representation of) any other gods. These commandments were also the basis of the scribal Fourth Philosophy's refusal to pay the tribute in Judea in 6 CE and of Jesus of Nazareth's clever (non-)answer to the Pharisees' attempt to entrap him on whether it was lawful (it was not!) to pay tribute to Caesar. Most remarkable about this strike was the peasants' ability to organize such a disciplined and sustained collective action across village communities, some of which were physically separated by the ridges that run east–west across Galilee. This strike is noteworthy also for what must have been local and, in effect, collective leadership, apparently with no central prophet or other "charismatic" figure leading the way.

### Jesus of Nazareth and His Movement(s)

The social movement for which the most extensive sources are available emerged in response to Jesus of Nazareth. In the last generation, it has become common to speak of the Jesus movement(s) in vague reference to the followers of Jesus after his mission and crucifixion. The Gospel sources indicate rather that a movement of disciples, women, and others first coalesced around Jesus during his mission in Galilee and was already under way there before the crucifixion in Jerusalem.[6] To make this presentation manageable, I focus on key episodes and speeches in the Gospel of Mark and in the Jesus-speeches that are closely parallel in Matthew and Luke (standardly attributed to their common "source," Q).[7]

---

6. Recognition of this evidence is usually blocked by the deeply rooted theological scheme of Christian origins that determines the way Gospel materials are filtered. In this controlling scheme of how a new, more universal religion broke away from an older, more parochial religion, Jesus was a revealer-teacher of individual followers in Galilee who, inspired by the resurrection ("Easter faith") formed a community ("church") in Jerusalem from whose missionary activity other communities soon started. This scheme is a modern scholarly construct based partly on a reading of the book of Acts and certain passages in Paul's letters. But it is not attested in the Gospel sources for Jesus, which are sustained stories comprising traditions of Jesus' teaching and activity that emerged in the context of Galilean village life. See further the discussion in Richard A. Horsley, *The Prophet Jesus and the Renewal of Israel: Moving Beyond a Diversionary Debate* (Grand Rapids: Eerdmans, 2012), chapters 6 and 8.

7. To use the Gospels as sources for Jesus movement(s) it is necessary to abandon and move beyond the highly problematic assumptions, concepts, and approaches that have become deeply entrenched in study of the Gospel tradition and "the historical Jesus." This standard study is the product of modern print culture, of Enlightenment skepticism of narrative and anything that is not natural, and of modern Western individualism. Jesus scholars thus assume that Jesus' teaching and its transmission did not involve (a) genuine communication (people cannot communicate merely in one-liners) (b) in the interactive context of the fundamental social forms of his society (the families and village communities of Galilee and Judea). Such a Jesus, of course, could not have been a historical figure. Recent researches in a number of interrelated areas (largely independent of one another), however, have challenged some of the key assumptions (and thus approaches) of New Testament, Gospel, and Jesus scholarship. See further the provisional attempts to discern the implications of these lines of research in Horsley, *Jesus and the Politics of Roman Palestine* (Columbia: University of South Carolina Press, 2013), chapter 1.

In many of the episodes, Jesus steps into or is understood in the role of a prophet like Moses and/or Elijah: in commissioning protégés (disciples), in sea crossings, and in wilderness feedings or healings. It is clear that the people as well as Herod Antipas take him as a prophet in the long Israelite tradition of prophets. His prophetic role as the new Moses and Elijah is confirmed in the appearance to the leading disciples on the mountain (Mark 9:2-8).

The Gospel of Mark portrays Jesus not only as beginning and focusing his movement of the renewal of Israel in Galilee, but focusing on life in the villages, the fundamental social form of the people's existence. In episode after episode and in several summary passages, Jesus works in villages and nearby places, proclaiming the rule of God and healing sicknesses and casting out unclean spirits. In the first exorcism episode, for example, he pointedly encounters and casts out the spirit in the village assembly (*synagogue*, συναγωγή; see Mark 1:21-29), the form of local community cohesion and self-governance. Jesus sends the disciples into village communities to expand his proclamation of the kingdom and exorcism of spirits and healing of sickness (Mark 6:7-12). In yet another indication of the base of Jesus' movement in villages, in the healing episodes he welcomes the support networks that the sick already have in family and friends, and restores them to their village communities (for example, Mark 2:2-5).

Both of the earliest Gospel texts, the one a sustained narrative (the Gospel of Mark) and the other in the very different form of a series of Jesus-speeches (source Q), portray Jesus as generating a movement based in villages, which were the fundamental social form in which the people lived. Numerous names, symbols, and allusions in both Gospel texts indicate that the agenda of the movement was a renewal of the people of Israel. But place-names in both texts indicate that Jesus and his movement originated in the villages of Galilee. The Q speeches, which know nothing of Jesus as a king or "messiah," represent him throughout as the greatest in the long line of Israelite prophets and as a new Moses, in particular in the covenant renewal speech. The Gospel of Mark consistently represents Jesus as a new Moses and Elijah, and pointedly criticizes or rejects the view that he was/is a "messiah" as a (the disciples') misunderstanding. Both of these earliest Gospel texts, moreover, portray Jesus' renewal of Israel in opposition to (condemnation of) the rulers, specifically the Jerusalem ruling house, the high priests, and their Roman patrons.

The prophet Jesus and the movement he generated in Galilee, like that of his "predecessor" John the Baptist, follow the same cultural pattern of prophets like Moses that was so deeply rooted in Israelite tradition and very much alive in the villages of Judea and Samaria, judging from the contemporary movements led by the Samaritan prophet and the Judean prophets Theudas and "the Egyptian" (Josephus, *Ant.* 18.85–87; 20.97–98, 169–71; *J.W.* 2.261–63). All of these were movements of villagers, evidently of Israelite heritage. The principal difference of the Jesus movement(s) from the two movements in Judea and the one in Samaria is that, while the latter drew the people out of their villages to experience a new act of deliverance by God (after which a renewed people would emerge), Jesus catalyzed a renewal of the people in their village communities in the confidence that God stood in judgment on the oppressive rulers.

## Bibliography

Horsley, Richard A. "Ancient Jewish Banditry and the Revolt against Rome." *CBQ* 43 (1981): 409–32.

———. *Jesus and the Politics of Roman Palestine.* Columbia: University of South Carolina Press, 2013.

———. *Jesus and the Spiral of Violence: Popular Jewish Resistance in Roman Palestine.* San Francisco: Harper & Row, 1987.

———. "Josephus and the Bandits." *JSJ* 10 (1979): 37–63.

———. "Popular Messianic Movements around the Time of Jesus." *CBQ* 46 (1984): 471–95.

———. *The Prophet Jesus and the Renewal of Israel: Moving Beyond a Diversionary Debate.* Grand Rapids: Eerdmans, 2012.

Horsley, Richard A., and John S. Hanson. *Bandits, Prophets, and Messiahs: Popular Movements at the Time of Jesus.* Minneapolis: Winston, 1985. Reprint, Harrisburg, Pa.: Trinity Press International, 1999.

Jonge, Marinus de. "The Use of the Word 'Anointed' in the time of Jesus." *NovT* 8 (1966): 132–48.

# VILLAGE LIFE

# 8

# THE GALILEAN VILLAGE IN THE LATE SECOND TEMPLE AND MISHNAIC PERIODS

## *David A. Fiensy*

If you lived in Galilee in the late Second Temple or Mishnaic period, you would most likely have lived in a village. There were only two cities, Sepphoris and Tiberias, and they were not large. What was it like to live in one of the villages? How large were they? When you walked around, what would you see? How would your family have made a living?

In a previous era of scholarship, we depended on Josephus and the Mishnah to describe life in Galilee in the time of Jesus. More recently, scholars have turned to the social sciences—ethnographies of traditional, contemporaneous villages—to inform their understanding of ancient Galilee. In the last thirty years, however, more and more archaeological work has been done in the region. This work sometimes confirms the older views and sometimes leads to a reassessment. The survey below relies mostly on the material remains to draw a picture of village life in the late Second Temple and Mishnaic periods.

### Village and Town Sizes

Most residents of Lower Galilee lived in villages. Josephus wrote that there were 204 cities and villages (πόλεις καὶ κῶμαι) in all of Galilee (*Life* 235). Whether this figure represents an

A previous version of this chapter was published under the title "Population, Architecture, and Economy in Lower Galilean Villages and Towns in the First Century AD: A Brief Survey," in *My Father's World: Celebrating the Life of Reuben G. Bullard* (ed. John D. Wineland, Mark Ziese, and James Riley Estep Jr.; Eugene, Ore.: Wipf & Stock, 2011), 101–19. Used by permission of Wipf and Stock Publishers. www.wipfandstock.com.

actual administrative count or merely his estimate is unclear, but the precision of the number might suggest the former.[1] At any rate, if we calculate the population of first-century Galilee at 175,000 persons,[2] and if we calculate the populations of the two cities, Sepphoris and Tiberias, at around 10,000 persons each,[3] then that leaves between 135,000 and 160,000 persons living in villages and towns in both Upper and Lower Galilee.

## *Terminology*

In defining ancient Galilean village sizes, we must first deal with the Greek and Hebrew terms for village and city. The two Greek terms that, in the main, are found in Josephus and the Gospels—πόλις (*polis*), usually translated "city," and κώμη (*kōmē*) usually translated "village"—were used in a confusing way. Technically, a *polis* had its own constitution, coinage, territory, and town council (βουλή, *boulē*).[4] But these texts often seem to refer to villages as cities and

---

1. On this, see Douglas R. Edwards, "Identity and Social Location in Roman Galilean Villages," in *Religion, Ethnicity, and Identity in Ancient Galilee: A Region in Transition* (ed. Jürgen Zangenberg, Harold W. Attridge, and Dale B. Martin; WUNT 210; Tübingen: Mohr Siebeck, 2007), 357–74. Edwards notes (p. 357) that a survey of Upper Galilee showed evidence of 108 Early Roman settlements. He further states (p. 358) that a study of Lower Galilee lists over 400 sites (from all periods of antiquity). Edwards then concludes that Josephus's figure of 204 villages "seems entirely plausible."

2. See Eric M. Meyers, "Jesus and His Galilean Context," in *Archaeology and the Galilee: Texts and Contexts in the Graeco-Roman and Byzantine Periods* (ed. Douglas R. Edwards and C. Thomas McCollough; South Florida Studies in the History of Judaism 143; Atlanta: Scholars Press, 1997), 59; and Harold W. Hoehner, *Herod Antipas* (SNTSMS 17; Cambridge: Cambridge University Press, 1972), 53. Hoehner prefers the figure 200,000, and Meyers prefers 150,000 to 175,000. Meyers accepts Josephus's figure of 204 villages in Galilee and multiplies this number by 500 residents per village. That number plus the populations of the two cities give his final population figure. C. C. McCown cites an older figure of 400,000 for Galilee ("The Density of Population in Ancient Palestine," *JBL* 66 [1947]: 426). His own estimate was 100,000 (p. 436), based on an estimate of 150 persons per square mile. This estimate he derives from a comparison with other population densities in the modern period.

3. The figures of Jonathan Reed are 8,000 to 12,000 in each city (*Archaeology and the Galilean Jesus: A Re-examination of the Evidence* [Harrisburg, Pa.: Trinity Press International, 2000], 117). Meyers suggests 18,000 for Sepphoris and 24,000 for Tiberias ("Jesus and His Galilean Context," 59). J. Andrew Overman offered 30,000 to 40,000 for Tiberias and 30,000 for Sepphoris ("Who Were the First Urban Christians?" in *SBL 1988 Seminar Papers* [Atlanta: Scholars Press, 1988], 160–68). Richard A. Horsley maintained that both cities together had a population of 15,000 (*Archaeology, History, and Society in Galilee: The Social Context of Jesus and the Rabbis* [Valley Forge, Pa.: Trinity Press International, 1996], 45). If we adhere to the general rule that 10 percent of the population in the ancient world lived in the cities, then a population of 175,000 for Galilee needs around 10,000 in each of the two cities. But see the calculation below.

4. See Emil Schürer, *The History of the Jewish People in the Age of Jesus Christ (175 B.C.–A.D. 135)* (rev. and ed. Geza Vermes, Fergus Millar, Matthew Black, and Martin Goodman; 3 vols. in 4 parts; Edinburgh: T&T Clark, 1973–87), 2:86–87; A. H. M. Jones, "The Urbanization of Palestine," *JRS* 21 (1931): 78–85; Victor Ehrenberg, "Polis," *OCD*, 851–52. A. N. Sherwin-White suggested that the solution to the problem was to consider the city (*polis*) in both Josephus and the Gospels as a capital of a toparchy (or region), even if the place was not technically a city (*Roman Society and Roman Law in the New Testament* [Oxford: Clarendon, 1963], 129–30). Cf. Schürer, *History of the Jewish People,* 2:188. The term κωμοπόλεις (Mark 1:38) in reference to the villages of Galilee may

cities as villages. The New Testament Gospels, for example, often use the term *polis* to refer to what must have been very small villages.[5] Thus, one must read cautiously when the New Testament uses the terms.

The rabbinic terms for cities, towns, and villages are *kerak* (כרך), *'ir* (עיר), *'irah* (עירה), *qiryah* (קריה), and *kaphar* (כפר). The places designated by the middle three terms appear to have been roughly equivalent in size, representing a median between *kerak*, the large walled city, and *kaphar*, the small unwalled village. Samuel Krauss affirmed that the Hebrew *kerak* was the equivalent of the Greek *polis* in the technical sense.[6] But—to complicate matters more—the word *'ir* could have a wide range of meaning, from a large city to a small town to even a country estate.[7]

The simplest procedure is to refer to the three most common usages in the rabbinic literature: the כרך (*kerak*), the עיר (*'ir*), and the כפר (*kaphar*). The Mishnah distinguishes among these three terms. *M. Megillah* 1:1–2, for example, observes that the scroll of Esther is read in the *kerak* on the fifteenth of Adar but in the *'ir* and *kaphar* on the fourteenth.[8] Of these three terms, the most frequently used in the Mishnah is *'ir*.[9] Thus, it could be concluded that in the Mishnaic period most people lived in a town or large village, in population midway between the small village (*kaphar*) and the city (*kerak*). Whether that conclusion is also appropriate for the late Second Temple period must be determined based on material remains.

---

indicate the same as the phrase πόλεις καὶ κῶμαι (Matt. 9:35). See Martin Goodman, *State and Society in Roman Galilee, A.D. 132–212* (Totowa, N.J.: Rowman & Allenheld, 1983), 27. The term πολίχνη, which Josephus used frequently (*J. W.* 1.22, 41, 334; 3.20, 134, 430; 4.84, etc.) seems to be a word for a town or a large village.

5. See Reed, *Archaeology and the Galilean Jesus*, 167.

6. Samuel Krauss "City and Country," *He-Atid* 3 (1923): 50–61, cited in Shimon Dar, *Landscape and Pattern: An Archaeological Survey of Samaria, 800 B.C.E.–636 C.E.* (2 vols.; BAR International Series 308; Oxford: BAR, 1986), 1.21. Dar agrees with Krauss.

7. See Shimon Applebaum, "Economic Life in Palestine," in *The Jewish People in the First Century: Historical Geography, Political History, Social, Cultural and Religious Life and Institutions*, vol. 2 (ed. Shmuel Safrai and Menahem Stern; CRINT, section 1, vol. 2; Assen: Van Gorcum, 1976), 643; and Applebaum, "The Settlement Pattern of Western Samaria from Hellenistic to Byzantine Times," in Dar, *Landscape and Pattern*, 263. Applebaum is followed in this view by Dar. See Dar, *Landscape and Pattern*, 21–22. But Martin Goodman was unconvinced; see his *State and Society*, 28. See also *m. Erub.* 5:6 and *t. B. Bat.* 3:5 on selling an *'ir*. Applebaum further asserts that the terms *'irah* and *qiryah* referred to settlements linked to large administrative centers, in a tenurial relationship either to the center of a vast estate or to an urban center. See Applebaum, "Economic Life in Palestine," 644. See also Shaye J. D. Cohen, "The Rabbi in Second-Century Jewish Society," in *The Cambridge History of Judaism*, vol. 3, *The Early Roman Period* (ed. William Horbury, W. D. Davies, and John Sturdy; Cambridge: Cambridge University, 1999), 929.

8. See further *m. Erub.* 5:1, 3, 6; *m. Shek.* 1:1; *m. Meg.* 1:1, 2, 3; 2:3; 3:1; *m. Ket.* 1:1; *m. Arak.* 9:6; *m. Kelim* 1:7. See Schürer, *History of the Jewish People*, 2:188–89.

9. Goodman (*State and Society*, 28) affirms that the term *'ir* is used in the Mishnah over one hundred times, *kerak* only eleven times, and *kaphar* twelve times. See also Evan Fry, "Cities, Towns, and Villages in the Old Testament," *Bible Translator* 30 (1979): 434–38, who affirms that the word *'ir* (the most common term) appears around one thousand times in the Hebrew Bible.

## *Archaeological Surveys*[10]

The most informed way to answer the question, How large were most villages in Galilee during our time period? is to consult the archaeological surveys. For comparison we will also note villages surveyed in the adjoining territories of the Golan and Samaria.

Archaeologists are only now clarifying the number of inhabitants of a typical town and village. Ze'ev Yeivin discussed ten towns in Galilee and the Golan falling mainly into the following categories: large towns (22 to 25 acres), middle-sized towns (10 to 17 acres), and one village with 2.5 acres.[11] Dan Urman's survey of the Golan discovered one site of over 175 acres but also 87 sites of 5 acres or less that were either small villages/hamlets or single farms.[12] Shimon Dar gives the measurement of six villages in Samaria ranging from 2.4 acres to 10 acres.[13]

The team of Rafael Frankel has recently made a survey of Upper Galilee.[14] Although the survey identified settlements from the Neolithic through the Ottoman periods, we can select out the settlements that are relevant to our study.[15] The survey indicates that of the 74 sites that relate to our inquiry, 37 were less than 2.5 acres; 27 were 2.5 to 5 acres; seven sites were 5 to 10 acres; and three sites were 10 to 30 acres.

Uzi Leibner surveyed sites in eastern Galilee, dividing them into six categories based on his estimate of their area. Most of them (27 sites) were less than 5 acres, with thirteen of them over 5 acres in size.[16]

Finally, we might add a few sites from Lower Galilee that have been excavated, some of them some time ago, others more recently. Nazareth, Jesus' hometown, is somewhat difficult to measure, since the ancient village lies beneath two churches today. John Dominic Crossan and Jonathan Reed suggest that the village covered 10 acres but that much of it was empty space because of gardens, orchards, and places for livestock.[17] Stanislao Loffreda calculates the size of

---

10. The Israeli scholars measure space in dunams (4 dunams = 1 acre). Europeans use hectares (1 hectare = 2.47 acres). For convenience I will convert all measurements into acres.

11. Ze'ev Yeivin, "Survey of Settlements in Galilee and the Golan from the Period of the Mishnah in Light of the Sources" (PhD diss., Hebrew University, 1971), VI.

12. Dan Urman, *The Golan: A Profile of a Region during the Roman and Byzantine Periods* (BAR International Series 269; Oxford: BAR, 1985), 87–88, 93.

13. Dar, *Landscape and Pattern*, 51, 53, 42, 47, 36, 231.

14. Rafael Frankel, Nimrod Getzov, Mordechai Aviam, and Avi Degani, *Settlement Dynamics and Regional Diversity in Ancient Upper Galilee: Archaeological Survey of Upper Galilee* (IAA Reports 14; Jeruslaem: Israel Antiquities Authority, 2001).

15. I have selected only settlements that include Hellenistic and/or Roman occupation and that did not continue past the Byzantine period.

16. Uzi Leibner, *Settlement and History in Hellenistic, Roman, and Byzantine Galilee: An Archaeological Survey of the Eastern Galilee* (TSAJ 127; Tübingen: Mohr Siebeck, 2009), 102–306. He found 50 sites but did not give size estimates for 10 of them.

17. John Dominic Crossan and Jonathan Reed, *Excavating Jesus: Beneath the Stones, Behind the Texts* (San Francisco: HarperSanFrancisco, 2001), 34. On the other hand, James F. Strange surmises that it covered an area of 60 acres ("Nazareth," *ABD* 4:1050).

Capernaum to have been between 10 and 12 acres.[18] Peter Richardson has likewise estimated that Cana (8 to 9 acres) as well as Yodefat (10 acres) were in this same size range.[19] Finally, Crossan and Reed estimate the size of Sepphoris at 100 to 150 acres.[20]

It appears from these findings[21] that most people lived in towns or villages ranging from less than 2.5 acres to 10 acres (see table 2). The ten towns examined by Yeivin may not then be typical of Galilean life, at least for the late Second Temple period. We presume that the same conditions that prevailed in Upper Galilee, the Golan, and Samaria also existed in Lower Galilee, as our brief survey of a few villages and towns seems to confirm.

### Calculating City and Village Population

The population of these towns and villages may be figured by counting the number of houses and multiplying by five, for five inhabitants on average to a dwelling, then subtracting 25 percent to allow rooms for storage and animals. Yeivin has, in this manner, estimated the population of several cities in Galilee and the Golan (see Table 1).

Most of these towns appear to have flourished in the Mishnaic period, and thus we must hesitate in affirming that they also give us an appropriate sample in size of a typical late Second Temple village or town. Further, the method of counting dwellings is not always appropriate because many villages are not preserved enough to identify the living quarters.

---

18. Stanslao Loffreda, "Capernaum," *NEAEHL* 1:292. But Crossan and Reed (*Excavating Jesus*, 81) suggest that 25 acres was the size of Capernaum and that it had a population of 1,000. In another publication, Reed suggests that the population of Capernaum was 1,700 (*Archaeology and the Galilean Jesus*, 83). See my calculation below.

19. Peter Richardson, *Building Jewish in the Roman East* (Waco, Tex.: Baylor University Press, 2004), 81. Douglas Edwards gives the size of the upper village of Khirbet Qana as 5 to 7 hectares (12 to 17 acres) "at its zenith," that is, in the Byzantine era, and Yodefat as 4.7 hectares (11 acres). See Edwards, "Khirbet Qana: From Jewish Village to Christian Pilgrim Site," in *The Roman and Byzantine Near East: Some Recent Archaeological Research*, vol. 3, *Late-Antique Petra, Nile Festival Building at Sepphoris, Deir Qal'a Monastery, Khirbet Qana Village and Pilgrim Site, 'Ain-'Arrub Hiding Complex and Other Studies* (edited by J. H. Humphrey; Journal of Roman Archaeology Supplementary Series 49; Ann Arbor, Mich.: Journal of Roman Archaeology, 2002), 101–32, esp. 106. C. Thomas McCollough prefers 7 hectares (17 acres). See his "City and Village in Lower Galilee: The Import of the Archeological Excavations at Sepphoris and Khirbet Qana (Cana) for Framing the Economic Context of Jesus," in *The Galilean Economy in the Time of Jesus* (ed. David A. Fiensy and Ralph K. Hawkins; Early Christianity and Its Literature 11; Atlanta: Society of Biblical Literature, 2013), 49–74, esp. 58.

20. Crossan and Reed, *Excavating Jesus*, 81.

21. The site of Shikhin (Asochis) has now been identified (see below). The survey team of James F. Strange, Dennis E. Groh, and Thomas R. W. Longstaff estimates the total area of the hill on which this important industrial town was situated at 27 acres, but the actual occupation area is so far uncertain. Thus, it will not be considered in these population estimates. See Strange, Groh, and Longstaff, "University of South Florida Excavations at Sepphoris: The Location and Identification of Ancient Shikhin (Asochis)," *IEJ* 44 (1994): 216–27; 45 (1995): 171–87.

| Town | Population |
|------|-----------|
| Juhadr | 5250 |
| Mazraat Kuneitra | 900 |
| Khirbet Shema | 1250 |
| Arbel | 5000 |
| Usha | 3000 |

**Table 1:** Yeivin's Population Estimates[22]

Another method of determining population is to multiply the number of acres of the site times the supposed number of people that on average lived on one acre in antiquity. This method appears to be the most common one used by historians.[23] This method too is problematic because, in the first place, we cannot always tell exactly the total area an ancient village covered; and, in the second place, the estimates of population density vary. Wolfgang Reinhardt, who has done a detailed study of ancient population calculations, notes that one should not expect all villages/cities to have had the same population density.[24] Nevertheless, calculating populations can be a helpful heuristic exercise to compare villages. I do not claim below to know the actual population—a literal head count—of these ancient villages. I only present these figures as a good guess in general to help the reader picture what an ancient village was like.

The figure accepted by both Magen Broshi and Yigal Shiloh is 160 to 200 people per acre.[25] The higher number seems to me too many persons per acre since there must have been, in most villages, spaces for threshing floors, perhaps gardens, and even areas where nomadic folk and travelers stayed in tents.[26] I incline, therefore, toward the lower number of 160 per-

---

22. Yeivin, "Survey of Settlements," VI.

23. See Wolfgang Reinhardt, "The Population Size of Jerusalem and the Numerical Growth of the Jerusalem Church," in *The Book of Acts in Its Palestinian Setting* (ed. Richard Bauckham; Book of Acts in Its First Century Setting 4; Grand Rapids: Eerdmans, 1995), 237–65, esp. 214: "The most common method is calculation by means of the product of area and density."

24. Ibid.

25. That is, 40 to 50 persons per dunam. See Magen Broshi, "The Population of Western Palestine in the Roman-Byzantine Period," *BASOR* 236 (1979): 1–10; Yigal Shiloh, "The Population of Iron Age Palestine in the Light of a Sample Analysis of Urban Plans, Areas, and Population Density," *BASOR* 239 (1980): 25–35. Yet William G. Dever has calculated populations of eighth-century BCE towns and villages using a slightly lower estimate of population density (*The Lives of Ordinary People in Ancient Israel: Where Archaeology and the Bible Intersect* [Gand Rapids: Eerdmans, 2012] 48–49). His estimate appears to be 100 persons per acre. At the other end of the time spectrum, Ze'ev Safrai speculates that 10 families could live on a dunam (or 40 families on an acre) of ground in the Talmudic period (200–500 CE) (*The Economy of Roman Palestine* [London: Routledge, 1994] 65). If we assume five persons per family, then we reach the upper limit of Broshi's calculations.

26. See the work on a modern village in the Middle East: Louise E. Sweet, *Tel Toqaan: A Syrian Village* (Anthropological Papers 14; Ann Arbor: University of Michigan, 1974), 52.

sons per acre.[27] Certainly the population figures obtained by this method are speculative, but they are often the only figures we have. At least they offer some comparisons among contemporaneous villages.

Thus, using the lower number, we obtain the population figures given in table 2 (see p. 178). Also using this calculation method, Sepphoris would have numbered around 16,000 persons.[28] But since Sepphoris had more open spaces than most villages—a marketplace, wide streets, much larger houses for the same number of family members as in a village house—perhaps we should estimate it even lower. Thus, 10,000 to 12,000 seems more feasible. One can easily discern the difficulty of simply using Broshi's and Shiloh's calculations.[29] Yet we offer these calculations here simply by way of comparing villages and towns using the most common method of determining population.

The dates for most of the villages cited by Dar are the Hasmonean through the Herodian (one through Byzantine) periods. The towns in the Golan range from the Early Roman to the Byzantine period. All of those selected from the Upper Galilee survey are Hellenistic or Roman. All of those from the eastern Galilean survey are Early Roman to Middle Roman. All of those listed from Lower Galilee are Herodian (or Early Roman = 37 BCE to 70 CE). Thus, it appears that most persons in the two Galilees, the Golan, and Samaria during the Roman period lived in villages with fewer than 2,000 inhabitants.

Arieh Ben David has attempted to define the Hebrew terms for town in the Mishnaic period by assigning to each a population figure:

1. A hamlet (עיר) – 50 inhabitants or fewer
2. A village (כפר) – 400 to 600 inhabitants
3. A country town (עירה) – 600 to 7,500 inhabitants
4. A large city (כרך) – 10,000 to 60,000 inhabitants[30]

His figures seem to harmonize roughly with what we have discussed above. It is interesting that Ben-David's four categories also fit with the depictions of towns and cities in the Madaba Map. Small villages are depicted as buildings having two towers, larger villages with three towers, small cities with four or five towers (for example, Jericho, Azotus), and large

27. Reinhardt inclines toward a higher population density, at least for Jerusalem ("Population Size," 253–55).

28. Compare the calculation given at the beginning of this essay. This figure is closer to that of Eric Meyers. The size of Tiberias is yet to be determined, since most of it lies now under the modern city.

29. Compare Reed (*Archaeology and the Galilean Jesus*, 152), who wants to assign a population of 150 to one hectare (not one acre) and perhaps even 100 persons per hectare. He is thinking here mostly of Capernaum, which was spread out and not confined by city walls, which tend to squeeze people together.

30. Arieh Ben-David, *Talmudische Ökonomie: Die Wirtschaft des jüdischen Palästina zur Zeit der Mischna und des Talmud* (Hildesheim: Georg Olms, 1974), 49.

| | Site in Acres | Population (160 persons/acre) |
|---|---|---|
| Yeivin | 22–25 acres | 3,520–4,000 |
| | 10–17 acres | 1,600–2,720 |
| | 2.5 acres | 400 |
| Urman | 1 site 175 acres | 28,000 |
| | 4 sites 30–50 acres | 4,800–8,000 |
| | 14 sites 10–30 acres | 1,600–4,800 |
| | 28 sites 5–10 acres | 800–1,600 |
| | 54 sites 2.5–5 acres | 400–800 |
| | 33 sites less than 2.5 acres | Fewer than 400 |
| Frankel et al. | 3 sites 10–30 acres | 1,600–4,800 |
| | 7 sites 5–10 acres | 800–1,600 |
| | 27 sites 2.5–5 acres | 400–800 |
| | 37 sites less than 2.5 acres | Fewer than 400 |
| Leibner[31] | 5 sites .5 acre | 80 |
| | 14 sites 1.7 acres | 300 |
| | 8 sites 3.7 acres | 592 |
| | 7 sites 7.5 acres | 1,200 |
| | 4 sites 12.5 acres | 1,900 |
| | 2 sites 18.7 acres | 3,000 |
| Dar[32] | 4–5 acres | 640–800 |
| | 3.5 acres | 560 |
| | 6 acres | 960 |
| | 6–7.5 acres | 960–1,200 |
| | 2.4 acres | 384 |
| | 10 acres | 1,600 |
| Lower Galilee Sites | 3 sites 10 acres[33] | 1,600 |
| | 1 site 5–10 acres | 800–1,600 |
| | 1 site 100–150 acres | 16,000–24,000 (10,000–12,000) |

**Table 2:** Villages in Galilee, Golan, and Samaria

---

31. Leibner gives a range of sizes (for example, 5–3 dunams). I have averaged his site sizes and converted them into acres. See Leibner, *Settlement and History,* 313.

32. Dar often estimates the population, however, at more than these amounts. For example, the population of Hirbet Hajar would be, at most, 1,000 persons using Broshi's method, but Dar estimates the population at 1,500 to 2,000. See Dar, *Landscape and Pattern,* 51. The average village in Egypt may have been somewhat larger. See Naphtali Lewis, *Life in Egypt under Roman Rule* (Oxford: Clarendon, 1983), 68.

33. But Crossan and Reed (*Excavating Jesus,* 34) estimate the population of Nazareth at 200 to 400 persons in spite of their suggested 10-acre size for the village. Strange ("Nazareth," 1050) calculates the population of Nazareth at 480 or fewer. Richardson (*Building Jewish,* 76) suggests that Yodefat had a population of 1,000.

cities as aerial sketches showing actual walls and buildings (for example, Jerusalem, Jamnia, Ascalon).[34]

Therefore, I suggest the following categories based on Ben David[35]:

| Village | κώμη | כפר | 2,000 inhabitants or | E.g., Nazareth, Cana, |
|---------|------|-----|---------------------|----------------------|
|         | komē | kaphar | fewer | Yodefat, Capernaum |
| Town | κώμη | עיר | 2,000 to 6,000 | The medium-sized |
|      | komē | 'ir | inhabitants | towns discussed by |
|      |      |     |             | Yeivin |
| City | πόλις | כרך | Over 6,000 | E.g., Sepphoris, |
|      | polis | kerak | inhabitants | Tiberias |

**Table 3:** Categories of Villages, Towns, and Cities in Galilee in the Herodian Period

Thus, although Josephus states that even the smallest village in Galilee had over 15,000 inhabitants (*J. W.* 3.43), the archaeological data indicate that most folk in Samaria, Golan, and Upper and Lower Galilee lived in villages (כפרים) that included only a few hundred to 2,000 persons.

## What Was in a Village, Town, or City?

I will describe a typical Galilean small town or village by comparing the hypothetical "medium-sized town" in the Mishnaic period that Yeivin has constructed with an actual village in Samaria of the Herodian period described by Dar and a Roman-era village of Lower Galilee (Khirbet Qana) excavated in the last twenty years.

### *Composite Town Plan*

Yeivin has put together a composite of a town of medium size based on the plans of Chorazin and Einan in Galilee, Nahef and Naaran in the Golan, and Horvat Susia in Judea. Although

---

34. See Michael Avi-Yonah, *The Madaba Mosaic Map: With Introduction and Commentary* (Jerusalem: Israel Exploration Society, 1954), 21–22.

35. Cf. Anne E. Killebrew, "Village and Countryside," in *The Oxford Handbook of Jewish Daily Life in Roman Palestine* (ed. Catherine Hezser; Oxford: Oxford University Press, 2010), 189–209, esp. 189, 195, who lists four categories of settlements in a period of "seven centuries" (evidently ca. 200 BCE–500 CE): urban settlements; towns (12 acres or more, thus around 2,000 persons); small villages (less than 12 acres, thus fewer than 2,000 persons); and farmhouses (that is, "a few structures around an open courtyard"). Also see Dever, *Lives of Ordinary People*, 48–49, who lists eighth-century BCE cities and villages in four "Tiers." He offers: capital cities/administrative centers; cities (with over 1,000 persons); towns (300–1000 population); and villages (50–300 population). Thus, my summary here, based largely on Ben David, is consistent with these other two analyses.

**Figure A. Yeivin's composite Mishnaic town.** Ze'ev Yeivin, "On the Medium-Sized City" (in Hebrew with English summary), *Eretz Israel* 19 (1987): 59–71. The town plan is on p. 60. Used by permission of the Israel Exploration Society.

these towns flourished in the late second century CE, they do not seem to differ markedly from the late Second Temple villages in their layout and the types of buildings found in them.

Yeivin's composite town indicates no street planning. The streets were haphazardly determined, often leaving open areas (G and H in fig. A) that became public domain. This arrangement can be observed in several of the villages in Lower Galilee[36] and is often noted by

---

36. For example, in Capernaum. See Crossan and Reed, *Excavating Jesus*, 81. Cf. Killebrew, "Village and Countryside," 196: "Natural topography, and not a master plan that typified the *polis*, played a key role in the general layout and network of streets of these unfortified 'medium-sized cities.'" Cf. also Ze'ev Safrai, *Economy of Roman Palestine,* 46: "The Jewish city or town was not planned. Therefore its streets and thoroughfares often meandered with no clear purposes." For open areas as public domain, see also Sweet, *Tell Toqaan*, 55. But contrast Stanislao Loffreda, "Capernaum," 291–95, who sees some order to the streets of Capernaum.

observers of modern Middle Eastern villages.[37] (Contrast Sepphoris, which had streets running parallel and perpendicular in an orthogonal grid pattern, often called a "Hippodamian grid.")

The town had no gates or fortified walls, but the houses were often built touching each other so that they formed a kind of *de facto* protective outer wall (A and B). Yeivin's hypothetical town had a synagogue (K), and it appears that buildings Q and R were also public buildings. Probably many of the towns also had commercial buildings.[38] Also near the town was the cemetery (the trapezoidal figure in the bottom right). According to Yeivin's previous estimates, a "medium-sized town" would have an area of 10 to 17 acres and thus a population of 1,600 to 2,720 people. Although the composite village is of the Mishnaic period, the buildings and their arrangement surely did not change that much from the late Second Temple to the Mishnaic period.

On the other hand, the one public building we cannot be sure existed in first century CE Galilean villages was the synagogue. Certainly synagogues existed in the Herodian period, but that most villages had a separate building for them is unproven. Most of the remains of the oldest synagogues are from the end of the second century or beginning of the third century CE.[39]

In the photograph below of a model of a typical Mishnaic Galilean village, the reader is urged to note how closely the houses were situated, how narrow the streets look, and how unplanned the entire village seems (see Figure B, p. 182).

### *Khirbet Karqush*

The village in Samaria known as Khirbet Karqush will serve as our second example, this one of an actual village from the late Second Temple period. This village, although not in Galilee, is a helpful model because so many of its structures are well preserved. Shimon Dar was able to date the village from the tombs in the nearby cemetery.[40] The village covers an area of 3.5 acres and thus would have had a population of from 560 to 700 persons—according to Broshi's method of computing population, a typical size for the Herodian period. Dar used Yeivin's method of determining the population and concluded that the village held around 600 people. Dar divides the village structures into two main blocks: A and B. Block A, which may be a later (Byzantine) section of the village, contained several courtyard houses. Across the street

---

37. See J. W. McGarvey, *Lands of the Bible* (Nashville: Gospel Advocate, 1966), 105, 108; Sweet, *Tell Toqaan*, 51, 54 (the streets [of contemporary Palestinian villages] are mere "cow paths"); and Abdulla M. Lutfiyya, *Baytin, a Jordanian Village: A Study of Social Institutions and Social Change in a Folk Community* (Studies in Social Anthropology 1; The Hague: Mouton, 1966), 20.

38. Such as the building found at Nabratein by Eric M. Meyers, James F. Strange, and Carol L. Meyers ("Second Preliminary Report on the 1981 Excavations at en-Nabratein, Israel," *BASOR* 246 (1982): 35–54.

39. On this subject, see Lee I. Levine, "'Common Judaism': The Contribution of the Ancient Synagogue," in *Common Judaism: Explorations in Second Temple Judaism* (ed Wayne O. McCready and Adele Reinhartz; Minneapolis: Fortress Press, 2008), 27–46; and Hershel Shanks, *Judaism in Stone: The Archaeology of Ancient Synagogues* (Jerusalem: Steinmatzky, 1979), 17–30. See also Levine's contribution on synagogues in this volume.

40. Dar, *Landscape and Pattern*, 42–46.

**Figure B. Model of a Galilean village in the Mishnaic period.** The model is in the museum of the Galilee Boat, Kibbutz Ginosar, Israel. Photo © David A. Fiensy.

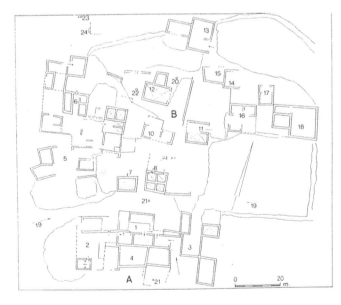

**Figure C. Khirbet Karqush.** Image from Shimon Dar, *Landscape and Pattern: An Archaeological Survey of Samaria, 800 B.C.E.–636 C.E.* (Oxford: BAR, 1986), part 2, figure 32. Copyright © 1986 Shimon Dar. Used by permission.

from Block A (in Block B) were several additional courtyard houses (numbers 6, 9, 16, 18, and probably also 12 and 13). Dar believes that building 11 was a water reservoir. Another building (10) had an unknown function and was built in the Hellenistic period. There were also several parts of an oil press found in the village that were not *in situ* (numbers 20, 23, and 24).

Dar believes that two of the structures (7 and 8) were public buildings. He found several other examples of such buildings in Samaritan villages,[41] and from other evidence we know that most villages in Syria, even small ones, had public buildings of some sort.[42] The buildings were evidently financed not from taxes but from donations of wealthy families when such families lived in or near the village, and perhaps also from the revenues of village-owned land.

Southeast of the village of Khirbet Karqush lay the cemetery with both *kokh* (Hebrew; Latin, *loculus*: a burial slot cut into a rock-cut cave) type of burial and open cist graves. Dar found 16 systems of *kokhim* tombs and 20 dwelling units in the village. Thus, he concludes that most families had a *hypogeum* (an underground family tomb). Evidently, however, the poorer families did not.

There was some evidence that one family was wealthier than the others. Dar found an ornamental tomb in the cemetery and a larger-than-usual courtyard house. Yet the difference in economic status must have been small, argues Dar, so that this family is only *primus inter pares*. In other words, this family probably did not own the village.

Just north of the supposed water reservoir was a large open square. One wonders if this area had a specific purpose such as a village marketplace, the center for exchange in ancient Palestine.[43] The Synoptic Gospels indicate that most small towns and villages had markets (Mark 6:56; 7:4; 12:28; Matt. 11:16 = Luke 7:32; Matt. 20:3; Matt. 23:7 = Luke 11:43) in addition to major market centers such as Jerusalem, Sepphoris, Shechem, Lydda, and Antipatris.[44] It is possible that such open areas served as temporary marketplaces in villages on the market day.[45] Alternatively, open areas may have been tent cities for seasonal nomadic visitors. Such village areas are known in modern Middle Eastern villages.[46]

### Khirbet Qana

The third village we will consider is Khirbet Qana, which lies on the northern edge of the western end of the Bet Netofa Valley in Lower Galilee. This village, as stated above, covered

---

41. For example, Dar, *Landscape and Pattern*, 49.

42. George McLean Harper, "Village Administration in the Roman Province of Syria," *Yale Classical Studies* 1 (1928): 105–68; and A. H. M. Jones, *The Greek City from Alexander to Justinian* (Oxford: Clarendon, 1940), 286.

43. See the chapter by Ze'ev Safrai in this volume. The marketplace was called שוק (*shuk*) in the rabbinic literature (see Marcus Jastrow, *A Dictionary of the Targumim, the Talmud Babli and Yerushalmi, and the Midrashic Literature* [2 vols.; New York: Pardes, 1950]) and ἀγορά (*agora*) in the Gospels (Mark 6:56). See also Goodman, *State and Society*, 54.

44. Applebaum, "Economic Life in Palestine," 687.

45. The pre-Mishnaic market day was Friday. See Applebaum, "Economic Life in Palestine," 687; and Goodman, *State and Society*, 54.

46. Sweet, *Tel Toqaan*, 52.

8 or 9 acres.[47] Like Yeivin's composite village and like Khirbet Karqush, Khirbet Qana had no wall in our period of occupation. There were two *columbaria* (dovecotes[48]). There has been found, so far, one olive press, a water reservoir, over 60 cisterns, and one "industrial complex" (fig. 4), identified by Peter Richardson as a wool dyeing installation.[49] There were two "public buildings," one of which may have been a synagogue, and 13 tombs.[50] Douglas Edwards, the lead excavator of this site, estimated that the total population by the second century (the Mishnaic period) was between 750 and 1400 persons.[51] Richardson thinks that in Khirbet Qana (as well as in parts of Yodefat and Gamla) some of the streets on the acropolis were arranged in an "informal or quasi-Hippodamian" grid, that is, running north to south and east to west as opposed to meandering and winding.[52] Thus, if Richardson is correct, these villages/towns may have had a bit more planning, at least in some areas of them, than most.

### *Common Patterns*

Yeivin's hypothetical medium-sized town, the village in rural Samaria described by Dar, and Khirbet Qana, the village in Lower Galilee, indicate common patterns. Most villages of any size had not only residences but also public and commercial buildings, agricultural structures

---

47. But see above. Edwards ("Khirbet Qana," 106) gives the site dimensions as 12 to 17 acres for Khirbet Qana "at its zenith," that is, in the Byzantine era.

48. For other dovecotes in Israel in the late Second Temple period, see Oded Lipschits, Yuval Gadot, Benjamin Arubas, and Manfred Oeming, "Palace and Village, Paradise and Oblivion: Unraveling the Riddles of Ramat Rahel," *NEA* 74 (2011): 2–49, esp. 38; Mordechai Aviam, *Jews, Pagans, and Christians in the Galilee: 25 Years of Archaeological Excavations and Surveys, Hellenistic to Byzantine Periods* (Land of Galilee 1. Rochester, N.Y.: University of Rochester Press, 2004), 31–40; and Boza Zissu, "Two Herodian Dovecotes: Horvat Abu Haf and Horvat 'Aleq," in *The Roman and Byzantine Near East: Some Recent Archaeological Research*, vol. 1 (Journal of Roman Archaeology Supplementary Series 14; Ann Arbor, Mich: Journal of Roman Archaeology, 1995), 56–69. As Aviam points out, so far nine *columbaria* have been found in Galilee. For dovecotes in general, see Ze'ev Safrai, *Economy of Roman Palestine,* 174–79.

49. McCollough also offers that the installation could have been used for tanning leather or as a fullery ("City and Village in Lower Galilee," 65).

50. Peter Richardson estimates that the tombs could have held around "100 loculi" ("What Has Cana to Do with Capernaum?" *NTS* 48 [2002]: 314–31, at 327). Thus, there must have been other graves (cist or trench graves?) elsewhere if the population of the village approached anything like the estimates given above (that is, around 1,600 persons in Table 2 or Edwards' estimate of between 750 and 1,400 persons). On this issue, see Jodi Magness, *Stone and Dung, Oil and Spit: Jewish Daily Life in the Time of Jesus* (Grand Rapids: Eerdmans, 2011), 155–64.

51. Edwards, "Khirbet Qana," 101–32; see esp. his maps on 106, 108. Also Peter Richardson, "Khirbet Qana (and Other Villages) as a Context for Jesus," in *Jesus and Archaeology* (ed. James H. Charlesworth; Grand Rapids: Eerdmans, 2006), 120–44. McCollough estimates the population in the first century CE at 1,200 ("City and Village in Lower Galilee," 58).

52. Richardson, "Khirbet Qana," 123. Loffreda saw a similar possibility of town planning at Capernaum ("Capernaum," 291–95). But contrast Crossan and Reed (*Excavating Jesus*, 81; and Reed, *Archaeology and the Galilean Jesus*, 152–53), who think that Capernaum shows no evidence of planning at all.

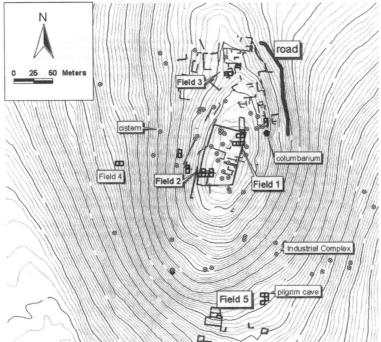

**Figure D. Khirbet Qana.** Map by Douglas Edwards in "Khirbet Qana: From Jewish Village to Christian Pilgrim Site," in *The Roman and Byzantine Near East: Some Recent Archaeological Research*, vol. 3 (Journal of Roman Archaeology Supplementary Series 49; Ann Arbor, Mich.: Journal of Roman Archaeology, 2002), 108. Used by permission of the *Journal of Roman Archaeology*.[53]

(oil or wine presses), water reservoirs, and cemeteries outside the village. Yeivin's composite village and the village in Samaria had an open space perhaps used on market days as temporary markets. (But as the reader will note below in table 5, none of the Galilean villages has exhibited such space for temporary markets.) They also had narrow, unpaved streets (that is, not paved with stone pavers) arranged in haphazard patterns, and no gates or walls.[54] The exception to the haphazard streets may have been some parts of Khirbet Qana and Yodefat. One Galilean town—Yodefat—in addition was fortified (given walls) in preparation for the revolt of 66–73 CE.[55]

---

53. The tombs lie outside the boundaries of the map.

54. See, for example, Capernaum (Crossan and Reed, *Excavating Jesus*, 81) and Nazareth (Reed, *Archaeology and the Galilean Jesus*, 131, 152–53).

55. David Adan-Bayewitz and Mordechai Aviam report that the excavations of Yodefat revealed that its walls were begun in the Hellenistic period but were strengthened by Josephus. Thus, this town had walls—at least in some areas—from the beginning (Adan-Bayewitz and Aviam, "Iotapata, Josephus, and the Siege of 67: Preliminary Report on the 1992–1994 Seasons," *Journal of Roman Archaeology* 10 [1997]: 131–65). Gamla, in the Golan, was also fortified during the revolt.

By way of contrast, the Galilean cities Sepphoris and Tiberias were planned with streets in a grid pattern and with a *Cardo* or main street over 40 feet wide in each. Tiberias had a stadium for athletic games, a monumental gate, possibly a gymnasium, and a hippodrome. Sepphoris had a large basilica (115 x 130 ft), that is, a building used for government purposes (administration or law courts).[56] Finally, there may have been a theater built in Sepphoris in the first century CE, but the date of this structure is now debated.[57] The cities had spacious streets, formally designated marketplaces, large public buildings, large domestic quarters, and more comforts of life such as entertainment. To go from village to city was to cross into a new subculture.

The following table contrasts the Galilean cities and villages:

| **Villages** | **Cities** |
| --- | --- |
| Most were unwalled. Exception: Yodefat (and Gamla in the Golan) | Walled |
| No formal marketplaces, but open spaces may have served informally | Clearly designated marketplaces |
| Topography determined how the streets were laid out. They were done in "traditional ways." | The cities were laid out in Hippodamian grids. |
| Cisterns were the main source of water, but there were some water reservoirs (at Khirbet Qana and Yodefat). | The cities had aqueducts. |
| There was no architecture for entertainment. | There were theaters in both Sepphoris and Tiberias, and Tiberias had a stadium and at some point perhaps a hippodrome. |

**Table 4.** Village and City Contrasts[58]

---

56. See Crossan and Reed, *Excavating Jesus*, 60–67; Moshe Dothan, *Hammath Tiberias* (2 vols.; Ancient Synagogue Studies; Jerusalem: Israel Exploration Society, 1983), 1:16; and Ze'ev Weiss, "Theatres, Hippodromes, Amphitheatres, and Performances," in *The Oxford Handbook of Jewish Daily Life in Roman Palestine* (ed. Catherine Hezser; Oxford: Oxford University Press, 2010), 623–40. On the basilica in Sepphoris, see James F. Strange, "The Eastern Basilical Building," in *Sepphoris in Galilee: Crosscurrents of Culture* (ed. Rebecca Martin Nagy, Carol L. Meyers, Eric M. Meyers, and Ze'ev Weiss; Raleigh: North Carolina Museum of Art; Winona Lake, Ind.: Eisenbrauns, 1996), 117–21. The building consisted of rows of offices or shops, all with floor mosaics. One room had a stepped pool.

57. For a date in the early first century (thus the time of Antipas and Jesus), see James F. Strange, "Six Campaigns at Sepphoris," in *The Galilee in Late Antiquity* (ed. Lee I. Levine; New York: Jewish Theological Seminary of America, 1992), 342; and Richard A. Batey, *Jesus and the Forgotten City: New Light on Sepphoris and the Urban World of Jesus* (Grand Rapids: Baker, 1991), 83–103. For a date in the late first or early second century for the theater, see: Ze'ev Weiss and Ehud Netzer, "Hellenistic and Roman Sepphoris: The Archaeological Evidence" in Nagy et al., *Sepphoris in Galilee*, 32; Carol L. Meyers and Eric M. Meyers, "Sepphoris," *OEANE* 4:533; and Eric M. Meyers, "Jesus and His World: Sepphoris and the Quest for the Historical Jesus," in *Saxa loquentur: Studien zur Archäologie Palästinas/Israels: Festschrift für Volkmar Fritz zum 65. Geburtstag* (ed. Cornelis G. den Hertog, Ulrich Hübner, and Stefan Münger; AOAT 302; Münster: Ugarit, 2003), 185–97.

58. The table was constructed based on ideas in Richardson, "Khirbet Qana," 127–28.

**Figure E. Cistern opening, Khirbet Qana.**
Photograph © David A. Fiensy.

What, then, was in the typical village? We may summarize our results for this section in the following table (table 5). All of the villages/towns are in Galilee (Meiron is in Upper Galilee). We include as well, for comparison, Yeivin's composite village. This table must be read with discretion. I have marked only those features attested archaeologically. But common sense will tell us that virtually all of the villages planted grain, olives, and grapes, and most of them (except for those located on the Sea of Galilee) must have had cisterns. And, of course, they all must have had cemeteries. They simply have not all been located yet. There are probably baths for rendering people and objects ritually pure (*mikva'ot*) in villages such as Shikhin and Nazareth, but none has yet been uncovered. Capernaum, located on the Sea of Galilee, would have little need of them. Thus, the table indicates only what has been discovered; it cannot be used to demonstrate what was not in the villages. At most, it can show only what has not (yet) been excavated.

The reader will notice that none of the Galilean villages excavated so far seems to have had an open space for a temporary market. Indeed, Richardson points out that the makeshift market is absent from most late Second Temple Galilean villages.[59] Here may be another difference between late Second Temple and Mishnaic villages (along with the absence, for the most part, of synagogue buildings and the presence of some sort of street planning).

---

59. Richardson, *Building Jewish*, 60. He specifically lists Cana, Yodefat, Gamla, Capernaum, and Chorazin along with "most other villages."

| Features | Meiron | Capernaum | Khirbet Qana | Yodefat | Shikhin | Nazareth | Yeivin's Composite |
|---|---|---|---|---|---|---|---|
| Synagogue | 3rd cent. | 4th cent., perhaps 1st | ? | | X | 4th cent. | X |
| Olives | X | X | X | X | X | X | |
| Grapes | | | X | | X | X | |
| Pottery production | | | | X | X | | |
| Grain production | X | X | | X | X | X | |
| Wool (loom weights) | | X | | X | X | | |
| Other industry | Cooperage | | Dyeing | | | | |
| Glass production | | | X | | | | |
| Quarries | | | X | X | X | X | |
| *Columbaria* | | | X | | | | |
| An open space | | | | | | | X |
| Tombs | X | | X | | X | X | X |
| Ritual baths | X | | X | X | X | X | |
| Water reservoir | | | X | X | | | |
| Cisterns | X | | X | X | X | X | |
| Public building | | | X | | | | |

**Table 5.** Features in ancient Galilean villages[60]

---

60. The table has been constructed based on information from the following: Edwards, "Khirbet Qana"; Richardson, "Khirbet Qana (and Other Villages)," 120–44; McCollough, "City and Village in Lower Galilee"; B. Bagatti, "Nazareth, Excavations," *NEAEHL* 3:1103–5; Adan-Bayewitz and Aviam, "Iotapata, Josephus, and the Siege of 67"; Reed, *Archaeology and the Galilean Jesus*, 131–32, 143–59; Stephen Pfann, Ross Voss, and Yehudah Rapuano, "Surveys and Excavations at the Nazareth Village Farm (1997–2002): Final Report," *BAIAS* 25 (1997): 19–79; Yeivin, "On the Medium-Sized City," 59–71; Eric M. Meyers and Carol L. Meyers, "Digging the Talmud in Ancient Meiron," *BAR* 4/2 (1978): 32–42; Eric M. Meyers, James F. Strange, and Carol L. Meyers, *Excavations at Ancient Meiron, Upper Galilee, Israel 1971–72, 1974–75, 1977* (Meiron Excavation Project 3; Cambridge, Mass.: American Schools of Oriental Research, 1981), xviii, 44, 107–20; Loffreda, "Capernaum"; anon. "Capernaum: The

**Figure F. Tomb with niches (Khirbet Qana).** This tomb is on the north side of the site. Photograph © David A. Fiensy.

## What Did They Do for a Living?

The first thing we should say about the ancient economy of Galilee, like that of every other economy of the ancient Mediterranean and Middle East, is that it was agrarian. This observation is so common as to be beyond dispute.[61] An agrarian economy was based on land ownership and farm production. Thus, most villages were supported by agriculture. If Dar's findings in Samaria are typical, the individual farm plots (one for each nuclear family) were marked off in the fields surrounding the village. The farmer, then, did not reside on his farm plot but walked out to it from the village to work it. The village residents huddled together in close quarters in the village. A good example of this arrangement can be seen in the village of

Town of Jesus," online: http://www.christusrex.org/www1/ofm/sites/TScpvill.html; James Riley Strange, "Report of the 2011 Survey and 2012 Excavation Seasons at Shikhin," American Schools of Oriental Research annual meeting, 2012, Chicago, Illinois. Online: http://www.samford.edu/uploadedFiles/2012_AS_Shikhin/ASOR_Shikhin2012.pdf

61. Michael Rostovtzeff, *A Large Estate in Egypt in the Third Century B.C.: A Study in Economic History* (University of Wisconsin Studies in the Social Sciences and History 6; Madison: University of Wisconsin Press, 1922), 270; Gerhard Lenski, *Power and Privilege: A Theory of Social Stratification* (New York: McGraw-Hill, 1966); Moses I. Finley, *The Ancient Economy* (updated ed.; Sather Classical Lectures 43; Berkeley: University of California Press, 1985); P. R. Bedford, "The Economy of the Near East in the First Millennium BC," in *The Ancient Economy: Evidence and Models* (ed. J. G. Manning and Ian Morris; Stanford: Stanford University Press, 2005), 58–83; Bruce J. Malina and Richard L. Rohrbaugh, *Social Science Commentary on the Synoptic Gospels* (Minneapolis: Fortress Press, 1992), 3–6; Douglas E. Oakman, *Jesus and the Peasants* (Matrix: The Bible in Mediterranean Context 4; Eugene, Ore.: Cascade, 2008); J. K. Davies, "Hellenistic Economies," in *The Cambridge Companion to the Hellenistic World* (ed. G. R. Bugh; Cambridge: Cambridge University Press, 2008), 73–92; Michael Avi-Yonah, *The Holy Land* (Grand Rapids: Baker, 1966), 188–89. See also the results of the survey of the Golan by Urman (*Golan*, 93), who notes that most of the villages and towns had an agricultural economy. Cf. Lewis, *Life in Egypt*, 65.

Qawarat Bene-Hassan in Samaria described by Dar.[62] There the ruins of the village and surrounding farm plots, marked off by stone walls, are still visible. Dar's survey team discovered similar farm plot systems in several other villages.[63]

But the agricultural base does not mean that there was no industry in late Second Temple and Mishnaic Palestine, especially in Galilee. As a matter of fact, there may have been more industry in Lower Galilee than elsewhere in Palestine. Yitzhak Magen's work on stoneware production has brought to light, for example, two quarry workshops in Lower Galilee—one in Bethlehem of Galilee (just southwest of Sepphoris) and the other in Kefar Reina (just east of Sepphoris). These were major producers of stone cups and other vessels. Stoneware has been discovered throughout Galilee as well (in twelve villages and cities).[64]

Further, the pottery of two villages, Kefar Hananya and Kefar Shikhin, already well known from the rabbinic sources (*m. Kelim* 2:2; *b. Baba Meṣ.* 74a; *b.Šabb.* 120b), has now been discovered archaeologically. David Adan-Bayewitz and Isadore Perlman have established that the tiny village of Kefar Hananya (located on the border between Lower Galilee and Upper Galilee) exported its common pottery up to twenty-four kilometers away into Galilee and the Golan. The pottery manufactured in this village has shown up in Nazareth, Capernaum, Kefar Kanna (a different site from Khirbet Qana), Tiberias, and Magdala in Lower Galilee, and in Meiron, Khirbet Shema' and Tel Anafa in Upper Galilee, among other sites. It also appears in the ruins of gentile cities such as Acco-Ptolemais, Hippos, Pella, and Scythopolis.[65] Further, it is clear that 75 percent of the first-century common table wares excavated at Sepphoris so far (cooking bowls) were made in Kefar Hananya. In addition, 15 percent of the storage jars or kraters discovered thus far in Sepphoris originated in the nearby town of Shikhin. As a matter of fact, the Shikhin storage jars account for the majority of pottery of that type in Galilee.[66] The conclusions usually drawn from these data are the following: (1) The cities with their rich people must not have completely exploited the peasants who lived in the villages but rather must have given them opportunities for marketing their goods and thus enhanced their economic situation. (2) The villages not only engaged in farming but had industries as well.[67]

---

62. Dar, *Landscape and Pattern*, 230–45.

63. For example, see Dar, *Landscape and Pattern*, figures 43 and 45 (Khirbet Burqa). See also Ben-David, *Talmudische Ökonomie*, 49; and the maps of village farm allotments in Ze'ev Safrai, *Economy of Roman Palestine*, 360–63.

64. Yitzhak Magen, *The Stone Vessel Industry in the Second Temple Period: Excavations at Ḥizma and the Jerusalem Temple Mount* (Judea and Samaria Publications 1; Jerusalem: Israel Exploration Society, 2002), 160.

65. David Adan-Bayewitz and Isadore Perlman, "The Socio-Economic and Cultural Ethos of the Lower Galilee in the First Century: Implications for the Nascent Jesus Movement," in Levine, *Galilee in Late Antiquity*, 53–91.

66. Strange, Groh, and Longstaff, "Excavations at Sepphoris," 216–27. The process that resulted in these conclusions is called neutron activation analysis. The scientific test allows the excavators to determine the chemical content of the clay used in making the pottery. The clay content of many of the wares found in the villages and cities of Galilee indicates that much of the pottery came from the area of Kefar Hananya and that many of the large jars came from the town of Shikhin (1.5 km from Sepphoris).

67. See David Adan-Bayewitz, *Common Pottery in Roman Galilee: A Study of Local Trade* (Bar-Ilan Studies

Shikhin (Asochis in Greek) was located on a hill with three peaks that cover 27 acres. Surely, however, the actual village was not that large. Based on surveys and two seasons of excavations, it appears that the village lay on the northern hilltop. The pottery count so far indicates that the village reached its apex during the Early Roman period. The abundance of pottery and pottery wasters indicates that the village, as celebrated in the Talmud, supported a major pottery-producing industry. The village's potters also made oil lamps.[68] Clearly, the residents of the village also engaged in agriculture, since the implements of farming are readily observed: grinding stones, oil presses, and grape presses.[69] There are many caves and underground rooms in the village area. Presumably the residents used them for food storage, perhaps also for living quarters. Excavation is ongoing at this site and should reveal more insights in the future.

Further archaeological evidence as to the economies of the villages in Lower Galilee comes from the excavation of five villages. The first two villages—Khirbet Qana[70] and Yodefat (or Jotapata)—were somewhat more prosperous than the other three.[71] Cana had some small industry: two *columbaria* (dovecotes) have been found, and a wool-dyeing installation[72] has been identified. Furthermore, at Khirbet Qana there were three types of houses representing evidently three tiers of economic prosperity in the village. But most residents lived in the simple terrace houses that shared walls with one another. The houses were made of unhewn stones and had beaten earth floors. Their roofs were of beams, brush, and plaster.[73]

Likewise, the houses of Yodefat were one or two stories of rough masonry. The walls were filled with mud plaster, and the floors were beaten earth. There was little evidence of public buildings in Yodefat. There were some large cisterns and two large open pools evidently for community use. This village was walled. One large house in Yodefat had rather elaborate frescoes in a style similar to those in the Herodian palace at Masada and in the houses of the wealthy in Jerusalem.[74] Thus, at least one family there had attained a measure of wealth. Near

---

in Near Eastern Languages and Culture; Ramat-Gan: Bar-Ilan University Press, 1993), 23–41, 216–36; Adan-Bayewitz, "Kefar Hananya, 1986," *IEJ* 37 (1987): 178–79; Adan-Bayewitz and Isadore Perlman, "The Local Trade of Sepphoris in the Roman Period," *IEJ* 40 (1990): 153–72; James F. Strange, "First Century Galilee from Archaeology and from the Texts," in Edwards and McCollough, *Archaeology and the Galilee*, 41; Douglas R. Edwards, "First Century Urban/Rural Relations in Lower Galilee: Exploring the Archaeological and Literary Evidence," *SBL 1988 Seminar Papers* (Atlanta: Scholars Press, 1988), 169–82; Meyers, "Jesus and His Galilean Context," 57–66.

68. Mordechai Aviam and James Riley Strange, "Pottery Production at the Ancient Galilean Jewish Village of Shikhin. Preliminary Studies: Oil Lamp Production" (forthcoming).

69. J. R. Strange, "Report of the 2011 Survey."

70. Probably the Cana of the New Testament, but see the essay "Kefar Kanna" in volume 2 for another view.

71. Richardson, *Building Jewish*, 57–71.

72. Richardson identifies the installation as a wool-dyeing industry. McCollough allows that it also could have been used for tanning or as a fullery ("City and Village in Lower Galilee," 65)..

73. The other two types of houses were side courtyard houses (the second tier) and central courtyard houses (the upper tier). See Richardson, *Building Jewish*, 103–4.

74. Mordechai Aviam, "Yodefat," *Hadashot Arkheologiyot* 112 (2000): 18–19.

Yodefat was a cave that had an "industrial-scale double press olive oil station." This installation seems to indicate more olive oil production than simply for private use. There was, therefore, probably an olive oil business in Yodefat. The numerous spindle whorls and loom weights found in and around the destroyed houses also attest to a "vigorous home industry of wool materials."[75] The most important industry in Yodefat, however, seems to have been pottery making because several kilns are evident among the ruins.[76]

**Figure G. The author in covered *mikveh*, near industrial installation, Khirbet Qana.** Photograph © David A. Fiensy.

We might also compare these two villages with three others: Nazareth, Capernaum, and Jalame. Nazareth was probably exclusively an agricultural village. So far, the excavations under the two churches in modern Nazareth (Church of St. Joseph and Church of the Annunciation) and on the Nazareth Village Farm have revealed granaries, pits, vaulted cells for storing wine and oil, wine presses, rock quarries, and oil presses.[77] Only slight traces of the houses have been left, leading one scholar to suggest that they must have been made of fieldstones and mud.[78] In addition, many of the houses were constructed around caves (that is, the caves were used for dwellings). These villagers do not seem to have been as prosperous as those at Yodefat and Khirbet Qana, nor do they seem to have had any industry or way to make a living beyond farming.

---

75. Mordechai Aviam, "People, Land, Economy, and Belief in First-Century Galilee and Its Origins: A Comprehensive Archaeological Synthesis," in *The Galilean Economy in the Time of Jesus* (ed. David A. Fiensy and Ralph K. Hawkins; Early Christianity and Its Literature 11; Atlanta: Society of Biblical Literature, 2013), 5–48, esp. 27.

76. Richardson, *Building Jewish*, 57–71.

77. Bagatti, "Nazareth, Excavations," 1103–5; and Pfann, Voss, and Rapuano, "Surveys and Excavations at the Nazareth Village Farm (1997-2002)," 19–79.

78. Reed, *Archaeology and the Galilean Jesus*, 132.

**Figure H. Wine Press, Nazareth village.**
Photograph © David A. Fiensy.

Capernaum was a medium-sized fishing and agricultural village. The private houses were built of undressed basalt fieldstones stacked without mortar. Small house-rooms (in *insula* fashion) surrounded large courtyards (the largest is 24 x 19.5 ft).[79] The walls are so weak that Virgilio Corbo surmised that they could never have held a stone slab roof. The roofs must have been beams, brush, and plaster. Finally, there are no houses such as those of the upper tier at Khirbet Qana, and certainly none discovered thus far with elaborate and expensive frescoes such as the one at Yodefat. There is no evidence of industry.

**Figure I. Artist's conception of Capernaum, including the synagogue and a house.** Photograph of Capernaum model used courtesy of the Virtual Bible, Inc.

---

79. Virgilio Corbo, *The House of Saint Peter at Capharnaum: A Preliminary Report of the First Two Campaigns of Excavations, April 16–June 19, Sept. 12–Nov. 26, 1968* (Publications of the Studium Biblicum Franciscanum, Collectio minor 5; Jerusalem: Franciscan Printing Press, 1969), 35–52; James F. Strange and Hershel Shanks, "Has the House Where Jesus Stayed in Capernaum Been Found?" *BAR* 8, no. 6 (1982): 26–37; Loffreda, "Capernaum," 291–95. Cf. similar findings in nearby Et Tel (probably New Testament Bethsaida), just outside the territory of Galilee: R. Arav, "Bethsaida Excavations: Preliminary Report, 1994–1996," in *Bethsaida: A City by the North Shore of the Sea of Galilee* (ed. Rami Arav and Richard A. Freund; Kirksville, Mo.: Truman State University Press, 1999), 2:3–113.

Finally, Jalame, located in western Lower Galilee, was a glass-manufacturing village. Glass was manufactured in two stages: First, the glass slabs were created by heating sand, soda, and lime. Next, raw glass from the slabs was made (or blown) into glass vessels. These vessels—usually rather small—held liquids, oils, perfumes, and ointments.[80] They may also have been used to collect tear drops from mourners.[81]

So, most residents of Lower Galilee in the first century CE would have lived in a village with a few hundred to 2,000 inhabitants and would have been engaged in agriculture, but some would have been involved in industry. It was not uncommon for entire villages to be dedicated to one type of industry,[82] such as the villages above devoted to pottery or stoneware vessels.

We should perhaps think of these village residents as existing in two categories: "pure agriculturalists" and "mixed agriculturalists."[83] The mixed agriculturalists combined farming with a craft. It appears that at least four of the villages of Galilee—Khirbet Qana, Yodefat, Kefar Hananya, and Shikhin—were composed of quite a large percentage of mixed agriculturalists. Those studying contemporary traditional villages have noted that the mixed agriculturalists generally fare better economically than the pure agriculturalists since they are not as dependent on luck and the weather.[84] The presence of so much industry in these villages might explain their apparent prosperity in comparison with Nazareth, Capernaum, and Bethsaida.

By way of contrast, if one lived in one of the two cities of Lower Galilee, Sepphoris or Tiberias, life would have been quite different. Many of those living in the cities were either the richest of the rich or their "retainers," those hired to meet the administrative needs of the rich. The houses of some of these wealthy persons may have been discovered in Sepphoris in the domestic quarter on the western slope of the acropolis. Eric Meyers, one of the excavators of Sepphoris, believes that it was inhabited by "well-to-do aristocratic Jews."[85] The houses in this quarter date from the early first century CE. These were multi-room dwellings with courtyards. Many of the houses were furnished with fresco wall paintings of floral scenes (no animals or human depictions) and a few had mosaic floors. Several of the houses were multi-storied, and

---

80. Uzi Leibner, "Arts and Crafts, Manufacture and Production," in Hezser, *Oxford Handbook of Jewish Daily Life*, 264–96, esp. 275; and Dan Barag, "Two Roman Glass Bottles with Remnants of Oil," in *Israel Exploration Journal Reader* (ed. Harry M. Orlinsky; Library of Biblical Studies; New York: Ktav, 1981), 674–76.

81. See Alexander Scheiber, "Lacrimatoria and the Jewish Sources," in Orlinsky, *Israel Exploration Journal Reader*, 678–79; and, in the same volume, Alexander Zeron, "Lacrimatoria and Pseudo-Philo's Biblical Antiquities," 677.

82. See Joseph Klausner, *Jesus of Nazareth: His Life, Times, and Teachings* (New York: Macmillan, 1925), 178; Avi-Yonah, *Holy Land*, 193.

83. These are the terms used by Joel M. Halpern to describe the residents of the village he studied (*A Serbian Village* [New York: Columbia University Press, 1958], 71).

84. Ibid., 95–96. The pure agriculturalist may boast of being such but his/her household "has no assured steady livelihood" (p. 95).

85. Eric M. Meyers, "Roman Sepphoris in Light of New Archaeological Evidence and Recent Research," in Levine, *Galilee in Late Antiquity*, 322.

many of them had ritual bath installations (stepped pools). By the size of houses and by the furnishings, we know that these were houses of those who were well-off.[86]

Yet, although the houses were of the well-to-do, they were not the houses of the extravagantly rich. They do not, for example, compare with the large and elaborately furnished mansions found in the Jewish Quarter of old Jerusalem[87] dating to the same period. By comparison of the houses alone, we would say that these are modestly rich persons. They may be the richest in Lower Galilee but not in all of Palestine/Israel in the Herodian period. Further, the small items found inside the houses do not indicate great wealth. The inhabitants used bone instead of ivory for cosmetic applications; they employed common pottery, not fine ware; they imported no wines.[88]

Thus, based on the evidence of the houses from first-century Sepphoris discovered so far (Tiberias has not been excavated adequately for such an assessment),[89] we have to say that a small percentage of the inhabitants of Lower Galilee lived in an urban setting and in plush but not extravagantly lavish houses. Houses in the villages ranged from rather comfortable to very simple structures. Probably there were also the very poor residents of villages and those who dwelled on the outskirts of the cities who lived in huts, tents, or caves.

## Conclusion

If the reader had lived in Lower Galilee in the first century CE, chances are he or she would have lived in a village of fewer than 2,000 inhabitants. The village would have consisted mostly of simply made houses, haphazardly planned, unpaved streets, perhaps a public building or two, and a few open areas used on market day or by nomadic persons for pitching their tents. If the reader was fortunate enough to have lived in one of the two cities, he or she would have known wide thoroughfares, impressive architecture, and various forms of entertainment. If the reader had lived in a village, he or she would probably have been engaged in agriculture, but certain kinds of industry would also not have been out of the question.

---

86. See Ehud Netzer and Ze'ev Weiss, *Zippori* (Jerusalem: Israel Exploation Society, 1994), 21–23; Meyers and Meyers, "Sepphoris," 531–32; Reed, *Archaeology and the Galilean Jesus*, 126; and Weiss and Netzer, "Hellenistic and Roman Sepphoris," 29–37; Kenneth G. Hoglund and Eric M. Meyers, "The Residential Quarter on the Western Summit," in Nagy et al., *Sepphoris in Galilee*, 40.

87. See Nahman Avigad, "How the Wealthy Lived in Herodian Jerusalem," *BAR* 2 (1976): 22–35. Eric M. Meyers indicates that the "Great Mansion" of Jerusalem had a living area of 600 square meters while a large house excavated at Sepphoris (building 84.1) had an area of 300 square meters ("The Problems of Gendered Space in Syro-Palestinian Domestic Architecture," in *Early Christian Families in Context: An Interdisciplinary Dialogue* [ed. David L. Balch and Carolyn Osiek; Religion, Marriage and Family; Grand Rapids: Eerdmans, 2003], 51, 67).

88. Reed, *Archaeology and the Galilean Jesus*, 126.

89. See Yizhar Hirschfeld, "Tiberias," *NEAEHL* 4:1466–67.

# Bibliography

Adan-Bayewitz, David. *Common Pottery in Roman Galilee: A Study of Local Trade.*. Bar-Ilan Studies in Near Eastern Languages and Culture. Ramat-Gan: Bar-Ilan University Press, 1993.

———. "Kefar Hananya, 1986." *IEJ* 37 (1987): 178–79.

Adan-Bayewitz, David, and Isadore Perlman. "The Local Trade of Sepphoris in the Roman Period." *IEJ* 40 (1990): 153–72.

Anonymous. "Capernaum: The Town of Jesus." N.p. Online: http://www.christusrex.org/www1/ofm/sites/TScpvill.html. Cited December 3, 2013.

Applebaum, Shimon. "Economic Life in Palestine." In *The Jewish People in the First Century: Historical Geography, Political History, Social, Cultural and Religious Life and Institutions*, vol. 2., edited by Shmuel Safrai and Menahem Stern, 631–700. CRINT, section 1, vol. 2. Assen: Van Gorcum, 1976.

———. "The Settlement Pattern of Western Samaria from Hellenistic to Byzantine Times." In Shimon Dar, *Landscape and Pattern: An Archaeological Survey of Samaria, 800 B.C.E.– 636 C.E.* 2 vols. BAR International Series 308. Oxford: BAR, 1986.

Arav, Rami. "Bethsaida Excavations: Preliminary Report, 1994–1996." In *Bethsaida: A City by the North Shore of the Sea of Galilee*, edited by Rami Arav and Richard A. Freund, 2:3–113. Kirksville, Mo.: Truman State University Press, 1999.

Aviam, Mordechai. *Jews, Pagans, and Christians in the Galilee: 25 Years of Archaeological Excavations and Surveys, Hellenistic to Byzantine Periods.* Land of Galilee 1. Rochester, N.Y.: University of Rochester Press, 2004.

———. "People, Land, Economy, and Belief in First-Century Galilee and Its Origins: A Comprehensive Archaeological Synthesis." In *The Galilean Economy in the Time of Jesus*, edited by David A. Fiensy and Ralph K. Hawkins, 5–48. Early Christianity and Its Literature 11. Atlanta: Society of Biblical Literature, 2013.

———. "Yodefat." *Hadashot Arkheologiyot* 112 (2000): 18–19.

Aviam, Mordechai, and James Riley Strange. "Pottery Production at the Ancient Galilean Jewish Village of Shikhin. Preliminary Studies: Oil Lamp Production." Forthcoming.

Avi-Yonah, Michael. *The Holy Land.* Grand Rapids: Baker, 1966.

———. *The Madaba Mosaic Map: With Introduction and Commentary.* Jerusalem: Israel Exploration Society, 1954.

Bagatti, Bellarmino. "Nazareth, Excavations." *NEAEHL* 3:1103–05.

Barag, Dan "Two Roman Glass Bottles with Remnants of Oil." In *Israel Exploration Journal Reader*, edited by Harry M. Orlinsky, 674–76. Library of Biblical Studies. New York: Ktav, 1981.

Batey, Richard A. *Jesus and the Forgotten City: New Light on Sepphoris and the Urban World of Jesus.* Grand Rapids: Baker, 1991.

Bedford, P. R. "The Economy of the Near East in the First Millennium BC." In *The Ancient Economy: Evidence and Models*, edited by J. G. Manning and Ian Morris, 58–83. Social Science History. Stanford: Stanford University Press, 2005.

Ben-David, Arye *Talmudische Ökonomie: Die Wirtschaft des jüdischen Palästinas zur Zeit der Mischna und des Talmud.* Hildesheim: Georg Olms, 1974.

Broshi, Magen. "The Population of Western Palestine in the Roman-Byzantine Period." *BASOR* 236 (1979): 1–10.

Cohen, Shaye J. D. "The Rabbi in Second-Century Jewish Society." In *The Cambridge History of Judaism*, vol. 3, *The Early Roman Period*, edited by William Horbury, W. D. Davies, and John Sturdy. Cambridge: Cambridge University Press, 1999.

Corbo, Virgilio. *The House of Saint Peter at Capharnaum: A Preliminary Report of the First Two Campaigns of Excavations, April 16–June 19, Sept. 12–Nov. 26, 1968.* Publications of the Studium Biblicum Franciscanum, Collectio minor 5. Translated by Sylvester Saller. Jerusalem: Franciscan Printing Press, 1972.

Crossan, John Dominic, and Jonathan Reed. *Excavating Jesus: Beneath the Stones, Behind the Texts.* San Francisco: Harper SanFrancisco, 2001.

Dar, Shimon. *Landscape and Pattern: An Archaeological Survey of Samaria, 800 B.C.E.–636 C.E.* 2 vols. BAR International Series 308. Oxford: BAR, 1986.

Davies, J. K. "Hellenistic Economies." In *The Cambridge Companion to the Hellenistic World*, edited by G. R. Bugh. Cambridge: Cambridge University Press, 2008.

Dever, William G. *The Lives of Ordinary People in Ancient Israel: Where Archaeology and the Bible Intersect.* Grand Rapids: Eerdmans, 2012.

Dothan, Moshe. *Hammath Tiberias.* 2 vols. Ancient Synagogue Studies. Jerusalem: Israel Exploration Society, 1983.

Edwards, Douglas R. "First Century Urban/Rural Relations in Lower Galilee: Exploring the Archaeological and Literary Evidence." In *SBL 1988 Seminar Papers*, edited by David J. Lull, 169–82. Atlanta: Scholars Press, 1988.

———. "Identity and Social Location in Roman Galilean Villages." In *Religion, Ethnicity, and Identity in Ancient Galilee: A Region in Transition*, edited by Jürgen Zangenberg, Harold W. Attridge, and Dale B. Martin, 357–74. WUNT 210. Tübingen: Mohr Siebeck, 2007.

———. "Khirbet Qana: From Jewish Village to Christian Pilgrim Site." In *The Roman and Byzantine Near East: Some Recent Archaeological Research*, vol. 3, *Late-Antique Petra, Nile Festival Building at Sepphoris, Deir Qal'a Monastery, Khirbet Qana Village and Pilgrim Site, 'Ain-'Arrub Hiding Complex and Other Studies* (edited by J. H. Humphrey; Journal of Roman Archaeology Supplementary Series 49; Ann Arbor, Mich.: Journal of Roman Archaeology, 2002), 101–32.

———. "The Socio-Economic and Cultural Ethos of the Lower Galilee in the First Century: Implications for the Nascent Jesus Movement." In *The Galilee in Late Antiquity*, edited by Lee I. Levine, 53–74. New York: Jewish Theological Seminary, 1992.

Fiensy, David A. "Population, Architecture, and Economy in Lower Galilean Villages and Towns in the First Century AD: A Brief Survey." In *My Father's World: Celebrating the Life of Reuben G. Bullard*, edited by. John D. Wineland, Mark Ziese, and James Riley Estep Jr., 101–19. Eugene, Ore.: Wipf & Stock, 2011.

Finley, Moses I. *The Ancient Economy.* Updated ed. Sather Classical Lectures 43. Berkeley: University of California Press, 1985.

Frankel, Rafael, Nimrod Getzov, Mordechai Aviam, and Avi Degani. *Settlement Dynamics and Regional Diversity in Ancient Galilee.* IAA Reports 14. Jerusalem: Israel Antiquities Authority, 2001.

Fry, Evan. "Cities, Towns, and Villages in the Old Testament." *Bible Translator* 30 (1979): 434–38.

Goodman, Martin. *State and Society in Roman Galilee, A.D. 132–212.* Totowa, N.J.: Rowman & Allenheld, 1983.

Halpern, Joel M. *A Serbian Village.* New York: Columbia University Press, 1958.

Harper, George McLean. "Village Administration in the Roman Province of Syria." *Yale Classical Studies* 1 (1928): 105–68.

Hoehner, Harold W. *Herod Antipas.* SNTSMS 17. Cambridge: Cambridge University Press, 1972.

Horsley, Richard A. *Archaeology, History, and Society in Galilee: The Social Context of Jesus and the Rabbis.* Valley Forge, Pa.: Trinity Press International, 1996.

Jones, A. H. M. *The Greek City from Alexander to Justinian.* Oxford: Clarendon, 1940.

———. "The Urbanization of Palestine." *JRS* 21 (1931): 78–85.

Killebrew, Anne E. "Village and Countryside." In *The Oxford Handbook of Jewish Daily Life in Roman Palestine*, edited by Catherine Hezser, 189–209. Oxford: Oxford University Press, 2010.

Leibner, Uzi. "Arts and Crafts, Manufacture and Production." In *The Oxford Handbook of Jewish Daily Life in Roman Palestine*, edited by Catherine Hezser, 264–96. Oxford: Oxford University Press, 2010.

———. *Settlement and History in Hellenistic, Roman, and Byzantine Galilee: An Archaeological Survey of the Eastern Galilee.* TSAJ 127. Tübingen: Mohr Siebeck, 2009.

Lenski, Gerhard E. *Power and Privilege: A Theory of Social Stratification.* New York: McGraw-Hill, 1966.

Levine, Lee I. "'Common Judaism': The Contribution of the Ancient Synagogue." In *Common Judaism: Explorations in Second Temple Judaism*, edited by Wayne O. McCready and Adele Reinhartz, 311–43. Minneapolis: Fortress Press, 2008.

Lewis, Naphtali. *Life in Egypt under Roman Rule.* Oxford: Clarendon Press, 1983.

Lipschits, Oded, Yuval Gadot, Benjamin Arubas, and Manfred Oeming. "Palace and Village, Paradise and Oblivion: Unraveling the Riddles of Ramat Rahel." *NEA* 74 (2011): 2–49.

Loffreda, Stanislao. "Capernaum." *NEAEHL* 1:292.

Lutfiyya, Abdulla M. *Baytin, A Jordanian Village: A Study of Social Institutions and Social Change in a Folk Community.* Studies in Social Anthropology 1. The Hague: Mouton, 1966.

Magen, Yitzhak. *The Stone Vessel Industry in the Second Temple Period: Excavations at Ḥizma and the Jerusalem Temple Mount.* Judea and Samaria Publications 1. Jerusalem: Israel Exploration Society, 2002.

Magness, Jodi. *Stone and Dung, Oil and Spit: Jewish Daily Life in the Time of Jesus.* Grand Rapids: Eerdmans, 2011.

Malina, Bruce J., and Richard L. Rohrbaugh. *Social Science Commentary on the Synoptic Gospels.* Minneapolis: Fortress Press, 1992.

McCollough, C. Thomas. "City and Village in Lower Galilee: The Import of the Archeological Excavations at Sepphoris and Khirbet Qana (Cana) for Framing the Economic Context of Jesus." In *The Galilean Economy in the Time of Jesus*, edited by David A. Fiensy and Ralph K. Hawkins, 49–74. Early Christianity and Its Literature 11. Atlanta: Society of Biblical Literature, 2013.

McGarvey, J. W. *Lands of the Bible.* Nashville: Gospel Advocate, 1966.

Meyers, Carol L., and Eric M. Meyers. "Sepphoris." *OEANE* 4:533.

Meyers, Eric M. "Jesus and His Galilean Context." In *Archaeology and the Galilee: Texts and Contexts in the Graeco-Roman and Byzantine Periods*, edited by Douglas R. Edwards and C. Thomas McCollough, 57–66. South Florida Studies in the History of Judaism 143. Atlanta: Scholars Press, 1997.

———. "Jesus and His World: Sepphoris and the Quest for the Historical Jesus." In *Saxa loquentur: Studien zur Archäologie Palästinas/Israels. Festschrift für Volkmar Fritz zum 65. Geburtstag*, edited by Cornelis G. den Hertog, Ulrich Hübner, and Stefan Münger, 185–97. AOAT 302. Münster: Ugarit, 2003.

Meyers, Eric M., and Carol L. Meyers. "Digging the Talmud in Ancient Meiron." *BAR* 4, no. 2 (1978): 32–42.

Meyers, Eric M., James F. Strange, and Carol L. Meyers. "Second Preliminary Report on the 1981 Excavations at en-Nabratein, Israel." *BASOR* 246 (1982): 35–54.

———. *Excavations at Ancient Meiron, Upper Galilee, Israel 1971–72, 1974–75, 1977.* Meiron Excavation Project 3. Cambridge, Mass.: American Schools of Oriental Research, 1981.

Netzer, Ehud, and Ze'ev Weiss. *Zippori.* Jerusalem: Israel Exploation Society, 1994.

Oakman, Douglas E. *Jesus and the Peasants.* Matrix: The Bible in Mediterranean Context 4. Eugene, Ore.: Cascade, 2008.

Overman, J. Andrew. "Who Were the First Urban Christians?" In *SBL 1988 Seminar Papers*, edited by David J. Lull, 160–68. Atlanta: Scholars Press, 1988.

Pfann, Stephen, Ross Voss, and Yehudah Rapuano. "Surveys and Excavations at the Nazareth Village Farm (1997–2002): Final Report." *BAIAS* 25 (2997): 19–79.

Reed, Jonathan. *Archaeology and the Galilean Jesus: A Re-Examination of the Evidence.* Harrisburg, Pa.: Trinity Press International, 2000.

Reinhardt, Wolfgang. "The Population Size of Jerusalem and the Numerical Growth of the Jerusalem Church." In *The Book of Acts in Its Palestinian Setting*, edited by Richard Bauckham, 237–65. Book of Acts in Its First Century Setting 4. Grand Rapids: Eerdmans, 1995.

Richardson, Peter. *Building Jewish in the Roman East.* Waco, Tex.: Baylor University Press, 2004.

———. "Khirbet Qana (and Other Villages) as a Context for Jesus." In *Jesus and Archaeology*, edited by James H. Charlesworth, 120–44. Grand Rapids: Eerdmans, 2006.

———. "What Has Cana to Do with Capernaum?" *NTS* 48 (2002): 314–31.

Rostovtzeff, Michael. *A Large Estate in Egypt in the Third Century B.C.: A Study in Economic History.* University of Wisconsin Studies in the Social Sciences and History 6. Madison: University of Wisconsin Press, 1922.

Safrai, Ze'ev. *The Economy of Roman Palestine.* London: Routledge, 1994.

Scheiber, Alexander. "Lacrimatoria and the Jewish Sources." In *Israel Exploration Journal Reader*, edited by Harry M. Orlinsky, 678–79. New York: Ktav, 1981.

Schürer, Emil. *The History of the Jewish People in the Age of Jesus Christ (175 B.C.–A.D. 135).* Revised and edited by Geza Vermes, Fergus Millar, Matthew Black, and Martin Goodman. 3 vols. in 4 parts. Edinburgh: T&T Clark, 1973–87.

Shanks, Hershel. *Judaism in Stone: The Archaeology of Ancient Synagogues.* Jerusalem: Steinmatzky, 1979.

Sherwin-White, A. N. *Roman Society and Roman Law in the New Testament.* Oxford: Clarendon Press, 1963.

Shiloh, Y. "The Population of Iron Age Palestine in the Light of a Sample Analysis of Urban Plans, Areas, and Population Density." *BASOR* 239 (1980): 25–35.

Strange, James F. "The Eastern Basilical Building." In *Sepphoris in Galilee: Crosscurrents of Culture*, edited by Rebecca Martin Nagy, Carol L. Meyers, Eric M. Meyers, and Ze'ev Weiss, 311–43. Raleigh: North Carolina Museum of Art; Winona Lake, Ind.: Eisenbrauns, 1996.

———. "First Century Galilee from Archaeology and from the Texts." In *Archaeology and the Galilee: Texts and Contexts in the Graeco-Roman and Byzantine Periods*, edited by Douglas R. Edwards and C. Thomas McCollough, 39–48. South Florida Studies in the History of Judaism 143. Atlanta: Scholars Press, 1997.

———. "Nazareth." *ABD* 4:1050.

———. "Six Campaigns at Sepphoris: The University of South Florida Excavations, 1983–1989." In *The Galilee in Late Antiquity*, edited by Lee I. Levine, 311–43. New York: Jewish Theological Seminary of America, 1992.

Strange, James F., Dennis E. Groh, and Thomas R. W. Longstaff. "University of South Florida Excavations at Sepphoris: The Location and Identification of Shikhin." *IEJ* 44 (1994): 216–27; 45 (1995): 171–87.

Strange, James F., and Hershel Shanks. "Has the House Where Jesus Stayed in Capernaum Been Found?" *BAR* 8, no. 6 (1982): 26–37.

Strange, James Riley. Online: http://www.samford.edu/uploadedFiles/2012_AS_Shikhin/ASOR_Shikhin2012.pdf.

Sweet, Louise E. *Tel Toqaan: A Syrian Village.* Anthropological Papers 14. Ann Arbor: University of Michigan, 1974.

Urman, Dan. *The Golan: A Profile of a Region during the Roman and Byzantine Periods.* BAR International Series 269. Oxford: BAR, 1985.

Weiss, Ze'ev. "Theatres, Hippodromes, Amphitheatres, and Performances." In *The Oxford Handbook of Jewish Daily Life in Roman Palestine*, edited by Catherine Hezser, 623–40. Oxford: Oxford University Press, 2010.

Weiss, Ze'ev, and Ehud Netzer. "Hellenistic and Roman Sepphoris: The Archaeological Evidence." In *Sepphoris in Galilee: Crosscurrents of Culture*, edited by Rebecca Martin Nagy, Carol L. Meyers, Eric M. Meyers, and Ze'ev Weiss, 29–37. Raleigh: North Carolina Museum of Art; Winona Lake, Ind.: Eisenbrauns, 1996.

Yeivin, Ze'ev. "On the Medium-Sized City." *Eretz Israel* 19 (1987): 59–71.

———. "Survey of Settlements in Galilee and the Golan from the Period of the Mishnah in Light of the Sources." PhD diss., Hebrew University, 1971.

Zeron, Alexander "Lacrimatoria and Pseudo-Philo's Biblical Antiquities." In *Israel Exploration Journal Reader*, edited by Harry M. Orlinsky, 677. New York: Ktav, 1981.

Zissu, Boaz. "Two Herodian Dovecotes: Horvat Abu Haf and Horvat 'Aleq." In *Roman and Byzantine Near East: Some Recent Archaeological Research*, vol. 1, 56–69. Journal of Roman Studies Supplementary Series 14. Ann Arbor, Mich: Journal of Roman Studies, 1995.

# 9

# HOUSEHOLD JUDAISM

*Andrea M. Berlin*

Household Judaism is the practice, beginning in the early first century BCE, whereby people living in the regions of Judea, the Lower Galilee, and southern Gaulanitis adopted identical new household goods that distinguished their homes, and therefore their daily lives, from those of people living in adjacent regions. These new goods comprised an array of ceramic vessels for the daily tasks of cooking, dining, and storing and shipping oil and wine. Appearing at the same time as these vessels, and in the same places, were neighborhood and household *mikva'ot*. Household Judaism allowed people throughout a large region to live in similar fashion and so project a shared identity; in effect, it allowed a *Ioudaios*, or a Judean, meaning somebody from the specific geographic region of Judea, to be regarded instead as a Jew, meaning somebody who maintained a specific lifestyle. At the end of the first century BCE and in the early first century CE, *Ioudaioi* also adopted a new type of plain oil lamp and vessels made of soft chalk. In addition, throughout these years most *Ioudaioi* in Jerusalem and Judea also followed identical burial practices, with understated funerals at undecorated family tombs. Household Judaism developed outside legal or priestly concerns. The practice reflects a broad desire for material possessions that encoded a singular lifestyle and ethnic affiliation.

## The Background to Household Judaism

From the middle to the end of the second century BCE, meaning in the first two generations of Hasmonean rule, Judea was a rural society. People lived dispersed throughout the region's hills and valleys, with Jerusalem the only settlement of significant size. In both city and countryside, people were self-sufficient and acquired essentially no imported goods. Theirs was a culture of material simplicity, marked more by items that were absent than by those that were present. Two pieces of evidence suggest that the absence was purposeful. First, earlier residents

208

of Jerusalem did have imported goods, indicating geographic access. Second, in contemporary settlements adjacent to early Hasmonean Judea, such goods continued to appear in quantity.

Evidence that earlier residents of Jerusalem possessed more than local utilitarian items comes from fourth- and third-century BCE fills from the City of David and the Armenian Garden. Here excavators found Aegean wine jars and black slipped and painted plates, bowls, and drinking cups from Athens, Antioch, Alexandria, and other producers in the eastern Mediterranean. A few luxury objects also occur, such as an ivory box carved with a rendition of Zeus, in the guise of an eagle, and the youth Ganymede. These show that some residents admired and acquired Mediterranean cultural goods.[1]

Evidence that in the middle and later second century BCE the supply of imported goods remained strong comes from sites in Idumea, along the coast, and in Samaria. People here lived in a fundamentally different economic and social world. Urbanized settlement patterns, Greek styles of house décor, Aegean wines and imported plates, figurines in Greek styles and subjects—such goods reveal a population intimately connected to the wider Mediterranean world and its dominant hellenizing culture.[2]

This period of purposefully simple households in Judea is concurrent with the rise of the Hasmonean state. In 142 BCE, Simon captured the Akra and expelled the Seleucid garrison. He died eight years later and his son John Hyrcanus took over, a dynastic succession that marked the transformation of a small native rebellion into an independent polity. Five years later, in 129 BCE, the Seleucid king Antiochus VII Sidetes died while on campaign in Parthia, an event that relieved the new ruler of his obligation to fund and supply troops on behalf of imperial Seleucid aims. The manner in which Hyrcanus chose to deploy his now available resources is well reflected in the archaeological record: in 112/111 BCE, Marisa was destroyed and essentially abandoned, followed by Mount Gerizim in 110, Samaria in 108, and Beth Shean-Scythopolis in 108/107. By 103 BCE, when Hyrcanus's son Alexander Jannaeus took the throne, the Hasmoneans controlled Idumea, Judea, Samaria, and Perea across the Jordan.

### The Appearance of Household Judaism

This is the background to the new cultural practice of household Judaism, which appeared in the early first century BCE and then continued to develop into the first century CE. Two physical aspects mark this earliest stage. The first concerns common, utilitarian goods. Throughout the newly expanded Hasmonean kingdom, potters began manufacturing household ceramic vessels with identical typological details, meaning simply that they all looked alike. Large jars

---

1. See Andrea M. Berlin, "Manifest Identity: From *Ioudaios* to Jew. Household Judaism as Hellenization in the Late Hasmonean Era," in *Between Cooperation and Hostility: Multiple Identities in Ancient Judaism and the Interaction with Foreign Powers* (ed. Rainer Albertz and Jakob Wöhrle; Journal of Ancient Judaism Supplements 11; Göttingen: Vandenhoeck & Ruprecht, 2013), 157–60.

2. Berlin, "Manifest Identity," 160–64.

for shipping and storing wine, oil, and water all had an elongated sacklike body and a wide, flat band around the mouth (fig. A).

**Figure B. Cooking pots, first century BCE.**
*Top left*, Jerusalem, Binyane Ha'Uma production site. Reprinted courtesy of the Israel Exploration Society. *Top right*, Beth Zur. Reprinted courtesy of the American Schools of Oriental Research. *Bottom*, Gamla, Area B. Photo provided by the author.

**Figure A. Storage jars from Jerusalem and Gamla.** Top image reprinted courtesy of the Israel Exploration Society. Bottom image provided by the author.

Cooking pots had a compact globular body, high, slightly canted neck, and plain lip (fig. B).

The forms of lamps, small bowls, and saucers were identical. Scientific clay analyses reveal that these basic household goods were made of different clays, local to the vicinities of the settlements in which they were found. Thus, their stylistic similarities were not due to production in a single manufacturing center.[3]

An important point is that these new household goods were not confined to Judea, but also now appeared at new settlements in Galilee and central Gaulanitis. The new sites were small, at least initially—a few houses clustered on low hills above valley land suitable for farm-

---

3. Berlin, "Manifest Identity," 168–69; Berlin, "Jewish Life before the Revolt: The Archaeological Evidence," *JSJ* 36 (2005): 420–29.

ing and grazing animals. Since most of the sites that had previously been occupied remained so, it is reasonable to conclude that new people moved into the region. With the new settlers came new market patterns. For several hundred years prior, people living in Galilee and Gaulanitis had purchased the bulk of their household pottery along with an array of luxury commodities from coastal suppliers, primarily from Akko and Tyre. In the early first century BCE, people living in the Upper Galilee and the Huleh Valley continued to acquire coastal products; a visitor to one of their houses could see Aegean wine jars, decorated dishes made near Antioch, and perfume bottles from Tyre. But a visitor to a settlement in Lower Galilee and Gaulanitis would see only jars, cooking vessels, and dishes made from local clays. Further, the household goods on these first-century BCE shelves were all shapes that had been common in Judea. The likeliest explanation for this phenomenon—Judean vessel forms in local Galilean clays—is that the new settlers and the new potters who supplied them had moved here from Judea. On this basis, the new population group can be called *Ioudaioi*—northern *Ioudaioi*. By the early first century BCE, in other words, "Judean" no longer denoted solely a geographical affiliation but rather indicated a kind of social or cultural identity.[4]

The second innovation is the sudden appearance of *mikva'ot*, stepped plastered pools, in the same settlements in Judea, the lower Galilee, and Gaulanitis where the new array of household goods now occurs (fig. C).

**Figure C. Mikva'ot, first century BCE.** *Left, Mikveh,* Jerusalem Upper City. Reprinted courtesy of the Israel Exploration Society. *Right, Mikveh,* Gamla, Area B. Reprinted courtesy of the Israel Antiquities Authority.

Before the early to mid-first century BCE there is no evidence for such installations anywhere where *Ioudaioi* lived. Now they occur everywhere, from the Hasmonean palaces at Jericho and the upper city of Jerusalem to rural villages such as Gezer and Gamla. The

---

4. Berlin, "Identity Politics in Early Roman Galilee," in *The Jewish Revolt against Rome: Interdisciplinary Perspectives* (ed. Mladen Popović; JSJSup 154; Leiden: Brill, 2011), 77–92.

widely scattered find-spots indicate that suddenly across a broad spectrum of society people had decided to build and use *mikva'ot* on some kind of regular basis and so needed to have this special installation available near their homes. The sudden appearance of *mikva'ot* does not mean that the belief in and rite of purifying immersion was itself new. But it does suggest that people now practiced such immersion outside of the temple rites for which it was traditionally mandated. In other words, the appearance of *mikva'ot* in places far removed from the Jerusalem temple indicates that in the early first century BCE *Ioudaioi* transformed a special rite into regular practice. Further, since *mikva'ot* were distinctive and easily recognizable, both the installations and the practice they allowed advertised ethnic identity and proclaimed cultural separation.[5]

To appreciate the message of both *mikva'ot* and the new vessels one had to enter private household space—hence the term *household Judaism* to describe this new practice. Four points must be made. First, this was *visible practice*, conscious, specific behavior carried out via material objects. Second, the specific objects were *new*, first appearing in the early years of the last century BCE but not before. Third, the objects were *domestic*; they represented the choices and supported the activities of private individuals. Finally, these objects were *not mandated by halakhah*. Unlike the material lifestyle of early Hasmonean times, household Judaism was active: it depended on regular and widespread demand for and supply of specific goods as well as the construction of *mikva'ot*. Jewish identity in the last century BCE and first century CE has been described as an "ideological complex" founded on "three pillars—the one God, the one Torah, and the one Temple."[6] Household Judaism comprised a fourth pillar, one that allowed individuals to craft a distinct home and lifestyle. With its practice, Judeans lived as one people, no matter where they actually resided within the Hasmonean kingdom. In effect, household Judaism was one of the practices that transformed a Judean into a Jew.

### Household Judaism in the First Century CE

In the early years of the first century CE, Jews living in Judea, Galilee, and Gaulanitis added two new categories of utilitarian objects to their household goods: plain knife-pared lamps and stone vessels made from soft chalk. Both the lamps and the stone vessels were distinctive in style, recognizably different from other contemporary objects that had the same function. As with the changes in material culture in the previous century, people seem to have adopted these new objects in order to communicate group identity, and even solidarity.

---

5. See Berlin, "Jewish Life before the Revolt," 451–53; Berlin, "Identity Politics," 92–95.

6. Seth Schwartz, *Imperialism and Jewish Society 200 B.C.E. to 640 C.E.* (Jews, Christians, and Muslims from the Ancient to the Modern World; Princeton: Princeton University Press, 2001), 49.

### Plain Knife-pared Lamps

The new lamp form was a stylistic amalgam, a combination of the double-convex body of Hellenistic mold-made lamps with a short flaring nozzle similar to a popular Italian form. Potters made the body of the lamp on a wheel and formed the nozzle by hand, paring away the sides of the nozzle in order to better simulate the pinched contours of the Italian originals. Immediately upon their invention at the very end of the first century BCE/beginning of the first century CE, these lamps appear throughout Judea, Galilee, and Gaulanitis; they are often the only lamp type found in first-century CE levels. Clay analyses of knife-pared lamps from Jerusalem, Khirbet Qumrân, Masada, and Gamla indicate that most were made of clay from Jerusalem, indicating that the city was the major supplier even for lamps found far to the north.[7]

Knife-pared lamps were deliberately plain; they carried no decoration save for an occasional line or impressed circles on the nozzle. The lack of decoration is unusual and unnecessary, at least in terms of technique or expense. For two centuries previously, lamps had been made by an inexpensive molding process that allowed adornment from palmettes and schematic foliage to winged Erotes. The Italian lamps whose nozzles Jerusalem potters copied almost always displayed images or scenes. Further, the molding process had been used by Judean lamp makers in the first century BCE. All of this indicates that potters could easily have decorated knife-pared lamps but chose not to do so. Instead, they designed a new form that was purposely plain.

### Stone Vessels

A variety of stone vessel shapes appear at the same time and at the same sites as do the new knife-pared lamps. Most fall into one of four functional groups: (1) cylindrical mugs (so-called measuring cups with chiseled exteriors); (2) deep, wide-mouthed jars; (3) dishes suitable for serving food and drink, such as trays, bowls, and mugs (fig. D); and (4) small miscellaneous items such as stoppers, lids, and inkwells.

**Figure D. Small stone dishes for table use from the Jerusalem Upper City excavations.** Image reprinted courtesy of the Israel Exploration Society.

Many scholars attribute the popularity of stone vessels at Jewish sites to an increased attentiveness to concerns of ritual purity. Aside from a single mention in John 2:6 of stone jars used to store water for purification, however, there is no textual evidence delineating how any of the many other types of vessels would have been used. Mishnah *Parah* 3:2 refers to the use

---

7. Berlin, "Jewish Life before the Revolt," 434–36.

of stone cups to take water from the Siloam Pool, but that text does not link the cups to any specific rituals, and the citation may simply reflect the common use of such vessels at that time. Several rabbinic rulings deemed stone vessels among a select group that were able to maintain and transmit purity to water, but all of these rulings actually postdate the archaeologically attested appearance of the vessels and could as easily represent the codifying of a popular idea.

Since they appear in such a variety of shapes and sizes, there is no reason that all forms of stone vessels were necessarily regarded and used in the same way. The cylindrical mugs and large jars were new shapes and may well have been designed to accommodate religious uses such as washing hands and holding water for "purification rites" (as indicated in John 2:6). On the other hand, vessels for serving food and drink, along with lids, inkwells, and the like, were designed for table and utilitarian uses; no evidence exists for "nonpriestly" personal or household rites that might have required any specific household object, no matter the material.

Over sixteen stone vessel workshops of varying sizes have been discovered. Five large operations were in the environs of Jerusalem; a sixth workshop was at Reina just north of Nazareth in the Lower Galilee. In addition to these larger operations, there were also "household" workshops in rural Judea, the Shephelah, the Lower Galilee, and Gaulanitis. One noticeable absence in the list is the region of Samaria. Here no workshops are known, and stone vessels occur at only two sites: Samaria itself and Khirbet el-Hammam, at the edge of the Jezreel Valley.

In view of the number of workshops and suppliers, the fact that stone vessels occur in settlements of every type and class, and the availability of the stone itself, stone dishes were probably not very expensive. The impetus behind their sudden popularity at this time probably springs from their most obvious characteristic, which is the material from which they were made. Stone dishes were recognizably local, part of the land itself. Their usage would have communicated a pride of place, a place suffused with an increasingly visible and material Jewish identity.[8]

## Household Judaism and the Revolt against Rome

The practice of household Judaism developed in the early first century BCE, probably during the time of the Hasmonean king Alexander Jannaeus. By the early years of the first century CE, three to four generations of Jews in Judea, Galilee, and Gaulanitis had been living surrounded by its material markers: identical household pottery, lamps, stone vessels, and *mikva'ot*. By these items, Jews infused their private lives with a unified sense of ethnic pride and solidarity.

Throughout these years the majority of Jews in Jerusalem and Judea followed identical burial practices, with understated funerals and the placement of the deceased in undecorated

---

8. Berlin, "Jewish Life before the Revolt," 429–34.

family tombs. Also at this time Jews began building in their villages synagogues, places in which they could gather to discuss and read from the Torah. In addition to their practical functions, synagogues provided an assertive structural advertisement of communal identity.[9]

Along with similar burial practices and regular gathering in synagogues, household Judaism formed a key part of Jewish daily life in the years leading up to the revolt. By following these practices Jews in Judea, Galilee, and Gaulanitis created a separate world for themselves. They made the deliberate and active choice to live in a manner specific to them alone and recognizable as such to outsiders. By the middle of the first century CE no Jew living in this region would have remembered a way of life that did not emphatically reify a distinctive ethnic and religious identity. While such a lifestyle was not necessarily radical in and of itself, it may well have contributed to a sharply delineated worldview, a sense of separation from others. It was a view, a sense, and a lifestyle that contributed in part to the decision in 66 CE to revolt against Rome. Neither the view nor the lifestyle survived intact beyond the Roman victory in the year 70 CE. The sense of separation that household Judaism enabled has, however, lived on.

## Bibliography

Berlin, Andrea M. *Gamla: Final Reports.* Vol. 1, *The Pottery of the Second Temple Period.* IAA Reports 29. Jerusalem: Israel Antiquities Authority, 2006.

———. "Identity Politics in Early Roman Galilee." In *The Jewish Revolt against Rome: Interdisciplinary Perspectives,* edited by Mladen Popović, 69–106. JSJSup 154. Leiden: Brill, 2011.

———. "Jewish Life before the Revolt: The Archaeological Evidence." *JSJ* 36 (2005): 417–70.

———. "Manifest Identity: from *Ioudaios* to Jew. Household Judaism as Hellenization in the Late Hasmonean Era." In *Between Cooperation and Hostility: Multiple Identities in Ancient Judaism and the Interaction with Foreign Powers,* edited by Rainer Albertz and Jakob Wöhrle, 171–75. Journal of Ancient Judaism Supplements 11. Göttingen: Vandenhoeck & Ruprecht, 2013.

Schwartz, Seth. *Imperialism and Jewish Society 200 B.C.E. to 640 C.E.* Jews, Christians, and Muslims from the Ancient to the Modern World. Princeton: Princeton University Press, 2001.

---

9. Berlin, "Identity Politics," 99.

# 10

# THE GALILEAN HOUSE IN THE LATE SECOND TEMPLE AND MISHNAIC PERIODS

*David A. Fiensy*

If you lived in Galilee in the late Second Temple or Mishnaic period, what sort of house would you live in? To a great extent the answer to this question would depend on your means, your location, and your own skills. The Galileans' situation cannot have been much different from the pioneers in the old American frontier. Materials for building were at hand, free for the taking (wood or sod), but the wealthier could hire professionals to do it for them. Likewise, in the first century BCE through the second century CE in Galilee, there were plenty of materials (stone, wood, plaster, and mud) that could have been accessed presumably free of charge, but some inhabitants wanted and could afford to hire professional carpenters and stone masons to build their house for them, or at least to direct its construction by volunteer laborers.

When we speak of a "house," what do we mean? We are here referring to the total domestic area: the buildings under roof, the open-air courtyard, and the subterranean silos and animal stalls. Most houses in the ancient Near East and Mediterranean world were associated with an outdoor courtyard.[1] Likewise, many, if not most, houses contained underground passageways that led to their store of goods or even to their accommodations for livestock.[2]

---

1. See H. K. Beebe, "Domestic Architecture and the New Testament," *BA* 38 (1975): 89–104: From the Middle Bronze period on, the courtyard was the central feature of houses in Palestine (p. 91).

2. See the excavations at Nazareth, which are visible today under the courtyard of the Church of the Annunciation and under the Church of St. Joseph. See also below.

## House Types

Scholars studying Palestinian houses have organized the structures into architectural styles. The village house underwent a change from the typical four-room house of the Israelite period, in which an extended family lived, to the "courtyard house" of the Hellenistic and Roman periods.[3] The four-room house consisted of "a back room the width of the building, with three long rooms stemming from it."[4] The house style that succeeded the four-room house usually had an internal courtyard and probably developed under foreign influence.[5]

Ze'ev Yeivin, examining excavation and survey reports for Galilee and the Golan, places houses into four categories.[6] Yizhar Hirschfeld also found four types, though his types were somewhat different from Yeivin's.[7] Santiago Guijarro suggests five types.[8] Peter Richardson has discovered nine forms of housing in rural areas and eleven in urban settings.[9] I will combine several of these types and seek to explore the following housing styles:[10]

- The simple house
- The complex house (both urban apartments and rural farmhouses)

---

3. Shimon Dar, *Landscape and Pattern: An Archaeological Survey of Samaria, 800 B.C.E.–636 C.E.* (2 vols.; BAR International Series 308; Oxford: BAR, 1986), 1:80–81.

4. Yigal Shiloh, "The Four-Room House: Its Situation and Function in the Israelite City," *IEJ* 20 (1970): 180–90. See also Hartmut Rösel, "Haus" in *Biblisches Reallexikon* (ed. Kurt Galling; 2nd ed.; Handbuch zum Alten Testament 1.1; Tübingen: Mohr Siebeck, 1977), 138–41.

5. As Dar suggests (*Landscape and Pattern*, 1:80).

6. Ze'ev Yeivin, "Survey of Settlements in Galilee and the Golan from the Period of the Mishnah in Light of the Sources" (PhD diss., Hebrew University, 1971) XI–XII. For floor plans, see pp. 186–89. His four types are the following: houses whose entrance is directly on the street and whose courtyard is usually in the back of the house; houses with exterior courtyards that open out into the street (see *t. B. Bat.* 3:1); houses whose courtyards are inside the house (the rooms then are built around the courtyard; this style is parallel to the buildings at Ostia, Pompeii, and Herculaneum); nonsymmetric buildings compiled from two squares or more. All of Yeivin's house types are courtyard houses.

7. Yizhar Hirschfeld, *The Palestinian Dwelling in the Roman-Byzantine Period* (SBF Collectio minor 34; Jerusalem: Franciscan Printing Press, 1995), 21–107. Hirschfeld lists the simple house, the complex house, the courtyard house, and the peristyle house.

8. Santiago Guijarro, "The Family in First-Century Galilee," in *Constructing Early Christian Families: Families as Social Reality and Metaphor* (ed. Halvor Moxnes; London: Routledge, 1997), 42–65. His housing types are simple house, courtyard house, mansion, farmhouse, and house with a shop.

9. Richardson, "Towards a Typology of Levantine/Palestinian Houses," *JSNT* 27 (2004): 47–68. Richardson's typology has been by far the most comprehensive. The nine rural types are cave, tent, beehive house, workshop house, farmhouse, villa, fortress-palace, apartment, and monastery. His urban typology includes one-room house, shop-dwelling, row shop, terrace house, side courtyard house, central courtyard house, peristyle house, axial peristyle house, communal courtyard house, apartment, and insula.

10. I will omit types that are not actually relevant to our time period and location. For example, Richardson notes that the beehive house is found in Syria, that urban apartments were rare, and that the shop dwelling and row-shop house were not part of villages in the late Second Temple period.

- The courtyard house (both side and central courtyard types and the peristyle house)
- The terrace house
- The "insula"
- Miscellaneous types (caves, tents, fortress-palaces, villas-rural mansions, monasteries, and so on)

### The Simple House

The simple house is "the most basic and commonly found of the Roman-Byzantine dwelling types."[11] It is basically a one-room building (or sometimes a building divided into two or more small rooms) attached to a courtyard. This domestic space minimized the amount of roofed area but still maintained a significant barrier from the public by way of its open-air courtyard. In the example below (see fig. A), two series of rooms enclose the courtyard (10 x 15 m). On the northeast there is a living room and two storage rooms or closets, and on the southwest, a tower. Based on the pottery, Dar dated the dwelling to the first century BCE.[12]

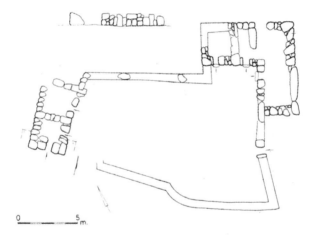

0        5 m.

**Figure A. Plan of farmhouse near Umm Rihan (Samaria) [see fig. B], first century BCE.** Dar, *Landscape and Pattern* (Oxford: BAR, 1986), part 2, figure 10. Copyright © 1986 Shimon Dar. Used by permission.

There would be virtually no personal or individual privacy in such a house but a great deal of family privacy behind the walls of the courtyard. The total area of the domicile tended to be smaller than in most of the other types of houses.[13]

---

11. Hirschfeld, *Palestinian Dwelling*, 21.
12. Dar, *Landscape and Pattern*, 1:8–9.
13. Hirschfeld, *Palestinian Dwelling*, 21; Guijarro, "Family in First-Century Galilee," 50–51.

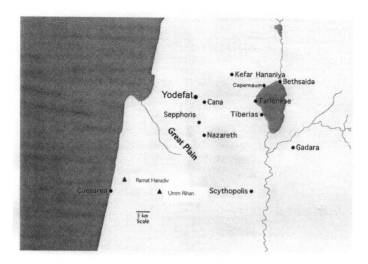

**Figure B. Galilee and northern Samaria.** Map created by
author using Accordance software.

### *The Complex House*

This architectural type, an expansion of the simple house, adds more rooms around the courtyard. Hirschfeld divides this type into urban apartment houses and rural farmhouses. The
former appear to be phenomena mostly later than our period of concern, ranging in date
from the Middle Roman (second–third centuries CE) to the Umayyad period (seventh–eighth
centuries CE).

Rural farmhouses as complex houses, however, were known in our period. In these cases
a farmhouse was simply gradually enlarged by adding more and more buildings to the compound. A farmhouse at Kalandiya, which dates from the late Second Temple period, illustrates
this sort of house. The courtyard still dominates the domestic space, but multiple rooms have
been added over the years to the courtyard until the floor space of the rooms is more than the
space of the courtyard.[14]

### *Courtyard Houses*[15]

This building pattern is found in three forms: houses with side courtyards, houses with inner
courtyards but no columns, and peristyle courtyards.

---

14. Hirschfeld, *Palestinian Dwelling*, 52.
15. Ibid., 22, 57–85.

*Side courtyards.* According to Richardson, this form of the courtyard house was the standard.[16] It consisted of a roofed house that could be multistoried plus a small courtyard to one side of it (see fig. C). Examples of such houses are found from our period at Gamla, Yodefat, Khirbet Qana, Sepphoris, and Jerusalem. The example below is from a mid-sized village.

**Figure C. Khirbet Qana (Cana) House with Side Courtyard.** Peter Richardson, *Building Jewish in the Roman East* (Waco, Tex.: Baylor University Press, 2004), plate 11. Reprinted by permission.

Houses with side courtyards could also be a feature in urban settings, as the house known as "Insula IV" in Sepphoris illustrates (see fig. D). This house included residences, storage rooms, rooms for animals, and a courtyard (letter D) to the southwest.

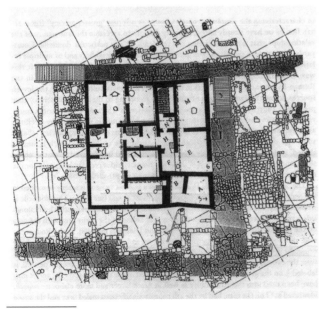

**Figure D. Insula IV, Sepphoris.** Eric M. Meyers, "Roman-Period Houses from the Galilee: Domestic Architecture and Gendered Spaces," in *Symbiosis, Symbolism, and the Power of the Past* (ed. William G. Dever and Seymour Gitin; Winona Lake, Ind.: Eisenbrauns, 2003), 487–99 (house plan on p. 491). Used by permission.

---

16. Richardson, "Typology," 60.

*Inner courtyards.* These were usually larger houses. They consisted of central courtyards with rooms on all sides. They have been found at Gamla, Yodefat, Khirbet Qana, Jerusalem, and Sepphoris. One such house in Jerusalem (see fig. E), often called the "Palatial Mansion," is a good illustration. It covered around 600 sq m and its central courtyard was surrounded with living rooms and other rooms (including a large "reception hall"), and held an indoor *mikveh*.[17] No houses of this size and grandeur have been found so far in Galilee.

**Figure E. The "Palatial Mansion" in Jerusalem, first century CE.** Photograph by the author of a model located in Wohl Archaeological Museum, Jewish Quarter, Old Jerusalem.

*Peristyle houses.* These houses are like those with inner or central courtyards but add roofed colonnades to the courtyard. Hirschfeld calls these house types "atrium houses."[18] They were an even more elaborate style of the central courtyard house. One such house was discovered at Sepphoris, the so-called Villa (see fig. F). This was a partially two-story building with an

---

17. Nahman Avigad, *Discovering Jerusalem* (Nashville: Thomas Nelson, 1983), 95–120. The artist's construction of the reception hall is on p. 102. See also Hirschfeld, *Palestinian Dwelling*, 59–62; Richardson, "Typology" 60–61.

18. Hirschfeld, *Palestinian Dwelling*, 85.

interior, columned courtyard and a roof around three sides of the courtyard. The excavators estimate its size as around 500 sq m.[19]

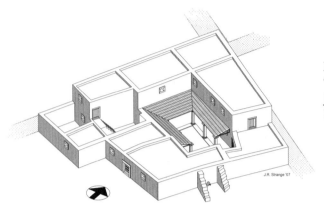

**Figure F. Isometric Sketch of the "Villa," Sepphoris.** Drawing by James Riley Strange. Used by permission.

### Terrace Houses

These houses were usually constructed without courtyards and were typical in villages and towns built on steep hillsides. They shared common walls with the house up the hill, and the roof of the lower house was also the patio of the upper house. Examples are known in Pella, Gamla, Yodefat, and Khirbet Qana (see fig. G).

### The "Insula" (or Houses with Communal Courtyards)

In this arrangement, several one-room or perhaps two-room houses surrounded a common courtyard. Some authors call these housing clusters *insulae*.[20] *Insulae* have been discovered in Rome, Pompeii, Ostia, and other Italian sites.[21] The term has also been used of buildings in

19. James F. Strange, Thomas R. W. Longstaff, and Dennis E. Groh, *Excavations at Sepphoris*, vol. 1, *University of South Florida Probes in the Citadel and Villa* (Brill Reference Library of Judaism 22; Leiden: Brill, 2006), 73, 116–18.

20. Beebe defines what he calls *insulae*: "An architectural design requiring the construction of a group of buildings standing together in a block or square isolated by streets on four sides constituted the *insula* style of houses" ("Domestic Architecture," 96). Guijarro defines *insulae* as high-rise apartments like those in Rome ("Family in First-Century Galilee," 55). Richardson agrees ("Typology," 61).

21. For *insulae* in Rome, see Jérôme Carcopino, *Daily Life in Ancient Rome: The People and the City at the Height of the Empire* (1940; repr., New Haven: Yale University Press, 1968), 22–44. On so-called *insulae* in Palestine, see also A. C. Bouquet, *Everyday Life in New Testament Times* (London: Batsford, 1953), 36–37.

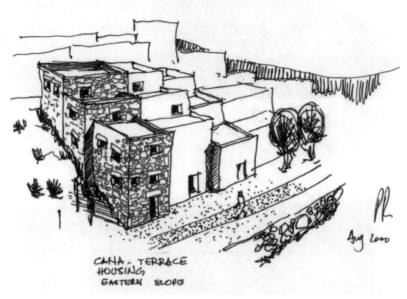

**Figure G. Terrace Houses at Khirbet Qana (Cana).** Peter Richardson, *Building Jewish in the Roman East* (Waco, Tex.: Baylor University Press, 2004), plate 12. Reprinted by permission.

Palestine in the Roman period at sites such as Samaria,[22] Capernaum,[23] Meiron,[24] Arbel,[25] and in the Negev,[26] as well as at Dura-Europos in Syria.[27] It seems wisest here, however, to

22. See J. W. Crowfoot, Kathleen M. Kenyon, and E. L. Sukenik, *The Buildings at Samaria* (London: Palestine Exploration Fund, 1942), 128, 137; also Dar, *Landscape and Pattern*, 1:42–46.

23. Virgilio C. Corbo, *The House of Saint Peter at Capharnaum: A Preliminary Report of the First Two Campaigns of Excavations, April 16–June 19, Sept. 12–Nov. 26, 1968* (trans. Sylvester Saller; Publications of the Studium Biblicum Franciscanum, Collectio minor 5; Jerusalem: Franciscan Printing Press, 1972); and Corbo, *Carfarnao*, vol. 1, *Gli edifici della città* (Studium Biblicum Franciscanum, Collectio maior 44; Jerusalem: Franciscan Printing Press, 1975). See also James F. Strange and Hershel Shanks, "Has the House Where Jesus Stayed in Capernaum Been Found?" *BAR* 8, no. 6 (1982): 26–37.

24. Eric M. Meyers, James F. Strange, and Carol L. Meyers, *Excavations at Ancient Meiron, Upper Galilee, Israel 1971–72, 1974–75, 1977* (Meiron Excavation Project 3; Cambridge, Mass.: American Schools of Oriental Research, 1981), 25–51.

25. Martin Goodman, *State and Society in Roman Galilee, A.D. 132–212* (Totowa, N.J.: Rowman & Allenheld, 1983), 30.

26. Yoram Tsafrir and Kenneth G. Holum, "Rehovot in the Negev: Preliminary Report, 1986," *IEJ* 38 (1988): 117–27.

27. Michael I. Rostovtzeff et al., *The Excavations at Dura-Europos Conducted by Yale University and the French Academy of Inscriptions and Letters. Final Report* (New Haven: Yale University Press, 1943–68).

use Richardson's term "houses with communal courtyards"[28] to designate this housing type. Virgilio Corbo calls these houses "clan dwellings."[29] *Insulae* proper were high-rise apartment buildings (up to seven stories high) in urban settings such as Rome. Villages with one-room houses clustered around a common courtyard are not the same architectural form.

Shimon Dar suggests that the houses with communal courtyards were originally built separately from each other, but as the villages grew and space became scarce, the buildings began to touch each other.[30] This suggestion might help explain the appearance of communal courtyards in several Palestinian villages and cities. At any rate, perhaps due both to lack of space and to foreign influence, the development of communal courtyards in Palestine is a peculiarly Roman-period phenomenon.

A good example of a communal courtyard house in Herodian Palestine is that at Capernaum described by Corbo—if we accept his interpretation of the material remains. The house we illustrate here (see fig. H), which Corbo calls *Insula* II, is just north of the one made famous by his claim that the house of Peter is preserved in it (his *Insula* I). According to one historian, *Insula* II consisted of around fifteen individual family rooms or house-rooms—holding around one hundred persons in all—which shared a courtyard.[31] The houses (single rooms according to this view) were constructed of crude, undressed basalt stones that were stacked without mortar. Corbo called these houses "very poor habitations" and thought that the walls were so weak that they could never have held the kind of stone slab roof that the rabbinic sources often allude to.[32] Each nuclear family would have lived in a single room and shared the courtyard with other (unrelated?) families or perhaps with other kin. This architectural style was typical for most of the houses in first-century Capernaum. Thus, the other residences seem to indicate similar economic and social conditions.

But the material remains have received another interpretation. Sharon Lea Matilla sees the structure as comprising three medium-sized houses, perhaps with two small shops attached. The area of two of them would be around 200 sq m and 120 sq m each—substantial dwellings. The third house has not been completely excavated and so its total area is unknown.[33]

---

28. Richardson, "Typology," 61.

29. Virgilio Corbo, "Capernaum," *ABD* 1:866–69, esp. 867.

30. Dar, *Landscape and Pattern*, 1:83. On lack of space, see Shmuel Safrai, "Home and Family," in *The Jewish People in the First Century: Historical Geography, Political History, Social, Cultural and Religious Life and Institutions*, vol. 2 (ed. Shmuel Safrai and Menahem Stern; CRINT, section 1, vol. 2; Assen: Van Gorcum, 1976), 728–92, esp. 730.

31. Jerome Murphy-O'Connor, *The Holy Land: An Oxford Archaeological Guide from Earliest Times to 1700* (5th rev. and expanded ed.; Oxford: Oxford University Press, 2008), 254.

32. Corbo, *House of Saint Peter*, 75. See also Strange and Shanks, who agree that the houses were poorly constructed ("House Where Jesus Stayed," 26–37). One must note, however, that there is evidence of second floors over some of the house-rooms since the bases of stairways have been preserved

33. Sharon Lea Matilla, "Revisiting Jesus' Capernaum: A Village of Only Subsistence-Level Fishers and Farmers?" in *The Galilean Economy in the Time of Jesus* (ed. David A. Fiensy and Ralph Hawkins; Early Christianity and Its Literature 11; Atlanta: Society of Biblical Literature, 2013).

Thus, she sees *Insula* II as containing three large, multiroom houses and not fifteen one-room dwellings.[34]

**Figure H. Capernaum "Insula" II.**
Photo © David A. Fiensy.

### Miscellaneous Housing Styles

Several types of housing played a small role in the life of the ordinary Jewish village or urban dweller. Therefore, these houses are of least importance for our study but deserve a brief mention. Among these are the cave houses. References in the ancient literature to caves as houses usually have in mind hideouts for bandits or revolutionaries.[35] But there are cave dwellings among contemporaneous traditional Palestinians as well.[36] Traditional people use whatever natural resources are available for their housing. Therefore, not all cave dwellers were necessarily bandits or revolutionaries. Also included in this section are tents.[37] Contemporaneous

---

34. See also Corbo, *House of Saint Peter,* 35–52; and Strange and Shanks, "House Where Jesus Stayed," 26–37. See further "Complex A" of single-room houses at Chorazin (Ze'ev Yeivin, "Ancient Chorazin Comes Back to Life," *BAR* 13, no. 5 [1987]: 22–36), which consists of fourteen one-room houses around a common central courtyard.

35. See Josephus, *J.W.* 1.304–11= *Ant.* 14.421–30 (Herod's campaign against the rebel forces of Antigonus in 38 BCE); *J.W.* 2.573, *Life* 188 (Josephus's preparations for the great war of 66–73 CE); Cassius Dio 69.12.3 (the Bar Kokhba war of 132–135 CE). See also Richardson, "Typology" 55–56, 58; Richardson and Douglas Edwards, "Jesus and Palestinian Social Protest: Archeological and Literary Perspectives," in *Handbook of Early Christianity: Social Science Approaches* (ed. Anthony J. Blasi, Jean Duhaime, and Paul-André Turcotte; Walnut Creek, Calif.: Altamira, 2002), 247–66, esp. 252; James D. Anderson, "The Impact of Rome on the Periphery: The Case of Palestina-Roman Period (63 BCE–324 CE)," in *The Archaeology of Society in the Holy Land* (ed. Thomas E. Levy; New Approaches in Anthropological Archaeology; London: Leicester University Press, 1998), 446-68, esp. 453.

36. Hirschfeld, *Palestinian Dwelling,* 135, 139, 146, 150–51.

37. Richardson ("Typology," 58) affirms that tents were being used in Galilee in antiquity.

traditional villages still often leave open spaces for itinerant—or permanent—tent dwellers.[38] Monasteries might also be mentioned here. The only example of a monastery from our period of investigation would be Khirbet Qumran.[39] Since the (presumably Essene) membership of this monastery was low, it had a relatively small influence on the Early Roman Palestinian people.

The final type of house we will discuss under the heading *Miscellaneous* is the rural mansion (sometimes referred to as a villa) and its related structure, the fortified palace. These were the huge dwellings of the very rich and the rulers of Palestine. One such mansion was located near Caesarea Maritima. This estate, on the Ramat Ha-Nadiv ridge (see Map, fig. B, p. 213), controlled 2,500 acres, according to Hirschfeld, and was occupied in the Hellenistic–Roman periods. The most impressive ruins originate from the era that stretches from Herod the Great to the beginning of the Great Revolt (37 BCE–66 CE). Hirschfeld speculated that this estate belonged to a member of the Herod family. On the estate were two complexes of buildings. The eastern complex, Horvat Eleq (see fig. I), had 150 rooms and was decorated in elaborate marble floor panels. The prominent feature of this mansion was its high tower, which may have reached five stories. Hirschfeld surmised that the tower was for defense against irate agricultural workers and bandits. The "manor" house of the estate was also equipped with a Roman bath and a swimming pool. This was clearly the estate of a very wealthy person.[40] The residents were evidently Jewish, since there was an absence of pig bones and a presence of stoneware vessels originating from Jerusalem. Again, we must point out that Ramat Ha-Nadiv is not located in Galilee and that no such country estates have so far been discovered in Galilee.

The mansion at Ramat Ha-Nadiv was fortified somewhat (the tower) but not effectively against an army. Other rural mansions were fortified heavily. These include the palaces of the Hasmonean and Herodian rulers at Masada, Herodium, Machaerus, and Jericho.[41]

### How Did They Build Houses?

Hirschfeld interviewed several residents in the Hebron hills in the course of his research for his monograph on Palestinian houses. He found that when twentieth-century traditional villagers

---

38. Louise E. Sweet, *Tell Toqaan: A Syrian Village* (Anthropological Papers 14; Ann Arbor, Mich.: University of Michigan, 1974), 52–53.

39. Richardson, "Typology," 59. See also Jodi Magness, *The Archaeology of Qumran and the Dead Sea Scrolls* (Studies in the Dead Sea Scrolls and Related Literature; Grand Rapids: Eerdmans, 2002).

40. See also Yizhar Hirschfeld, "The Early Roman Bath and Fortress at Ramat Hanadiv near Caesarea," in *The Roman and Byzantine Near East: Some Recent Archaeological Research*, vol. 1 (Journal of Roman Archaeology Supplementary Series 14; Ann Arbor, Mich: Journal of Roman Archaeology 1995), 28–55; Hirschfeld, *Ramat Hanadiv Excavations* (Jerusalem: Israel Exploration Society, 2000).

41. For a summary of Herod the Great's building program, see Duane W. Roller, *The Building Program of Herod the Great* (Berkeley: University of California Press, 1998), 125–238.

**Figure I: Horvat Eleq "Mansion."** Artist's reconstruction by Balage Balough and first used in Yizhar Hirschfeld and Miriam Feinberg-Vamosh, "A Country Gentleman's Estate," *BAR* 31, no. 2 (2005): 18–31, at 18–19. Used by permission.

built a new house, they almost always employed a professional mason or "master builder." The family to whom the house belonged did the actual work, but the master builder supervised the work. The professional builder lived in the community and served the local needs, having learned his profession from his father and grandfather. He used a standard plan (which he kept in his head), but could vary it somewhat according to the needs of the family.[42] One is tempted to think of Jesus of Nazareth's family, said to have been carpenters (Mark 6:3; Matt 13:55). Did they function in the same way as master builders for the community?

Hirschfeld also believed that most ancient houses in Palestine were built under the supervision of a master builder or stone mason.[43] The rabbinic literature refers to several builders/masons (carpenters?) by name, and the rabbis held these builders in high regard. One story illustrates the work of such experts. Students were told to ask Abba Joseph, the builder, a question about the creation of the world. They went to ask him and found him standing on a scaffold. He responded to the students that he could not come down but would try to answer their questions from the scaffold (*Midrash Rabbah on Exodus* 13:1).[44] The point is, the rabbis regarded master builders as very clever people.

---

42. Hirschfeld, *Palestinian Dwelling*, 113, 115, 120.
43. Ibid., 226–29.
44. Quoted in ibid., 228.

Hirschfeld notes that these craftsmen/builders are often mentioned in the Greco-Roman literature and even depicted in wall paintings and sculptures. He assumes that the builders of ancient Palestine/Israel were similar to these.[45]

But in other areas in the Middle East the building of houses has been done traditionally and exclusively by the extended family, rather like a barn-raising in early rural America. It would be finished in only a few days, and no one paid any money for the labor.[46] So, one's house could be built at no cost whatsoever, except for the land underneath it.[47]

The first task in building a house was to gather materials. The main materials were stone, mortar (clay soil mixed with water), and wood (for the roof). Builders of houses in nineteenth- and twentieth-century traditional Palestinian villages would pile up the soil in huge heaps and bring in the quarried stones to stack in storage while waiting for the beginning of the construction. The stones might then be cut into "worked stones" (flat-surfaced blocks) or into "hammered" stones (hewn stones from a quarry that were not dressed or fieldstones with minimal dressing). The stones might also not be worked at all but merely picked up from the ground, especially from a wadi bed, and used as they were.[48]

Building in nineteenth- and twentieth-century villages began with laying out the dimensions of the new house, usually with string. Next came the excavation of the wall foundations down to the bedrock. The construction of the walls came next: workers laid stones in the foundation trenches directly on bedrock and then sealed the trenches with packed earth. They continued to build the walls by cleverly stacking large and small stones very tightly without mortar, and then they sealed the exteriors of the walls with mortar plaster. This kind of

---

45. Ibid., 227. See his sketch of a mosaic from North Africa depicting a master builder (p. 229) and of a relief sculpture from southern France depicting the architect (p. 231).

46. As reported by Sweet, *Tell Toqaan*, 117. See also Suad Amiry and Vera Tamari, *The Palestinian Village Home* (London: British Museum, 1989) 20. They write, "House building was a cooperative venture, and involved both men and women."

47. What would a house cost if one were to buy it completely finished? The prices preserved for us show varied costs. Ian Morris notes that in fourth century BCE Greece one could pay from 230 drachmas to 5,300 drachmas for a house ("Archaeology, Standards of Living, and Greek Economic History," in *The Ancient Economy: Evidence and Models* [ed. Ian Morris and J. G. Manning; Social Science History; Stanford: Stanford University Press, 2005], 126). Isaeus (2.35) stated that a small house in his day (fourth century BCE) cost 300 drachmas. Morris concludes that a poor, simple house would cost from 200 to 300 drachmas in fourth-century BCE Greece. Daniel Sperber lists prices for two houses in Palestine in the era of 200 to 400 CE: 200 denarii and 250 denarii (*Roman Palestine 200–400: Money and Prices* [Bar-Ilan Studies in Near Eastern Languages and Culture; Ramat-Gan: Bar-Ilan University Press, 1974], 106). These prices roughly coincide with Morris's price for a small and simple house. Richard Alston gives a table of house prices gleaned from the papyri ("Houses and Households in Roman Egypt," in *Domestic Space in the Roman World: Pompeii and Beyond* [ed. Ray Laurence and Andrew Wallace-Hadrill; Journal of Roman Archaeology Supplementary Series 22; Portsmouth, R.I.: Journal of Roman Archaeology, 1997], 25–39, esp. 32). Urban houses in the first century CE averaged 853 drachmas; village houses averaged 488 drachmas. In the second century CE the prices were 1200 drachmas and 500 drachmas, respectively. Since the Egyptian drachma may have been worth less than the Greek drachma, these prices are not too far out of line with the other two sources.

48. Hirschfeld, *Palestinian Dwelling*, 217–19, 222.

construction resulted in essentially human-made caves: compared to the outdoors, house interiors would be significantly cooler in the summer and warmer in the winter. Builders used the native stone from the area (limestone in Judea and Galilee, basalt in the Golan). Those doing the building would plaster the interior of the walls next and then build the roof, which kept out the weather, formed a working and living space above the house, and served to stabilize the walls. Typical roofs used wooden beams woven with smaller branches and then covered with a thick layer of plaster. More expensive roofs were made of stone slabs.[49]

Most of the traditional nineteenth- and early-twentieth-century houses Hirschfeld surveyed in the Hebron hills had one room.[50] The house-room was usually divided into three parts: upstairs there was the living space and the storage space, often divided by a window-wall or an elevated area. The living space was where the family ate, entertained, and slept. There were no chairs and no mattresses on frames, just mats for sitting and bedding, which were unrolled at night. Those houses without the underground stables housed the livestock in the first floor of the house with the family. If there was an excavated area under the floor of the house, it was for the livestock.[51] We know from excavations, especially in Nazareth (see, for example, the so-called Grotto of St. Joseph, the underground area of an ancient house), that the ancients also utilized all available space, including the space under the floor of their house to give shelter to their livestock. The photograph below (fig. J) is from the excavations beneath the courtyard of the Church of the Annunciation in Nazareth. It illustrates an underground stable.

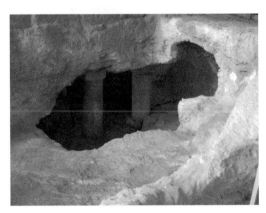

**Figure J. Underground Animal Stable, Church of the Annunciation, Nazareth.** Photograph © David A. Fiensy.

For most houses in Herodian Palestine, stone was the primary building material: either the white limestone so abundant in much of Palestine or the black basalt found north of the Sea of Galilee. The exception was in the Sharon Plain and other lower-lying areas, where houses

49. Ibid., 120–34; Sweet, *Tell Toqaan*, 114–15; William M. Thompson, *The Land and the Book* (1877; Hartford, Conn.: Scranton, 1910), 1:132, 386; 2:434.

50. See also Amiry and Tamari, *Palestinian Village Home*, 27.

51. Hirschfeld, *Palestinian Dwelling*, 120–34; Amiry and Tamari, *Palestinian Village Home*, 25–29.

were built of bricks.[52] The use of bricks in building houses seems to have been both a necessity for those living in certain regions where stones were not readily available, and a local tradition, as the following text from the Mishnah indicates.

> A place where people are accustomed to build with rough stones, hewn stones, rafters, or bricks, they build (that way). Everything is done according to the custom of the region. (*m. B. Bat.* 1:1)[53]

According to Hirschfeld, the ancients used two types of bricks: sun-dried and fired. By far the most commonly used brick was the sun-dried. The disadvantage of this sort of construction was that, if the house was left unplastered, after a heavy rain there could be a great deal of damage to the construction. The house might even collapse totally.[54]

A. C. Bouquet also suggested that very poor peasants even in the hill country must have had huts built entirely of perishable material (branches, straw, and mud), so that no trace of them has survived.[55] In extreme cases, people may have had no houses at all, but merely wandered from place to place.[56] Homelessness was known in antiquity also.

Some roofs in ancient Palestine also were made of limestone slabs, like those in the traditional contemporary Palestinian houses reported above.[57] Nevertheless, houses such as those at Capernaum apparently had roofs of wooden beams and smaller tree branches covered with bundles of brush and mud-plaster (cf. Mark. 2:4).[58] These flat roofs were very common in ancient Palestine/Israel. Since the plaster has to be frequently smoothed down, in modern-day traditional houses there is a stone roller left in place on the roof to flatten it on occasion.[59] The ancients had the same technique. The owners of flat-roofed houses regarded the roofs as extensions of the courtyard. One could use the roof for eating, praying, drying food, storing items, and sleeping.

---

52. Shmuel Safrai "Home and Family," 732; and Hirschfeld, *Palestinian Dwelling*, 24. See *m. Sotah* 8:3 and *m. B. Bat.* 1:1 for mud-brick houses. For the technology of ancient brick building, see Robert S. Homsher, "Mud Bricks and the Process of Construction in the Middle Bronze Age Southern Levant," *BASOR* 368 (2012): 1–27.

53. Translation from the Hebrew text in Obadiah Mabratnora, *The Six Orders of the Mishnah* (Jerusalem: Eschol, n.d.), 2:67.

54. Hirschfeld, *Palestinian Dwelling*, 221–22.

55. Bouquet, *Everyday Life in New Testament Times*, 27.

56. *M. Peah* 8:7. See Goodman, *State and Society*, 39.

57. Samuel Krauss, *Talmudische Archäologie* (3 vols.; Hildesheim: Georg Olms, 1966), 1.27; Beebe, "Domestic Archecture," 101; Safrai, "Home and Family," 732; Yeivin, "Survey of Settlements," XIV; Yeivin describes the basalt roofs of ancient Chorazin ("Ancient Chorazin Comes Back to Life," 25).

58. Strange and Shanks, "House Where Jesus Stayed," 26–37; Corbo, *House of Saint Peter*, 37.

59. Hirschfeld, *Palestinian Dwelling*, 244.

Often, when the walls were made strong enough to support it, the flat roofs held an upper room, either the full size of the room below or as a partial second story.[60] Yeivin's survey found several ancient two-story houses still in use by Arabs.[61] The contemporary, traditional village dwellers in Palestine use the upper room for resting in private and for hosting guests and leaders of the clan. It is a place apart from the noise of the rest of the household.[62] Was the upper room in Jerusalem that Jesus and his disciples borrowed for the Passover meal used in this way (Mark 14:15; Luke 22:12)?

Although flat roofs were much more common (and less expensive) in the period of concern in this chapter, the residents of ancient Palestine/Israel also sometimes built with vaulted stone roofs. Hirschfeld reports finding several such roofs from the third to the first centuries BCE. The stones were fitted together to form the vault in such a manner that no mortar was necessary.[63]

The floors of Herodian-period houses were most commonly packed earth. One can also find floors of stone slabs and plastered floors. The elaborate houses of the wealthy might have mosaic floors. Under the floors, people were accustomed to hide treasures, whether food or coins, usually stashed in clay jars. Hirschfeld reports that some houses in Jerusalem have been found that contained stone compartments under the floor, cut into the bedrock, that served as a kind of safe.[64]

### How Many Rooms?

The individual house (בית *bayit*) held the nuclear family, the smallest social unit in the rural village. Many historians have concluded that most ancient Palestinian/Israeli folk lived in houses that were only one room. This conclusion seems evident because the common inhabitants of traditional villages today live in such houses.[65] Yeivin estimates that, on average, the typical village room could house five people.[66] Thus, it is doubtful that anyone more than the nuclear

---

60. See Safrai, "Home and Family," 730; Krauss, *Talmudische Archäologie*, 1.29; and Jdt. 8:5; Mark 14:15; Acts 1:3; 20:8; *m.Šabb.* 1:4, *m. B. Bat.* 2:2–3; *m. Ned.* 7:4. For an example of a flat roof, see Meyers, Strange, and Meyers, *Excavations at Ancient Meiron*, 40.

61. Yeivin, "Survey of Settlements," XIV.

62. Hirschfeld, *Palestinian Dwelling*, 246–47.

63. Ibid., 239–40.

64. Ibid., 270–72.

65. Bouquet notes that poor Arabs of Palestine still live in only one room (*Everyday Life in New Testament Times*, 28). See also Amiry and Tamari, *Palestinian Village Home*, 27; and Hirschfeld, *Palestinian Dwelling*, 120–34, 259.

66. Yeivin, "Survey of Settlements," XV. Cf. Lawrence E. Stager, "The Archaeology of the Family," *BASOR* 260 (1985): 18. This figure is close to the average family size (six) suggested by Arieh Ben-David, *Talmudische Ökonomie: Die Wirtschaft des jüdischen Palästina zur Zeit der Mischna und des Talmud* (Hildesheim: Georg Olms, 1974), 45. See also Israel Finkelstein, who estimated that the average house in premodern Palestine held 4.4 to 6 persons ("A Few Notes on Demographic Data From Recent Generations and Ethnoarchaeology," *PEQ* 122 [1990]:

family lived in a house under usual circumstances. Families with more than five people might be compelled to build a smaller upper room. Nevertheless, some evidence does exist that the extended families occasionally lived together in the same room (*m. B. Bat.* 9:8–10; Mark 1:29).[67] Dar notes that the Mishnah describes a small house as 4.48 x 3.36 meters (15 sq m) and a large house as 4.48 x 5/6 meters (22–27 sq m; *m. B. Bat.* 6:4). Dar found these same measurements commonly in his survey of Samaria, and he therefore concludes that they represent house sizes generally in Palestine in the Herodian period.[68] We must remember, however, that by "house size" Dar means the dimensions of the covered portions of the domestic area, not including the courtyard. In the one-room house everything—eating, entertaining, and sleeping—was done in the same place. At night they unrolled mats for sleeping. By day, the family sat on the floor for eating and entertaining. But even if we exclude the courtyards from these measurements, Dar's average figures do not harmonize well with those we will present below from Hirschfeld's survey. Dar's house sizes are smaller (see below).

Yet Hirschfeld maintains that, although today the residents in traditional villages of Israel live in one-room houses, it was not the case in the Roman and Byzantine eras. He has found that the houses of those periods usually contained two rooms: the טריקלין (*triclin*) from the Latin *triclinium* (dining room) and the קיטון (*qiton*) from the Greek word κοιτών (*koitōn*, bedroom).[69] With two rooms for a house there would be space for beds and not just mats that were unrolled at night. There are references to beds being used in our period, although several people apparently slept together in them.[70] But the presence of actual beds, not just bedrolls, argues for multiroom houses. Hirschfeld's literary evidence is mostly Mishnaic, and his archaeological examples for the two-room house as the most common all come from the Byzantine era (fourth to sixth centuries CE). Yet his argument does have merit, and therefore one must conclude that many two-room houses were known during our period (37 BCE through the second century CE).

---

47–52). But see also Hirschfeld, *Palestinian Dwelling*, 135, whose table 5 gives much larger numbers for the houses he surveyed.

67. Safrai, "Home and Family," 733. That extended families lived in one house supports Hirschfeld's findings, where as many as twenty-five persons lived in one house (which had 93 sq m). See Hirschfeld, *Palestinian Dwelling*, 135. Alston ("Houses and Households," 34) gives a table of "House Occupancy and Household Sizes" (gleaned from tax records) in which he finds that the average number of persons per house in ancient Philadelphia (Egypt) was seven to eight. This number, he found, represented more than one household. Thus, many houses were occupied by more than one household.

68. Dar, *Landscape and Pattern*, 1:85. Goodman maintained that the standard house sizes in the Mishnah are pure "theory" (*State and Society*, 31).

69. Hirschfeld, *Palestinian Dwelling*, 260–61.

70. *M. Niddah* 9:4 refers to three women sleeping in one bed (מטה *mittah*). *1 Enoch* 83:6 has the seer Enoch recounting a dream he had while sleeping with his grandfather. Luke 11:7 narrates a parable in which the entire family is in the same bed (κοίτη, *koitē*) asleep (and cf. Luke 17:34, "two in one κλίνη," *klinē*). This term for bed must be distinguished from the Greek word κράββατος (*krabbatos*), the poor man's mat or bedroll, which is referred to ubiquitously in the New Testament (Mark 2:4, 9, 11, 12; 6:55; John 5:8, 9, 10, 11; Acts 5:15; 9:33), and the κλίνη (*klinē*) "dining couch," "bier," or "stretcher," which could also be used for a bed.

## The Courtyard

The courtyard (חצר, *ḥatser*; αὐλή, *aulē*), has been especially important in both ancient and modern (traditional) Palestinian houses. It was the place of both domestic work and leisure—the place to find privacy from the street and to meet and talk to neighbors and kinfolk. For most of the year the family ate in the courtyard and even slept there in the hot months. Krauss described the courtyard as follows:

> The courtyard was occasionally dug up and planted with decorative trees and fruit trees or vines. One walked around at leisure, ate, did the wash, and took care of all business necessary in life in the courtyard.[71]

Hirschfeld also emphasized that the courtyard was as important as the roofed portion of the house itself in the activities of the family. "It seems that the (roofed) house functioned primarily as a storehouse and pantry in the summer months, while the family lived outside in the courtyard both day and night."[72] Local informants commonly report that the traditional Middle Eastern folk live mostly out of doors, except when weather forbids it.[73] It helps to remember that, compared to the outdoors, during daylight hours house interiors were relatively dim because of the small size of windows, and at night the flames from oil lamps offered feeble illumination by today's standards. Hence, another reason for spending most of one's time outside is simply that you can see better.

Most courtyards appear to have been encircled with a wall at least two meters (about six feet) high.[74] Hirschfeld observes that maintaining privacy was an important reason for the courtyard walls. The Mishnah refers to a courtyard in which a man is not ashamed to eat (*m. Maʿaś.* 3:5), meaning a courtyard in which one can eat without outsiders observing.[75] Courtyards, as in Meiron,[76] might have had flagstone pavements, or, more often, were simply packed dirt.

Some courtyards must have been quite small. The Mishnah (*m. B. Bat.* 1:6) rules that the smallest one could make a courtyard by dividing it up was four cubits or two meters (2 x 2 m).[77] But most courtyards were much larger. The Tosefta (*t. Erub.* 7:9) refers to a courtyard of ten cubits or five meters (that is, 5 x 5 m.?) as "small." The courtyard in Meiron Field I was

---

71. Krauss, *Talmudische Archäologie*, 1:46. Krauss cites *t. Maʿaś.* 2:8, 2:20, *y. B. Bat.* 2:7, *y.* Šabb. 6:1

72. Hirschfeld, *Palestinian Dwelling*, 139.

73. See, for example, Abraham Mitrie Rihbany, *The Syrian Christ* (Boston: Houghton Mifflin, 1916), 241–313.

74. Safrai, "Home and Family," 729; *m. Erub.* 7:1, *m. B. Bat.* 1:4, *t. Erub.* 6:13–14. For archaeological evidence, see, for example, Meiron in Meyers, Strange, and Meyers, *Excavations at Meiron*; and Corbo, *House of Saint Peter*. See also Krauss, *Talmudische Archäologie*, 1:45.

75. Hirschfeld, *Palestinian Dwelling*, 272.

76. Meyers, Strange, and Meyers, *Excavations at Meiron*, 40.

77. Herbert Danby (*The Mishnah* [Oxford: Oxford University, 1933], 366) understands the size to be 4 x 4 cubits.

7.5 x 5 m. [78] A typical courtyard described by Dar for the village of Hirbet Buraq in Samaria was of similar size. Most of the ancient rural houses surveyed by Hirschfeld had rather large courtyards (See figs. A and C).

According to the Mishnah, communal courtyards appear to have been shared by two to three houses. *M. Arakin* 9:6 describes a walled city as needing at least three courtyards with two houses in each. [79] In Samaria, Dar found that most courtyards contained five or six living quarters or houses, but he notes that the later courtyard houses (Roman-Byzantine) tended to be smaller. [80] Hirschfeld found houses (he calls them "apartments") in Hebron that shared courtyards. [81] Yet at Capernaum and Chorazin, there were clusters of fourteen to fifteen one-room houses sharing a courtyard (see above). The Tosefta refers to those sharing a common courtyard as "members of the courtyard" (*t. Erub.* 7:7, 14).

In addition to the living quarters that were attached to the courtyard, one could find other buildings used for crafts or for animals (cattle barns), straw sheds, woodsheds, and storage houses for wine and oil. [82] Krauss maintained that the animals would have been kept in buildings behind the living quarters, or when there were two courtyards, in the second courtyard. [83] Lawrence E. Stager, however, suggests that livestock were usually brought into a room close to the living quarters at night, either under the living quarters or in an adjacent room. The practice was maintained in the Israelite period and is done by Arabs today. He suggests that side rooms found at Capernaum with "fenestrated walls" actually contained not windows but storage niches for animals. If Stager is correct, then animals often slept on the ground floor or adjoining room to the living quarters. As mentioned, there were many houses with stables underground. [84]

As the archaeological remains and literature show, ovens, cisterns, millstones, gardens, ponds, chicken coops, and dovecotes were also in the courtyard. Krauss suggests that many of these things were the common property of all sharing the courtyard. [85] The Mishnah refers to several uses of courtyards:

---

78. Meyers, Strange, Meyers, *Excavations at Meiron*, 40.

79. Cf. *m. Arak.* 9:7, *t. Ma'aś* 2:20.

80. Dar, *Landscape and Pattern*, 1:85.

81. Hirschfeld, *Palestinian Dwelling*, 273.

82. See Meyers, Strange, and Meyers, *Excavations at Ancient Meiron,* 33–37; Safrai, "Home and Family," 729; Yeivin, "Survey of Settlements," XV; *b. Pes.* 8a; *m. Erub.* 8:4; *m. B. Bat.* 2:2–3; 4:4.

83. Krauss, *Talmudische Archäologie* 1:46. See *b. Yoma* 11a, *b. Pes.* 8a.

84. Stager, "Archaeology of the Family," 11–14. For animals sleeping either in the living quarters of the family or under the living quarters, see Hirschefeld, *Palestinian Dwelling*, 149, 158–59; Amiry and Tamari, *Palestinian Village Home*, 27.

85. *M. B. Bat.* 3:5; *m. Pes.* 1:1; *m. Erub.* 8:6; *m. Ohol.* 5:6; *t. Ma'aś* 3:8, 2:20; *t. B. Bat.* 2:14, 16; 3:1. See Safrai, "Home and Family," 730; Krauss, *Talmudische Archäologie* 1:46; Strange and Shanks, "House Where Jesus Stayed," 34; Yeivin, "Survey of Settlements," XVII. For chicken coops and dovecotes, see Hirschfeld, *Palestinian Dwelling*, 141, 142, 145, 153, 154–55,

He puts in the courtyard cattle, an oven, stoves, and a millstone; and he raises chickens and puts his compost in the courtyard . . . .(*m. B. Bat.* 3:5).[86]

Thus, the courtyard was the main living area for a family. For most families, except the wealthy, the indoor areas were for escaping from inclement weather.

## House Sizes and Standard of Living

Ian Morris has argued for an increase in the standard of living in the Early Roman to Late Roman periods and has appealed to housing to make his case.[87] The archaeological remains of houses demonstrate to him that the standard of living increased in Greece from the eighth to the third centuries BCE. His study of three hundred houses indicates, remarkably, that house sizes increased fivefold in that span, and he therefore concludes that there must have been "a dramatic improvement in the standard of living." Table 1 presents Morris's evidence. Morris gives both the mean and median sizes of the houses for each period. He distrusts using simply the mean sizes, since a few very large houses in the fourth century would skew the evidence. But even considering mostly the median sizes, the increase in size is remarkable. Therefore, Morris rejects the standard model of the ancient economy in which scholars believe that there was "essentially static economic performance"[88] and instead concludes that the standard of living was on the rise.

| Period | Mean Size of Houses | Median Size of Houses |
|---|---|---|
| 800–700 BCE | 53 m$^2$ | 51 m$^2$ |
| ca. 700 BCE | 69 m$^2$ | 56 m$^2$ |
| 700–600 BCE | 53 m$^2$ | 45 m$^2$ |
| 600–500 BCE | 92 m$^2$ | 67 m$^2$ |
| 500–400 BCE | 122 m$^2$ | 106 m$^2$ |
| 400–300 BCE | 325 m$^2$ | 240 m$^2$ |

**Table 1: Morris's Evidence for the Rise in Standards of Living in Greece
From 800 BCE to 300 BCE**[89]

---

86. Translation from the text of Mabratnorah, *Six Orders of the Mishnah*, 2:75.
87. Ian Morris, "Archaeology, Standards of Living," 107.
88. Ibid., 123, 107,
89. Ibid., 110.

Morris's study of housing size is most interesting, and I will follow his lead in comparing housing sizes in Palestine between the Hellenistic and the Byzantine eras to determine if the size (square meters) of the domestic space increased. By "domestic space" I mean not only the buildings under roof but the courtyards as well.

### Did Domestic Space Increase?

Our base of data will be the work of Yizhar Hirschfeld, who gathered dimensions on more than fifty houses spanning the Hellenistic to the Byzantine periods.[90] The tables presented here are based mostly on his work. I must offer several cautions before we look at these results. First, one may ask if Hirschfeld's sample size is adequate. Analyzing fifty-plus houses is certainly not as satisfying as Morris's analysis of over three hundred houses. Second, one may ask about Hirschfeld's selection of the houses he has described. How and why did he select the houses included in his monograph? Thus, one cannot claim to be comparing Hirschfeld's results with an equal sampling given by Morris. Yet this work does offer at least a preliminary comparison.

The advantages of choosing Hirschfeld's data include the following. First, he presents a wide assortment of houses from the Golan, Upper Galilee, Lower Galilee, Samaria, Judea, and the Negev. Second, his houses cover the periods from the Hellenistic through the Byzantine periods (and five houses from later periods), which is exactly the time period of interest to us in our investigation of the standard of living in Galilee in the late Second Temple through the Mishnaic periods. Thus, Hirschfeld is comprehensive in scope, if not exhaustive.

The second table gives the mean and median house sizes by archaeological periods in imitation of Morris's example in table 1.[91] The difference between Hirschfeld and Morris is that Morris gave only housing dimensions of those portions "probably roofed." Hirschfeld included the courtyards as well, a significant difference. According to these figures, the Early Roman period saw the largest house sizes on average. There is no evidence of house sizes gradually improving as Morris found in his study. Based on this comparison, if one wants to tie standard of living to average house sizes, the standard of living fluctuated rather freely in ancient Palestine. If we follow the median sizes (preferred by Morris), there was a decline in standard of living from the Early Roman period through the Late Roman period.

### Complicating Factors

But analyzing housing sizes by chronological periods is complicated because it fails to consider other factors. One of these factors is architectural type. Table 3, also derived from Hirschfeld's data, shows this complication.

---

90. Hirschfeld, *Palestinian Dwelling*.
91. Morris, "Archaeology, Standards of Living," 108.

| Archaeological period | Mean Size of Houses[92] | Median Size of Houses | Sample size |
|---|---|---|---|
| Hellenistic | 297 m² | 925m² | 5 houses |
| Early Roman | 761 m² | 1425m² | 13 houses |
| Middle Roman | 380 m² | 1065m² | 11 houses |
| Late Roman | 180 m² | 190m² | 6 houses |
| Byzantine | 348 m² | 460m² | 14 houses |

**Table 2: Average Size of Palestinian Houses by Period[93]**

As noted above (p. 211), Hirschfeld found four main housing types. The simple house—the most basic and common type—consisted of one main structure built onto an open courtyard. The complex house was simply an expansion of a simple house type. The courtyard house was a courtyard surrounded on all four sides by dwelling structures. The peristyle house or atrium house was a Greco-Roman innovation. It consisted of an inner garden surrounded by columns and rooms.[94] As table 3 shows, the complex house, by virtue of its architecture, usually occupied the most space. Yet would one maintain that the complex houses were more expensive or lavish than the courtyard houses, or especially the peristyle houses? One can also note that the simple and courtyard houses were the most popular (at least according to Hirschfeld's data).

| House type | Average size | Sample size | Houses by chronological period |
|---|---|---|---|
| Simple houses | 130 m² | 19 houses | 2 ER, 2 MR, 5 LR, 7 Byz, 3 other |
| Complex houses | 1,010 m² | 8 houses | 3 ER, 1 MR, 2 Byz, 2 other |
| Courtyard houses | 569 m² | 21 houses | 4 Hell, 5 ER, 7 MR, 4 Byz, 1 other |
| Peristyle houses | 793 m² | 8 houses | 1 Hell, 3 ER, 1 MR, 1 LR, 2 Byz |

**Table 3: Hirschfeld's Architectural Typoplogy[95]**

---

92. Hirschfeld usually includes the courtyard in the measurement of the house size.

93. Based on Hirschfeld, *Palestinian Dwelling*, 21–101. Compare Hirschfeld's data with that collected by Richard Alston, who compared housing sizes in Roman Egypt. He found very little change in size from one level (lower) of excavation of the village of Karanis to a later level. The mean area went from 73 sq m to 75 sq m. See Alston, "Houses and Households," 28.

94. Hirschfeld, *Palestinian Dwelling*, 85–99, 101.

95. Ibid., 100–101.

Another complicating factor was the location. One needs to ask where the houses were built: in a city, town, village, or on an isolated farm. Table 4 indicates that the largest houses tended to be built in the towns and on the isolated farms. Was this because the cities and villages tended to squeeze the houses together and thus leave less ground space for building? According to this table, the cities had house sizes similar to the village houses. At any rate, estimating standard of living based only on house sizes can be quite deceptive.

| City | 299 m$^2$ |
| Town | 607 m$^2$ |
| Village | 298 m$^2$ |
| Farmhouse | 867 m$^2$ |
| Villa | 961 m$^2$ |

**Table 4: Average Size of Palestinian Houses Arranged by Location**[96]

## Conclusion

If you, the reader, had lived in Galilee in the Herodian through the Mishnaic period, what sort of house would you probably have had? You would likely have lived in a house with plastered stone walls, a dirt floor, and a flat roof made with wooden beams, other smaller branches, and mud plaster. Your house would have been one room—possibly two rooms—and it would have shared a courtyard with other nuclear families, most likely your cousins. You would have built your house with materials you gathered locally at no cost: stones, wood, and clay soil for mortar. Your family would have provided the labor to build the house, but you may have employed a master builder to supervise the work. Weather permitting, your family basically would have lived out of doors for most of the year in the courtyard. Your courtyard would have afforded you privacy from outsiders but still would have taken you out into the open air. Indoors would mainly have been used only for shelter from inclement weather and for storage. Your house may have had a cave beneath it for storage of food and for sheltering animals. If you lived in a village (which would be probable) your house, including courtyard, would have been around 300 sq m (about 3,230 sq ft) in size.

## Bibliography

Alston, Richard. "Houses and Households in Roman Egypt." In *Domestic Space in the Roman World: Pompeii and Beyond*, edited by Ray Laurence and Andrew Wallace-Hadrill, 25–39.

---

96. Ibid.

Journal of Roman Archaeology Supplementary Series 22. Portsmouth, R.I.: Journal of Roman Archaeology, 1997.

Amiry, Suad, and Vera Tamari. *The Palestinian Village Home.* London: British Museum, 1989.

Anderson, James D. "The Impact of Rome on the Periphery: The Case of Palestina-Roman Period (63 BCE–324 CE)." In *The Archaeology of Society in the Holy Land,* edited by Thomas E. Levy, 446–68. New Approaches in Anthropological Archaeology. London: Leicester University Press, 1998.

Aviam, Mordechai. "Economy and Social Structure in First-Century Galilee: Evidence from the Ground—Yodefat and Gamla." Paper presented at the annual meeting of the Society of Biblical Literature, Boston, Massachusetts, November 2008.

Avigad, Nahman. *Discovering Jerusalem.* Nashville: Thomas Nelson, 1983.

Beebe, H. K. "Domestic Architecture and the New Testament." *BA* 38 (1975): 89–104.

Ben-David, Arieh. *Talmudische Ökonomie: Die Wirtschaft des jüdischen Palästina zur Zeit der Mischna und des Talmud.* Hildesheim: Georg Olms, 1974.

Bouquet, A. C. *Everyday Life in New Testament Times.* London: Batsford, 1953.

Carcopino, Jérôme. *Daily Life in Ancient Rome: The People and the City at the Height of the Empire.* 1940. Reprint, New Haven: Yale University Press, 1968.

Corbo, Virgilio C. *Cafarnao,* vol. 1, *Gli edifici della città.* Studium Biblicum Franciscanum, Collectio maior 44. Jerusalem: Franciscan Printing Press, 1975.

———. "Capernaum." *ABD* 1:866–69.

———. *The House of Saint Peter at Capharnaum: A Preliminary Report of the First Two Campaigns of Excavations, April 16–June 19, Sept. 12–Nov. 26, 1968.* Translated by Sylvester Saller. Studium Biblicum Franciscanum, Collectio minor 5. Jerusalem: Franciscan Printing Press, 1972).

Crowfoot, J. W., Kathleen M. Kenyon, and E. L. Sukenik. *The Buildings at Samaria.* London: Palestine Exploration Fund, 1942.

Danby, Herbert. *The Mishnah: Translated from the Hebrew with Introduction and Brief Explanatory Notes.* Oxford: Oxford University Press, 1933.

Dar, Shimon. *Landscape and Pattern: An Archaeological Survey of Samaria, 800 B.C.E.–636 C.E.* 2 vols. BAR International Series 308. Oxford: BAR, 1986.

Finkelstein, Israel "A Few Notes on Demographic Data from Recent Generations and Ethnoarchaeology." *PEQ* 122 (1990): 47–52.

Goodman, Martin. *State and Society in Roman Galilee, A.D. 132–212.* Totowa, N.J.: Rowman & Allenheld, 1983.

Guijarro, Santiago. "The Family in First-Century Galilee." In *Constructing Early Christian Families: Families as Social Reality and Metaphor,* edited by Halvor Moxnes, 42–65. London: Routledge, 1997.

Hachlili, Rachel, and Patricia Smith. "The Genealogy of the Goliath Family." *BASOR* 235 (1979): 67–71.

Hirschfeld, Yizhar. "The Early Roman Bath and Fortress at Ramat Hanadiv near Caesarea." *The Roman and Byzantine Near East: Some Recent Archaeological Research*, vol. 1, 28–55. Journal of Roman Archaeology Supplementary Series 14. Ann Arbor, Mich: Journal of Roman Archaeology, 1995.

———. *The Palestinian Dwelling in the Roman-Byzantine Period.* Studium Biblicum Franciscanum, Collectio minor 34. Jerusalem: Franciscan Printing Press, 1995.

———. *Ramat Hanadiv Excavations.* Jerusalem: Israel Exploration Society, 2000.

Hirschfeld, Yizhar and Miriam Feinberg-Vamosh. "A Country Gentleman's Estate." *BAR* 31, no. 2 (2005): 18–31.

Homsher, Robert S. "Mud Bricks and the Process of Construction in the Middle Bronze Age Southern Levant." *BASOR* 368 (2012): 1–27.

Krauss, Samuel. *Talmudische Archäologie.* 3 vols. Hildesheim: Georg Olms, 1966.

Mabratnora, Obadiah. *The Six Orders of the Mishnah.* Jerusalem: Eschol, n.d.

Magness, Jodi. *The Archaeology of Qumran and the Dead Sea Scrolls.* Studies in the Dead Sea Scrolls and Related Literature. Grand Rapids: Eerdmans, 2002.

Matilla, Sharon Lea. "Revisiting Jesus' Capernaum: A Village of Only Subsistence-Level Fishers and Farmers?" In *The Galilean Economy in the Time of Jesus*, edited by David A. Fiensy and Ralph K. Hawkins, 75–138. Early Christianity and Its Literature 11. Atlanta: Society of Biblical Literature, 2013.

Meyers, Eric M. "Roman-Period Houses from the Galilee: Domestic Architecture and Gendered Spaces." In *Symbiosis, Symbolism, and the Power of the Past: Canaan, Ancient Israel, and Their Neighbors from the Late Bronze Age through Roman Palaestina. Proceedings of the Centennial Symposium, W. F. Albright Institute of Archaeological Research and American Schools of Oriental Research, Jerusalem, May 29/31, 2000*, edited by William G. Dever and Seymour Gitin, 487–99. Winona Lake, Ind.: Eisenbrauns, 2003.

Meyers, Eric M., James F. Strange, and Carol L. Meyers. *Excavations at Ancient Meiron, Upper Galilee, Israel 1971–72, 1974–75, 1977.* Meiron Excavation Project 3. Cambridge, Mass.: American Schools of Oriental Research, 1981.

Morris, Ian. "Archaeology, Standards of Living, and Greek Economic History." In *The Ancient Economy: Evidence and Models*, edited by Ian Morris and J. G. Manning, 91–126. Social Science History. Stanford: Stanford University, 2005.

Murphy-O'Connor, Jerome. *The Holy Land: An Oxford Archaeological Guide from Earliest Times to 1700.* 5th rev. and expanded ed. Oxford: Oxford University Press, 2008.

Oakman, Douglas E. *Jesus and the Economic Questions of His Day.* Studies in the Bible and Early Christianity 8. Lewiston, N.Y.: Mellen, 1986.

Richardson, Peter. *Building Jewish in the Roman East.* Waco, Tex.: Baylor University Press, 2004.

———. "Towards a Typology of Levantine/Palestinian Houses." *JSNT* 27 (2004): 47–68.

Richardson, Peter, and Douglas Edwards. "Jesus and Palestinian Social Protest: Archeological and Literary Perspectives." In *Handbook of Early Christianity: Social Science Approaches*, edited by Anthony J. Blasi, Jean Duhaime, and Paul-André Turcotte. Walnut Creek, Calif.: Altamira, 2002.

Rihbany, Abraham Mitrie. *The Syrian Christ*. Boston: Houghton Mifflin, 1916.

Roller, Duane W. *The Building Program of Herod the Great*. Berkeley: University of California Press, 1998.

Rösel, Hartmut. "Haus." In *Biblisches Reallexikon*, edited by Kurt Galling, 138–41. 2nd ed. Handbuch zum Alten Testament 1.1. Tübingen: Mohr Siebeck, 1977.

Rostovtzeff, Michael I. *The Excavations in Dura-Europos Conducted by Yale University and the French Academy of Inscriptions and Letters. Final Report*. New Haven: Yale University Press, 1943–68.

Safrai, Shmuel. "Home and Family." In *The Jewish People in the First Century: Historical Geography, Political History, Social, Cultural and Religious Life and Institutions*, vol. 2, edited by Shmuel Safrai and Menahem Stern, 728–92. CRINT, section 1, vol. 2. Assen: Van Gorcum, 1976.

Shiloh, Yigal. "The Four-Room House: Its Situation and Function in the Israelite City." *IEJ* 20 (1970): 180–90.

Smith, Patricia, Elizabeth Bornemann, and Joe Zias. "The Skeletal Remains." In *Excavations at Ancient Meiron, Upper Galilee, Israel 1971–72, 1974–75, 1977*, edited by Eric M. Meyers, James F. Strange, and Carol L. Meyers, 110–20. Meiron Excavation Project 3. Cambridge, Mass.: American Schools of Oriental Research, 1981.

Sperber, Daniel. *Roman Palestine 200–400: Money and Prices*. Bar-Ilan Studies in Near Eastern Languages and Culture. Ramat-Gan: Bar-Ilan University, 1974.

Stager, Lawrence E. "The Archaeology of the Family." *BASOR* 260 (1985): 1–35.

Strange, James F., Thomas R. W. Longstaff, and Dennis E. Groh. *Excavations at Sepphoris*. Vol. 1, *University of South Florida Probes in the Citadel and Villa*. Brill Reference Library of Judaism 22. Leiden: Brill, 2006.

Strange, James F., and Hershel Shanks. "Has the House Where Jesus Stayed in Capernaum been Found?" *BAR* 8, no. 6 (1982): 26–37.

Sweet, Louise E. *Tell Toqaan: A Syrian Village*. Anthropological Papers 14. Ann Arbor, Mich.: University of Michigan Press, 1974.

Thompson, William M. *The Land and the Book*. 1877. Reprint, Hartford, Conn.: Scranton, 1910.

Tsafrir, Yoram, and Kenneth G. Holum. "Rehovot in the Negev: Preliminary Report, 1986." *IEJ* 38 (1988): 117–27.

Yeivin, Ze'ev. "Ancient Chorazin Comes Back to Life." *BAR* 13, no. 5 (1987): 22–36.

———. "Survey of Settlements in Galilee and the Golan from the Peiod of the Mishnah in Light of the Sources." PhD diss., Hebrew University, 1971.

# 11

# MORTALITY, MORBIDITY, AND ECONOMICS IN JESUS' GALILEE

*Jonathan L. Reed*

This chapter intends to examine the social stability of Galilee by drawing on the hitherto neglected field of historical demography.[1] In particular, the tightly interrelated aspects of mortality-morbidity and economics will be examined with an eye toward assessing internal migration. To anticipate the conclusions at the outset, life in first-century Galilee—though not necessarily dissimilar to other parts of the Mediterranean—was substantially different from the modern world and cannot be characterized as stable. Chronic and seasonal disease, especially malaria, cut down significant segments of the population and left even the healthy quite often ill. The ancient Mediterranean was as a whole, in Walter Scheidel's words, a place "of frequent pregnancy and sudden death."[2] Galilee in particular, in the wake of Hasmonean settlment and under Antipas's urbanization projects, witnessed considerable internal migration. Galilee was not demographically stable.

## Life Expectancy

The evidence for low life expectancy in antiquity, albeit circumstantial, is abundant. Funerary inscriptions noting the deceased's age—none exist from Galilee—tend to round numbers

---

1. Noted forcefully by Glen W. Bowersock, "Beloch and the Birth of Demography," *TAPA* 127 (1997): 373–79; for an overview, see Walter Scheidel, "Problems and Progress in Roman Demography," in *Debating Roman Demography* (ed. Walter Scheidel; Mnemosyne 211; Leiden: Brill, 2001), 1–81.

2. Walter Scheidel, "Population and Demography," Version 040604, Princeton/Stanford Working Papers in Classics. Online: http://www.princeton.edu/~pswpc.

and favor wealthy men. Even so, for example, the mean age of Latin epitaphs in the city of Rome is a paltry twenty-three.[3] Similarly, skeletal remains beyond puberty cannot always be aged precisely, and burials suffer from class, age, and gender distortion. Even so, a few tomb complexes in and near Galilee have been examined; in one Roman-Byzantine tomb complex (197 individuals) at Upper Galilean Meiron nearly 50 percent of the interred died before reaching adulthood, and, of those, 70 percent died in the first few years of life.[4] In a study of Hellenistic-Roman complexes (227 individuals) around the Shephelah, the age distribution showed an average life span of twenty-four years.[5] Interestingly, those latter rural Jews were about as well off in terms of life expectancy as the Roman imperial family—assassinations and suicides excluded.[6]

### Seasonal Mortality Rates

High mortality rates in antiquity are clear also from the monthly spikes in the number of deaths. In contrast to modern developed societies, where degenerative diseases such as heart attack, cancer, or stroke are the main killers and are evenly spread across the calendar, prior to advances in medicine and sanitation, acute infectious diseases active in particular months were the big killers (see charts A and B).[7] These leave few clear traces in the osteoarchaeological record, although the prevalence of porotic hyperostosis and criba orbitalia in Roman-era skulls

---

3. Keith Hopkins was suspicious of funerary epigraphy ("On the Probable Age Structure of the Roman Population," *Population Studies* 20 (1966): 245–64; also Tim G. Parkin, *Demography and Roman Society* (Ancient Society and History; Baltimore: Johns Hopkins University Press, 1992), 5–19.

4. Patricia Smith, Elizabeth Bornemann, and Joe Zias, "The Skeletal Remains," in *Excavations at Ancient Meiron, Upper Galilee, Israel, 1971–72, 1974–75, 1977* (ed. Eric M. Meyers, James F. Strange, and Carol L. Meyers; Meiron Excavation Project 3; Cambridge, Mass.: American Schools of Oriental Research, 1981), 110–11.

5. Yossi Nagar and Hagit Torgeé, "Biological Characteristics of Jewish Burial in the Hellenistic and Early Roman Periods," *IEJ* 53 (2003): 164-71; Christian burials in the Negev show similar numbers, with life expectancy of twenty-six at birth and thirty after age ten (Yossi Nagar and Flavia Sonntag, "Byzantine Period Burials in the Negev: Anthropological Description and Summary," *IEJ* 58 [2008]: 79–93). See also Bruce W. Frier, "Roman Life Expectancy: The Pannonian Evidence," *Phoenix* 37 (1983): 328–44; Mirko D. Grmek, *Diseases in the Ancient Greek World* (Baltimore: Johns Hopkins University Press, 1989), 99–105. For skeptical views of osteoarchaeological remains, see Scheidel, "Progress and Problems," 19; Parkin, *Demography and Roman Society*, 41–58; and Ian Morris, *Death-Ritual and Social Structure in Classical Antiquity* (Key Themes in Ancient History; Cambridge: Cambridge University Press, 1992), 72–91.

6. Walter Scheidel, "Emperors, Aristocrats, and the Grim Reaper: Towards a Demographic Profile of the Roman Élite," *CQ* 49 (1999): 255–66.

7. Grmek lists the three great killers of antiquity as tuberculosis, malaria, and typhoid fever (*Diseases in the Ancient Greek World*, 86–89). Epidemics were commonplace, and there were three well-known pandemics: the Antonine Plague (165–180 CE), the Plague of Cyprian (251–266 CE), and the Justinian Plague (451–750 CE). See Susan Scott and Christopher J. Duncan, *Biology of Plagues: Evidence from Historical Populations* (Cambridge: Cambridge University Press, 2001); and *Plague and the End of Antiquity: The Pandemic of 541–750* (ed. Lester K. Little; Cambridge: Cambridge University Press, 2006).

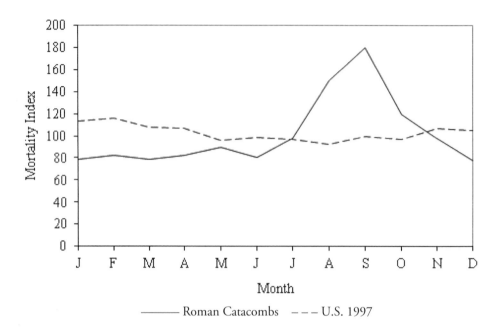

**Chart A. Monthly rates of death.** Sources: Brent D. Shaw, "Seasons of Death: Aspects of Mortality in Imperial Rome," *JRS* 96 (1996): 118–21; and Centers for Disease Control and Prevention.

indicates that anemia was widespread, with malaria likely in many cases.[8] The seasonal rhythm of death means that Mediterranean populations suffered from a plethora of quick-killing gastrointestinal and respiratory diseases such as dysentery, typhus, typhoid, tuberculosis, plague, and especially malaria. For example, inscriptions from Roman catacombs reveal that twice as many people died in August and September as was typical of other months, when hot weather made contagious malarial fevers acute and exacerbated gastrointestinal diseases (see chart A).[9] Coptic epitaphs and Greek papyri from Egypt likewise reveal the grim reaper's seasonality,

---

8. The issue is complex; see Grmek, *Diseases in the Ancient Greek World*, 245–83; Patty Stuart-Macadam, "Porotic Hyperostosis: Representative of a Childhood Condition," *American Journal of Physical Anthropology* 66 (1985): 391–98; and Scheidel, *"Progress and Problems,"* 27. See also Robert Sallares, *Malaria and Rome: A History of Malaria in Ancient Italy* (Oxford: Oxford University Press, 2002).

9. See the original data in Brent D. Shaw, "Seasons of Death: Aspects of Mortality in Imperial Rome," *JRS* 96 (1996): 118–21, esp. tables 5, 9–12; Shaw, "Seasonal Mortality in Imperial Rome and the Mediterranean: Three Problem Cases," in *Urbanism in the Preindustrial World: Cross-Cultural Approaches* (ed. Glenn R. Storey; Tuscaloosa: University of Alabama Press, 2006), 86–109. With further discussion on seasonality and malaria, see Sallares, *Malaria and Rome*, 201–34; and Walter Scheidel, "Germs for Rome," in *Rome the Cosmopolis* (ed. Catharine Edwards and Greg Woolf; Cambridge: Cambridge University Press, 2003), 158–76.

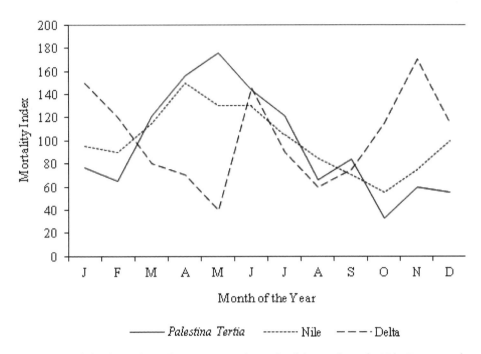

**Chart B. Rates of death on the Nile.** Sources: Walter Scheidel, *Death on the Nile: Disease and Demography of Roman Egypt* (Leiden: Brill 2001), 4–10, 16–25; and Evelyne Patlagean, *Pauvreté économique et pauvretésociale à byzance 4ᵉ–7ᵉ siècles* (Paris: Mouton, 1977), 94.

with those living along the Nile dying in April–May from typhoid fever, and those living in the Delta dying more frequently in winter and summer because of tuberculosis and dysentery, respectively.[10] Concrete evidence from the Levant is singular but similar, with monastic deaths peaking in early summer (see chart B).[11]

## Malaria as the Cause of Seasonal Mortality Rates

Notwithstanding the geographical, microbiological, and seasonal variations across the Mediterranean, Scheidel underscores the main point: "high amplitudes of seasonality . . . coincide with high mortality *per se*."[12] Richard Sallares has proposed that the preponderance of malaria

---

10. The issue is nuanced by Walter Scheidel, *Death on the Nile: Disease and the Demography of Roman Egypt* (Mnemosyne 228; Leiden: Brill, 2001), 25–35, 51–109.

11. Evelyne Patlagean *Pauvreté économique et pauvreté sociale à byzance 4ᵉ–7ᵉ siècles* (Civilisations et Sociétés 48; Paris: Mouton, 1977), 92–94.

12. Scheidel, *Death on the Nile*, 116.

across wide swaths of the Mediterranean lowered the average life expectancy to just over twenty years.[13] This bleak picture seems to be the case in the Egyptian Fayum, a region with a reputation from antiquity to modernity for substandard health conditions and malaria.[14] And this was probably also the case in Galilee, especially the areas near the lake or Lower Galilean valleys that resemble the Fayum. Both had higher annual rainfalls, areas where rain wound up either in marshes, in standing pools at the end of wadis, or seeping into moist alluvial soil atop hard limestone formations, all breeding grounds for anopheles, the mosquitoes that carry malaria.[15] One need only recall the notoriously high death rates of Jewish settlers due to malaria in the early twentieth century, from the Huleh Valley down past the Gennesar Plain to Tiberias and over along the Bet Netofah Valley, which, until modern irrigation, flooded often. These well-watered areas with alluvial soil eventually became Galilee's prime agricultural tracts, but they were areas that nineteenth-century century travelers described as malarial and that early-twentieth-century Zionist settlers viewed as death traps until malaria was eradicated.[16]

Evidence from antiquity confirms that malaria was a problem in and around Galilee. Josephus at one point describes the areas south of the lake as pestilent and disease ridden (*J. W.* 4.457).[17] The rabbis frequently discuss various fevers, and even distinguish different types of fever cycles typical of malaria.[18] Of course, the Gospels mention fevers with Peter's mother-in-law at Capernaum (Mark 1:30-31 and parallels), and John specifies that the Capernaum centurion's son suffered from a fever as well (4:52); both seem to have been life-threatening and hence malarial, rather than benign fevers.[19] Several amulets from late-antique Galilee also ward

13. Sallares, *Malaria and Rome,* 277–78. Ulpian's Table might approximate malarial Rome. See Roger S. Bagnall and Bruce W. Frier, *The Demography of Roman Egypt* (Cambridge Studies in Population, Economy, and Society in Past Time 23; Cambridge: Cambridge University Press, 1994), 88–90; Scheidel, "Progress and Problems," 14–21.

14. Scheidel, *Death on the Nile,* 16–19, 82–89; Sallares, *Malaria and Rome,* 160–64.

15. Robert Sallares, "Ecology," in *The Cambridge Economic History of the GReco-Roman World* (ed. Walter Scheidel, Ian Morris, and Richard P. Saller; Cambridge: Cambridge University Press, 2007), 21–25.

16. In 1902, John Cropper described Banias, Tiberias, and the Sea of Galilee as crippled with malaria ("The Geographical Distribution of Anopheles and Malarial Fever in Upper Palestine," *Journal of Hygiene* 2 [1902]: 47–57). See further the chilling reports by Israel J. Kligler, *The Epidemiology and Control of Malaria in Palestine* (Chicago: University of Chicago Press, 1930). Yossi Nagar notes that over half of the skeletal remains from Tel Tanim had criba orbitalia, which he attributes primarily to malaria (personal communication).

17. Josephus describes Alexander Jannaeus as suffering from quartan fever, that is, malaria, and dying in the region of Gergasa (*Ant.* 15.398).

18. Among them some Galilean sages, for example, Ḥanina ben Dosa (*b. Ber.* 34b); see further Julius Preuss, *Biblical and Talmudic Medicine* (trans. and ed. Fred Roser; New York: Sanhedrin, 1978), 160–64; and Avraham Steinberg, *Encyclopedia of Jewish Medical Ethics: A Compilation of Jewish Medical Law on All Topics of Medical Interest* (3 vols.; Jerusalem: Feldheim, 2003), 2:538–39.

19. Luke 4:38 specifies it as a πυρετῷ μεγάλῳ, commonly diagnosed as malaria.

off "great fevers," a common term for malaria, like one from Sepphoris and two from Horvat Kanaf, two miles northeast of the lake.[20]

## Ancient Defenses against Malaria

Of course a better defense against malaria than such amulets was living away from standing water and at higher altitudes—anopheles become rarer as the elevation increases and disappear completely above fifteen hundred meters. Thus, much of Upper Galilee offered some safety, as did Lower Galilean hilltops with late summer winds at dusk when anopheles are most active.[21] Since they are weak flyers and rarely travel more than a few miles, pockets of malaria could exist with devastating results in one village with a particular topography while leaving others a few miles away relatively unscathed.[22] Over centuries, indigenous knowledge accumulated— without anyone's ever recognizing the cause of malaria—and the most insidious locales were avoided.[23] One presumes that Jews in the late Hellenistic period settled hilltops for defensive purposes but in the process avoided malarial areas, into which they eventually moved in the Early Roman period. These were conveniently closer to crops, fishing, or trade, but increased the risk of malaria.[24] Thus, we should expect much higher rates of malaria in villages like Capernaum or Magdala near the Gennesar Plain than in, say, Nazareth or Cana, which were on a slope and atop a hill above the valley.[25] And surely Sepphoris, atop a hill, was better off than hot and humid Tiberias right on the lake, at least in terms of malaria.[26]

Another defense against malaria was living in more isolated locations with lower population densities, which would curtail its spread via anopheles and also decrease the transmission of other diseases. As sites increased in size and density, Galilee's rapid population growth would

---

20. Joseph Naveh and Shaul Shaked, *Amulets and Magic Bowls: Aramaic Incantations of Late Antiquity* (Jerusalem: Magnes, 1985), 44–55; C. Thomas McCullough and Beth Glazier-McDonald, "Magic and Medicine in Byzantine Galilee: A Bronze Amulet from Sepphoris," in *Archaeology and the Galilee: Texts and Contexts in the Graeco-Roman and Byzantine Periods* (ed. Douglas R. Edwards and C. Thomas McCollough; South Florida Studies in the History of Judaism 143; Atlanta: Scholars Press, 1997), 143–49; and Irina Wandrey, "Fever and Malaria 'for Real' or as a Magical-Literary Topos," in *Jewish Studies between the Disciplines/Judaistik zwischen den Disziplinen: Papers in Honor of Peter Schäfer on the Occasion of His 60th Birthday* (ed. Klaus Herrmann et al.; Leiden: Brill, 2003), 257–66.

21. Kligler, *The Epidemiology and Control*, 50–86.

22. Sallares, *Malaria and Rome*, 201–34; Kligler, *Epidemiology and Control*, 19–86.

23. See further François Retief and Louise Cilliers, "Malaria in Graeco-Roman Times, *Acta Classica* 47 (2004): 127–37.

24. Sallares. *Malaria and Rome*, 279.

25. Kligler classified Migdal, Kinnereth, and Degania on the lake as "intensely malarious," and even Nazareth was categorized in the lesser but still serious "malarious" category (*Epidemiology and Control*, 88).

26. Judah ha-Nasi left the lower-lying Beth She'arim after an unspecified illness for Sepphoris's salubrious air (*b. Ketub.* 103b, and *y. Kil.* 9:32b). The reluctance among Jews to settle in Tiberias, which according to Josephus was due to its being built atop tombs, might actually have been due to malaria (*Ant.* 18.36-38).

eventually wane as malaria increased the mortality rate, since it viciously attacks pregnant mothers, fetuses, and newborns.[27] Malaria's effects on morbidity are equally pernicious. Victims suffer from alternating fevers and chills, severe muscle and joint pain, and often headaches and diarrhea; also common are an enlarged spleen, anemia, lung or kidney failure, and cognitive impairment leading to brain damage and even coma.[28] Fatality rates are one in five. Even after survivors build up childhood immunities, malarial strands morph and recur with a vengeance. Over the course of several generations, populations can develop a genetic predisposition against malaria—but in the form of sickle cell anemia or thalassemia, conditions that have their own complications, including chronic anemia that renders sufferers vulnerable to other infections and shortens life spans. For these reasons, over so much of the Mediterranean where malaria was endemic, though not the main cause of death, it interacted with other diseases to increase overall mortality rates by as much as 50 percent.[29]

## The Effect of Disease on Economic Conditions

Disease represented the most significant demographic factor in the ancient world. As Scheidel has forcefully argued in his body of work, "In the long term, the nature and prevalence of endemic infectious disease acted as the principal environmental determinant of local age structure."[30] High mortality and morbidity created considerable social instability, with a significant impact on socioeconomics. In terms of labor alone, if modern underdeveloped countries with malaria are comparable, the average amount of time any person lived in ill health or disability was close to 20 percent.[31] Malaria, therefore, depressed economic productivity generally, and had an especially adverse effect on labor-intensive crops such as grains and grapes, harvested in late summer and early autumn.[32] Disease, death, mourning, and funerals would contribute to poorer harvests, higher malnutrition in the subsequent year, and then greater susceptibility to disease. Sallares emphasizes the negative correlation between malaria-infested areas and per-capita growth rates, and Roman agronomists were keenly aware of the problem, even if they could not diagnose the cause. Consider Varro's advice:

---

27. Sallares, *Malaria and Rome*, 125–27; Retief and Cilliers, "Malaria in Graeco-Roman Times," 129. Arab villages in Galilee are still built on the slopes that are wind-swept on summer evenings, a common malaria avoidance strategy found also in Italy (Sallares, *Malaria and Rome*, 91–92, 279). Herodotus describes Egyptian dwellings in the Delta as elevated to avoid "gnats" (2.95).

28. On malaria's various strands, see Sallares, *Malaria and Rome*, 7–22.

29. Ibid., 120–21.

30. Scheidel, "Demography," 39.

31. Ibid., 41, citing the WHO 2003 World Health Report.

32. According to Kligler, malarial occurrences in Palestine in the 1920s spiked in July; the most malignant strains rose in September and exploded in late October (*Epidemiology and Control*, 111, 122, 124).

on land that is pestilent, no matter how fertile it is, disaster does not allow the farmer to achieve a profit. For, where the reckoning is with death, not only is the profit uncertain there, but even the lives of the farmers are at risk. In an unhealthy location farming is a lottery in which the life and possession of the owner are in danger. (*Rust.* 1.4.3)[33]

In the same vein, Cato noted that a full quarter of the cost should be added when estimating the labor for constructing a villa "in a pestilential locality" (Cato, *Agr.* 14.5), a cost he accounts for in purely financial terms but which slaves must have paid for with ruined health and even death. The areas on the Sea of Galilee where Jesus was most active, as well as other portions of Lower Galilee, were similarly "pestilential," that is to say, malarial. A measure of pessimism on Galilee's economic activity and relative prosperity under Antipas is in order, perhaps not only vis-à-vis modern expectations but also compared to more salubrious areas in the ancient Mediterranean.[34]

## Conclusion

On the issue of Antipas's urbanization, it is clear that a much more nuanced discussion of the socioeconomic impact of Sepphoris and Tiberias is necessary in light of demographic insights. On the one hand, it bears stressing that Galilee's population growth and construction of cities in the Early Roman period are not themselves evidence of an overall Galilean prosperity. In fact, overall population growth, newly built cities, considerable migration, and extensive malaria caution against an optimistic view of economic life under Antipas. This is not to imply the opposite, namely, that Galileans fared terribly and were destitute under Antipas, just that any widespread socioeconomic improvement is questionable. On the other hand, although many Galilean urbanites seem better off than rural villagers in terms of their houses, in terms of their mortality and morbidity they were worse off. But the significance of these two cities' negative growth rates in the context of overall Galilean growth in the Early Roman period goes far beyond issues of health and comfort. The newly built cities' contribution to social instability must be stressed: Sepphoris and Tiberias fueled internal migration from villages to the cities. Thus, the rural–urban divide was often crossed, and we cannot assume a rigid division between rural peasants in villages and urban elites in the cities. Surely Jesus had some extended family in Sepphoris.

At the same time that the Galilean cities were built, many smaller sites were settled in malarial areas. Significant numbers of people moved from healthier areas with higher birth

---

33. Quoted in Sallares with a valuable discussion also of Cato's *Agr.* 14.5 and Columella's *Rust.* 1.4.2–3.

34. Kligler describes Lower Galilee as "one of the most malarious [regions] in Palestine" (*Epidemiology and Control*, 41; generally for Galilee, 40–44).

rates into less healthy ones, due to the competition over land in the former and for the sake of opportunities, however menial, in the latter. A large number of migrants were younger male villagers moving to the cities, but also to the lake where fishing might provide opportunities. Even if such internal mobility was not out of line with other areas of the Mediterranean, descriptions of life under Antipas as stable miss the mark. Sudden death, rampant disease, frequent pregnancy, and impulsive yet increasing migration would make for a rather unstable environment with volatile households whose compositions were constantly and abruptly changing. The negative socioeconomic impact of this instability has only been implied here, and its cultural and religious implications, whether in terms of the ephemeral nature of patriarchal households or the necessity of reciprocity between village households, merit further consideration.[35]

## Bibliography

Bowersock, Glen W. "Beloch and the Birth of Demography." *TAPA* 127 (1997): 373–79.

Cropper, John. "The Geographical Distribution of Anopheles and Malarial Fever in Upper Palestine." *Journal of Hygiene* 2 (1902): 47–57.

Ery, K. K. "Investigations on the Demographic Source Value of Tombstones Originating from the Roman Period." *Alba Regia* 10 (1969): 51–67.

Frier, Bruce W. "Roman Life Expectancy: The Pannonian Evidence." *Phoenix* 37 (1983): 328–44.

Grmek, Mirko D. *Diseases in the Ancient Greek World*. Baltimore: Johns Hopkins University Press, 1989.

Hopkins, Keith. "On the Probable Age Structure of the Roman Population." *Population Studies* 20 (1966): 245–64.

Kligler, Israel J. *The Epidemiology and Control of Malaria in Palestine*. Chicago: University of Chicago Press, 1930.

Little, Lester K., ed. *Plague and the End of Antiquity: The Pandemic of 541–750*. Cambridge: Cambridge University Press, 2006.

McCollough, C. Thomas, and Beth Glazier-McDonald. "Magic and Medicine in Byzantine Galilee: A Bronze Amulet from Sepphoris." In *Archaeology and the Galilee: Texts and*

---

35. Halvor Moxnes suggests that Jesus created an alternative space that subverted powerful patriarch-dominated households; yet perhaps the unpredictable health of older males made such alternative space attractive (*Putting Jesus in His Place: A Radical Vision of Household and Kingdom* [Louisville: Westminster John Knox, 2003]). A good starting point on the ephemeral nature of patriarchy would be the essays in *Growing Up Fatherless in Antiquity* (ed. Sabine R. Hübner and David M. Ratzan; Cambridge: Cambridge University Press, 2009). Milton Moreland stresses the importance of household networks ("The Jesus Movement in the Villages of Roman Galilee: Archaeology, Q, and Modern Anthropological Theory," in *Oral Performance, Popular Tradition, and Hidden Transcript in Q* [ed. Richard A. Horsley; Semeia Studies 60; Atlanta: Society of Biblical Literature, 2006], 159–80).

*Contexts in the Graeco-Roman and Byzantine Periods*, edited by Douglas R. Edwards and C. Thomas McCollough, 143–49. South Florida Studies in the History of Judaism 143. Atlanta: Scholars Press, 1997.

Morris, Ian. *Death-Ritual and Social Structure in Classical Antiquity*. Key Themes in Ancient History. Cambridge: Cambridge University Press, 1992.

Moxnes, Halvor. *Putting Jesus in His Place: A Radical Vision of Household and Kingdom*. Louisville: Westminster John Knox, 2003.

Nagar, Yossi, and Flavia Sonntag. "Byzantine Period Burials in the Negev: Anthropological Description and Summary." *IEJ* 58 (2008): 79–93.

Nagar, Yossi, and Hagit Torgeé. "Biological Characteristics of Jewish Burial in the Hellenistic and Early Roman Periods." *IEJ* 53 (2003): 164–71.

Naveh, Joseph, and Shaul Shaked. *Amulets and Magic Bowls: Aramaic Incantations of Late Antiquity*. Jerusalem: Magnes, 1985.

Parkin, Tim G. *Demography and Roman Society*. Ancient Society and History. Baltimore: Johns Hopkins University Press, 1992.

Patlagean, Evelyne. *Pauvreté économique et pauvreté sociale à byzance 4ᵉ–7ᵉ siècles*. Civilisations et Sociétés 48. Pairs: Mouton, 1977.

Preuss, Julius. *Biblical and Talmudic Medicine*. Translated and edited by Fred Roser. New York: Sanhedrin, 1978.

Retief, François, and Louise Cilliers. "Malaria in Graeco-Roman Times." *Acta Classica* 47 (2004): 127–37.

Sallares, Robert. "Ecology." In *The Cambridge Economic History of the Greco-Roman World*, edited by Walter Scheidel, Ian Morris, and Richard P. Saller, 15–37. Cambridge: Cambridge University Press, 2007.

———. *Malaria and Rome: A History of Malaria in Ancient Italy*. Oxford: Oxford University Press, 2002.

Scheidel, Walter. *Death on the Nile: Disease and the Demography of Roman Egypt*. Mnemosyne 228. Leiden: Brill, 2001.

———. "Demography." In *The Cambridge Economic History of the Greco-Roman World*, edited by Walter Scheidel, Ian Morris, and Richard Saller, 38–86. Cambridge: Cambridge University Press, 2007.

———. "Emperors, Aristocrats, and the Grim Reaper: Towards a Demographic Profile of the Roman Élite." *CQ* 49 (1999): 255–66.

———. "Germs for Rome." In *Rome the Cosmopolis*, edited by Catharine Edwards and Greg Woolf, 158–76. Cambridge: Cambridge University Press, 2003.

———. "Population and Demography," Version 040604, Princeton/Stanford Working Papers in Classics. Online: http://www.princeton.edu/~pswpc.

———. "Problems and Progress in Roman Demography." In *Debating Roman Demography*, edited by Walter Scheidel, 1–81. Mnemosyne 211. Leiden: Brill 2001.

Scott, Susan, and Christopher J. Duncan. *Biology of Plagues: Evidence from Historical Populations.* Cambridge: Cambridge University Press, 2001.

Shaw, Brent D. "Seasonal Mortality in Imperial Rome and the Mediterranean: Three Problem Cases." In *Urbanism in the Preindustrial World: Cross-Cultural Approaches,* edited by Glenn R. Storey, 86–109. Tuscaloosa: University of Alabama Press, 2006.

———. "Seasons of Death: Aspects of Mortality in Imperial Rome." *JRS* 96 (1996): 118–21.

Smith, Patricia, Elizabeth Bornemann, and Joe Zias. "The Skeletal Remains." In *Excavations at Ancient Meiron, Upper Galilee, Israel, 1971–72, 1974–75, 1977,* edited by Eric M. Meyers, James F. Strange, and Carol L. Meyers. Meiron Excavation Project 3. Cambridge, Mass.: American Schools of Oriental Research, 1981.

Steinberg, Avraham. *Encyclopedia of Jewish Medical Ethics: A Compilation of Jewish Medical Law on All Topics of Medical Interest.* 3 vols. Jerusalem: Feldheim, 2003.

Stuart-Macadam, Patty. "Porotic Hyperostosis: Representative of a Childhood Condition." *American Journal of Physical Anthropology* 66 (1985): 391–98.

Wandrey, Irina. "Fever and Malaria 'for Real' or as a Magical-Literary Topos." In *Jewish Studies between the Disciplines/Judaistik zwischen den Disziplinen: Papers in Honor of Peter Schäfer on the Occasion of His 60th Birthday,* edited by Klaus Herrmann et al., 257–66. Leiden: Brill, 2003.

# 12

# EDUCATION/LITERACY IN JEWISH GALILEE: WAS THERE ANY AND AT WHAT LEVEL?

*John C. Poirier*

### Introduction

The story of education among Galilean Jews in the Second Temple era and the Tannaitic era has been told differently by different scholars. The difference is more than one of accents. The disagreements turn on the creditability of foundation stories in the two Talmuds and (less centrally) on the proper interpretation of Josephus's claim that all the Jews of his day knew the law (*C. Ap.* 2.18, 178). The Talmuds claimed that a system of primary schools was established in the first century BCE (*y. Ketub.* 8:11, 32c) or the first century CE (*b. B. Bat.* 21a). Beginning with Wilhelm Bacher in 1903, a long string of scholars took these claims at face value (or nearly so), arguing that, while the temple still stood, the land was filled with schools to equip Jewish boys with the ability to read Scripture.[1] Beginning with Nathan Morris in 1937, an

---

1. Wilhelm Bacher, "Das altjüdische Schulwesen," *Jahrbuch für Jüdische Geschichte und Literatur*, vol. 6 (Berlin: A. Katz, 1903), 48–81. Bacher's portrayal of community-wide primary schools would be upheld, in one form or another, by William Rosenau, "The Rabbinical Era," in *The Chautauqua System of Jewish Education* (ed. Abram Simon and William Rosenau; Philadelphia: Jewish Chautauqua Society, 1912), 41–58; Louis Ginzberg, *Students, Scholars and Saints* (Philadelphia: Jewish Publication Society of America, 1928), 1–34; Towa Perlow, *L'éducation et l'enseignement chez les juifs à l'époque talmudique* (Paris: Leroux, 1931), 23–45; Max Arzt, "The Teacher in Talmud and Midrash," in *Mordecai M. Kaplan: Jubilee Volume on the Occasion of His Seventieth Birthday* (ed. Moshe Davis; New York: Jewish Theological Seminary of America Press, 1953), 35–47; Eliezer Ebner, *Elementary Education in Ancient Israel during the Tannaitic Period (10–220 C.E.)* (New York: Bloch, 1956); Birger Gerhardsson, *Memory and Manuscript: Oral Tradition and Written Transmission in Rabbinic Judaism and Early Christianity* (Acta Seminarii Neotestamentici Upsaliensis 22; Uppsala: Almqvist & Wiksell, 1961); and Shmuel Safrai, "Elementary Education, Its Religious and Social Significance in the Talmudic Period," *Cahiers d'Histoire Mondiale* 11 (1968): 148–69. See

overlapping string of scholars has challenged this view, noting its reliance on post-Tannaitic traditions, with later scholars noting the dearth of archaeological support for that reading.[2] As Catherine Hezser points out, there is no mention of schools in Josephus (ca. 90 CE), the Mishnah (ca. 200–210 CE), the Tosefta (ca. 300 CE), or the Tannaitic Midrashim (ca. 10–210 CE), nor is there any "unambiguous" archaeological evidence that school-based education took place prior to the Amoraic period (ca. 220–500 CE).[3] At most, the early writings refer only to parents or private teachers equipping (male) children with basic reading skills.[4]

Although some scholars continue to speak of widespread education among early Jews, others have argued that the rabbis had a pronounced tendency to "rabbinize" the past, and that their assertions about the origins of widespread primary education were not exempt from this tendency: they wrote their own educational goals into a past society that largely had lacked those goals. (Education would become more widespread in the third century CE.) Of course, that does not mean that education was nonexistent among Galilean Jews. Although estimates of a region's *illiteracy* have occasionally been overstated, the issues surrounding Palestinian Jewish education are more or less responsive to William Harris's signal account of literacy among the Jews' Roman contemporaries. (Harris estimated an overall literary literacy level of 5–10 percent for Rome's western provinces during our period.[5])

Before I attend to the varieties of evidence, I should clarify what I mean by an unqualified reference to *education*. When education *was* pursued, it was basically for Hebrew literacy—for the sake of reading Scripture. Only occasionally was grapho-literacy the goal (viz., the ability to read *and write*).[6] Even fewer Jewish students were afforded the opportunity to learn tradi-

---

the review in Marc Hirshman, *The Stabilization of Rabbinic Culture, 100 C.E. –350 C.E.: Texts on Education and Their Late Antique Context* (Oxford: Oxford University Press, 2009), 121–26. Alan Millard continues to support a similar view, albeit with a greater appreciation of the problems with that opinion (*Reading and Writing in the Time of Jesus* [New York: New York University Press, 2000]).

2. See Nathan Morris, *The Jewish School: An Introduction to the History of Jewish Education* (London: Eyre & Spottiswoode, 1937); Catherine Hezser, *Jewish Literacy in Roman Palestine* (TSAJ 81; Tübingen: Mohr Siebeck, 2001). More generally, see Martin Goodman, *State and Society in Roman Galilee, A.D. 132–212* (2nd ed.; Parkes-Wiener Series on Jewish Studies; London: Valentine Mitchell, 2000), 71–81.

3. Hezser, *Jewish Literacy*, 48, 88.

4. *Sifre Deuteronomy* 46 proscribes the education of daughters, but see Arzt, "Teacher in Talmud and Midrash," 47.

5. William V. Harris, *Ancient Literacy* (Cambridge, Mass.: Harvard University Press, 1989), 272. Harris says little about ancient Judaism in his book. See Seth Schwartz, *Imperialism and Jewish Society, 200 BCE to 640 CE* (Jews, Christians, and Muslims from the Ancient to the Modern World; Princeton: Princeton University Press, 2001), 11 n. 15.

6. *Grapho-literacy* is Chris Keith's term for the ability to read *and write* ("'In My Own Hand': Grapho-Literacy and the Apostle Paul," *Bib* 89 [2008]: 39–58). See the chapter entitled "Who Read and Who Wrote" in Millard, *Reading and Writing*, 154–84. Cf. M. C. A. MacDonald, "Literacy in an Oral Environment," in *Writing and Ancient Near Eastern Society: Papers in Honour of Alan R. Millard* (ed. Piotr Bienkowski, Christopher Mee, and Elizabeth Slater; Library of Hebrew Bible/Old Testament Studies 426; New York: T&T Clark, 2005), 49–118, esp. 64–65.

tional "Greek" subjects, such as Homer, philosophy, and rhetoric. Indeed, there was even some opposition to the very idea of providing a "Greek" education for Jewish boys.[7]

## Literary Evidence

Mention is often made of Josephus's reference to his people's knowledge of the law, but that reference mentions only their *hearing* the law as read to them on the Sabbath. By contrast, the Fourth Gospel's Pharisees take a bleaker view, complaining that a crowd "does not know the law" (John 7:47-49). Context counts a great deal in both cases.

Two Talmudic passages are more central to the debate, as they present two competing accounts of the founding of a widespread primary education system. The first passage credits Shimon b. Shetach (first century BCE) with the establishment of compulsory education for children (*y. Ketub.* 8:11, 32c). This is probably an overambitious rabbinizing of the past by backdating later developments. The second passage has a better prospect of being based on a historical core; it alleges, in the name of Rav, that the high priest Yehoshua b. Gamla (ca. 60-70 CE) instituted a system of primary schools, to wit, that teachers "should be appointed in each district and in each town" for the education of boys beginning at age six or seven (*b. B. Bat.* 21a). This arrangement replaced an earlier one, which in turn replaced a custom of fathers sending their sons to learn in Jerusalem. There may be a kernel of truth in this account, but, if so, it more likely describes an educational apparatus designed especially for the sons of *priests and Levites*.[8] That it was instituted by a high priest, and that it was a secondary improvement on going to school in Jerusalem, makes better sense if the students in view belonged to the priestly class. And it would not be unusual for Rav to "rabbinize" the accomplishments of the temple's priestly administration.[9] The best alternative to limiting this passage to the education of priests is to suppose that it too is a pure fabrication, or that the schools in question were poorly attended. To take it as evidence of a widespread system of education only renders the silence of so many other sources a problem. (For example, we might wonder why Josephus never said anything about this accomplishment of Yehoshua b. Gamla.)

## Archaeological Findings

The relative paucity of inscriptions in Jewish Galilee may indicate that few people apart from scribal functionaries could write. I have already noted, however, that education existed

---

7. See Josephus, *C. Ap.* 1.9, 51; Goodman, *State and Society*, 76; Hezser, *Jewish Literacy*, 92.

8. This is essentially the view of Hirshman, *Stabilization of Rabbinic Culture*, 87–88. Safrai opines that the story's "core is certainly historical" ("Elementary Education," 149), but he does not consider that the core originally had a priestly focus. See Morris, *Jewish School*, 18–19. On the literacy of priests and Levites, see E. P. Sanders, *Judaism: Practice and Belief 63 BCE –66 CE* (London: SCM, 1992), 179.

9. Hirshman writes, "It is not surprising that our *sugya* in Bava Batra continues with detailed instructions about the governance of primary education in 'contemporary' Babylonia" (*Stabilization of Rabbinic Culture*, 86).

primarily for *reading* skills, so the lack of inscriptions might not be related to typical educational opportunities in the region.[10] Of more direct relevance, perhaps, is the lack of identifiable school buildings, although Hezser notes that several synagogues from the rabbinic period feature annexes that might have served as classrooms (for example, Capernaum, Khirbet Shema', Meroth, Nabratein, Chamat Gader, and Beth Alpha).[11]

The only finds sometimes regarded as concrete evidence of schools are the alphabetic inscriptions (*abecedaries*) found at several locations throughout Palestine, including Beth She'arim and Cana in the Galilee.[12] As with the Greeks and Romans, education among Galilean Jews began with learning the alphabet (see *'Avot de R. Nathan A* 6.15).[13] Thus, a number of scholars have explained the significance of the abecedaries in terms of the first steps in a child's education. The difficulty with this line of interpretation is that the alphabet was often written out for the sake of a magical or apotropaic effect.[14] Many of the abecedaries, including those from Beit She'arim, were found in a funerary setting—on ossuaries or in burial niches—certainly the strangest of settings for a schoolboy to practice writing his ABCs.[15] It

---

10. See Hezser, *Jewish Literacy*, 488; Mark A. Chancey, "The Epigraphic Habit of Hellenistic and Roman Galilee," in *Religion, Ethnicity, and Identity in Ancient Galilee: A Region in Transition* (ed. Jürgen Zangenberg, Harold W. Attridge, and Dale B. Martin; WUNT 210; Tübingen: Mohr Siebeck, 2007), 83–98 (including a list of non-numismatic inscriptions in the region).

11. See Hezser, *Jewish Literacy*, 52–53. Hezser notes that the Jerusalem Talmud and Amoraic Midrashim envision education taking place in the synagogue and in study houses (p. 51).

12. See Moshe Schwabe and Baruch Lifshitz, *Beth She'arim*, vol. 2, *The Greek Inscriptions* (New Brunswick, N.J.: Rutgers University Press, 1974), 46–47 (no. 73); Alice Bij de Vaate, "Alphabet-Inscriptions from Jewish Graves," in *Studies in Early Jewish Epigraphy* (Jan Willem van Henten and Pieter Willem van der Horst, eds., AGAJU 21; Leiden: Brill, 1994), 149–50; Douglas R. Edwards, "Khirbet Qana: From Jewish Village to Christian Pilgrim Site," in *The Roman and Byzantine Near East: Some Recent Archaeological Research*, vol. 3, *Late-Antique Petra, Nile Festival Building at Sepphoris, Deir Qal'a Monastery, Khirbet Qana Village and Pilgrim Site, 'Ain-'Arrub Hiding Complex and Other Studies* (ed. J. H. Humphrey; Journal of Roman Archaeology Supplementary Series 49; Ann Arbor, Mich.: Journal of Roman Archaeology, 2002), 101–32. Some of the abecedaries found at Beth She'arim have not been published.

13. See Hezser, *Jewish Literacy*, 83–84; Hirshman, *Stabilization of Rabbinic Culture*, 106. On abecedaries in general, see Aaron Demsky, "Abecedaries," in *The Context of Scripture*, vol. 1, *Canonical Compositions from the Biblical World* (ed. William W. Hallo; Leiden: Brill, 1997), 362–65; Esther Eshel and Douglas R. Edwards, "Language and Writing in Early Roman Galilee: Social Location of a Potter's Abecedary from Khirbet Qana," in *Religion and Society in Roman Palestine: Old Questions, New Approaches* (ed. Douglas R. Edwards; New York: Routledge, 2004), 49–55, esp. 52–53; Hezser, *Jewish Literacy*, 85–87.

14. It is now well known that Palestinian Jews engaged in magical practices. See Franz Dornseiff, *Das Alphabet in Mystik und Magie* (2nd ed.; Stoicheia 7; Leipzig: Teubner, 1925), 70–71; Javier Teixidor, "Bulletin d'Épigraphie Sémitique 1978–1979," *Syria* 56 (1979): 353–400, esp. 354–55; Bij de Vaate, "Alphabet-Inscriptions," 148–61, esp. 158.

15. See Doron Ben-Ami and Yana Tchekhanovets, "A Greek Abecedary Fragment from the City of David," *PEQ* 140 (2001): 197–98. Dornseiff's "Corpus der ABC-Denkmäler" includes a number of abecedaries found in funerary contexts, for example, "Vasen" nos. 2, 4, 14; "Steine" nos. 11, 14, 15, 28, 30 (*Das Alphabet in Mystik und Magie*, 158–68).

has been noted that "all published abecedaries discovered outside of Israel are clearly cultic in context," which raises the question of why abecedaries found *within* Israel should be the only ones that (purportedly) served a pedagogical end.[16] The pedagogical interpretation of the abecedaries also fails to explain why so many inscriptions contain only a partial alphabet: it would be odd (to say the least) for so many schoolboys to become fatigued before completing the whole alphabet.[17] Of course, even if we did not know that abecedaries usually had magical applications, we still would have little reason to infer the existence of a *communal* school from the discovery of an abecedary. Whether education was carried on in a communal setting or in a one-to-one setting within the home, learning the alphabet would have been a foundation for literacy, and one would have to find multiple abecedaries within a *single* setting to justifiably suggest the existence of communal school.[18]

Sociological modeling is a third field of data that could stand beside literary evidence and archaeological findings, but its role should be limited to testing models more firmly based on the literary and the archaeological. Failure so to limit it has sometimes resulted in artificially low literacy estimates for Palestine and/or the Galilee—estimates as low, in fact, as 3–5 percent.[19] In most cases an estimate this low reflects a failure to account for the existence of a hereditary priestly class, a significant presence in the populace with more than the farmer's and artisan's incentive (and opportunity) for at least partial literacy.

---

16. Ben-Ami and Tchekhanovets, "Greek Abecedary Fragment," 199.

17. Scholars have sometimes supposed that the poor letter formation found on many of the abecedaries is an indication of students' rudimentary writing skills, but poor morphology is also to be expected in the case of an illiterate's attempt to write the alphabet for magical effect. See, for example, Roland de Vaux, "Fouilles au Khirbet Qumrân," *RB* 61 (1954): 206–36, esp. 229; André Lemaire, "A Schoolboy's Exercise on an Ostracon at Lachish," *Tel Aviv* 3 (1976): 109–10, esp. 109; Lemaire, "Abécédaires et exercices d'écolier en épigraphie nord-ouest sémitique," *Journal Asiatique* 266 (1978): 221–35, esp. 223, 231–32; Lemaire, *Les écoles et la formation de la Bible dans l'ancien Israël* (OBO 39; Fribourg: Editions Universitaires; Göttingen: Vandenhoeck & Ruprecht, 1981), 10. See Bij de Vaate, "Alphabet-Inscriptions," 154. Poor letter formation is noted (but not interpreted) in Yigael Yadin and Joseph Naveh, "The Aramaic and Hebrew Ostraca and Jar Inscriptions," in *Masada: The Yigael Yadin Excavations 1963–1965. Final Reports*, vol. 1 (Jerusalem: Israel Exploration Society, 1989), 61 (nos. 606–7).

18. To my knowledge, the only attempt to establish the existence of a communal school on the basis of multiple abecedaries is connected to an eighth-century BCE date: Lemaire interprets the finding of two abecedaries near a palace in Lachish as evidence of a school at that location ("Schoolboy's Exercise," 110). Unfortunately for Lemaire, one of the abecedaries in question was inscribed *on a staircase*, and is more easily explained as a protective device, while his identification of the other abecedary was immediately questioned by Yohanan Aharoni in an appended "Editor's Note." Lemaire's refusal to consider a magical context for the abecedaries he discusses is so headstrong that he even passes up a magical interpretation in the case of an abecedary appearing on a *bowl* ("Abécédaires et exercices d'écolier," 226)—a clear instance of a magical application.

19. The 3–5 percent claim is advanced in Meir Bar-Ilan, "Illiteracy in the Land of Israel in the First Centuries C.E.," in *Essays in the Social Scientific Study of Judaism and Jewish Society*, vol. 2 (ed. Simcha Fishbane and Stuart Schoenfeld; Hoboken, N.J.: Ktav, 1992), 46–61.

## A Possible Upswing in Literacy in the Second Century CE

It is widely accepted that the beginnings of a school system existed in the third century CE, which raises the question whether the factors leading to that development were active in the second century CE. Hirschman's explanation (although centering more on the later Babylonian Jewish situation) probably taps into one true cause of the development: he cites hellenization and the failure of two revolts as "engender[ing] a deep sense of anxiety among the rabbis and sages as to the sustainability of their culture."[20] It seems unlikely that such an effect would not manifest at all until the third century, regardless of who was or was not in control of the synagogue (and religious life in general) in the third century. After the destruction of the temple in 70 CE, and especially after the Bar Kokhba Revolt in 132–135 CE, the migration of priests to Galilee would have increased the percentage of those who could read and/or write.[21] This might even have improved the educational opportunities for others living in the Galilee.

### Grapho-literacy

What about the ability to write? Grapho-literacy was rarer but not unknown in most parts of Jewish Palestine. The title "scribe" evokes thoughts of public functionaries and experts in legal matters. Regardless of whether the title was worn only by those who practiced their scribalism on a professional basis, scribes were needed throughout Palestine. The temple itself needed many scribes for its daily activities, but the remote towns in Galilee also needed a means of generating paperwork at watershed moments in a person's life. Putting the temple functionaries and the town functionaries together, E. P. Sanders estimates (as something one "may assume") that there were thousands of scribes in the land before the destruction of the temple.[22] How many were in Galilee? It is difficult to say, but there is no reason to assume that Galilean towns needed fewer scribes than other nonpriestly locales.[23] A scribe was probably within reach (relatively speaking) of just about anyone who needed one, but that is no reason to include grapho-literacy as an expectation of a run-of-the-mill education at any point during our period.

### Bibliography

Aharoni, Yohanan. "Editor's Note." *Tel Aviv* 3 (1976): 110.

Arzt, Max. "The Teacher in Talmud and Midrash." In *Mordecai M. Kaplan: Jubilee Volume on the Occasion of His Seventieth Birthday*, edited by Moshe Davis, 35–47. New York: Jewish Theological Seminary of America Press, 1953.

---

20. Hirshman, *Stabilization of Rabbinic Culture*, 120.

21. The idea of priests migrating to the Galilee does not depend on the veracity of the "list of settlements of the priestly courses"; see Uzi Leibner, *Settlement and History in Hellenistic, Roman, and Byzantine Galilee: An Archaeological Survey of the Eastern Galilee* (TSAJ 127; Tübingen: Mohr Siebeck, 2009), 404–19.

22. Sanders, *Judaism: Practice and Belief*, 181.

23. See the section "Galilee a Backwater?" in Millard, *Reading and Writing*, 179–82.

Bacher, Wilhelm. "Das altjüdische Schulwesen." In *Jahrbuch für Jüdische Geschichte und Literatur*, 6:48–81. Berlin: A. Katz, 1903

Bar-Ilan, Meir. "Illiteracy in the Land of Israel in the First Centuries C.E." In *Essays in the Social Scientific Study of Judaism and Jewish Society*, edited by Simcha Fishbane and Stuart Schoenfeld, 2:46–61. Hoboken, N.J.: Ktav, 1992.

Ben-Ami, Doron, and Yana Tchekhanovets. "A Greek Abecedary Fragment from the City of David." *PEQ* 140 (2001): 197–98.

Bij de Vaate, Alice. "Alphabet-Inscriptions from Jewish Graves." In *Studies in Early Jewish Epigraphy*, edited by Jan Willem van Henten and Pieter Willem van der Horst, 148–61. AGAJU 21. Leiden: Brill, 1994.

Chancey, Mark A. "The Epigraphic Habit of Hellenistic and Roman Galilee." In *Religion, Ethnicity, and Identity in Ancient Galilee: A Region in Transition*, edited by Jürgen Zangenberg, Harold W. Attridge, and Dale B. Martin, 83–98. WUNT 210. Tübingen: Mohr Siebeck, 2007.

Demsky, Aaron. "Abecedaries." In *The Context of Scripture*, vol. 1, *Canonical Compositions from the Biblical World*, edited by William W. Hallo, 362–65. Leiden: Brill, 1997.

Dornseiff, Franz. *Das Alphabet in Mystik und Magie.* 2nd ed. Stoicheia 7. Leipzig: Teubner, 1925.

Ebner, Eliezer. *Elementary Education in Ancient Israel during the Tannaitic Period (10–220 C.E.).* New York: Bloch, 1956.

Edwards, Douglas R. "Khirbet Qana: From Jewish Village to Christian Pilgrim Site." In John H. Humphrey, ed., *The Roman and Byzantine Near East: Some Recent Archaeological Research*, vol. 3, *Late-Antique Petra, Nile Festival Building at Sepphoris, Deir Qal'a Monastery, Khirbet Qana Village and Pilgrim Site, 'Ain-'Arrub Hiding Complex and Other Studies*, edited by J. H. Humphrey, 101–32. Journal of Roman Archaeology Supplementary Series 49. Ann Arbor, Mich.: Journal of Roman Archaeology, 2002.

Eshel, Esther, and Douglas R. Edwards. "Language and Writing in Early Roman Galilee: Social Location of a Potter's Abecedary from Khirbet Qana." In *Religion and Society in Roman Palestine: Old Questions, New Approaches*, edited by Douglas R. Edwards, 49–55. New York: Routledge, 2004.

Gerhardsson, Birger. *Memory and Manuscript: Oral Tradition and Written Transmission in Rabbinic Judaism and Early Christianity.* Acta Seminarii Neotestamentici Upsaliensis 22. Uppsala: Almqvist & Wiksell, 1961.

Ginzberg, Louis. *Students, Scholars and Saints.* Philadelphia: Jewish Publication Society of America, 1928.

Goodman, Martin. *State and Society in Roman Galilee, A.D. 132–212.* 2nd ed. Parkes-Wiener Series on Jewish Studies. London: Valentine Mitchell, 2000.

Harris, William V. *Ancient Literacy.* Cambridge, Mass.: Harvard University Press, 1989.

Hezser, Catherine. *Jewish Literacy in Roman Palestine.* TSAJ 81. Tübingen: Mohr Siebeck, 2001.

Hirshman, Marc. *The Stabilization of Rabbinic Culture, 100 C.E.–350 C.E.: Texts on Education and Their Late Antique Context.* Oxford: Oxford University Press, 2009.

Keith, Chris. "'In My Own Hand': Grapho-Literacy and the Apostle Paul." *Bib* 89 (2008): 39–58.

Leibner, Uzi. *Settlement and History in Hellenistic, Roman, and Byzantine Galilee: An Archaeological Survey of the Eastern Galilee.* TSAJ 127. Tübingen: Mohr Siebeck, 2009.

Lemaire, André. "Abécédaires et exercices d'écolier en épigraphie nord-ouest sémitique." *Journal Asiatique* 266 (1978): 221–35.

———. *Les écoles et la formation de la Bible dans l'ancien Israël.* OBO 39. Fribourg: Editions Universitaires; Göttingen: Vandenhoeck & Ruprecht, 1981.

———. "A Schoolboy's Exercise on an Ostracon at Lachish." *Tel Aviv* 3 (1976): 109–10.

MacDonald, M. C. A. "Literacy in an Oral Environment." In *Writing and Ancient Near Eastern Society: Papers in Honour of Alan R. Millard,* edited by Piotr Bienkowski, Christopher Mee, and Elizabeth Slater, 49–118. Library of Hebrew Bible/Old Testament Studies 426. New York: T&T Clark, 2005.

Millard, Alan. *Reading and Writing in the Time of Jesus.* New York: New York University Press, 2000.

Morris, Nathan. *The Jewish School: An Introduction to the History of Jewish Education.* London: Eyre & Spottiswoode, 1937.

Perlow, Towa. *L'éducation et l'enseignement chez les juifs à l'époque talmudique.* Paris: Leroux, 1931.

Rosenau, William. "'The Rabbinical Era.'" In *The Chautauqua System of Jewish Education,* edited by Abram Simon and William Rosenau, 41–58. Philadelphia: Jewish Chautauqua Society, 1912.

Safrai, Shmuel. "Elementary Education, Its Religious and Social Significance in the Talmudic Period." *Cahiers d'Histoire Mondiale* 11 (1968): 148–69.

Sanders, E. P. *Judaism: Practice and Belief, 63 BCE –66 CE.* London: SCM, 1992.

Schwabe, Moshe, and Baruch Lifshitz. *Beth She'arim.* Vol. 2, *The Greek Inscriptions.* New Brunswick, N.J.: Rutgers University Press, 1974.

Schwartz, Seth. *Imperialism and Jewish Society, 200 BCE to 640 CE.* Jews, Christians, and Muslims from the Ancient to the Modern World. Princeton: Princeton University Press, 2001.

Teixidor, Javier. "Bulletin d'Épigraphie Sémitique 1978–1979." *Syria* 56 (1979): 353–400.

Vaux, Roland de. "Fouilles au Khirbet Qumrân." *RB* 61 (1954): 206–36.

Yadin, Yigael, and Joseph Naveh. "The Aramaic and Hebrew Ostraca and Jar Inscriptions." In *Masada: The Yigael Yadin Excavations 1963–1965. Final Reports,* 1:61. Jerusalem: Israel Exploration Society, 1989.

# Economics

# 13

# The Galilean Road System

## *James F. Strange*

The earliest biblical reference to travel in what is evidently Galilee is in Genesis 12:5-6, where Abraham comes to Canaan. The text omits Abraham's travel across Galilee and the Plain of Jezreel but mentions his arrival at Shechem. A later and clearer reference to a road in the Galilee is Isaiah 9:1 (Heb. 8:23): ". . . in the later time he will honor *the Way of the Sea*, the Land beyond the Jordan [as seen from east of the Jordan], Galilee of the Nations." The "Way of the Sea" is the name of the main coastal highway in Canaan and of the eighth-century BCE Assyrian province formed from the territories of Dor, Megiddo, and Gilead on both sides of the Jordan.[1] Twenty kilometers south of Megiddo the "Way of the Sea" divides into two branches moving north. The west branch skirts the base of Mount Carmel and leads to Acco and eventually to Tyre. The eastern branch leads to Megiddo, crosses the Plain of Jezreel to Mount Tabor, and continues to the biblical city of Hazor southeast of Lake Huleh, now drained. From there it leads eighty kilometers to Damascus (for roads and locations in Galilee, see the "Maps Gallery").

Galilee shares its name with the "Sea of Galilee," usually given in the Hebrew Bible as *Chinnerith* or "the Sea of Chinnereth" (Num. 34:11; Deut. 3:17; Josh. 13:27; 19:35). The name is derived from Hebrew *kinnor* ("harp") and describes its shape. The Apocrypha gives us the name Gennesareth in 1 Maccabees 11:67 ("the Waters of Gennesaret"). It is also in Luke 5:1 (Jesus stood by the "Lake of Gennesaret"). The town of Gennesaret on the northwest shore of the lake appears in Matthew 14:34 and Mark 6:53.[2] Otherwise in the New Testament this body is called "the Sea of Galilee" (Matt. 4:18 = Mark 1:16; Matt. 15:29; Mark 7:31). Another New Testament name is the "Sea of Tiberias" (John 21:1), after the city of Tiberias, which

---

1. Yohanan Aharoni, *The Land of the Bible: A Historical Geography* (trans. and ed. Anson F. Rainey; 2nd rev. and enlarged ed.; Philadelphia: Westminster, 1979), 45.

2. Michael Avi-Yonah believes that the town of Gennesaret gave its name to the lake ( *Gazetteer of Roman Palestine* (Qedem 5; Jerusalem: Institute of Archaeology, Hebrew University, and Carta, 1976), 60.

Herod Antipas built on the western shore about 18 CE. Once, in John 6:1, it is called "the Sea of Galilee of Tiberias." A road on the shore surrounds the entire lake.

Josephus gives a description of the Galilee in *Jewish War* 3.35. He knows that Mount Carmel (which belonged to Tyre) and the independent city of Ptolemais-Acco occupied western Galilee and the shoreline. The small, independent city of Geba, or Gaba, stood between Carmel and Galilee at the foot of Mount Carmel.[3] To the south Galilee borders on the independent city-territory of Scythopolis and on Samaria.

Josephus traces the borders of Upper and Lower Galilee in his *Jewish War* (3.35–36). He knows village names that mark the borders of the region. These include Meroth, Thella, Baca, and Barsabe (Beer-sheba north). Michael Avi-Yonah fit these limits to a map of Upper Galilee by drawing a border westward from Thella on Lake Huleh to Baca (modern Pik'in). He suggested that Upper Galilee reached south from Meroth (Marun er-Ras in Lebanon) to Barsabe at the border with Lower Galilee.[4] Thus, Upper Galilee reached 27 km west from Thella to Baca and 19 km south to Barsabe (Beer-sheba north). Lower Galilee would extend from Tiberias on the Sea of Galilee to borders with Gaba and Ptolemais-Acco in the west, or about 39 km. Lower Galilee ranges south from Barsabe (Beer-sheba north) to Ginae at the ascent to Samaria, a distance of 53 km.[5]

In the same passage, Josephus knows that there is an Upper Galilee and a Lower Galilee. The mountains of Upper Galilee extend upward to 1,208 m at Mount Meiron, while the elevation of Lower Galilee at Mount el-Sikh 5 km northeast of Nazareth is 573 m. The hills intensified effort in travel and therefore impeded trade.

Josephus in his *Life* (*Vita*) mentions the distances between certain villages. In *Life* 265 Sogane is 20 stadia (3.7 km) from Gabara. The actual distance is 4.4 km.[6] In *Life* 234 Jotapata is 40 stadia (7.4 km) from Chabalo (Cabul), which equals the measured distance. In *Life* 157 he locates Taricheae (Magdala) 30 stadia (5.6 km) from Tiberias, which compares well with the measured distance.

---

3. Josephus, *Ant.* 15.294: "Moreover [Herod] chose certain select horsemen and placed them in the great plain and built for them a place in Galilee known as Geba." The earliest coins minted at Geba date to 36 BCE, which suggests that this locality predates Herod the Great. See Ya'akov Meshorer, *City Coins of Eretz-Israel and the Decapolis in the Roman Period* (Jerusalem: Israel Museum, 1985), 38 ("Gaba").

4. Michael Avi-Yonah, *The Holy Land, from the Persian to the Arab Conquest, 536 B.C.–A.D. 640: A Historical Geography* (rev. ed.; Baker Studies in Biblical Archaeology; Grand Rapids: Baker, 1977), 133–35.

5. Mordechai Aviam infers the extent of Jewish settlement by archaeological methods in *Jews, Pagans, and Christians in the Galilee: 25 Years of Archaeological Excavations and Surveys, Hellenistic to Byzantine Periods* (Land of Galilee 1; Rochester, N.Y.: University of Rochester Press, 2004). See also Aviam, "Galilee: The Hellenistic to Byzantine Periods," *NEAEHL* 2:453–58.

6. The Roman stadium (Greek *stadion*) as a unit of measure is 625 Roman feet. If the Roman foot is 0.296 m, then the stadium is 185 m, which is our conversion factor.

Some scholars estimate the total land area of Galilee as low as 1,400 and as high as 1,600 sq km.[7] Careful measurement and digitization of the first-century CE borders of Galilee as presented in Aharoni and Avi-Yonah yield 2,073 sq km.[8] This measurement omits the territory of Beth Shean-Scythopolis, which is part of the Decapolis.[9]

## Research into the Galilean Road System of the Roman Period

Research into the Roman-era road system in the Galilee is limited. Many scholars investigate Israelite settlement, the place-names in the Gospels, and identification of sites in the Hebrew Bible, the Apocrypha, and the New Testament, but understanding the road system was not a top priority. Nevertheless, certain scholars made contributions to the knowledge of the road system, principally Gustaf Dalman, Albrecht Alt, Michael Avi-Yonah, Willibald Bösen, Yosef Stepansky, John Wilkinson, and James F. Strange,[10] culminating in Isaac and Roll.[11]

7. Willibald Bösen, *Galiläa als Lebensraum und Wirkungsfeld Jesu: Eine zeitgeschichtliche und theologische Untersuchung* (Biblische Sachbuch; Freiburg: Herder, 1985), 58. Bösen follows Arieh Ben-David's suggestion that the land area of all Galilee was 1,500 sq km. Bösen's maps 10 and 11 show the city territory of Beth Shean-Scythopolis as part of Galilee. Ben-David estimates 1,500 sq km in *Talmudische Ökonomie: Die Wirtschaft des jüdischen Palästina zur Zeit der Mischna und des Talmud* (Hildesheim: Georg Olms, 1974), 48. Perhaps he is only counting *tillable farmland*. Bösen also cites G. Bertram and Theodor Klauser, "Galiläa," in *Reallexikon für Antike und Christentum: Sachwörterbuch zur Auseinandersetzung des Christentums mit der Antiken Welt* (ed. Theodor Klauser; Stuttgart: Anton Hiersemann, 1972), 8: 796–821. They give 2,000 sq km, but Bösen reduces this by 320 sq km included from the Jezreel Plain by mistake, leaving 1,680 sq km.

8. Yohanan Aharoni and Michael Avi-Yonah, *The Macmillan Bible Atlas* (3rd rev. ed., ed. Anson F. Rainey and Ze'ev Safrai; Jerusalem: Carta, 1993), 164. Digitization and measurement by James F. Strange.

9. The inclusion of Scythopolis would add another 490 sq km to Galilee.

10. Gustaf Dalman, *Sacred Sites and Ways: Studies in the Topography of the Gospels* (trans. Paul P. Levertoff; New York: Macmillan, 1935); Albrecht Alt, *Where Jesus Worked: Towns and Villages of Galilee Studied with the Help of Local History* (trans. Kenneth Grayston; London: Epworth, 1961); Michael Avi-Yonah, "The Roman Road System," in Avi-Yonah, *Holy Land* (1966), 181–87; Bösen, *Galiläa,* 30; Yosef Stepansky, "Kefar Nahum Map, Survey," *HA-ESI* 10 (1991): 87–90; Stepansky, "Rosh Pinna Map, Survey–1992," *HA-ESI* 14 (1995): 13–15; Stepansky, "Map of Rosh Pinna, Survey–1993," *HA-ESI* 15 (1996): 14–17; Stepansky, "Horvat Mishlah," *HA-ESI* 16 (1997): 30–32; John Wilkinson, *Jerusalem Pilgrims before the Crusades* (Warminster: Aris & Phillips, 1977); James F. Strange, "First Century Galilee from Archaeology and from the Texts," in *Archaeology and the Galilee: Texts and Contexts in the Graeco-Roman and Byzantine Periods* (ed. Douglas R. Edwards and C. Thomas McCollough; South Florida Studies in the History of Judaism 143; Atlanta: Scholars Press, 1997), 39–48; James Riley Strange, "John and the Geography of Palestine," in *Archaeology and the Fourth Gospel* (ed. Paul N. Anderson; Grand Rapids: Eerdmans, forthcoming).

11. See Yoram Tsafrir, Leah Di Segni, and Judith Green, *Tabula Imperii Romani, Eretz Israel in the Hellenistic, Roman, and Byzantine Periods. Iudaea-Palestina: Maps and Gazetteer* (Jerusalem: Israel Academy of Sciences and Humanities, 1994), with five maps in color.

## The Galilean Road System in the Nineteenth Century

It is a commonplace in archaeological research to test hypotheses and generate new ones by appealing to comparative data. In 1871–77, the officers and enlisted men of *The Survey of Western Palestine* (henceforth SWP) gathered comparative data in a first-time survey of Ottoman Palestine.[12] They produced a map in twenty-six sheets at a scale of 1:63,360. There was no map grid such as the Palestine Grid.[13] Our interest lies in the thousands of surveyed footpaths, donkey caravan paths, trails, cart tracks, and "roads" of the time in Galilee. The nineteenth-century people who used the paths traveled without electricity, steam, or fossil fuels, matching the practice in the Roman period.

The accompanying volumes of *The Survey of Western Palestine* contain notes on archaeology, topography, mountains and mountain ridges (orography), and water sources (hydrography), with notes on the footpaths or trails connecting localities. *Galilee* is the title of volume 1 of the set and its related sheets (I–VI).

| Col 1 | Col 2 | Col 3 | Col 4 | Col 5 | Col 6 | Col 7 | Col 8 | Col 9 | Col 10 |
|---|---|---|---|---|---|---|---|---|---|
| Sheet | Major Site[14] | Square Miles | Square kms in Sheet | No. of Villages in Sheet | Density Villages per km$^2$ | Rank in Villages per km$^2$ | Census numbers | Density: Persons per km$^2$ | Rank: Persons per km$^2$ |
| I | Tyre | 60.8 | 157.5 | 39 | 0.25 | 1 | 8,500 | 54.0 | 1 |
| II | Dan | 203 | 525.8 | 92 | 0.17 | 2 | 19,670 | 37.4 | 2 |
| III | Acco | 201.6 | 522.1 | 51 | 0.10 | 3 | 17,000 | 32.6 | 4 |
| IV | Safed | 307 | 795.1 | 60 | 0.08 | 4 | 18,170 | 22.9 | 5 |
| V | Sepphoris | 316 | 818.4 | 39 | 0.05 | 6 | 28,890 | 35.3 | 3 |
| VI | Tiberias | 252.8 | 654.8 | 33 | 0.05 | 5 | 10,000 | 15.3 | 6 |
| Total/ Average | | 1341.2 | 3473.7 | 314 | Av = 0.09 | | 102,230 | Av. = 29.4 | |

### Chart A. A Summary of Information from SWP Sheets I–VI

The SWP reported the area of each sheet in square miles (column 3), which appears as km$^2$ in column 4. The number of villages in each sheet appears in column 5. Column 6 displays the density of each sheet as the number of villages per km$^2$. The distributions of the nineteenth-century villages and footpaths were not uniform. The number of villages per km$^2$

---

12. Charles R. Conder and H. H. Kitchener, *Palestine Exploration Fund Maps I–VII* (Southampton: Ordinance Survey Office, 1878–79; copyright is now held by Todd Bolen, Bibleplaces.com).

13. The Palestine Grid emanated from the British Mandate of Palestine in 1922. It was based on grid lines ten kilometers apart with a central east–west and a central north–south meridian through Jerusalem. See Dov Gavish, *A Survey of Palestine under the British Mandate, 1920–1948* (RoutledgeCurzon Studies in Middle East History 3; New York: RoutledgeCurzon, 2005), 66.

14. Column 2 contains the name of a major site in each sheet, supplied by the present author.

decreased on a line from Tyre toward Sepphoris. Sheets I and II to the north have the most villages per square kilometer, while Sheets V and VI contain the fewest.

The SWP also published a census for all villages, citing Guérin for comparison.[15] One might expect to find more footpaths with higher populations. Census numbers including the total appear in column 8. Column 9 contains the calculated density of each sheet. Sheet I is the most densely populated. The villages were larger in Lower Galilee. The SWP reports that Nazareth, at "nearly 6,000," is the largest town in Sheet V, larger than Haifa, the port city.[16] The SWP reports the population of Saffûrieh (Sepphoris) as most reasonably 2,500 people.[17]

Sheet VI is the least densely populated.[18] The SWP gives the population of Tiberias as "about 2000 inhabitants."[19]

### Roads in Roman Galilee

Paved, Roman imperial roads mostly date from the second century CE. They are broad, hard-surfaced, featuring curb stones, sometimes center stones, and even milestones. Such is not the case for village ways or paths.

The four-part composite Maps 4A–4D in the Maps Gallery show the villages and footpaths mapped by the SWP in 1881 and show the Palestine grid as an overlay. The ancient names of villages appear when known. The thick, dashed line is the boundary for Roman period Galilee, which is 40% smaller than the total territory the SWP called "the Galilee." The major source for the paths and ways is the SWP Map of 1878–9. These maps synthesize data from Aharoni (1979), Avi-Yonah (1976), Dorsey (1991), and Leibner (2006).

Each 10 x 10 km map square is designated by the intersection of grid lines at its northeast corner. The northeast corner of randomly selected Square 200/240 (see Map 4D) is the crossing of north–south grid line 200 and east–west grid line 240 in Sheet VI. This area of 100 sq km of mountains and valleys slopes downhill to the south-southeast. It contains fifteen villages with Roman-period remains. The SWP map shows six trails across the territory following the fretted terrain. A second group of thirteen trails crosses the first group nearly at right angles. They form a kind of network following the land. The trails average nearly 5 km long, but the longest is 11 km long. One would not walk more than 3 km on any trail without encountering

---

15. Victor Guérin was privately commissioned in 1863 to visit Ottoman Palestine and report village and city populations. He did so in seven volumes after eight visits: Victor Guérin, *Description géographique, historique, et archéologique de la Palestine*, *Judée* I–III (1869), *Samarie* I–II (1874–75), *Galilée* I–II (1880) (Paris, Imprimée Impériale, 1868–80).

16. Charles R. Conder and H. H. Kitchener, *The Survey of Western Palestine: Memoirs of the Topography, Orography, Hydrography, and Archaeology* (London: Palestine Exploration Fund, 1881), 275 and 278.

17. Conder and Kitchener, *SWP*, 280.

18. There were no census data available for Sheet VI, so the *SWP* used "approximately estimated" numbers (Conder and Kitchener, *SWP*, 360).

19. Conder and Kitchener, *SWP*, 361.

a crossing with another trail or an intersection on one side or the other with a new trail. Often paths lead *near* a village, but seldom directly to it.

Some trails follow the tops of ridges, but others follow the valleys on one or both sides of a ridge. They also sometimes follow wadis. A trail may fork anywhere the terrain allows and intersect with a third trail. Some of these are shortcuts between two trails, and the traveler saves a few minutes by following the shortcut.

## Walking Speeds and Distances

The walk from Meiron to the Sea of Galilee (see Map 4B), a distance of 16 km, takes from two to five hours.[20] Therefore, the walker travels at 3.2 to 8 kph. From Meiron, the path drops more than one km to the shore of the lake (1,253 m), which adds to the effort.[21]

If villagers travel to the next village, buy and sell, then return that day, there is a constraint on travel. If one travels for two hours in the morning and returns in the afternoon, one could travel 6.4 to 9.6 km over two hours. Therefore, from the center of Map 4D: Square 200/240, one could travel to every village within the 100 sq km in two hours. At this same rate, one could walk to within a kilometer of Tiberias and could easily reach Philoteria on the south end of the lake. The trek would reach west to Mount Tabor. One could walk 3 km into the city territory of Sepphoris.[22]

## Travel from Nazareth to Cana

John 2:1-12 narrates a story of Jesus transforming water into wine at a wedding in Cana. I prefer the identification of "Cana of Galilee" with the Khirbet Qana east of Jotapata.[23]

The most direct route would take Jesus, his mother, and the disciples 14 km to Cana. Using the *SWP* data, we see a 2.5 km trail descend to the northeast from Nazareth to Reina (see Map 4C), whose ancient name is not known. (A Sepphoris aqueduct starts in Reina.) From Reina, at 300 m above sea level, they could continue northeast about 1.5 km to a point near Gath Hepher, skirting to the east of Sepphoris. The shortest route leads through 1.2 km of light forest across the main east–west road from Tiberias. From there the trail would lead north 5 km to Rimmon on the south edge of the Bet Netopha Valley. From Rimmon one could see the hilltop of Cana (see Maps 4A and 4B) on the far north edge of the valley 4 km away and 66 m above the valley floor. One might simply walk from there across the flat valley, because the

20. Anna Dintaman and David Landis, *Hiking the Jesus Trail and Other Biblical Walks in the Galilee* (Harleysville, Pa.: Village to Village Press, 2013).

21. Lake elevation in Conder and Kitchener, *SWP*, 33.

22. See similar figures in Wilkinson, *Jerusalem Pilgrims before the Crusades*, 16–28.

23. Gustaf Dalman, "Cana in Galilee," in Dalman, *Sacred Sites and Ways*, 101–6.

marsh is 2 km to the east. This trip takes four to four and one-half hours of steady walking.[24] If there were breaks to rest or eat it would take longer. One might conclude that the invitees to the wedding were expected to spend the night.[25]

### Travel from Cana to Capernaum

A healing story in John 4:46-54 tells of a "royal man" (*basilikos*) from Capernaum who comes to Cana and petitions Jesus to heal his son. Jesus grants healing, and the man returns to Capernaum. He begins his return around the great marsh (see Map4A), which is depicted as 6 x 1.5 km. He starts 0.7 km south of Cana on the east–west trail. From that point he walks nine km east to Bet Netopha (see Map 4B). At Bet Netopha the way turns southeast 2.8 km to the Ailabon–H. Amudim footpath. (The ancient name of H. Amudim is not known.) From this intersection he proceeds 0.6 km to intersect the east–west trail leading uphill from Beth Anath-Bu'ina past Umm el Amed to Kefar Hittaia. From there he descends steeply eastward for 4.4 km to Kefar Hittaia, which may be where he met his servants coming to tell him his son was well. From Kefar Hittaia it is 2.4 km to the Wadi Hammam trail, on which one walks 3.7 km eastward toward Magdala and the International Way or "highway" next to the Sea of Galilee. This highway leads past Magdala and Gennesaret, past the relatively uninhabited area between Gennesaret and Capernaum, and finally to Capernaum itself. The total distance from Cana is 30–31 km, which is a trip of about six to nine hours.[26] The walk is a descent of 380 m to the shores of the Sea of Galilee. One can see that it could take parts of two days.[27]

One can readily see that a dense network of trails, tracks, and footpaths probably covered Roman-period Galilee. The network was the imprint of everyday travel in the Galilee for trade, some of it from cities like Sepphoris or Tiberias and some from villages like Nazareth or Shikhin.[28] Part of the network is international, but the majority is formed of local trails. Some have wondered how Jesus gathered crowds, but it is simpler to imagine given such a solid web of footpaths, ways, and roads.

### Bibliography

Adan-Bayewitz, David, and Isadore Perlman. "The Local Trade of Sepphoris in the Roman Period." *IEJ* 40 (1990): 153–72.

---

24. We use the slow rate to accommodate families.

25. Cf. James Riley Strange, "John and the Geography of Palestine" (forthcoming).

26. The modern hiking trail through Arbel is 60 km (Dintaman and Landis, *Hiking the Jesus Trail*, 15).

27. Cf. James Riley Strange, "John and the Geography of Palestine" (forthcoming).

28. See David Adan-Bayewitz and Isadore Perlman, "The Local Trade of Sepphoris in the Roman Period," *IEJ* 40 (1990): 153–72; and James F. Strange, Dennis E. Groh, and Thomas R.W. Longstaff, "University of South Florida Excavations at Sepphoris: The Location and Identification of Shikhin, Parts 1 & 2," *IEJ* 44 (1994): 216–27; 45 (1995): 171–87.

Aharoni, Yohanan. *The Land of the Bible: A Historical Geography*. Translated and edited by Anson F. Rainey. 2nd rev. and enlarged ed. Philadelphia: Westminster, 1979.

Aharoni, Yohanan, and Michael Avi-Yonah. *The Macmillan Bible Atlas*. 3rd rev. ed. Edited by Anson F. Rainey and Ze'ev Safrai. Jerusalem: Carta, 1993.

Alt, Albrecht. *Where Jesus Worked: Towns And Villages of Galilee Studied with the Help of Local History*. Translated by Kenneth Grayston. London: Epworth, 1961.

Aviam, Mordechai. "Galilee: The Hellenistic to Byzantine Periods." *NEAEHL* 2:453–58.

———. *Jews, Pagans, and Christians in the Galilee: 25 Years of Archaeological Excavations and Surveys, Hellenistic to Byzantine Periods*. Land of Galilee 1. Rochester, N.Y.: University of Rochester Press, 2004.

Avi-Yonah, Michael. *Gazetteer of Roman Palestine*. Qedem 5. Jerusalem: Institute of Archaeology, Hebrew University and Carta, 1976.

———. *The Holy Land, from the Persian to the Arab Conquests, 536 B.C. to A.D. 640: A Historical Geography*. Baker Studies in Biblical Archaeology. Grand Rapids: Baker, 1966. Rev. ed., 1977.

Ben-David, Arieh. *Talmudische Ökonomie: Die Wirtschaft des jüdischen Palästina zur Zeit der Mischna und des Talmud*. Hildesheim: Georg Olms, 1974.

Bertram, Georg, and Theodor Klauser. "Gallilää." In *Reallexikon für Antike und Christentum: Sachwörterbuch zur Auseinandersetzung des Christentums mit der Antiken Welt*, edited by Theodor Klauser, 8:796–821. Stuttgart: Anton Hiersemann, 1972.

Bösen, Willibald. *Galiläa als Lebensraum und Wirkungsfeld Jesu: Eine Zeitgeschichtliche und theologische Untersuchung*. Freiburg: Herder, 1985.

Conder, Charles R., and H. H. Kitchener. *Palestine Exploration Fund Maps I–VII*. Southampton: Ordinance Survey Office, 1878–79. Copyright now held by Todd Bolen, Bibleplaces. com.

———. *The Survey of Western Palestine: Memoirs of the Topography, Orography, Hydrography, and Archaeology*. London: Palestine Exploration Fund, 1881.

Dalman, Gustaf. *Sacred Sites and Ways: Studies in the Topography of the Gospels*. Translated by Paul P. Levertoff. New York: Macmillan, 1935.

Dintaman, Anna, and David Landis. *Hiking the Jesus Trail and Other Biblical Walks in the Galilee*. Harleysville, Pa.: Village to Village Press, 2013.

Dorsey, David A. *The Roads and Highways of Ancient Israel*. Baltimore: Johns Hopkins University Press, 1991.

Gavish, Dov. *A Survey of Palestine under the British Mandate, 1920-1948*. RoutledgeCurzon Studies in Middle East History 3. New York: RoutledgeCurzon, 2005.

Guérin, Victor. *Description géographique, historique, et archéologique de la Palestine. Judée I–III* (1868–69); *Samarie I–II* (1874–75); *Galilée I–II* (1880). Paris, Imprimée Impériale, 1868–80.

Isaac, Benjamin, and Israel Roll. *Roman Roads in Judaea I: The Legio-Scythopolis Road*. London: BAR International Series 141. Oxford: BAR, 1982.

Leibner, Uzi. "Settlement and Demography in Late Roman and Byzantine Eastern Galilee." In *Settlements and Demography in the Near East in Late Antiquity: Proceedings of the Colloquium, Matera, 27–29 October 2005*, edited by Ariel S. Lewin and Pietrina Pellegrini. Biblioteca di Mediterraneo antico 2. Pisa: Istituti Editoriali e Poligrafici Internazionali, 2006.

Meshorer, Ya'akov. *City Coins of Eretz-Israel and the Decapolis in the Roman Period*. Jerusalem: Israel Museum, 1985.

Roll, Israel. "Between Damascus and Megiddo: Roads and Transportation in Antiquity across the Northeastern Approaches to the Holy Land." In *Man Near a Roman Arch: Studies Presented to Prof. Yoram Tsafrir*, edited by Leah Di Segni, Yizhar Hirschfeld, Joseph Patrich, and Rina Talgam, 1–20. Jerusalem: Israel Exploration Society, 2009.

———. "Survey of Roman Roads in Lower Galilee." *HA-ESI* 14 (1995): 38–40.

Stepansky, Yosef. "Horvat Mishlah." *HA-ESI* 16 (1997): 30–32.

———. "Kefar Nahum Map, Survey." *HA-ESI* 10 (1991): 87–90.

———. "Map of Rosh Pinna, Survey–1993." *HA-ESI* 15 (1996): 14–17.

———. "Rosh Pinna Map, Survey–1992." *HA-ESI* 14 (1995): 13–15.

Strange, James F. "First Century Galilee from Archaeology and from the Texts." In *Archaeology and the Galilee: Texts and Contexts in the Graeco-Roman and Byzantine Periods*, edited by Douglas R. Edwards and C. Thomas McCollough, 39–48. South Florida Studies in the History of Judaism 143. Atlanta: Scholars Press, 1997.

Strange, James F., Dennis E. Groh, and Thomas R. W. Longstaff, "University of South Florida Excavations at Sepphoris: The Location and Identification of Shikhin, Parts 1 & 2." *IEJ* 44 (1994): 216–27; 45 (1995): 171–87.

Strange, James Riley. "John and the Geography of Palestine." In *Archaeology and the Fourth Gospel*, ed. Paul N. Anderson. Grand Rapids: Eerdmans, forthcoming.

Tsafrir, Yoram, Leah Di Segni, and Judith Green. *Tabula Imperii Romani, Eretz Israel in the Hellenistic, Roman, and Byzantine Periods. Iudaea-Palestina: Maps and Gazetteer*. Jerusalem: Israel Academy of Sciences and Humanities, 1994.

Wilkinson, John. *Jerusalem Pilgrims before the Crusades*. Warminster: Aris & Phillips, 1977.

# 14

# URBANIZATION AND INDUSTRY IN MISHNAIC GALILEE

## *Ze'ev Safrai*

This chapter deals with cities, the urbanization process, and industry in the Galilee during the Tannaitic period, from 70 to 220 CE. The end of the Tannaitic period is of great significance for Jewish culture and religion, but less important for the economy and local administration. Limiting the discussion to the Tannaitic period enables us to distinguish clearly between the period as it is reflected in sources that were redacted during the Tannaitic period and other, later sources (Amoraic and post-Amoraic, c. 220–500 CE).

We can assume that the structure of the economy and the city did not change much between the third and fourth centuries. If, however, the only literary evidence for a certain situation is from the Amoraic literature (largely the Talmuds and some midrashic literature), we must consider whether we have only late evidence through coincidence, or whether this is a late situation. I date the sources according to the texts in which they appear, rather than according to the names of the sages who are mentioned or the definition of the source as a *baraita*: the words of Tannaim (early sages) that were preserved only in the Talmuds (literature of later, Amoraic sages). A *baraita* that was preserved only in the Talmuds reflects the views of the Amoraim, unless it has a Tannaitic source or parallel.[1]

The problems with using the rabbinic literature should be a lever for research rather than a source of paralysis, as has been the case for a number of scholars. Of course, parallel to the

---

1. In this chapter a Talmudic source, generally speaking, is treated like any other literary historical source. It reflects the reality within the limitations familiar to any historian. Among other things, it includes exaggeration, forgetting, bias, and subjectivity, and it promotes an ideology. This subject is in dispute in the research, and it deserves an in-depth and systematic discussion, as I have concluded after fifteen years of joint work on a systematic commentary on the six books of the Mishnah. See Shmuel Safrai and Ze'ev Safrai, *Mishnat Eretz Israel I* (Jerusalem, E.M. Lipshitz, 2008), 27–31.

rabbinic literature I use the archaeological findings, including excavations that have yet to be published in detail.

## Settlement Structure before and after 70 CE

In the early first century CE the communities in the Galilee were divided into three levels: cities, villages, and field structures.[2] Although this distinction among levels of settlement is crucial to understanding the socioeconomic situation in every region in every period, when describing a particular settlement, none of the available sources—the Gospels,[3] Josephus, and rabbinic sources[4]—uses the correct term with any precision. When they refer to the settlement hierarchy, however, they use the terms more precisely. Since a similar situation is found in all these types of literature, their authors probably knew the precise terminology but did not feel that it was always important to use it.

Josephus describes the Galilee as a region with 204 cities and villages (*Life* 235). Three of the cities are Tiberias, Sepphoris, and Gabara (*Life* 124), and probably also Taricheae (Magdala), which was the center of the Galilee before Tiberias was established. Herod Antipas built Sepphoris and Tiberias, and Taricheae and Gabara were apparently the earlier centers. In addition to these four, we should include Bethsaida, which Philip rebuilt as a city named Julias. To this list we should probably also add Gischala as a central community ("city") of the Jewish Upper Galilee, and Gamla, which was the capital of the southern Golan and is always called a city. Possibly we should add Beit Yerah (Philoteria; Polybius 5.70.3).[5]

These cities were not ordinary Greek-Roman *poleis* (πόλεις). In this chapter I maintain that there were two types of cities in the provincial area:[6]

---

2. Ze'ev Safrai, *The Economy of Roman Palestine* (London: Routledge, 1994), 19–103.

3. Gospel passages listing settlements of different levels use precise terminology, for example, "cities, towns, and field buildings" (κώμας, πόλεις, ἀγρούς) in Mark 6:56; cf. 5:14. However, in other places in the narratives the terms are not used precisely. Nazareth and Capernaum are called "cities" in Mark 1:33 and 2:1, although they were certainly no more than rural towns, and the same settlement is sometimes called a "village" and at other times a "city." Similarly, Josephus mentions Kadasa once as a village and once as a city (*Ant.* 13.154; *J.W.* 2.111, 459), Arbel once as a fortified village and once as a city (*Ant.* 12.421; 14.416), and Kadasa both as a village and as a city (*J.W.* 4.1; 123). In addition, he calls Yodefat an ordinary village-town that he describes as a main fortress under his command (*J.W.* 2.111), and a *polis* when it is in the center of action (*J.W.* 3.114, 135). It may be that this "upgrading" aims at enhancing Roman military superiority (*J.W.* 1.505; 2.129, 421, 504, 568, and many more). In a more general context, he relates that Vespasian appointed decurions in the villages and centurions in the cities (*J.W.* 4.442). Here, "villages" seem to be medium-sized towns or small villages.

4. Ze'ev Safrai, *The Jewish Community in the Talmudic Period* (in Hebrew; Jerusalem, 1995), 31–49.

5. See Stephanus Byzantinus, *Ethnica* 666–67; Georgius Syncellus, *Chronogr.* 355.

6. See Ze'ev Safrai, "The Hasmonean and Herodian Family Villages," in *Ehud Netzer Memorial Volume* (ed. Hillel Geva et al., *Eretz Israel* 31; in press).

*a. Roman cities.* These are characterized by an urban level of construction, a Greek-speaking population, full municipal administration, a non-Jewish majority and leadership, buildings for leisure-time culture (a theater, a forum, a gymnasium etc.), minting coins (limited to some cities), issuing weights in Greek, and control over the surrounding *chora* (region). There were probably additional urban phenomena, such as a social and work-related class structure and other characteristics of the Roman *polis*. There were, of course, poor neighborhoods where the construction was inferior.

*b. Local cities.* In these cities the population was local (Jews in Jewish areas), they did not mint coins, they ruled their surroundings as at least toparchic capitals, they had a partial municipal administration and several buildings for leisure-time culture, and the city government used both Greek and Aramaic as the official languages. In general, these cities were of a more rural character, and construction was on a rural standard.

A main point of this chapter is the existence of this intermediate level of "local cities." The distinction between the cities of the first level and the towns is clear, but the difference between the first- and second-level cities (*poleis* as opposed to "local cities") is flexible, as is the distinction between local cities and large villages. I have suggested that the local cities had several components that were absent from the villages (rural towns):

- Regional rule (most of the rural towns did not have this status).
- Public buildings. See, for example, Tiberias and Taricheae (Magdala).
- Little penetration of Hellenism, and local rule with little evidence of Hellenistic influences.
- Aqueducts (found in Gamla, Tiberias, Sepphoris [date unclear] and Beit Yerah [Philoteria]). At this stage no aqueducts have been found in a settlement that is not a *polis* or a local city.
- Paved streets (discovered in Taricheae, Gamla, and Beit Yerah). The first-century ruins of Khirbet Bteicha contain streets (see figs. A and B), but they are far inferior.[7] Of course, attractive streets have been found in Herodion and Antipatris, where they are constructed on an urban standard.
- Imported vessels (in Sepphoris, Antipatris, Herodion, a few in Gamla, many in Taricheae). There are no imported ceramics in the rural Jewish settlements.[8]

---

7. Rami Arav excavated a large settlement from the period under discussion; he believes it is Bethsaida. See Rami Arav and Richard A. Freund, *Bethsaida: A City on the North Shore of the Sea of Galilee* (4 vols.; Kirksville, Mo. Truman State University Press, 2004–9).

8. See Andrea M. Berlin, "Romanization and Anti-Romanization in Pre-Revolt Galilee," in *The First Jewish Revolt: Archaeology, History, and Ideology* (ed. Andrea M. Berlin and J. Andrew Overman; London: Routledge, 2002), 57–73; Gerald Finkielsztejn, "Hellenistic Jerusalem: The Evidence of the Rhodian Amphora, Stamps," *New Studies on Jerusalem* 5 (1999): 21–23. Berlin thought that the reason was nationalist. On the other hand, Safrai and Safrai suggested that the reason is halakhic-religious, although it is possible that the motives behind the halakhic decision were nationalist. See Ze'ev Safrai and Chana Safrai, "Were the Sages an elite class," in *Ohev Shalom: Studies*

**Figure A. Paved street at Khirbet Bteicha.**
Photo by author.

**Figure B. Paved street at Gamla.**
Photo by author.

---

*in Honor of Israel Friedman Ben-Shalom* (ed. Dov Gera and Miryam Ben Ze'ev; Be'er Sheva: Universitat Ben Guryon ba-Negev, 2005) 423–24. The suggestion was examined at length by Yonatan Adler, "The Archaeology of Purity: Archaeological Evidence for the Observance of Ritual Purity in Ereṣ-Israel from the Hasmonean Period until the End of the Talmudic Era (164 BCE–400 CE) (PhD diss., Bar-Ilan University, 2011), 223–82. Adler also believes that the meticulous observance of the impurity of "Eretz Ha'amim" (non-Jewish territories) is the best explanation for the paucity of imported ceramics in the Jewish community.

A number of characteristics that are usually considered "urban" have been found in both the cities and the towns. For example, wealthy people lived in both rural and urban areas. The Jewish community was active in both of these settlement levels. Construction was mainly from simple materials: local stones, without mosaics or marble, and without decorated column capitols and the like.

The gentile population was not well represented either in the towns or in the local cities, as opposed to the Roman *polis*, whose public character was gentile with a Jewish minority. Only some *poleis* were granted the right to mint coins, and of course they had more luxurious private buildings and a greater number of public buildings. All these generalizations are based on the present state of the findings. It is possible that in the future we will be able to reach more precise parameters regarding all these distinctions.

Most of the local cities ruled their *chōra* (regions), but there may have been exceptions, such as Antipatris, built in full Roman style with a wide paved *cardo maximus* (main north–south street) and more.[9] All the cities in first-century Galilee were "local cities."[10] Toward the end of the Second Temple period, Sepphoris became stronger and received the Roman name Neronias. In Tiberias, however, no change is evident during the entire Second Temple period.

### Urbanization in the Galilee after the First Revolt

After the First Revolt almost all the local cities in the land of Israel declined. In the Galilee, Tiberias and Sepphoris proved to be exceptions by becoming ordinary Roman cities. Both were granted the right to mint coins and had non-Jewish leadership, as we will see below. The other settlements became ordinary villages: some were damaged in the revolt (Gamla in the Golan, and perhaps Taricheae as well), and some declined without any known external crisis. In contrast to the other parts of the province, no new cities were built in the Galilee until the fourth century, when Helenopolis was founded.[11] This phenomenon is unique to the Galilee and requires an explanation.

---

9. Yuval Gadot, *Aphek-Antipatris II: The Remains on the Acropolis. The Moshe Kochavi and Pirhiya Beck Excavations* (Emily and Claire Yass Publications in Archaeology; Tel Aviv: Institute of Archaeology, Tel Aviv University, 2009).

10. See also Ze'ev Weiss, "Tiberias and Sepphoris in the First Century CE: Urban Topography and Construction Projects of Herod Antipas in the Galilee" (in Hebrew), *Cathedra* 120 (2006): 11–32. The data about Sepphoris are also indicated by the detailed report of the excavations of the city. For Taricheae, see Stefano De Luca, "La città ellenistico-romana di Magdala/Taricheae: Gli scavi del Magdala project 2007 e 2008. Relazione preliminare e prospettive di indagine," *Studium Biblicum Franciscanum Liber Annuus* 59 (2009): 343–562.

11. Helenopolis is identified with Kafr Kama, but without any real proof. R. Steven Notley and Ze'ev Safrai estimated that it inherited the Sharon toparchy mentioned by Eusebius. See Notley and Ze'ev Safrai, *Eusebius, Onomasticon: The Place Names of Divine Scripture, Including the Latin Edition of Jerome* (Jewish and Christian Perspectives 9; Leiden: Brill, 2005), no. 888, p. 152.

The process of building a city is somewhat familiar from other Roman provinces. Officially, the emperor decides to build a city. In practice, local leaders or governors lobbied for new cities in order to develop the province. The locals wanted to upgrade the status of their community and to receive the prestigious title and the economic and territorial rights to rule the surrounding *chōra*. For its part, the Roman government acceded to the request of the residents, or to their pressure. It also, however, saw the building of a *polis* as a way to develop the economy in the region and the province and, through these, the empire's economy.

The third component in deciding to build a city was the geographical and historical conditions of the site (lobbying was probably based on this third component). The geographical conditions included the situation in the region that was in need of a major city and the nature of the designated settlement. The historical conditions were the glorious past of the site (perhaps only for declaration), and mainly its size, the state of its development, its wealth, the level of Hellenization, its public institutions, and other matters. In the province of Judea, cities were built only in places that had been local toparchic capitals in the past. These towns were upgraded to the level of a *polis*, but not rebuilt.

Tiberias and Sepphoris became the main cities before the revolt. Consequently, after the revolt both cities had an influx of gentiles. We do not know if this strengthening of the gentile population resulted from some of the residents defining themselves as non-Jews, or if there was an influx of gentiles from other provinces. We have no direct information about whether the government encouraged immigration to the country, nor do we have any real evidence of such immigration. This is a central question that has yet to be examined in the research.

Very few new cities were built in the heart of the central mountains. In Samaria, Vespasian built Neapolis ("new city"). In Judea a new urban settlement,[12] Antipatris, which was designated a *polis* sometime in the second century, began on the fringes of the mountains, and Hadrian rebuilt Jerusalem as Aelia Capitolina. Later, at the end of the second century, additional cities were built on the fringes of the mountains: Nicopolis, Eleutheropolis, and Diospolis. Cities were also established on the margins of the Galilee (Paneas, Hippos, Scythopolis, Gabae, Ptolemais), but in the interior of the Galilee were only Sepphoris and Tiberias.

Consequently, there are two questions that confront us: Why were no more new cities built in the Galilee? And why did the "local cities" decline? I begin with the first. I can understand why Vespasian (r. 69–79 CE) did not rehabilitate additional cities in the Galilee. In all the other regions he built no more than one city, but I believe that no new cities were built in the Galilee because of a combination of factors.

The local residents, virtually all of whom were Jewish, apparently did not push for the construction of new cities. The lobbying ability of the country's Jews was great, but evidently the Jewish leadership was not interested in foreign influence despite the economic advantages.

---

12. The excavations were published only initially in Rachel Bar-Nathan and Deborah A. Sklar-Parnas, "A Jewish Settlement in Orine between the Two Revolts," *New Studies in the Archaeology of Jerusalem and Its Region* 1 (2007): 54–64.

For their part, the Romans apparently felt that planting another city in the Jewish Galilee would violate the equilibrium and the quiet of the region. Construction of highways was connected to the process of urbanization, and only a few roads in Lower Galilee, and none in Upper Galilee, were constructed.

Not until the fourth century were two new cities built: Maximianopolis, based on the Roman army camp at Legio, and Helenopolis, perhaps based on the capital of the Sharon toparchy. It is interesting that the process of Christianization in the Galilee was also slower than in the other parts of the province, but that is outside our discussion. In any case, the relatively slow pace of Romanization-Hellenization in the Galilee probably explains the delay in urbanization.

Hence, the Galilee became polarized. Either the local settlements that experienced Hellenistic influence declined and the Hellenistic influence dwindled, or they became Roman cities and lost their role as a bridge between cultures and religions.[13] We will be able to learn how this process came about when the results of the excavations at Taricheae (Magdala) are published.

### The Urban Distribution

Sepphoris is located in the center of the Lower Galilee. All the other cities are located on the margins of the Galilee, whether they lie within the Galilee's borders or outside of them. No rural settlement in the Galilee was more than 27 km/17 miles (a one-day walk) from a city, but the distances by road or path are greater due to the hilly conditions. In the fourth century, in the northern part of the Jezreel Plain, the founding of Helenopolis and the cluster formed by Exaloth, Nain, and Mount Tabor/Habyrium reduced the walking distances from the cities to the villages in the Lower Galilee. Hence, theoretically, the cities and the villages in the Lower Galilee could maintain a close relationship, as described in ordinary hierarchical settlement systems. By contrast, the entire Upper Galilee had no urban center and was over a day's walk from the nearest city.[14]

#### *Ethnography*

Both Sepphoris and Tiberias had gentile communities alongside their Jewish ones. Of course, we cannot determine the percentage of Jewish residents in the cities, nor which was the majority population. At the same time, many scholars have noted that Tiberian coins

---

13. See Ze'ev Safrai, "Socio-Economic and Cultural Developments in the Galilee, from the Late First to the Early Third Century CE," in *Jews and Christians in the First and Second Centuries: How to Write Their History*, Peter J. Tomsen and Joshua Schwartz, eds. (CRINT 13; Leiden: Brill, forthcoming) 278–310.

14. See the chapter by James F. Strange on the Galilean road system in this volume.—Ed.

included pagan symbols during the reign of Trajan, as opposed to the Sepphorean coins of the same period, which included no such symbols. Later, the coins of both cities were typically Roman in nature and included pagan symbols.[15] Throughout the Roman and Byzantine periods, the grave inscriptions in Tiberias were in Greek, whereas those in the Sepphoris region were in Hebrew.[16]

There probably was at least one pagan temple in a Roman city like Diocaesarea (as Sepphoris was renamed under Hadrian), but none has been published and none is mentioned in the sources.[17] By contrast, in Tiberias, which has been only partially excavated, we know of a temple from Hadrian's reign whose remains may have been discovered.[18]

The Jewish presidency and leadership in the Galilee were initially based in the rural centers (Usha, Shefar'am and Beth She'arim),[19] and even when they moved to cities they were initially located in Sepphoris and only later (in the third century) did they gradually wander to Tiberias (first the *beit din* [Sanhedrin?] and later the presidency). It should be mentioned that at least from what we know so far, the Jewish settlement was concentrated in its own neighborhoods.

### *Architecture*

As mentioned, Sepphoris has been thoroughly excavated. The second- to third-century neighborhood has yet to be published in detail, but we know it had a central street (*cardo maximus*) on a local standard (paved, but with ordinary stones rather than marble), and "rural" construction with local stones (see fig. C).[20]

---

15. Alla Kushnir-Stein, "Reflection of Religious Sensitivities on Palestinian City Coinage," *Israel Numismatic Research* 3 (2008): 125–36; Aharon Oppenheimer, *Galilee in the Mishnaic Period* (in Hebrew; Jerusalem: Merkaz Zalman Shazar, 1991), 81–82; and many more.

16. Mordechai Aviam and Aharoni Amitai, "The Cemetries of Sepphoris" (in Hebrew), *Cathedra* 141 (2011): 7–26. But see also Baruch Lifschitz, "Notes d'épigraphie grecque," *RB* 77 (1969): 78 for three Greek grave inscriptions from Sepphoris.

17. Despite the large-scale excavations in Sepphoris, only one possible pagan temple has been discovered there. For a partial publication see http://www.antiquities.org.il/article_heb.aspx?sec_id=17&sub_subj_id=532 (in Hebrew).

18. Yizhar Hirschfeld and Katharina Galor, "New Excavations in Roman-Byzantine Tiberias," in *Religion, Ethnicity, and Identity in Ancient Galilee: A Region in Transition* (ed. Jürgen Zangenberg, Harold W. Attridge, and Dale B. Martin; WUNT 210; Tübingen: Mohr Siebeck, 2007), 207–29. Unfortunately there is no archaeological basis for this identification. There is a wall of a large structure there, but in a Roman city there were many such structures.

19. There is a great deal of literature on the subject. An up-to-date (for its time) summary can be found in Oppenheimer, *Galilee in the Mishnaic Period*, 45–52 (in Hebrew).

20. Such streets are in Beth She'arim and Hurvat Hamam.

**Figure C. Paved street on Sepphoris's acropolis.** Photo by author.

A wealthy family's luxurious home with a mosaic floor in Hellenistic style sat at the top of the hill. The municipal center of early Roman Sepphoris has yet to be found. The excavations reveal that the city was only partially planned: the theater was located on the outskirts of the city and was not arranged in a suitable way for a private building of the wealthy. The same is true of the quarter where the synagogue was located. There too a street paved according to a local standard (fig. D) and simple houses have been found. The synagogue at Sepphoris is unique in having fewer signs of Hellenistic influence than rural synagogues.[21] This may be evidence either of a relative lack of Hellenistic culture or of a greater tension with Hellenistic culture and a demonstrative battle against the symbols of assimilation.

Whereas the city of Sepphoris grew from a rural town, Tiberias was planned to some extent. In Tiberias, despite the small number of excavations, excavators have found a central *cardo* with public buildings, a magnificent gate, and later a wall. As mentioned, these differences between the cities stem from their different histories.

---

21. Ze'ev Weiss, *The Sepphoris Synagogue: Deciphering an Ancient Message through Its Archaeological and Socio-Historical Contexts* (Jerusalem: Israel Exploration Society, 2005).

**Figure D. Paved street near Sepphoris's synagogue.** Photo by author.

### *Industry*[22]

We have to separate industry for export beyond the borders of the village in general and the Galilee in particular from industries for self-consumption. The major export industries in the Galilee are treated here.

*Pressing olives* was done for domestic use and for export. Evidence for this industry has been found in almost every village of any size. In fact, four to five olive presses have been found in small villages. Clearly, the production capacity surpassed local consumption. The oil was marketed via the coastal cities and the ports, west to Egypt and north to Lebanon (Tyre, Sidon, and elsewhere; see *t. Demai* 1:11 and many other sources).

*Wine* was produced for both local consumption and export. Farmers produced wine on the site of the vineyards, and of course they marketed it via the cities to regions outside the Galilee as well.

*Processing and grinding grains* was agricultural processing, and the grinding was done at home or by the *nahtom* (baker). In Sepphoris, for example, there was a guild of grinders of wheat and barley (*y. Pes.* 4:1, 30d; *b. Moed Qatan* 13b).[23]

*Textile production.* The textile industry was based primarily on processing flax, but also wool. The flax industry was centered in Scythopolis, and rabbinic sources mention a center in Arbel (*Bereshit Rabba* 19a, Albeck edition, p. 170 and parallels). Scythopolis appears as the most

---

22. Uzi Leibner, "Arts and Crafts, Manufacture and Production," in *The Oxford Handbook of Jewish Daily Life in Roman Palestine* (ed. Catherine Hezser; Oxford: Oxford University Press, 2010), 264–96.

23. In the Talmudic sources there are alternative traditions regarding the specific role of each guild; see below.

| "Normal" *Polis* | Tiberias | | Sepphoris | |
|---|---|---|---|---|
| | Archaeological finds[24] | Historical sources[25] | Archaeological finds[26] | Historical sources[27] |
| Planning | ✓ | | partly | |
| *Cardo* | ✓ | | ✓ | |
| *Decumanus* | | | ✓ | |
| Wall | ✓ | ✓ | | ✓ |
| Gates | ✓ | ✓ | | |
| *Agora* | | | ✓ | |
| Market | | ✓ | ✓ | ✓ |
| Forum | ? | | ✓ | |
| Temple | ✓? | ✓ | | |
| *Tetrapylon* | | | | |
| *Stoa* | ✓ | | ✓ | ✓ |
| Bath | ✓ | ✓ | ✓ | ✓ |
| Gymnasium | | | | |
| Theater | ✓ | | ✓ | |
| Circus | | | | |
| Stadium | | ✓ | | ✓ |
| Aqueduct + Castelum | ✓ | ✓ | ✓ | ✓ |
| Castrum | | ✓ | | ✓ |
| Hellenistic population | ✓ | ✓ | ✓ | ✓ |
| Rich citizens | ✓ | ✓ | ✓ | ✓ |
| Paved streets | ✓ | ✓ | ✓ | ✓ |

**Table 1: Public Building in Galilean *Poleis***

---

24. Yizhar Hirschfeld, *Archaeological Sites in Tiberias* (Jerusalem: Israel Antiquities Authority, 1992).

25. The best "supermarket" list is in Samuel Klein, *The Land of the Galilee* (Jerusalem: Mosad Ha-Rav Kook, 1967), 94–100; M. D. Yudelevitz, *Tiberias: The Jewish Life During the Talmudic Era* (Jerusalem: Mosad Harav Kook, 1946), 6–8.

26. Weiss, *Sepphoris Synagogue*; Eric M. Meyers, "Roman Sepphoris in Light of New Archeological Evidence and Recent Research," in *The Galilee in Late Antiquity* (ed. Lee I. Levine; New York: Jewish Theological Seminary of America, 1992), 321–38; Hirschfeld and Galor, "New Excavations in Roman-Byzantine Tiberias," 207–29.

27. See Yehuda Ne'eman, *Sepphoris in the Period of the Second Temple, the Mishnah and the Talmud* (in Hebrew; Jerusalem: Shem, 1993), 82–97; Klein, *Galilee*, 85–94.

important international center and produced the highest quality clothes in the entire Roman Empire. Because the sources for the large-scale flax industry are from Byzantine literature,[28] it is not clear when the flax industry began in the Galilee. We have no direct evidence for a beginning in the second century, but there are indications in the rabbinic literature that flax was a common crop as early as the Mishnaic period, perhaps only after the Bar Kokhba Revolt.[29]

Amoraic texts tell us that the entire Sea of Galilee was surrounded by facilities for treating flax (*b. Moed Qatan* 18a; *y. B. Meṣ.* 5:6; 10c).[30] In Sepphoris there was a guild of flax processors, which is described as a group composed of Jews (*y. Peah* 1:1, 16a).

Next to Gabae, archaeologists have excavated a series of installations that are believed to be the remains of retting canals for flax dating from the third to fourth centuries. Because these installations belonged to the farmers themselves, villagers not only manufactured the fabrics and wove the threads in the city but also grew the flax. An earlier stage of these installations was found in Area 4. That means that manufacture began at the site before the third century, and the design of the facilities was changed during the course of work.

*Glass production.* In many towns in the Galilee vestiges of raw glass have been found, attesting to a glass industry. The places include Nahf,[31] Beth She'arim,[32] along Nahal Na'aman (in Phoenician Galilee),[33] 'Illut,[34] Hurvat Zagag near modern Carmiel,[35] Kafr Yasif,[36] Carmiel itself,[37] most of the villages on Mount Carmel,[38] and many more. In Khirbet Jalame in the Zebulun Valley (on the margins of the Galilee), an excavated estate included a large furnace for manufacturing glass, and in Beth She'arim one of the largest slabs of glass in the world was found, weighing almost nine tons. Other remains have been discovered in a surface survey of the area.

The raw material was brought from the Acco coast, and the Galileans transported it to towns for processing and producing vessels. Most of the facilities mentioned in the literature,

---

28. *Expositio Totius Mundi* 1882 (= *Totius Orbis Descriptio*) *Geographi Graecis Minores* (ed. C. W. L. Muller; 2 vols.; Paris: Firmin Didot, 1882), vol. 2, chapter 31.

Leibner, "Arts and Crafts"; Safrai, *Economy of Roman Palestine*, 155–63.

29. See *m. B. Qam.* 10:9; *m. Moed Qatan* 2:3; *m. Bekhorot* 4:8; *t. Parah* 12:16.

30. See also a Byzantine source in Sebastian Brock, "An Early Syriac Life of Maximus the Confessor," *Analecta Bollandiana* 91 (1973): 299–346.

31. R. Abu Raya, "Kafr Nahf," *HA-ESI* 125 (2013): electronic version (from volume 116 on in electronic version), www.hadashot-esi.org.il/report_detail.aspx?id=4347.

32. "The Mystery Slab of Beth She'arim," online at http://www.cmog.org/article/mystery-slab-Beth-Shearim. (Corning Museum of Glass website).

33. *HA-ESI*, http://www.iaa-conservation.org.il/Projects_Item_heb.asp?site_id=64&subject_id=6.

34. Edna Amos, "Illut," *HA-ESI* 121 (2009).

35. Mordechai Aviam, personal communication, yet unpublished.

36. R. Abu Raya, "Kafr Yasif," *HA-ESI* 122 (2010); Abu Raya, "Nahal Na'aman, Survey," ibid.

37. http://www.limudim-info.co.il/one_studi.asp?IDNews=8198#.UrauR_RdURo.

38. Shimon Dar, *Rural Settlements on Mount Carmel in Antiquity* (in Hebrew; Jerusalem: Israel Exploration Society, 2012).

and those that have been found, were in the rural towns. The rabbinic literature also indicates that there were groups (families or guilds?) of glaziers in the towns (*y. 'Avod. Zar.* 2:1, 40c). At the same time, there is literary evidence of a glass industry in Tiberias as well (*b. Nidah* 21a; *y. Nidah* 2:7, 50b).

Dating glass installations is difficult. The slab in Beth She'arim is from the early fifth century, whereas the factory in Jalama closed in the fourth century and was active mainly in the third century. It is difficult to date the period of operation of many of these factories because they have not yet been excavated, and most of the sources we have are Amoraic. This is not proof that this manufacture did not begin in the Tannaitic period, but manufacture probably spread during the Amoraic period.

*Pottery manufacturing* was a common and crucial trade, and producing pottery clearly demanded significant manpower. Potters threw pots mainly for local use but also manufactured jars for wine and oil export. The main factories in the Jewish Galilee were at Kfar Hananya and Kfar Shikhin. One pottery kiln at Kfar Hananya has been investigated and excavated, and the product of the factory has been chemically analyzed and examined. Specific types of pottery were produced only in Kfar Hananya, and some types were produced only in Kfar Shikhin. Kfar Hananya had a large number of factories, which are also mentioned in the rabbinic sources, and which operated from the first to the fourth centuries.[39]

David Adan-Bayewitz has analyzed vessels from a surface survey of Shikhin. The village has been excavated for three seasons, and the dig is turning up much evidence of pottery and oil lamp production.[40]

In contrast to the glass industry, the pottery described in the rabbinic literature (primarily the Talmuds) precisely matches the archaeological information about the main centers, the techniques, and so on.

*Fishing.* Tiberias and other cities around the Sea of Galilee were centers of fishing. The fishermen in the Acco-Ptolemais region of the Mediterranean coast also supplied the Galilee and the interior of the country.[41] Due to their short shelf life and the challenges with selling live fish, fish were sold dried, salted, or crushed as a kind of paste. This required a system of facilities of a type that has yet to be found, unless the pools in Magdala-Taricheae were used for drying fish.[42]

Conversely, along the Mediterranean, and mainly on the rocky coast between today's Kibbutz Habonim and Dor, pools have been found for immersing fish and drying them on the rocky beach (not yet published). In this case, the centers of fishing were in the cities, but along the Sea of Galilee many additional piers have been found, the largest in Hellenistic

---

39. David Adan-Bayewitz, "Manufacture and Local Trade in the Galilee of Roman-Byzantine Palestine: A Case Study" (PhD diss., Hebrew University, Jerusalem, 1985).

40. Thanks to Prof. James Riley Strange for the permission to publish this information.

41. Acco-Ptolemais fishermen and Tiberias fishermen had an association (*b. Tagarim*; *y. Pes.* 4:1, 30d; *b. Mo'ed Qat.* 13b).

42. See De Luca, "La città ellenistico-romana di Magdala."

and Roman Taricheae (Magdala). Additional piers have been found in surveys but cannot be securely dated.

*Mat weaving.* The Talmuds mention the mats of Usha and Tiberias (*y. Sukkah* 1:12; *b. Sukkah* 20b). This important information attests to an industry in both the *polis* and the rural towns. The Talmuds compare the two places, favoring the mats from Usha over those from Tiberias. Because the information is limited to Amoraic sources, there is no way of knowing whether the industry flourished as early as the second century.

*Agriculture.* Parallel to the presence of industry, crafts, and services in the villages, there was also agriculture in the cities. There are many sources attesting to this phenomenon, and both Sepphoris and Tiberias are portrayed as rich agricultural centers whose residents worked directly in agriculture.[43]

## The Nature of Galilean Industry

Nowhere in the ancient world was there any significant industry in the modern sense. Craftspeople had no need of large and expensive facilities. Similarly, cloth producers relied on many independent spinners and weavers.

The flax industry facilities near Gabae were scattered haphazardly over the area and relied on a common infrastructure of water cisterns. This is apparently a model parallel to that in Beth She'arim, where the huge slab of glass was found. The size of the slab indicates an industrial stage in which glass was purified for the needs of many craftspeople. During the second stage the work was given to private glaziers.[44]

In Kfar Hananya we find a different method. At the site there were vestiges of dozens of small private furnaces, one of which was excavated. Apparently the small manufacturers had friendly reciprocal relations and were willing to sell merchandise for one another. In Jalama, by contrast, there was one large, independent furnace. However, it still cannot be defined as a factory; it was, rather, a large workshop. This organization is reflected in *t. Baba Meṣi'a* 6:3, which describes a situation in which every potter ran a private shop, but all the factories were friendly neighbors who helped each other.

In most of our sources the factories are in the towns, allowing us to conclude that the industrial center was not located in the cities. Nevertheless, the sources point to the city's involvement in the industries through guilds that coordinated the various manufacturers.

---

43. For Sepphoris, see *y. Kilaim* 1:4; 27a; *t. Demai* 1:1; *t. Šebi'it* 6:13; *t. Makširin* 3:5; *y. Peah* 7:3 20a; 7:3 20b; *y. Kilaim* 9:4, 38b; *Sifrei Deut.* 316, p. 358; *y. Ma'aśer Šeni* 5:2, 56b; *Eicha Rabba* 3:9, Buber edition, p. 125; *y. Šebi'it* 5:1, 35d; Yehuda Ne'eman, *Sepphoris in the Mishna and Talmud Period* (Jerusalem: Schem, 1993), 319–24. For Tiberias, see *m. Kilayim* 1:4; Yudelevitz, *Tiberias*, 10–13.

44. A similar example was excavated in Beit Eliezer (in Hadera), where seventeen glass furnaces were found alongside one another. This find has not yet been published in a scientific version. For a short summary, without the writer's name, see Eli Schiller, ed., *Ariel* 95–96 (1993): 15–19.

Because they facilitated taxation and collection, guilds were an important component of the Roman city. The manufacturers in the villages may have belonged to a regional guild, or they may have been independent producers. We can assume that the villagers sold their wares in the shops in the city. Since the shops were part of the guild, the villagers probably belonged to the same guild.

Guild members were independent craftsmen and private citizens who organized in order to regulate work relations and to collect taxes for the products, but they manufactured privately. The activity of the various guilds has been examined in the literature for some time, and we know that in that sense the Galilee is no exception in the Roman Empire.

We can assume that the guilds of the fishermen of Acco-Ptolemais and Tiberias included all the fishermen of the region. In Tiberias, Moshe Schwabe deciphered a grave inscription as referring to a member of the weavers' guild.[45] In Sepphoris there was a millers' guild and a flax workers' guild (*y. Peah*, 1:1, 16a). Another tradition tells about someone who was the "head" of the cooks of Sepphoris, perhaps an indication of a guild of cooks (*b. Ḥulim* 6b). The guild of coppersmiths (Hebrew *tarsi'im*) had a synagogue in Hamat in the second century (*y. Šeqal.* 2:5, 47a).

The centers of commerce and marketing were therefore located in the cities, and the guild centers were probably found there too. The factories themselves were dispersed throughout both the cities and the villages.

In all these cases, the guild operated as an internal Jewish organization that remained faithful to the *halakhah*. Because the guild was part of the organizational system in the *polis*, one of its roles was tax collection, whereas in the *polis*, tax collection was the job of the council. This indicates that the Jewish public was recognized as an independent entity within the *polis* system, which we will discuss further below.

All the archaeological evidence of guilds comes from the Late Roman period (third through fourth centuries). I assume that such an arrangement was in effect also during the Middle Roman period (second and third centuries)

### Commerce

Both Tiberias and Sepphoris were commercial centers. In Sepphoris, a wheat market operated all year round, not only during the harvest season (*y. B. Meṣ.* 5b; 10c), serving as a link in the Galilean commercial system.

There is a story of a honey merchant, Rabbi Hananya, who was active in Sepphoris and who once sold wasp honey by mistake. With the money he received he built the *beit midrash* (literally, "house of study," a place for Torah study) in the city. Despite the story's legendary elements, it reflects large-scale commerce (*y. Peah* 7:3b). A parallel story about large-scale com-

---

45. Moshe Schwabe, "Tiberias Revealed—Through Inscriptions," in *All the Land of Naphtali* (in Hebrew; ed. H. Z. Hirschberg; Jerusalem: ha-Ḥevrah la-ḥakirat Erets-Yiśra'el va-'atiḵoteha, 1968), 180–91, esp. 181. But see also Leah Di Segni, "The Inscription from Tiberias," in *Tiberias from Its Beginning until the Muslim Conquest* (ed. Yizhar Hirschfeld; Jerusalem: Isaac ben Zvi, 1988), 70–95.

merce tells of an old man who sold oil in large quantities in Gischala/Gush Halav, which was the capital of a toparchy (*Sifrei Deut.* 325, p. 421).

We know of additional markets in Sepphoris: an upper market, a lower market, and an "ordinary market" (*y. Eruvin* 54c; *y. Ket.* 13:1, 35d; *y. Ber.* 4:6, 8c; *b. Yoma* 11a). In rabbinic language, *shuk* means a commercial quarter (the Greek *emporium*) or a commercial center parallel to the agora in a *polis* but without the Roman architectural structures. In both instances from the Palestinian Talmud the subject is definitely a commercial center. A passage from the Babylonian Talmud attributed to Rabbi Yose, a native of Sepphoris who lived in the Usha generation (138–180 CE), exaggerates the number of markets in Sepphoris, but it indicates that Sepphoris enjoyed an image of having an abundance of shops (*b. B. Bat.* 75b).

In Tiberias there is more evidence for commerce. Tiberias was located on the coast of the lake, with merchandise and people arriving from Babylonia via the Golan or Transjordan and entering the country through the gate of Tiberias.[46] The Tiberians had a commercial outpost in Rome,[47] and some Tiberians participated in the silk commerce that developed in southern Syria on the Damascus–Beirut route.[48]

### City and Village, or the Cities and Jewish Settlement

Relations between the city and the village are an important subject in the study of cities in every period, and they have implications for various economic and cultural issues. In ancient times, there was usually a lack of contact between the urban, Hellenistic culture and the autochthonous (that is, indigenous or local), rural culture. In the province of Judea, there was a unique tension in addition to the intercultural conflict between Hellenistic and Jewish culture.

In the classical research of preceding generations, scholars assumed that the Hellenistic-Roman culture thoroughly marginalized the local culture: Greek (in the East) or Latin (in the West) replaced the ancient local languages. Today, after the studies by Fergus Millar and Ramsay MacMullen,[49] it is clear that in all the provinces the local culture was not eradicated, and local languages continued to be used among the masses, albeit below the radar of the scholars.

The major difference between the Jewish community in Judea and autochthonous communities in other provinces was that Jewish culture was preserved in writing, while in other regions the local cultures remained oral; hence, today the inhabitants representing the other

---

46. *y. Šebi'it* 4:7, 35c; *Bereshit Raba* 32:9, p. 296; 96:5, p. 1198 [compare *Ruth Raba* 3; *Qohelet Zuta* 2; *Qohelet Raba* 3:9. Imports also came from the Golan and the Perea through Hippos (*y. Demai*, 2:1, 22a; *y. Ned.* 8:4, 41a; *y. Šebi'it* 8:3; 38a; *y. B. Meṣ.* 5:6, 10c). For an exaggerated list, see Yudelevitz, *Tiberias*, 13–15.

47. Di Segni, "Inscription from Tiberias," 70–95.

48. For example, see *Bereshit Raba* 77b, pp. 910–11; *Vayikra Raba* 34:12, p. 796; *y. B. Meṣ.* 4:2, 9c; and more.

49. Fergus Millar, "Empire, Community and Culture in the Roman Near East: Greeks Syrians, Jews and Arabs," *JJJ* 38 (1987): 143–64; Millar, "Paul of Samosata, Zenobia and Aurelian," *JRS* 61 (1971): 1–13; Ramsay MacMullen, "Provincial Languages in the Roman Empire," in Macmullen, *Changes in the Roman Empire: Essays in the Ordinary* (Princeton: Princeton University Press, 1990), 32–40.

local cultures are a "silent population," lost to us. Many of those who researched the land of Israel also ignored the Aramaic-speaking, pagan population, but it was clearly a significant element in the villages and cities of Judea.[50]

In the province of Judea, and in any case in the Galilee, at least until the fourth century, the Jewish component was strong and large, and the intercultural (and political) tension between the city and the village, and the Jewish village in particular, was stronger than in other provinces. The tension was of a religious nature, in addition to the usual social and cultural gaps found all over the empire.

In the research it is usually assumed that the city was the economic and cultural center of the rural area. The locals came to the city often, bought goods there that they did not produce for themselves, and sold their agricultural produce. The wealthy residents of the city were the owners of the estates surrounding the city,[51] and in this way there was a constant flow of capital from the village to the city.

At the same time, the assumption is that the city also provided regular goods and services to the village. Industry and crafts were concentrated in the city, and a considerable percentage of the city residents made a living from the village, as landowners, as providers of services, or as consumers of the agricultural produce. Indeed, this is the picture all over the empire, and during most of the historical periods as well, although the strength of the ties between city and village naturally depended on the structure of the economy (more open or more closed), the conditions of transportation in the region, and other realities.

The picture in the rabbinic sources is somewhat different. According to them, the supplying of goods from the city to the village was carried out mainly by a merchant (*tagar* תגר) who lived in the city and visited the villages as part of a convoy of donkey drivers (*ḥameret* חמרת) that left the *polis* and circulated among the villages for a week or two, returning to the city for Shabbat.[52] In the rabbinic sources that describe the life of the simple villager, the *polis* (*kerak* in the rabbinic literature) is a hostile place, and anyone who visits the city should say a blessing and the "prayer upon entering," lest he be harmed by the residents of the *polis*, and a prayer of thanksgiving when he leaves. In the opinion of another Tanna one should recite four blessings, two upon entering and two upon leaving (*m. Ber.* 9:5). The Mishnah reflects the social and national tension in the country.

Jewish villagers could encounter dangers in the city on two levels. The first was social: in the city the villager encountered Roman rule, which always involved some risk. A person who came to the city was likely to be taken for *angareia* work (compulsory service): forced to perform a public service by participating in a procession, digging, or carrying loads. One famous

---

50. Ze'ev Safrai, "The Aramaic Population in Palestine in the Roman-Byzantine Period," in *Jews and Gentiles in the Holy Land in the Days of the Second Temple, the Mishnah, and the Talmud: A Collection of Articles* (ed. Aharon Oppenheimer, et al.; Jerusalem: Yad Ben-Zvi, 2003), 82–101.

51. This was the situation everywhere in the empire. For an example in the Galilean *polis,* see *t. Šabb.* 13:9; *b. Šabb.* 121a; *b. Sukkah* 27a.

52. Safrai, *Economy of Roman Palestine,* 28, 234–37.

case is that of Simon of Cyrene, who came to Jerusalem during the Second Temple period and was obligated to carry the cross during the execution of a political criminal (Matt. 27:32; Luke 23:26; Mark 15:21). A meeting with a soldier was liable to lead to a violent clash, and there were other, similar dangers.

The rabbis mention the fear of the *angareia* often. They do not always connect it to the city, but in the city the danger is greater and more frequent. The Midrash also accuses the Roman government: "Everything you did you did for your own needs," and "cities . . . impose the *angareia*, bridges for collecting tax" (*Tanḥuma Buber, Shoftim* 9, p. 31; *Tanḥuma Judges* 9). In the city, the villager met rich people, which aroused fear and suspicion in itself. In addition, often a villager arrived in the *polis* in order to make some arrangements to meet with government representatives. Of course, the negotiations with them were not always crowned with success.

The second level was antireligious. In the *polis*, the Jewish villager encountered the Roman-Hellenistic way of life with its many temptations, on the one hand, and the fear of an encounter with non-Jews, on the other (*Tanḥuma Shoftim* 10; *Midrash on Psalm 118* 18, p. 486). Another *mishnah* in the laws of Eruv can apparently be explained on the basis of the sages' desire to prevent residents of a small town from visiting the big city on Shabbat: to be more precise, visits made by the residents of Hamat near Tiberias (*m. Eruvin* 5:8).[53]

We can assume that reciprocal visits of townspeople to the rural sector and of villagers to the city were rare. In general, there was little geographical mobility, and contact among the various social classes was limited. The residents of villages that were near the city, within one or two hours' walk, came to the city more often, of course. The sages use a definition of someone who was "nearby and seen," in which "nearby" means a one-hour walk. Those who lived at this short distance were considered townspeople (*y. Meg.* 1:1, 70a; *b. Meg.* 2b, 3b), and they followed the laws of the city. But those who lived a greater distance away were farther removed from city life.

Another *halakhah* in the Mishnah (*m. Ket.* 13:10) states that a man is permitted to force his wife to change her place of residence, on the condition that it will not constitute a change in the sociocultural nature of the settlement (this wording is modern, of course). The accepted ruling was that the man is permitted to change his place of residence from one city to another in the same region, but not to change the type of residential area: "but not from the city to the town and not from the town to the city." A move from the town to the *polis* constitutes a change in lifestyle. There were, however, neighborhoods in the *polis* in which the autochthonous lifestyle was preserved and the Greek language and Hellenistic culture were not dominant.

Another *mishnah* explains that a husband misleading his bride by telling her that he was a townsman while he was actually the resident of a *polis*, or vice versa, was grounds for canceling

---

53. Shmuel Safrai and Ze'ev Safrai, *Mishnat Eretz Israel Eruvin,* 175–82.

the marriage, even if she did not demand it (*m. Qidd.* 2:3). Once again, the distance between the rural town and the *polis* is evident.

How did the lifestyle in the town differ from that in the city? The *halakhah* brings several examples. In the towns, people rarely wore shoes, and in the city they wore them every day (*y. Ket.* 7:4, 31b); in the *polis* there was running water, and in the towns they had to draw water (*t. Nidah* 6:9).[54] In reality, even in the *polis* most of the residents did not have running water in their homes; both in the *polis* and in the village the residents drew water from the water cisterns in their yards. The rabbis' contrast is therefore exaggerated and artificial.

The doors in the city were more attractive and had a bell attached (*t. Kelim*; *t. B. Meṣ.* 1:14). The *polis* residents shaved far more often than the villagers (*t. Soṭah* 3:16). In the *polis* there were luxurious public facilities and buildings, some of which are mentioned in the sources.[55] In the cities, the main characteristics, of course, were the Hellenistic culture itself, the presence of gentiles, and widespread polytheism. There is some reflection of these phenomena in the sources, and they certainly existed. Of course, the differences themselves do not create an emotional distance between the town and the *polis*, and they could even have been a source of attraction to the *polis*. In fact, everywhere in the Roman world we find movement from the village to the *polis*, but the sages of course consider this migration a disadvantage.[56] All the stories we have mentioned are examples of the inherent tension between the city and the village expressed in the rabbinic literature. They are all symptoms of hostility and tension, but are not the main reasons for the basic intercultural tension.[57]

The rural settlements near the *polis* were naturally in more frequent contact with the city. For halakhic purposes, it was determined that a settlement a mile away from the city was considered "near the city" (*t. Meg.* 1:1, according to the interpretation in *b. Meg.* 2:2). The example in the Babylonian Talmud is "as from Hamat to Tiberias." This example probably originated in

---

54. This statement is attributed to R. Eleazar the son of R. Zadok, who was a native of Tivoʻin in the Lower Galilee.

55. Daniel Sperber, *The City in Roman Palestine* (New York: Oxford University Press, 1998); and see table 1 above.

56. See, for example, *Mechilta D' Rabbi Yishmael, Masechta D' Pascha*, Bo, in Saul Horovitz and Israel A. Rabin, eds., *Mechilta D'Rabbi Yishmael* (in Hebrew; Jerusalem: Bamberger et Vahrman, 1960), p. 2; *Mechilta D' Rabbi Shimon b. Yochai*, ed. Ezra Z. Melamed (in Hebrew; Jerusalem: Sumptibus Mekize Nirdamim adiuvante American Academy for Jewish Research, 1955), XII, 1, p. 7; *b. Pes.* 40a; *b. Avodah Zarah* 41a; *m. 'Uqsin* 3:2; *t. 'Uqsin* 3:2.

57. In my opinion, the social distance between the city and the townships in rural areas in an earlier period is reflected in the tales about Jesus. All the traditions about his activity in the holy land are connected to the rural sector, except for the Holy City. There is no tradition about him visiting the nearby local city Magdala-Taricheae, or Sepphoris or Tiberias. Bethsaida-Julias was founded after his ministry or in the last years of his life. The stories about his activity in the gentile regions, outside Judea, are late and mention only cities (Hippos, Caesarea Philippi/Paneas, and Tyre). Therefore, they are suspect from a historical point of view; they appears only in some of the Gospels, and they are not part of the main Christian memories of the historical Jesus. This statement is crucial for understanding the history of the first Christian community, and it is part of the larger debate about this period. This is not the place to discuss it in detail.

the Amoraic discussion of the land of Israel, since only the Amoraim used examples from life in the Galilee. The prohibition against walking from Hamat to Tiberias on Shabbat was meant to prevent walking from the suburb to the *polis* on Shabbat, even though the distance allows for it, according to the *halakhah*.

As we have said, the *halakhah* reflects the distance to, and the fear of, the city felt by the village residents, even in this instance of a suburb that provided bathing services from a hot water spring to the residents of the *polis*.[58] This *halakhah* reflects the very limited range of movement of our ancestors. The actual background of these *halakhot* is the geographical and social distance between the city and the village, a concept that is difficult for contemporary readers to appreciate. These were two societies that shared the same geography yet differed in their natures and behaviors. This difference existed independent of the ethnic tension in the country and formed the infrastructure that influenced the state of mind, the economic connection, and the problem of assimilation and Hellenization of rural Galilee in that period.[59]

This evidence joins the picture that emerges from the *mishnayot*, and in this sphere almost certainly there are no differences between the later Amoraic and earlier Mishnaic periods. Of course, the sages also characterize the *polis* as a place of sexual depravity,[60] so that the sages describe separation and tension, and incidentally paint an exaggerated picture of the differing conditions in the city and the village.

The rural town had almost the entire variety of services available in the city: baker, shops, glaziers, and carpenters. There was a money changer (*trapezis*) only in the *polis* (*m. B. Meṣ.* 4:6; *t. B. Meṣ.* 3:2; and more). In the rural town, the money changer was replaced by the shopkeeper or the experienced merchant (*tagar*), who came to the rural town at least once a week. The market in the *polis* was, of course, more developed, but the picture from the rabbinic tradition downplays even that.

The Mishnah contains a *halakhah* ruling that a man who pledged an item to the temple or perhaps for another purpose but then had to sell it must wait for an increase in prices. This he can do by waiting to sell at the *atliz* (אטליז, "fair"). A cow is not usually sold in the rural town, where the price is cheap, because there is little demand (*m. Parah* 6:5). That is why it is worth waiting for the big market day (the *yarid* or *atliz*). A pearl should be sold in the *polis*, but according to the Mishnah, ordinary agricultural merchandise is probably the same price in the town or the *polis*.

---

58. The Babylonian Talmud worded the practical example as a legal rule, which is its way of turning every case into a legal rule with clear boundaries.

59. For an example of social hostility from Jerusalem without an ethnic-religious aspect, see *y. Ta'an.* 4:8, 69a.

60. See, for example, *b. Pesaḥ.* 113a. Of course it can be claimed that this is the actual situation only in Babylon, and is even perhaps exaggerated. This argument is part of the approach of sages to the gentile world, which by definition was considered sexually depraved. This should not be accepted as an objective evaluation, but rather as a reflection of contempt and hostility.

Needless to say, there was more for sale in the *polis*; this is reflected in the rabbinic literature, but in incidental contexts. We can assume that the public considered the greater inventory a major advantage of the *polis*, and it may have been a source of attraction as well, but not in the opinion of the sages.

## The Galilean Cities and the Rabbinic Leadership

As we know, during the Second Temple period the religious leadership of both the Pharisees and the Sadducees lived and worked in Jerusalem. In the Jamnia generation (70–135 CE), the rabbinic leadership was located in Jamnia in Judea. Sages from the Galilee participated in study and in halakhic decisions, but mainly Galilean students studied in the Jamnia-Lydda region. After the Bar Kokhba Revolt, most of the *batei midrash* (houses of study) moved to the Galilee. Contrary to what we might expect, after the revolt there were sages both in the cities and in the rural areas.

The Sanhedrin, the central Jewish body, roamed in the Galilee from Usha to Shefar'am to Beth She'arim. At the end of the second century it moved to Sepphoris and then back to Beth She'arim. I will not discuss here whether there really was such an entity. Suffice it to say that even if the description of the Sanhedrin as a center of study and as a legislative and decision-making body is exaggerated and legendary, there was a central court. It may have been only a *beit va'ad* (rabbinic council) surrounding the president, but there was some kind of active central body in a specific location.

I accept the prevailing opinion in the research that the rabbis and their council convened in the rural towns due both to the Roman demand that the *polis* be isolated from the influence of sages and to the sages' desire to keep their distance from the influence of the *polis*. It reflects the tension between the city and the village and between the economic elite and the sages.

Rabbi Yehuda ha-Nasi (late second century and early third century; responsible for codifying the Mishnah; often simply called "Rabbi") worked to reduce the tension and would "respect the rich." Therefore, he was able to move to Sepphoris, with the excuse of what today we would call a "diplomatic illness."[61]

What was the situation in Sepphoris before the president's residence was transferred there? Although there was a large concentration of Jews in Sepphoris, there was one active sage during the time of Rabbi: R. Yishmael b. R. Yose, whose father was also an important sage. R. Yishmael was a famous judge and apparently also participated in the city leadership in an unknown role. We also hear of "the judges of Sepphoris" (*m. B. Bat.* 6:7), a leadership-judicial body whose connection to the institutions in the *polis* is unclear.[62]

---

61. Oppenheimer, *Rabbi Judah ha-Nasi* (Jerusalem: Zalman Shazar Center, 2007).

62. In another place I plan to discuss the question of the place and integration of the Jewish community as a component of the administration of the *polis*.

During the entire Tannaitic period the sages were active mainly in the villages. Although there were sages in Sepphoris, as well as in Tiberias,[63] there was no special concentration of sages in the cities. The city had no advantage in the number of its sages, although the Jewish communities in Tiberias and Sepphoris were larger than those in villages or towns. Later on, during Amoraic times, many rabbis moved from the villages to the cities, and the number of sages active in the cities increased.[64]

It is interesting to note that in the Jamnia generation, although there were Galilean sages (for example, *t. Ta'an.* 1:13), there are stories about "students" who taught *halakhah* to the residents of Tiberias and Sepphoris (*y. Kilaim* 1:4, 27a). In other words, students rather than the great scholars came to these cities. Nevertheless, according to the sages themselves, regardless of whether they followed the *halakhah* beforehand, the Galileans accepted the opinion of the sages.[65] Whether this conclusion is realistic or reflects the sages' hopes for how a Jewish community should behave, the sages criticized the Jewish community for its ignorance rather than for any lack of loyalty.

Over time the tension between the city and the village (parallel to the tension between the Hellenistic culture and the Judaism of the period) weakened, and the sages were less afraid to be involved in urban activity. Earlier, during the Tannaitic period, the centers of learning were not in the *polis*, and the system in which the *polis* was the regional center did not apply to the internal Jewish organization. On the contrary, the urban Jewish communities were somewhat distant from the learning atmosphere of the sages. Later on, during the Amoraic period, this phenomenon disappeared.

## Conclusion

According to the rabbinic literature there was a significant lack of communication between the *polis* and the rural sector. Consequently, the rural sector was independent from the *polis* in terms of supplying services. The commercial ties that were important to both sides were carried out by means of intermediaries (most of them described as Jews), residents of the *polis* who went out to the rural sector. By contrast, I assume that elsewhere the empire was characterized by the rural sector's dependence on the *polis*. That was the way of the world, but the situation in the Galilee in the second and third centuries was more complicated.

The image presented in the rabbinic literature reveals a distinctive situation in every part of the picture. Although one can maintain that the picture is distorted due to the sages' desire to exaggerate the disadvantages of the *polis* and to describe as reality what they wished to see

---

63. For example, *t. Ta'an.* 1:13; *b. Moed Qatan* 21a; *b. Sanh.* 32b.

64. For the list, see Ben-Zion Rosenfeld, *Torah Centers and Rabbinic Activity in Palestine, 70–400 CE: History and Geographic Distribution* (JSJSup; Leiden: Brill, 2010); Rosenfeld, "Places of Rabbinic Settlements in the Galilee 70–400 C.E.," *HUCA* 69 (1998): 349–84.

65. For example, see *m. Eruvin* 10:10; *m. Šabb.* 3:4; *b. Šabb.* 39b.

happen, nevertheless, after a perusal of the sources, we can conclude that most disadvantages are presented without polemics. The description of the sexual depravity in the cities might be tendentious, but this is not the case with the simple descriptions in which the *polis* appears only as unimportant background to the halakhic or ideological content. I assume, therefore, that the picture in the rabbinic literature is somewhat extreme, but social tensions did help to shape a model of city–village relations that was exceptional in the Roman Empire.

## Bibliography:

Abu Raya, Rafeh. "Kafr Yasif." *HA-ESI* 122 (2010): On line: http://www.hadashot-esi.org.il/ report_detail_eng.aspx?id=1325&mag_id=117.

———. "Nahf." *HA-ESI* 125 (2013): On line: www.hadashot-esi.org.il/report_detail.eng. aspx?id=2265&mag_id=120.

Adan-Bayewitz, David. "Manufacture and Local Trade in the Galilee of Roman-Byzantine Palestine: A Case Study." PhD diss., Hebrew University, Jerusalem, 1985.

Adler, Yonatan. "The Archaeology of Purity: Archaeological Evidence for the Observance of Ritual Purity in Ereṣ-Israel from the Hasmonean Period until the End of the Talmudic Era (164 bce–400 ce)." PhD diss., Bar-Ilan University, 2011.

Amos, Edna. "Illut." *HA-ESI* 121 (2009). Online: http://www.hadashot-esi.org.il/report_ detail_eng.aspx?id=1038&mag_id=115.

Arav, Rami, and Richard A. Freund. *Bethsaida: A City on the North Shore of the Sea of Galilee.* 4 vols.; Kirksville, Mo: Truman State University Press, 2004–9.

Aviam, Mordechai, and Aharoni Amitai. "The Cemetries of Sepphoris" (in Hebrew), *Cathedra* 141 (2011): 7–26.

Bar-Nathan, Rachel, and Deborah A. Sklar-Parnas. "A Jewish Settlement in Orine between the Two Revolts." *New Studies in the Archaeology of Jerusalem and Its Region* 1 (2007): 54–64.

Berlin, Andrea M. "Romanization and Anti-Romanization in Pre-Revolt Galilee." In *The First Jewish Revolt: Archaeology, History, and Ideology*, ed. Andrea M. Berlin and J. Andrew Overman, 57–73. London: Routledge, 2002.

Brock, Sebastian. "An Early Syriac Life of Maximus the Confessor." *Analecta Bollandiana* 91 (1973): 299–346.

Dar, Shimon. *Rural Settlements on Mount Carmel in Antiquity.* Jerusalem: Israel Exploration Society, 2012 (in Hebrew).

De Luca, Stefano. "La città ellenistico-romana di Magdala/Taricheae: Gli scavi del Magdala project 2007 e 2008. Relazione preliminare e prospettive di indagine." *Studium Biblicum Franciscanum Liber Annuus* 59 (2009): 343–562.

Di Segni, Leah. "The Inscription from Tiberias." In *Tiberias from Its Beginning until the Muslim Conquest,* ed. Yizhar Hirschfeld, 70–95. Jerusalem: Isaac ben Zvi, 1988.

Finkielsztejn, Gerald. "Hellenistic Jerusalem: The Evidence of the Rhodian Amphora, Stamps." *New Studies on Jerusalem* 5 (1999): 21–23.

Gadot, Yuval. *Aphek-Antipatris II: The Remains on the Acropolis. The Moshe Kochavi and Pirhiya Beck Excavations.* Emily and Claire Yass Publications in Archaeology; Tel Aviv: Institute of Archaeology, Tel Aviv University, 2009.

Hirschfeld, Yizhar. *Archaeological Sites in Tiberias.* Jerusalem: Israel Antiquities Authority, 1992.

Hirschfeld, Yizhar, and Katharina Galor. "New Excavations in Roman-Byzantine Tiberias." In *Religion, Ethnicity, and Identity in Ancient Galilee: A Region in Transition*, ed. Jürgen Zangenberg, Harold W. Attridge, and Dale B. Martin, 207–29. WUNT 210; Tübingen: Mohr Siebeck, 2007.

Klein, Samuel. *The Land of the Galilee.* Jerusalem: Mosad Ha-Rav Kook, 1967.

Kushnir-Stein, Alla. "Reflection of Religious Sensitivities on Palestinian City Coinage." *Israel Numismatic Research* 3 (2008): 125–36.

Leibner, Uzi. "Arts and Crafts, Manufacture and Production." In *The Oxford Handbook of Jewish Daily Life in Roman Palestine*, ed. Catherine Hezser, 264–96. Oxford: Oxford University Press, 2010.

Lifschitz, Baruch. "Notes d'épigraphie grecque." *RB* 77 (1969): 78.

MacMullen, Ramsay. "Provincial Languages in the Roman Empire." In *Changes in the Roman Empire: Essays in the Ordinary*, ed. Ramsay Macmullen, 32–40. Princeton: Princeton University Press, 1990.

Meyers, Eric M. "Roman Sepphoris in Light of New Archeological Evidence and Recent Research." In *The Galilee in Late Antiquity*, ed. Lee I. Levine, 321–38. New York: Jewish Theological Seminary of America, 1992.

Millar, Fergus. "Paul of Samosata, Zenobia and Aurelian." *JRS* 61 (1971): 1–13.

_____. "Empire, Community, and Culture in the Roman Near East: Greeks Syrians, Jews and Arabs." *JJJ* 38 (1987): 143–64.

Muller, C. W. L., ed. *Geographi Graecis Minores.* 2 vols.; Paris: Firmin Didot, 1882.

"The Mystery Slab of Beth She'arim." Online at: http://www.cmog.org/article/mystery-slab-Beth-Shearim.

Ne'eman, Yehuda. *Sepphoris in the Period of the Second Temple, the Mishnah and the Talmud.* Jerusalem: Shem, 1993 (in Hebrew).

Notley, R. Steven, and Ze'ev Safrai. *Eusebius, Onomasticon: The Place Names of Divine Scripture, Including the Latin Edition of Jerome.* Jewish and Christian Perspectives 9; Leiden: Brill, 2005.

Oppenheimer, Aharon. *Galilee in the Mishnaic Period.* Jerusalem: Merkaz Zalman Shazar, 1991 (in Hebrew).

_____. *Rabbi Judah ha-Nasi.* Jerusalem: Zalman Shazar Center, 2007.

Rosenfeld, Ben-Zion. "Places of Rabbinic Settlements in the Galilee 70–400 C.E." *HUCA* 69 (1998): 349–84.

_____. *Torah Centers and Rabbinic Activity in Palestine, 70–400 CE: History and Geographic Distribution.* JSJSup; Leiden: Brill, 2010.

Safrai, Shmuel, and Ze'ev Safrai. *Mishnat Eretz Israel I.* Jerusalem: E.M. Lipshitz, 2008.

Safrai, Ze'ev, and Shmuel Safrai. "Were the Sages an elite class?" In *Ohev Shalom: Studies in Honor of Israel Friedman Ben-Shalom*, ed. Dov Gera and Miryam Ben Ze'ev, 423–24. Be'er Sheva: Universitat Ben Guryon ba-Negev, 2005.

Safrai, Ze'ev. *The Economy of Roman Palestine.* London: Routledge, 1994.

_____. *The Jewish Community in the Talmudic Period.* Jerusalem, 1995 (in Hebrew).

_____. "The Aramaic Population in Palestine in the Roman-Byzantine Period." In *Jews and Gentiles in the Holy Land in the Days of the Second Temple, the Mishnah, and the Talmud: A Collection of Articles*, ed. Aharon Oppenheimer, et al., 82–101. Jerusalem: Yad Ben-Zvi, 2003,

_____. "The Hasmonean and Herodian Family Villages." In *Ehud Netzer Memorial Volume*, ed. Hillel Geva et al.; *Eretz Israel* 31. Forthcoming.

_____. "Socio-Economic and Cultural Developments in the Galilee, from the Late First to the Early Third Century CE." In *Jews and Christians in the First and Second Centuries: How to Write Their History*, Eds. Peter J. Tomsen and Joshua Schwartz, 278-310. CRINT13; Leiden: Brill, Forthcoming.

Schwabe, Moshe. "Tiberias Revealed—Through Inscriptions." In *All the Land of Naphtali*, edited by H. Z. Hirschberg, 180–81. Jeruslaem: ha-Hevrah la-haḳitat Erets-yiśra'el va-'atiḳotela, 1968.

Sperber, Daniel. *The City in Roman Palestine.* New York: Oxford University Press, 1998.

Weiss, Ze'ev. *The Sepphoris Synagogue: Deciphering an Ancient Message through Its Archaeological and Socio-Historical Contexts.* Jerusalem: Israel Exploration Society, 2005.

_____. "Tiberias and Sepphoris in the First Century CE: Urban Topography and Construction Projects of Herod Antipas in the Galilee" (in Hebrew). *Cathedra* 120 (2006): 11–32.

Yudelevitz, M. D. *Tiberias: The Jewish Life During the Talmudic Era.* Jerusalem: Mosad Harav Kook, 1946.

# 15

# NEVER THE TWO SHALL MEET? URBAN–RURAL INTERACTION IN LOWER GALILEE

*Agnes Choi*

## The Urban–Rural Relationship in Lower Galilee

The nature of the urban–rural relationship in Lower Galilee has been the subject of much debate. In spite of this, no consensus has been reached regarding the quality of that relationship, as evidenced by the extensive corpus of secondary literature, in which the urban–rural relationship is described in a startling variety of ways.

At one end of the spectrum, the urban–rural relationship is depicted as amicable, with the urban and the rural populations coexisting in an interdependent and cooperative relationship. Peasant surpluses were voluntarily exchanged for urban goods and services. For example, the distribution of the kitchen ware of Kefar Hananya throughout and even beyond Lower Galilee has frequently been adduced as evidence for urban–rural interdependence, not only between the village of production at Kefar Hananya and the city of distribution at Sepphoris, but also between Sepphoris and the villagers who frequented its market.[1] Urban–rural reci-

---

1. David Adan-Bayewitz and Isadore Perlman, "The Local Trade of Sepphoris in the Roman Period," *IEJ* 40 (1990): 153–72; Adan-Bayewitz, *Common Pottery in Roman Galilee: A Study of Local Trade* (Bar-Ilan Studies in Near Eastern Languages and Culture; Ramat-Gan: Bar-Ilan University Press, 1993).

James F. Strange argues for an interdependent and amicable urban–rural relationship on the basis of rabbinic texts that indicate that certain villages were wheat production centers, while others specialized in wine production. He concludes that villages specialized in a particular agricultural or manufactured product and that "an extensive specialized agricultural and industrial production implies a vigorous trade network" (James F. Strange, "First-Century Galilee from Archaeology and from the Texts," in *Society of Biblical Literature 1994 Seminar Papers* [ed. Eugene H. Lovering Jr.; SBLSP 33; Atlanta: Scholars Press, 1994], 84; see also Strange, "First Century Galilee from Archaeology and from the Texts," in *Archaeology and the Galilee: Texts and Contexts in the Graeco-Roman and Byzantine Periods* [ed. Douglas R. Edwards and C. Thomas McCollough; South Florida Studies in the History of Judaism 143; Atlanta: Scholars Press, 1997], 39–48).

procity developed as a result of common interests: both urban and rural populations benefited from stable trade networks and the development of productive agricultural areas.[2]

At the other end of the spectrum, the urban–rural relationship is depicted as one of animosity, with the urban population exploiting the rural population through the collection of excessive rents and taxes. Jonathan L. Reed argues that the urban–rural relationship was strained because of the changes that the cities had caused in rural areas with respect to land-holding patterns and kinship.[3] Seán Freyne argues for urban–rural animosity arising from peasant debt and the conflicting value systems of the rural and urban areas, specifically the orthogenetic orientation of the rural population and the heterogenetic orientation of the urban population.[4] Richard A. Horsley maintains that urban–rural interaction was "minimal," as opportunities for direct interaction were limited to occasions such as court appearances in the city or visits from members of the urban population who went to the rural areas only to collect taxes, interest, and rent.[5] Nevertheless, he argues that the urban–rural relationship was one of animosity: "The general impact of the cities on the Galilean populace [that is, the rural population] in the first two-thirds of the first century was such as to have evoked *an unusual degree of hostility*."[6]

---

2. Douglas R. Edwards, "Identity and Social Location in Roman Galilean Villages," in *Religion, Ethnicity, and Identity in Ancient Galilee: A Region in Transition* (ed. Jürgen Zangenberg, Harold W. Attridge, and Dale B. Martin; WUNT 210; Tübingen: Mohr Siebeck, 2007), 362–68. See also Edwards, "First Century Urban/Rural Relations in Lower Galilee: Exploring the Archaeological and Literary Evidence," in *SBL 1988 Seminar Papers* (ed. David J. Lull; SBLSP 27; Atlanta: Scholars Press, 1988), 182; and Edwards, "The Socio-Economic and Cultural Ethos of the Lower Galilee in the First Century: Implications for the Nascent Jesus Movement," in *The Galilee in Late Antiquity* (ed. Lee I. Levine; New York: Jewish Theological Seminary of America, 1992), 53–73.

In the absence of meaningful urban–rural interaction, Seán Freyne argues that "a peaceful coexistence was possible" (*Galilee from Alexander the Great to Hadrian, 323 B.C.E. to 135 C.E.: A Study of Second Temple Judaism* [University of Notre Dame Center for the Study of Judaism and Christianity in Antiquity 5; Wilmington, Del.: Michael Glazier; Notre Dame: University of Notre Dame Press, 1980], 128).

3. Jonathan L. Reed, *Archaeology and the Galilean Jesus: A Re-Examination of the Evidence* (Harrisburg, Pa.: Trinity Press International, 2000), 98.

4. Seán Freyne, "Urban-Rural Relations in First-Century Galilee: Some Suggestions from the Literary Sources," in *The Galilee in Late Antiquity* (ed. Lee I. Levine; New York: Jewish Theological Seminary of America, 1992), 75–91; Freyne, "Jesus and the Urban Culture of Galilee," in *Texts and Contexts: Biblical Texts in Their Textual and Situational Contexts. Essays in Honor of Lars Hartman* (ed. Tord Fornberg and David Hellholm; Oslo: Scandinavian University Press, 1995), 597–622; Freyne, "Town and Country Once More: The Case of Roman Galilee," in Freyne, *Galilee and Gospel: Collected Essays* (Leiden: Brill, 2002), 59–72.

5. See chapter 8 by Richard Horsley in the present volume. See also Richard A. Horsley, *Galilee: History, Politics, People* (Valley Forge, Pa.: Trinity Press International, 1995), 179–80. In spite of the substantial literary evidence for villagers selling their produce in cities throughout the Roman Empire, Horsley warns against "imagin[ing] Galileans as having entered one of the cities every so often to sell their produce, that is, projecting a modern market economy back into ancient Palestine" (p. 179).

6. Horsley, *Galilee: History*, 181 (emphasis added). See also Horsley, *Archaeology, History, and Society in Galilee: The Social Context of Jesus and the Rabbis* (Valley Forge, Pa.: Trinity Press International, 1996), 118–30.

The existence of a relationship, regardless of its quality, presupposes interaction. Thus, it is surprising that the urban–rural *relationship* has received so much attention when urban–rural *interaction* has received so little. As urban and rural populations interacted most frequently for economic reasons, this study will consider urban–rural economic interaction in Lower Galilee. As it is generally agreed that the economy of first-century CE Lower Galilee was predominantly agrarian in nature, the task of this study will be to consider the production and distribution of agricultural goods. As agricultural goods will not flourish equally under all conditions, it will be necessary to consider the physical environment and its impact on production. It will also be necessary to consider the process of distribution, specifically, the respective roles of the urban and rural populations in this process, as this will illuminate not only urban–rural interaction but also the urban–rural relationship.

## The Production of Agricultural Goods: Pedology, Archaeology, and Lower Galilee

The study of the production of agricultural goods requires serious consideration of the soil in which crops are planted. Thus, pedology, that is, the study of soil, must be introduced into the conversation concerning the economy of Lower Galilee. The types and distribution of soils in first-century CE Lower Galilee will be identified with a view to determining which crops would have been best suited to the available soils. Soil types and crop needs will then be compared with the available material evidence with a view to determining whether those possibilities were, in fact, realized.

### *Soil Classification and Formation*

Soil can be defined as "the collection of natural bodies, formed on the Earth's surface containing living matter and supporting or capable of supporting plants."[7] Throughout the history of pedology, various criteria have been proposed as the basis for a system of soil classification, not only as a means to facilitate the study of soils, but also for the purpose of creating soil maps. The debate over soil classification is also reflected in the history of pedology in Israel. One of the difficulties of detailed soil mapping is that soils are not discrete, but are a continuum, changing laterally from one to another.[8] The soil units grade into each other, and their precise

---

In studies of the urban–rural relationship throughout the Roman Empire, the same spectrum of descriptions may be found, ranging from reciprocal and amicable (see, for example, Donald Engels, *Roman Corinth: An Alternative Model for the Classical City* [Chicago: University of Chicago Press, 1990]) to hostile and parasitic (see, for example, Moses I. Finley, *The Ancient Economy* [2nd ed.; Sather Classical Lectures 43; Berkeley: University of California Press, 1985]).

7. E. M. Bridges, *World Soils* (3rd ed.; Cambridge: Cambridge University Press, 1997), 3.

8. Ibid., *World Soils*, 44.

separation is actually impossible.[9] Thus, in the 1975 Soil Map of Israel, "soil associations" were introduced as the basic mapping unit.[10] Soil associations "describe soils which occur together in a regular pattern on the landscape" and "are created by specific combinations of landscape elements, such as lithology and physiography."[11] Because of the great variation in environmental conditions within Israel, twenty-three soil associations were introduced, and it was this classification system that was accepted by the Israel Soils Classification Committee.[12]

As Israel launched a project of soil reclamation in the mid-twentieth century, the factors that contribute to the formation of soil must be considered in order to determine whether modern soil maps reflect the types and distribution of soils in first-century CE Lower Galilee.[13] Five major factors influence soil formation, namely, parent material, climate, relief, organisms, and time.[14] In the formation of soils in Israel, parent material and climate are the most significant influencing factors.[15]

Parent material of soils originated from rock minerals formed in the earth's crust at temperatures and pressures very different from those at the surface. Through geological action, these minerals were revealed at the earth's surface through the Palaeozoic, Mesozoic, and Cenozoic ages, and they have remained unchanged since that time, approximately six million years ago.[16] The parent material becomes soil through the processes of weathering, a geological process that produces the regolith (the layer of rock material that typically overlies or covers the bedrock,[17] and soil formation, a pedological process that "modif[ies] the regolith and give[s] it the acquired characteristics which distinguish soil from parent material."[18]

---

9. Arieh Singer, *The Soils of Israel* (Berlin: Springer, 2007), 253.

10. A soil map of Israel was published in 1969 at a scale of 1:250,000; however, this map did not map soils by their soil association.

11. Bridges, *World Soils*, 141; cf. Singer, *Soils of Israel*, 253.

12. Singer, *Soils of Israel*, 253. The twenty-three soil associations are as follows: Terra Rossas, Brown Rendzinas and Pale Rendzinas; Brown Rendzinas and Pale Rendzinas; Pale Rendzinas; Basaltic Protogrumusols, Basaltic Brown Grumusols and Pale Rendzinas; Hamra soils; Basaltic Brown Mediterranean soils and Basaltic Lithosols; Hydromorphic and Gley soils; Grumusols; Pararendzinas; Dark Brown soils; Calcareous Serozems; Brown Lithosols and Loessial Arid Brown soils; Loessial and Arid Brown soils; Alluvial Arid Brown soils; Solonchaks; Loessial Serozems; Brown Lithosols and Loessial Serozems; Sandy Regosols and Arid Brown soils; Sand dunes; Regosols; Bare Rocks and Desert Lithosols; Reg soils and coarse Desert Alluvium; Fine-grained Desert Alluvial soils.

13. See also W. C. Lowdermilk, N. Gil, and Z. Rosenzaft, "An Inventory of the Land of Israel: Land Classification for Use with Soil Conservation," *IEJ* 3 (1953): 162–77.

14. Bridges, *World Soils*, 20–30.

15. Singer, *Soils of Israel*, 251.

16. Bridges, *World Soils*, 33. For a discussion of the geological history of Palestine, see Singer, *Soils of Israel*, 8–15; Efraim Orni and Elisha Efrat, *Geography of Israel* (2nd ed.; Jerusalem: Israel Program for Scientific Translations, 1966), 6–13, 49, 63–64; Michael Zohary, *Geobotany* (Ma'anit: Sifriat Hapoalim, 1955), 67; and Zohary, *Plant Life of Palestine: Israel and Jordan* (Chronica Botanica New Series of Plant Science Books 33; New York: Ronald, 1962), 65, 67.

17. Klaus K. E. Neuendorf, James P. Mehl Jr., and Julia A. Jackson, eds., *Glossary of Geology* (5th ed.; Alexandria: American Geological Institute, 2005), 543–44.

18. Bridges, *World Soils*, 28, 33.

Climate, too, influences the formation of soils. Throughout the Mediterranean, the climate is marked by winter rains and summer droughts; thus, when thinking about the impact of rainfall on soil formation, one must consider not only the annual amounts but also season, intensity, and microclimate.[19] The current annual rainfall in Lower Galilee ranges from 400 to 700 mm.[20] Winter begins in mid-October, when the rains begin, and lasts through the end of April.[21] Rainfall steadily increases from the beginning of the season, peaks during the months of December, January, and February, and declines thereafter. The rainfall during the three peak months accounts for two-thirds of the annual rainfall.[22] Both rainfall and rainfall regularity increase from south to north and, to a lesser extent, from east to west.[23] Further, slopes facing west or southwest, and thus exposed to Mediterranean winds, receive more rain than slopes facing the opposite direction, that is, east, southeast, and northeast.[24]

That this situation was typical of the climate of first-century CE Galilee is supported by dendroarchaeological analyses. Plant materials recovered in Tel Beer Sheba, Arad, and Tel Ta'anach were analyzed, the earliest samples dating to the tenth century BCE and the latest to the seventh to eighth centuries CE.[25] In each case it was found that the flora of the region had remained stable from ancient times to the present, for the plant species represented in the ancient plant material corresponded to the plant species of the present. That the same results were obtained from both arid and humid regions of Israel indicates that "the macroclimate has remained stable for the past 4,500 years."[26] *Macroclimatic* stability is not synonymous with the absence of *microclimatic* variation. Nevertheless, we can conclude that the climate of first-century CE Lower Galilee was similar to that of modern times, that is, that the circumstances in which soil formation took place were comparable. It follows, then, that modern soil maps *are* accurate reflections of the soils of first-century CE Lower Galilee, for Israel's young soils retain

---

19. Orni and Efrat, *Geography of Israel*, 105; David C. Hopkins, *The Highlands of Canaan: Agricultural Life in the Early Iron Age* (Social World of Biblical Antiquity 3; Sheffield: JSOT Press, 1985), 79–81, 84; Michael Zohary, *Geobotanical Foundations of the Middle East* (Stuttgart: Gustav Fischer, 1973), 16–18; Adolf Reifenberg, *The Soils of Palestine: Studies in Soil Formation and Land Utilisation in the Mediterranean* (2nd ed.; trans. C. L. Whittles; London: Thomas Murby, 1947), 18–22; Bridges, *World Soils*, 8–22.

20. Orni and Efrat, *Geography of Israel*, 121–22.

21. Hopkins, *Highlands of Canaan*, 84; Reifenberg, *Soils of Palestine*, 19.

22. Hopkins, *Highlands of Canaan*, 86; Orni and Efrat, *Geography of Israel*, 114; Singer, *Soils of Israel*, 6. There is rainfall data for Jerusalem dating back to 1846 (see Naftali Rosenan, "One Hundred Years of Rainfall in Jerusalem," *IEJ* 5 [1955]: 137–53); however, it cannot be used to determine annual amounts of rain in Lower Galilee, for rainfall is location-specific.

23. Hopkins, *Highlands of Canaan*, 84; Orni and Efrat, *Geography of Israel*, 111.

24. Hopkins, *Highlands of Canaan*, 84–85; Orni and Efrat, *Geography of Israel*, 112; Singer, *Soils of Israel*, 6. Orni and Efrat compare Sha'ar Ha-Gay Gorge, on the western slope of the Judean Hills, with Ein Fari'a, on the eastern slope, "both at the same latitude, and at an altitude of 330 m (1,000 ft): the former receives 516 mm (20³/₅ in) of annual rainfall, the latter 276 mm (11 in)" (*Geography of Israel*, 112).

25. Nili Liphschitz and Yoav Waisel, "Dendroarchaeological Investigations in Israel," *IEJ* 23 (1973): 30–36; Liphschitz and Waisel, "Dendroarchaeological Investigations in Israel (Taanach)," *IEJ* 30 (1980): 132–36.

26. Liphschitz and Waisel, "Dendroarchaeological Investigations," 133.

the features of the parent material from which they developed some six million years ago and, in the absence of macroclimatic changes, the soils have developed in comparable climates.

### Soil Types and Crops in Lower Galilee

In spite of Israel's small area, its soils are very diverse; thus, "in Israel it is not unusual to find several types of soil within the area of a single settlement."[27] Within Lower Galilee, five soil types are represented: Terra Rossa soils, Pale Rendzina soils, Brown Rendzina and Calcimorphic Brown Forest (CBF) soils, Vertisols, and basalt-derived soils. A detailed examination of each soil type lies beyond the scope of this study, but Table A presents the main features of the soils as they relate to agriculture.

Table B presents the optimal soil conditions and soils for wheat, barley, grapes, and olives—staples in the ancient diet and crops for which material evidence in the first centuries BCE and CE have been excavated.

We cannot assume, however, that a crop *would* be cultivated on a particular soil simply because it *could* be. When the extant agricultural installations and implements are mapped onto a soil map, however, in all but three Lower Galilean rural sites one finds evidence of the practice of agricultural determinism, that is, the crops that were best suited to the soils were indeed cultivated there (see Table C).

One would have expected the cultivation of vines at Asochis/Shikhin, not the (limited) cultivation of olives; however, its proximity to Sepphoris may have allowed its residents to purchase agricultural products from the markets in Sepphoris and to remain extensively involved in the manufacturing of pottery instead. That agricultural determinism does not appear to have been practiced at Capernaum and Bethsaida can be explained by their proximity to the lake and, hence, their involvement in the fishing industry. Agricultural determinism appears to have been practiced at Sepphoris and Tiberias, though the material evidence dates to a later period.

Agricultural determinism ought not to be confused with specialization, however, for the cultivation of soil-appropriate crops was not to the exclusion of all others. For example, while the soils at Nazareth are not particularly suitable for cereals, the presence of the threshing floor indicates that cereals were cultivated there nonetheless.

It seems reasonable to conclude, then, that during the first century CE the agrarian economy of Lower Galilee with its practice of agricultural determinism made a certain degree of inter-village trade necessary. Cereals were probably cultivated around each village, but none of the excavated villages cultivated both grapes and olives. The dearth of agricultural material evidence at Sepphoris and Tiberias probably indicates their dependence on the villages for agricultural products, though further excavations at these sites may uncover material evidence to the contrary.

---

27. Singer, *Soils of Israel*, 1; Ḥayyim Halperin, *Changing Patterns in Israel Agriculture* (London: Routledge & Kegan Paul, 1957), 1.

| | Content | Associated Physiography | Agriculture-Related Features |
|---|---|---|---|
| Terra Rossa[28] | • Macro- & micronutrients present<br>• Low $CaCO_3$ levels<br>• Clay > 60% | Steep mountains | • Shallow to moderately deep soil<br>• Gravelly to limited degree |
| Pale Rendzina[29] | • Micronutrient-deficient (frequently), esp. iron<br>• High $CaCO_3$ levels | Rounded hills, separated by wide valleys | • Shallow to moderately deep<br>• Well-aerated<br>• Low plant-available water |
| Brown Rendzina, CBF[30] | • Little to no $CaCO_3$ | Hills and plateaus, with moderate to steep slopes | • Shallow soil<br>• Well-drained and well-aerated |
| Vertisols[31] | • Clay > 50%<br>• Low to moderate carbonate levels | Valleys, plains, & plateaus (e.g., Jezreel and Bet Netofa Valleys) | • Macronutrient-deficient (esp. phosphorus)<br>• Prone to flooding<br>• Requires fertilizer and extensive human activity |
| Basalt-derived soils[32] | • Clay > 40% | Lower Eastern Galilee (N and W of Kinneret) | • Shallow soil (usu. less than 50 cm)<br>• Basalt rock protrusions in 10-30% of soil mantle |

**Table A. Soil Types in Lower Galilee**

| Crop | Optimal Soil Conditions | Optimal Soil(s) |
|---|---|---|
| Wheat | well-drained, stiff clay loams that hold and conserve water and provide conditions favorable for nitrate formation | Pale Rendzina soils |
| Barley | well-drained, fertile deep loam soils, particularly soils with high nitrogen content | Pale Rendzina soils |
| Grapes | heavy soils with a high proportion of stones or gravel (which therefore retain moisture) | Pale Rendzina, Brown Rendzina, and Calcimorphic Brown Forest soils |
| Olives | calcareous, sandy or even rocky soils, in well-drained situations | Terra Rossa and basalt-derived soils |

**Table B. Optimal Soil Conditions for Various Crops**

---

28. Singer, Soils of *Israel*, 91–106.
29. Ibid., 106–13.
30. Ibid., 113–23.
31. Ibid., 181–206; Bridges, *World Soils,* 67–70.
32. Singer, *Soils of Israel,* 181–206.

| Location | Soil | Material Evidence |
|---|---|---|
| Arbel | Terra Rossa, Brown Rendzina, and Pale Rendzina | winery (T961),[33] with a beam niche (T85) and a tethering ring (T855), in one-axis plan with intermediate vat |
| Asochis/Shikhin[34] | Brown and Pale Rendzina | fragment of olive press and a screw-type olive press |
| Bethsaida | border of Vertisols and basalt-derived | none from I CE |
| Capernaum | border of basalt-derived and Pale Rendzina | none from I CE |
| Chorazim | basalt-derived and Pale Rendzina | three screw-press bases: one from the early Arab period (T741), one from the Roman-Byzantine period (II–IV CE; T732), and one from the Roman period (II CE; T732)[35] |
| Kefar Hananya | Terra Rossa, Brown Rendzina, and Pale Rendzina | two screw weights (T62111 and T625111), a small lever and weights press (T201121101) with niche (T2111), press bed (T2622210), collecting vat (T2721), and crushing mortar (T1152)[36] |
| Magdala | border of Vertisols and basalt-derived | reversed-T weight (T5323) |
| Nazareth[37] (Area A) | Brown Rendzina | winepress |
| Nazareth (Area B) | Terra Rossa, Brown Rendzina, and Pale Rendzina | threshing floor |
| Sepphoris | Brown and Pale Rendzina | rotating-screw press base (T7413) → post-I CE winepress |
| Tiberias | Vertisols, with basalt-derived soils nearby | screw weight (T62111) → post-I CE |
| Yodefat | Terra Rossa | an olive-press complex and an oil press of the lever and weights style (T401146302), with a simple beam niche (T4111), a square press bed (T46411), a collecting vat (T47111), and a crushing basin (T31) |

**Table C. Agricultural Installations and Implements in Lower Galilee**

---

33. The presses will be labeled according to the system in Rafael Frankel, *Wine and Oil Production in Antiquity in Israel and Other Mediterranean Countries* (JSOT/ASOR Monograph Series 10; Sheffield: Sheffield Academic Press, 1999).

34. James F. Strange, Dennis E. Groh, and Thomas R. W. Longstaff, "University of South Florida Excavations at Sepphoris: The Location and Identification of Shikhin, Part 2," *IEJ* 45 (1995): 171–87.

35. The installation and channel of the third were probably set up already in the first century CE (Ze'ev Yeivin, "Korazim – 1983/1984," *HA-ESI* 3 [1984]: 66–71).

36. This type of press could be used for both wine and oil production, but was more frequently used to produce the latter. In the absence of either a treading floor (for grapes) or a crushing basin (for olives), it is difficult to be certain.

37. Stephen Pfann, Ross Voss, and Yehudah Rapuano, "Surveys and Excavations at the Nazareth Village Farm (1997–2002): Final Report," *BAIAS* 25 (2007): 19–79.

## The Distribution of Agricultural Goods

As production took place in the rural domain and as the populations of both the rural and the urban domains consumed these goods, some degree of trade or distribution of agricultural goods was necessary. As a result, the process of distribution involved both the urban and the rural domains; thus, it will certainly have been the case that the process involved the interaction of the urban and rural populations. An understanding of the process of distribution, then, will allow us to determine the frequency of and the domain in which urban–rural interaction occurred.

In order to understand the process of distribution, it is necessary to address two issues, namely, the *mechanics of distribution* and the *organization of distribution*. When we consider the mechanics of distribution, the main question in view is, How did distribution work? This encompasses such questions as: Who moved the goods? By what means? In which direction? How far and how frequently? As regards the organization of distribution, the main question is, Why did distribution work that way? This encompasses such questions as: Who directed the process of distribution? Who was under their direction? What reasons might have motivated or compelled those under direction to follow those directions?

The documentary papyri of Egypt can shed light on all of these questions, for they contain a wealth of information about short-haul land transport. While a range of variation undoubtedly existed among the provinces of the Roman Empire and "whilst the papyri may reveal details which are not literally applicable to provinces other than Egypt, they may, sanely applied, illuminate administrative, social and economic features of the Empire as a whole."[38] Further, since the technological capabilities of Lower Galilee and Egypt were comparable, distribution would have functioned in much the same way. Thus, Egypt's documentary evidence can illuminate both the mechanics and the organization of the process of distribution in Lower Galilee.

Customs-house registers reveal a great deal about the mechanics of distribution. To date, approximately four hundred individual receipts and fourteen customs registers have been recovered, totalling nearly one thousand receipts, the earliest dating to 18 CE and the latest to 214 CE.[39] They reveal that all manner of agricultural goods, including but not limited to cereals, wine, and oil, were transported from the villages of the Fayum throughout the year by the labor of donkeys, camels, and their drivers. The regular but small volume of agricultural exports suggests that the goods were not intended for interregional transport, but for local sale or consumption. In landlocked regions of the empire, including much of Egypt and Lower Galilee, the distribution of goods could have taken place only by land transport. The roads used for intraregional transport in Egypt were not well-constructed roads but simply dyke

---

38. Alan K. Bowman, "Papyri and Roman Imperial History, 1960–75," *JRS* 66 (1976): 161.

39. P. J. Sijpesteijn, *Customs Duties in Graeco-Roman Egypt* (Studia Amstelodamensia ad epigraphicam ius antiquum et papyrologicam pertinentia 17; Zutphen: Terra, 1987), 85–86. Many of the customs-house registers and receipts have been collected in Sijpesteijn, *Customs Duties*. To these should be added *P.Louvre* 1.27-29, *P.Oxy.* 69.4740–44, *O.Eleph.Wagner* 55–61, and the two receipts published in Colin E. P. Adams and Nikolaos Gonis, "Two Customs-House Receipts from the Bodleian Library," *ZPE* 126 (1999): 213–18.

tops that existed between floodings of the Nile. In the same way, the roads used for intrare-gional transport in Lower Galilee were simple footpaths, since the Romans developed much of the road network in Israel only after the First Revolt.[40] Thus, the mechanics by which land transport occurred and the roads used for this transport both in Egypt and in Lower Galilee were comparable, and the documentary papyri of Egypt provide a model for the mechanics by which land transport in Lower Galilee was possible.

A rather complex picture of the organization of distribution emerges from Egypt's docu-mentary evidence. Agricultural goods were transported over land not only for the purpose of local sale or export but also as a result of the fragmentation of estates and the management of transport resources. These have implications for our understanding of urban–rural interaction.

As a result of the fragmentation of estates, rural-to-rural movement of goods and animals took place between the various units of an estate and was conducted by members of the rural population. As a result of the residence of estate owners or the centralization of administra-tors in urban centers, rural-to-urban movement resulted when goods were transported to the urban center.[41] If the goods were delivered, then a member of the rural population would have interacted with a member of the urban population in the urban domain. If the goods were retrieved, however, then a member of the urban population would have interacted with a member of the rural population in the rural domain.

That estate owners or administrators were to be found in the urban domain allows us to conclude that the process of distribution was directed by members of the urban population. Those under direction were predominantly members of the rural population, though members of the urban population received such instructions as well. Those who issued instructions were concerned to minimize the costs associated with transport.[42] Thus, estates typically maintained only as many animals as were needed to meet the average transport needs of the estate, hiring other animals and drivers when the need arose.[43]

---

40. Benjamin Isaac and Israel Roll, *Roman Roads in Judaea I: The Legio-Scythopolis Road* (BAR International Series 141; Oxford: BAR, 1982), 3–14; Israel Roll, "The Roman Road System in Judaea," *Jerusalem Cathedra* 3 (1983): 138. See chapter 13 in this volume, by James F. Strange.

41. Instances of both rural-to-rural and rural-to-urban transport may be found throughout the archives of the estate of Lucius Bellenus Gemellus (the archive consists of *P.Fay.* 91, 102, 110–123, 248, 249, 252, 254, 255, 259–261, 265, 273–277), the descendants of Laches (documents included in this archive include *P.Mil.Vogl.* 1.23–28, 2.50–72, 3.129–54, 4.209–19, 6.264–82, 7.301–8, and *PSI* 8.961A and 961B), and Heroninos (on which see Dominic W. Rathbone, *Economic Rationalism and Rural Society in Third-Century A.D. Egypt* [Cambridge Classical Studies; Cambridge: Cambridge University Press, 1991]).

42. For example, *P.Flor.* 2.176 states: "If anyone sends up even the most trifling item he should send it up with a note and make clear what is being sent up through whom. What you sent up was not worth the wasting of the time of a man and an ass, all for four little baskets of bitter little figs. . . . And the one at Euhemeria (sc. Eirenaios) sent up another (ass) with a few things when both of you, if one had informed the other, could have sent up through the one" (translation in Rathbone, *Economic Rationalism*, 273).

43. See, for example, the frequent hiring of transport resources in the archives of the estate of Epimachos (Anna Świderek, *La propriété foncière privée dans l'Égypte de Vespasien et sa technique agricole d'après P. Lond. 131 recto* [Bibliotheca Antiqua 1; Wrocław: Zakład Narodowy Imienia Ossolińskich/Wydawnictwo Polskiej Akademii

Those who were permanent employees of an estate would certainly have heeded the instructions issued concerning the transport of goods, if only to remain employed by the estate. Those who were hired for a particular transport task, however, would have had a slightly different motivation to carry out these instructions. A number of archives, including those of Soterichos and Kronion, reveal that tenants were expected to provide the animals required to carry out their agricultural tasks.[44] Thus, tenants, as well as small farmers, possessed the human and animal labor required during peak agricultural periods.[45] During off-peak times, then, small farmers had an excess of human and animal labor available, which could be employed in land transport of goods from their own farm or from neighboring farms or estates.[46]

The similarities between Egypt and Lower Galilee with respect to landholding would very likely have resulted in similar patterns of transport and urban–rural interaction; that is, rural-to-rural transport would have been carried out by members of the rural population as a result of the rise of fragmented large estates, and rural-to-urban transport would have been carried out by members of the urban and the rural populations as a result of the urban residence of estate owners or centralization of administration. The retrieval of goods from the rural domain by a member of the urban population would have resulted in urban–rural interaction in the rural domain; however, the more frequent delivery of goods by a member of the rural population points to urban–rural interaction as a feature of the urban domain instead.

To conclude, the volume of rural-to-urban traffic in Lower Galilee must be considered. The average yearly consumption of grain, wine, and oil was 200 kilograms, 250 liters, and 20 kilograms per capita.[47] On the basis of the area and population densities of Sepphoris and Tiberias during the Herodian period, Reed calculates that the population of Sepphoris was 8,000

---

Nauk, 1960]), Sarapion (Jacques Schwartz, *Les archives de Sarapion et de ses fils: Une exploitation agricole aux environs d'Hermoupolis Magna [de 90 à 133 P.C.]* [Institut français d'archéologie orientale bibliothéque d'étude 29; Cairo: Imprimerie de l'Institut français d'archéologie orientale, 1961]), the descendants of Laches (see n. 41), and Heroninos (see n. 41).

Three more documents, *PSI* 6.688 recto (117 CE), *P.Cairo.Goodspeed* 30 (191–192 CE), and *BGU* 1.14 (255 CE), may also be cited as evidence that "the hire of animals supplemented the existing capacity of estate animals, allowing the estate-owners to maximize profits" (Colin Adams, *Land Transport in Roman Egypt: A Study of Economics and Administration in a Roman Province* [Oxford Classical Monographs; Oxford: Oxford University Press, 2007], 273–75; quotation from 275).

44. On the archive of Soterichos, see Sayed Omar, *Das Archiv des Soterichos* (Papyrologica Coloniensia 8; Opladen: Westdeutscher Verlag, 1979); and Omar, "Neue Kopfsteuerquittungen aus dem Archiv des Soterichos," *ZPE* 86 (1991): 215–29. On the archive of Kronion, see Daniele Foraboschi, *L'Archivio di Kronion* (Milan: Istituto Editoriale Cisalpino, 1971).

45. Paul P. M. Erdkamp, "Agriculture, Underemployment, and the Cost of Rural Labour in the Roman World," *CQ* 49 (1999): 558.

46. Ibid., 566.

47. Lin Foxhall states that the consumption of oil for an individual in an elite household was 25 to 35 kilograms per capita; thus, the calculations here use a slightly lower number (Lin Foxhall, *Olive Cultivation in Ancient Greece: Seeking the Ancient Economy* [Oxford: Oxford University Press, 2007], 86–91, esp. table 4.1).

to 12,000 and that of Tiberias was 6,000 to 12,000.[48] Using the lower population estimate for Sepphoris, 8,000 people would have consumed 1,600,000 kilograms of wheat, 2,000,000 liters of wine, and 160,000 kilograms of oil each year. Egypt's customs-house receipts reveal that a donkey could carry at least three artabae of wheat, which weighs approximately 90 kilograms. Assuming that wine weighed as much as water, Sepphoris required 48.7 donkey-loads of wheat, 60.9 loads of wine, and 4.9 loads of oil to be delivered on each day of the year; that is, 114.5 donkey-loads. If, however, no deliveries were made on the Sabbath, then the total would increase to 133.5 donkey-loads of food per weekday.

Using the lower population estimate for Tiberias, 6,000 people would have consumed 1,200,000 kilograms of wheat, 1,500,000 liters of wine, and 120,000 kilograms of oil each year. Thus, Tiberias required 36.5 donkey-loads of wheat, 45.7 loads of wine, and 3.7 loads of oil to be delivered on each day of the year, that is, 85.9 donkey-loads. If, however, no deliveries were made on the Sabbath, then the total would increase to 100.5 donkey-loads of food per weekday (see table D).

| | Sepphoris (population = 8,000) | | Tiberias (population =6,000) | |
|---|---|---|---|---|
| **Deliveries/year** | 365 | 313 | 365 | 313 |
| **Food** | | | | |
| Wheat | 48.7 | 56.8 | 36.5 | 43.0 |
| Wine | 60.9 | 71.0 | 45.7 | 53.2 |
| Oil | 4.9 | 5.7 | 3.7 | 4.3 |
| **Donkey-loads/day** | 114.5 | 133.5 | 85.9 | 100.5 |

**Table D. Food Consumption in Sepphoris and Tiberias**

Feeding the populations of Sepphoris and Tiberias, then, required at least 114.5 and 85.9 donkey-loads of food to be delivered each day, respectively, from the villages no more than ten kilometers away. Evidence that it was possible to move this volume of foodstuffs in antiquity may be found in the Heroninos archive, which reveals that in an average year, 7,100 monochora of wine (that is, 49,700 liters, the equivalent of 552 donkey-loads) was transported from Theadelphia to Arsinoe, a distance of approximately eleven kilometers.[49] Thus, it was certainly possible to carry out the land transport of foodstuffs required to feed the urban populations of Sepphoris and Tiberias. Since this food would have been transported by members of the rural population, the volume of rural-to-urban movement, as well as the levels of urban–rural interaction, would have been substantial.

---

48. Reed, *Archaeology and the Galilean Jesus*, 77–82.

49. To be precise, camels were the transport animal of choice at this estate. Since a camel could carry twice as much as a donkey, this volume of wine was equivalent to only 276 camel-loads.

## Conclusion

An examination of a single arena of urban–rural interaction, namely, the agricultural sector of the economy, reveals that agricultural goods were produced in the villages by ancient farmers whose practice of agricultural determinism necessitated some level of inter-village trade. While this would seem to support the argument for a cooperative and interdependent urban–rural relationship, our study of the mechanics and organization of distribution reveals that agricultural goods were distributed primarily by members of the rural population under the direction of members of the urban population, who were concerned with minimizing their costs of transportation. As a result, the distribution process was structured in such a way that the rural population, specifically tenants and small farmers, bore the brunt of transportation costs. In short, in economic interactions between the urban and rural populations of Lower Galilee, the rural population was at a distinct disadvantage.

More can certainly be said about urban–rural interaction and the urban–rural relationship. While pedology has been introduced into this conversation, the impact of the fishing industry on the Kinneret should also be considered. Urban and rural populations may have interacted for legal, religious, familial, or other reasons, and these await further study. Consideration should be given to interregional trade as well, for Lower Galilee did not exist in isolation from Upper Galilee, Judea, or the Decapolis. Nevertheless, it is clear from this study that urban–rural interaction can and must be considered in evaluating Lower Galilee's urban–rural relationship.

## Bibliography

Adams, Colin. *Land Transport in Roman Egypt: A Study of Economics and Administration in a Roman Province*. Oxford Classical Monographs. Oxford: Oxford University Press, 2007.

Adams, Colin E. P., and Nikolaos Gonis. "Two Customs-House Receipts from the Bodleian Library." *ZPE* 126 (1999): 213–18.

Adan-Bayewitz, David. *Common Pottery in Roman Galilee: A Study of Local Trade*. Bar-Ilan Studies in Near Eastern Languages and Culture. Ramat-Gan: Bar-Ilan University Press, 1993.

Adan-Bayewitz, David, and Isadore Perlman. "The Local Trade of Sepphoris in the Roman Period." *IEJ* 40 (1990): 153–72.

Bowman, Alan K. "Papyri and Roman Imperial History, 1960–75." *JRS* 66 (1976): 153–73.

Bridges, E. M. *World Soils*. 3rd ed. Cambridge: Cambridge University Press, 1997.

Edwards, Douglas R. "First Century Urban/Rural Relations in Lower Galilee: Exploring the Archaeological and Literary Evidence." In *SBL 1988 Seminar Papers*, edited by David J. Lull, 169–82. SBLSP 27. Atlanta: Scholars Press, 1988.

————. "Identity and Social Location in Roman Galilean Villages," In *Religion, Ethnicity, and Identity in Ancient Galilee: A Region in Transition*, edited by Jürgen Zangenberg, Harold W. Attridge, and Dale B. Martin, 357–74. WUNT 210. Tübingen: Mohr Siebeck, 2007.

————. "The Socio-Economic and Cultural Ethos of the Lower Galilee in the First Century: Implications for the Nascent Jesus Movement." In *The Galilee in Late Antiquity*, edited by Lee I. Levine, 53–73. New York: Jewish Theological Seminary of America, 1992.

Engels, Donald. *Roman Corinth: An Alternative Model for the Classical City*. Chicago: University of Chicago Press, 1990.

Erdkamp, Paul P. M. "Agriculture, Underemployment, and the Cost of Rural Labour in the Roman World." *CQ* 49 (1999): 556–72.

Finley, Moses I. *The Ancient Economy*. 2nd ed. Sather Classical Lectures 43. Berkeley: University of California Press, 1985.

Foraboschi, Daniele. *L'Archivio di Kronion*. Milan: Istituto Editoriale Cisalpino, 1971.

Foxhall, Lin. *Olive Cultivation in Ancient Greece: Seeking the Ancient Economy*. Oxford: Oxford University Press, 2007.

Freyne, Seán. *Galilee from Alexander the Great to Hadrian, 323 B.C.E. to 135 C.E.: A Study of Second Temple Judaism*. University of Notre Dame Center for the Study of Judaism and Christianity in Antiquity 5. Wilmington, Del: Michael Glazier; Notre Dame: University of Notre Dame Press, 1980.

————. "Jesus and the Urban Culture of Galilee." In *Texts and Contexts: Biblical Texts in Their Textual and Situational Contexts. Essays in Honor of Lars Hartman*, edited by Tord Fornberg and David Hellholm, 597–622. Oslo: Scandinavian University Press, 1995.

————. "Town and Country Once More: The Case of Roman Galilee." In *Galilee and Gospel: Collected Essays*. WUNT 125. Tübingen: Mohr Siebeck, 2000. Reprint, Leiden: Brill, 2002. Originally published in *Archaeology and the Galilee: Texts and Contexts in the Graeco-Roman and Byzantine Periods*, edited by Douglas R. Edwards and C. Thomas McCollough, 49–56. South Florida Studies in the History of Judaism 143. Atlanta: Scholars Press, 1997.

————. "Urban–Rural Relations in First-Century Galilee: Some Suggestions from the Literary Sources." In *The Galilee in Late Antiquity*, edited by Lee I. Levine, 75–91. New York: Jewish Theological Seminary of America, 1992.

Hopkins, David C. *The Highlands of Canaan: Agricultural Life in the Early Iron Age*. Social World of Biblical Antiquity 3. Sheffield: JSOT Press, 1985.

Horsley, Richard A. *Archaeology, History, and Society in Galilee: The Social Context of Jesus and the Rabbis*. Harrisburg, Pa.: Trinity Press International, 1996.

————. *Galilee: History, Politics, People*. Valley Forge, Pa.: Trinity Press International, 1995.

Isaac, Benjamin, and Israel Roll. *Roman Roads in Judaea I: The Legio-Scythopolis Road*. BAR International Series 141. Oxford: BAR, 1982.

Liphschitz, Nili, and Yoav Waisel. "Dendroarchaeological Investigations in Israel." *IEJ* 23 (1973): 30–36.

———. "Dendroarchaeological Investigations in Israel (Taanach)." *IEJ* 30 (1980): 132–36.

Lowdermilk, W. C., N. Gil, and Z. Rosenzaft. "An Inventory of the Land of Israel: Land Classification for Use with Soil Conservation." *IEJ* 3 (1953): 162–77.

Neuendorf, Klaus K. E., James P. Mehl Jr., and Julia A. Jackson, eds. *Glossary of Geology*. 5th ed. Alexandria, Va.: American Geological Institute, 2005.

Omar, Sayed. *Das Archiv des Soterichos*. Papyrologica Coloniensia 8. Opladen: Westdeutscher Verlag, 1979.

———. "Neue Kopfsteuerquittungen aus dem Archiv des Soterichos." *ZPE* 86 (1991): 215–29.

Orni, Efraim, and Elisha Efrat. *Geography of Israel*. 2nd ed. Jerusalem: Israel Program for Scientific Translations, 1966.

Rathbone, Dominic W. *Economic Rationalism and Rural Society in Third-Century A.D. Egypt*. Cambridge Classical Studies. Cambridge: Cambridge University Press, 1991.

Reed, Jonathan L. *Archaeology and the Galilean Jesus: A Re-Examination of the Evidence*. Harrisburg, Pa.: Trinity Press International, 2000.

Reifenberg, Adolf. *The Soils of Palestine: Studies in Soil Formation and Land Utilisation in the Mediterranean*. Translated by C. L. Whittles. 2nd ed. London: Thomas Murby, 1947.

Roll, Israel. "The Roman Road System in Judaea." *Jerusalem Cathedra* 3 (1983): 136–61.

Rosenan, Naftali. "One Hundred Years of Rainfall in Jerusalem." *IEJ* 5 (1955): 137–53.

Schwartz, Jacques. *Les archives de Sarapion et de ses fils: Une exploitation agricole aux environs d'Hermoupolis Magna (de 90 à 133 P.C.)*. Institut français d'archéologie orientale bibliothéque d'étude 29. Cairo: Imprimerie de l'Institut français d'archéologie orientale, 1961.

Sijpesteijn, P. J. *Customs Duties in Graeco-Roman Egypt*. Studia Amstelodamensia ad epigraphicam ius antiquum et papyrologicam pertinentia 17. Zutphen: Terra, 1987.

Singer, Arieh. *The Soils of Israel*. Berlin: Springer, 2007.

Strange, James F. "First Century Galilee from Archaeology and from the Texts." In *Archaeology and the Galilee: Texts and Contexts in the Graeco-Roman and Byzantine Periods*, edited by Douglas R. Edwards and C. Thomas McCollough, 39–48. South Florida Studies in the History of Judaism 143. Atlanta: Scholars Press, 1997.

———. "First-Century Galilee from Archaeology and from the Texts." In *SBL 1994 Seminar Papers*, edited by Eugene H. Lovering Jr., 81–90. SBLSP 33. Atlanta: Scholars Press, 1994.

Świderek, Anna. *La propriété foncière privée dans l'Égypte de Vespasien et sa technique agricole d'après P. Lond. 131 recto*. Bibliotheca Antiqua 1. Wrocław: Zakład Narodowy Imienia Ossolińskich/Wydawnictwo Polskiej Akademii Nauk, 1960.

Zohary, Michael. *Geobotanical Foundations of the Middle East*. 2 vols. Geobotanica Selecta 3. Stuttgart: Gustav Fischer, 1973.

———. *Geobotany*. Ma'anit: Sifriat Hapoalim, 1955.

———. *Plant Life of Palestine: Israel and Jordan*. Chronica Botanica New Series of Plant Science Books 33. New York: Ronald, 1962.

# 16

# INNER VILLAGE LIFE IN GALILEE: A DIVERSE AND COMPLEX PHENOMENON

## *Sharon Lea Mattila*

Much research on life in the Greco-Roman world has taken a "top-down" approach. It has focused first on the activities of the rulers, temple authorities, and other members of the elite, only then taking into account those who lived outside these spheres. Moreover, it has been common to depict most of the non-elite as a homogeneous mass of "peasants": members of self-provisioning "peasant family farms" who lived in tradition-bound, autarchic village communities just above the level of subsistence after the ruling, parasitic, urban elite extracted rents and taxes. Market exchange was peripheral and harmful to this mode of existence, for subsistence-oriented peasant production was not geared toward markets. When peasants did exchange goods with each other, it was usually through barter. According to this received wisdom, few, if any, people existed between the self-sufficient, subsistence-level masses living in the villages, on the one hand, and the parasitic, ruling elite based in the cities, on the other.[1]

To my knowledge, there has been no serious attempt properly to demonstrate, on the basis of hard evidence from ancient rural contexts, the existence of such masses of "peasants," or of a related "peasant economy" (often also called a "natural economy"). Instead, what one routinely encounters are either assumptions or assertions, backed only by appeals to the influential theories of certain social scientists and economic historians of the last century, as though

I would like to thank my student research assistant, Mary Tess Johnson, for her invaluable assistance with the final research and editing of this chapter. This help was very timely as the hard deadline for this chapter's submission arrived.

1. An attempt to document this brief summary would be overwhelmed by the quantity of secondary literature involved.

the heuristic value and at least the rough empirical accuracy of these theories must now be accepted as established.

The data I survey cover roughly the period from 200 BCE to 450 CE, somewhat beyond the time span of this volume, but the archaeological evidence in particular requires this broader span, as should become evident in my discussion. In this chapter I date the beginning of the Byzantine period to the reign of Constantine I, and I designate the last century or so of the time span considered here Early Byzantine. I focus mainly on the Galilee, in line with the emphasis of this volume, but I also consider pertinent data from elsewhere in Palestine. Given the broad time span covered, I make no pretense at being comprehensive within the confines of a book chapter, although I do aim to highlight the most salient features of these data, and to underscore both the discontinuity and continuity that they exhibit over time.

I will demonstrate that *all* of the data consistently undermine the conventional wisdom outlined above. This is why, over the decades during which I have been familiarizing myself with this evidence, I have found it increasingly imperative to seek alternative interpretive frameworks that provide both a much better fit to the data on the ground and a more lucid explanation of what these data do indicate. The evidence surveyed should show that alternative premises deserve further consideration in future study of village life in Greco-Roman and Early Byzantine Palestine.

## A Survey of the Evidence from Middle Roman–Byzantine Times

### *What Was a Village?*

There remains one further methodological question that must be addressed. This is the simple one of what, precisely, was a village, and how does one distinguish an ancient village from a city or a town? The question is simple but the answer is not, as was already recognized by ancient authors, such as the rabbis and Eusebius, who attempted to classify the settlements of Palestine. Ze'ev Safrai has devoted some discussion to this issue and has proposed a typology based on the rabbinic categories: (1) the *polis*, whether a capital of a province or toparchy, a large urban trading center, or a smaller city of some importance; (2) the "town," which he in turn divides into three categories—(a) the "large town," or "local center"; (b) the "medium-size town," or "large village"; and (c) the "small town" or "small village town"; and finally (3) the "village" (כפר, *kfr*, "kefar"), which he confines to settlements consisting of no more than "a small number of private houses" or to "the private '*yr*' or Roman villa, usually a house or a number of houses belonging to a wealthy landowner."[2]

According to this typology, the majority of settlements in Greco-Roman and Byzantine Galilee would have to be classified as "towns," including even those whose very names designate them as villages, such as Kefar Nahum ("Village of Nahum"), or Capernaum. The termi-

---

2. Ze'ev Safrai, *The Economy of Roman Palestine* (London: Routledge, 1994), 17–19.

nology, moreover, is confusing, given that by Safrai's own definition many of these "towns" are villages, whether "large villages," or "small village towns." Finally, it is best not to designate a villa a "village," as it is surely a different kind of rural settlement, while what Safrai classifies as a "village" is probably better described as a hamlet.

It is thus preferable, I would submit, to employ the concept of an urban–rural spectrum, ranging from large cities with all the usual urban amenities (and confining the term *city* largely to these) to small towns to large villages to small villages to hamlets, and including as separate categories the villas and large agricultural complexes that have been found in Palestine (although the last-mentioned complexes have not yet been found in the Galilee).[3] This avoids collapsing the important distinction between urban and rural settlements altogether, while allowing for the diversity that characterized both. It is a concept that also recognizes that sometimes a large village could be very similar to a small town and may be referred to using both designations without serious confusion.

### Why I Begin with the Later Evidence

As our database from Greco-Roman and Byzantine Palestine grows, and as more of it is published, it is becoming increasingly clear that throughout the Hellenistic, Roman, and Byzantine periods Galileans living in settlements of virtually all sizes along the urban–rural spectrum participated in market exchange with each other. There is, of course, no space here to survey all of this abundant data. I will only be able to highlight some of the most salient features of this evidence, beginning with the Middle Roman–Byzantine periods, for which our database is more abundant, and then moving backward to the Hasmonean–Early Roman periods, where it is less abundant but growing. For the earlier period I will focus in particular on the numismatic data, which, together with other archaeological indicators, demonstrate that local trade thrived as much in late Second Temple times as it did in later periods. Nevertheless, the data are also clear that there were important shifts in trade patterns, which I will also highlight.

### The Rabbis as a Source for Rural Socioeconomic Life

Ze'ev Safrai's claim that the Palestinian rabbinic traditions "are unique in that they allow examination and analysis of a rural sector" is well founded.[4] Shaye Cohen's meticulous compilation of the Tannaitic evidence (evidence from rabbis who lived from 10 to 220 CE) has shown that about two-thirds of the early rabbis lived in villages.[5] Space constraints force me to leave aside

---

3. For a survey of these, see Yizhar Hirschfeld, "Jewish Rural Settlement in Judaea in the Early Roman Period," in *The Early Roman Empire in the East* (ed. Susan E. Alcock; Oxbow Monograph 95; Oxford: Oxbow Books, 1997), 72–88.

4. Safrai, *Economy of Roman Palestine*, 340.

5. Shaye J. D. Cohen, "The Rabbi in Second-Century Jewish Society," in *The Cambridge History of Judaism*, vol. 3, *The Early Roman Period* (ed. William Horbury, W. D. Davies, and John Sturdy; Cambridge: Cambridge University Press, 1999), 922–90. A shorter version of this study, without the appendixes, is found in Cohen, "The

any detailed defense of using the rabbinic literature as an indispensable source for reconstructing socioeconomic life in rural Roman Palestine. I must confine myself to a couple of important points.

First, seeking information in these texts on the world in which the rabbis lived is an enterprise quite apart from trying to determine how widespread rabbinic regulations reached among the general Jewish population. I see no reason to question the new growing consensus that rabbinic movement was "part of an ongoing cultural struggle by a segment of a Roman provincial population in a political and administrative setting where they would have had no official authority and possibly little popular appeal."[6] The texts themselves suggest as much in their frequent criticisms and distrust of the infamous עמי הארץ ('amê ha'aretz, "the people of the land"), who were clearly Jews themselves, on account of their lax observance.[7] Alexei Sivertsev's well-worded general methodological conclusion is surely sound, however, that, "[i]n order to be properly understood by their readers and/or listeners rabbinic texts . . . could not feature totally fictional institutions or refer to completely imaginative life circumstances . . . [but] had to be grounded in the historical reality familiar to their audience."[8] Second, the view that none of the traditions preserved in these texts predates its writing, that all are the invention of their editors and that all of the biographical details associated with the rabbis whose sayings they record must be considered fictitious is, in my view, too extreme to be credible. There is therefore adequate reason to trust the result of Cohen's analysis, mentioned above.

This does not mean, of course, that one can dispense with critical judgment in evaluating what these texts say about the rabbis and their world. Seth Schwartz is certainly correct, for instance, that one cannot at all take at face value the patently exaggerated rabbinic declarations of average grain crop yields in ancient Palestine, which have been accepted uncritically by some scholars.[9] It is a specious argument, however (of which, to be fair, Schwartz is not alone guilty), that: (1) in the absence of large quantities of agricultural surplus, trade and specialized production must have been limited and the bulk of economic activity subsistence-oriented; and (2) any other conclusion is "unrealistic" and even "impossible."[10]

---

Place of the Rabbi in Jewish Society of the Second Century," in *The Galilee in Late Antiquity* (ed. Lee I. Levine; New York: Jewish Theological Seminary of America, 1992), 157–73.

   6. Ḥayim Lapin, "The Origins and Development of the Rabbinic Movement in the Land of Israel," in *The Cambridge History of Judaism*, vol. 4, *The Late Roman–Rabbinic Period* (ed. Steven T. Katz; Cambridge: Cambridge University Press, 2006), 206–29, esp. 225.

   7. The classic study of these is Aharon Oppenheimer, *The 'Am Ha-Aretz. A Study in the Social History of the Jewish People in the Hellenistic-Roman Period* (trans. I. H. Levine; Arbeiten zur Literatur und Geschichte des hellenistischen Judentums 8; Leiden: Brill, 1977).

   8. Alexei Sivertsev, *Private Households and Public Politics in 3rd–5th Century Jewish Palestine* (TSAJ 90; Tübingen: Mohr Siebeck, 2002) 16.

   9. Seth Schwartz, "Political, Social, and Economic Life in the Land of Israel, 66–c. 235," in Katz, *Cambridge History of Judaism*, 4: 23–52, esp. 38–41.

   10. Ibid., esp 40 n. 54 and 41 n. 57. It is surely no accident that the secondary literature Schwartz cites in support of this contention all dates to the 1970s and '80s (ibid., 39 nn. 48 and 49).

The more complex picture is, in fact, quite possible. The rhythms of the ancient agricultural calendar left plenty of time for people to do other things. Given that it was probably only during harvest season that a large proportion of available labor needed to be devoted to grain crops, David A. Warburton has estimated, on the basis of various mathematical calculations, that producing enough grain to feed a given population required a far lower percentage of the people to be engaged in full-time agricultural pursuits than is commonly assumed.[11]

Schwartz is also misleading when he declares that the evidence for alternative views is "restricted . . . to a handful of passages in rabbinic literature."[12] Ben-Zion Rosenfeld and Joseph Manirav report that the rabbinic literature mentions markets in everyday situations in different types of settlements over 120 times, and if we include parallels to the literature the number is well over one thousand.[13] It is unlikely that all of these references stem merely from rabbinic fantasies.

### *The Rabbinic Testimony to Market Exchange and Specialization of Production*

Rosenfeld and Manirav discuss this large body of rabbinic evidence in some detail, as does Ze'ev Safrai. They demonstrate that these sources frequently attest not only to permanent markets in the larger settlements but also to periodic markets and fairs, as well as traveling large-scale wholesalers, convoys of donkey drivers, and itinerant peddlers. All of these in combination apparently provisioned both the cities and the countryside with a wide variety of goods, even down to the smallest settlements.[14]

Indeed, early rabbinic (Tannaitic) texts attest to a wide variety of specialized products and specialists involved in producing them, and there is no sound methodological reason to confine all to urban contexts, especially in light of Cohen's carefully substantiated argument that most of the tradents of these traditions were villagers. Even the most cursory reading of the Mishnah's tractate *Kelim* ("Vessels"), for instance, unmistakably reveals the rich variety of commodities that were manufactured out of clay, straw, reeds, bone, leather, linen, wool, wood, glass, metal, and combinations of these. Safrai, moreover, compiles a large quantity of evidence

---

11. David A. Warburton, *Macroeconomics from the Beginning: The General Theory, Ancient Markets, and the Rate of Interest* (Civilisations du Proche-Orient, Série 4, Histoire-essais 2; Neuchâtel: Recherches et publications, 2003), 200–203. Warburton focuses on Egypt, where the yields were definitely higher than in Palestine, and thus comes up with an estimate of only 20 percent of the population so engaged. Presumably it would have been higher in Palestine, given lower yields, but his basic reasoning surely applies beyond Egypt.

12. Schwartz, "Political, Social, and Economic Life," 41.

13. Ben-Zion Rosenfeld and Joseph Menirav, *Markets and Marketing in Roman Palestine* (trans. Chava Cassel; JSJSup 99; Leiden: Brill, 2005), 1.

14. Rosenfeld and Menirav, *Markets and Marketing*, passim; Safrai, *Economy of Roman Palestine*, 224–321. Rosenfeld and Menirav disagree with Safrai's argument that the Monday and Thursday markets held in towns and villages disappeared after the Bar Kochba Revolt (*Markets and Marketing*, 44–45).

from the larger rabbinic corpus and from archaeology attesting to a wide variety of products and services in Palestine from Middle Roman to Byzantine times.[15]

The various specialists include craftsmen, agricultural and manual laborers with various skills, shepherds, as well as individuals involved in transport of goods, the provision of services, and other diverse aspects of trade. Confined to the Tannaitic literature alone, without pretending to provide an exhaustive list of the specialists mentioned, there occur in these texts, in addition to the frequently mentioned donkey drivers, bakers, potters, shops, and shopkeepers:[16] butchers (*t. B. Qam.* 10:9–10); tanners (*t. B. Meṣiʿa* 11:16–17); millers (*m. Demai* 3:4; *t. B. Qam.* 10:9); carpenters (*m. B. Qam.* 9:3; 10:10; *t. B. Qam.* 10:8; 11:15); joiners (*t. B. Qam.* 10:8); smiths (*t. B. Qam.* 6:26); craftsmen who repair utensils (*t. B. Meṣiʿa* 10:7); craftsmen who make plows, yokes, winnowing fans, mattocks, scythes, sickles, and wagons (*m. Šeb.* 5:6); craftsmen who make doors, bolts, and locks (*m. B. Meṣiʿa* 8:7); stone cutters (*t. B. Qam.* 11:18; *t. B. Meṣiʿa* 11:5); builders (*m. B. Qam.* 9:3); barbers (*m. Kil.* 9:3; *m. Šeb.* 8:5; *t. B. Meṣiʿa* 10:11); bathhouse keepers (*m. Šeb.* 8:5); laundry men (*m. B. Qam.* 10:10; *t. B. Qam.* 11:13; *t. B. Bat.* 2:6); sailors (*m. Šeb.* 8:5); shipmasters (*t. B. Meṣiʿa* 11:26); mistresses of inns (*m. Demai* 3:5); tavern keepers (*t. B. Meṣiʿa* 11:30); measurers (*t. B. Meṣiʿa* 11:30); diggers of wells or ditches (*t. B. Qam.* 6:5; *t. B. Meṣiʿa* 11:18, 30); pipers for a bride or a corpse (*m. B. Meṣiʿa* 6:1); vine trimmers, shrub trimmers, weed cutters (*t. B. Meṣiʿa* 11:18); watchmen over produce, fruit trees, or vegetable gardens (*m. B. Qam.* 8:1; 10:9; *m. B. Meṣiʿa* 7:8; *t. B. Qam.* 11:8; *m. B. Bat.* 4:8–9); herdsmen (*m. Ḥal.* 1:8; *m. B. Qam.* 10:9); shepherds (*t. B. Qam.* 6:20; 11:9–10; *t. B. Meṣiʿa* 8:17–18; *t. B. Bat.* 2:5); camel drivers (*t. B. Meṣiʿa* 11:5); porters (*t. B. Meṣiʿa* 11:5); wagon drivers and litter bearers (*m. B. Meṣiʿa* 6:1); wholesale dealers, dealers in grain, provision dealers, and merchants (*m. B. Meṣiʿa* 4:4, 11–12; *m. B. Bat.* 5:10; 6:5; *m. Demai* 2:4; 5:4, 6); middlemen (*m. B. Bat.* 5:8); householder's "agents" (*m. Ter.* 4:4); "pedlars that go around from town to town" (*m. Maas.* 2:3); and large-scale dealers (*monopol*) who buy from many bakers (*m. Demai* 5:4) and/or from multiple threshing floors and/or wine presses (*m. B. Meṣiʿa* 4:12). Money changers are also frequently mentioned (for example, *m. Maʿaś. Š.* 4:2; *m. B. Meṣiʿa* 2:4; 3:11; 4:6; 9:12; *t. B. Meṣiʿa* 4:2, 9; *t. B. Qam.* 10:10). The oft-mentioned donkey drivers apparently frequently doubled as small-scale merchants, who bought up produce, oil, and wine from householders and sold it at a higher price (*t. B. Meṣiʿa* 3:25; 4:8).

In the textile industry alone, there were weavers (הַגַּרְדִּי [cf. Greek γέρδιος and Latin *gerdius*]; *m. Demai* 1:4; *t. B. Qam.* 11:11; *t. B. Meṣiʿa* 7:15–17), wool workers or weavers (הצמרין; *t. B. Meṣiʿa* 11:24, 30), wool combers (הסורק; *m. Demai* 1:4; *m. B. Qam.* 10:10; *t. B. Qam.* 11:12), dyers (הצבעין; *m. B. Qam.* 9:4; *m. B. Meṣiʿa* 8:6; *t. B. Qam.* 11:12; *t. B. Meṣiʿa* 11:24, 30), tailors (החייט or תּוֹפְרֵי כְסוּת; *m. Kil.* 9:6; *m. B. Qam.* 10:10; *t. B. Qam.* 11:17), and garment vendors (מוֹכְרֵי כְסוּת; *m. Kil.* 9:5).

---

15. Safrai, *Economy of Roman Palestine*, 104–221.

16. A very partial list of references to shops and shopkeepers includes *m. Demai* 2:4; 5:4; *m. Šeb.* 10:1; *m. Maʿaś. Š.* 4:2; *m. B. Qam.* 6:6; *m. B. Meṣiʿa* 2:4; 3:11; 4:12; 5:4; 8:6; 9:12; *m. B. Bat.* 2:3; 5:9–10; *t. B. Qam.* 6:26, 28; 7:8; *t. B. Meṣiʿa* 2:14; 3:27–28; 4:11–13; 7:16; 8:27, 29; 11:16; *t. B. Bat.* 1:4, 2:6, 15.

It appears that most of these specialists were male. While the early rabbinic texts present both men and women as weaving, they sequester "women to an older form of loom that was possibly extinct by the time these texts were circulated." This older form of loom was the warp-weighted loom that the two-beam loom replaced by the second century. Whereas the Tannaim depict both men and women as working at the older form of loom, they represent only men as working at the newer, more efficient loom.[17] This suggests that by the second century, weaving, already practiced by male specialists in the earlier period, had become so much the domain of male specialized production that women rarely conducted it in their homes.

Spinning, however, the Mishnah assigns predominantly to women. In the textile industry of ancient Palestine there apparently was a symbiosis between housewife and specialized production, which also often took place in people's homes (see further below). According to the Mishnah, one of the wife's duties to her husband is "to work in wool" (לַעֲשׂוֹת בַּצֶּמֶר; *m. Ketub.* 5:5). This is patently a reference to spinning, for the stipulation is that the woman must produce for her husband "the weight of five *selaim* of warp [שְׁתִי] in Judea, which are ten *selaim* in the Galilee; or the weight of ten *selaim* of woof [עֶרֶב] in Judea, which are twenty *selaim* in the Galilee" (*m. Ketub.* 5.9). Warp consists of the thinner, harder-to-spin longitudinal threads, and woof of the thicker latitudinal threads. Spinning is also manifestly meant when the Tosefta adds that a woman's husband "cannot force her to work in flax, for it makes the mouth stink and stiffens the lips" (*t. Ketub.* 5:4). Unlike wool, flax must be dampened as it is being spun, and this was usually done by "wiping the ball of the thumb on the lower lip."[18]

The Mishnah expects the woman to sell her spun thread and to give the proceeds to her husband or, under certain circumstances, to use the proceeds to support herself. This is plain from the fact that, if her husband does not give her the prescribed allowance of a "silver *maah* for her needs," then "her handiwork is hers" to sell in order to procure her own necessities (*m. Ketub.* 5:9). If her husband steps outside his authority and "consecrates his wife's handiwork" to the temple, "she works and eats" (*m. Ketub.* 5:4). That is, she sells her spun woof and warp and buys her own food.

The likelihood that women of this time routinely spun but did not themselves generally weave either their own clothing or that of their family is corroborated by the Mishnah's ruling regarding a wife's minimum maintenance. Along with food allotments and other necessities, the husband must give her clothes to the value of fifty *zuz* every winter (*m. Ketub.* 5.8). The ruling does not state that she is to be furnished with wool in order to make her own clothes, but that she is to be provided yearly with new, finished garments of a certain monetary value, which could be purchased in the marketplace (*t. B. Meṣiʿa* 3:16).

The male specialists in the textile industry appear often to have formed guilds within their villages or towns. The sages therefore prescribe that "those who work in wool and the

---

17. Miriam Peskowitz, "Gender, Difference, and Everyday Life: The Case of Weaving and Its Tools," in *Religion and Society in Roman Palestine: Old Questions, New Approaches* (ed. Douglas R. Edwards; New York: Routledge, 2004), 129–45, esp. 134–35.

18. Elsie G. Davenport, *Your Handspinning* (Pacific Grove, Calif.: Select Books, 1964), 82.

dyers have the power to say, 'Any purchase order which comes to town—all of us will share in it'" (*t. B. Meṣiʿa* 11:24).[19] The practitioners of other trades also appear to have organized themselves into guilds. "The bakers" of a village or town, the Tannaim declare, "are permitted to form a combination among themselves [setting the weight or price of bread]" (*t. B. Meṣiʿa* 11:25).[20] The donkey drivers are permitted to organize in order to establish a kind of mutual insurance fund, within which the guild will replace a dead animal, so long as it has not died through "flagrant neglect" (ibid.). Shipmasters can set up a similar mutual insurance fund to replace lost ships (*t. B. Meṣiʿa* 11:26).[21]

*Tosefta Baba Meṣiʿa* 11:27 confirms that specialists in Palestine were not confined to cities but could also be found in sometimes very small settlements. Here it is stipulated that, if there is only one bath attendant, barber, or baker in a community, he is not allowed to leave for a festival unless he first sets up someone to replace him during his absence. It appears that the Tannaim viewed the services of these specialists as essential. Another Toseftan ruling also shows unambiguously that bakers were present in villages as well as in cities. Whereas bakers in "the cities" (בכרכין) were expected to bake many times daily, those "in the villages" (בכפרים) were expected to bake once a day. The village bakers still baked far more frequently than the wives of householders (בעלי בתים), however, who would bake only once a week (*t. Pesaḥ.* 2:1).[22]

### *The Early Rabbinic Evidence for Rural Socioeconomic Differentiation*

In addition to providing ample evidence for local specialization and trade, the early rabbinic material strongly suggests rural socioeconomic stratification. Shaye Cohen has shown that virtually all of the early rabbis, two-thirds of whom were villagers as mentioned above, were well-to-do landowners.[23] The Tannaim were not the only members of this group. A number of passages clearly imply that some of the individuals whom the rabbis called עמי הארץ ("the people of the land"), from whom they carefully separated themselves, were also well-to-do.[24]

---

19. I have translated the word מקח as "purchase order," in line with its clear meaning of "purchase" in *t. B. Meṣiʿa* 4:3.

20. My translation follows that offered by Isaac Mendelsohn, "Guilds in Ancient Palestine," *BASOR* 80 (1940): 19. Much the same translation is suggested by Marcus Jastrow under his entry for רגיעה (*A Dictionary of the Targumim, the Talmud Babli and Yerushalmi, and the Midrashic Literature* [2 vols.; New York: Pardes, 1950]).

21. Actual guild registers among a variety of craftsmen, including weavers, have been unearthed from the Egyptian village of Tebtunis. See Richard Alston, "Trade and the City in Roman Egypt," in *Trade, Traders, and the Ancient City* (ed. Helen Parkins and Christopher Smith; London: Routledge, 1998), 168–202, esp. 175; and Arthur E. R. Boak, "The Organization of Gilds [*sic*] in Greco-Roman Egypt," *TAPA* 48 (1937): 212–20.

22. Ḥayim Lapin discusses these passages, along with various Amoraic passages, as instances of the typical market hierarchy predicted by central place market models in *Economy, Geography, and Provincial History in Later Roman Palestine* (TSAJ 85; Tübingen: Mohr Siebeck, 2001), 30–38.

23. Cohen, "Rabbi in Second-Century Jewish Society," 922–90; Cohen, "Place of the Rabbi," 157–73; cf. Ḥayim Lapin, *Early Rabbinic Civil Law and the Social History of Roman Galilee: A Study of Mishnah Tractate Baba' Meṣiʿa'* (BJS 307; Atlanta: Scholars Press, 1995), 193–94; cf. 123–24, 223, 232–33.

24. See the discussion and references in Oppenheimer, *'Am Ha-Aretz*, 18–22.

Importantly, however, it is not only the existence of a rural, leisured, land-owning class in the Galilee that the Tannaitic literature reveals. The "householder," whose concerns the Tannaitic rulings mainly reflect, stands at the center of a sizable circle of people of lesser economic means. These are people with whom the householder frequently interacts, and upon whose labor his leisured lifestyle depends—namely, slaves, other family members, tenants, day laborers of all sorts, and a multitude of specialized craftsmen, money changers and tradesmen, and a diverse range of providers of services (for example, bath keepers, bakers, barbers) and of transport. Not surprisingly, it is the householder whose interests are primarily represented in Tannaitic legislation concerning these interactions.

The concerns of an affluent rural class are the focus of the series of regulations in *m. B. Meṣiʿa* 5:8; 9:1–10. The passage delineates tenants' obligations to cultivate and weed the householder's land according to local customary practices, and to preserve it undamaged for him. If the quality of a given year's crop is excellent, the tenant is not to sell it in the marketplace and then purchase inferior produce with which to pay his rent. Also stipulated are the few very exceptional circumstances, such as a region-wide natural disaster, in which the landlord must accept a reduced rent.

A series of prescriptions about the hiring of laborers in *m. B. Meṣiʿa* 7:1–8; 9:11–12 likewise reflects the interests of prosperous landowners. This is despite the fact that the sages enjoin feeding laborers a basic meal in accordance with local custom and following the pentateuchal injunctions to pay wages promptly and to allow harvest laborers to eat as they reap. The following anecdote reveals the degree to which the concerns of the landowners are dominant, even among those respecting these injunctions.

A case happened in connection with R. Yohanen b. Mattiah [ca. 120–140 CE] who said to his son:

> "Go out and hire laborers for us." And he [the son] agreed on food with them. And when he came to his father he [the father] said: "Even if you make them [a meal] like a feast of Solomon in his time, you have not fulfilled your obligation with respect to them, for they are sons of Abraham, Isaac, and Jacob. Rather, before they begin working go out and tell them: 'On condition that you have [a claim to] only bread and pulse.'" (*m. B. Meṣiʿa* 7:1)[25]

In the case of slaves, however, not only the customary meals but even the biblical right to eat of the crop while reaping it could be completely bypassed. Another Mishnaic ruling allows householders hiring out the labor of their slaves to other householders to negotiate for monetary compensation for their slaves who are denied this right (*m. B. Meṣiʿa* 7:6). The Tosefta includes an impressive number of other rulings on the hiring of all kinds of agricultural laborers, as well

---

25. Translation is that of Lapin (with a few modifications) provided in his "Appendix," in *Early Rabbinic Civil Law*. The dates for R. Yohanen b. Mattiah are from Herbert Danby, *The Mishnah, Translated from the Hebrew with Introduction and Brief Explanatory Notes* (Oxford: Oxford University Press, 1933), 799.

as numerous regulations on the leasing out of fields, orchards, vineyards, olive groves, vegetable gardens, and so on (for example, *t. B. Meṣiʿa* 7:2–8; 8:1–3, 6–9; 9:1–33; 10:2–6). Laborers and tenants populated the world of the early rabbis in quite some abundance.

At the bottom of the socioeconomic spectrum lay the destitute, whose existence the Mishnah's tractate *Peah* and the parallel Toseftan tractate clearly indicate. These tractates are devoted to a slew of regulations ensuring the destitutes' rights to gleanings, the forgotten sheaf, the separated grape and defective cluster, the produce of the rear corner of the field, and poor men's tithes in the third and sixth years of the seven-year cycle;[26] in short, to basic subsistence guarantees. These were not self-sufficient "peasants" but people reliant on charity to survive. Indeed, the Mishnah takes care to ensure that only those truly in need benefit from these rights (*m. Peah* 8:8–9). The notion that a self-sufficient farmer, or even a self-sufficient tenant, would avail himself of them is anathema to the sages.

It should be evident that the portrait of village life emerging from the early rabbinic texts is not more optimistic than the standard view. It is optimistic only insofar as the relative sophistication of the economy and comfort of the rural well-to-do and those in the middling range were concerned. One must not forget those at the bottom of the spectrum. The circumstances of even those who owned small plots and cattle of their own could be quite dire, as another Tosephtan passage shows, once again reflecting the interests of the privileged:

> A worker has no right to do his own work by night and to hire himself out by day, to plow with his cow by night and to hire it out in the morning. Nor may he deprive himself of food and starve himself in order to give his food to his children, on account of the robbery of his labor, which belongs to the householder. (*t. B. Meṣiʿa* 8:2)

### *How These Data Fit into the Results of Anthropological Fieldwork*

What does all of this rabbinic material suggest about inner village life in Roman Palestine, including the Galilee? The results of anthropological fieldwork provide some insight. We seem to see the "structures of 'neighbourly' exploitation often linked within complex networks of 'patronage,'" which even a continuing advocate of the peasant model, Teodor Shanin, concedes exists in "*every* peasant community."[27]

"Yet," Shanin also insists, "to most of the peasants, inter-peasant inequality and exploitation is secondary to the extra-peasant one."[28] The observations recorded by James Scott, based on two years of ethnographic fieldwork (1978–80) in a Malaysian village, contradict this asser-

---

26. Jacob Neusner discusses these in "The Mishnah and Aristotle's Economics," in his *The Mishnah: Social Perspectives* (Handbuch der Orientalistik, Der Nahe und Mittlere Orient 46; Leiden: Brill, 1970), 189–90, 192–93. One who does not follow these regulations is explicitly said to be a "robber of the poor" (*m. Peah* 5:6; 7:3).

27. Teodor Shanin, "Defining Peasants: Conceptualisations and De-Conceptualisations: Old and New in a Marxist Debate," *Sociological Review* 30 (1982): 407–32, esp. 420 (emphasis added).

28. Ibid.

tion. The poor in this village, Scott reports, focused far more on the inequalities between themselves and their well-to-do neighbors than on those between themselves and wealthy people living outside the village. They tended to "dwell upon the *local and personal causes* of their distress," rather than on "the larger context of agrarian capitalism" in which they lived.[29] Nor did the people in this village share a similar peasant cognitive orientation. On the one hand, the well-to-do claimed that they were barely making do and generous to a fault to those less fortunate than themselves, while, on the other, the poor declared that the situation in the village was "one of great inequities, where a few privileged monopolize the land and income, where the poor live from hand to mouth and are without prospects, and where generosity is rare and insufficient."[30]

Based on her own field work in Anglophone West Africa and South India, Polly Hill likewise argues that the attitudes and motivations of "cultivators with one acre are bound to be very different from those with five, twenty, or forty acres."[31] She also observes that—while it is true that villages do feel corporate responsibility to assist those who are starving and that there are customary mechanisms for rendering communal assistance—in general "the rich are admired, feared and envied; and the gravely impoverished are pitied, despised and helped by some people."[32]

### An Overview of the Archaeological Data from Middle Roman–Byzantine Times

Uzi Leibner's recently published extensive survey of Eastern Galilee calls into question the consensus view (as framed by David Goodblatt) that Palestine, including the Galilee, "reached its highest population density ever (until the twentieth century) precisely in the Byzantine period."[33] Instead, at least in the Galilee, it appears that it was during the Middle Roman period that settlement reached its apex, and this increase over the Early Roman period was due mainly to a growth in the sizes of the already occupied settlements, with only a few new settlements being established.[34] Rather than continued growth into Byzantine times, there was apparently a dramatic decline in the number of settlements, beginning in the mid-third century but mainly in the fourth century (ca. 250–400 CE). The decline was steady, so it appears

29. James C. Scott, *Weapons of the Weak: Everyday Forms of Peasant Resistance* (New Haven: Yale University Press, 1985), 182 (emphases mine).

30. Ibid., 202–4.

31. Polly Hill, *Development Economics on Trial: The Anthropological Case for a Prosecution* (Cambridge: Cambridge University Press, 1986), 70.

32. Ibid., 71.

33. David Goodblatt, "The Political and Social History of the Jewish Community in the Land of Israel, c. 235–638," in Katz, *Cambridge History of Judaism*, 4:404–30; quotation from 406. Safrai also argues for this demographic peak in the Byzantine period (*Economy of Roman Palestine*, 436–58).

34. Uzi Leibner, *Settlement and History in Hellenistic, Roman, and Byzantine Galilee: An Archaeological Survey of the Eastern Galilee* (TSAJ 127; Tübingen: Mohr Siebeck, 2009), 345–49.

to have been an ongoing process rather than due to any specific event, although it is probably related to the mid-fourth-century crisis in the empire at large.[35]

Leibner's work is a valuable corrective to earlier views that saw the Byzantine period as a "golden age" in ancient Palestine. Nevertheless, Leibner's argument that the early Byzantine period was one of economic hardship also cannot be sustained. For, as Leibner himself concedes, along with the demographic decline came the development of considerable trade with distant regions that had been of negligible significance before.[36]

### An Example: The Upper Galilean Village of Ancient Meiron

I have examined in detail the example of the Lower Galilean village of Capernaum elsewhere.[37] Another well-published village site, exemplifying the above-mentioned features with some variations, is Meiron in Upper Galilee.[38] The excavators set the apogee of village life in the Late Roman period (250–360 CE), although the settlement also thrived in Middle Roman times. Significantly, however, in line with Leibner's survey results for Eastern Galilee, there was a sharp decline in settlement in the mid-fourth century.[39]

In comparison with Late Roman and Byzantine Meiron, the Middle Roman trade networks in which the village of Meiron participated were much more limited in extent. Nevertheless, it is also clear that the village already thrived in Middle Roman times, as is evident in the large, two-story domestic-industrial complex, including both living quarters and workshops, built in the Middle Roman period and renovated in the Late Roman Period (and thus occupied ca. 135–360 CE). The remains and finds clearly show that workshops and storage rooms were located on the ground floor surrounding the large central courtyard, while the living quarters, which included plastered walls and various luxury items, were located on the second floor.[40]

This building is a good example of the nature of much industrial and commercial activity in Roman Palestine, with workshops and shops located in domestic contexts. That is, although production was highly specialized, most of it was small-scale and took place within peoples' houses, with larger workshops and agricultural complexes having been more the exception than the rule. Still, such small-scale industry could reap decent returns. Indicators of some

---

35. Ibid., 351–89.

36. Ibid.

37. Sharon Lea Mattila, "Revisiting Jesus' Capernaum: A Village of Only Subsistence-Level Fishers and Farmers?" in *The Galilean Economy in the Time of Jesus* (ed. David A. Fiensy and Ralph K. Hawkins; Early Christianity and Its Literature 11; Atlanta: Society of Biblical Literature, 2013), 75–138. This article includes discussion of the later periods as well.

38. Eric M. Meyers, James F. Strange, and Carol L. Meyers, *Excavations at Ancient Meiron, Upper Galilee, Israel, 1971–72, 1974–75, 1977* (Meiron Excavation Project 3; Cambridge, Mass.: American Schools of Oriental Research, 1981).

39. Ibid., 23–41.

40. Ibid., 31–38.

wealth found among this Meiron building's remains include fine glassware, including decorated bowls, both molded and blown, bottles, and plates. Fine decorated lamps dating from the
Middle to Late Roman periods and some jewelry were also recovered.[41]

In the Late Roman period (ca. 250 CE), the Patrician House and the Lintel House were
founded on bedrock on what appears to have been virgin terrain farther up the hill. These
houses were abandoned around 360 CE. After this date, a smaller Byzantine structure was built
on top of the northwestern part of the now deserted and crumbling Late Roman Patrician
House.[42] The village declined but the long-distance trade continued, although in abated form.
Still, this is when most of the imported fine red-slipped wares arrived in the village.

### *Important Evidence for Local Trade in Roman Times*

The thriving nature of local production and trade in Roman Galilee, and even of interregional trade with the Golan, is indicated by the thousands of fragments of cooking vessels that
have been designated "Kefar Ḥananya" ware, on account of David Adan-Bayewitz's pioneering study, which attributed the production center of this ware to this village.[43] While Kefar
Ḥananya, a village situated on the border between the Upper and Lower Galilee, was no doubt
a major supplier of this ware, more recent work has shown that the ware was also apparently
produced at Yodefat/Jotapata, and probably at other Galilean villages.[44] Adan-Bayewitz further
found (in conjunction with Isadore Perlman) that the village of Shikhin adjacent to Sepphoris
was the manufacturing center of the common Galilean storage jar, starting in the first century
BCE until about the mid-third century CE.[45] This storage jar was also marketed in both the
Galilee and the Golan. Moreover, rabbinic sources single out these two Galilean villages, Shikhin explicitly for its storage jars and Kefar Ḥananya for its cooking ware. It was not until the
early Byzantine period that this marketing pattern began to be undermined, and by about the
fourth decade of the fifth century CE the extensive marketing network of Kefar Ḥananya wares
ceased to exist.[46]

It is no longer possible to dismiss the importance of this ware and its implications for
local production and trade.[47] Leibner refers to "thousands of cooking vessels from the Roman

---

41. See the plates in ibid., 221, 223–25, 228–30.

42. Ibid., 50–51. The Patrician House was not built all at once but underwent various additions and altera-
tions that the excavators were not able to trace out clearly (ibid., 55).

43. David Adan-Bayewitz, *Common Pottery in Roman Galilee: A Study of Local Trade* (Bar-Ilan Studies in
Near Eastern Languages and Culture; Ramat-Gan: Bar Ilan University Press, 1993).

44. Mordechai Aviam, "People, Land, Economy, and Belief in First-Century Galilee and Its Origins: A
Comprehensive Archaeological Synthesis," in Fiensy and Hawkins, *Galilean Economy in the Time of Jesus*, 5–48,
esp. 27–28.

45. David Adan-Bayewitz and Isadore Perlman, "The Local Trade of Sepphoris in the Roman Period," *IEJ*
40 (1990): 153–72. See the chapter by James Riley Strange on Kefar Shikhin in volume 2 of this series.

46. Adan-Bayewitz, *Common Pottery in Roman Galilee*, 23–41, 201–23, 248; Adan-Bayewitz and Perlman,
"Local Trade of Sepphoris," 153–72.

47. As does Schwartz, "Political, Social, and Economic Life," 40 n. 54.

period that were collected," the overwhelming majority of which were of the Kefar Ḥananya type. Only a relatively small number of further examples of the Shikhin storage jar, however, were found; hence, these appear to have been traded in more limited numbers over a much more limited range.[48]

Another indication of vibrant local trade is found in the number of structures excavated in village contexts that were probably shops. For instance, in his survey of ancient Palestinian villages, Yizhar Hirschfeld discusses various examples of excavated buildings that have been interpreted as shops, especially small structures associated with larger houses.[49] He concludes:

> The increasing number of houses with shops discovered to date in archaeological excavations may reflect the commonness of such structures in the Roman-Byzantine period, as implied in the rabbinic sources which suggest that several shops existed in every settlement.[50]

Peter Richardson classifies the "shop-dwelling" as a major type of structure commonly found from the Hellenistic through to the Byzantine periods "in small towns and villages, and even larger cities."[51]

### Was Ancient Galilean Village Life "Modern"?

From all of these data there emerges a portrait of Middle Roman–Byzantine Palestine that largely confirms the picture for this period painted by Safrai.[52] Is such a portrait, as Schwartz contends, "a modern-sounding characterization of the economy of rural Galilee," or an unconstrained "modernizing description of the ancient Palestinian economy"?[53]

There is nothing whatever "modern-sounding" or "modernizing" about it. While there was a large degree of division of labor and production was highly specialized, industrial activity was also small in scale, with most workshops located in people's houses. Textile production involved a symbiotic exchange between housewives and specialists. Overland transport of goods was by donkey and on foot, with the more international imports and exports of the Byzantine period making the large part of their journey by sea. All of the technology involved in food, wine, oil, and craft production was ancient.[54] Permanent and periodic markets and other forms of market exchange took place within the context of ancient social structures.

---

48. Leibner, *Settlement and History*, 52–54.

49. See, for example, Yizhar Hirschfeld, *The Palestinian Dwelling in the Roman-Byzantine Periods* (Jerusalem: Israel Exploration Society, 1995), 28–29, 33–38, 67, 78–79, 98–99.

50. Ibid., 99 n. 103.

51. Peter Richardson, "Towards a Typology of Levantine/Palestinian Houses," *JSNT* 27 (2004): 57–60.

52. Safrai, *Economy of Roman Palestine*, passim.

53. Schwartz, "Political, Social, and Economic Life," 40–41.

54. Rafael Frankel examines in meticulous detail the diverse technology involved in the preindustrial production of wine and oil in particular in Israel and elsewhere, covering the centuries from the Iron Age to the Middle

In sum, the relative sophistication and complexity of rural socioeconomic life in Roman and Byzantine Palestine were not "modern." They were ancient.

### Corroborating Evidence from the Very Early Rabbinic Period

Strictly speaking, of course, the Tannaitic literature is not a direct source of evidence for any period prior to the second century CE, and some would argue only late in that century. Yet the fact that local craftsmanship in Palestine was already highly specialized at the latest by the late first century to early second century CE is amply confirmed by the finds in the Cave of Letters, dating to before the end of the Bar Kokhba Revolt (135 CE). It is likely that many, if not most, of these objects once belonged to villagers because they were found in the vicinity of the archive of Babatha, from the village of Maḥoza.

Beautiful, high-quality woolen textiles were recovered, some bearing weavers' marks, often woven in various colors with "large quantities of decorative patterns," as Yigael Yadin reports. "All our finds show that textile manufacturing and dyeing were on a very high level among the Jews in the first centuries A.D."[55]

Discovered along with these finds was the archive of a relatively affluent Jewish woman from the village of Maḥoza on the southern shore of the Dead Sea, named Babatha (בבתא; βαβαθα).[56] The thirty-five documents of this archive—six Nabatean, three Aramaic, and twenty-six Greek (nine of which have subscriptions and signatures in Aramaic and Nabatean)—date from 93/94 to 132 CE (*P. Yadin* 1–35). They afford us a rare, detailed, and concrete snapshot of a series of legal property and business proceedings undertaken by a well-to-do rural Jewish woman and her family.

From Babatha's census declaration (*P. Yadin* 16), it is clear that a large amount of property eventually came into her possession. Four date groves are listed, and Babatha also states that she is "domiciled in my own private properties in the said Maoza" (line 14), clearly implying that she had also inherited the family real estate. Not only was Babatha a young woman of some means; she was also quite enterprising. She had loaned her second husband, Judah, a lump

---

Ages in *Wine and Oil Production in Antiquity in Israel and Other Mediterranean Countries* (JSOT/ASOR Monograph Series 10; Sheffield: Sheffield Academic Press, 1999).

55. Yigael Yadin, *The Finds from the Bar Kokhba Period in the Cave of Letters* (Judean Desert Studies; Jerusalem: Israel Exploration Society, 1963), 170, 176, 225. One must examine the colored plates to see how gorgeous some of the colored designs are: see plates 60–69. For the weavers' marks, see plates 69 and 85.

56. This archive has now been fully published in two volumes: Naphtali Lewis, Yigael Yadin, and Jonas C. Greenfield, eds., *The Documents from the Bar Kokhba Period in the Cave of Letters: Greek Papyri and Aramaic and Nabatean Signatures and Subscriptions* (Judean Desert Studies 2; Jerusalem: Israel Exploration Society, 1989); Yigael Yadin, Jonas C. Greenfield, Ada Yardeni, and Baruch A. Levine, eds., *The Documents from the Bar Kokhba Period in the Cave of Letters: Hebrew, Aramaic, and Nabatean-Aramaic Papyri* (Judean Desert Studies; Jerusalem: Israel Exploration Society, 2002). Another woman's archive, containing one Aramaic document and six Greek, was found in the Naḥal Ḥever: that of Salome Komaïse, daughter of Levi, who seems to have known Babatha, since "their families' properties were abutted by the same neighbours" (Hannah M. Cotton and Ada Yardeni, *Aramaic, Hebrew and Greek Documentary Texts from Naḥal Ḥever and Other Sites* [DJD 27; Oxford: Clarendon Press, 1997], 159).

sum of three hundred denarii toward the five-hundred-denarii dowry of her step-daughter, Shelamzion (*P. Yadin* 17 and 18). When he died and his estate failed to repay that loan and her own dowry, she seized three date groves that had been his (*P. Yadin* 21–24).

To be sure, this villager and her family were far from being as wealthy as a Roman senatorial family, nor did their affluence come close to matching that of the Herodian and high-priestly families who had lived a generation or two before them when Jerusalem was still the religious, and thus also the economic, center of late Second Temple Judaism. But they were also far removed from being subsistence-oriented "peasants," and not only on account of their relative affluence. It is also because their income was derived predominantly from the cultivation of a single, albeit lucrative, crop: dates. It is essential to keep in mind the degree of market dependence that this would have necessitated. Babatha and her family, of course, did not subsist on dates alone. Not only would they have had to sell the major part of their crop in the market, but they would also have been compelled to rely entirely on the market for all of their basic staple supplies of grain, oil, and wine—never mind more specialized goods.

Was it only in the Judean Desert that sophisticated craft and agricultural specialization existed so soon after the temple fell? The dry climate of the Judean Desert has preserved these important items from the late first to the early second centuries; they would have had little chance of surviving to the present day in the Galilee. It would be unreasonable, I would submit, to insist that it was only in the Judean Desert that the kind of sophisticated local production suggested above existed so soon after the temple fell. Parallels found in the Mishnah suggest that almost identical items were produced in the Galilee in the second century. In addition, the facts that many Galilean settlements continued to thrive after the revolt, and that all of the archaeological and literary evidence that the Galilee was far more fertile, productive, and densely populated than the Judean Desert and even reached its peak settlement in the second century, surely render such an argument highly suspect.

This leads us now to the earlier, Hasmonean–Early Roman periods, discussed in the next section. Did such highly developed local trade and specialization develop in a mere couple of generations out of the ruins of the Great Revolt?

## Discontinuity and Continuity with Earlier Times

### *Points of Discontinuity*

There are certainly some important respects in which Jewish Palestine of the late Second Temple period was different from later times. By Jewish Palestine, I mean many of the settlements in the Galilee and the lower Golan. There is no need for me to argue here that by the first century BCE these had become predominantly Jewish and closely interconnected culturally, religiously, and ideologically, with the then-great center of Jerusalem. This has already been done at length with such compelling force of evidence that I am frankly perplexed that it should be any longer a matter of debate.[57] The cumulative evidence overwhelmingly points to the Jewish nature of these settlements by the first century BCE and in some cases earlier.

The distinctive features of Hasmonean–Early Roman Jewish Palestine, evident in both the literary sources and the archaeological record from Jewish settlements in Judea, the Galilee, and the Golan, are now well known. First, in striking contrast to the later periods, figurative art was scrupulously avoided.[58] The zeal with which the Jews of these times adhered to the law forbidding images of "any living creatures" (Josephus, *Ant.* 17.151–52) is illustrated by the burning of Antipas's palace in Tiberias because it contained images of animals (Josephus, *Life* 65–66), and by the two "sages" and their young followers, who paid with their lives for tearing down the golden eagle over the great gate of the temple (Josephus, *J. W.* 1.651–55; *Ant.* 17.149–65). The latter incident is especially striking in contrast to how often eagles decorate the synagogues of late antiquity.

Second, an extensive—albeit not ubiquitous and certainly not uniform—concern for ritual purity spread throughout Jewish Palestine in Hasmonean–Early Roman times. The evidence for this stems not only from our primary literary sources but also from archaeological evidence, including stepped immersion pools for ritual cleansing (*mikva'ot*; singular, *mikveh*), some of which were associated with oil and wine presses, and locally produced stone vessels (unsusceptible to impurity), which appear at virtually all Jewish sites beginning in the first century BCE but proliferating especially during the first century CE.[59] Stone vessel production was a thriving local industry in this period, with a wide distribution all over Jewish Palestine and

---

57. The main study is Mark A. Chancey, *The Myth of a Gentile Galilee* (SNTSMS 118; Cambridge: Cambridge University Press, 2002). See also Jonathan L. Reed, "Galileans, 'Israelite Village Communities,' and the Sayings Gospel Q," in *Galilee through the Centuries: Confluence of Cultures* (ed. Eric M. Meyers; Duke Judaic Studies Series 1; Winona Lake, Ind.: Eisenbrauns, 1999), 87–108.

58. See, for example, Nahman Avigad, *Discovering Jerusalem* (Nashville: Thomas Nelson, 1983), 154–60; and Eric M. Meyers, "Jesus and His Galilean Context," in *Archaeology and the Galilee: Texts and Contexts in the Graeco-Roman and Byzantine Periods* (ed. Douglas R. Edwards and C. Thomas McCollough; South Florida Studies in the History of Judaism 143; Atlanta: Scholars Press, 1997), 57–66, esp. 59–60. For the few exceptions that prove the rule, see Jodi Magness, *Stone and Dung, Oil and Spit: Jewish Daily Life in the Time of Jesus* (Grand Rapids: Eerdmans, 2011) 221 n. 80.

59. This has been argued quite comprehensively by Thomas Kazen in his *Issues of Impurity in Early Judaism* (Coniectanea biblica: New Testament 45; Winona Lake, Ind.: Eisenbrauns, 2010) and *Jesus and Purity Halakah: Was Jesus Indifferent to Impurity?* (rev. ed.; Coniectanea biblica: New Testament 38; Winona Lake, Ind.: Eisenbrauns, 2010). For a brief and well-documented survey of the evidence for *mikva'ot* and the stone-vessel industry, see Magness, *Stone and Dung*, 16–17, 70–74. It must nevertheless be mentioned that the extent and nature of Jewish purity observance in late Second Temple times is still the subject of considerable debate. For a basic bibliography on Jewish purity laws representing the spectrum of opinion, see John P. Meier, *A Marginal Jew: Rethinking the Historical Jesus*, vol. 4, *Law and Love* (Anchor Yale Bible Reference Library; New Haven: Yale University Press, 2009), 415–26 (but see Kazen's critique of Meier's own discussion of Jesus and purity *halakhah* [*Issues of Impurity*, 151–67]). For a strong critique of the "minimalist" position in this debate, see John C. Poirier, "Purity beyond the Temple in the Second Temple Era," *JBL* 122 (2003): 247–65.

centers of production in Jerusalem, elsewhere in Judea, and even in the Galilee itself. Some of the stone items produced were of very high quality and no doubt quite expensive.[60]

As Mordechai Aviam has summed it up, also in marked contrast to later times, Jews avoided "almost all kinds" of imported vessels, "a distinctive phenomenon" of the Hasmonean-Herodian period, quite akin to the avoidance of figurative art.[61] While this avoidance was not at all absolute (and Aviam does not assert that it was), it was nevertheless marked.

A good example is the distribution pattern of a fine red-slipped table ware called Eastern Terra Sigillata A (ETSA), produced during the first centuries BCE and CE all along the eastern Mediterranean coast, with Antioch and Tyre serving as major production centers, but also with others, from just north of Antioch down through the Sharon Plain.[62] In contrast to Byzantine fine ware, which was ubiquitous at pagan and Jewish sites alike, at virtually all Jewish sites in Hasmonean and Early Roman times, ETSA was apparently nowhere near as popular as it was among pagans. For instance, 23,756 fragments of ETSA were recovered at pagan Tel Anafa, situated eight kilometers south of Tel Dan in the northern part of the Ḥula Valley east of the Jordan, a site that reached its *floruit* during the heyday of the independent Jewish Hasmonean kings (128–80 BCE).[63] In contrast, this ware is "conspicuous by its absence" from no less an edifice than the Hasmonean palace complex at Jericho.[64] During the time of Herod and his descendants (starting in ca. 31 BCE), some sherds of ETSA do show up at Jericho, although it must be underscored that even then their occurrence is still rather limited compared with pagan sites.[65] The finds thus far published from the Jewish Quarter of Jerusalem likewise sug-

---

60. Yitzhak Magen, *The Stone Vessel Industry in the Second Temple Period: Excavations at Ḥizma and the Jerusalem Temple Mount* (Judea and Samaria Publications 1; ed. Levana Tsfania; Jerusalem: Israel Exploration Society, 2002), passim; Mordechai Aviam, "Distribution Maps of Archaeological Data from the Galilee: An Attempt to Establish Zones Indicative of Ethnicity and Religious Affiliation," in *Religion, Ethnicity, and Identity in Ancient Galilee: A Region in Transition* (ed. Jürgen Zangenberg, Harold W. Attridge, and Dale B. Martin; WUNT 210; Tübingen: Mohr Siebeck, 2007), 115–32, esp. 119–20. Aviam mentions "the survey find of a Galilean stone-vessel workshop near Nazareth" ("First Century Jewish Galilee: An Archaeological Perspective," in *Religion and Society in Roman Palestine: Old Questions, New Approaches* [ed. Douglas R. Edwards; New York: Routledge, 2004], 7–27, esp. 20).

61. Aviam, "First Century Jewish Galilee," 23.

62. Andrea Berlin, personal communication, 2008.

63. See Kathleen Warner Slane, "The Fine Wares," in *Tel Anafa II.1: The Hellenistic and Roman Pottery* (ed. Sharon C. Herbert; Journal of Roman Archaeology Supplementary Series 10; Ann Arbor, Mich.: Kelsey Museum of the University of Michigan, 1997), 249–406, esp. 255, 261–64, 272. On the site of Tel Anafa in general, see Sharon C. Herbert, "Introduction," and "Occupational History and Stratigraphy," in *Tel Anafa I.1: Final Report on Ten Years of Excavation at a Hellenistic and Roman Settlement in Northern Israel* (ed. Sharon C. Herbert; Journal of Roman Archaeology Supplementary Series 10; Ann Arbor, Mich.: Kelsey Museum of the University of Michigan, 1994), 1–25, 26–182, esp. 16 and 32–33.

64. Rachel Bar-Nathan, *Hasmonean and Herodian Palaces at Jericho: Final Reports of the 1973–1987 Excavations*, vol. 3, *The Pottery* (Jerusalem: Israel Exploration Society, 2002), 119–20, 197. See the plans of the Hasmonean palace complex in Ehud Netzer, ed., *Hasmonean and Herodian Palaces at Jericho: Final Reports of the 1973–1987 Excavations* (3 vols. Jerusalem: Israel Exploration Society, 2001), vol. 1.

65. Bar-Nathan, *Hasmonean and Herodian Palaces at Jericho*, 3:119–20, 129, 190–91, 199–203.

gest that ETSA started to arrive in the city "probably not before the middle of the 1st century BCE," or not long before Herod's reign, and even afterwards "the ware was not as popular as on sites with Greek and Phoenician connections like Tel Anafa, Samaria and Maresha."[66]

This is especially remarkable, given that at pagan sites it was not only the people at the highest end of the socioeconomic stratum who purchased ETSA. For example, even the new, much humbler Early Roman settlers of Tel Anafa—who, after a settlement gap of over half a century, built much simpler dwellings on top of the abandoned late Hellenistic "villa"—continued to import substantial quantities of it.[67] Indeed, the fragments of ETSA are far fewer in number at Gamla, a much larger settlement, in comparison with the large quantities found at Tel Anafa.[68] ETSA is totally absent at Yodefat/Jotapata in the Galilee.[69]

Also striking is the dramatic decline in numbers, beginning in Hasmonean times, of the imported stamped amphorae of the earlier Hellenistic period at Capernaum, Jerusalem, and other Jewish sites.[70] As was the case for ETSA, the priestly elite of Jerusalem purchased some imported amphorae in the Herodian period, but in substantially fewer quantities than at pagan sites.[71] Neither ETSA nor stamped handles of imported amphorae have thus far been found in any of the excavations of rural settlements in the land of Benjamin (just north of Jerusalem), nor in excavations of the town of the Hellenistic period on Mount Gerizim (in Samaria). The large number of coins and substantial industrial installations for the production of wine and olive oil found in the Benjamin settlements surely indicate that the absence of these imported products was likewise not due to economic reasons.[72]

It was not only gentile luxury products like ETSA and imported wine that were avoided. "Galilean Coarse Ware" (GCW), a locally produced ware that occurs in Persian and pre-Hasmonean Hellenistic pagan contexts in Upper and northern Lower Galilee, disappears from the region in the Hasmonean period. Some of the GCW sites were abandoned in the wake of

---

66. Renate Rosenthal-Heginbottom, "Chapter 6 (b): Hellenistic and Roman Fine Ware and Lamps from Area A," in *The Finds from Areas A, W and X-2. FINAL REPORT*, vol. 2 of *Jewish Quarter Excavations in the Old City of Jerusalem Conducted by Nahman Avigad, 1969–1982* (ed. Hillel Geva; Jerusalem: Israel Exploration Society, 2003), 192–223, esp. 214, 219–20.

67. Slane, "Fine Wares," 264; and see Andrea M. Berlin, "Romanization and Anti-Romanization in Pre-Revolt Galilee," in *The First Jewish Revolt: Archaeology, History, and Ideology* (ed. Andrea M. Berlin and J. Andrew Overman; London: Routledge, 2002), 57–73, esp. 62, figure 4.1.

68. See Berlin, "Romanization and Anti-Romanization," 62, figure 4.1.

69. Aviam, "First Century Jewish Galilee," 19.

70. Donald T. Ariel and Aryeh Strikovsky, "Appendix," in *Excavations at the City of David 1978–1985 Directed by Yigal Shiloh*, vol. 2, *Imported Stamped Amphora Handles, Coins, Worked Bone and Ivory, and Glass* (ed. Donald T. Ariel; Qedem 30; Jerusalem: Institute of Archaeology, Hebrew University of Jerusalem, 1990), 25–29.

71. Magness, *Stone and Dung*, 54–58.

72. As observed by Yitzhak Magen, "The Land of Benjamin in the Second Temple Period," in *The Land of Benjamin* (ed. Yitzhak Magen et al.; Judea and Samaria Publications; Jerusalem: Israel Antiquities Authority, 2004), 1–28, esp. 18–21. Magen also notes that *mikva'ot* were discovered in conjunction with wine and oil presses in this region (ibid.).

the Hasmonean conquest, and others continued to exist but now with Hasmonean coins and no GCW.[73]

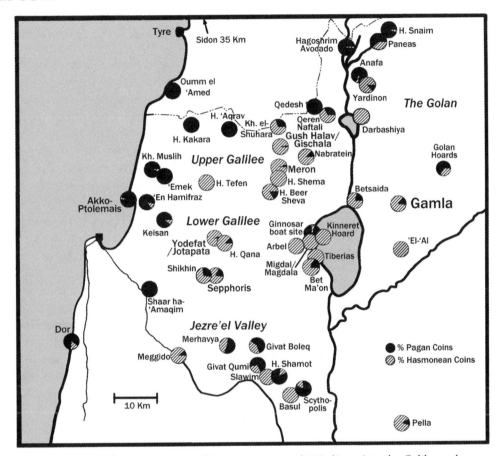

**Figure A.** Coins from pagan versus Hasmonean mints (125–40 BCE) in the Galilee and the Golan. Based on Danny Syon, "Tyre and Gamla: A Study in the Monetary Influence of Southern Phoenicia on Galilee and the Golan in the Hellenistic and Roman Periods" (PhD diss., Hebrew University, Jerusalem, 2004), p. 230, map 19, including only sites with n > 5. Map used by permission.

As many have recognized for some time now, and as Danny Syon has shown persuasively and in detail, the numismatic data also confirm this Jewish-versus-pagan profile.[74] See figure A for a distribution map of the coins minted in the Hasmonean period (125–40 BCE), indicating

73. See Aviam, "Distribution Maps," 115–18; and Aviam, "First Century Jewish Galilee," 7–15.
74. Syon, "Tyre and Gamla."

the relative proportions of pagan versus Hasmonean coins, specifically for the Galilee and the Golan, based on Syon's work. Whereas the sites that can be identified as Jewish on the basis of the other archaeological indicators mentioned above display what is often a large preponderance of Hasmonean coins in comparison with pagan issues, the pagan sites display precisely the opposite pattern.[75]

What is more, at Jewish sites occupied prior to Hasmonean times one sees a dramatic decline in the number of pagan coins arriving at these sites, which correlates with the arrival of the Hasmonean coins and with the emergence of other Jewish indicators. Beginning especially during the reign of Alexander Jannaeus, Hasmonean bronze coins almost entirely displaced those of gentile origin at Jewish sites throughout Judea, the Galilee, and the Golan.[76] Pagan sites, in contrast, exhibit few Hasmonean coins.[77] As Syon notes, however, "this phenomenon usually does not touch upon the circulation of silver coinage, as there was no Jewish alternative to the silver sheqels of Tyre until the Great Revolt, and these blatantly pagan sheqels were used by Jews even for the temple dues . . . and certainly for trade."[78]

This Jewish-versus-pagan contrast in the archaeological record of Hasmonean and Herodian Palestine most likely reflects not only the widespread Jewish concern for purity but also Jewish nationalism. What remains quite clear is that during late Second Temple times a widespread regard for *halakhah*, and probably a closely intertwined spirit of religious nationalism inherited from the Maccabean Revolt and the time of Jewish independence, gave rise to deliberately introverted trade patterns on the part of the Jews.

On the one hand, it is important not to exaggerate the extent of this introversion in trade. The presence of some pagan coins, ETSA, and other imported items at Jewish sites, for instance, attests to some trade with pagans. On the other hand, a marked preference on the part of the Jews of this period to trade with their fellow Jews and only comparatively seldom with pagans is the most reasonable conclusion to draw from this clear pattern displayed by all the data.

It is in this light that the oft-cited passage from Josephus, routinely adduced in support of the supposed economic backwardness of Palestine in the period, is best understood. In *Against Apion* 1.60, Josephus famously describes his homeland thus:

Well then, neither do we dwell in a coastal region [of the Mediterranean Sea], nor do we take delight in sea trade or the dealings with others that arise from it. Instead,

---

75. It is instructive to compare this distribution map with those for this period found in Aviam, "Distribution Maps," 118–19, esp. maps 3 and 4, showing the distribution of ritual baths and stone vessels.

76. For an overview of the numismatic evidence, which amply reflects this displacement in the Galilee, see Mark A. Chancey, *Greco-Roman Culture and the Galilee of Jesus* (SNTSMS 134; Cambridge: Cambridge University Press, 2005), 167–92.

77. Aviam, "First Century Jewish Galilee," 14–15.

78. Syon, "Tyre and Gamla," 104.

our cities have been built inland far from the Sea and, enjoying as our own possession a fertile land, this we cultivate. . . . (my translation)

I translate the passage in this way because Josephus's use of the word ἐμπορία in this context requires it. The context is one in which he is defending the antiquity of his homeland by comparing it with the Phoenicians, in order to explain why the early Greek historians make no mention of the Jews, and his use of the same word elsewhere in the same context consistently and clearly refers to sea trade. Moreover, while it is true that ἐμπορία can sometimes mean commerce in general, according to LSJ it is "mostly used of commerce or trade by sea," whether in the singular or in the plural.

As this Josephan passage indicates, Jewish Palestine of the Hasmonean Herodian period appears quite deliberately to have engaged in only limited trade with their pagan neighbors, and only limited long-distance trade. But what about local trade and production? Did the high degree of local specialization, trade, and monetization, for which there is evidence already in the very early rabbinic period, arise no earlier than after the fall of the temple?

### Exploring the Question of Whether There Were Points of Continuity

A passage singled out by Lapin to demonstrate the remarkable extent to which the Mishnah presupposes a monetary economy is important because it is attributed to Hillel, who lived in Jerusalem ca. 30 BCE–10 CE. It reads: "For Hillel used to say: 'Let a woman not lend a loaf to her fellow until she has calculated its monetary value, lest wheat become more expensive and they will commit usury.'" (*m. B. Meṣi'a* 5:9)[79] In Lapin's summary, Hillel decreed that "all loans of commodities (even a neighborly loan of a loaf of bread) should be made on the monetary value of the commodities."[80] We see here not only evidence of high monetization but also a fascinating example of how credit arrangements within communities operated, with money serving as the unit of account for the quantity of debt incurred in even small, relatively informal loans.

But can it really be dated back to the time of Hillel? Or is this Mishnaic anachronism? I will not undertake here the probably impossible task of attempting to prove it originated with Hillel; at any rate this is not the most important point. What I argue is that the numismatic data indicate that it could have. This is because the dictum is concerned with loans between fellow Jews residing in the same community, and the numismatic data strongly suggest that specifically the local Jewish economy, not just of Jerusalem but of all Jewish Palestine, had become quite highly monetized by Hillel's time.

The numismatic data indicate an intense infusion of small change into the local Jewish economy, beginning in Jerusalem but spreading quite rapidly to sites in the Galilee and the Golan, starting during the reign of John Hyrcanus and intensifying especially under Alexander Jannaeus. The coins in question were mostly bronze Hasmonean *prutot*, or small change, and

---

79. Translation and Hebrew from Lapin, *Early Rabbinic Civil Law*, 193–94.
80. Ibid.; cf. 123–24, 232.

hence this phenomenon was probably not related to tax collection by the new rulers because the high-value Tyrian shekel remained the standard silver currency in the region and was the coin explicitly required for payment of the temple tax.[81]

As underscored by H. S. Kim, from the earliest period of monetization, bronze coins were small change, the lowest common denominator in coinage, unlikely to have been used between members of the upper strata and predominantly geared toward local economic transactions.[82] As Constantina Katsari frames it in her study of the Roman monetary system, bronze coins "paid for a large part of the wages, food, clothing and other needs of the lower social strata"; she notes that "[t]he overall picture of the Roman provinces implies a highly monetized economy" by the time of the Principate.[83] These coins tend to show signs of being extremely worn and of having had a long circulation life, which is very common among the Hasmonean coins but also for bronze change throughout the empire,[84] and it argues strongly that they were used mostly for day-to-day local transactions.

### Other Evidence of Trade and Socioeconomic Differentiation

The strong economic connections of both Gamla and Yodefat with Jerusalem are evident not only in the abundance of Hasmonean coins but also in the very high percentage of oil lamps made in Jerusalem that were found at both sites.[85] At Jotapata, moreover, excavations have uncovered a magnificent mansion in the village. This mansion had not only frescoed walls, including "the most vividly painted intact first-century wall in Israel," but even a frescoed floor, "the first of its type to be found in a private house in the Land of Israel." Only one other place in Israel has so far been found with a frescoed floor—a theater in Caesarea! In keeping with other frescoes from this period, neither the walls nor the floor contained any figurative art.[86]

The village appears to have specialized in textile production. Aviam reports over 250 pyramidal loom weights that were discovered there, "the largest number of loom weights ever found in residential areas of the land of Israel from the Roman period." In contrast, at Gamla, "where the excavated area was twice as large, only about ninety loom weights were discovered." C. Cope's analysis of the animal bones supports the conclusion that there was vigorous

---

81. My analysis depends heavily on Danny Syon's recent work, but also on Donald T. Ariel and Jean-Philippe Fontanille, *The Coins of Herod: A Modern Analysis and Die Classification* (Ancient Judaism and Early Christianity; Leiden: Brill, 2012); Ḥaim Gitler, "Chapter Twenty-Two: The Coins," in Geva, *Finds from Areas A, W and X-2. FINAL REPORT*, 453–92.

82. H. S. Kim, "Small Change and the Moneyed Economy," in *Money, Labour and Land: Approaches to the Economies of Ancient Greece* (ed. Paul Cartledge, Edward E. Cohen, and Lin Foxhall; London: Routledge, 2002), 44–51.

83. Constantina Katsari, *The Roman Monetary System: The Eastern Provinces from the First to the Third Century AD* (Cambridge: Cambridge University Press, 2011), 225.

84. Katsari speaks of these coins having become so worn that they were "indistinguishable from small nuggets of metal" (*Roman Monetary System*, 250).

85. Aviam, "People, Land, Economy," 33–35.

86. Ibid., 23–26, and see figure 13 for a photograph of the wall frescos.

production of woolen textiles in the village. "According to her study, not only are there more sheep bones than goat bones, but most of the sheep were killed at an older age," indicating that "sheep were grazed for wool and milk rather than meat only."[87] The discovery of a "potter's quarter" in the village suggests that Yodefat may also have been a center for the production of Kefar Hananya–type cooking pots, as already mentioned above.[88]

Excavations at Gamla have likewise unearthed evidence of wealthy villagers. Excavators designated the residential block called the Western Quarter by Syon, located to the north and to the west of the Early Roman oil press (Areas R and S), the "wealthy residential quarter." As at Jotapata, the residents of this quarter were wealthy enough to have had frescoed walls in their houses.[89] The white plaster found there was also "of excellent quality," and in addition an ornate lintel was discovered. In general, "the buildings were of dressed stone and the quality of construction high."[90] Other signs of some villagers' wealth at Gamala include some imported red-slipped ETSA (although not in the same quantity as at pagan sites and not after the end of the first century BCE), a variety of luminous beads, seals, and semiprecious stones and gems, several of which exhibit delicately executed carvings. Bronze, bone, and ivory utensils were found, as were dice made from the hucklebones of sheep, called *astragali*. A hoard of twenty-seven silver coins, including twenty Tyrian shekels and seven tetradrachmas from Antioch, was unearthed near the oil press in this wealthy part of the village.[91]

Of course, it is clear that not all villagers in either Gamla or Jotapata were this prosperous. Humbler houses uncovered in both villages show that they were socioeconomically mixed. A similar pattern was found at the Galilean village of Khirbet Qana. Indeed, Peter Richardson has noted that archaeologists of the region "are gradually developing a three-item typology" of "differentiated neighborhoods": "terrace housing without courtyards, side courtyard houses, and central courtyard houses."[92]

We also find in Josephus's description of his time in the Galilee evidence of well-to-do villagers. He makes various references to "the village magistrates of the Galileans," local "powerful men" (*Life* 79; *J.W.* 2.569–71), "the principal men of the Galilee" (*Life* 220; cf. 266–68), the "leading men of the Galileans" (*Life* 305), the "rich people" of the Upper Galilean village of

---

87. Cope's report was given in Aviam, "People, Land, Economy," 27, n. 40.

88. Ibid., 27–28.

89. See Danny Syon, "Gamla: Portrait of a Rebellion," *BAR* 18, no. 1 (1992): 20–37; esp. 33, with photo; S. Gutman, "Gamala," in *NEAEHL* 2: 459–63, esp. 462–63. Also see the photograph in the Hebrew report (Shemaryah Gutman and Joel Rappel, *Gamla—A City in Rebellion* [in Hebrew; Tel Aviv: Misrad Habitahon, 1994], 128).

90. Gutman, "Gamala," 462. See the plans in Gutman, "Gamala," 459; Syon, "Gamla: Portrait of a Rebellion," 22; and in the Hebrew report (Gutman and Rappel, *Gamla*, 129).

91. Syon, "Gamla: Portrait of a Rebellion," 23–24, 34–35, with photos; Gutman, "Gamala," 463. The final full report on the pottery has recently been published. See Andrea I. Berlin, *Gamla: Final Reports*, vol. 1, *The Pottery of the Second Temple Period* (IAA Reports 29; Jerusalem: Israel Antiquities Authority, 2006).

92. Richardson, "Khirbet Qana (and Other Villages) as a Context for Jesus," in *Jesus and Archaeology* (ed. James H. Charlesworth; Grand Rapids: Eerdmans, 2006), 133–35.

Gischala (*J. W.* 2.590), the "powerful men" or "men of distinction" of the Lower Galilean village of Yodefat/Jotapata (*J. W.* 3.193, 341–42), whose wealth has been impressively confirmed by the archaeological record mentioned above, the owners of the houses at Chabulon in the Lower Galilee, "built in the style of those in Tyre, Sidon, and Berytus," whose beauty inspired the amazed admiration of no less a personage than the Roman general Cestius Gallus (*J. W.* 2.504), and Jesus of Gabara, whose house "was a great castle, no less imposing than an acropolis" (*Life* 246). There is also, of course, the famous story of John of Gischala, who was able to procure sufficient capital in Tyrian shekels to purchase the entire olive crop of a bumper year (*J. W.* 2.591–92; *Life* 73–74).

On the other end of the socioeconomic spectrum were the destitute mentioned in a saying that has a high likelihood of having originated with the historical Jesus:[93] "How fortunate are the destitute [οἱ πτωχοί]! For it is to them that the kingdom of God belongs. How fortunate are those who go hungry! For they shall be well fed" (Luke 6:20-21). These destitute people, Jesus' words make clear, were so impoverished that they suffered chronically from pangs of hunger.

In sum, all the data strongly suggest that there was socioeconomic differentiation among villagers and a high degree of integration of Jewish villages of all sizes into the flourishing intra-Jewish trade networks of the Hasmonean–Early Roman periods, with substantial small change available to facilitate local market and intraregional market exchange, which penetrated far into the countryside. In these regards, there is continuity between earlier and later times in Greco-Roman and Byzantine Galilee. There is also discontinuity, however, in that Jewish villagers and urbanites alike did engage in market exchange with their pagan neighbors far less frequently than in later times. The villagers among the latter were likewise not market-averse "peasants," but highly integrated into their own trade networks, usually centered on the Phoenician towns.

Regarding the pagan sites, there is space here to consider only one well-published example, namely, Tel Anafa, already mentioned above. The site was abandoned finally in the mid-first century CE, so it is quite informative for the Late Hellenistic to Early Roman periods.[94] Tel Anafa's heyday was in ca. 130–80 BCE, as indicated by ceramic, architectural, and numismatic remains. This late Hellenistic settlement was dominated by a large, quite finely constructed domestic complex, perhaps a kind of villa, whose rather wealthy and cosmopolitan inhabitants imported many luxury items: thousands of cast glass bowls, enormous quantities of

---

93. Even the Fellows of the Jesus Seminar, well known for their methodological skepticism and their hesitancy to trace back any of the words found in the Gospels with certainty to the historical Jesus, "were virtually unanimous in the view that Jesus" was the author of this proclamation (*The Five Gospels: The Search for the Authentic Words of Jesus. New Translation and Commentary* [ed. Robert W. Funk and Roy W. Hoover; New York: Macmillan, 1993], 290).

94. At Tel Anafa "all permanent Roman era occupation of the site seems to have ended by the middle of the first century CE or slightly later" (Herbert, "Introduction," 22). Only "a very few items" from the later Roman periods were found, "that are probably relics of sporadic later visits to the site" (ibid.).

the red-slipped fine ware ETSA, and hundreds of wine amphorae from the Greek island of Rhodes.[95] There was in this period virtually no trade with Hasmonean-dominated Palestine to the south, as the "truly extraordinary" distinctiveness of the late Hellenistic plain wares "*vis-à-vis* other Palestinian assemblages" shows.[96] The data also display a strong economic orientation toward the Phoenician cities of Tyre and Sidon.[97]

Another sign of their lavish lifestyle is the evidence of a high proportion of meat in their diet. On account of the fact that 60 percent of the sheep bones examined had been "killed before the age of 16 months"—a "pattern of mortality" that "is extremely unusual"—it appears that the Hellenistic residents had either imported or raised large numbers of young sheep primarily for food.[98] With respect to their basic staples, however, the occupants of late Hellenistic Tel Anafa were apparently relatively self-sufficient. The large number of storage jars and mortaria dating to this period "indicates that much of the food" had been "grown and processed by the residents themselves." They had therefore been "largely self-supplied and so self-sufficient."[99] Involved in intensive agriculture, they had also reared cattle, pigs, and goats locally.[100] The site was abandoned ca. 80/75 B.C.E. and remained unoccupied until the first century CE.

In contrast, the people who resettled Tel Anafa in the Early Roman period lived in much humbler socioeconomic circumstances. "The Roman era buildings are much smaller and simpler than their Hellenistic predecessors."[101] Interestingly, the new residents also appear to have been far less self-sufficient with respect to their staple supplies. Andrea Berlin remarks on

> the tremendous quantity of Early Roman–period amphoras; two new forms account for 75% of *all* identifiable jar rims (excluding Mediterranean wine amphoras) found at the site. The new forms occur in fabrics that come from the Lower Galilee, the Akko region, the Hula itself, and another unknown source. The shape of the jars reflects their function as transport vessels. . . . The abundance of such vessels for this relatively small population reveals their dependence on imported foodstuffs.[102]

---

95. Herbert, "Introduction," 16. On the late Hellenistic building and its various phases of construction, see Herbert, "Occupational History and Stratigraphy," 26–182. Slane, "Fine Wares," 255, 272.

96. Berlin, "The Plain Wares," in Herbert, *Tel Anafa II.1*, 29 n. 72.

97. See "Figure 1.4: Histogram of Dated Coins Found at Tel Anafa," in Herbert, "Introduction," 16; and also see Y. Meshorer, "Coins 1968–1986," in Herbert, *Tel Anafa I.1*, 241–60.

98. Richard W. Redding, "The Vertebrate Fauna," in Herbert, *Tel Anafa I.1*, 287, 292–93. Redding finds a different pattern in the faunal remains for the last phase of late Hellenistic occupation. On account of the high cattle to sheep-goat ratio, he posits that these last occupants "were involved with cattle pastoralism" (ibid., 292).

99. Berlin, "Plain Wares," 22.

100. Redding, "Vertebrate Fauna," 291–92.

101. Herbert, "Introduction," in 21–22. On the transition in the buildings at the site from the Late Hellenistic to Early Roman periods, see Herbert, "Occupational History and Stratigraphy," 26–182.

102. Berlin, "Plain Wares," 31–32 (emphasis in original).

She also notes "the surprisingly small number of mortaria found" from the Early Roman period, necessary for processing one's own grain.[103] All of this demonstrates that the Early Roman residents of Tel Anafa "imported a great quantity of foodstuffs."[104]

We also learn from Early Roman Tel Anafa that, whereas many Jews of this period preferred not to purchase gentile products, as discussed above, they were less hesitant to sell their own produce and wares to gentiles (as we also see in Acts 12:20-21, which claims that the people of Tyre and Sidon depended on Agrippa I's territory for food). No longer economically oriented toward Phoenicia, as their Hellenistic predecessors had been, the new inhabitants of Tel Anafa traded mainly with the south, especially the Lower Galilee.[105] "An astonishing 85% of all recognizable Early Roman cooking and kitchen/utility vessels (excluding jars)" were of the Kefar Hananya type.[106] Nevertheless, economic ties with the west and north continued, for they also imported a cosmopolitan range of fine ware, albeit in smaller quantities than had their wealthier Hellenistic predecessors. In addition, they imported cattle for meat, although they reared their own pigs.[107]

Their major economic activity is probably best indicated by the faunal remains. The survival rate of sheep utilized at the site during the Early Roman period was unusual. The proportion "that were beyond two years of age is high, 65%, and beyond three years is very high, 50%. The most likely explanation for this type of survivorship is that the residents at Tel Anafa were managing their flocks to maximize wool production."[108] Berlin postulates that the inhabitants were "Roman/Italic mercenaries in the employ of Herod Philip, settled at Anafa in the manner of an outpost." Friendly relations between Philip and Antipas would have permitted free exchange between the two Herodian territories.[109] Alternatively, they could simply have been shepherds specializing in producing wool for the market, which is how they raised the cash to purchase their flour or bread, wine, oil, and other supplies.

What this example shows is another important feature of life in rural areas. It could be the poorer inhabitants who were more reliant on market exchange for their basic necessities, while their richer counterparts could be more self-sufficient in such daily requirements, engaging in market exchange more for the purpose of acquiring luxuries.

---

103. Ibid.

104. Ibid., 14–15, 22–23, 29 n. 72, 31–32; Herbert, "Introduction," 21–22.

105. Berlin, "Plain Wares," 14–15, 22–23, 29 n. 72, 31–32.

106. Berlin, "Plain Wares," 14–15, 31–32.

107. Slane, "Fine Wares," 264. Toward the end of Early Roman occupation "the entire range of Italian and eastern fine wares found on any urban site is represented." The proportion of fine ware that is Eastern Sigillata A, however, is less than in the earlier period of occupation. "ESA represents only 54–70 percent of the Roman fineware assemblage . . . much reduced from the more than 90 percent it represented in the Hellenistic stage" (ibid.).

108. Redding, "Vertebrate Fauna," 287–88, 291–92.

109. Berlin, "Plain Wares," 30–32.

## Conclusion

I have surveyed above a mass of evidence indicating the relative sophistication of village life and the relative wealth of some villagers in the Galilee starting as early as Hasmonean times and continuing through the Roman and Byzantine periods, and this survey is far from exhaustive. While there were clear shifts in trade patterns over these centuries, the data give no indication that Galilean villagers were "peasants," innately averse to market exchange with other villagers, other villages, the Galilean towns, or in the earlier periods the city of Jerusalem. Indeed, the data clearly demonstrate quite the contrary: namely, that villagers were ready participants in such market exchange.

## Bibliography

Adan-Bayewitz, David. *Common Pottery in Roman Galilee: A Study of Local Trade*. Bar-Ilan Studies in Near Eastern Languages and Culture. Ramat-Gan: Bar Ilan University Press, 1993.

Adan-Bayewitz, David, and Isadore Perlman. "The Local Trade of Sepphoris in the Roman Period." *IEJ* 40 (1990): 153–72.

Alston, Richard. "Trade and the City in Roman Egypt." In *Trade, Traders, and the Ancient City*, edited by Helen Parkins and Christopher Smith, 168–202. London: Routledge, 1998.

Archibald, Zofia Halina. "Markets and Exchange: The Structure and Scale of Economic Behaviour in the Hellenistic Age." In *Making, Moving and Managing: The New World of Ancient Economies, 323–31 BC*, edited by Zofia H. Archibald, John K. Davies, and Vincent Gabrielsen, 1–26. Oxford: Oxbow Books, 2005.

Ariel, Donald T., and Jean-Philippe Fontanille. *The Coins of Herod: A Modern Analysis and Die Classification*. Ancient Judaism and Early Christianity 79. Leiden: Brill, 2012.

Ariel, Donald T., and Aryeh Strikovsky. "Appendix." In *Excavations at the City of David 1978–1985 Directed by Yigal Shiloh*. Volume 2, *Imported Stamped Amphorae Handles, Coins, Worked Bone and Ivory, and Glass*, edited by Donald T. Ariel, 25–29. Qedem 30. Jerusalem: Institute of Archaeology, Hebrew University of Jerusalem, 1990.

Aviam, Mordechai. "The Beginning of Mass Production of Olive Oil in the Galilee." In *Jews, Pagans, and Christians in the Galilee: 25 Years of Archaeological Excavations and Surveys, Hellenistic to Byzantine Periods*, 51–58. Land of Galilee 1. Rochester, N.Y.: University of Rochester Press, 2004.

———. "Distribution Maps of Archaeological Data from the Galilee: An Attempt to Establish Zones Indicative of Ethnicity and Religious Affiliation." In *Religion, Ethnicity, and Identity in Ancient Galilee: A Region in Transition*, edited by Jürgen Zangenberg, Harold W. Attridge, and Dale B. Martin, 115–32. WUNT 210. Tübingen: Mohr Siebeck, 2007.

————. "First Century Jewish Galilee: An Archaeological Perspective." In *Religion and Society in Roman Palestine: Old Questions, New Approaches*, edited by Douglas R. Edwards, 7–27. New York: Routledge, 2004.

————. "People, Land, Economy, and Belief in First-Century Galilee and Its Origins: A Comprehensive Archaeological Synthesis." In *The Galilean Economy in the Time of Jesus*, edited by David A. Fiensy and Ralph K. Hawkins, 5–48. Early Christianity and Its Literature 11. Atlanta: Society of Biblical Literature, 2013.

Avigad, Nahman. *Discovering Jerusalem*. Nashville: Thomas Nelson, 1983.

Bar-Nathan, Rachel. *Hasmonean and Herodian Palaces at Jericho: Final Reports of the 1973–1987 Excavations*. Volume 3, *The Pottery*. Jerusalem: Israel Exploration Society, 2002.

Berlin, Andrea M. *Gamla: Final Reports*. Volume 1, *The Pottery of the Second Temple Period*. Jerusalem: Israel Antiquities Authority, 2006.

————. "Romanization and Anti-Romanization in Pre-Revolt Galilee." In *The First Jewish Revolt: Archaeology, History, and Ideology*, edited by Andrea M. Berlin and J. Andrew Overman, 57–73. London: Routledge, 2002.

Boak, Arthur E. R. "The Organization of Gilds in Greco-Roman Egypt." *TAPA* 48 (1937): 212–20.

Cancian, Frank. "Economic Behavior in Peasant Communities." In *Economic Anthropology*, edited by Stuart Plattner, 127–70. Stanford: Stanford University Press, 1989.

Chancey, Mark A. *The Myth of a Gentile Galilee*. SNTSMS 134. Cambridge: Cambridge University Press, 2002.

Cohen, Shaye J. D. "The Place of the Rabbi in Jewish Society of the Second Century." In *The Galilee in Late Antiquity*, edited by Lee I. Levine, 157–73. New York: Jewish Theological Seminary of America, 1992.

————. "The Rabbi in Second-Century Jewish Society." In *The Cambridge History of Judaism*. Volume 3, *The Early Roman Period*, edited by William Horbury, W. D. Davies, and John Sturdy, 922–90. Cambridge: Cambridge University Press, 1999.

Cotton, Hannah. "Land Tenure in the Documents from the Nabataean Kingdom and the Roman Province of Arabia." *ZPE* 119 (1998): 1-11.

Cotton, Hannah M., and Ada Yardeni. *Aramaic, Hebrew and Greek Documentary Texts from Naḥal Ḥever and Other Sites*. DJD 17. Oxford: Clarendon Press, 1997.

Danby, Herbert. *The Mishnah, Translated from the Hebrew with Introduction and Brief Explanatory Notes*. Oxford: Oxford University Press, 1933.

Davenport, Elsie G. *Your Handspinning*. Pacific Grove, Calif.: Select Books, 1964.

De Callataÿ, François. "A Quantitative Survey of Hellenistic Coinages: Recent Achievements." In *Making, Moving and Managing: The New World of Ancient Economies, 323–31 BC*, edited by Zofia H. Archibald, John K. Davies, and Vincent Gabrielsen, 73–91. Oxford: Oxbow Books, 2005.

Dupont, Jacques. *Les Béatitudes*. Volume 1, *Le problème littéraire: Les deux versions du Sermon sur la montagne et des Béatitudes*. Bruges: Abbaye de Saint-André, 1958.

Feig, Nurit. "Meron." *HA-ESI* 7–8 (1988–89): 127–28.

Frankel, Rafael. *Wine and Oil Production in Antiquity in Israel and Other Mediterranean Countries.* JSOT/ASOR Monograph Series 10. Sheffield: Sheffield Academic Press, 1999.

Funk, Robert W., and Roy W. Hoover, eds. *The Five Gospels: The Search for the Authentic Words of Jesus. New Translation and Commentary.* New York: Macmillan, 1993.

Gemici, Kurtuluş. "Karl Polanyi and the Antinomies of Embeddedness." *SER* 6 (2008): 5–33.

Gitler, Ḥaim. "Chapter Twenty-Two: The Coins." In *Jewish Quarter Excavations in the Old City of Jerusalem Conducted by Nahman Avigad, 1969–1982. Volume 2, The Finds from Areas A, W and X-2: FINAL REPORT*, edited by Hillel Geva, 453–92. Jerusalem: Israel Exploration Society, 2003.

Goodblatt, David. "The Political and Social History of the Jewish Community in the Land of Israel, c. 235–638." In *The Cambridge History of Judaism. Volume 4, The Late Roman –Rabbinic Period*, edited by Steven T. Katz, 404–30. Cambridge: Cambridge University Press, 2006.

Groh, Dennis E. "The Finewares from the Patrician and Lintel Houses." In *Excavations at Ancient Meiron, Upper Galilee, Israel 1971–72, 1974–75, 1977*, edited by Eric M. Meyers, James F. Strange, and Carol L. Meyers, 129–38. Cambridge, Mass.: American Schools of Oriental Research, 1981.

———. "The Stratigraphic Chronology of the Galilean Synagogue from the Early Roman Period through the Early Byzantine Period (ca. 420 CE)." In *Ancient Synagogues: Historical Analysis and Archaeological Discovery*, edited by Dan Urman and Paul V. M. Flesher, 51–69. 2 vols. StPB 47. Leiden: Brill, 1995.

Gutman, Shemaryah. "Gamala." In *NEAEHL* 2: 459–63.

Gutman, Shemaryah, and Joel Rappel. *Gamla—A City in Rebellion.* In Hebrew. Tel Aviv: Misrad ha-biṭaḥon, 1994.

Herbert, Sharon C. "Introduction." In *Tel Anafa I, 1: Final Report on Ten Years of Excavation at a Hellenistic and Roman Settlement in Northern Israel*, edited by Sharon C. Herbert, 1–25. Journal of Roman Archaeology Supplementary Series 10. Ann Arbor, Mich.: Kelsey Museum, 1994.

———. "Occupational History and Stratigraphy." In *Tel Anafa I, 1: Final Report on Ten Years of Excavation at a Hellenistic and Roman Settlement in Northern Israel*, edited by Sharon C. Herbert, 26–182. Journal of Roman Archaeology Supplementary Series 10. Ann Arbor, Mich.: Kelsey Museum, 1994.

Hill, Polly. *Development Economics on Trial: The Anthropological Case for a Prosecution.* Cambridge: Cambridge University Press, 1986.

Hirschfeld, Yizhar. "Jewish Rural Settlement in Judaea in the Early Roman Period." In *The Early Roman Empire in the East*, edited by Susan E. Alcock, 72–88. Oxbow Monograph 95. Oxford: Oxbow Books, 1997.

———. *The Palestinian Dwelling in the Roman-Byzantine Period.* Jerusalem: Israel Exploration Society, 1995.

Johnson, Allen W., and Timothy Earle. *The Evolution of Human Societies: From Foraging Group to Agrarian State*. 2nd ed. Stanford: Stanford University Press, 2000.

Katsari, Constantina. *The Roman Monetary System: The Eastern Provinces from the First to the Third Century AD*. Cambridge: Cambridge University Press, 2011.

Kazen, Thomas. *Issues of Impurity in Early Judaism*. Coniectanea biblica: New Testament 45. Winona Lake, Ind.: Eisenbrauns, 2010.

———. *Jesus and Purity Halakah: Was Jesus Indifferent to Impurity?* Rev. ed. Coniectanea biblica: New Testament 38. Winona Lake, Ind.: Eisenbrauns, 2010.

Kearney, Michael. *Reconceptualizing the Peasantry: Anthropology in Global Perspective*. Boulder, Colo.: Westview, 1996.

Kim, H. S. "Small Change and the Moneyed Economy." In *Money, Labour, and Land: Approaches to the Economies of Ancient Greece*, edited by Paul Cartledge, Edward E. Cohen, and Lin Foxhall, 44–51. London: Routledge, 2002.

Kingsley, Sean A. "The Economic Impact of the Palestinian Wine Trade in Late Antiquity." In *Economy and Exchange in the East Mediterranean during Late Antiquity*, edited by Sean Kingsley and Michael Decker, 44–68. Oxford: Oxbow Books, 2001.

Lapin, Hayim. *Early Rabbinic Civil Law and the Social History of Roman Galilee: A Study of Mishnah Tractate Baba' Mesi'a'*. BJS 307. Atlanta: Scholars Press, 1995.

———. *Economy, Geography, and Provincial History in Later Roman Palestine*. TSAJ 85. Tübingen: Mohr Siebeck, 2001.

———. "The Origins and Development of the Rabbinic Movement in the Land of Israel." In *The Cambridge History of Judaism*. Volume 4, *The Late Roman–Rabbinic Period*, edited by Steven T. Katz, 206–29. Cambridge: Cambridge University Press, 2006.

Leibner, Uzi. *Settlement and History in Hellenistic, Roman, and Byzantine Galilee: An Archaeological Survey of the Eastern Galilee*. TSAJ 127. Tübingen: Mohr Siebeck, 2009.

Levine, Lee I. "Jewish Archaeology in Late Antiquity: Art, Architecture, and Inscriptions." In *The Cambridge History of Judaism*. Volume 4, *The Late Roman–Rabbinic Period*, edited by Steven T. Katz, 519–55. Cambridge: Cambridge University Press, 2006.

Lewis, Naphtali, Yigael Yadin, and Jonas C. Greenfield, eds. *The Documents from the Bar Kokhba Period in the Cave of Letters: Greek Papyri and Aramaic and Nabatean Signatures and Subscriptions*. Judean Desert Studies. Jerusalem: Israel Exploration Society, 1989.

Loffreda, Stanislao. *Cafarnao*. Volume 2, *La Ceramica*. Studium Biblicum Franciscanum, Collectio maior 44. Jerusalem: Franciscan Printing Press, 1974.

Magen, Yitzhak. "The Land of Benjamin in the Second Temple Period." In *The Land of Benjamin*, edited by Yitzhak Magen, Donald T. Ariel, Gabriela Bijovsky, Yoav Tzionit, and Orna Sirkis, 1–28. Judea and Samaria Publications. Jerusalem: Israel Antiquities Authority, 2004.

———. *The Stone Vessel Industry in the Second Temple Period: Excavations at Ḥizma and the Jerusalem Temple Mount*. Edited by Levana Tsfania. Judea and Samaria Publications 1. Jerusalem: Israel Exploration Society, 2002.

Magness, Jodi. *Stone and Dung, Oil and Spit: Jewish Daily Life in the Time of Jesus.* Grand Rapids: Eerdmans, 2011.

Mattila, Sharon Lea. "Jesus and the 'Middle Peasants': Problematizing a Social-Scientific Concept." *CBQ* 72 (2010): 291–313.

———. "Revisiting Jesus' Capernaum: A Village of Only Subsistence-Level Fishers and Farmers?" In *The Galilean Economy in the Time of Jesus*, edited by David A. Fiensy and Ralph K. Hawkins, 75–138. Early Christianity and Its Literature 11. Atlanta: Society of Biblical Literature, 2013.

———. "Towards Doffing a Methodological Straightjacket in the Study of Ancient Economies." In *City Set on a Hill: Essays in Honor of James F. Strange*, edited by Daniel Warner and Donald B. Binder. Mountain Home, Ariz.: BorderStone Press, forthcoming.

Meier, John P. *A Marginal Jew: Rethinking the Historical Jesus.* Volume 4, *Law and Love.* Anchor Yale Bible Reference Library. New Haven: Yale University Press, 2009.

Mendelsohn, Isaac. "Guilds in Ancient Palestine." *BASOR* 80 (1940): 17–21.

Meshorer, Yaakov. "Coins 1968–1986." In *Tel Anafa I, 1: Final Report on Ten Years of Excavation at a Hellenistic and Roman Settlement in Northern Israel*, edited by Sharon C. Herbert, 241–60. Journal of Roman Archaeology Supplementary Series 10. Ann Arbor, Mich.: Kelsey Museum, 1994.

———. *A Treasury of Jewish Coins: From the Persian Period to Bar Kokhba.* Jerusalem: Yad Yitshak ben-Zvi, 2001.

Meyers, Eric M. "Jesus and His Galilean Context." In *Archaeology and the Galilee: Texts and Contexts in the Graeco-Roman and Byzantine Periods*, edited by Douglas R. Edwards and C. Thomas McCollough, 57–66. South Florida Studies in the History of Judaism 143. Atlanta: Scholars Press, 1997.

Meyers, Eric M., and James F. Strange. *Archaeology, the Rabbis, and Early Christianity.* Nashville: Abingdon, 1981.

Meyers, Eric M., James F. Strange, and Dennis E. Groh. "The Meiron Excavations Project: Archaeological Survey in Galilee and Golan, 1976." *BASOR* 230 (1978): 1–24.

Meyers, Eric M., James F. Strange, and Carol L. Meyers, eds. *Excavations at Ancient Meiron, Upper Galilee, Israel 1971–72, 1974–75, 1977.* Meiron Excavation Project 3. Cambridge, Mass.: American Schools of Oriental Research, 1981.

Morris, Ian, and J. G. Manning, eds. *The Ancient Economy: Evidence and Models.* Social Science History. Stanford: Stanford University Press, 2005.

Nagy, Rebecca Martin, et al., eds. *Sepphoris in Galilee: Crosscurrents of Culture.* Raleigh: North Carolina Museum of Art; Winona Lake, Ind.: Eisenbrauns, 1996.

Neusner, Jacob. "Chapter Two: The Mishnah and Aristotle's Economics." In Neusner, *The Mishnah: Social Perspectives*, 85–197. Handbuch der Orientalistik, Der Nahe und Mittlere Orient 46. Leiden: Brill, 1999.

———. *The Mishnah. A New Translation.* New Haven: Yale University Press, 1988.

Oakman, Douglas. "Execrating? or Execrable Peasants!" In *The Galilean Economy in the Time of Jesus*, edited by David A. Fiensy and Ralph K. Hawkins, 139–64. Early Christianity and Its Literature 11. Atlanta: Society of Biblical Literature, 2013.

Oppenheimer, Aharon. *The 'Am Ha-Aretz. A Study in the Social History of the Jewish People in the Hellenistic-Roman Period*. Translated by I. H. Levine. Arbeiten zur Literatur und Geschichte des hellenistischen Judentums 8. Leiden: Brill, 1977.

Peskowitz, Miriam. "Gender, Difference, and Everyday Life: The Case of Weaving and Its Tools." In *Religion and Society in Roman Palestine: Old Questions, New Approaches*, edited by Douglas R. Edwards, 129–45. New York: Routledge, 2004.

Poirier, John C. "Purity beyond the Temple in the Second Temple Era." *JBL* 122 (2003): 247–65.

Rathbone, Dominic. "Monetisation, Not Price-Inflation, in Third-Century A.D. Egypt?" In *Coin Finds and Coin Use in the Roman World: The Thirteenth Oxford Symposium on Coinage and Monetary History, 25.–27.3.1993. A NATO Advanced Research Workshop*, edited by Cathy E. King and David G. Wigg, 321–39. Studien zu Fundmünzen der Antike 10. Berlin: Gebr. Mann, 1993.

Raynor, Joyce, and Yaakov Meshorer. *The Coins of Ancient Meiron*. Meiron Excavation 4. Winona Lake, Ind.: Eisenbrauns, 1988.

Redding, Richard W. "The Vertebrate Fauna." In *Tel Anafa I, 1: Final Report on Ten Years of Excavation at a Hellenistic and Roman Settlement in Northern Israel*, edited by Sharon C. Herbert, 279–322. Journal of Roman Archaeology Supplementary Series 10. Ann Arbor, Mich.: Kelsey Museum, 1994.

Reed, Jonathan L. "Galileans, 'Israelite Village Communities,' and the Sayings Gospel Q." In *Galilee through the Centuries: Confluence of Cultures*, edited by Eric M. Meyers, 87–108. Duke Judaic Studies Series 1. Winona Lake, Ind.: Eisenbrauns, 1999.

Richardson, Peter. "Khirbet Qana (and Other Villages) as a Context for Jesus." In *Jesus and Archaeology*, edited by James H. Charlesworth, 120–44. Grand Rapids: Eerdmans, 2006.

Rosenfeld, Ben-Zion, and Joseph Menirav. *Markets and Marketing in Roman Palestine*. Translated by Chava Cassel. JSJSup 99. Leiden: Brill, 2005.

Rosenthal-Heginbottom, Renate. "Chapter 6 (b): Hellenistic and Roman Fine Ware and Lamps from Area A." In *Jewish Quarter Excavations in the Old City of Jerusalem Conducted by Nahman Avigad, 1969–1982. Volume 2, The Finds from Areas A, W and X-2. FINAL REPORT*, edited by Hillel Geva, 192–223. Jerusalem: Israel Exploration Society, 2003.

Safrai, Ze'ev. *The Economy of Roman Palestine*. London: Routledge, 1994.

Saller, Richard. "Framing the Debate over Growth in the Ancient Economy." In *The Ancient Economy*, edited by Walter Scheidel and Sitta von Reden, 251–69. Edinburgh Readings on the Ancient World. Edinburgh: Edinburgh University Press, 2002.

Scheidel, Walter, and Sitta von Reden, eds. *The Ancient Economy*. Edinburgh Readings on the Ancient World. Edinburgh: Edinburgh University Press, 2002.

Schwartz, Seth. "Political, Social, and Economic Life in the Land of Israel, 66–c. 235." In *The Cambridge History of Judaism*. Volume 4, *The Late Roman–Rabbinic Period*, edited by Steven T. Katz, 23–52. Cambridge: Cambridge University Press, 2006.

Scott, James C. *Weapons of the Weak: Everyday Forms of Peasant Resistance.* New Haven: Yale University Press, 1985.

Shanin, Teodor. "Defining Peasants: Conceptualisations and De-Conceptualisations. Old and New in a Marxist Debate." *Sociol. Rev.* 30 (1982): 407–32.

Slane, Kathleen Warner. "The Fine Wares." In *Tel Anafa II, 1: The Hellenistic and Roman Pottery*, edited by Sharon C. Herbert, 249–406. Journal of Roman Archaeology Supplementary Series 10. Ann Arbor, Mich.: Kelsey Museum, 1997.

Syon, Danny. "Gamla: Portrait of a Rebellion." *BAR* 18, no. 1 (1992): 20–37.

———. "Tyre and Gamla: A Study in the Monetary Influence of Southern Phoenicia on Galilee and the Golan in the Hellenistic and Roman Periods." PhD dissertation, Hebrew University, Jerusalem, 2004.

Temin, Peter. Review of *The Ancient Economy: Evidence and Models*, ed. Ian Morris and Joseph G. Manning. *Journal of Interdisciplinary History* 37 (2006): 100–102.

Warburton, David A. "The Egyptian Economy: Sources, Models, and History." In *Commerce and Economy in Ancient Egypt: Proceedings of the Third International Congress for Young Egyptologists 25–27 September 2009, Budapest*, edited by András Hudecz and Máté Petrik, 165–75. Oxford: Archaeopress, 2010.

———. *Macroeconomics from the Beginning: The General Theory, Ancient Markets, and the Rate of Interest.* Civilisations du Proche-Orient, Série 4, Histoire-essais 2. Neuchâtel: Recherches et publications, 2003.

Yadin, Yigael. *The Finds from the Bar Kokhba Period in the Cave of Letters.* Judean Desert Studies. Jerusalem: Israel Exploration Society, 1963.

Yadin, Yigael, Jonas C. Greenfield, Ada Yardeni, and Baruch A. Levine, eds. *The Documents from the Bar Kokhba Period in the Cave of Letters: Hebrew, Aramaic, and Nabatean-Aramaic Papyri.* Judean Desert Studies. Jerusalem: Israel Exploration Society, 2002.

# 17

# DEBATE: WAS THE GALILEAN ECONOMY OPPRESSIVE OR PROSPEROUS?

## A. Late Second Temple Galilee: Socio-Archaeology and Dimensions of Exploitation in First-Century Palestine

*Douglas E. Oakman*

What did you go out into the wilderness to look at? a reed shaken by the wind? But what did you go out to see? A man clothed in soft garments? Behold, those bearing soft clothing are in royal houses.

—Q 7:24-25[1]

The scholarship of antiquity is often removed from the real world, of the voiceless masses, the 95% who knew how "the other half" lived in antiquity.

—Thomas Carney[2]

---

1. James M. Robinson, Paul Hoffmann, and John S. Kloppenborg, eds., *The Critical Edition of Q: Synopsis Including the Gospels of Matthew and Luke, Mark and Thomas with English, German, and French Translations of Q and Thomas* (Hermeneia; Minneapolis: Fortress Press, 2000), 128–30 (my translation; Q is cited according to Lukan chapter-and-verse numbers).

2. Thomas F. Carney, *The Shape of the Past: Models and Antiquity* (Lawrence, Kan.: Coronado, 1975), xiv.

Recent scholarship on Galilee has focused intently on social matters. This chapter examines whether Herodian Galilee can be characterized as "socially oppressive," and whether Jesus of Nazareth and his early followers were responding to perceived oppression.[3] While to date there is no consensus, the answers here will be *yes* to both issues.

The alternative raised by the question in the chapter title presents something of a false dilemma, since both prosperity and oppression can be true for first-century Galilee. The more appropriate question is *cui bono*? Who in fact benefitted from an obviously prosperous economic development in Herodian Galilee? Prosperity, if shared or controlled inequitably, could reasonably be perceived by some like Jesus of Nazareth as the other side of oppressive and exploitative social relations.

In this short essay, two main claims will be made: (1) Palestinian archaeology cannot ignore insights of comparative social science; in particular, Galilean archaeologists cannot simply work in pursuit of cultural artifacts; (2) early Roman Galilee was a hierarchically stratified society, and this social stratification is clearly visible in the archaeological record. In fact, specific archaeological features show the unequal distribution of power and wealth, and sensitive common people might feel oppressed and characterize their lot as exploitation. To support this second claim, appeals will also be made to the early Jesus material in the Q tradition.

### The Importance of Comparative Sociotheoretical Frameworks

Archaeology, like biblical studies, is an interpretive discipline. No interpretation is "innocent," that is, without preunderstandings or conditioning from the modern environment. Further, the archaeological record, like all historical records, is more or less incomplete, which is why interpretation is always needed. Historians, biblical scholars, and archaeologists have to "posit" what is missing. John Rogerson has put the matter well:

> while we do not invent the past, our narrative accounts of it are affected and shaped by factors such as our very limited knowledge of what happened in the past, and our situatednesses in nation, gender, class, political and religious commitment or lack of the same, and aims and interests in wanting to construct narratives about the past, in the first place.[4]

---

3. Morten Hørning Jensen, "Herod Antipas in Galilee: Friend or Foe of the Historical Jesus?" *JSHJ* 5 (2007): 7–32; for an earlier installment of this dialogue, largely concerned with Upper Galilee, see Richard A. Horsley, "Archaeology and the Villages of Upper Galilee: A Dialogue with Archaeologists," *BASOR* 297 (1995): 1–16; see also Eric M. Meyers, "An Archaeological Response to a New Testament Scholar," *BASOR* 297 (1995): 17–26.

4. John W. Rogerson, *A Theology of the Old Testament: Cultural Memory, Communication, and Being Human* (Minneapolis: Fortress Press, 2009), 18.

Comparative social sciences can help to correct anachronistic and ethnocentric interpretations, as well as to characterize typical social stratification patterns or other social relations.

A recent development in views on ancient social *realia* has been the declaration of a "post-Finley" thought world, bringing Roman antiquity much closer to the view that Roman rule was benign and Roman-period commerce and urbanization produced a kind of utilitarian greatest good for the greatest number. This shift would seem to rule out a view of oppression or exploitation in provincial settings, or at least call for a measured testing of social conditions in various areas through artifact, inscription, and text. Still, the post-Finley view itself highlights, just as much as Moses Finley, Gerhard Lenski, or John Kautsky, that larger conceptual frames are always involved in identifying and interpreting data.

Partly because of scholarly disputes about the use of Finley, Lenski, or Kautsky in elucidating social relations in such an agrarian context, I invoked in my recent *The Political Aims of Jesus* the approach of David Christian and Big History to show that a bird's-eye view of all (advanced) agrarian civilizations reveals fairly static social themes with variations.[5] These agrarian societies have been the prevalent type since the end of the last ice ages, with predictable population structures—with so-called surpluses able to support only about 10 percent of the populace as nonagricultural producing elites (Carney's "other half"). Even if the 10 percent were to become larger, there are still numerous village and town dwellers with minimal resources, high infant mortality rates, low life expectancies, and dependence on favors from the more powerful. A regular class of agrarian producers—invariably close to 90 percent—were compelled by adaptive necessities to produce or starve. Commerce complicates this picture but raises questions about who benefits and what or how things "trickle down" to small towns and villages.

It is important to see that "exploitation" can be typical, built into ordinary structures of agrarian societies. Exploitative oppression is objectively normal, whether the 90 percent are subjectively aware of it or not, and has been so for most of historical humanity who have lived in agrarian villages and small towns. Oppression could occasionally grow heavier through acute circumstances, for instance, in times of social stress brought on by natural disasters (drought, pestilence) or social disasters (warfare).

To evaluate properly the lead question of this chapter, then, it is helpful to distinguish structural oppression, "inarticulate felt-oppression," and "articulate perception" about oppression. Preindustrial agrarian societies were based on structural oppression in the form of exploitation of agrarian labor and so-called surpluses by relatively small leisured elites, with correspondingly constant food insecurity for the primary producers. Peasants could feel this oppression without necessarily being aware of its systemic causes; under certain circumstances, individuals could become conscious of the injustices of exploitation and speak out or decide to resist, or at least criticize salient social aspects. Armed insurrections are rare among rural

---

5. Douglas E. Oakman, *The Political Aims of Jesus: Peasant Politics in Herodian Galilee* (Minneapolis: Fortress Press, 2012); David Christian, *Maps of Time: An Introduction to Big History* (California World History Library 2; Berkeley: University of California Press, 2004).

peoples; banditry is a more likely course of protest. Both of these are dangerous for primary producers since insurrection or banditry makes an already precarious subsistence even more insecure.

## The Importance and Consequences of Social Stratification

Some years ago, Eric Meyers and James Strange emphasized the cultural overlays in Greco-Roman Palestine.[6] Their analysis remains helpful, but I prefer to speak of political overlays. While there are many cultural variables in the picture of Roman Galilee, the primary social variable for social stratification is power, especially expressed through patronage to or from privileged families and concomitant social structures and stratifications. The Herods in Galilee are a clear example, but the elite Judean priestly groups also had strong interests in Galilee (as Josephus's mission demonstrates). In my mind, politics is primary; culture is embedded (that is, a function of the preferences of the ruling family/ies). Moreover, culture can support politics, as in the case of religious legitimation of Roman power. Culture can become a powerful tool of empire!

Christian speaks of "important characteristics" that, despite diverse cultures, provide underlying coherence to all agrarian societies. These are societies "based on villages," open to "epidemic disease," that evidence "new forms of power and hierarchy" and develop "enduring relations with nonagrarian peoples." Further,

> Although the crops, the technologies, and the rituals of villagers varied greatly from region to region, all such peasant communities were affected by the annual rhythms of harvesting and sowing, the demands of storage, the need for cooperation within and among households, and the need to manage relations with outside communities.[7]

### *Agrarian Prosperity and Endangered Subsistence*

On the one hand, prosperity is indicated for Hellenistic-Roman Galilee in several respects. Josephus stresses that Galilee was intensively farmed and very productive (*J. W.* 3.41–44): wine development from the time of Ptolemy Philadelphus is attested in the Zenon Papyri (third century BCE); oil development in Galilee in the Hasmonean era, and for export, but in Judea and Philistia from the Iron Age.[8] The appearance of larger and multitudinous presses for wine and

---

6. Eric M. Meyers and James F. Strange, *Archaeology, the Rabbis, and Early Christianity* (Nashville: Abingdon, 1981).

7. David Christian, *This Fleeting World: A Short History of Humanity* (Great Barrington, Mass.: Berkshire, 2008), 32.

8. Mordechai Aviam, *Jews, Pagans, and Christians in the Galilee: 25 Years of Archaeological Excavations and Surveys, Hellenistic to Byzantine Periods* (Land of Galilee 1; Rochester, N.Y.: University of Rochester Press, 2004), 54, 56–57.

oil during the Greco-Roman era indicates specialization. City and state garnered grain stores. Josephus mentions royal and imperial grain stores (*Life* 71, 73, 119). Acts 12:20 mentions Herod Agrippa's grain supply for Tyre and Sidon. Mendel Nun calls attention to the grain supply of Tiberias from lands of Susita.[9] The solid prosperity of Sepphoris and Tiberias is attested by both Josephus and archaeology. Houses on the acropolis of Sepphoris have storerooms aplenty.[10] For Tiberias, the fish of the lake were a ready resource.

On the other hand, the commoner population would have good reasons for perennial concern about subsistence. For peasant villagers, whose primary productive activity was agriculture, and who always needed to procure annual food after rents, taxes, and other exchanges in kind, very little could be left of the annual harvest. Peter Brown recently has stressed that 60 percent of agrarian production by the 80 percent (according to Lenski, 86 percent of agrarian societies are peasants) ended up in the storehouses of the "wealthy decile," and that typically one-third of the harvest was left for the annual peasant food stock. Brown claims that "granaries emerge as the economic villains of the ancient world."[11] Jesus is well aware of the storehouse (Q 12:42-46 [that is, Luke 12:24–46]), and there is ample attestation of criticism (Q 16:13 "Mammon"; Q 9:58 "foxes have holes"; cf. Luke 12:16-20). One study suggests that the interannual storage in the ancient world may only have been 5 percent, meaning that most of the annual harvest was consumed in the year harvested.[12]

Some thought experiments can indicate important social variables in food security. Assume the arable land of Roman Palestine available for grain production to be 381,000 hectares.[13] If 5 hectares (= 12.35 acres) are an average subsistence plot in the Mediterranean world, then Roman Palestine would nominally support 76,200 subsistence farms. If land plots were less than 5 hectares, then farmers might have to draw in food resources from elsewhere. Eusebius (*Hist. eccl.* 3.20.1–2) says that Jesus' relatives held 39 *plethra* (*iugera* = 5 hectares) between two families. If some land were fallowed, then this would also mandate alternate food resources. If population grew beyond about 76,200 families (there are estimates of families five to ten persons in size and Roman-era population in Palestine of 250,000 to 1,000,000), then food insecurity might grow as well. If landlords put more area into commercial crops, leaving less production for subsistence, then this too would stress food security. Hence, land use and land tenure arrangements and population pressure could place a significant strain on basic food resources for many.

---

9. Mendel Nun, *Ancient Anchorages and Harbours around the Sea of Galilee* (Kibbutz Ein Gev, Israel: Kinnereth Sailing Co., 1988), 12.

10. Zeev Weiss, "Sepphoris," in *NEAEHL* 4: 1327.

11. Peter Brown, *Through the Eye of a Needle: Wealth, the Fall of Rome, and the Making of Christianity in the West, 350–550 AD* (Princeton: Princeton University Press, 2012), 12–13, 15.

12. Peter Foldvari, Bas van Leeuwen, and Reinhard Pirngruber, "Markets in Pre-Industrial Societies: Storage in Hellenistic Babylonia in the English Mirror," *CGEH Working Paper Series*, no. 0003, Utrecht University, Centre for Global Economic History, January 2011, http://www.cgeh.nl/working-paper-series/.

13. Gildas Hamel, *Poverty and Charity in Roman Palestine, First Three Centuries C.E.* (University of California Publications: Near Eastern Studies 23; Berkeley: University of California Press, 1990), 138.

Magen Broshi approaches the issue from a different angle.[14] He says that 381,000 hectares produce 230,000 tons of grain = 230,000,000 kilograms. With minimal average annual consumption (beggar = 200 kgs), this estimate arrives at maximum population in Roman Palestine of 1,150,000. This estimate ignores animal feed.

Natural disasters would only compound the social-structural factors working against secure subsistence for the many. According to Josephus (*Ant.* 15.299–316), in 25 BCE Herod imported 80,000 kors of grain from Egypt during a famine; 80,000 cors = 24,218,000 kilograms = enough to feed 121,090 minimally for a year. Gildas Hamel cites Tannaitic tradition: "The real difference between rich and poor people was in terms of security. Richer people had a wide margin of safety. . . . The Midrash on Lamentations puts it tersely: 'While the fat one becomes lean, the lean one is dead.'"[15] Thus, perennial food insecurity, based on the structural exploitation of an agrarian society, could lead to felt oppression and from time to time also to overt perception of oppressive arrangements. Bones from commoner graves would certainly shed light on how often subsistence crises were encountered in the first century. As is known, in Palestinian archaeology there are difficulties related to bone studies.

Social stratification is clearly evident in the archaeological record. Fieldstone walls are typical in villages and towns, while ashlars are common in city public buildings. Jotapata/Yodefat shows social stratification within the site, as commoner houses with unplastered fieldstone walls were found near a house with painted plaster.[16] The Herodian period witnessed numerous monumental building projects throughout Palestine (Jerusalem temple, Caesarea Maritima, Herod's villas at Jericho, the Herodium, Sepphoris, and Tiberias). These projects depended on available labor and siphoned off labor from the villages and away from agricultural work. Considering also that these building projects were tied into the demonstration of loyalty and honor toward Rome, their implications for social pressure on the village are clear.

### Downstream Patronage, Land Tenure, and Tenancy

Typically, peasant villagers engage in agricultural production with the aim of annual consumption. There is strong evidence that the Late Hellenistic and Early Roman periods produced changes in land-holding and labor commitments detrimental to the village peasant but positive for the urban landlord and Herodian building programs.

Careful studies of landholding patterns in various periods of Greco-Roman Palestine may eventually settle the distribution between "large estates" and commoner/village smallholdings.[17] One problem with this dichotomy, which may frustrate archaeological inferences

---

14. Broshi's estimates as reported by Hamel, *Poverty and Charity*, 136 n. 242, 138–39. Calculations aided by the privately distributed *Convert* program of Stefan Kloppenborg © 2001.

15. Hamel, *Poverty and Charity*, 55.

16. Mordechai Aviam, "Yodfat," in *NEAEHL: Supplementary Volume*, ed. Ephraim Stern (Jerusalem: Israel Exploration Society, 2008), 2077.

17. See David Fiensy, "Did Large Estates Exist in Lower Galilee in the First Half of the First Century CE?" *JSHJ* 10 (2012): 133–53; Yizhar Hirschfeld, "Fortified Manor Houses of the Ruling Class in the Herodian

about land tenure, is that "large estates" are often comprised of patchworks of smaller holdings worked by various villages, and it seems that elites thought of villages as belonging to estates or cities. This was a ready way to organize agrarian productive labor and, given traditional hostility between villages, to divide and conquer (hinder mass organized rebellion).

John S. Kloppenborg's careful study, perhaps the best available now, indicates the growth of tenancy relationships in Hellenistic-Roman Palestine, and this would accord well with the (re)organization of large estate holdings, absentee landowners dwelling in urban areas, and heightened dependence of agrarian labor.[18] Douglas Edwards substantially denies this picture (see below on coins, markets).[19]

### Upstream Patronage, Money, and Markets

Work of Keith Hopkins[20] has urged us to see that Roman provincial policy allowed a fair amount of the tax/rent proceeds to "buy" the loyalty of provincial elites. In the first century, this system worked for a good while for the Herods and elite Judean priestly families. Peter Brown concurs but sees urban town councillors as the heavy lifters in the later empire. All provincial elites expressed their loyalty by building monuments favorable to Rome, for example, Herod (Caesarea Maritima), Antipas (Tiberias), and Philip (Bethsaida). Moreover, the Herods shipped significant resources out of their territories in Palestine.[21]

The key issue in this picture is the elite control of productive decisions and resources, particularly control of agriculture, fishing, and small industry (*ergastēria*). Control of land by city elites and estate tenancy is indicated in the pages of Josephus and in the New Testament Gospels. Further, that Antipas built Tiberias on the lake suggests his interest in tighter control of the fishing industry.[22] Elites controlled production of ceramics and textiles, as evidenced in Galilee by common pottery made at Kefar Ḥananyah, Kefar Shikhin, and Yodefat. Loom weights may tie Sepphoris and Yodefat (Jotapata) together. Jerusalem interests controlled production and distribution of Herodian lamps, while chalk vessels seem to have been a concern

Kingdom of Judaea," in *The World of the Herods* (ed. Nikos Kokkinos; Oriens et occidens 14; Stuttgart: Franz Steiner, 2007), 197–226.

18. John S. Kloppenborg, "The Growth and Impact of Agricultural Tenancy in Jewish Palestine (III BCE–I CE)," *JESHO* 51 (2008): 33–66. Concerning the impact of the city of Tiberias on land tenure, see Fred Strickert, *Philip's City: From Bethsaida to Julias* (Collegeville, Minn.: Liturgical Press, 2011), 165.

19. Douglas R. Edwards, "Identity and Social Location in Roman Galilean Villages," in *Religion, Ethnicity, and Identity in Ancient Galilee: A Region in Transition* (ed. Jürgen Zangenberg, Harold W. Attridge, and Dale B. Martin; WUNT 210; Tübingen: Mohr-Siebeck, 2007), 362–63.

20. Keith Hopkins, "Rome, Taxes, Rents and Trade," in *The Ancient Economy*, ed. Walter Scheidel and Sitta von Reden (New York: Routledge, 2002), 190–230.

21. Oakman, *Political Aims of Jesus*, 66.

22. Strickert, *Philip's City*, 91, 165.

of priestly groups.[23] Ceramics have been central to discussions of markets and trade in Galilee, but they also hold information about social status and stratification. Commoner houses do not as a rule yield fine wares or stone vessels. It is interesting to consider that stone vessels are often found along with hard-fired ceramic vessels (subject to impurity). Yitzhak Magen gives information that the craftsmen at Ḥizma near Jerusalem prepared their lunches in common vessels![24] Stone vessels thus are also a mark of status and not simply an indication of purity concerns; they provide evidence of social differentiation.

With regard to money and markets, coin counts at Jotapata, Kefar Qana, and Gamla show that bronze coinage flowed to political centers, thus indicating its predominant function of keeping the countryside in debt.[25] Indeed, the bimetal money system of the early empire worked in accordance with Gresham's Law, that is, driving the good silver to political centers and leaving the countryside holding less-valuable copper money. Jesus was critical of money's power, and again warned of enslavement to Mammon (money on deposit or loan). So Jesus also said (Q 12:58), "As you are underway with your creditor, make a deal (take pains to be free of him), lest he remand you to the judge, and the judge hand you over to the bailiff, and you be thrown into (debt) prison." So Hamel is of the opinion, "Debt was a permanent feature of the economic structure. . . . From the point of view of the landowner, the existence of debt was a sign that the correct degree of extraction was being applied to his tenants."[26]

Markets too showed political overlay. While Ramsay MacMullen's 75 percent of ancient exchanges is perhaps correct—since peasants sometimes need to exchange for other necessities—commercial markets were under the control of royal or urban elites.[27] In Brown's judgment, "[f]armers could bring their produce into the nearest town. But the rich had privileged access to wider and more lucrative markets. They alone could defeat distance."[28] City markets and local fairs were controlled by elites (*agoranomoi*).[29] Again, Jesus lamented a situation in which everything now had a price: "Are not five sparrows sold for two *assaria*? And not one of

---

23. See Mordechai Aviam, "Distribution Maps of Archaeological Data from the Galilee: An Attempt to Establish Zones Indicative of Ethnicity and Religious Affiliation," in Zangenberg et al., *Religion, Ethnicity, and Identity in Ancient Galilee*, 120 (map includes twenty-five sites).

24. Yitzhak Magen, *The Stone Vessel Industry in the Second Temple Period: Excavations at Ḥizma and the Jerusalem Temple Mount* (Judea and Samaria Publications 1; Jerusalem: Israel Exploration Society, 2002), 52–61, 138–41.

25. Douglas E. Oakman, "Execrating? or Execrable Peasants!" in *The Galilean Economy in the Time of Jesus* (ed. David A. Fiensy and Ralph K. Hawkins; Early Christianity and Its Literature 11; Atlanta: Society of Biblical Literature, 2013), 139–64.

26. Hamel, *Poverty and Charity*, 156–57.

27. Ramsay MacMullen, "Market-Days in the Roman Empire," *Phoenix* 24 (1970): 333–41.

28. Brown, *Through the Eye of a Needle*, 14; this general picture is corroborated by Daniel C. Snell, "Trade and Commerce (ANE)," *ABD* 6:625–29; and Steven E. Sidebotham, "Trade and Commerce (Roman)," *ABD* 6:629–33.

29. Mark A. Chancey, *Greco-Roman Culture and the Galilee of Jesus* (SNTSMS 134; Cambridge: Cambridge University Press, 2005), 135.

them is forgotten before God. Indeed, even the hairs of your head are all numbered. Fear not; you are worth more than many sparrows" (Q 12:6-7).

There are good reasons, finally, for seeing both prosperity and oppressive exploitation as interrelated social realities conditioning the Galilean material record and the concerns and activities of the historical Jesus (and others). To a degree, the debate continues unresolved because of differing ways of viewing both textual and artifactual data. Neville Morley has written (as has John Rogerson):

> The problem with this long-running debate [about the "primitivism" of Finley, Paulina, *et al.*]—the reason why it has yet to be resolved, and why historians are becoming increasingly frustrated with it . . . is that the available evidence is inconclusive, because the interpretation of any individual example depends on prior assumptions about the nature of the ancient economy.[30]

The interpretation of Herodian Galilee through text and spade can show material prosperity, exploitative relations benefitting the power elites, and reasons to believe that the commoner felt oppression and sometimes perceived its social mechanisms with utter clarity. For the future, the fuller inclusion of comparative social sciences is necessary to test assumptions and pose more precise social questions. Both historians and archaeologists can benefit from "big picture deductions" as well as "induction from detail"—at the very least, having both types of approaches *in situ* will allow sharper questions. The kinds of social questions asked of excavation can sharpen the interpretive results, but *caveat lector*—interpretation must reckon always with an incomplete record!

## Bibliography

Aviam, Mordechai. "Distribution Maps of Archaeological Data From the Galilee: An Attempt to Establish Zones Indicative of Ethnicity and Religious Affiliation." In *Religion, Ethnicity and Identity in Ancient Galilee*, edited by Jürgen Zangenberg, Harold W. Attridge, and Dale B. Martin, 115–32. WUNT 210. Tübingen: Mohr Siebeck, 2007.

———. *Jews, Pagans, and Christians in the Galilee: 25 Years of Archaeological Excavations and Surveys, Hellenistic to Byzantine Periods*. Land of Galilee 1. Rochester, N.Y.: University of Rochester Press, 2004.

———. "Yodfat." In *NEAEHL: Supplementary Volume*, edited by Ephraim Stern, 2076–78. Jerusalem: Israel Exploration Society, 2008.

---

30. Neville Morley, *Trade in Classical Antiquity* (Key Themes in Ancient History; Cambridge Cambridge University Press, 2007), 5.

Brown, Peter. *Through the Eye of a Needle: Wealth, the Fall of Rome, and the Making of Christianity in the West, 350–550 AD*. Princeton: Princeton University Press, 2012.

Carney, Thomas F. *The Shape of the Past: Models and Antiquity*. Lawrence, Kan.: Coronado, 1975.

Chancey, Mark A. *Greco-Roman Culture and the Galilee of Jesus*. SNTSMS 143. Cambridge: Cambridge University Press, 2005.

Christian, David. *Maps of Time: An Introduction to Big History*. California World History Library 2. Berkeley: University of California Press, 2004.

———. *This Fleeting World: A Short History of Humanity*. Great Barrington, Mass.: Berkshire, 2008.

Edwards, Douglas R. "Identity and Social Location in Roman Galilean Villages." In *Religion, Ethnicity, and Identity in Ancient Galilee: A Region in Transition*, edited by Jürgen Zangenberg, Harold W. Attridge, and Dale B. Martin, 357–74. WUNT 210. Tübingen: Mohr Siebeck, 2007.

Fiensy, David. "Did Large Estates Exist in Lower Galilee in the First Half of the First Century CE?" *JSHJ* 10 (2012): 133–53.

Finley, Moses I. *The Ancient Economy*. Updated ed. Sather Classical Lectures 43. Berkeley: University of California Press, 1985.

Foldvari, Peter, Bas van Leeuwen, and Reinhard Pirngruber. "Markets in Pre-Industrial Societies: Storage in Hellenistic Babylonia in the English Mirror," *CGEH Working Paper Series* No. 0003, Utrecht University, Centre for Global Economic History, January 2011, http://www.cgeh.nl/working-paper-series.

Hamel, Gildas. *Poverty and Charity in Roman Palestine, First Three Centuries C.E.* University of California Publications: Near Eastern Studies 23. Berkeley: University of California Press, 1990.

Hirschfeld, Yizhar. "Fortified Manor Houses of the Ruling Class in the Herodian Kingdom of Judaea." In *The World of the Herods*, edited by Nikos Kokkinos, 197–226. Oriens et occidens 14. Stuttgart: Franz Steiner, 2007.

Hopkins, Keith. "Rome, Taxes, Rents and Trade." In *The Ancient Economy*, edited by Walter Scheidel and Sitta von Reden, 190–230. New York: Routledge, 2002.

Horsley, Richard A. "Archaeology and the Villages of Upper Galilee: A Dialogue with Archaeologists." *BASOR* 297 (1995): 1–16.

Jensen, Morten Hørning. "Herod Antipas in Galilee: Friend or Foe of the Historical Jesus?" *JSHJ* 5 (2007): 7–32.

Kautsky, John H. *The Politics of Aristocratic Empires*. Chapel Hill: University of North Carolina Press, 1982.

Kloppenborg, John S. "The Growth and Impact of Agricultural Tenancy in Jewish Palestine (III BCE–I CE)." *JESHO* 51 (2008): 33–66.

Lenski, Gerhard E. *Power and Privilege: A Theory of Social Stratification*. 2nd ed. Chapel Hill: University of North Carolina Press, 1984.

MacMullen, Ramsay. "Market-Days in the Roman Empire." *Phoenix* 24 (1970): 333–41.

Magen, Yitzhak. *The Stone Vessel Industry in the Second Temple Period: Excavations at Ḥizma and the Jerusalem Temple Mount.* Judea and Samaria Publications 1. Jerusalem: Israel Exploration Society, 2002.

Meyers, Eric M. "An Archaeological Response to a New Testament Scholar." *BASOR* 297 (1995): 17–26.

Meyers, Eric M., and James F. Strange. *Archaeology, the Rabbis, and Early Christianity.* Nashville: Abingdon, 1981.

Morley, Neville. *Trade in Classical Antiquity.* Key Themes in Ancient History. Cambridge: Cambridge University Press, 2007.

Nun, Mendel. *Ancient Anchorages and Harbours around the Sea of Galilee.* Kibbutz Ein Gev, Israel: Kinnereth Sailing Co., 1988.

Oakman, Douglas E. "Execrating? or Execrable Peasants!" In *The Galilean Economy in the Time of Jesus*, edited by David A. Fiensy and Ralph K. Hawkins, 139–64. Early Christianity and Its Literature 11. Atlanta: Society of Biblical Literature, 2013.

———. *The Political Aims of Jesus: Peasant Politics and Herodian Galilee.* Minneapolis: Fortress Press, 2012.

Robinson, James M., Paul Hoffmann, and John S. Kloppenborg, eds. *The Critical Edition of Q: Synopsis Including the Gospels of Matthew and Luke, Mark and Thomas with English, German, and French Translations of Q and Thomas.* Hermeneia. Minneapolis: Fortress Press, 2000.

Rogerson, John W. *A Theology of the Old Testament: Cultural Memory, Communication, and Being Human.* Minneapolis: Fortress Press, 2009.

Sidebotham, Steven E. "Trade and Commerce (Roman)." *ABD* 6:629–33.

Snell, Daniel C. "Trade and Commerce (ANE)." *ABD* 6:625–29.

Strickert, Fred. *Philip's City: From Bethsaida to Julias.* Collegeville, Minn.: Liturgical Press, 2011.

Weiss, Ze'ev. "Sepphoris." In *NEAEHL* 4:1324–28.

# B. Late Second Temple Galilee:
# A Picture of Relative Economic Health

## *J. Andrew Overman*

It is a difficult task to disaggregate a category like *the economy* from a range of other relative or absolute developments in our own day, much less in the Roman period. Political changes in the empire in the East surely had an economic impact, good and bad, though this is difficult to quantify. Political *dramatis personae* associated with the region, such as Pompey, John Hyrcanus, or Herod, had policies and took actions that affected the economy and livelihoods of Galileans. These include, of course, war. Galilee was a land that suffered more than its share of conflict from the time Rome laid claim to the eastern Mediterranean and Asia, as early as the Peace of Apamea, (188 BCE) through the First Jewish Revolt (66–70 CE), the period covered by this discussion. The climate, earthquakes, lack of rainfall, fire, all very common features of the eastern Mediterranean landscape then as today, surely had significant, at times devastating regional impact.

But our sources are scant. Galilee did not loom large in the minds of most Roman writers. Galilee's importance was definitely growing, but aside from Josephus, few Roman writers focus very extensively on it. This paucity of evidence, especially with respect to the question of the economy of Galilee, has led to the application of social and economic models by some scholars to help us better imagine what we have a hard time reconstructing.

Careful and critical readings of Josephus, our main literary source, the Gospels, and early rabbinic traditions have all been variously marshaled to hew out a portrait of Galilee and its economy in our period. What economic or social models best suit Galilee of our period, if appropriate at all? How do we construe the relationship between village and city in Galilee across the Roman period? Were most Galileans peasants? Anti-Roman? Were they oppressed by their Roman imperial realities? Do traditions about Jesus of Nazareth indeed reflect these very concerns, or are these thinly veiled modern political impositions that bear little on first-century Galilean life?

An impressive list of scholars has pursued these questions vigorously and has succeeded in placing the serious study of Roman Galilee much more in the forefront of the critical study of Jesus and the Jesus movements, early rabbinism, and the eastern Roman Empire. This is quite an accomplishment given how little attention was paid to Roman Galilee a mere thirty years ago.[1]

Though a recent endeavor, the archaeology of Galilee has provided much-needed new data that help us at times balance our limited literary sources, and begin to fill out more vividly the picture of Galilean life and material culture in this period. The amount of information uncovered and the dedicated fieldwork that has occurred in Galilee on Hellenistic and Roman sites over the last thirty years are nothing short of a revolution. We now have Galilean sites from this period that have been carefully excavated, and many published, so now we can talk about *realia* in Galilee. There is a material Galilean world that can be analyzed and assessed.[2]

## The Climate of Galilee

The climate of Galilee has been viewed as enviable, if not ideal, by many observers of the region for a long time. Josephus idealizes the land of Galilee in book 3 of his *Jewish War* as a place of very rich soil, pastures, and produce. There is a great variety of trees in Galilee, talented farmers, and a density of towns and villages due to the fertility (3.42–43). We are not surprised to find Josephus overstating things or using hyperbole, and this may be the case here. But even to the casual observer, when arriving in Galilee from the arid south or the moonscape of the eastern desert, Galilee does look at bit like a paradise. The presence and relative abundance of water, except in the hot months of a drought, are a striking feature of Galilee for any visitor. This continues to be a notable aspect of Galilean life and commerce to this day. Most parts of the Middle East are vulnerable to drought. Many areas remarkably survive on next to no water. But Galilee is different. Morten Jensen has recently drawn attention to the significant rainfall in Galilee. The annual rainfall, he says, is on a par with that of London.[3] Of course, inhabitants have to develop technologies to help them deal with inconsistencies and fluctuations. But this

---

1. Galilean scholars who have helped pave the way are Seán Freyne, whose first book on Galilee came out in 1980, and Richard A. Horsley, who followed with a series of articles in the 1980s and a number of important monographs. Mark A. Chancey, David A. Fiensy, Aaron Gale, Morten Hørning Jensen, Sharon Lea Mattila, Milton C. Moreland, and Douglas E. Oakman are a few of the important names in the serious historical and social-scientific study of the Galilee.

2. Archaeologists Eric M. Meyers and James F. Strange helped lead the way with their study of Upper Galilean villages and synagogues of the Meiron region. Mordechai Aviam, Moshe Hartal, Zvi Ma'oz, Vassilios Tzaferis, and many other Israeli archaeologists are among the leaders in this Galilean revolution. Saul Weinberg and Sharon Herbert directed the work at Tel Anafa around the same period, and then Herbert moved on to Kedesh with Andrea Berlin. Douglas Edwards and C. Thomas McCollough were early excavators at Sepphoris and then moved on to Cana across the valley. Jack Olive worked at all these sites except for Anafa but helped start the excavations at Horvat Omrit. Jürgen Zangenberg now leads excavations at Horvat Kur near the Kinneret excavations.

3. Morten H. Jensen, "Climate, Drought, Wars, and Famines in Galilee as a Background for Understanding the Historical Jesus," *JBL* 131 (2012): 311.

is exactly what farmers learn to do, and they become remarkably resourceful in dealing with these realities.

So Josephus's description is not as fanciful as some might think. It turns out that Galilee is a rich and productive land.[4] That does not mean there were not periods of significant swings and inconsistencies with respect to the climate. Of course, that was as true in the Roman period as it is now. But Galilee stands out in Israel and in the region as productive and fertile land. The accessibility and rare resource of fresh water in Galilee is itself a very significant feature of the region.

## Technology

Galilee's rainfall and relatively rich soil coincide in the Early Roman period with important advances in technologies related to water and agriculture. Water-lifting devices were developed and implemented during this period. Philo, among others, seems to have been familiar with these advances.[5] These improvements, as archaeologists have long recognized, included also water transport, storage, and irrigation. The remarkable water installations known to us in Sepphoris and at Caesarea, and Herod the Great's numerous projects involving water in fact reflect the larger breakthroughs in technology around the Mediterranean in the Early Roman period. The hydraulic plaster commonly known to archaeologists in the region working on Hellenistic and Roman sites is a discrete example of advances in water technologies, as are the many sophisticated drainage systems we know from excavated Galilean sites like Sepphoris, or smaller sites like Omrit and later Banias and many more.[6] From what we have said above, it is not surprising that Galilee too should reflect broader developments we know to be in existence around the Mediterranean basin. These developments have come to light in Galilee as a result of archaeological work over the last few decades.

Andrew Wilson, citing among others Keith Hopkins, is right in noting for us, "Agriculture remained fundamental to the Roman economy, but the Roman Empire in the early centuries A.D. saw both aggregate and *per capita* economic growth . . . due to significant technological progress."[7] Not long ago scholars assumed that Galilee was a backwater and an

---

4. Jensen is here utilizing the work of contemporary regional geographers such as Yair Goldreich, *The Climate of Israel: Observation, Research, and Application* (New York: Kluwer Academic/Plenum, 2003); and Yehudah Karmon, *Israel: A Regional Geography* (London: Wiley-Interscience, 1971).

5. Andrew Wilson, "Machines, Power and the Ancient Economy," *JRS* 92 (2002): 1–32.

6. Tsvika Tsuk, "The Aqueducts to Sepphoris," in *Galilee through the Centuries: Confluence of Cultures* (ed. Eric M. Meyers; Duke Judaic Studies; Winona Lake, Ind.: Eisenbrauns, 1999), 161–76; Joseph Patrich, *Studies in the Archaeology and History of Caesarea Maritima: Caput Judaeae, Metropolis Palaestinae* (Ancient Judaism and Early Christianity 77; Leiden: Brill, 2011), 36–37; Vassilios Tzaferis and Shoshana Israeli, *Paneas (Banias)*, vol. 1, *The Roman to Early Islamic Periods: Excavations in Areas A, B, E, F, G, and H* (IAA Reports 37; Jerusalem: Israel Antiquities Authority, 2008).

7. Wilson, "Machines, Power and the Ancient Economy," 30.

underdeveloped part of the eastern Roman world. We know differently now. We should not be surprised to see Galilee participating in many of the developments and advances we see more broadly in the Early Roman Empire. But it could not always have been good news for people in the cities and villages of the lush Galilee.

## Earthquakes

One aspect of the environment of Galilee that is belied by the rich soil is the occurrence of earthquakes. The seismic activity in Galilee is substantial and relatively frequent. Archaeologists of the Galilee are very familiar with the earthquakes of 363 CE and 749 CE. These two huge seismic shocks transformed the landscape. The collapse from these two events is evident in sites around the Galilee. In Beit She'ah the destruction is immediately apparent to visitors because the excavators preserved the collapse as part of the archaeological history of the site.[8] A report of the 363 earthquake sometimes attributed to Cyril of Jerusalem details the massive destruction. He lists the towns that were partially or completely destroyed. He mentions in excess of twenty. Galilee seemed to be hit particularly hard. A third of Banias was destroyed and part of Tiberias, where many died in a fire. The territory of Tiberias was also destroyed, as was Sepphoris and all its territory. Haifa, Cyril said, "flowed with blood for three days," and all of Japho perished.[9]

But Galilee suffered earthquakes before these two more famous shocks. The cataloguing of David Amiran shows the frequency of these powerfully destructive events. His work also indicates that Galilee in particular suffers from its location on and between several major rifts. Safed and Nablus are two major epicenters of activity. The Nazareth rift is also a major fault in the region. Amiran counts three major earthquakes in the first century BCE, including one in 31 BCE. Two of the three he records as very strong or major. In the first centuruy CE he counts five.[10]

At larger sites, or where there are monumental buildings as at Beit She'ah, or at the Omrit temple complex, it is easy to see the earthquake damage. But what about Galilean villages that do not have this larger architecture? Amiran did provide a report from an eyewitness account of an earthquake from an Egyptian governor of the region of Sidon who surveyed the damage in parts of Galilee from an earthquake of 1837. The houses in Safed were all destroyed, he said. Seventeen villages in the district of Tiberias were destroyed. Forty-nine villages around Haifa were destroyed. The destruction went south to Jerusalem and north to Damascus and Aleppo. The economic and personal impact of these shocks is unmistakable. And our scholar-

---

8. Visible now in Gabriel Mazor and Arfan Najjar, *Bet She'an I: Nysa-Scythopolis, The Caesareum and the Odeum* (IAA Reports 33; Jerusalem: Israel Antiquities Authority, 2007).

9. Gregory W. Stoehr, "The Potential for Earthquake Damage to Temple Two Architecture at Roman Omrit," in *The Roman Temple Complex at Horvat Omrit: An Interim Report* (ed. J. Andrew Overman and Daniel N. Schowalter; BAR International Series 2205: Oxford: Archaeopress, 2011), 87–89.

10. David H. K. Amiran, "A Revised Earthquake-Catalogue of Palestine," *IEJ* 2 (1952): 48–65.

ship and our sources do not give us much information. But we can see from our data that the destruction caused by these earthquakes, in the period under study here, was extreme. What was the broader economic impact of these earthquakes? We assume there were many refugees, as today. It must have meant the end of some villages, perhaps the beginning of others. But the suffering was clearly extensive and many people perished.

## Archaeological Finds

The number of excavations over the last few decades in Galilee has started to present a picture of a region with numerous villages, most with presses of several kinds, and houses with shared space or courtyards. Many of these sites are larger, at least in area if not population, than we previously thought, but this is difficult to determine and much debated. Work at the villages of Cana or Jotopata/Yodefat provides us with recent new data. The large and striking urban center of Sussita-Hippos on the western shore of the Sea of Galilee, or the newly discovered site Taricheae on the northwest shore show a Galilee growing, possessing larger centers than we once thought, and demonstrating signs of expanding economic growth. And the Israel Antiquities Authority is continuing work at Tiberias, where impressive finds from the first half of the first century CE are now uncovered.[11] Such findings have even prompted us to reassess some of the sites and finds from work conducted in the twentieth century, as in the case of Capernaum, for example.[12]

Jürgen Zangenberg has rightly commented that the volume and diversity of the archaeological finds in Galilee just over the last few years have made reconstructing Galilee ironically a greater challenge, more complex. Villages and cities have an economic range in their material remains; they are not economically homogenous. In addition, Zangenberg draws our attention to how Galilee now begins to emerge as a region that can be seen, in a way, as introducing the West to the Decapolis region and parts of the East. Galilee does begin to emerge as more of a crossroads when one takes this into account.[13]

---

11. For Jotopata/Yodefat, see Mordechai Aviam, "Socio-Economic Hierarchy and Its Economic Foundations in First Century Galilee: The Evidence from Yodefat and Gamla," in *Flavius Josephus: Interpretation and History* (ed. Jack Pastor, Pnina Stern, and Menahem Mor; JSJSup 146; Leiden: Brill, 2011), 29–38. For Cana, see C. Thomas McCollough, "City and Village in Lower Galilee: The Import of Archaeological Excavations at Sepphoris and Khirbet Qana (Cana) for Framing the Economic Context of Jesus," in *The Galilean Economy in the Time of Jesus* (ed. David A. Fiensy and Ralph K. Hawkins; Early Christianity and Its Literature 11; Atlanta: Society of Biblical Literature, 2013). 49–74. For Hippos-Sussita, see the reports edited by Arthur Segal and M. Eisenberg and produced by the Zinman Institute at the University of Haifa. For Taricheae/Migdal, see the full report by Stefano De Luca, "La citta ellenistico-romana di Magdala/Taricheae: Gli scavi del Magdala Project 2007 e 2008. Relazione preliminare e prospettive di indagine," *LASBF* 59 (2009): 343–62.

12. Sharon Lea Mattila, "Revisiting Jesus' Capernaum: A Village of Only Subsistence-Level Fishers and Farmers?" in Fiensy and Hawkins, *Galilean Economy in the Time of Jesus*, 75–138.

13. Jürgen Zangenberg, "Archaeological News from the Galilee: Tiberias, Magdala, and Rural Galilee," *Early Christianity* 1 (2010): 471–84.

Regional surveys have been and are being done in Galilee as well, with important results. The finds from this work do bear on the broader economic questions about Galilee. The survey work of at least three scholars, Uzi Leibner, Rafael Frankel, and Chaim Ben David, has focused on settlement patterns and growth, or decline, in different parts of Galilee in our period and later. [14] The independent research projects do end up comporting with the important demographic observation that Galilee was growing in population, not declining, in our period. It is also important to observe that this growth continues and even accelerates after the First Jewish Revolt and the destruction of the temple in Jerusalem. Now these data do not help us understand income distribution in this time period or where Galileans might fall on the so-called happiness index. But the survey data seems to support what we see on the ground archaeologically. That is, Galilee is growing and developing in our period.

## Conclusions

The broader observations that Susan E. Alcock has made about the eastern Mediterranean economically hold also for Galilee, as we suspect they should. Her survey reflects a modest measure of sustained economic growth. Much of the east is more urbanized than the west. In addition, she observes that, in the eastern Mediterranean setting, growing rural settlements develop and maintain connections with larger towns and cities in their area. This is often done through landowners who might live in cities or towns but own larger tracts of land beyond the towns. Veterans' colonies, or so-called royal lands, might fit this description. [15]

A picture of Galilee has emerged slowly over the last several decades of work in the field that obviously and reasonably positions Galilee economically in the broader eastern Mediterranean world. Galilee was not unusual in this respect.

Shipping amphora and Terra Sigillata pottery are virtually ubiquitous in most Galilean excavations. Roman-period technologies, trade patterns, and infrastructure became part of Galilean life as well. As Galilee was enveloped into or ensconced in the broader Roman East, so the systems and advances associated with this period became part of Galilean life. What we see

---

14. Uzi Leibner, "History of Settlement in the Eastern Galilee during the Hellenistic, Roman, and Byzantine Periods in Light of an Archaeological Survey" (PhD diss., Bar Ilan University, 2004), summarized in "Settlement and Demography in Late Roman and Byzantine Galilee," in *Settlements and Demography in the Near East in Late Antiquity: Proceedings of the Colloquium, Matera, 27–29 October 2005* (Biblioteca di Mediterraneo antico 2; Pisa: Istituti Editoriali e Poligrafici Internazionali, 2006), 105–9; Rafael Frankel, *Settlement Dynamics and Regional Diversity in Ancient Upper Galilee: Archaeological Survey of Upper Galilee* (IAA Reports 14; Jerusalem: Israel Antiquities Authority, 2001); Chaim Ben David, "Settlement Patterns in the Lower Golan at the End of the Second Temple, Roman, and Byzantine Periods" (PhD diss., Bar Ilan University, 1999).

15. Susan E. Alcock, "The Eastern Mediterranean," in *Cambridge Economic History of the Greco-Roman World* (ed. Walter Scheidel, Ian Morris, and Richard Saller; Cambridge: Cambridge University Press, 2007), 671–97ff.

on the ground is a developing, productive, growing Galilean economy. Numerous villages and cities were founded or expanded during our period. It is a picture of relative economic health.

But economic health is relative, and in every economy there are people who profit more than others, and profit from others. It is hard to imagine an economy in which this is not also a reality. Moreover, economic data and development are not the same as economic justice. Sometimes these two topics conflate. What is just or fair is not the same as economic trends or developments. There were, precisely during our period, several Galileans who attempted to draw people's attention to this distinction and obdurate datum.

## Bibliography

Amiran, David H. K. "A Revised Earthquake-Catalogue of Palestine." *IEJ* 2 (1952): 48–62.

Aviam, Mordechai. "Socio-Economic Hierarchy and Its Economic Foundations in First Century Galilee: The Evidence from Yodefat and Gamla. In *Flavius Josephus: Interpretation and History*, edited by Jack Pastor, Pnina Stern, and Menahem Mor, 29–38. JSJSup 146. Leiden: Brill, 2011.

Bencivenni, Alice. "Massima considerazione: Forma dell' ordine e immagini del potere nella corrispondenza di Seleuco IV." *ZPE* 176 (2011): 139–53.

Ben David, Chaim. "Settlement Patterns in the Lower Golan at the End of the Second Temple, Roman and Byzantine Periods." PhD dissertation, Bar Ilan University, 1999.

Biran, Avraham. "Dan." *IEJ* 26 (1976): 204.

Cotton, Hannah, and Michael Wörrle. "Seleukos IV to Heliodoros: A New Dossier of Royal Correspondence from Israel." *ZPE* 159 (2007): 191–95.

De Luca, Stefano. "La citta ellenistico-romana di Magdala/Taricheae. Gli scavi del Magdala Project 2007 e 2008. Relazione preliminare e prospettive di indagine." *LASBF* 59 (2009): 343–62.

Derow, Peter. "Polybius, Rome, and the East." *JRS* 69 (1979): 1–15.

Dothan, Moshe. "Akko: Interim Excavation Report, First Season 1973/4." *BASOR* 224 (1976): 21–22.

Fischer, Thomas. "Zur Seleukideninschrift von Hefzibah." *Zeitschrift fur Theologie und Kirche* 33 (1979): 133–38.

Frankel, Rafael. *Settlement Dynamics and Regional Diversity in Ancient Upper Galilee: Archaeological Survey of Upper Galilee*. IAA Reports 14. Jerusalem: Israel Antiquities Authority, 2001.

Gordon, Robert. "The Stucco Wall Decoration at Tel Anafa." PhD dissertation, University of Missouri, 1977.

Grainger, John D. *The Syrian Wars*. Mnemosyne 320. Leiden: Brill, 2010.

Habicht, Christian. "Royal Documents in Maccabees II." *Harvard Studies in Classical Philology* 8 (1976): 1–18.

Herbert, Sharon C. *Tel Anafa: Final Report of Ten Years of Excavation at a Hellenistic and Roman Settlement in Northern Israel.* JRASS 10. Ann Arbor: University of Michigan Press, 1994.

Herbert, Sharon C., and Andrea M. Berlin. "A New Administrative Center for Persian and Hellenistic Galilee: Preliminary Report of the University of Michigan and Minnesota Excavations at Kedesh." *BASOR* 329 (2003): 13–59.

Jensen, Morten Hørning. "Climate, Drought, Wars, and Famines in Galilee as a Background for Understanding the Historical Jesus." *JBL* 131 (2012): 307–24.

Jones, A. H. M. *The Cities of the Eastern Roman Provinces.* 1937. Reprint, Oxford: Clarendon Press, 1971.

Leibner, Uzi. "History of Settlement in the Eastern Galilee during the Hellenistic, Roman, and Byzantine Periods in Light of an Archaeological Survey." PhD dissertation, Bar Ilan University, 2004.

———. "Settlement and Demography in Late Roman and Byzantine Galilee." In *Settlements and Demography in the Near East in Late Antiquity: Proceedings of the Colloquium, Matera, 27–29 October 2005*, edited by Ariel S. Lewin and Pietrina Pellegrini, 105–9. Biblioteca di Mediterraneo antico 2. Pisa: Istituti Editoriali e Poligrafici Internazionali, 2006.

Ma, John. *Antiochus III and the Cities of Western Asia Minor.* Oxford: Oxford University Press, 2002.

Mattila, Sharon Lea. "Revisiting Jesus' Capernaum: A Village of Only Subsistence-Level Fishers and Farmers?" In *The Galilean Economy in the Time of Jesus*, edited by David A. Fiensy and Ralph K. Hawkins, 74–138. Early Christianity and Its Literature 11. Atlanta: Society of Biblical Literature, 2013.

Mazor Gabriel, and Arfan Najjar. *Bet She'an I: Nysa-Scythopolis, The Caesareum and the Odeum.* IAA Reports 33. Jerusalem: Israel Antiquities Authority, 2007.

McCollough, C. Thomas. "City and Village in Lower Galilee: The Import of Archaeological Excavations at Sepphoris and Khirbet Qana (Cana) for Framing the Economic Context of Jesus." In *The Galilean Economy in the Time of Jesus*, edited by David A. Fiensy and Ralph K. Hawkins, 49–74. Early Christianity and Its Literature 11. Atlanta: Society of Biblical Literature, 2013.

McDonald, A. H. "The Treaty of Apamea (188 BC)." *JRS* 57 (1967): 1–8.

McGing, Brian C. "Illegal Salt in the Lycopolite Nome." *APF* 48 (2002): 42–66.

———. *Polybius' Histories.* Oxford: Oxford University Press, 2010.

Millar, Fergus. *The Roman Near East, 31 B.C.–A.D. 337.* Cambridge, Mass.: Harvard University Press, 1993.

Overman, J. Andrew. "Between Rome and Parthia: Galilee and the Implications of Empire." In *A Wandering Galilean: Essays in Honour of Seán Freyne*, edited by Zuleika Rogers et al., 279–300. JSJSup 132. Leiden: Brill, 2011.

Overman J. Andrew, and Daniel N. Schowalter, eds. *The Roman Temple Complex at Horvat Omrit: An Interim Report.* BAR International Series 2205. Oxford: Archaeopress, 2011.

Patrich, Joseph. *Studies in the Archaeology and History of Caesarea Maritima: Caput Judaeae, Metropolis Palaestinae*. Ancient Judaism and Early Christianity 77. Leiden: Brill, 2011.

Rajak, Tessa. "The Parthians in Josephus." In *Das Partherreich und seine Zeugnisse/The Arsacid Empire: Sources and Documentation. Beiträge des internationalen Colloquiums, Eutin (27.–30. Juni 1996)*, 309–24. Historia. Einzelschriften 2. Stuttgart: Franz Steiner, 1996.

Richardson, Peter. *Herod: King of the Jews and Friend of the Romans*. Studies on Personalities of the New Testament. Columbia: University of South Carolina Press, 1996.

Rose, Charles B. "Parthians in Augustan Rome." *AJA* 109 (2005): 21–36.

Scheidel, Walter, Ian Morris, and Richard Saller, eds. *The Cambridge Economic History of the Greco-Roman World*. Cambridge: Cambridge University Press, 2007.

Schlude, Jason M. "Pompey and the Parthians." *Athenaeum* 101 (2013): 163–82.

Tsuk, Tsvika. "The Aqueducts to Sepphoris." In *Galilee through the Centuries: Confluence of Cultures*, edited by Eric M. Meyers, 161–76. Winona Lake, Ind.: Eisenbrauns, 1999.

Tzaferis, Vassilios, and Shoshana Israeli. *Paneas (Banias). Volume I, The Roman to Early Islamic Periods: Excavations in Areas A, B, E, F, G, and H*. IAA Reports 37. Jerusalem: Israel Antiquities Authority, 2008.

Weinberg, Saul S. "Tel Anafa: The Hellenistic Town." *IEJ* 21 (1971): 86–109.

Wilson, Andrew. "Machines, Power and the Ancient Economy." *JRS* 92 (2002): 1–32.

Zangenberg, Jürgen. "Archaeological News from the Galilee: Tiberias, Magdala, and Rural Galilee." *EC* 3 (2010): 471–84.

# 18

# TAXATION AND OTHER SOURCES OF GOVERNMENT INCOME IN THE GALILEE OF HEROD AND ANTIPAS

*Fabian Udoh*

### Introduction: The Problem with Taxes in Early Roman Palestine

A lucid analysis of taxation and sources of income under Herod the Great and Antipas comes up against several challenges. First, the dearth of evidence prevents a detailed reconstruction of the tax systems under the two rulers, or, in fact, of the various systems of taxation that the Jews were under from Pompey's conquest in 63 BCE to the revolt of 66 CE. Second, although the general social and economic conditions of Judea in the Early Roman period have received some attention from scholars of Roman imperial administration, discussions of these conditions are more often undertaken in the contexts of the heated debates about the causes of the revolt of 66 CE and, especially, the rise of the Christian movement. In the various "factors of explanation" theories proposed, taxation under both rulers is the decisive factor that explains the socioeconomic deterioration and spiraling conflicts that "*must have*" characterized Judea in the early Roman period. [1]

Third, perhaps because of these two problems, confusion persists on fundamental issues of Herodian taxation: the kinds of taxes paid, by whom, and how they were characterized. For

---

1. See, recently, Douglas E. Oakman, *The Political Aims of Jesus* (Minneapolis: Fortress Press, 2012); for the discussion of the problem see Morten Hørning Jensen, *Herod Antipas in Galilee: The Literary and Archaeological Sources on the Reign of Herod Antipas and Its Socio-Economic Impact on Galilee* (WUNT 2.215; Tübingen: Mohr Siebeck, 2010), 3–47, 257–59; especially Fabian E. Udoh, *To Caesar What Is Caesar's: Tribute, Taxes, and Imperial Administration in Early Roman Palestine (63 B.C. E.–70 C.E.)* (Brown Judaic Studies 343; Providence, RI: Brown University Press, 2005), 1–7, 279–87.

instance, Samuel Rocca, who thinks that Herod the Great merely continued the Hellenistic tax system, cites Josephus, *Antiquities* 15.303 as evidence that Herod levied "the '*phoros*,' or tribute," on his subjects. In the Hasmonean period, Jews did not pay the "tribute" because it "had been an obligation solely associated with the Gentile population." In the last years of his rule, however, Herod, "like the Hasmoneans before him, probably exempted the Jews from payment of the tribute, since the economic situation was stable enough."[2] Moreover, "[a]ll of Herod's subjects had to pay the *epikephaleion* [*sic*], the capitation or poll tax." Yet Rocca concludes that "Herod favored his Jewish subjects. Jewish subjects paid only a tribute, while the gentile subjects probably had to pay both a tribute and a poll tax."[3]

For the sake of clarity, we use the term *tribute* to refer to imposts levied on a subject people by a foreign power either directly on an annual basis or indirectly in the form of tolls and duties, for example. *Taxes* refer to payments made to local authorities of a state or subject state. Jews paid tribute to the Ptolemies, then to the Seleucids, and afterwards to the Romans. Scholars frequently propose that there was a consistent, cumulative continuum of tax policy from the Ptolemaic, Seleucid, Hasmonean, and the various phases of Roman rule, to the Herodian period. This assumption is entirely without basis.

### *The Background to Herod the Great and Antipas: The Ptolemaic Period*

Little information exists about Ptolemaic taxation in Palestine, and not very much more is known of Seleucid taxation. Besides, in 142 BCE, Simon the Hasmonean is said to have freed the Jews from subjection and tribute to the Seleucids.[4] Before this liberation and thereafter, the Jews paid taxes, first to the high-priestly aristocracy and, afterwards, to the Hasmoneans. Although we have no records of what these taxes were, two factors seem evident. First, it is not reasonable to assume that the Hasmoneans reimposed on the Jews the Hellenistic tax system from which they are said to have freed them. Second, by the time of its conquest by Pompey in 63 BCE, the Jewish state had been an independent regional power for almost eighty years. Therefore, when it became tributary to Rome, the Jewish state's only "traditional" tax structure was the Hasmonean tax system, on which we have no records.

---

2. Samuel Rocca, *Herod's Judaea: A Mediterranean State in the Classical World* (Texts and Studies in Ancient Judaism; Tübingen: Mohr Siebeck, 2008), 206.

3. Rocca, *Herod's Judaea*, 208. Similarly, Oakman: "It cannot be stressed often enough that 'taxation' or tribute-taking included state taxes, tolls, rents, liens, tributes of various kinds, religious dues, labor levies, and the like. . . . Early imperial taxes were fixed and levied in imperial silver. Every adult male owed the head tax (*tributum capitis*) and all agricultural soil was taxed (*tributum soli*)." Oakman, *Political Aims*, 64; see p. 63. In Oakman's imagination all taxation in the early Roman empire was "coordinated" and directed to Rome. See Figure 3.1 ("The Herodian tax system") on p. 65.

4. *Ant.*13.113–114; *J.W.* 1.50–53; 1 Macc. 13:13-14.

## *The Background to Herod the Great and Antipas:*
## *The Roman Reorganization*

Since, in 63 BCE, the Jews in Palestine became for the first time subject to Rome's imperial administration and taxation, attention should be paid to four factors that are relevant to the discussion of Herodian taxation. First, the reduced Jewish state became tributary to Rome by virtue of its incorporation into the province of Syria.[5] Although we have no record of the tribute imposed by Pompey,[6] there is ample evidence that the senate contracted the tribute to one of Rome's public companies, the *societates publicanorum*.[7] Second, on account of the numerous revolts in Palestine and Rome's inability to pacify Syria generally, the *publicani* were unable to collect tribute for much of the territory and for much of the time. Third, consequently, and also because of the instability of Rome itself during the late Republic and early Principate, "Roman tribute" in practice consisted of "exactions," that is, amounts extracted from the Jews as "gifts," war contributions and indemnities, advance taxation, and open robbery. Fourth, subsequent to 48 BCE the system of taxation in Palestine depended on the political status of the Jewish state and on the extent of the territory controlled by Jewish rulers. The political status determined what tribute, if any, the Jews paid to Rome; the extent of the territory determined the kinds and amounts of revenue they could raise and the tribute and taxes they paid.[8]

Julius Caesar is credited with reorganizing and regulating the chaotic situation in the Jewish state. The decrees issued by Caesar and the senate confirming grants made to the Jewish state, Hyrcanus II, and Antipater (Herod's father) give us the most direct information about Roman taxation in the territory. Josephus, who cites these decrees in fragmentary and disorderly fashion,[9] presents the grants as favors and privileges given to the Jews and their rulers by Caesar as rewards for the services they rendered to him in the winter of 47 BCE during his Alexandrian campaign against Pompey's partisans.

Caesar appointed Hyrcanus II ethnarch, recognized the Jews as an *ethnos* with the legal right to live according to their customs (Josephus, *Ant.* 14.194–96), granting the Jewish authorities in Judea the *de iure* right to collect the temple tax even from Jews living outside of

---

5. Pompey reduced the Hasmonean state to eastern Idumea, Judea proper, Perea, and Galilee (*J.W.* 1.154–157; *Ant.* 13.395–397; 14.74–77; Dio, *Hist.* 39.56.6).

6. See, for instance, E. Badian, *Roman Imperialism in the Late Republic* (Ithaca, N.Y.: Cornell University Press, 1968), 75: "We do not know for certain what Pompey did with the taxes of Syria; or, for that matter, with those of Bithynia-Pontus, which he also organized as a province."

7. Cicero, *Prov. con.* 5.10; *Flac.* 69.

8. See Udoh, *To Caesar What Is Caesar's*, 10–30.

9. *Ant.* 14.190–195, 200–210. For a full discussion of the decrees, see Udoh, *To Caesar What Is Caesar's*, 31–99; also Miriam Pucci Ben Zeev, *Jewish Rights in the Roman World: The Greek and Roman Documents Quoted by Josephus Flavius* (Tubingen: Mohr Siebeck, 1998); Arnaldo Momigliano, *Ricerche sull'organizzazione della Giudea sotto il dominio romano, 63 a. C.–70 d. C.* (Bologna: Annali della R. Scuola Normale Superiore di Pisa, 1934; repr., Amsterdam: Hakkert, 1967).

Judea. He granted Roman citizenship to Antipater, with exemption from taxation everywhere, and appointed him procurator (*epitropos*) of Judea.[10] Further, Caesar restored the seaport city of Joppa to the Jews, together with the fertile and strategic land between Joppa and Lydda in "the Great Plain" of Sharon.[11] Thus, treating Judea as a city-state comprising two principal cities, Caesar imposed a tribute "for the city of Jerusalem" to be paid "every year except in the seventh year. . . . And that in the second year they shall deliver the tribute at Sidon, consisting of one-fourth of the produce sown" (*Antiquities* 14.202–3). Caesar and the senate, in other words, established a tax cycle for Judea consisting of six taxable years and recommencing at the end of each sabbatical year. Hyrcanus was to deliver to the seaport at Sidon one-quarter of the produce of his territory in the second, fourth, and sixth years. It is not known whether Hyrcanus demanded from his subjects 25 percent of the produce biannually or collected half that amount annually (except in the seventh year), as *Ant.* 14.202 seems to stipulate. Further, Hyrcanus was to deliver 20,670 *modii* of grain every year at Sidon, except for the sabbatical year, for the "city of Joppa." This was tribute "on the land, the harbor, and exports" (*Ant.*14.205–6), that is, compensation to the Romans for the loss of the tolls and duties (*portoria*) from the seaport at Joppa and the overland trade route. In 44 BCE the Senate granted a reduction of "one (?) *kor*" from the biannual tribute (*Ant.* 14.200–201), which makes it impossible to know how much the Jews subsequently paid.[12]

Modern scholars have noted that, although in general both provincial tribute and the various indirect taxes were considerable, more onerous were the exactions, corvées, and requisitions that were part of Roman provincial administration. It is noteworthy that Caesar exempted the Jews from the most notorious of these: billeting (*Ant.* 14.195, 204), military service (that is, the obligation to contribute troops to the Roman auxiliary forces),[13] and "molestation," including the requisition of transport animals for soldiers and officials (*angareia,* or

---

10. *Ant.* 14.137, 143 (επιτροπον αυτον αποδεικνυσι της Ιουδαιας); *J. W.* 1.194, 199.

11. See Fabian E. Udoh, "*Jewish Antiquities* XIV. 205, 207–08 and 'the Great Plain'," *PEQ* 134 (2002): 130–43; Udoh, *To Caesar What Is Caesar's,* 60–75.

12. See Udoh, *To Caesar What Is Caesar's,* 41–57; also Fabian E. Udoh, "Tribute and Taxes," in *The Eerdmans Dictionary of Early Judaism* (ed. John J. Collins and Daniel C. Harlow; Grand Rapids: Eerdmans, 2010), 1320–21.

13. *Ant.* 14.204: "no one, whether magistrate or pro-magistrate, praetor or legate, shall raise auxiliary troops (συμμαχιαν) in the territories of the Jews. . . ." The exemption is confirmed by Dolabella after Caesar's death (*Ant.* 14.226). Earlier (49 BCE), Lucius Lentulus granted exemption from conscription into the Roman army to the Jews resident in Asia who were Roman citizens (*Ant.*14.228–229, 234, 237–240). This grant is also confirmed by Dolabella in 43 BCE (*Ant.* 233–227). When Oakman (*Political Aims,* 60–61) writes that the "*chiliarchoi,* 'commanders of one thousand'" in Mark 6:21 "head the Galilean (auxiliary) army" in "Herod's realm," he is, at the very least, indulging in deliberate equivocation. There were no Galilean *auxiliary* troops in Herod's (and Antipas's) Galilee. It has long been established that the Jews did not contribute to the (Roman) garrisoning of their land. See Emil Schürer, *The History of the Jewish People in the Age of Jesus Christ, 175 B.C.–A.D. 135* (3 vols. in 4 parts; rev. and ed. Geza Vermes, et al.; Edinburgh: T&T Clark, 1973–87), 1:362–67; also Mark A. Chancey, *Greco-Roman Culture and the Galilee of Jesus* (Society for New Testament Studies Monograph Series 134; Cambridge: Cambridge University Press, 2005), 47–56.

forced labor), and the confiscation of the temple tax (*Ant.* 14.204).[14] No extant evidence suggests that, before 70 CE, Rome considered any part of the Jewish territory to be "public land" (*ager publicus;* that is, land belonging to the Roman people), nor did any mines exist. The Jews cannot be said to have been paying *vectigal*, that is, "rent" paid for farming public (government owned) lands or working mines, or "fees" (*scriptura*) for grazing rights on public lands.

Caesar, in other words, established a rational tax system that was beneficial both to the Romans and, considered together with the grants and exemptions, to the Jews. Provincial tribute during the Republic and early Principate was neither "coordinated" nor "fixed": it varied widely from place to place, from one period to the next in a territory's history. According to Cicero (*Verr.* 3.6.12–15), direct provincial tribute was divided into *vectigal certum* ("set rent") or *stipendium* ("tax") and *censoria locatio* ("public lease"). The *stipendium*, being a fixed yearly amount, would have been easy to collect by either local authorities or Roman governors and quaestors. When assessed as a percentage of the total valuation of landed property, it was profitable to the Romans but disastrous for farmers in the event of a bad harvest. Tribute in Asia and Sicily was a *decumae* ("tithe"), a variable percentage of the annual harvest. Whereas the right to collect the tithes in Sicily was sold by Roman quaestors to private contractors *(decumani)* in Sicily itself, C. Gracchus's law of 123 BCE gave the collection of the Asian tithes to the *societates publicanorum* ("companies of tax collectors"), who bid for and bought the right from censors in Rome. The province of Asia is the only extant example of the *censoria locatio,* that is, of direct tribute contracted out to the *publicani* by censors in Rome. Caesar reformed the taxation in Asia by turning over to the local authorities the collection of tribute from the farmers.[15]

Caesar did for Judea what he had done for Asia: he required the Jews to pay a *decumae* ("tithe") and he abolished the *publicani*, turning over collection and delivery to the Jewish authorities. The local authorities in Asia probably contracted with Roman quaestors for the amounts due for each year. There was no Roman quaestor in Judea with whom a contract could be made, though Hyrcanus's procurator, Antipater, may have represented Roman financial interests in the region. As in Asia, Caesar's tax reform in Judea was a favor, with the added bonus for Judea, namely, that the Romans had to be content with what the Jewish leaders delivered as tribute. The inhabitants of Judea paid local taxes to Hyrcanus (*Ant.* 14.196), including tolls and duties at Joppa.

Caesar's arrangement was interrupted by the civil war that followed his assassination in 44 BCE. Arriving in Syria in 43 BCE, Cassius imposed a (one-year) tribute of seven hundred talents on the Jewish state. Herod helped to raise a portion of this tribute from Galilee, which he governed.[16] This was another instance of extraordinary exactions and belonged in the context of Cassius's and Brutus's treatment of other cities of Syria and of the East in general. After their defeat by the *Triumviri* in 42 BCE, the Jewish authorities, portraying themselves as victims of Cassius's

---

14. Udoh, *To Caesar What Is Caesar's,* 75–99.

15. Appian, *Bell. civ.* 5.4; Dio, *Hist.* 42.6.3; Caesar, *Bell. civ.* 3.3, 31, 103.

16. *Ant.* 14.272–276; *J.W.* 1.218–222.

brutality, secured from Antony (who dominated the East until his defeat in 31 BCE) confirmation that the Jewish state would continue to pay the same tribute that Caesar had demanded.[17]

## Taxation under Herod the Great and Antipas

This summary discussion of taxation in the Jewish state prior to Herod the Great's appointment as king, following the Parthian invasion of Palestine in 40 BCE, has enabled us to set the terms of taxation in early Roman Palestine. Moreover, we can more clearly establish the context of Herodian taxation. If Herod "inherited" a tax system, it was the system that Julius Caesar organized in 47 BCE, which was confirmed by Antony, and which Herod ("who was still quite young") helped to operate as governor of Galilee.[18] That context includes important changes to the status of the Jewish state within Rome's imperial administration, resulting from Herod's appointment as "King of the Jews" (Josephus, *J.W.* 1.282). Herod became a "client king," whose primary duties included helping Rome to recapture from the Parthians the territory that he was to rule; acting as a buffer against further Parthian incursion into Syria; assuring his own personal loyalty; and assuring the continued loyalty of his subjects and preventing internal turmoil (such as tax revolts).[19] For the first time, the Jewish state became a "client kingdom," that is, removed from the *provincia* and direct *imperium* of the governor of Syria.[20]

Appian's garbled account of Herod's appointment (*Bell. civ.* 5.75) notwithstanding,[21] the scholarly consensus is that in the Republic and early Principate no client kingdom was tributary.[22] There is preponderant evidence that the Jewish state, or any part of it, did not pay

17. Josephus, *Ant.* 14.304–323; 217–227; Udoh, *To Caesar What Is Caesar's*, 100–112.

18. Josephus, *Ant.* 14.158–164; *J.W.* 1.203–207. According to Josephus (*Ant.* 14.326; *J.W.* 1.244), Antony later (41 BCE) appointed Herod and his brother Phasael "tetrarchs" (τετραρχαι) "and entrusted to them the government of the Jews." Gabba, for instance, writes: "It has been very well shown that the king 'did not change, or changed only slightly, the tax yield as it was established in Judaea at the death of Caesar." See Emilio Gabba, "The Social, Economic and Political History of Palestine 63 BCE–CE 70," in *The Cambridge History of Judaism*, vol. 3 (eds. William Horbury, W. D. Davies, and John Sturdy; Cambridge: Cambridge University Press, 1999), 118.

19. For discussions of the "duties" of Roman client kings see David C. Braund, *Rome and the Friendly King: The Character of the Client Kingship* (London: Croom Helm, 1984), 55–122; David M. Jacobson, "Three Roman Client Kings: Herod of Judaea, Archelaus of Cappadocia and Juba of Mauretania," *PEQ* 133 (2001): 25–27; P. C. Sands, *The Client Princes of the Roman Empire Under the Republic* (Cambridge: Cambridge University Press, Cambridge Historical Essays 16, 1908; repr., New York: Arno Press, 1975), 49–139.

20. For the detailed analysis of the evolution of the status of Jewish Palestine under Roman hegemony from 63 BCE to Herod's appointment, see Udoh, *To Caesar What Is Caesar's*, 122–36 and the literature cited there.

21. For an analysis of the passage, see Udoh, *To Caesar What Is Caesar's*, 137–43. Ironically, ancient historians pointed at Herod's Judea as the evidence that client kingdoms paid tribute. Udoh, *To Caesar What Is Caesar's*, 118–22; Braund, *Rome and the Friendly King*, 65; Andrew Lintott, *Imperium Romanum: Politics and Administration* (London: Routledge, 1993), 35.

22. See Udoh, *To Caesar What Is Caesar's*, 143–44 and n. 152; also, especially, Braund, *Rome and the Friendly King*, 63–73; David C. Braund, "Client Kings," in *The Administration of the Roman Empire, 241 BC–AD 193* (ed. David C. Braund; Exeter: University of Exeter Press, 1988), 92; Jacobson, "Client Kings," 25.

tribute to Rome while it was ruled either by Herod or by his children.[23] This is, obviously, true of Antipas's Galilee. It is worth repeating, with Emilio Gabba: "The often painted picture of a kingdom tragically oppressed by the double weight of taxes due to the king and the tribute paid to Rome, is tendentious in both of its elements."[24]

Herod was, personally, a "friend and ally of the Roman people" (*socius et amicus populi romani*).[25] Since the privileges attached to the grant of this status to individuals during the Republic must be verified in each individual case, it cannot be assumed that Herod's status implied immunity from taxation. However, Antipater's descendants, by virtue of the hereditary grant made to him by Caesar, were Roman citizens with immunity from taxation everywhere.[26] Thus, the territories ruled by Herod and his descendants were free from tribute as such, and their revenues, considered the income of full Roman citizens, were also free from taxation. The fact that Herod and his descendants ruled with complete financial independence (within the limits of Rome's hegemony), can be verified, for example, in the manner in which Herod dealt with his territory[27] and Tiberius's treatment of the taxes that were raised in Philip's tetrarchy after the latter's death.[28]

---

23. There is now also a growing consensus on this point among scholars of Roman imperial administration in Palestine. See Rocca, *Herod's Judaea*, 54, 209; Jack Pastor, *Land and Economy in Ancient Palestine* (London: Routledge, 1997), 109–10; Gabba, "Social, Economic and Political History," 116, 121–22; Emilio Gabba, "The Finances of King Herod," in *Greece and Rome in Eretz Israel: Collected Essays* (eds. Aryeh Kasher, Uriel Rappaport, and Gideon Fuks; Jerusalem: Yad Izhak Ben-Zvi, Israel Exploration Society, 1990), 164; Schürer, *History*, 1:316–17.

24. Gabba, "Social, Economic and Political History," 121.

25. φιλου και συμμαχου (Josephus, *Ant.* 17.246) = (*rex*) *sociusque et amicus*. Similarly, he is known as φιλορωμαιος = *amicus populi romani*, see *Ant.* 15.387; Wilhelm Dittenberger, ed., *Orientis graeci inscriptiones selectae* (2 vols.; Leipzig: Hirzel, 1903–5), no. 414; and as φιλοκαισαρ = *amicus caesaris*, see *J.W.* 1.400, Dittenberger, *OGIS*, no. 427. See Peter Richardson, *Herod, King of the Jews and Friend of the Romans* (Columbia, S.C.: University of South Carolina Press, 1996; repr., Minneapolis: Fortress Press, 1999), 204–8; Braund, *Rome and the Friendly King*, 23–25, 105–7; Jacobson, "Client Kings," 25–26.

26. By virtue of the grant Herod and all his descendants, to quote Sullivan, "could properly bear the *nomen* Julius, in that Herod's father Antipater had obtained Roman citizenship from Julius Caesar." See Richard D. Sullivan, "The Dynasty of Judaea in the First Century," *ANRW* 2.8:313; also pp. 296–354. Evidence that Herod bore the *tria nomina* appears in the statue base from Kos honoring "King Gaius Julius Herodes." See David M. Jacobson, "King Herod, Roman Citizen and Benefactor of Kos," *BAIAS* 13 (1993/94): 31–35. For Herod's descendants, see Udoh, *To Caesar What Is Caesar's*, 148–49, n. 181.

27. Herod gave Perea to Pheroras (Josephus, *Ant.* 15.362; *J.W.* 1.483); settled three thousand Idumeans in the garrison in Trachonitis (*Ant.* 16.285); and, most significantly (in 7/6 BCE), settled Babylonian Jews in Batanea, promising "that this land should be free of taxes and that they should be exempt from all the customary forms of tribute [εισφορων, that is, 'taxes'], for he would permit them to settle on the land without obligation." According to Josephus, Jews from all parts were attracted by the territory's "immunity from all taxation" to settle there (*Ant.* 17. 23–27). Josephus goes on to narrate how the inhabitants gradually lost their immunity from taxation under Herod's son (Philip) and grandson (Agrippa I), until they were completely crushed "by the imposition of tribute" by the Romans (*Ant.* 17.27–28). See Udoh, *To Caesar What Is Caesar's*, 144–45.

28. Philip died in 33/34 CE. Josephus writes: "Since he had died childless, Tiberius took over his territory and annexed it to the province of Syria. Nonetheless, he ordered that the tribute (φορους) which was collected in his tetrarchy should be held on deposit" (Josephus, *Ant.* 18.108). Annexation should have meant that the territory's

It may be argued that taxation in Herod's kingdom mirrored certain specific patterns that are notable in the early Roman Empire. Those patterns were, as we observed, adaptable and varied widely. Different provinces, city-states, groups, and individuals within provinces and city-states developed a great variety of tax obligations with Rome. The usual procedure of attributing to Herod and Antipas any tax that might be encountered in the Ptolemaic, Seleucid, and Roman empires, is obviously arbitrary.[29] Some scholars have argued that Herod maintained Caesar's tax system unchanged, and that the tax revenue of Herod's kingdom remained static from 47 BCE to 4 BCE.[30] This is impossible.[31] Thus, rather than assume the collect taxes witnessed elsewhere, or conjecture a consistency, it is much more reasonable to expect that Herod imposed such taxes as were suited to his economic circumstances and political agenda.

### *Land and Property Taxes*

Herod's direct taxation fell on landed property, a *tributum soli*. This can be deduced from Josephus's narrative of Herod's reign. He frequently links Herodian taxation with agricultural produce. Early in Herod's reign, when he needed to raise large sums of money to give to Antony, he collected valuables and despoiled the rich.[32] Josephus notes that Herod later found the resources to send help to Antony at the beginning of the battle of Actium (31 BCE) because Herod had brought stability to his kingdom "and the countryside had been furnishing him much good pasture already for some time."[33] Although Herod might have sent cash along with grain to Antony (*Ant.* 15.189), Josephus only specifically mentions the "many thousand measures of corn" (*J.W.* 1.388). Similarly, Josephus specifically mentions the water and wine that Herod furnished to Octavian's troops when Octavian passed through Syria on his way to his campaign in Egypt against Antony and Cleopatra (*Ant.* 15.198–200).[34] According to the account in *Antiquities*, it was especially the cash gift of eight hundred talents that Herod made to Octavian that gave everyone the impression that Herod's munificence was beyond what his

---

taxes be turned into tribute to Rome. Yet, by Tiberius's extraordinary action, the revenues waited in deposit for Philip's Herodian successor: the territory paid no tribute while Rome administered it; none was paid while Philip lived. Udoh, *To Caesar What Is Caesar's*, 153–54.

29. See, among many others, Harold W. Hoehner, *Herod Antipas* (Cambridge: Cambridge University Press, 1972), 75–77.

30. Principally, Momigliano, *Ricerche*, 45–50, followed by, among others, Gabba, "Finances," 161 and n. 1; Gabba, "Social, Economic and Political History," 118 and n. 107. Gabba's view is adopted by Rocca, *Herod's Judaea*, 208–9 and n. 36.

31. See Udoh, *To Caesar What Is Caesar's*, 43–48, 182–89.

32. Josephus, *Ant.* 5–7; also 15.264; *J.W.* 1.358. "Valuables" (κοσμον in both *J.W.* 1.358 and *Ant.* 15.5) is, unfortunately rendered "equipment" in the LCL edition of *Antiquities*. Later (9 BCE), when Herod was said again to be short of cash, he robbed David's tomb. Finding no money, however, he carried away "many ornaments of gold and other valuable deposits" (*Ant.* 16.179–183; according to *Ant.* 7.394, Herod "took away a large sum of money").

33. *Ant.* 15.109: και της χωρας ευβοτουμενης αυτω πολυν ηδη χρονον.

34. See *J.W.* 1.394–395, where the wine goes unmentioned.

restricted and landlocked kingdom could afford.[35] Herod might have remained short of cash seven years into his reign. Octavian responded to Herod's "generous spirit" by extending his territory.

What Josephus says of the drought and famine of 27/26 BCE further confirms the fact that Herod taxed landed property: Herod was in want, "for he was deprived of the taxes which he received from the (product of) the earth."[36] Josephus distinguishes these taxes from Herod's "money," which he says that the king had spent "in the lavish reconstruction of cities."[37] In this instance Herod remedied his cash shortage by turning his own valuables into cash (*Ant.* 15.305–6).[38] Josephus reports that five to seven years later, Herod remitted a third of the taxes paid by the Jews "under the pretext of letting them recover from a period of lack of crops."[39]

We noted, with reference to Cicero, that the *tributum soli* (paid in the form of *vectigal* or *stipendium*) may be assessed either as a percentage of the annual produce or as a percentage of the total valuation of landed property. We do not know if Herod's taxes applied to produce or to landed property as such, that is, according to the size of arable land. We do not know if Herod demanded a fixed percentage or a variable percentage of the annual harvest (*decumae*), as Caesar had. Though wheat was certainly taxed, we do not know what other crops—barley, grapes, olives, and so on—were taxed, and we do not know what initial rates applied, that is, before Herod began to reduce taxes. When the *tributum soli* was assessed on the value of the farmland, the tax may have been levied (elsewhere in the empire) also on its appurtenances (*instrumentum fundi*): slaves, animals, equipment used for cultivation and processing of crops, boats, wagons, farm buildings and storage facilities, and so on.[40] We have, of course, no evidence that either Herod or Antipas conducted the valuation necessary for levying such taxes. Thus, on the basis of the extant evidence we cannot say if either Herod or Antipas levied direct taxes on other kinds of property than agricultural land. Some have attributed the so-called "house tax" that, according to Josephus, Agrippa I remitted to the inhabitants of Jerusalem when he received Judea (the region, Archelaus's former ethnarchy) from Claudius.[41] I have argued that it was unlikely that this tax was imposed by Herod. It was more probably imposed

---

35. In *J. W.* 1.394–395, Josephus does not mention the cash gift.

36. *Ant.* 15.303: των τε φορων ους ελαμβανεν απο της γης αφηρημενω.

37. *Ant.* 15.303: και τα χρηματα δεδαπανηκοτι προς φιλοτιμιαν ων τας πολεις επεσκευαζεν.

38. See Pastor, *Land and Economy*, 115–27; Richardson, *Herod*, 222–23. Richardson (p. 223 n.18) suggests that Herod probably turned the metal (silver and gold) into bullion for trade, rather than mint coins, as Josephus intimates.

39. *Ant.* 15.365: προφασιν μεν ως αναλαβοιεν εκ της αφοριας. See Udoh, *To Caesar What Is Caesar's*, 162–63; Richardson, *Herod*, 236.

40. See, for example, Tacitus, *Ann.* 13.51 and P. A. Brunt, "The Revenues of Rome," *JRS* 71 (1981): 164–66.

41. Josephus, *Ant.* 19.299: "the king recompensed the inhabitants of Jerusalem for their goodwill to him by remitting to them the tax on every house (τα υπερ εκαστης οικιας). . . ." For the origin of the view, see F. M. Heichelheim, "Roman Syria," in *An Economic Survey of Ancient Rome*, vol. 4 (ed. Tenney Frank; Baltimore, Md.: Johns Hopkins University Press, 1938), 236.

on the inhabitants of Jerusalem by one of the Roman *preafecti*, who governed the territory from 6 CE until Agrippa I received it in 41 CE.[42]

As far as we know, Herodian direct taxes were land taxes, paid in produce, which furnished Herod with produce. The possibility remains that Herod and Antipas might have imposed, at least occasionally, some taxes apart from tolls and duties that required cash payments. Some New Testament scholars, in particular, have continued to propose that both Herod and Antipas required that taxes be paid in coins. Herod and Antipas minted coins in order to monetize the economy of Jewish Palestine and, by increasing the money supply, facilitated the efficient collection of taxes.[43] This contention is not supported by the evidence. Both Herod and Antipas, as client rulers, minted only bronze coins. As Mark A. Chancey correctly notes with respect to Antipas, the coins he (and Herod) minted were "relatively small change; it is unlikely that their main purpose was to make taxation and the transfer of wealth easier, since silver would have been preferable for both purposes."[44] It has been shown that the coins served not an economic "market" need but rather as propaganda, expressing ideological, political, and cultural values.[45] We must reassert here Richard Duncan-Jones's cautionary conclusion that, where the evidence exists, the land-tax "visibly remained a tax in kind in a number of the provinces."

> This apparently recognized the limited extent to which money could be extracted from an agricultural population in which ownership of money was sporadic. Cicero's comments on attempts to exact money from the Sicilian farmer are worth recalling: he says that for a farmer to hand over something which he could not grow would mean selling off his equipment.[46]

---

42. Although the exact meaning of Josephus's tax is not clear, the closest instances of similar imposts are Roman and include: Appius Claudius's house tax on the province of Cilicia (Cicero, *Fam.* 3.8.3–5; also *Att.* 5.16.2) and Scipio's—Pompey's general's— house tax on the inhabitants of Asia, part of his extraordinary exactions at the beginning of the civil war against Pompey in 49 BCE (Caesar, *Bell. civ.* 3.32). The Roman taxes appear under an assortment of names: *ostiarium* or *exactio ostiorum* (a door tax), and *columnarium* (a pillar tax). They seem to have been imposed in cases of emergency or as a punishment. See Udoh, *To Caesar What Is Caesar's*, 177–80.

43. See, for instance, William Arnal, *Jesus and the Village Scribes* (Minneapolis: Fortress Press, 2001), 134–46; also Oakman, *Political Aims*, 64–66.

44. Chancey, *Greco-Roman Culture*, 181. Oakman (*Political Aims*, 66) claims: "The requirement of tax payments in silver 'leveraged' bronze money and agricultural production."

45. For a comprehensive discussion of Herodian coinage, see Morten Hørning Jensen, "Message and Minting: The Coins of Herod Antipas in Their Second Temple Context as a Source for Understanding the Religio-Political and Socio-Economic Dynamics of Early First Century Galilee," in *Religion, Ethnicity, and Identity in Ancient Galilee: A Region in Transition* (ed. Jürgen Zangenberg, Harold W. Attridge, and Dale B. Martin; WUNT 210; Tübingen: Mohr Siebeck, 2007), 277–313; also Jensen, *Herod Antipas in Galilee*, 187–217.

46. *Nummos vero ut det arator, quos non exarat, quos non aratro ac manu quaerit, boves et aratrum ipsum atque omne instrumentum vendat necesse est* (Cicero, *Verr.* 2.3.199). Richard Duncan-Jones, *Structure and Scale in the Roman Economy* (Cambridge: Cambridge University Press, 1990), 198, also from p. 187. Udoh, *To Caesar What Is Caesar's*, 164.

### Sales Taxes, Tolls, and Duties on Goods in Transit

Herod imposed taxes "upon public purchases and sales." After his death, demands were made that Archelaus remove these taxes.[47] The taxes appear to have affected a variety of items sold in the marketplace.[48] However, we do not know what kinds of sales were taxed, the rate that was assessed, or which parts of his kingdom were affected. One might suspect that Archelaus removed the taxes.[49] In any event, when Vitellius (governor of Syria) is said, in 37 CE, to have "remitted to the inhabitants of the city [Jerusalem] all taxes on the sale of agricultural produce,"[50] these taxes, like the "house tax," are best considered to have been imposed by one of the Roman *praefecti*.[51] Unlike Herod's sales taxes, they appear to have been imposed on produce and food items that were brought into the city for sale, and only Jerusalem was affected.

The lead weight (possibly from Tiberias) inscribed "of Gaius Julius . . ." belonging to his term of office as *agoranomos* testifies to the fact that Antipas regulated the markets in his tetrarchy.[52] Equally, according to Josephus, Antipas had appointed the young Agrippa I market inspector for Tiberias.[53] It is possible that Antipas also levied sales taxes in the marketplace, though this is not the duty of the *agoranomos*.[54]

Herod derived his tax income primarily from tolls and duties (*portoria*), which constituted a major source of income for provinces and city-states.[55] Octavian extended Herod's kingdom in 30 BCE to include not only Jericho and Joppa, previously excised from his kingdom by Antony and Cleopatra, but also the semi-autonomous city-states Samaria, Gadara, Hippus (in the interior), Gaza, Anthedon, and Strato's Tower (on the Mediterranean coast).[56] Azotus and Jamneia were also coastal cities. Herod founded and rebuilt Samaria-Sebaste, Anthedon

47. *Ant.* 17.205: των τελων α επι πρασεσιν η ωναις δημοσιαις; The taxes were, according to the protesters, "ruthlessly exacted." In *J. W.* 2.4, they demanded "the abolition of duties" (αναιρειν τα τελη).

48. Schalit's view that Herod's tolls were collected in the marketplaces is plausible. However, his often repeated idea that this implies that Herod registered all sales in the kingdom and kept records of them in Jerusalem is without merit. See Abraham Schalit, *König Herodes: der Mann und sein Werk* (Berlin: Walter de Gruyter, 1969), 286–88.

49. According to Josephus, Archelaus "by no means opposed" (*Ant.* 17.205); "readily assented" (*J. W.* 2.4).

50. *Ant.* 18.90: τα τελη των ωνουμενων καρπων.

51. *Contra* Heichelheim, "Roman Syria," 238, whose view is often repeated. See, for instance, Seán Freyne, *Galilee from Alexander the Great to Hadrian: 323 B.C.E. to 235 C.E.* (Notre Dame: University of Notre Dame Press, 1980), 190–91. See Udoh, *To Caesar What Is Caesar's*, 175–77.

52. See Jensen, *Herod Antipas in Galilee*, 145–46; Marcus Sigismund, "Coins and Weights as a Mirror of Ethnic, Religious and Political Identity in First and Second Century C.E. Tiberias," in *Religion, Ethnicity, and Identity in Ancient Galilee: A Region in Transition* (ed. Jürgen Zangenberg, Harold W. Attridge, and Dale B. Martin; WUNT 210; Tübingen: Mohr Siebeck, 2007), 332–36.

53. *Ant.* 18.149: αγορανομια τε της Τιβεριαδος ετιμησαν.

54. See, for example, the *agoranomoi* in Ephesus (*Ant.* 14.261).

55. On tolls and duties in the Roman Empire, see Siegfried J. de Laet, *Portorium: études sur l'organisation douanière chez les Romains, surtout a l'époque du haut-empire* (Brugge: De Tempel, 1949); Lintott, *Imperium Romanum*, 83–85.

56. *Ant.* 15.96, 217; *J. W.* 1.361–362, 396.

(Agrippias), Pegae (Antipatris), Strato's Tower (Caesarea), Geba, and Esbus.[57] The expanded territory, apart from increasing his revenues from direct taxes, gave him access to the tolls and duties paid for trade within and for goods transiting the cities.[58] Much more income came from the control Herod exercised over seaports and the overland long-distance trade routes that traversed his vast kingdom. When Julius Caesar restored Joppa and the surrounding territory to Hyrcanus and the Jewish state he not only gave them access to the sea, but also control at this point over the coastal trade route, running from Egypt northward to Syria and beyond: the *via maris* ("the highway of the sea"). Herod greatly extended and reinforced his control over the trade route, vastly increasing his revenues, by rebuilding Pegae (Antipatris) and Strato's Tower (Caesarea). The continued importance of tolls and duties as sources of income at the seaport at Caesarea can be seen by the fact that one of the city's Jewish principal citizens in 66 CE, long after Herod, was John "the toll collector."[59]

Herod's new seaport city, Anthedon (Agrippias), stood between Ascalon (where Herod had a palace)[60] and Gaza. Gaza, an important commercial center, was the meeting point between the *via maris* and the southern trade routes from Arabia, providing these latter with an outlet to the sea.[61] Frankincense and myrrh, spices, cotton, and probably silk were transported on the southern trade routes from southern Arabia, eastern Africa, India, and China through Nabatean Arabia and Idumea to Gaza.[62] Herod, an Idumean, had long-standing ties with Gaza and the Nabatean trade.[63] When Octavian added Gaza to Herod's kingdom in 30 BCE he gave him full control over the trade routes together with the vast income that came from them. After Herod died, Gaza was reannexed to the province of Syria, and the income reverted to the Romans.[64] Moreover, when in 23 BCE Octavian (now Augustus) added Aurantis, Batanea, and

---

57. See Richardson, *Herod*, 188–91 for the commercial importance of Herod's projects.

58. For discussions of tolls and duties in Judea, see Schürer, *History*, 1:373–76; de Laet, *Portorium*, 333–44.

59. *J. W.* 2.287: οι δυνατοι των Ιουδαιων συν οις Ιωαννης ο τελωνης.

60. *Ant.* 17.321; *J. W.* 2.98.

61. See Udoh, *To Caesar What Is Caesar's*, 172–73, and the literature cited in n. 293.

62. On frankincense and myrrh, the route through Gaza, the tolls and duties paid en route, and the importance of the aromatics in the first century, see Pliny, *Nat.* 12.32.51–71; Strabo, *Geogr.* 16.4.24; Gus W. Van Beek, "Frankincense and Myrrh," *BA* 23 (1960): 70–95; Manfred G. Raschke, "New Studies in Roman Commerce with the East," *ANRW* 2.9.2:604–1361; Nigel Groom, *Frankincense and Myrrh: A Study of the Arabian Incense Trade* (London: Longman, 1981); Magen Broshi, "The Role of the Temple in the Herodian Economy," *JJS* 38 (1987): 33–35.

63. Herod's grandfather was "the governor of the whole of Idumea," appointed by Alexander Janneus and his successor wife, Alexandra. According to Josephus, Antipater, Herod's father, "made friends of the neighboring Arabs and Gazaeans and Ascalonites, and completely won them over by many gifts" (*Ant.* 14.10). This connection between Idumea and Arabia, which Antipater cemented by marrying into the Arabian aristocracy, explains Antipater's wealth (*Ant.* 14.8, 121–122; *J. W.* 1.123, 181). Herod himself appointed the Idumean Costobarus "governor of Idumea and Gaza," marrying him to his sister (*Ant.* 15.254). This position accounted for Costobarus's wealth (*Ant.* 15.257). See Aryeh Kasher, *Jews, Idumaeans and Ancient Arabs* (Tübingen: Mohr Siebeck, 1988), 89–90, 109; Udoh, *To Caesar What Is Caesar's*, 173–75.

64. Josephus, *Ant.* 17.320; *J. W.* 2.97; Pliny, *Nat.* 12.32.64–65.

Trachonitis to Herod's kingdom, he granted him control over the trade route that went north across Transjordania to Damascus.

### *The "Head Tax"*

Prior to 70 CE, when Vespasian converted the temple tax into a poll tax imposed on all Jews,[65] the Jews in Palestine did not pay an annual "head tax." They did not pay it under John Hyrcanus II; they did not pay it under Herod, or in Galilee under Antipas, or in Judea (Archelaus's ethnarchy) after it was annexed in 6 CE. The topic of the Roman *tributum capitis* or capitation tax (ἐπικεφάλαιον) is complicated. The Greek term *epikephalaion* was used in the Republic to designate various capitation charges imposed on individuals, *per caput*, and generally paid in cash. These were ad hoc exactions, such as the house taxes imposed by Scipio on the inhabitants of Asia or by Appius Claudius on the inhabitants of the province of Cilicia, noted above. Herod's punitive imposition of one hundred talents on the cities of Galilee in 37 BCE would be an instance of such a tax (Josephus, *Ant.* 14.433; *J.W.* 1.314). He is reported to have similarly punished the Pharisees, though in this instance the impost was paid by Pheroras's (Herod's brother's) wife (*Ant.* 17.42–43).

These taxes are easily confused with the *tributum capitis*, properly so called, which made its appearance in the Principate. This *tributum capitis* or *phoros tōn sōmatōn* was the annual head tax assessed through a census at a flat rate on qualifying members of the population.[66] The *tributum capitis* was not introduced into the provinces until after the necessary and appropriate census had been conducted in them. The first known census was conducted by Augustus in Gaul (and probably Spain) in 27 BCE. This new administrative tool, it would appear, was used when Rome needed to assess the revenues of newly acquired territories. Extant evidence suggests that censuses were not widespread and were used haphazardly in the early Principate.[67] Moreover, a population census—a registration of persons in a household[68]—is necessary for the imposition of a poll tax. Of course, the proper assessment of the tax requires that a population registration be conducted periodically. This census format is encountered only in Egypt. Elsewhere, although there was no uniformity, the format appears to have been a registration of property, particularly farmland, leading to the imposition of a *tributum soli*.[69]

---

65. Josephus, *J.W.* 7.218 (see *Ant.* 3.194; 7.318); Dio, *Hist* 65.7.2.

66. See φορος των σωματων; see Dio (*Hist.* 62.3.3), who also refers to the tax as κεφαλας υποτελεις. The tax is known in Egypt as λαογραφια. On the use of the terms, see Dominic W. Rathbone, "Egypt, Augustus and Roman Taxation," *CahGlotz* 4 (1993): 86–97; Udoh, *To Caesar What Is Caesar's*, 220–21.

67. Dio, *Hist.* 53.22.5. Rathbone, "Egypt, Augustus and Roman Taxation," 94–99; P. A. Brunt, *Roman Imperial Themes* (Oxford: Clarendon, 1990), 533, correcting his previous views in Brunt, "Revenues of Rome," 163–66, 171–72. For other instances of censuses in the early Principate and discussion, see Udoh, *To Caesar What Is Caesar's*, 208–10.

68. That is, κατ' οικιαν απογραφη.

69. See Brunt, "Revenues of Rome," 163 and 166–67; Udoh, *To Caesar What Is Caesar's*, 212–13.

This "registration" of property is what Quirinius conducted in Judea in 6 CE, following the banishment of Archelaus and the annexation of his ethnarchy.[70] It was also the format of the census conducted in 127 CE in Arabia, which was annexed in 106 CE.[71] The scholars who propose that Jews paid a poll tax in Herod's kingdom and in Galilee under Antipas ("in Jesus' time") often do not specify how Herod and Antipas assessed the tax.[72] Others, relying either on the Egyptian model or on Luke 2:1-7, have argued that Herod conducted regular censuses in his kingdom.[73] The many attempts to date Quirinius's census to the time of Herod have been futile.[74] There is no shred of evidence that Herod conducted a census in his kingdom or that Antipas did so in Galilee.[75]

### *Partial Summary*

One can say with certainty that Herod derived tax revenues from three kinds of taxes: (1) a land tax assessed either as a percentage of the annual yield or on the value of property; (2) a tax on sales, probably levied in the marketplace; and (3) tolls and duties. We do not know what rates applied in any of these taxes. We do know, however, that Herod understood the political, social, and economic significance of tax cuts. Thus, in 28/27 BCE he received no revenue from direct taxes because of the drought and famine that devastated his kingdom (*Ant.* 15.303–6). In 20 BCE, while his building program was approaching its zenith, he reduced the taxes paid by his Jewish subjects by one-third (*Ant.* 15.365), and in 14 BCE he further reduced them by a quarter (*Ant.* 16.62–65). Unless this latter reduction was only for that year, Herod reduced the taxes paid by the Jews by 50 percent in the six-year period. The reductions suggest that the Jews paid less, rather than more, in direct taxes as Herod's reign progressed. Nevertheless, because of the bitter and persistent opposition among some of his Jewish subjects, Herod's tax policies failed to achieve the political results that he desired (*Ant.* 16.63–65): to avert the charges

---

70. Josephus, *Ant.* 18.1–4; 17.355; 18.4, 26. See discussion in Udoh, *To Caesar What Is Caesar's*, 211–15.

71. Returns from this census are preserved in the Babatha archive. See Naphtali Lewis, Yigael Yadin, and Jonas C. Greenfield, eds., *The Documents from the Bar Kokhba Period in the Cave of Letters: Greek Papyri* (Judean Desert Studies 2; Jerusalem: Israel Exploration Society, the Hebrew University of Jerusalem, & the Shrine of the Book, 1989), no. 16; Udoh, *To Caesar What Is Caesar's*, 215–18.

72. For instance, Seán Freyne, "The Geography, Politics, and Economics of Galilee and Quest for the Historical Jesus," in *Studying the Historical Jesus: Evaluations of the State of Current Research* (eds. Bruce Chilton and Craig A. Evans; Leiden: Brill, 1994), 87.

73. For instance, Schalit, *König Herodes*, 272–78; Brook W. R. Pearson, "The Lucan Censuses, Revisited," *CBQ* 61 (1999): 262–82. See Udoh, *To Caesar What Is Caesar's*, 165–71.

74. There has, of course, been a long debate on the subject. See Udoh, *To Caesar What Is Caesar's*, 155–56, and the literature cited there.

75. Fergus Millar observes correctly that Luke is "wholly misleading and unhistorical" in implying that a "Roman census was imposed in Galilee," which was under Antipas. See Fergus Millar, *The Roman Near East: 31 BC –AD 337* (Cambridge, Mass.: Harvard University Press, 1993), 46.

that were later brought against him, namely, that he taxed the Jews to "helpless poverty" and despoiled them to enrich Greek cities.[76]

Galilee (and Perea), Antipas's tetrarchy, was a fraction of his father's kingdom, even at the beginning of Herod's reign. The territory was landlocked and excluded the Greek cities, Antipas had no access to the major trade routes to the south, to the east, and on the Mediterranean coast. It is possible that a larger percentage of his tax revenues derived from direct land tax. However, we have noted that it is probable that Antipas also levied taxes on sales. The continual importance of tolls and duties in Galilee might be attested to, on the evidence of the Gospels, by the presence of Jewish toll collectors (τελῶναι) in the tetrarchy.[77] Antipas would have continued to benefit from the cross-border trade with the neighboring cities, with Judea in the south, and with Philip's territory in the east and beyond.[78] By founding Tiberias on the shore of the Sea of Galilee, Antipas might have sought to increase his tax base and control the trade, including the fishing industry, flowing through the lake.[79]

## Other Sources of Income

Herod obviously did not pay, and could not have paid, for his numerous enterprises (including the temple) and benefactions from the direct taxes he imposed on Jewish "peasants." Besides

76. Josephus, *Ant.* 16.154–156; 17.191; 19.329; 17.204–205 (*J. W.* 2.4); 17.306–308 (*J. W.* 2.85–86). Scholars who view the tax policies of Herod (and Antipas) as the causes of conflict and decay in Palestine accept this assessment of Herod's rule. See Udoh, *To Caesar What Is Caesar's*, 115–17, 180–209.

77. Known by name is Levi/Matthew, whom Jesus calls from his toll office by the Sea of Galilee—Lake Tiberias (Mark 2:17 // Luke 5:27-32; Matt 9:9-13). Zacchaeus, the rich ἀρχιτελώνης, is located in Jericho (Luke 19:1-10), and John, the toll collector, is one of the leading men of Caesarea (Josephus, *J. W.* 2.287, 292). Both cities were outside of Antipas's territory. On toll collectors see John R. Donahue, "Tax Collectors and Sinners: An Attempt at Identification," *CBQ* 33 (1971): 39–61; Udoh, *To Caesar What Is Caesar's*, 241.

78. The largest number of Antipas's coins to date has been found in Gamala, on the northeast shore of Lake Tiberias, in Philip's tetrarchy. This suggests that Gamala's trade was more with Tiberias than with Paneas. Archaeological finds indicate that Gamala produced ritually pure olive oil. The hills of Galilee, according to Josephus, were a special home to the olive tree (*J. W.* 2.592; 3.516), In the Hellenistic and early Roman periods, Jews of Palestine and the Diaspora could not use foreign, that is, Grecian oil (*Ant.* 12.119–120; *J. W.* 2.591; *Life* 74). The requirement that Jews use "pure oil"—bought from other Jews—made it possible for John of Gischala (during the revolt of 66 CE) to make enormous profits by exporting oil from Galilee to the Jews of Caesarea Philippi (*J. W.* 2.591–592; *Life* 74–76). See Jensen, *Herod Antipas in Galilee*, 175–76, 212; Mordechai Aviam, "People, Land, Economy, and Belief in First-Century Galilee and Its Origins: A Comprehensive Archaeological Synthesis," in *The Galilean Economy in the Time of Jesus* (ed. David A. Fiensy and Ralph K. Hawkins; Early Christianity and Its Literature 11; Atlanta: Society of Biblical Literature, 2013), 28–29.

79. Scholars now, correctly, see the foundation of Tiberias as "a great royal investment." What Jonathan Reed says of Capernaum must also be true of Tiberias, to which it was connected, namely, that it "would have witnessed considerable regional and some interregional traffic, which would become a prominent feature of its character during the first half of the first century C.E." See, J. L. Reed, *Archaeology and the Galilean Jesus* (Harrisburg, Pa.: Trinity Press International, 2000), 148; Aviam, "People, Land, Economy, and Belief," 20; Jensen, *Herod Antipas in Galilee*, 96, 171.

revenue derived from direct and, especially, indirect taxes, Herod had at his disposition other vast resources.

### Family and Personal Wealth

Herod, we noted, came from a wealthy Idumean family. He came into sole possession of his family fortune after the death of his brothers Phasael and Joseph.[80] Herod's status as a Roman citizen permitted him, before and after he became king, to be involved in Roman imperial administration within and beyond the Jewish state: governor of Galilee and Coele-Syria and (the city of) Samaria under Caesar,[81] governor of Coele-Syria under Cassius,[82] and tetrarch of the Jewish state under Antony.[83] According to Josephus (*J. W.* 1.399), Augustus made Herod "procurator of all Syria" (in 20 BCE), subjecting all procurators to his authority.[84] This claim is exaggerated, although Augustus certainly gave Herod, as king, some procuratorial responsibilities in the region.[85] In addition, the persistent view that Herod was an imperial procurator in his kingdom is untenable.[86] Finally, in the 12 BCE exchange of gifts with Augustus, Herod received "half the revenue from the copper mines of Cyprus" and was entrusted with the management of the other half.[87] Herod was individually wealthy, even before he became king.[88]

### Money-Lending Ventures

Revenues earned by Herod from money lending come to light in his dealing with the Arabs. He lent five hundred talents to the viceroy Syllaeus[89] and is said to have lent sixty talents to the Arab king Obadas, through Syllaeus.[90] Herod probably lent money to other dignitaries and cit-

---

80. Phasael died in 40 BCE during the Parthian invasion (*Ant.* 14.367–368; *J.W.* 1.271–272), Joseph in 38 BCE, in the subsequent war to recover Herod's kingdom from Antigonus (*Ant.* 14.448–450; *J.W.* 1.323–325).

81. In 47/46 BCE (*J.W.* 1.229, 213; *Ant.* 14.284, 180); see Richardson, *Herod*, 112; Millar, *Roman Near East*, 423–24.

82. *Ant.* 14.280: στρατογον αυτον κοιλης Συριας εποιησαν. That was in 43/42, probably reaffirming the earlier appointment. Josephus's assertion (*J. W.* 1.225) that Herod was at this time "procurator of all Syria (Συριας απασης επιμελητην) is doubtful.

83. 41 BCE (*Ant.* 14.326; *J. W.* 1.244). Richardson, *Herod*, 121–24.

84. Συριας ολης επιτροπον; see also *Ant.* 15.360.

85. Richardson, *Herod*, 234; Braund, *Rome and the Friendly King*, 84–85; Schürer, *History*, 1:319 and n. 122.

86. For example, Oakman, *Political Aims*, 64: "If Herod the Great had tax-farming contracts in Nabataea and Asia (Dar), he certainly had them in his Palestinian kingdom. These arrangements were undoubtedly passed on to Herod Antipas and Archelaus." See Udoh, *To Caesar What Is Caesar's*, 148–50.

87. *Ant.* 16.128. Herod is said to have presented the Emperor with three hundred talents. See Udoh, *To Caesar What Is Caesar's*, 190–91.

88. See *Ant.* 14.364; *J. W.* 1.268.

89. *Ant.* 16.279, 220–225; see *J. W.* 1.487; Strabo, *Geogr.* 16.4.23–24.

90. *Ant.* 16.280–285, 343–355; *J.W.* 1.574–577. Default on the loan is given as the reason why Herod invaded Arab territory around 9 BCE. See Richardson, *Herod*, 279–81; Kasher, *Jews, Idumaeans, and Ancient Arabs*, 156–73.

ies in need. Evidence for this comes from Josephus's report of the numerous debts and taxes he is said to have discharged. Josephus specifically mentions that Herod "lightened the burden of their annual taxes for the inhabitants of Phaselis, Balanea and various minor towns in Cilicia" (*J.W.* 1.428). Gabba, linking Josephus's statement to Herod's procuratorial duties, proposes that the present statement by Josephus "should be understood to mean that Herod held the contract from the Roman state in these areas for the domanial revenues (*vectigalia*) and/or the taxes both direct (*stipendium*) and indirect (*vectigalia*), and that he could afford the generosity of giving up part of his collection rights."[91] This often-repeated view is not tenable.[92] Josephus's statement that Herod relieved some communities of their "debts and taxes" more likely means that Herod paid off the money owed. He did so for the inhabitants of Chios in Asia.[93] Some of the debts he forgave might have been for money that he himself had lent.

### The Estate of the Extinct Hasmonean Dynasty and Others

Herod acquired land, palaces, treasures, and cash. In addition, he confiscated the property of the (pro-Hasmonean) Jewish aristocracy and/or those who were for other reasons opposed to him.[94] He also acquired the property of the demised dynasts—Zenodorus, for example—whose territories were added to his kingdom by Augustus.

### Revenues from Landed Estates and Other Natural Resources

The extent to which large "private estates" existed in Jewish Palestine remains debatable.[95] I have rejected the generally held view that the Hasmoneans, first, and then the Herods held the farmlands of Esdraelon ("the Great Plain" of Jezreel) as their private estate, since Caesar restored the domain to them in 47 BCE. I have argued, instead, that "the villages in the Great Plain" that Caesar restored to "Hyrcanus and the Jews" (*Ant.* 14.207) were not in Esdraelon, but the plain of (south) Sharon, along with the grant of the seaport of Joppa (*Ant.* 14.205–7). Moreover, Caesar's grant of the territory was not a recognition by Caesar that it had been an ancient private crown estate, belonging to Jewish kings. Caesar was reaffirming a previous Jewish claim (going back to Simon the Hasmonean) to Joppa and the surrounding territory lying between Pegae and Gezer (*Ant.* 14.207–8; 13.261; 14.249–50).[96]

91. Gabba, "Social, Economic and Political History," 210 and Gabba, "Finances," 163.

92. See Udoh, *To Caesar What Is Caesar's*, 192 and n. 386.

93. *Ant.* 16.26. Gabba rejects this reading of the text. See, however, Richardson, *Herod*, 272–73 and n. 46.

94. See *Ant.* 15.5–6; 17.307; *J.W.* 1.358; 2.84.

95. See Shimon Applebaum, "Judaea as a Roman Province: The Countryside as a Political and Economic Factor," *ANRW* (1977): 2.8:355–95; David A. Fiensy, *The Social History of Palestine in the Herodian Period: The Land is Mine* (Lewiston, N.Y.: Edwin Mellen, 1991); David A. Fiensy, *Jesus the Galilean: Soundings in a First Century Life* (Piscataway, NJ: Gorgias Press, 2007), 34; Udoh, *To Caesar What Is Caesar's*, 61–62, and the literature cited there.

96. See above; Udoh, "The Great Plain"; Udoh, *To Caesar What Is Caesar's*, 60–75.

There can be no doubt, however, that Herod owned and exploited farmlands within his kingdom. The balsam and date palm estates in Jericho and Phaselis are the best known. Josephus underlines on numerous occasions that the region around Jericho and the Jordan Valley was the most fertile in Judea, interjecting that "it would be no misnomer to describe it as divine."[97] The revenue that Herod derived from the region was such that, rather than lose it when Antony made a gift of it to Cleopatra soon after 37 BCE, he preferred to retain it and pay an annual tribute of two hundred talents to Cleopatra, until it was restored to him in 30 BCE by Octavian.[98] Herod appears also to have exploited land outside his kingdom. He owned land in or near Arabia, part of which was rented as grazing land by the Arabs.[99]

Although one may assume that Antipas received a portion of the family wealth and engaged, at least indirectly, in some form of business transactions, we have no record that he actually did. Despite his Roman citizenship and being "friend (*amicus*)" of Tiberius,[100] he is not reported to have held an administrative post outside his domain. Antipas is not known to have sought to increase his revenues by developing the agricultural potential of his territory, as Herod did in Jericho and Phaselis, and Archelaus did in the same Jordan Valley by founding Archelaïs and planting date palms "in very great numbers and the dates are of the highest quality" (*Ant.* 18.31; 17.340). In spite of the repeated claims that "Antipas, himself, evidently received an annual income of 200 talents both from taxes and from his large estates in Perea and on the Great Plain" (*Ant.* 17.318), there is no actual evidence linking Antipas to "large estates."[101]

## Summary

Josephus sometimes distinguishes between "public funds" and the king's "private" revenues. By "public funds," Josephus means only the temple treasury.[102] Proceeds from royal exploitation of estates, mines, quarries, and other natural resources within Herod's kingdom and Antipater's

---

97. *J.W.* 4.469; see, for example *J.W.* 1.361; *Ant.* 15.96; *J.W.* 1.138; *Ant.* 14.54; 4.100.

98. *Ant.* 15.93–96, 106–107, 132; *J.W.* 1.361–362; *Ant.*15.217; *J.W.* 1.396. With the foundation of the city and the palm groves of Phaselis, Josephus says, Herod "made the surrounding region, formerly a wilderness, more productive through the industry of its inhabitants" (*Ant.* 16.145; see *J.W.* 1.418; 2.167). Pliny (*Nat.Hist.* 12.111–113), after observing that the region's balsam groves belonged formerly to the kings, comments on the groves' importance to the Romans and the steps they took to protect the plants during the revolt of 66 CE. See Udoh, *To Caesar What Is Caesar's*, 65–66.

99. *Ant.* 16.291. Josephus claims that Herod "dedicated groves and meadow-land to communities," while "[m]any cities, as though they had been associated with his realm, received from him grants of land" (*J.W.* 1.422–423). Besides, in his penultimate will Herod left "large tracts of territory" to his relatives (*J.W.* 1.646; see *Ant.* 17.147). We do not know where these territories are located.

100. *Ant.* 18.36.

101. The quote from Fiensy, *Jesus the Galilean: Soundings in a First Century Life*, 34 is emblematic. See the passages he cites (n. 87) from Josephus's works in support of this claim. If the "the Great Plain" (of Jezreel) is removed from this picture, there is nothing left.

102. See, for instance, *Ant.* 14.113; 19.326–327; *J.W.* 2.218–219; 5.147–152.

tetrarchy belonged to their revenues. Their wealth was one and the same thing as government (state) revenues. Generations of scholars have claimed to know the amount of revenues that Herod derived from his kingdom, and Antipas from Galilee. This claim is based on Arnaldo Momigliano's attempt to demonstrate that the figures presented by Josephus, specifically in *Ant.* 17.318–21,[103] for the various parts of Herod's kingdom, at the moment of its partition by Augustus, added up to the sum total of the tax revenues of Herod's kingdom.[104] According to this view, Antipas's annual revenue (during his forty-three-year rule) was two hundred talents. I have shown that Josephus's figures and the calculations that derive from them are not reliable. We cannot, with the extant evidence, accurately determine how much revenue Herod and his sons derived from their domains.[105]

Nonetheless, it is evident that Herod disposed of vast resources; Antipas, on the contrary, had limited resources. This is not to say that Galilee was more prosperous under Herod than it was under Antipas. The limits to his resources help to explain why Antipas's impact on the socioeconomic conditions of early first-century Galilee was moderate.[106]

## Bibliography

Applebaum, Shimon. "Judaea as a Roman Province: The Countryside as a Political and Economic Factor." *ANRW* 2.8.2 (1977): 355–96.

Arnal, William E. *Jesus and the Village Scribes: Galilean Conflicts and the Setting of Q.* Minneapolis: Fortress Press, 2001.

Aviam, Mordechai. "People, Land, Economy, and Belief in First-Century Galilee and Its Origins: A Comprehensive Archaeological Synthesis." In *The Galilean Economy in the Time of Jesus*, edited by David A. Fiensy and Ralph K. Hawkins, 5–48. Early Christianity and Its Literature 11. Atlanta: Society of Biblical Literarute, 2013.

Badian, E. *Roman Imperialism in the Late Republic.* 2nd ed. Ithaca, N.Y.: Cornell University Press, 1968.

Braund, David C. "Client Kings." In *The Administration of the Roman Empire, 241 BC–AD 193*, edited by David C. Braund, 69–96. Exeter Studies in History 18. Exeter: University of Exeter Press, 1988.

---

103. In *Antiquities*, Archelaus: 600 talents; Antipas: 200 talents; Philip: 100 talents; Salome: 60 talents. Total = 960 talents. In *War*, Archelaus: 400 talents. Total: 760 talents.

104. See, for instance, Rocca, *Herod's Judaea*, 208–9. Rocca appeals to Gabba, "Social, Economic and Political History," 118. Gabba notes (n. 107) that his "conclusion is reached through a complex argument based primarily on Jos. *Bell.*=*J.W.* II.94–8 and *Ant.* XVII.318–20," and that he follows Momigliano, *Ricerche*, 46–48; see also Gabba, "Finances," 161 and n. 1.

105. Udoh, *To Caesar What Is Caesar's*, 181–99.

106. See Jensen, *Herod Antipas in Galilee*, 254–59.

————. *Rome and the Friendly King: The Character of the Client Kingship*. London: Croom Helm, 1984.

Broshi, Magen. "The Role of the Temple in the Herodian Economy." *JJS* 38 (1987): 31–37.

Brunt, Peter A. "The Revenues of Rome." *JRS* 71 (1981): 161–72.

————. *Roman Imperial Themes*. Oxford: Clarendon Press, 1990.

Chancey, Mark A. *Greco-Roman Culture and the Galilee of Jesus*. SNTSMS 134. Cambridge: Cambridge University Press, 2005.

Dittenberger, Wilhelm, ed. *Orientis graeci inscriptiones selectae: Supplementum Sylloges inscriptionum graecarum*. 2 vols. Leipzig: Hirzel, 1903–5.

Donahue, John R. "Tax Collectors and Sinners: An Attempt at Identification." *CBQ* 33 (1971): 39–61.

Duncan-Jones, Richard. *Structure and Scale in the Roman Economy*. Cambridge: Cambridge University Press, 1990.

Fiensy, David A. *Jesus the Galilean: Soundings in a First Century Life*. Piscataway, N.J.: Gorgias, 2007.

————. *The Social History of Palestine in the Herodian Period: The Land is Mine*. Studies in the Bible and Early Christianity 20. Lewiston, N.Y.: Mellen, 1991.

Freyne, Seán. *Galilee from Alexander the Great to Hadrian, 323 B.C.E. to 235 C.E.: A Study of Second Temple Judaism*. University of Notre Dame Center for the Study of Judaism and Christianity in Antiquity 5. Wilmington, Del.: Michael Glazier; Notre Dame: University of Notre Dame Press, 1980.

————. "The Geography, Politics, and Economics of Galilee and the Quest for the Historical Jesus." In *Studying the Historical Jesus: Evaluations of the State of Current Research*, edited by Bruce Chilton and Craig A. Evans, 75–121. NTTS 19. Leiden: Brill, 1994.

Gabba, Emilio. "The Finances of King Herod." In *Greece and Rome in Eretz Israel: Collected Essays*, edited by Aryeh Kasher, Uriel Rappaport, and Gideon Fuks, 160–68. Jerusalem: Yad Izhak Ben-Zvi, Israel Exploration Society, 1990.

————. "The Social, Economic and Political History of Palestine 63 B.C.E.–C.E. 70." In *The Cambridge History of Judaism*. Volume 3, *The Early Roman Period*, edited by William Horbury, W. D. Davies, and John Sturdy, 94–168. Cambridge: Cambridge University Press, 1999.

Groom, Nigel. *Frankincense and Myrrh: A Study of the Arabian Incense Trade*. London: Longman, 1981.

Heichelheim, F. M. "Roman Syria." In *An Economic Survey of Ancient Rome*, edited by Tenney Frank, 4:121–257. Baltimore: Johns Hopkins University Press, 1938.

Hoehner, Harold W. *Herod Antipas*. SNTSMS 17. Cambridge: Cambridge University Press, 1972.

Jacobson, David M. "King Herod, Roman Citizen and Benefactor of Kos." *BAIAS* 13 (1993–94): 31–35.

————. "Three Roman Client Kings: Herod of Judaea, Archelaus of Cappadocia and Juba of Mauretania." *PEQ* 133 (2001): 22–38.

Jensen, Morten Hørning. *Herod Antipas in Galilee: The Literary and Archaeological Sources on the Reign of Herod Antipas and Its Socio-Economic Impact on Galilee.* WUNT 2.215. Tübingen: Mohr Siebeck, 2010.

————. "Message and Minting: The Coins of Herod Antipas in Their Second Temple Context as a Source for Understanding the Religio-Political and Socio-Economic Dynamics of Early First Century Galilee." In *Religion, Ethnicity, and Identity in Ancient Galilee: A Region in Transition*, edited by Jürgen Zangenberg, Harold W. Attridge, and Dale B. Martin, 277–313. WUNT 210. Tübingen: Mohr Siebeck, 2007.

Kasher, Aryeh. *Jews, Idumaeans, and Ancient Arabs: Relations of the Jews in Eretz-Israel with the Nations of the Frontier and the Desert during the Hellenistic and Roman Era (332 BCE–70 CE).* TSAJ 18. Tübingen: Mohr Siebeck, 1988.

Laet, Siegfried J. de. *Portorium: Études sur l'organisation douanière chez les Romains, surtout a l'époque du haut-empire.* Brugge: De Tempel, 1949.

Lewis, Naphtali, Yigael Yadin, and Jonas C. Greenfield, eds. *The Documents from the Bar Kokhba Period in the Cave of Letters: Greek Papyri.* Judean Desert Studies 2. Jerusalem: Israel Exploration Society, Hebrew University of Jerusalem, and Shrine of the Book, 1989.

Lintott, Andrew. *Imperium Romanum: Politics and Administration.* London: Routledge, 1993.

Millar, Fergus. *The Roman Near East: 31 BC–AD 337.* Cambridge, Mass.: Harvard University Press, 1993.

Momigliano, Arnaldo. *Ricerche sull'organizzazione della Giudea sotto il dominio romano, 63 a. C.–70 d. C.* Bologna: Annali della R. Scuola Normale Superiore di Pisa, 1934. Reprint, Amsterdam: Hakkert, 1967.

Oakman, Douglas E. *The Political Aims of Jesus: Peasant Politics and Herodian Galilee.* Minneapolis: Fortress Press, 2012.

Pastor, Jack. *Land and Economy in Ancient Palestine.* London: Routledge, 1997.

Pearson, Brook W. R. "The Lucan Censuses, Revisited." *CBQ* 61 (1999): 262–82.

Pucci Ben Zeev, Miriam. *Jewish Rights in the Roman World: The Greek and Roman Documents Quoted by Josephus Flavius.* TSAJ 74. Tübingen: Mohr Siebeck, 1998.

Raschke, Manfred G. "New Studies in Roman Commerce with the East." *ANRW* 2.9.2 (1980): 604–1378.

Rathbone, Dominic W. "Egypt, Augustus and Roman Taxation." *CahGlotz* 4 (1993): 81–112.

Reed, Jonathan L. *Archaeology and the Galilean Jesus: A Re-Examination of the Evidence.* Harrisburg, Pa.: Trinity Press International, 2000.

Richardson, Peter. *Herod: King of the Jews and Friend of the Romans.* Studies on Personalities of the New Testament. Columbia: University of South Carolina Press, 1996. Reprint, Minneapolis: Fortress Press, 1999.

Rocca, Samuel. *Herod's Judaea: A Mediterranean State in the Classical World*. TSAJ 122. Tübingen: Mohr Siebeck, 2008.

Sands, P. C. *The Client Princes of the Roman Empire under the Republic*. Cambridge Historical Essays 16. Cambridge: Cambridge University Press, 1908. Reprint, New York: Arno Press, 1975.

Schalit, Abraham. *König Herodes: Der Mann und sein Werk*. Studia Judaica 4. Berlin: de Gruyter, 1969.

Schürer, Emil. *The History of the Jewish People in the Age of Jesus Christ (175 B.C.–A.D. 135)*. Revised and edited by Geza Vermes, Fergus Millar, Martin Goodman, and Matthew Black, 3 vols. in 4 parts. Edinburgh: T&T Clark, 1973–87.

Sigismund, Marcus. "Coins and Weights as a Mirror of Ethnic, Religious and Political Identity in First and Second Century C.E. Tiberias." In *Religion, Ethnicity, and Identity in Ancient Galilee: A Region in Transition*, edited by Jürgen Zangenberg, Harold W. Attridge, and Dale B. Martin, 315–36. WUNT 210. Tübingen: Mohr Siebeck, 2007.

Sullivan, Richard D. "The Dynasty of Judaea in the First Century." *ANRW* 2.8.2 (1977): 296–354.

Udoh, Fabian E. "*Jewish Antiquities* XIV. 205, 207–08 and 'the Great Plain.'" *PEQ* 134 (2002): 130–43.

———. *To Caesar What Is Caesar's: Tribute, Taxes, and Imperial Administration in Early Roman Palestine (63 B.C.E.–70 C.E.)*. BJS 343. Providence, R.I.: Brown Judaic Studies, 2005.

———. "Tribute and Taxes." In *The Eerdmans Dictionary of Early Judaism*, edited by John J. Collins and Daniel C. Harlow, 1320–23. Grand Rapids: Eerdmans, 2010.

Van Beek, Gus W. "Frankincense and Myrrh." *BA* 23 (1960): 70–95.

# CONTRIBUTORS

ANDREA M. BERLIN
James R. Wiseman Chair in Classical Archaeology, Director of Graduate Studies, Department of Archaeology, Boston University

THOMAS SCOTT CAULLEY
Associate Professor of New Testament, Kentucky Christian University

MARK A. CHANCEY
Professor of Religious Studies, Dedman College of Humanities and Sciences, Southern Methodist University

AGNES CHOI
Assistant Professor of New Testament, Pacific Lutheran University

ROLAND DEINES
Professor in New Testament, Faculty of Arts, Department of Theology and Religious Studies, University of Nottingham

DAVID A. FIENSY
Dean and Professor of New Testament, Graduate School of Bible and Ministry, Kentucky Christian University

RICHARD HORSLEY
Emeritus Professor, University of Massachusetts, Boston

MORTEN HØRNING JENSEN
Adjunct Professor, MF Norwegian School of Theology, Oslo, Norway, and Associate Professor, Lutheran School of Theology, Aarhus, Denmark

LEE I. LEVINE
Institute of Archaeology, Department of Jewish History, Hebrew University of Jerusalem

SHARON LEA MATTILA
Assistant Professor, Department of Philosophy & Religion, University of North Carolina at Pembroke

DOUGLAS E. OAKMAN
Professor of Religion, Pacific Lutheran University

J. ANDREW OVERMAN
Harry M. Drake Distinguished Professor in the Humanities and Fine Arts, Macalester College

JOHN C. POIRIER
Chair of Biblical Studies, Kingswell Theological Seminary

JONATHAN L. REED
Dean, College of Arts and Sciences and Professor of Religion, University of La Verne

ZE'EV SAFRAI
Professor in the Martin Szuss Department of Land of Israel Studies and Archaeology, Bar-Ilan University

JAMES F. STRANGE
Distinguished University Professor, University of South Florida

JAMES RILEY STRANGE
Associate Professor, Department of Religion, Samford University

FABIAN UDOH
Affiliate Faculty, McGill University

# ABBREVIATIONS

| | |
|---|---|
| AASOR | Annual of the American Schools of Oriental Research |
| *ABD* | *The Anchor Bible Dictionary*. Edited by David Noel Freedman. 6 vols. New York: Doubleday, 1992. |
| AGAJU | Arbeiten zur Geschichte des antiken Judentums und des Urchristentums |
| *AJA* | *American Journal of Archaeology* |
| *AJP* | *American Journal of Philology* |
| *AJSR* | *Association for Jewish Studies Review* |
| *ANRW* | *Aufstieg und Niedergang der römischen Welt: Geschichte und Kultur Roms im Spiegel der neueren Forschung*. Edited by H. Temporini and W. Haase. Berlin: de Gruyter, 1972–. |
| AOAT | Alter Orient und Altes Testament |
| *APF* | *Archiv für Papyrusforschung* |
| *BA* | *Biblical Archaeologist* |
| *BAIAS* | *Bulletin of the Anglo=Israel Archeological Society* |
| *BASOR* | *Bulletin of the American Schools of Oriental Research* |
| *BAR* | *Biblical Archaeology Review* |
| BETL | Bibliotheca ephemeridum theologicarum lovaniensium |
| *Bib* | *Biblica* |
| BJS | Brown Judaic Studies |
| *BTB* | *Biblical Theology Bulletin* |
| CahGlotz | Cahiers du Centre Gustave-Glotz |
| *CBR* | *Currents in Biblical Research* |
| *CBQ* | *Catholic Biblical Quarterly* |
| CHANE | Culture and History of the Ancient Near East |
| ConBNT | Coniectanea biblica: New Testament |
| *CQ* | *Classical Quarterly* |
| *CurBS* | *Currents in Research: Biblical Studies* |
| DJD | Discoveries in the Judaean Desert |
| *DSD* | *Dead Sea Discoveries* |
| *EC* | *Early Christianity* |
| *EncJud* | *Encyclopedia Judaica*. 16 vols. Jerusalem, 1972. |
| FRLANT | Forschungen zur Religion und Literatur des Alten und Neuen Testaments |

| | |
|---|---|
| *HA-ESI* | *Hadashot Arkheologiyot—Excavations and Surveys in Israel* |
| *HUCA* | *Hebrew Union College Annual* |
| IAA | Israel Antiquities Authority |
| *IEJ* | *Israel Exploration Journal* |
| *Int* | *Interpretation* |
| *JAC* | *Jahrbuch für Antike und Christentum* |
| *JBL* | *Journal of Biblical Literature* |
| *JESHO* | *Journal of the Economic and Social History of the Orient* |
| *JIH* | *Journal of Interdisciplinary History* |
| *JJS* | *Journal of Jewish Studies* |
| *JQR* | *Jewish Quarterly Review* |
| *JR* | *Journal of Religion* |
| JRASS | Journal of Roman Archaeology Supplementary Series |
| *JRS* | *Journal of Roman Studies* |
| *JSHJ* | *Journal for the Study of the Historical Jesus* |
| *JSJ* | *Journal for the Study of Judaism in the Persian, Hellenistic, and Roman Period* |
| JSJSup | Journal for the Study of Judaism: Supplement Series |
| *JSNT* | *Journal for the Study of the New Testament* |
| JSNTSup | Journal for the Study of the New Testament: Supplement Series |
| *JSOT* | *Journal for the Study of the Old Testament* |
| JSOTSup | Journal for the Study of the Old Testament: Supplement Series |
| JSPSup | Journal for the Study of the Pseudepigrapha: Supplement Series |
| *JTS* | *Journal of Theological Studies* |
| *LASBF* | *Liber annuus Studii biblici franciscani* |
| LCL | Loeb Classical Library |
| LSJ | Liddell, H. G., R. Scott, and H. S. Jones. *A Greek-English Lexicon.* 9th ed. with revised supplement. Oxford: Clarenton, 1966. |
| LXX | Septuagint |
| MT | Masoretic Text |
| *NEA* | *Near Eastern Archaeology* |
| *NEAEHL* | *The New Encyclopedia of Archaeological Excavations in the Holy Land.* Edited by Ephraim Stern. 4 vols. Jerusalem: Israel Exploration Society and Carta, 1993 |
| *Neot* | *Neotestamentica* |
| NIGTC | New International Greek Testament Commentary |
| *NovT* | *Novum Testamentum* |
| NovTSup | Supplements to Novum Testamentum |
| *NTS* | *New Testament Studies* |
| NTTS | New Testament Tools and Studies |
| OBO | Orbis biblicus et orientalis |

| | |
|---|---|
| *OCD* | *The Oxford Classical Dictionary.* Edited by Simon Hornblower and Antony Spawforth. 3rd ed. Oxford: Oxford University Press, 1996. |
| *OEANE* | *The Oxford Encyclopedia of Archaeology in the Near East.* Edited by Eric M. Meyers. New York: Oxford University Press, 1997. |
| *RB* | *Revue biblique* |
| *RevQ* | *Revue de Qumrân* |
| *RQ* | *Römische Quartalschrift für christliche Altertumskunde und Kirchengeschichte* |
| SBLDS | Society of Biblical Literature Dissertation Series |
| SBLMS | Society of Biblical Literature Monograph Series |
| SBLSP | Society of Biblical Literature Seminar Papers |
| SBT | Studies in Biblical Theology |
| SemeiaSt | Semeia Studies |
| *SER* | *Socio-Economic Review* |
| SJLA | Studies in Judaism in Late Antiquity |
| SNTSMS | Society for New Testament Studies Monograph Series |
| *Sociol. Rev.* | *Sociological Review* |
| *ST* | *Studia Theologica* |
| STDJ | Studies on the Texts of the Desert of Judah |
| StPB | Studia Post-Biblica |
| TANZ | Texte und Arbeiten zum neutestamentlichen Zeitalter |
| *TAPA* | *Transactions of the American Philological Association* |
| *TBei* | *Theologische Beiträge* |
| *TLZ* | *Theologische Literaturzeitung* |
| *TRE* | *Theologische Realenzyklopädie.* Edited by G. Krause and G. Müller. Berlin: de Gruyter, 1977. |
| TSAJ | Texte und Studien zum antiken Judentum/Texts and Studies in Ancient Judaism |
| *TTKi* | *Tidsskrift for Teologie og Kirke* |
| *TynBul* | *Tyndale Bulletin* |
| VTSup | Supplements to Vetus Testamentum |
| *WUB* | *Welt und Umwelt der Bibel* |
| WUNT | Wissenschaftliche Untersuchungen zum Neuen Testament |
| *ZDPV* | *Zeitschrift des deutschen Palästina-Vereins* |
| *ZPE* | *Zeitschrift für Papyrologie und Epigraphik* |
| *ZThK* | *Zeitschrift für Theologie und Kirche* |

# INDEX OF ANCIENT SOURCES

**HEBREW BIBLE**

Genesis
12:5-6     263

Exodus
18:21     154

Numbers
34:11     263

Deuteronomy
3:17     263
12:5     104
17:8-11     90
26:13     92

Joshua
13:27     263
19:35     263

1 Samuel
22:1-2     170

2 Samuel
2:1-4     170
4:1-4     170

2 Kings
15:29     53, 113

Isaiah
8:23—9:1     53
8:31     112
9:1     112, 263

Hosea
6:6     88

Joel
4:4     53

Habakkuk
2:1     154

1 Chronicles
5:26     53

2 Chronicles
19:8-11     90

**APOCRYPHA**

Judith
8:5     231

1 Maccabees
1:15     36
5:9-23     54, 115
5:14-24     82
5:14-23     17
5:15     54
5:22     54
5:23     54
9:2     54
11:60-74     115
11:63-74     51
11:67     263
12:24-53     115
13:13-14     367

2 Maccabees     54

**NEW TESTAMENT**

Q (= Luke)
7:24-25     346
9:58     350
12:6-7     354
12:42-46     350
12:58     353
16:13     350

Matthew
2:13-14     84
2:22-23     84
3:7     87
3:17     87
4:14-15     112
4:17     87
4:18     263
4:23     140
5:17-26     87
5:17     83
5:21-48     3
6:2     88
6:5     88
7:28-29     88
7:36-50     87
8:4     87
8:5-15     133
8:5-13     123, 133
9:1-8     87
9:9-13     380
9:11-13     86

Matthew (*continued*)
9:11        87
9:13        88
9:14        87, 88
9:33-34     88
9:34        87, 88
9:35        121, 140, 179
11:16       189
11:20-24    15
12:1-8      86
12:2        88
12:4-5      87
12:7        88
12:9-14     86, 88, 132
12:9        88
12:14       88, 141
12:22-28    87
12:23-24    88
12:28       88
12:34       88
12:38-42    87
12:38-39    86
12:54-56    86
13:54-58    130
13:54       121
14:3-12     156
14:4        157
14:34       263
15:1-12     87
15:1-2      88
15:1        86, 90
15:2        78
15:12       87
15:29       263
16:1-2      86
16:1        87
16:6-12     88
16:6        87
16:12       87
16:21       87
19:3        87
20:3        189
21:45       87

22:15-22    87
22:34       87
22:41       87
23:1-36     87
23:2        79, 88
23:6        88
23:7        189
23:13       88
23:23       95
26:69       11, 13
26:73       13
27:32       289
27:62       87
28:7        98
28:10       98
28:18-20    112

Mark
1:16        263
1:21-29     132, 173
1:21-28     140
1:22        88
1:23-29     121
1:29        232
1:30-31     246
1:33        273
1:38        178
1:39        140
1:44        87
2:1-12      87
2:1         273
2:2-5       173
2:4         230, 232
2:9         232
2:11-12     232
2:15-16     86
2:16        85, 87, 88
2:17        380
2:18        87, 88
2:23-28     86
2:26        87
2:24        88
2:25-26     88

3:1-6       86, 88
3:1         140
3:6         21, 88
3:22        88
5:14        273
5:20        87
6:1-6       130
6:2         121, 140
6:7-12      173
6:17-29     156
6:53        263
6:55        232
6:56        189, 273
7:1-5       86
7:1-2       88
7:1         85, 86, 90
7:3-4       88, 95
7:3         79
7:4         189
7:5         85
7:31        263
8:11-13     86
8:15        87, 88, 89
9:2-8       173
10:2        87
11:9-10     15
12:13-17    87
12:13       90
12:28       189
14:15       231
14:28       98
14:70       13
15:21       289
16:7        98

Luke
2:1-7       379
2:41-50     33
3:10-17     88
4           142
4:15-44     140
4:16-30     131
4:16        121

| | | | | | | | |
|---|---|---|---|---|---|---|---|
| 4:31-38 | 132 | 19:39 | 87 | 19:29 | 135 |
| 4:33-39 | 121 | 20:20-26 | 87 | 22:5 | 92 |
| 4:38 | 246 | 20:46 | 88 | 23:8 | 88 |
| 4:44 | 140 | 22:12 | 231 | 24:5 | 78 |
| 5:1 | 263 | 23:6-12 | 156 | 24:14 | 78 |
| 5:14 | 87 | 23:6-9 | 87 | 25:13—26:32 | 159, 160 |
| 5:27-32 | 380 | 23:6 | 13 | 26:5 | 78 |
| 5:30-32 | 86 | 23:26 | 289 | 26:10 | 92 |
| 5:30 | 87 | 26:5 | 87 | 26:28 | 159 |
| 5:33 | 87, 88 | | | 28:22 | 78 |
| 6:1-5 | 86 | John | | | |
| 6:2 | 88 | 2:1-12 | 268 | Hebrews | |
| 6:4 | 87 | 2:6 | 88, 119 | 8:23 | 263 |
| 6:6-11 | 86, 88 | 4:44-53 | 93 | | |
| 6:7 | 88 | 4:46-54 | 269 | Old Testament | |
| 6:20-21 | 336 | 4:52 | 246 | Pseudepigrapha | |
| 7:1-10 | 121, 133 | 5:8-11 | 232 | *1 Enoch* | |
| 7:1-5 | 133 | 6:1 | 264 | 83:6 | 232 |
| 7:5 | 121, 133 | 6:35-59 | 132, 140 | | |
| 7:30 | 86 | 7:47-49 | 255 | *Psalms of Solomon* | |
| 7:32 | 189 | 18:20 | 140 | 17 | 170 |
| 7:36-39 | 87 | 21:1 | 263 | | |
| 8:28f. | 21 | | | Dead Sea Scrolls | |
| 9:51-53 | 86 | Acts | | CD | |
| 10:13-15 | 15 | 1:3 | 231 | VI, 5 | 84 |
| 11:7 | 232 | 1:11 | 98 | | |
| 11:14-15 | 88 | 4:1-6 | 92 | 4QpNah 3–4 | |
| 11:37-53 | 87 | 5:15 | 232 | II, 4–5 | 84 |
| 11:43 | 189 | 5:17-18 | 92 | II, 8–9 | 88 |
| 12:1 | 87, 88 | 5:17 | 78 | III, 5 | 88 |
| 12:16-20 | 350 | 5:34 | 87, 92 | | |
| 13:10-21 | 140 | 5:37 | 65, 153 | Philo | |
| 13:14 | 141 | 9:2 | 92 | *Against Flaccus* | |
| 13:31 | 65, 86 | 9:31 | 98 | 40 | 158 |
| 14:1 | 86 | 9:33 | 232 | | |
| 14:3 | 86 | 10:37 | 98 | *On the Embassy to Gaius* | |
| 15:2 | 86 | 12:1-4 | 159 | 276–329 | 158 |
| 16:14 | 86 | 12:20-23 | 159 | | |
| 17:7-24 | 132 | 12:20-21 | 338 | Josephus | |
| 17:20 | 86 | 12:20 | 350 | *Against Apion* | |
| 17:34 | 232 | 13:15-16 | 132 | 1.9, 51 | 255 |
| 18:10-11 | 86, 87 | 13:31 | 98 | 1.60 | 332 |
| 19:1-10 | 380 | 15:5 | 78, 87 | 2.18, 178 | 253 |

*Antiquities*

| | |
|---|---|
| 3.194 | 378 |
| 4.100 | 383 |
| 5–7 | 373 |
| 7.394 | 373 |
| 12.119–120 | 380 |
| 12.257–58 | 19 |
| 12.289 | 83 |
| 12.292 | 83 |
| 12.313–19 | 19 |
| 12.318–19 | 53 |
| 12.421 | 54, 55, 273 |
| 13.113–14 | 367 |
| 13.154 | 51, 273 |
| 13.171 | 78 |
| 13.261 | 382 |
| 13.288 | 78 |
| 13.293 | 78 |
| 13.296–97 | 83 |
| 13.297 | 79 |
| 13.301 | 81 |
| 13.318–19 | 115 |
| 13.320–404 | 84 |
| 13.322 | 35, 82, 115 |
| 13.324–97 | 116 |
| 13.337 | 51 |
| 13.338 | 51 |
| 13.372–83 | 84 |
| 13.377 | 85 |
| 13.395–97 | 368 |
| 13.408 | 79 |
| 13.409 | 84 |
| 14.8 | 377 |
| 14.10 | 377 |
| 14.18 | 116 |
| 14.22–24 | 154 |
| 14.22 | 84 |
| 14.54 | 383 |
| 14.73 | 58 |
| 14.77–78 | 58 |
| 14.74–77 | 368 |
| 14.74–76 | 57 |
| 14.74 | 58 |

| | |
|---|---|
| 14.91 | 58 |
| 14.92–97 | 59 |
| 14.92 | 64 |
| 14.101–102 | 59 |
| 14.113 | 383 |
| 14.120 | 59 |
| 14.121–22 | 377 |
| 14.127–33 | 58 |
| 14.137 | 59, 369 |
| 14.143–44 | 59 |
| 14.143 | 369 |
| 14.156–58 | 59 |
| 14.158–64 | 371 |
| 14.158–59 | 151 |
| 14.158 | 59 |
| 14.159 | 11, 62, 151 |
| 14.165–84 | 59 |
| 14.167–74 | 11 |
| 14.180 | 59, 381 |
| 14.190–216 | 58 |
| 14.190–95 | 368 |
| 14.194–96 | 368 |
| 14.195 | 369 |
| 14.196 | 370 |
| 14.200–210 | 368 |
| 14.200–201 | 369 |
| 14.202–3 | 369 |
| 14.204 | 369, 370 |
| 14.205–7 | 382 |
| 14.205–6 | 369 |
| 14.205 | 58 |
| 14.207–8 | 382 |
| 14.207 | 58, 382 |
| 14.217–27 | 371 |
| 14.226 | 369 |
| 14.228–29 | 369 |
| 14.234 | 369 |
| 14.237–40 | 369 |
| 14.249–50 | 382 |
| 14.261 | 158, 376 |
| 14.272–76 | 370 |
| 14.280 | 59, 381 |
| 14.284 | 381 |

| | |
|---|---|
| 14.297–99 | 59 |
| 14.303 | 59 |
| 14.304–23 | 371 |
| 14.326 | 381 |
| 14.342 | 61 |
| 14.364 | 381 |
| 14.367–68 | 381 |
| 14.388 | 60 |
| 14.395 | 60 |
| 14.413–30 | 169 |
| 14.414 | 60 |
| 14.415–16 | 60 |
| 14.420–30 | 60 |
| 14.430–33 | 60 |
| 14.431–33 | 165 |
| 14.432 | 60 |
| 14.433 | 378 |
| 14.448–50 | 381 |
| 14.450 | 60 |
| 14.452–53 | 60 |
| 14.468 | 61 |
| 14.484 | 60 |
| 15.3 | 91 |
| 15.5–6 | 382 |
| 15.5 | 373 |
| 15.9–10 | 60 |
| 15.11 | 159 |
| 15.93–96 | 383 |
| 15.96 | 376, 383 |
| 15.106–7 | 383 |
| 15.109 | 373 |
| 15.132 | 383 |
| 15.189 | 373 |
| 15.198–200 | 373 |
| 15.217 | 376, 383 |
| 15.254 | 377 |
| 15.257 | 377 |
| 15.266–76 | 61 |
| 15.268 | 373 |
| 15.294 | 264 |
| 15.299–316 | 351 |
| 15.303 | 367, 374 |
| 15.305–6 | 374 |

| | | | | | |
|---|---|---|---|---|---|
| 15.328–41 | 61 | 17.306–8 | 380 | 18.274 | 171 |
| 15.328 | 60 | 17.307 | 382 | 18.283–84 | 171 |
| 15.360 | 381 | 17.318–21 | 384 | 18.312 | 378 |
| 15.362 | 372 | 17.318 | 383 | 19.36–39 | 156 |
| 15.365 | 374, 379 | 17.320 | 378 | 19.236–45 | 159 |
| 15.373 | 78 | 17.321 | 377 | 19.274–75 | 159 |
| 15.387 | 372 | 17.340 | 383 | 19.276–77 | 160 |
| 15.398 | 246 | 17.355 | 379 | 19.326–27 | 383 |
| 16.26 | 382 | 18.1–4 | 379 | 19.329 | 380 |
| 16.62–65 | 371 | 18.4–6 | 170 | 19.350–52 | 67 |
| 16.63–65 | 379–80 | 18.4 | 65, 91, 153, | 19.351 | 159 |
| 16.128 | 381 | | | 379 | 19.354 | 159 |
| 16.136–49 | 61 | 18.9–10 | 170 | 19.363 | 159 |
| 16.145 | 383 | 18.9 | 78 | 20.1 | 159 |
| 16.154–56 | 380 | 18.11 | 78 | 20.97–98 | 173 |
| 16.179–83 | 373 | 18.23–25 | 153, | 20.104 | 160 |
| 16.220–25 | 381 | 18.23–24 | 170 | 20.118–36 | 67 |
| 16.279 | 381 | 18.23 | 65, 78, 91 | 20.145 | 160 |
| 16.280–85 | 381 | 18.25 | 78 | 20.146 | 160 |
| 16.285 | 372 | 18.26 | 379 | 20.159 | 67, 159 |
| 16.343–55 | 381 | 18.27 | 64, 156 | 20.169–71 | 173 |
| 17.23–27 | 372 | 18.31 | 383 | 20.199 | 78 |
| 17.27–28 | 372 | 18.36–38 | 247 | | |
| 17.42–43 | 378 | 18.36 | 383 | *Jewish War* | |
| 17.146 | 155 | 18.85–87 | 173 | 1.50–53 | 367 |
| 17.147 | 383 | 18.90 | 376 | 1.65 | 81 |
| 17.149–65 | 326 | 18.108 | 373 | 1.70 | 83 |
| 17.149 | 91 | 18.113–15 | 65 | 1.77 | 81 |
| 17.151–52 | 326 | 18.116–20 | 157 | 1.85–106 | 84 |
| 17.191 | 380 | 18.116–19 | 63, 65, 156 | 1.85 | 83 |
| 17.204–5 | 380 | 18.119 | 65 | 1.86–97 | 116 |
| 17.205 | 376 | 18.143–47 | 158 | 1.86 | 51 |
| 17.213–18 | 62 | 18.149 | 134, 158, 376 | 1.93 | 85 |
| 17.224–27 | 62 | 18.161–236 | 158 | 1.98 | 84 |
| 17.224 | 156 | 18.165 | 157, 158 | 1.104–5 | 116 |
| 17.246 | 372 | 18.237 | 158 | 1.111 | 84 |
| 17.269–85 | 62 | 18.240–55 | 157 | 1.120–22 | 58 |
| 17.271–72 | 62, 152, 169 | 18.240–46 | 158 | 1.123 | 377 |
| 17.271 | 60, 62, 156 | 18.252 | 67 | 1.138 | 383 |
| 17.273–84 | 169 | 18.253–55 | 158 | 1.153 | 58 |
| 17.285 | 62 | 18.257–309 | 171 | 1.154–57 | 368 |
| 17.289 | 62, 156 | 18.257–60 | 158 | 1.155–58 | 57 |
| 17.299 | 62 | 18.269 | 67 | 1.155 | 58 |

*Jewish War* (continued)

| | |
|---|---|
| 1.160–178 | 58 |
| 1.170 | 58 |
| 1.171–74 | 59 |
| 1.177 | 59 |
| 1.180 | 59 |
| 1.193–203 | 59 |
| 1.193–94 | 58 |
| 1.194 | 369 |
| 1.199 | 369 |
| 1.201–5 | 151 |
| 1.203–7 | 371 |
| 1.203 | 59, 151 |
| 1.204 | 11, 59, 62 |
| 1.205–11 | 59 |
| 1.213 | 59, 381 |
| 1.218–22 | 370 |
| 1.221 | 59 |
| 1.225 | 381 |
| 1.229 | 381 |
| 1.238–39 | 59 |
| 1.242 | 59 |
| 1.244 | 371, 381 |
| 1.256 | 61 |
| 1.268 | 381 |
| 1.271–72 | 381 |
| 1.282 | 371 |
| 1.285 | 60 |
| 1.291 | 60 |
| 1.303 | 60 |
| 1.304–13 | 169 |
| 1.305–6 | 60 |
| 1.305 | 168 |
| 1.309–13 | 60 |
| 1.314–16 | 168 |
| 1.315–16 | 60 |
| 1.323–25 | 381 |
| 1.326 | 60 |
| 1.327 | 61 |
| 1.329–30 | 60 |
| 1.355 | 60 |
| 1.358 | 373, 382 |
| 1.361–62 | 376, 383 |

| | |
|---|---|
| 1.361 | 383 |
| 1.388 | 373 |
| 1.394–95 | 373, 374 |
| 1.396 | 376, 383 |
| 1.399 | 381 |
| 1.400 | 372 |
| 1.401–28 | 61 |
| 1.418 | 383 |
| 1.422–23 | 383 |
| 1.428 | 382 |
| 1.483 | 372 |
| 1.487 | 381 |
| 1.505 | 273 |
| 1.574–77 | 381 |
| 1.646 | 155, 383 |
| 1.648 | 91 |
| 1.651–55 | 326 |
| 2.4–13 | 62 |
| 2.4 | 376, 380 |
| 2.20–32 | 62 |
| 2.20–22 | 156 |
| 2.20 | 155 |
| 2.55–65 | 62 |
| 2.56 | 62, 65, 152, 156, 168 |
| 2.57–59 | 169 |
| 2.60–65 | 169 |
| 2.65 | 62 |
| 2.68 | 62, 156 |
| 2.79 | 62 |
| 2.84 | 382 |
| 2.85–86 | 380 |
| 2.98 | 377 |
| 2.111 | 273 |
| 2.116 | 170 |
| 2.118 | 65, 78, 91, 152, 153 |
| 2.119 | 78 |
| 2.122 | 78 |
| 2.124–25 | 91 |
| 2.129 | 273 |
| 2.137 | 78 |
| 2.142 | 78 |

| | |
|---|---|
| 2.162 | 78 |
| 2.166 | 78 |
| 2.167 | 156, 383 |
| 2.178–80 | 158 |
| 2.183–203 | 171 |
| 2.183 | 67, 158 |
| 2.193 | 67 |
| 2.215–16 | 159 |
| 2:218–19 | 159, 383 |
| 2.219 | 67, 159 |
| 2.220 | 159 |
| 2.221–23 | 160 |
| 2.232–35 | 67 |
| 2.252 | 67, 159 |
| 2.261–63 | 173 |
| 2.287 | 377, 380 |
| 2.292 | 380 |
| 2.360 | 160 |
| 2.390–91 | 160 |
| 2.407 | 161 |
| 2.412 | 273 |
| 2.418–21 | 68 |
| 2.418 | 68 |
| 2.426 | 159, 161 |
| 2.427–48 | 163 |
| 2.433–35 | 163 |
| 2.447–48 | 163 |
| 2.457–59 | 162 |
| 2.499–556 | 68 |
| 2.500–503 | 160 |
| 2.504 | 273, 336 |
| 2.510–12 | 68 |
| 2.511 | 69 |
| 2.523–25 | 160 |
| 2.527–75 | 34 |
| 2.533 | 68 |
| 2.566–3.203 | 5 |
| 2.568–564 | 68 |
| 2.568 | 68, 273 |
| 2.569–71 | 335 |
| 2.573–75 | 69 |
| 2.585–94 | 168 |
| 2.590 | 336 |

| | | | |
|---|---|---|---|
| 2.591–92 | 336, 380 | 7.47 | 135 |
| 2.592 | 380 | 7.252–55 | 163 |
| 2.598 | 160 | | |
| 2.599 | 134 | *Life* | |
| 2.604–9 | 69 | 10–12 | 78 |
| 2.615 | 134 | 10 | 78 |
| 2.618 | 64 | 12 | 78, 91 |
| 2.632–34 | 163 | 17–23 | 68 |
| 2.641 | 134 | 23–24 | 68 |
| 2.652–53 | 169 | 23 | 68 |
| 3.29–43 | 68 | 28–413 | 68 |
| 3.30–34 | 69 | 28–29 | 68 |
| 3.35–44 | 34 | 28 | 69 |
| 3.35–36 | 264 | 30–31 | 69 |
| 3.41–44 | 349 | 32 | 69 |
| 3.41–42 | 30 | 34 | 69 |
| 3.42–43 | 358 | 37–38 | 64, 67 |
| 3.59–4.120 | 70 | 37 | 162 |
| 3.59–63 | 68 | 39 | 69 |
| 3.110–542 | 68 | 41 | 162 |
| 3.114 | 273 | 46–61 | 69 |
| 3.128–31 | 69 | 49 | 160 |
| 3.135 | 273 | 64–69 | 64 |
| 3.401–2 | 69 | 65–67 | 123 |
| 3.516 | 380 | 65–66 | 326 |
| 3.539 | 64 | 69 | 134 |
| 3.622 | 160 | 71 | 350 |
| 4.1–120 | 68 | 73–74 | 336 |
| 4.1 | 273 | 73 | 350 |
| 4.11–54 | 70 | 74 | 380 |
| 4.62–83 | 70 | 79 | 335 |
| 4.100–102 | 162 | 85 | 64 |
| 4.123 | 273 | 91 | 135 |
| 4.128–61 | 168 | 92 | 64 |
| 4.134–61 | 159 | 119 | 350 |
| 4.389–90 | 162 | 124 | 273 |
| 4.442 | 273 | 134 | 134 |
| 4.457 | 246 | 136–44 | 69 |
| 4.469 | 383 | 157 | 264 |
| 4.503–13 | 169 | 187–88 | 69 |
| 4.529–34 | 169 | 189–335 | 69 |
| 5.147–52 | 383 | 191–92 | 90 |
| 5.155 | 163 | 191 | 78, 91 |

| | |
|---|---|
| 196–98 | 90 |
| 197 | 78 |
| 220 | 335 |
| 235 | 34, 177, 264, 273 |
| 246 | 336 |
| 265 | 264 |
| 266–68 | 335 |
| 271 | 134 |
| 277–80 | 121 |
| 277 | 64, 134 |
| 278 | 134 |
| 279 | 134 |
| 280 | 134 |
| 290–303 | 134 |
| 294 | 134 |
| 296 | 134 |
| 305 | 335 |
| 331 | 64, 135 |
| 340–44 | 162 |
| 346–48 | 69 |
| 384 | 69 |
| 394 | 69 |
| 411 | 70 |

RABBINIC LITERATURE
Mishnah
*'Abot*

| | |
|---|---|
| 1:7 | 84 |
| 6:8 | 164 |

*'Arakin*

| | |
|---|---|
| 9:6 | 234 |

*Baba Batra*

| | |
|---|---|
| 1:1 | 230 |
| 1:4 | 233 |
| 1:6 | 233 |
| 2:2–3 | 231, 234 |
| 2:3 | 317 |
| 3:5 | 234, 235 |
| 4:4 | 234 |
| 4:8–9 | 317 |

*Baba Batra (continued)*
| | |
|---|---|
| 5:8–10 | 317 |
| 6:4 | 232 |
| 6:7 | 292 |
| 9:8–10 | 232 |

*Baba Meṣiʿa*
| | |
|---|---|
| 2:4 | 317 |
| 3:11 | 317 |
| 4:4 | 317 |
| 4:6 | 291, 317 |
| 4:11–12 | 317 |
| 5:4 | 317 |
| 5:8 | 320 |
| 5:9 | 333 |
| 6:1 | 317 |
| 7:1–8 | 320 |
| 7:1 | 320 |
| 7:6 | 320 |
| 7:8 | 317 |
| 8:6 | 317 |
| 8:7 | 317 |
| 9:1–10 | 317 |
| 9:11–12 | 320 |
| 9:12 | 317 |

*Baba Qamma*
| | |
|---|---|
| 6:6 | 317 |
| 8:1 | 317 |
| 9:3 | 317 |
| 9:4 | 317 |
| 10:9 | 317 |
| 10:10 | 317 |

*Berakot*
| | |
|---|---|
| 5:5 | 155 |
| 9:5 | 288 |

*Demai*
| | |
|---|---|
| 1:4 | 317 |
| 2:4 | 317 |
| 3:4 | 317 |
| 3:5 | 317 |

| | |
|---|---|
| 5:4 | 317 |
| 5:6 | 317 |

*ʿErubin*
| | |
|---|---|
| 5:8 | 289 |
| 7:1 | 233 |
| 8:4 | 234 |
| 8:6 | 234 |
| 10:10 | 293 |

*Ḥallah*
| | |
|---|---|
| 1:8 | 317 |

*Kelim*
| | |
|---|---|
| 2:2 | 196 |

*Ketubbot*
| | |
|---|---|
| 5:4 | 318 |
| 5:5 | 318 |
| 5:8 | 318 |
| 5:9 | 318 |
| 13:10 | 289 |

*Kilaʾyim*
| | |
|---|---|
| 1:4 | 285 |
| 9:3 | 317 |
| 9:5 | 317 |
| 9:6 | 317 |

*Maʿaśer Šeni*
| | |
|---|---|
| 4:2 | 317 |

*Maʿaśerot*
| | |
|---|---|
| 2:3 | 317 |
| 3:5 | 233 |

*Megillah*
| | |
|---|---|
| 1:1–2 | 179 |

*Nedarim*
| | |
|---|---|
| 7:4 | 231 |

*Niddah*
| | |
|---|---|
| 9:4 | 232 |

*ʾOhalot*
| | |
|---|---|
| 5:6 | 234 |

*Parah*
| | |
|---|---|
| 3:3 | 119 |
| 6:5 | 291 |

*Peʾah*
| | |
|---|---|
| 5:6 | 321 |
| 7:3 | 321 |
| 8:7 | 230 |
| 8:8–9 | 321 |

*Pesahim*
| | |
|---|---|
| 1:1 | 234 |

*Qiddušin*
| | |
|---|---|
| 2:3 | 290 |

*Šabbat*
| | |
|---|---|
| 3:4 | 293 |

*Šebiʿit*
| | |
|---|---|
| 5:6 | 317 |
| 8:5 | 317 |
| 10:1 | 317 |

*Soṭah*
| | |
|---|---|
| 9:15 | 155, 164 |

*Taʿanit*
| | |
|---|---|
| 3:8 | 154 |

*ʿUqṣin*
| | |
|---|---|
| 3:2 | 290 |

Tosefta
*Baba Batra*
| | |
|---|---|
| 1:4 | 317 |
| 2:6 | 317 |
| 2:14 | 234 |
| 2:15 | 317 |
| 2:16 | 234 |
| 3:1 | 234 |

*Baba Meṣiʿa*
| | |
|---|---|
| 1:14 | 290 |
| 2:14 | 317 |
| 3:2 | 291 |
| 3:16 | 318 |
| 3:25 | 317 |
| 3:27–28 | 317 |
| 4:2 | 317 |
| 4:8 | 317 |
| 4:9 | 317 |
| 4:11–13 | 317 |
| 6:3 | 285 |
| 7:2–8 | 321 |
| 7:15–17 | 317 |
| 8:1–3 | 321 |
| 8:2 | 321 |
| 8:6–9 | 321 |
| 9:1–33 | 321 |
| 9:102–6 | 321 |
| 10:7 | 317 |
| 10:11 | 317 |
| 11:5 | 317 |
| 11:15–17 | 317 |
| 11:18 | 317 |
| 11:24 | 317, 318 |
| 11:25 | 317 |
| 11:26 | 317, 318 |
| 11:27 | 317, 319 |
| 11:30 | 317 |

*Baba Qamma*
| | |
|---|---|
| 6:5 | 317 |
| 6:20 | 317 |
| 6:26 | 317 |
| 6:28 | 317 |
| 7:8 | 317 |
| 9:3 | 317 |
| 10:8 | 317 |
| 10:9–10 | 317 |
| 11:8 | 317 |
| 11:9–10 | 317 |
| 11:11 | 317 |
| 11:12 | 317 |

| | |
|---|---|
| 11:13 | 317 |
| 11:15 | 317 |
| 11:17 | 317 |
| 11:18 | 317 |

*Berakot*
| | |
|---|---|
| 3:20 | 154 |

*Demai*
| | |
|---|---|
| 1:1 | 285 |
| 1:11 | 281 |

*ʿErubin*
| | |
|---|---|
| 6:13–14 | 233 |
| 7:7 | 234 |
| 7:9 | 233 |
| 7:14 | 233 |

*Ḥulin*
| | |
|---|---|
| 2:22–23 | 101 |
| 2:24 | 101 |

*Kilʾayim*
| | |
|---|---|
| 38b | 285 |

*Maʿaśerot*
| | |
|---|---|
| 2:20 | 234 |
| 3:8 | 234 |

*Makširin*
| | |
|---|---|
| 3:5 | 285 |

*Megillah*
| | |
|---|---|
| 1:1 | 290 |
| 3 | 142 |

*Niddah*
| | |
|---|---|
| 6:9 | 290 |

*Peʾah*
| | |
|---|---|
| 20a–b | 285 |

*Pesaḥim*
| | |
|---|---|
| 2:1 | 319 |

*Šabbat*
| | |
|---|---|
| 1:4 | 231 |
| 13:9 | 288 |

*Sanhedrin*
| | |
|---|---|
| 2:6 | 92 |

*Sotah*
| | |
|---|---|
| 3:16 | 290 |

*Sukkah*
| | |
|---|---|
| 4:6 | 135 |

*Taʿanit*
| | |
|---|---|
| 1:13 | 293 |

Talmud of Israel
*ʿAbodah Zarah*
| | |
|---|---|
| 40c | 284 |

*Baba Batra*
| | |
|---|---|
| 2:7 | 233 |
| 10c | 281 |

*Baba Meṣiʿa*
| | |
|---|---|
| 5b | 286 |
| 9c | 287 |
| 10c | 286, 287 |

*Berakot*
| | |
|---|---|
| 7c | 93 |
| 8c | 287 |

*Demai*
| | |
|---|---|
| 22a | 287 |

*ʿErubin*
| | |
|---|---|
| 54c | 287 |

*Ketubbot*
| | |
|---|---|
| 31b | 290 |
| 32c | 253, 255 |
| 35d | 287 |

*Kil'ayim*
27a          293
32b          247
38b          285

*Ma'aśer Šeni*
56b          285

*Megillah*
70a          289

*Nedarim*
41a          287

*Niddah*
50b          284

*Pe'ah*
16a          281, 286
7:1          6
7:3b         286

*Pesaḥim*
30d          281, 284

*Qiddušin*
66a          83

*Šabbat*
4d           87
6.1          233
15d          20, 93

*Šebi'it*
35c          287
38a          287

*Šeqalim*
47a          286

*Sukkah*
1:12         285

*Ta'anit*
3:4          6
69a          291

Talmud of Babylonia
*'Abodah Zarah*
41a          290

*Baba Batra*
21a          253, 255
74b          155
75b          287

*Baba Meṣi'a*
74a          196

*Berakot*
33a          154
34b          93, 246
61b          154

*'Erubin*
53b          13

*Ḥagigah*
14a          154–55

*Ḥulim*
6b           286

*Ketubbot*
35a          164
103b         164, 247
104a         164

*Megillah*
2b           289
2:2          290
3b           289
11a          164

*Mo'ed Qaṭan*
13b          281, 284
18a          281

21a          293

*Niddah*
21a          284

*Pesaḥim*
8a           234
40a          290
113a         291

*Roš Haššanah*
31b          5

*Šabbat*
39b          293
120b         196
121a         288

*Sanhedrin*
32b          293
107b         84

*Sotah*
47a          84

*Sukkah*
20b          285
27a          288

*Ta'anit*
23a          154
24b–25a      155
25a          155

*Yoma*
11a          234, 287

OTHER RABBINIC WORKS
*'Abot de R. Nathan A*
6.15         256

*Midrash on Psalms*
93           134
(Ps. 118) 18  289

*Sifre Deuteronomy*
46            254
316           285
325           287

*Breshit Rabbah*
19a           281
32:9          281
77b           281
96:5          287

*Vayikra Rabbah*
34:12         287

*Ruth Rabbah*
3             287

*Eicha Rabba*
3:9           285

*Qohelet Rabbah*
3:9           287

*Qohelet Zuta*
2             287

*Tanḥuma Buber, Shoftim*
9             289
10            289

*Tanḥuma Judges*
9             289

CLASSICAL AND ANCIENT
CHRISTIAN WRITINGS
Anonymous
*Epitome de Caesaribus*
10.4.7        161

Appian
*Bella civilia (Civil Wars)*
5.4           370

Cassius Dio
*Roman History*
39.56.6       368
42.6.3        370
53.22.5       378
59.8.2        158
60.8.2        158
62.3.3        378
64.15.3–5     161
65.7.2        378
66.18.1       161

Cato
*Agriculture*
14.5          149

Cicero
*Epistulae ad familiares*
*(Letters to Friends)*
3.8.3–5       375

*In Verrem (Against Verres)*
2.3.199       375
3.6.12–15     370

*Letters to Atticus*
5.16.2        375

*Pro Flacco (For Flaccus)*
69            368

*Provinciis consularibus*
*(On the Consular Provinces)*
5.10          368

Epiphanius
*Panarion*
30.4.1        101
30.4.5        101
30.5.5        101

Eusebius
*Historia ecclesiastica*
1.7.14        101

3.5.2–3       99
3.20.1–2      350

Georgius Syncellus
*Chronography*
355           273

*Itinerarium Burdigalense*
              101

Justin Martyr
*Dialogue with Trypho*
108           13

Julius Caesar
*De bello civile*
*(On the Civil War)*
3.3           370
3.31          370
3.32          375
3.103         370

Juvenal
*Satirae*
6.156–58      161

Pliny the Elder
*Natural History*
5.70          79
5.71          156
12.32.51–71   377
12.111–13     383

Polybius
5.70.3        273

Stephanus Byzantinus
*Ethics*
666–67        273

Strabo
*Geography*
16.2.2        79

*Geography* (*continued*)
| | |
|---|---|
| 16.2.10 | 81 |
| 16.2.18 | 81 |
| 16.2.20 | 81 |
| 16.2.21 | 79 |
| 16.2.32 | 79 |
| 16.2.34 | 79 |
| 16.2.40 | 79 |
| 16.2.41–45 | 79 |
| 16.2.45 | 79 |
| 16.4.23–24 | 381 |
| 16.4.24 | 377 |

Suetonius
*Claudius*
| | |
|---|---|
| 11 | 159 |

Tacitus
*Annales*
| | |
|---|---|
| 12.54 | 67 |

*Historiae*
| | |
|---|---|
| 2.1–2 | 160 |
| 2.79 | 160 |
| 2.81–88 | 160 |

| | |
|---|---|
| 2.81.2 | 161 |
| 5.2–13 | 162 |
| 5.9.1 | 158 |

Varro
*De re rustica*
| | |
|---|---|
| 1.4.3 | 249 |

PAPYRI
*BGU*
| | |
|---|---|
| 1.14 | 307 |

*P.Cairo.Goodspeed*
| | |
|---|---|
| 30 | 307 |

*P.Fay*
| | |
|---|---|
| 91 | 306 |
| 102 | 306 |
| 110–23 | 306 |
| 248 | 306 |
| 249 | 306 |
| 252 | 306 |
| 254 | 306 |
| 255 | 306 |
| 259–61 | 306 |

| | |
|---|---|
| 265 | 306 |
| 273–77 | 306 |

*P.Flor.*
| | |
|---|---|
| 2.176 | 306 |

*P.Mil.Vogl.*
| | |
|---|---|
| 1.23–28 | 306 |
| 2.50–72 | 306 |
| 3.129–54 | 306 |
| 4.209–19 | 306 |
| 6.264–82 | 306 |
| 7.301–8 | 306 |

*PSI*
| | |
|---|---|
| 6.688 recto | 307 |
| 8.961A and B | 306 |

*P. Yadin*
| | |
|---|---|
| 1–35 | 326 |
| 16 | 326 |
| 17 | 326 |
| 18 | 326 |
| 21–24 | 326 |

# Index of Subjects

abecedaries, 36, 256–57
agrarian, 4, 169, 171, 195,
    299, 302, 322, 348–52
Agrippa I, xiii, 19, 67, 134,
    157–59, 171, 338, 350,
    372, 374–76
Agrippa II, xiii, 69, 159–63
Akko, 28, 56, 211, 337
Alexander Jannaeus, xii, 35,
    55, 81–85, 104, 115–16,
    136, 209, 214, 246,
    332–33
Amoraic, 254, 256, 272,
    283–85, 291, 293, 319
anthropology, cultural, 3, 37
Antigonus, xii, 58–60, 81, 225,
    381
Antiochus IV (Epiphanes), xii,
    36, 83–84, 95
Antipas, xi, xiii, xvii, 5, 29–31,
    33–35, 52, 61–67, 73,
    123, 134, 155–59, 173,
    192, 242, 249–50, 264,
    273, 328, 338, 352,
    366–69, 371–81, 383–84
Arbel, G-1, 55, 60–61, 84, 97,
    168, 182, 223, 269, 273,
    281, 304
archaeological surveys, 5, 55,
    81, 97, 113, 180
Aristobulus I, xii, 52, 81, 115
Aristobulus II, xii, 58–59, 67,
    154

Athronges, 62, 169

Babatha, 326–27, 379
banditry, 30–31, 104, 151,
    167–71, 225–26, 349
Bar Kokhba, xi, xv, 28, 72,
    74, 80, 86, 94–97,
    102–3, 119–20, 142,
    146, 225, 258, 283,
    292, 326
Bernice, 160–61
Bethsaida, 82, 123, 199, 200,
    273–74, 290, 302, 304,
    352
Byzantine, ix, xvii, 121, 180,
    183, 187, 190, 218, 232,
    234, 236–37, 243, 279,
    283, 294, 304, 313–14,
    317, 322–26, 329, 336,
    339

Cana, G-7, 93, 119, 137, 181,
    185, 193, 197, 220,
    223, 247, 256, 268–69,
    283, 358, 361. See also
    Khirbet Qana
Capernaum, G-4, G-5, 7, 95,
    100, 119, 121, 123,
    129–33, 144, 181,
    183, 185–86, 190–91,
    193–94, 196, 198–200,
    223–25, 230, 234,
    246–47, 256, 269, 273,

302, 304, 313, 323, 330,
    361, 380
Cardo, 192, 276, 279–80,
    282
Cave of Letters, 326
Christians (Jewish), 98, 100
cities, xvii, 4–5, 7, 15, 18, 19,
    23, 28–29, 32, 34–35,
    62, 64, 69–73, 81–82,
    95, 97, 101, 103, 121,
    140, 156, 162, 171,
    177–79, 181–83, 185–
    86, 189, 192, 196, 200–
    201, 224, 238, 249–50,
    269, 272–74, 276–81,
    284–90, 292–94, 298,
    312, 314, 316, 319, 325,
    333, 337, 352, 360–63,
    369–70, 374, 376–78,
    380, 383
coins, numismatics, 56, 64–65,
    70–72, 96, 116, 124,
    231, 256, 264, 274,
    278–79, 314, 330–36,
    352, 374–75, 380
commerce, 286–87, 333, 348,
    358. See also trade
courtyard, 185, 187, 189, 197,
    199, 200, 216–22, 224–
    25, 229–30, 232–38,
    323, 335, 361
craftsmen, 32–33, 228, 286,
    317, 319–20, 353

customs, 305, 308. *See also*
    tolls
Cynics, Cynicism, 4, 19, 21,
    24–26

Early Roman, ix, 56, 115–16,
    119, 121, 178, 183, 197,
    226, 235–37, 247, 249,
    280, 315, 322, 327–30,
    335–38, 347, 351,
    359–60, 366–67, 371,
    373, 380
earthquakes, 357, 360–61, 363
Eastern Terra Sigillata A
    (ETSA), 329–30, 332,
    335, 337, 362
economics, 242, 248
education, 7, 17, 20–21, 23,
    35–36, 89, 156, 253–58
ethnicity, 6, 26, 112
Essenes, 14, 21, 78, 86, 91,
    133, 226
Evangelists, 85–88. *See also*
    Synoptic Gospels

Fourth Philosophy 78, 80, 91,
    153, 163, 172

Gadara, 23, 34, 58, 376
Galilean Coarse Ware, 114,
    116, 330
Gamaliel, 90–93, 102, 153
Gamla, xi, 67, 70–71, 82,
    91, 118–19, 121, 130,
    135–37, 144, 170,
    190–93, 210–11, 213,
    220–22, 255, 273–76,
    330–31, 334–35, 353
Gischala. *See* Gush Halav
glass, 194, 200, 283–85, 316,
    324, 336
Great Revolt, 226, 327, 332.
    *See also* Jewish Revolt

guilds, 284–86, 318–19
Gush Halav (Gischala), xvii,
    287

*Halakhah*, 13, 88, 143, 212,
    286, 289–91, 293, 328,
    332
Ḥanina ben Dosa, 92, 104,
    154–55, 246
Hasmonean, xii, 5, 19, 22–23,
    29, 35, 51–54, 56–58,
    60, 67, 73, 80–84, 94,
    97, 104, 115–19, 122,
    129, 161, 168, 183,
    208–9, 211–12, 214,
    226, 242, 314, 327,
    328–34, 336–37, 339,
    349, 367, 368, 382
Hellenistic, ix, xii, xvii, 23–24,
    26–27, 34, 36, 55, 62,
    95, 97, 113, 115–16,
    129, 134, 137, 162, 180,
    183, 189, 191, 213, 217,
    226, 236–37, 243, 247,
    274, 278, 280, 282, 284,
    287, 289–90, 283, 314,
    325, 330–31, 336–38,
    349, 351–52, 358–59,
    367, 380
Herod the Great, xi, xiii,
    58–59, 61, 67, 73, 119,
    152–53, 155–57, 159,
    226, 264, 359, 366–68,
    371, 381
Herodian, xiii, 34–35, 52,
    60–62, 66–67, 73,
    89–90, 120, 133, 163,
    170–71, 183, 185, 187,
    197, 201, 224, 226,
    229, 231–32, 238, 307,
    327, 329–30, 332–33,
    338, 347, 351–52, 354,
    366–68, 371, 373, 375

Hezekiah (Ezekias), 11, 59, 60,
    62, 65, 104, 151–52,
    156, 168–70
Hillel, 13, 101, 164, 333
Ḥoni the Circle Drawer, 92,
    154
household/house, 7, 26, 32,
    94–95, 98, 100, 121–22,
    130, 146, 181, 183, 185,
    187, 189, 197–201,
    208–12, 214–15,
    216–38, 249–50, 280,
    307, 313, 317, 319,
    320, 321, 323, 324–25,
    334–36, 346, 349–51,
    353, 360–61, 374–76,
    378
Hyrcanus II, xii, 58, 154, 368,
    378

industry, 194, 196–201, 272,
    281, 283–85, 288, 302,
    309, 317–18, 323, 328,
    352, 380, 383
*insula*, G-5, 199, 217–18, 220,
    222, 224–25
*Ioudaios*, 117–18, 208, 211–12
Itureans, 53–54, 56, 81, 115

Jalame, 198, 200, 283
Jamnia. *See* Yavneh
Jerusalem, xi, xv, 11, 13–15,
    19–23, 27, 29–30,
    32–35, 37–38, 55,
    57–62, 65, 67–69, 71,
    73, 79, 81, 83–96,
    98–99, 102–4, 120,
    122–23, 129–30, 133,
    138–39, 142, 146, 151,
    154, 156, 158–59,
    161–63, 169, 171–73,
    183, 185, 189, 197, 201,
    208–14, 220–21, 226,

231, 255–56, 266, 277, 289, 291–92, 301, 327, 329, 330, 333, 339, 351–53, 360, 362, 369, 374–76

Jesus of Nazareth, 12, 65, 73, 98, 172, 227, 347, 357

Jesus Seminar, 336

Jewish Revolt, xi, 80, 133, 160, 357, 362. *See also* Great Revolt

John, Gospel of, 87, 119

John of Gischala, 161–62, 168, 336, 380

John Hyrcanus I, xii, 58, 154, 368, 378

Josephus, 378, 380–84

Jotapata. *See* Yodefat

Judah Ha-Nasi, 5, 72, 164, 247, 292

Judas the Galilean, 65, 91, 98, 104, 152–53, 163

Judas son of Hezekiah, 65, 152, 156, 169–70

Julius Caesar, 368, 371–72, 377

Justus of Tiberias, 68, 133, 162

Kedesh, G-9, 82, 115, 124, 358

Kefar Hananya, 196, 200, 284–85, 297, 304, 335, 338

Khirbet Qana, xvii, 36, 94, 130, 137–38, 181, 185, 189–200, 220–23, 256, 268, 335. *See also* Cana

lamps, 120, 124, 197, 210, 212–14, 233, 324, 334, 352

large estates, 307, 351–52, 383

Late Roman, ix, 235–37, 286, 323–24

literacy, 36, 253–54, 256–58

Luke, Gospel of, 85–87, 98–99, 131–33, 140, 172, 379

Magdala, xi, xvii, 57, 97, 121, 138, 143, 196, 247, 264, 269, 273, 278, 284–85, 290, 304

malaria, 242–49

mansion, 119, 201, 217–18, 221, 226–27, 334

Mark, Gospel of, 85, 87, 98, 131–33, 140, 172

market(s), 7, 19, 91, 96, 158, 183, 189, 191–93, 196, 201, 211, 281–82, 286–87, 291, 297–98, 302, 312, 314, 316, 318–20, 324–25, 327, 336, 338–39, 352–53, 375–76, 379

Matthew, Gospel of, 85–89, 90, 98, 131–33, 140–41, 172

Meiron, G-7, 193–94, 196, 223, 233, 243, 264, 268, 323–24, 358

Menahem, 163

merchants, 286, 288, 291, 317

Messiahs, messianic, 13, 22, 20, 65, 132, 163, 169, 170, 173

Middle Roman, ix, 183, 219, 237, 286, 313–14, 317, 322–23, 325

Midrash, 72, 92, 134, 227, 254–56, 272, 286, 289, 292, 351

*Mikveh, mikva'ot*, 32, 94, 118, 120, 135, 137, 193, 198, 208, 211–12, 214, 221, 328, 330

Mishnah, xi, 6, 36, 72, 74, 103, 143, 164, 167, 177, 179, 213, 230, 232–34, 254, 272, 288–89, 291–92, 316, 318, 321, 327, 333

Mishnaic Period, xi, xviii, 112, 177, 179, 181, 183, 185, 187–88, 190, 216–17, 236, 238, 283, 291

money, 228, 286, 291, 317, 320, 333, 352–53, 373–75, 381–82. *See also* coins

morbidity, 242, 248–49

mortality, 242, 248–29

movement(s), socio-religious, 6, 22, 24–25, 30, 33, 63, 73, 78–81, 85–86, 91–92, 95, 98, 100, 103, 134, 163, 167, 169–73, 290–91, 298, 306, 308, 315, 357, 366

Nazareth, G-2, G-3, 3, 5, 7, 12, 23, 33, 35, 37, 65, 73, 95, 98, 100–101, 119, 121, 129–33, 170, 172, 180, 184–85, 191, 193–94, 196, 198–200, 214, 216, 227, 229, 247, 264, 267–69, 273, 302, 304, 329, 347, 357, 360

olive press(es), 63, 190, 281, 304

ossuaries, 94, 120, 256

patronage, 321, 349, 351–52

peasant(s)/peasantry, 4, 19, 21, 36, 53, 57, 63, 168–69, 171–72, 196, 230, 249, 297–98, 312, 321, 327, 336, 339, 348–51, 353, 357, 380 pedology, 299, 309

Pharisees, Pharisaic, 13, 17–18, 20, 26, 30, 33, 35, 78–81, 83–93, 95–96, 98, 102, 104, 133, 141, 153, 161, 172, 255, 292, 378

*polis*, 134, 156, 178–79, 185–86, 273–74, 276–77, 282, 285–94, 313

Pompey, xi, 57–59, 73, 357, 366–68, 375

population, xvii, 4, 17–19, 27, 29–35, 53–54, 56–57, 69, 62–63, 79, 82–83, 93, 95, 101, 112–14, 122, 142, 129, 140, 162, 178–79, 181–87, 190, 209, 211, 242, 244, 247–49, 267, 274, 276–78, 282, 288, 297–99, 305–9, 315–16, 322, 337, 348, 350–51, 361–62, 367, 375, 378

prayer hall (*proseuchē*), 99–100, 121, 134–35, 139

priest(s), priestly, xii, 11, 18, 21, 29, 58–59, 72, 81, 83–84, 87–92, 94–95, 154–55, 159, 164, 168, 173, 208, 214, 255, 257–58, 327, 330, 349, 352–53, 367

purity, 33, 87–88, 94–95, 118–19, 213–14, 275, 328, 332, 353

Q (source), 5, 15–17, 22–25, 33, 35, 37, 86, 172–73, 346–47

Qumran, 36–37, 79, 84, 88, 95, 97, 130, 164, 226

rabbis/rabbinic, xi, xvii, 5–6, 17–21, 28, 36–37, 72, 74, 79–80, 83–86, 89, 91–96, 98, 100–104, 112, 119, 124, 129, 134–35, 140, 142–43, 154, 164, 179, 198, 196, 214, 224, 227, 246, 253–56, 258, 272–73, 281, 283–84, 286–94, 297, 313–19, 321, 324–26, 333, 357

road, G-6, 7, 52, 57, 155, 263–69, 278, 305–6

roof(s), 124, 138, 145, 154, 197, 199, 216, 218, 220–22, 224, 228–31, 233, 236, 238

room(s), G-9, 136–39, 146, 155, 181, 192, 197, 200, 217–22, 224–26, 229, 231–32, 234, 237–38, 256, 323, 350

rural, 4, 7, 11, 17, 20, 26, 30–31, 56, 58, 62–64, 119, 140–41, 190, 208, 211, 214, 217–19, 226, 228, 231, 234, 243, 249, 273–74, 276, 278–80, 284–85, 287–93, 297–99, 302, 305–9, 312, 314–15, 319–21, 325–26, 330, 338, 348, 362

Sabbath, 32, 55, 88, 131–35, 140–41, 155, 255, 308

Sadducees, 78, 86–88, 159, 292

sages, xvii, 7, 22, 80, 102, 154, 167, 246, 258, 272, 289–93, 318, 320–21, 328

school(s), 23, 35–37, 78, 164, 253–58

scribes, 35, 85, 87–90, 95, 98, 132–33, 258

Scythopolis, 24, 28, 34, 58, 101, 123, 196, 209, 264–65, 277, 281

Second Quest, 17–18

sect, 24, 37, 78, 122, 153

Sepphoris, ix, xi, xvii, G-2, 4–7, 18–20, 23, 27–28, 32–34, 36–37, 55, 57–58, 60–64, 69–74, 91, 95, 100–102, 118–19, 122–24, 137, 152, 156, 162, 164, 169–70, 177–78, 181, 183, 185, 187, 189, 192, 196, 200–201, 220–22, 247, 249, 266–69, 273–74, 276–87, 290, 292–93, 297, 302, 304, 307–8, 324, 350–52, 358–60

Shikhin, ix, G-6, 181, 193–94, 196–97, 200, 269, 284, 302, 304, 324–25, 352

Simon (Maccabee), xii, 54, 115, 209, 367, 382

Simon of Perea, 62, 169–79

soil, 31, 228, 299–304, 358–60, 367

stone vessels, 32, 63, 93–95, 97, 119–20, 212–14, 328, 332, 353

stratification (archaeological), 55

stratification (social), 30, 319, 347–49, 351, 353

subsistence, 312, 315, 321, 327, 349–51

synagogue/synagogal, G-5, 6–7, 18, 64, 88–89, 94, 97, 118, 121–22,

129–46, 173, 187, 190, 193–94, 199, 215, 256, 258, 280–81, 286, 328, 358
Synoptic Gospels, 85, 130, 189. *See also* Evangelists

table fellowship, 87
Talmud, xviii, 36, 72, 74, 154–55, 164, 182, 197, 253, 255–56, 272, 281, 284–85, 287, 290–91
Tannaitic, 92, 143, 253–54, 272, 284, 293, 314, 316–17, 320, 326, 351
tax(es)/taxation/tax collector, 7, 21, 29–30, 57–58, 86–87, 163, 189, 232, 286, 289, 298, 312, 334, 350, 352, 366–83. *See also* tribute
Tel Anafa, 196, 329–30, 336–38, 358
tenancy, 164, 351–52
textiles, 326, 335, 352
Third Quest, 12, 16–17
Third Reich, 51–52
Tiberias, xi, xvii, 4–5, 7, 18, 28–29, 33–34, 36, 64, 66–70, 72–74, 82, 97, 101, 114, 121–24, 129, 133–35, 138–39, 156, 158, 162, 171, 177–78, 183, 185, 192, 196, 200–201, 246–47, 249, 263–64, 266, 69, 273–74, 277–80, 282, 284–87, 289–91, 293,

302, 304, 307–8, 328, 350–52, 360–61, 376, 380
tolls, 367, 369–70, 375–77, 379–80. *See also* customs
Torah, 20–22, 38, 79, 89, 122, 132, 136, 138–40, 146, 212, 215, 286
Tosefta, 100, 135, 143, 233–34, 254, 318–21
trade, 7, 26–27, 32, 67, 122, 247, 264, 269, 284, 297–98, 302, 305, 309, 314–17, 319–20, 323–25, 327, 332–39, 353, 362, 369, 374, 377–78, 380. *See also* commerce
trail, G-7, 266–69
tribute, 153, 170–72, 367–73, 383. *See also* taxes
Tyre, 28, 54, 56, 211, 263–64, 266–67, 281, 290, 329, 331–32, 336–38, 350

urban/urbanization, xvii, 7, 17, 23, 26–28, 33–35, 64–65, 71, 73, 102, 119, 140, 179, 185, 201, 209, 217, 219–20, 224–25, 228, 242, 249, 272, 274, 276–78, 287, 293, 297–99, 305–9, 312–16, 336, 338, 348, 351–53, 361–62
Usha, xi, 5, 102, 182, 279, 285, 287, 292

village(s), xvii, G-3, 4, 6–7, 18–19, 32–35, 57, 63, 95, 119, 121, 123, 129, 137, 140, 161, 168–73, 177–201, 211, 215, 217, 220, 222, 224–26, 228, 231–32, 234, 237–38, 247–50, 264, 266–69, 273–74, 276, 278, 281, 283–94, 297–98, 302, 305, 308–9, 312–14, 316, 318–19, 321–27, 334–36, 339, 348–52, 357–58, 360–61, 362, 382

wine press, 191, 198–99, 304, 317, 328

Yavneh (Jamnia), 5, 72, 102–3, 185, 292–93
Yodefat (Jotapata), xi, xvii, 56, 67, 69, 94, 116, 118, 181, 184–85, 190–94, 197–200, 220–22, 264, 268, 273, 304, 324, 330, 334–36, 351–53, 361
Yohanan ben Zakkai, 20–21, 92–93, 100, 102, 104, 154

zealots, 80, 98, 153, 162–63, 168